Toyota Tacoma, 4Runner & T100 Automotive Repair Manual

by Robert Maddox, Mike Stubblefield and John H Haynes

Member of the Guild of Motoring Writers

Models covered:

2WD and 4WD Toyota Tacoma (1995 thru 2004),
4Runner (1996 thru 2002) and T100 (1993 thru 1998)

(2N10 - 92076)

ABCDE
FGHIJ

2

Haynes Publishing Group
Sparkford Nr Yeovil
Somerset BA22 7JJ England

Haynes North America, Inc
861 Lawrence Drive
Newbury Park
California 91320 USA

About this manual

Its purpose

The purpose of this manual is to help you get the best value from your vehicle. It can do so in several ways. It can help you decide what work must be done, even if you choose to have it done by a dealer service department or a repair shop; it provides information and procedures for routine maintenance and servicing; and it offers diagnostic and repair procedures to follow when trouble occurs.

We hope you use the manual to tackle the work yourself. For many simpler jobs, doing it yourself may be quicker than arranging an appointment to get the vehicle into a shop and making the trips to leave it and pick it up. More importantly, a lot of money can be saved by avoiding the expense the shop must pass on to you to cover its labor and overhead costs. An added benefit is the sense of satisfaction and accomplishment that you feel after doing the job yourself.

Using the manual

The manual is divided into Chapters. Each Chapter is divided into numbered Sections, which are headed in bold type between horizontal lines. Each Section consists of consecutively numbered paragraphs.

At the beginning of each numbered Section you will be referred to any illustrations which apply to the procedures in that Section. The reference numbers used in illustration captions pinpoint the pertinent Section and the Step within that Section. That is, illustration 3.2 means the illustration refers to Section 3 and Step (or paragraph) 2 within that Section.

Procedures, once described in the text, are not normally repeated. When it's necessary to refer to another Chapter, the reference will be given as Chapter and Section number. Cross references given without use of the word "Chapter" apply to Sections and/or paragraphs in the same Chapter. For example, "see Section 8" means in the same Chapter.

References to the left or right side of the vehicle assume you are sitting in the driver's seat, facing forward.

Even though we have prepared this manual with extreme care, neither the publisher nor the author can accept responsibility for any errors in, or omissions from, the information given.

NOTE

A **Note** provides information necessary to properly complete a procedure or information which will make the procedure easier to understand.

CAUTION

A **Caution** provides a special procedure or special steps which must be taken while completing the procedure where the Caution is found. Not heeding a Caution can result in damage to the assembly being worked on.

WARNING

A **Warning** provides a special procedure or special steps which must be taken while completing the procedure where the Warning is found. Not heeding a Warning can result in personal injury.

Acknowledgements

We are grateful for the help and cooperation of the Toyota Motor Company for their assistance with technical information and certain illustrations. Technical consultants who contributed to this project include James Cota and John Wegman. Wiring diagrams were provided exclusively for Haynes North America, Inc. by Valley Forge Technical Communications.

A book in the Haynes Automotive Repair Manual Series

Printed in the U.S.A.

ISBN-10: 1-56392-626-1
ISBN-13: 978-1-56392-626-6

Library of Congress Control Number: 2006921481

Contents

Haynes mechanic, author and photographer with Toyota T100

Introduction to the Toyota T100, Tacoma and 4Runner

The T100 was manufactured beginning in 1993 and is equipped with either the 2.4L or 2.7L four-cylinder engine or the 3.0L or 3.4L V6 engine. The Tacoma was manufactured beginning in 1995 and is equipped with either the 2.4L or 2.7L four-cylinder engine or the 3.4L V6 engine. The 4Runner was manufactured beginning in 1996 through 1998 and is equipped with either the 2.7L four cylinder or the 3.4L V6 engine.

All engines are equipped with the Electronic Fuel Injection (EFI) system.

The engine drives the rear wheels through either a manual or automatic trans-mission via a driveshaft and solid rear axle. A transfer case and driveshaft are used to drive the front axle. All models are equipped with either 2WD or 4WD.

The front suspension is fully independent; it consists of upper and lower control arms, and a stabilizer bar. T100 models use torsion bars and shock absorbers; Tacoma 2WD models use coil springs and shock absorbers; Tacoma 4WD models and 4Runner models use an integral coil spring/shock absorber assembly. A solid axle at the rear is suspended by leaf springs and shock absorbers (T100 and Tacoma models) or coil springs and shock absorbers (4Runner models). 4Runner models have four rear suspension arms (two upper and two lower arms) and a lateral rod.

The steering box on 4WD T100 models is mounted to the left of the engine and is connected to the steering arms through a series of rods. The steering gear on all other models is a rack-and-pinion type and is connected to the steering knuckles by tie-rods.

The front brakes are disc brakes and the rear brakes are drums, with power assist standard. Some models are equipped with anti-lock brakes.

Vehicle identification numbers

Modifications are a continuing and unpublicized process in vehicle manufacturing. Since spare parts manuals and lists are compiled on a numerical basis, the individual vehicle numbers are essential to correctly identify the component required.

Vehicle Identification Number (VIN)

This very important identification number is stamped on a plate attached to the left side of the dashboard just inside the windshield on the driver's side of the vehicle (see illustration). The VIN also appears on the Vehicle Certificate of Title and Registration. It contains information such as where and when the vehicle was manufactured, the model year and the body style.

Engine identification number

The engine ID number on four-cylinder engines is located on a machined surface on the left side of the block (see illustration).

On V6 engines, the ID number is also located on the left side of the engine block, near the oil filter (see illustration).

Manufacturer Certification label

The Manufacturer Certification label is affixed to the front door pillar. The plate contains the name of the manufacturer, the month and year of production, the Gross Vehicle Weight Rating (GVWR) and the certification statement (see illustration).

Vehicle Emissions Control Information (VECI) label and Vacuum Schematic

The emissions control information label and vacuum schematic is found under the hood. This label contains information on the emissions control equipment installed on the vehicle, as well as tune-up specifications (see illustration).

Transfer case and transmission identification number

The transfer case and manual transmission identification number is stamped into the case of the component. Automatic transmission numbers are stamped onto ID plates (see illustrations).

The Vehicle Identification Number (VIN) is visible through the driver's side of the windshield

5VZ-FE Engine

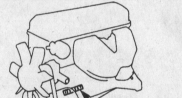

The engine identification number on four-cylinder engines is stamped on the left side of the engine block

The engine identification number on V6 engines is also stamped onto a pad on the left side of the engine block, above the oil filter cartridge

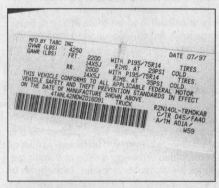

The manufacturer's certification label is affixed to the end of the driver's side door

The Vehicle Emissions Control Information (VECI) label is located on the underside of the hood

The identification number on manual transmissions is stamped into the bottom of the case

The identification number on automatic transmissions is stamped into a plate located on the side of the transmission

Buying parts

Replacement parts are available from many sources, which generally fall into one of two categories - authorized dealer parts departments and independent retail auto parts stores. Our advice concerning these parts is as follows:

Retail auto parts stores: Good auto parts stores will stock frequently needed components which wear out relatively fast, such as clutch components, exhaust systems, brake parts, tune-up parts, etc. These stores often supply new or reconditioned parts on an exchange basis, which can save a considerable amount of money. Discount auto parts stores are often very good places to buy materials and parts needed for general vehicle maintenance such as oil, grease, filters, spark plugs, belts, touch-up paint, bulbs, etc. They also usually sell tools and general accessories, have convenient hours, charge lower prices and can often be found not far from home.

Authorized dealer parts department: This is the best source for parts which are unique to the vehicle and not generally available elsewhere (such as major engine parts, transmission parts, trim pieces, etc.).

Warranty information: If the vehicle is still covered under warranty, be sure that any replacement parts purchased - regardless of the source - do not invalidate the warranty!

To be sure of obtaining the correct parts, have engine and chassis numbers available and, if possible, take the old parts along for positive identification.

Maintenance techniques, tools and working facilities

Maintenance techniques

There are a number of techniques involved in maintenance and repair that will be referred to throughout this manual. Application of these techniques will enable the home mechanic to be more efficient, better organized and capable of performing the various tasks properly, which will ensure that the repair job is thorough and complete.

Fasteners

Fasteners are nuts, bolts, studs and screws used to hold two or more parts together. There are a few things to keep in mind when working with fasteners. Almost all of them use a locking device of some type, either a lockwasher, locknut, locking tab or thread adhesive. All threaded fasteners should be clean and straight, with undamaged threads and undamaged corners on the hex head where the wrench fits. Develop the habit of replacing all damaged nuts and bolts with new ones. Special locknuts with nylon or fiber inserts can only be used once. If they are removed, they lose their locking ability and must be replaced with new ones.

Rusted nuts and bolts should be treated with a penetrating fluid to ease removal and prevent breakage. Some mechanics use turpentine in a spout-type oil can, which works quite well. After applying the rust penetrant, let it work for a few minutes before trying to loosen the nut or bolt. Badly rusted fasteners may have to be chiseled or sawed off or removed with a special nut breaker, available at tool stores.

If a bolt or stud breaks off in an assembly, it can be drilled and removed with a special tool commonly available for this purpose.

Most automotive machine shops can perform this task, as well as other repair procedures, such as the repair of threaded holes that have been stripped out.

Flat washers and lockwashers, when removed from an assembly, should always be replaced exactly as removed. Replace any damaged washers with new ones. Never use a lockwasher on any soft metal surface (such as aluminum), thin sheet metal or plastic.

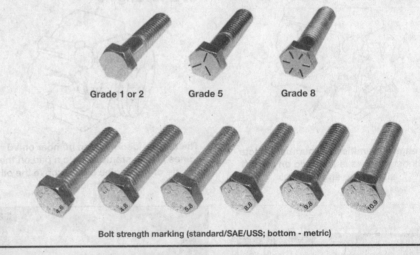

Grade 1 or 2   Grade 5   Grade 8

Bolt strength marking (standard/SAE/USS; bottom - metric)

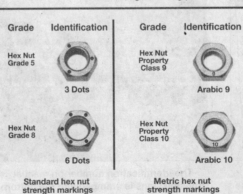

Grade	Identification
Hex Nut Grade 5	3 Dots
Hex Nut Grade 8	6 Dots

Standard hex nut strength markings

Grade	Identification
Hex Nut Property Class 9	Arabic 9
Hex Nut Property Class 10	Arabic 10

Metric hex nut strength markings

Class 10.9   Class 9.8   Class 8.8

Metric stud strength markings

00-1 HAYNES

Fastener sizes

For a number of reasons, automobile manufacturers are making wider and wider use of metric fasteners. Therefore, it is important to be able to tell the difference between standard (sometimes called U.S. or SAE) and metric hardware, since they cannot be interchanged.

All bolts, whether standard or metric, are sized according to diameter, thread pitch and length. For example, a standard 1/2 - 13 x 1 bolt is 1/2 inch in diameter, has 13 threads per inch and is 1 inch long. An M12 - 1.75 x 25 metric bolt is 12 mm in diameter, has a thread pitch of 1.75 mm (the distance between threads) and is 25 mm long. The two bolts are nearly identical, and easily confused, but they are not interchangeable.

In addition to the differences in diameter, thread pitch and length, metric and standard bolts can also be distinguished by examining the bolt heads. To begin with, the distance across the flats on a standard bolt head is measured in inches, while the same dimension on a metric bolt is sized in millimeters (the same is true for nuts). As a result, a standard wrench should not be used on a metric bolt and a metric wrench should not be used on a standard bolt. Also, most standard bolts have slashes radiating out from the center of the head to denote the grade or strength of the bolt, which is an indication of the amount of torque that can be applied to it. The greater the number of slashes, the greater the strength of the bolt. Grades 0 through 5 are commonly used on automobiles. Metric bolts have a property class (grade) number, rather than a slash, molded into their heads to indicate bolt strength. In this case, the higher the number, the stronger the bolt. Property class numbers 8.8, 9.8 and 10.9 are commonly used on automobiles.

Strength markings can also be used to distinguish standard hex nuts from metric hex nuts. Many standard nuts have dots stamped into one side, while metric nuts are marked with a number. The greater the number of dots, or the higher the number, the greater the strength of the nut.

Metric studs are also marked on their ends according to property class (grade). Larger studs are numbered (the same as metric bolts), while smaller studs carry a geometric code to denote grade.

It should be noted that many fasteners, especially Grades 0 through 2, have no distinguishing marks on them. When such is the case, the only way to determine whether it is standard or metric is to measure the thread pitch or compare it to a known fastener of the same size.

Standard fasteners are often referred to as SAE, as opposed to metric. However, it should be noted that SAE technically refers to a non-metric fine thread fastener only. Coarse thread non-metric fasteners are referred to as USS sizes.

Since fasteners of the same size (both standard and metric) may have different

Metric thread sizes	Ft-lbs	Nm
M-6	6 to 9	9 to 12
M-8	14 to 21	19 to 28
M-10	28 to 40	38 to 54
M-12	50 to 71	68 to 96
M-14	80 to 140	109 to 154

Pipe thread sizes		
1/8	5 to 8	7 to 10
1/4	12 to 18	17 to 24
3/8	22 to 33	30 to 44
1/2	25 to 35	34 to 47

U.S. thread sizes		
1/4 - 20	6 to 9	9 to 12
5/16 - 18	12 to 18	17 to 24
5/16 - 24	14 to 20	19 to 27
3/8 - 16	22 to 32	30 to 43
3/8 - 24	27 to 38	37 to 51
7/16 - 14	40 to 55	55 to 74
7/16 - 20	40 to 60	55 to 81
1/2 - 13	55 to 80	75 to 108

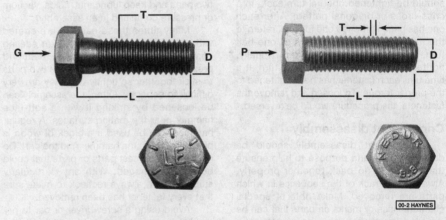

Standard (SAE and USS) bolt dimensions/grade marks

G   Grade marks (bolt strength)
L   Length (in inches)
T   Thread pitch (number of threads per inch)
D   Nominal diameter (in inches)

Metric bolt dimensions/grade marks

P   Property class (bolt strength)
L   Length (in millimeters)
T   Thread pitch (distance between threads in millimeters)
D   Diameter

strength ratings, be sure to reinstall any bolts, studs or nuts removed from your vehicle in their original locations. Also, when replacing a fastener with a new one, make sure that the new one has a strength rating equal to or greater than the original.

Tightening sequences and procedures

Most threaded fasteners should be tightened to a specific torque value (torque is the twisting force applied to a threaded component such as a nut or bolt). Overtightening the fastener can weaken it and cause it to break, while undertightening can cause it to eventually come loose. Bolts, screws and studs, depending on the material they are

made of and their thread diameters, have specific torque values, many of which are noted in the Specifications at the beginning of each Chapter. Be sure to follow the torque recommendations closely. For fasteners not assigned a specific torque, a general torque value chart is presented here as a guide. These torque values are for dry (unlubricated) fasteners threaded into steel or cast iron (not aluminum). As was previously mentioned, the size and grade of a fastener determine the amount of torque that can safely be applied to it. The figures listed here are approximate for Grade 2 and Grade 3 fasteners. Higher grades can tolerate higher torque values.

Fasteners laid out in a pattern, such as cylinder head bolts, oil pan bolts, differential cover bolts, etc., must be loosened or tigh

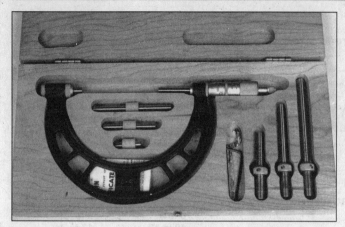

Micrometer set

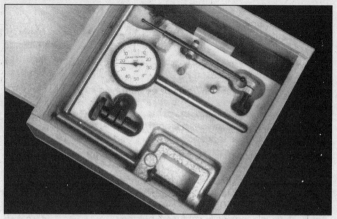

Dial indicator set

ened in sequence to avoid warping the component. This sequence will normally be shown in the appropriate Chapter. If a specific pattern is not given, the following procedures can be used to prevent warping.

Initially, the bolts or nuts should be assembled finger-tight only. Next, they should be tightened one full turn each, in a criss-cross or diagonal pattern. After each one has been tightened one full turn, return to the first one and tighten them all one-half turn, following the same pattern. Finally, tighten each of them one-quarter turn at a time until each fastener has been tightened to the proper torque. To loosen and remove the fasteners, the procedure would be reversed.

Component disassembly

Component disassembly should be done with care and purpose to help ensure that the parts go back together properly. Always keep track of the sequence in which parts are removed. Make note of special characteristics or marks on parts that can be installed more than one way, such as a grooved thrust washer on a shaft. It is a good idea to lay the disassembled parts out on a clean surface in the order that they were removed. It may also be helpful to make sketches or take instant photos of components before removal.

When removing fasteners from a component, keep track of their locations. Sometimes threading a bolt back in a part, or putting the washers and nut back on a stud, can prevent mix-ups later. If nuts and bolts cannot be returned to their original locations, they should be kept in a compartmented box or a series of small boxes. A cupcake or muffin tin is ideal for this purpose, since each cavity can hold the bolts and nuts from a particular area (i.e. oil pan bolts, valve cover bolts, engine mount bolts, etc.). A pan of this type is especially helpful when working on assemblies with very small parts, such as the carburetor, alternator, valve train or interior dash and trim pieces. The cavities can be marked with paint or tape to identify the contents.

Whenever wiring looms, harnesses or connectors are separated, it is a good idea to identify the two halves with numbered pieces of masking tape so they can be easily reconnected.

Gasket sealing surfaces

Throughout any vehicle, gaskets are used to seal the mating surfaces between two parts and keep lubricants, fluids, vacuum or pressure contained in an assembly.

Many times these gaskets are coated with a liquid or paste-type gasket sealing compound before assembly. Age, heat and pressure can sometimes cause the two parts to stick together so tightly that they are very difficult to separate. Often, the assembly can be loosened by striking it with a soft-face hammer near the mating surfaces. A regular hammer can be used if a block of wood is placed between the hammer and the part. Do not hammer on cast parts or parts that could be easily damaged. With any particularly stubborn part, always recheck to make sure that every fastener has been removed.

Avoid using a screwdriver or bar to pry apart an assembly, as they can easily mar the gasket sealing surfaces of the parts, which must remain smooth. If prying is absolutely necessary, use an old broom handle, but keep in mind that extra clean up will be necessary if the wood splinters.

After the parts are separated, the old gasket must be carefully scraped off and the gasket surfaces cleaned. Stubborn gasket material can be soaked with rust penetrant or treated with a special chemical to soften it so it can be easily scraped off. A scraper can be fashioned from a piece of copper tubing by flattening and sharpening one end. Copper is recommended because it is usually softer than the surfaces to be scraped, which reduces the chance of gouging the part. Some gaskets can be removed with a wire brush, but regardless of the method used, the mating surfaces must be left clean and smooth. If for some reason the gasket surface is gouged, then a gasket sealer thick enough to fill scratches will have to be used during reassembly of the components. For most applications, a non-drying (or semi-drying) gasket sealer should be used.

Hose removal tips

Warning: *If the vehicle is equipped with air conditioning, do not disconnect any of the A/C hoses without first having the system depressurized by a dealer service department or a service station.*

Hose removal precautions closely parallel gasket removal precautions. Avoid scratching or gouging the surface that the hose mates against or the connection may leak. This is especially true for radiator hoses. Because of various chemical reactions, the rubber in hoses can bond itself to the metal spigot that the hose fits over. To remove a hose, first loosen the hose clamps that secure it to the spigot. Then, with slip-joint pliers, grab the hose at the clamp and rotate it around the spigot. Work it back and forth until it is completely free, then pull it off. Silicone or other lubricants will ease removal if they can be applied between the hose and the outside of the spigot. Apply the same lubricant to the inside of the hose and the outside of the spigot to simplify installation.

As a last resort (and if the hose is to be replaced with a new one anyway), the rubber can be slit with a knife and the hose peeled from the spigot. If this must be done, be careful that the metal connection is not damaged.

If a hose clamp is broken or damaged, do not reuse it. Wire-type clamps usually weaken with age, so it is a good idea to replace them with screw-type clamps whenever a hose is removed.

Tools

A selection of good tools is a basic requirement for anyone who plans to maintain and repair his or her own vehicle. For the owner who has few tools, the initial investment might seem high, but when compared to the spiraling costs of professional auto maintenance and repair, it is a wise one.

To help the owner decide which tools are needed to perform the tasks detailed in this manual, the following tool lists are offered: *Maintenance and minor repair, Repair/overhaul* and *Special*.

The newcomer to practical mechanics

Dial caliper

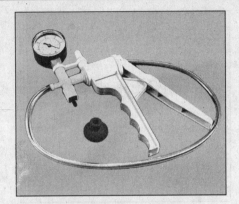

Hand-operated vacuum pump

Timing light

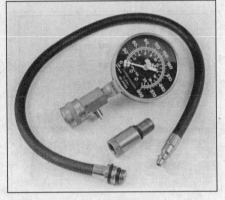

Compression gauge with spark plug
hole adapter

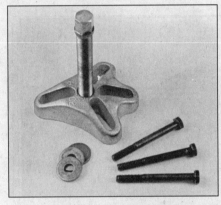

Damper/steering wheel puller

General purpose puller

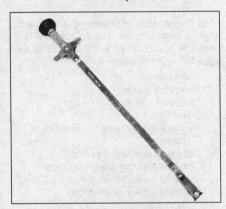

Hydraulic lifter removal tool

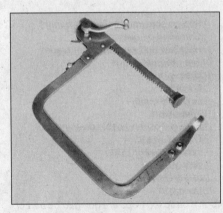

Valve spring compressor

Valve spring compressor

Ridge reamer

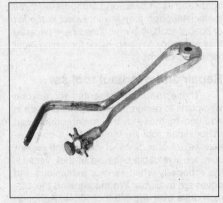

Piston ring groove cleaning tool

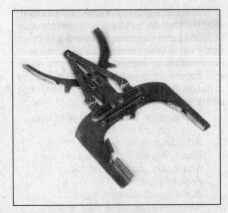

Ring removal/installation tool

Ring compressor

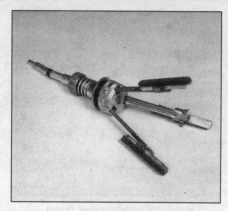

Cylinder hone

Brake hold-down spring tool

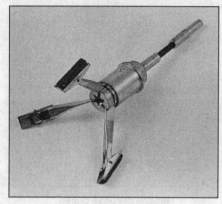

Brake cylinder hone

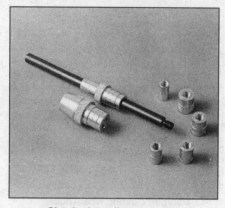

Clutch plate alignment tool

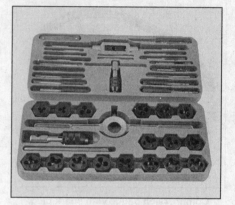

Tap and die set

should start off with the *maintenance and minor repair* tool kit, which is adequate for the simpler jobs performed on a vehicle. Then, as confidence and experience grow, the owner can tackle more difficult tasks, buying additional tools as they are needed. Eventually the basic kit will be expanded into the *repair and overhaul* tool set. Over a period of time, the experienced do-it-yourselfer will assemble a tool set complete enough for most repair and overhaul procedures and will add tools from the special category when it is felt that the expense is justified by the frequency of use.

Maintenance and minor repair tool kit

The tools in this list should be considered the minimum required for performance of routine maintenance, servicing and minor repair work. We recommend the purchase of combination wrenches (box-end and open-end combined in one wrench). While more expensive than open end wrenches, they offer the advantages of both types of wrench.

> *Combination wrench set (1/4-inch to 1 inch or 6 mm to 19 mm)*
> *Adjustable wrench, 8 inch*
> *Spark plug wrench with rubber insert*
> *Spark plug gap adjusting tool*
> *Feeler gauge set*
> *Brake bleeder wrench*
> *Standard screwdriver (5/16-inch x 6 inch)*

> *Phillips screwdriver (No. 2 x 6 inch)*
> *Combination pliers - 6 inch*
> *Hacksaw and assortment of blades*
> *Tire pressure gauge*
> *Grease gun*
> *Oil can*
> *Fine emery cloth*
> *Wire brush*
> *Battery post and cable cleaning tool*
> *Oil filter wrench*
> *Funnel (medium size)*
> *Safety goggles*
> *Jackstands (2)*
> *Drain pan*

Note: *If basic tune-ups are going to be part of routine maintenance, it will be necessary to purchase a good quality stroboscopic timing light and combination tachometer/dwell meter. Although they are included in the list of special tools, it is mentioned here because they are absolutely necessary for tuning most vehicles properly.*

Repair and overhaul tool set

These tools are essential for anyone who plans to perform major repairs and are in addition to those in the maintenance and minor repair tool kit. Included is a comprehensive set of sockets which, though expensive, are invaluable because of their versatility, especially when various extensions and drives are available. We recommend the 1/2-inch drive over the 3/8-inch drive. Although the larger drive is bulky and more expensive,

it has the capacity of accepting a very wide range of large sockets. Ideally, however, the mechanic should have a 3/8-inch drive set and a 1/2-inch drive set.

> *Socket set(s)*
> *Reversible ratchet*
> *Extension - 10 inch*
> *Universal joint*
> *Torque wrench (same size drive as sockets)*
> *Ball peen hammer - 8 ounce*
> *Soft-face hammer (plastic/rubber)*
> *Standard screwdriver (1/4-inch x 6 inch)*
> *Standard screwdriver (stubby - 5/16-inch)*
> *Phillips screwdriver (No. 3 x 8 inch)*
> *Phillips screwdriver (stubby - No. 2)*
> *Pliers - vise grip*
> *Pliers - lineman's*
> *Pliers - needle nose*
> *Pliers - snap-ring (internal and external)*
> *Cold chisel - 1/2-inch*
> *Scribe*
> *Scraper (made from flattened copper tubing)*
> *Centerpunch*
> *Pin punches (1/16, 1/8, 3/16-inch)*
> *Steel rule/straightedge - 12 inch*
> *Allen wrench set (1/8 to 3/8-inch or 4 mm to 10 mm)*
> *A selection of files*
> *Wire brush (large)*
> *Jackstands (second set)*
> *Jack (scissor or hydraulic type)*

Note: *Another tool which is often useful is an electric drill with a chuck capacity of 3/8-inch and a set of good quality drill bits.*

Special tools

The tools in this list include those which are not used regularly, are expensive to buy, or which need to be used in accordance with their manufacturer's instructions. Unless these tools will be used frequently, it is not very economical to purchase many of them. A consideration would be to split the cost and use between yourself and a friend or friends. In addition, most of these tools can be obtained from a tool rental shop on a temporary basis.

This list primarily contains only those tools and instruments widely available to the public, and not those special tools produced by the vehicle manufacturer for distribution to dealer service departments. Occasionally, references to the manufacturer's special tools are included in the text of this manual. Generally, an alternative method of doing the job without the special tool is offered. However, sometimes there is no alternative to their use. Where this is the case, and the tool cannot be purchased or borrowed, the work should be turned over to the dealer service department or an automotive repair shop.

Valve spring compressor
Piston ring groove cleaning tool
Piston ring compressor
Piston ring installation tool
Cylinder compression gauge
Cylinder ridge reamer
Cylinder surfacing hone
Cylinder bore gauge
Micrometers and/or dial calipers
Hydraulic lifter removal tool
Balljoint separator
Universal-type puller
Impact screwdriver
Dial indicator set
Stroboscopic timing light (inductive pick-up)
Hand operated vacuum/pressure pump
Tachometer/dwell meter
Universal electrical multimeter
Cable hoist
Brake spring removal and installation tools
Floor jack

Buying tools

For the do-it-yourselfer who is just starting to get involved in vehicle maintenance and repair, there are a number of options available when purchasing tools. If maintenance and minor repair is the extent of the work to be done, the purchase of individual tools is satisfactory. If, on the other hand, extensive work is planned, it would be a good idea to purchase a modest tool set from one of the large retail chain stores. A set can usually be bought at a substantial savings over the individual tool prices, and they often come with a tool box. As additional tools are needed, add-on sets, individual tools and a larger tool box can be purchased to expand the tool selection. Building a tool set gradually allows the cost of the tools to be spread over a longer period of time and gives the mechanic the freedom to choose only those tools that will actually be used.

Tool stores will often be the only source of some of the special tools that are needed, but regardless of where tools are bought, try to avoid cheap ones, especially when buying screwdrivers and sockets, because they won't last very long. The expense involved in replacing cheap tools will eventually be greater than the initial cost of quality tools.

Care and maintenance of tools

Good tools are expensive, so it makes sense to treat them with respect. Keep them clean and in usable condition and store them properly when not in use. Always wipe off any dirt, grease or metal chips before putting them away. Never leave tools lying around in the work area. Upon completion of a job, always check closely under the hood for tools that may have been left there so they won't get lost during a test drive.

Some tools, such as screwdrivers, pliers, wrenches and sockets, can be hung on a panel mounted on the garage or workshop wall, while others should be kept in a tool box or tray. Measuring instruments, gauges, meters, etc. must be carefully stored where they cannot be damaged by weather or impact from other tools.

When tools are used with care and stored properly, they will last a very long time. Even with the best of care, though, tools will wear out if used frequently. When a tool is damaged or worn out, replace it. Subsequent jobs will be safer and more enjoyable if you do.

How to repair damaged threads

Sometimes, the internal threads of a nut or bolt hole can become stripped, usually from overtightening. Stripping threads is an all-too-common occurrence, especially when working with aluminum parts, because aluminum is so soft that it easily strips out.

Usually, external or internal threads are only partially stripped. After they've been cleaned up with a tap or die, they'll still work. Sometimes, however, threads are badly damaged. When this happens, you've got three choices:

1) *Drill and tap the hole to the next suitable oversize and install a larger diameter bolt, screw or stud.*
2) *Drill and tap the hole to accept a threaded plug, then drill and tap the plug to the original screw size. You can also buy a plug already threaded to the original size. Then you simply drill a hole to the specified size, then run the threaded plug into the hole with a bolt and jam nut. Once the plug is fully seated, remove the jam nut and bolt.*
3) *The third method uses a patented thread repair kit like Heli-Coil or Slimsert. These easy-to-use kits are designed to repair damaged threads in straight-through holes and blind holes. Both are available as kits which can handle a variety of sizes and thread patterns. Drill the hole, then tap it with the special included tap. Install the Heli-Coil and the hole is back to its original diameter and thread pitch.*

Regardless of which method you use, be sure to proceed calmly and carefully. A little impatience or carelessness during one of these relatively simple procedures can ruin your whole day's work and cost you a bundle if you wreck an expensive part.

Working facilities

Not to be overlooked when discussing tools is the workshop. If anything more than routine maintenance is to be carried out, some sort of suitable work area is essential.

It is understood, and appreciated, that many home mechanics do not have a good workshop or garage available, and end up removing an engine or doing major repairs outside. It is recommended, however, that the overhaul or repair be completed under the cover of a roof.

A clean, flat workbench or table of comfortable working height is an absolute necessity. The workbench should be equipped with a vise that has a jaw opening of at least four inches.

As mentioned previously, some clean, dry storage space is also required for tools, as well as the lubricants, fluids, cleaning solvents, etc. which soon become necessary.

Sometimes waste oil and fluids, drained from the engine or cooling system during normal maintenance or repairs, present a disposal problem. To avoid pouring them on the ground or into a sewage system, pour the used fluids into large containers, seal them with caps and take them to an authorized disposal site or recycling center. Plastic jugs, such as old antifreeze containers, are ideal for this purpose.

Always keep a supply of old newspapers and clean rags available. Old towels are excellent for mopping up spills. Many mechanics use rolls of paper towels for most work because they are readily available and disposable. To help keep the area under the vehicle clean, a large cardboard box can be cut open and flattened to protect the garage or shop floor.

Whenever working over a painted surface, such as when leaning over a fender to service something under the hood, always cover it with an old blanket or bedspread to protect the finish. Vinyl covered pads, made especially for this purpose, are available at auto parts stores.

Jacking and towing

Jacking

The jack supplied with the vehicle should only be used for raising the vehicle when changing a tire or placing jackstands under the frame. **Warning:** *Never work under the vehicle or start the engine while this jack is being used as the only means of support.*

The vehicle should be on level ground with the hazard flashers on, the wheels blocked, the parking brake applied and the transmission in Park (automatic) or Reverse (manual). If a tire is being changed, loosen the lug nuts one-half turn and leave them in place until the wheel is raised off the ground.

Place the jack under the vehicle (**see illustrations**):

Front:

2WD models: Under the frame rail, where the crossmember is attached.
4WD models: Under the front suspension crossmember.

Rear (all models): Under the rear axle housing.

Operate the jack with a slow, smooth motion until the wheel is raised off the ground. Remove the lug nuts, pull off the wheel, install the spare and thread the lug nuts back on with the beveled sides facing in. Tighten them snugly, but wait until the vehicle is lowered to tighten them completely.

Lower the vehicle, remove the jack and tighten the nuts (if loosened or removed) in a criss-cross pattern.

Front jacking point (2WD model)

Towing

As a general rule, the vehicle should be towed with professional towing equipment. If towed from the front, the rear wheels should be placed on a towing dolly. If towed from the rear, the front wheels should be placed on a towing dolly. If towed with either two or four wheels on the ground, disconnect the driveshaft(s) from the differential(s).

When a vehicle is towed with the rear wheels raised, the steering wheel must be clamped in the straight ahead position with a special device designed for use during towing. The ignition key must be in the OFF posi-

Rear jacking point (all models)

tion, since the steering lock mechanism isn't strong enough to hold the front wheels straight while towing.

Equipment specifically designed for towing should be used. It should be attached to the main structural members of the vehicle, not the bumpers or brackets. Safety is a major consideration when towing and all applicable state and local laws must be obeyed. A safety chain system must be used at all times. Remember that power steering and power brakes will not work with the engine off.

Booster battery (jump) starting

Observe these precautions when using a booster battery to start a vehicle:

a) *Before connecting the booster battery, make sure the ignition switch is in the Off position.*
b) *Turn off the lights, heater and other electrical loads.*
c) *Your eyes should be shielded. Safety goggles are a good idea.*
d) *Make sure the booster battery is the same voltage as the dead one in the vehicle.*
e) *The two vehicles MUST NOT TOUCH each other!*
f) *Make sure the transaxle is in Neutral (manual) or Park (automatic).*
g) *If the booster battery is not a maintenance-free type, remove the vent caps and lay a cloth over the vent holes.*

Connect the red jumper cable to the positive (+) terminals of each battery (**see illustration**).

Connect one end of the black jumper cable to the negative (-) terminal of the booster battery. The other end of this cable should be connected to a good ground on the vehicle to be started, such as a bolt or bracket on the body.

Start the engine using the booster battery, then, with the engine running at idle speed, disconnect the jumper cables in the reverse order of connection.

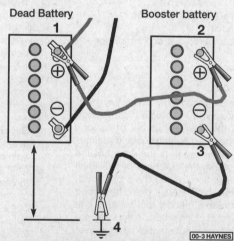

Make the booster battery cable connections in the numerical order shown (note that the negative cable of the booster battery is NOT attached to the negative terminal of the dead battery)

Automotive chemicals and lubricants

A number of automotive chemicals and lubricants are available for use during vehicle maintenance and repair. They include a wide variety of products ranging from cleaning solvents and degreasers to lubricants and protective sprays for rubber, plastic and vinyl.

Cleaners

Carburetor cleaner and choke cleaner is a strong solvent for gum, varnish and carbon. Most carburetor cleaners leave a dry-type lubricant film which will not harden or gum up. Because of this film it is not recommended for use on electrical components.

Brake system cleaner is used to remove brake dust, grease and brake fluid from the brake system, where clean surfaces are absolutely necessary. It leaves no residue and often eliminates brake squeal caused by contaminants.

Electrical cleaner removes oxidation, corrosion and carbon deposits from electrical contacts, restoring full current flow. It can also be used to clean spark plugs, carburetor jets, voltage regulators and other parts where an oil-free surface is desired.

Demoisturants remove water and moisture from electrical components such as alternators, voltage regulators, electrical connectors and fuse blocks. They are non-conductive and non-corrosive.

Degreasers are heavy-duty solvents used to remove grease from the outside of the engine and from chassis components. They can be sprayed or brushed on and, depending on the type, are rinsed off either with water or solvent.

Lubricants

Motor oil is the lubricant formulated for use in engines. It normally contains a wide variety of additives to prevent corrosion and reduce foaming and wear. Motor oil comes in various weights (viscosity ratings) from 0 to 50. The recommended weight of the oil depends on the season, temperature and the demands on the engine. Light oil is used in cold climates and under light load conditions. Heavy oil is used in hot climates and where high loads are encountered. Multi-viscosity oils are designed to have characteristics of both light and heavy oils and are available in a number of weights from 5W-20 to 20W-50.

Gear oil is designed to be used in differentials, manual transmissions and other areas where high-temperature lubrication is required.

Chassis and wheel bearing grease is a heavy grease used where increased loads and friction are encountered, such as for wheel bearings, balljoints, tie-rod ends and universal joints.

High-temperature wheel bearing grease is designed to withstand the extreme temperatures encountered by wheel bearings

in disc brake equipped vehicles. It usually contains molybdenum disulfide (moly), which is a dry-type lubricant.

White grease is a heavy grease for metal-to-metal applications where water is a problem. White grease stays soft under both low and high temperatures (usually from -100 to +190-degrees F), and will not wash off or dilute in the presence of water.

Assembly lube is a special extreme pressure lubricant, usually containing moly, used to lubricate high-load parts (such as main and rod bearings and cam lobes) for initial start-up of a new engine. The assembly lube lubricates the parts without being squeezed out or washed away until the engine oiling system begins to function.

Silicone lubricants are used to protect rubber, plastic, vinyl and nylon parts.

Graphite lubricants are used where oils cannot be used due to contamination problems, such as in locks. The dry graphite will lubricate metal parts while remaining uncontaminated by dirt, water, oil or acids. It is electrically conductive and will not foul electrical contacts in locks such as the ignition switch.

Moly penetrants loosen and lubricate frozen, rusted and corroded fasteners and prevent future rusting or freezing.

Heat-sink grease is a special electrically non-conductive grease that is used for mounting electronic ignition modules where it is essential that heat is transferred away from the module.

Sealants

RTV sealant is one of the most widely used gasket compounds. Made from silicone, RTV is air curing, it seals, bonds, waterproofs, fills surface irregularities, remains flexible, doesn't shrink, is relatively easy to remove, and is used as a supplementary sealer with almost all low and medium temperature gaskets.

Anaerobic sealant is much like RTV in that it can be used either to seal gaskets or to form gaskets by itself. It remains flexible, is solvent resistant and fills surface imperfections. The difference between an anaerobic sealant and an RTV-type sealant is in the curing. RTV cures when exposed to air, while an anaerobic sealant cures only in the absence of air. This means that an anaerobic sealant cures only after the assembly of parts, sealing them together.

Thread and pipe sealant is used for sealing hydraulic and pneumatic fittings and vacuum lines. It is usually made from a Teflon compound, and comes in a spray, a paint-on liquid and as a wrap-around tape.

Chemicals

Anti-seize compound prevents seizing, galling, cold welding, rust and corrosion in fasteners. High-temperature ant-seize, usu-

ally made with copper and graphite lubricants, is used for exhaust system and exhaust manifold bolts.

Anaerobic locking compounds are used to keep fasteners from vibrating or working loose and cure only after installation, in the absence of air. Medium strength locking compound is used for small nuts, bolts and screws that may be removed later. High-strength locking compound is for large nuts, bolts and studs which aren't removed on a regular basis.

Oil additives range from viscosity index improvers to chemical treatments that claim to reduce internal engine friction. It should be noted that most oil manufacturers caution against using additives with their oils.

Gas additives perform several functions, depending on their chemical makeup. They usually contain solvents that help dissolve gum and varnish that build up on carburetor, fuel injection and intake parts. They also serve to break down carbon deposits that form on the inside surfaces of the combustion chambers. Some additives contain upper cylinder lubricants for valves and piston rings, and others contain chemicals to remove condensation from the gas tank.

Miscellaneous

Brake fluid is specially formulated hydraulic fluid that can withstand the heat and pressure encountered in brake systems. Care must be taken so this fluid does not come in contact with painted surfaces or plastics. An opened container should always be resealed to prevent contamination by water or dirt.

Weatherstrip adhesive is used to bond weatherstripping around doors, windows and trunk lids. It is sometimes used to attach trim pieces.

Undercoating is a petroleum-based, tar-like substance that is designed to protect metal surfaces on the underside of the vehicle from corrosion. It also acts as a sound-deadening agent by insulating the bottom of the vehicle.

Waxes and polishes are used to help protect painted and plated surfaces from the weather. Different types of paint may require the use of different types of wax and polish. Some polishes utilize a chemical or abrasive cleaner to help remove the top layer of oxidized (dull) paint on older vehicles. In recent years many non-wax polishes that contain a wide variety of chemicals such as polymers and silicones have been introduced. These non-wax polishes are usually easier to apply and last longer than conventional waxes and polishes.

Conversion factors

Length (distance)
Inches (in)	X	25.4	= Millimetres (mm)	X	0.0394	= Inches (in)
Feet (ft)	X	0.305	= Metres (m)	X	3.281	= Feet (ft)
Miles	X	1.609	= Kilometres (km)	X	0.621	= Miles

Inches (in) X 25.4 = Millimetres (mm) X 0.0394 = Inches (in)
Feet (ft) X 0.305 = Metres (m) X 3.281 = Feet (ft)
Miles X 1.609 = Kilometres (km) X 0.621 = Miles

Volume (capacity)
Cubic inches (cu in; in^3) X 16.387 = Cubic centimetres (cc; cm^3) X 0.061 = Cubic inches (cu in; in^3)
Imperial pints (Imp pt) X 0.568 = Litres (l) X 1.76 = Imperial pints (Imp pt)
Imperial quarts (Imp qt) X 1.137 = Litres (l) X 0.88 = Imperial quarts (Imp qt)
Imperial quarts (Imp qt) X 1.201 = US quarts (US qt) X 0.833 = Imperial quarts (Imp qt)
US quarts (US qt) X 0.946 = Litres (l) X 1.057 = US quarts (US qt)
Imperial gallons (Imp gal) X 4.546 = Litres (l) X 0.22 = Imperial gallons (Imp gal)
Imperial gallons (Imp gal) X 1.201 = US gallons (US gal) X 0.833 = Imperial gallons (Imp gal)
US gallons (US gal) X 3.785 = Litres (l) X 0.264 = US gallons (US gal)

Mass (weight)
Ounces (oz) X 28.35 = Grams (g) X 0.035 = Ounces (oz)
Pounds (lb) X 0.454 = Kilograms (kg) X 2.205 = Pounds (lb)

Force
Ounces-force (ozf; oz) X 0.278 = Newtons (N) X 3.6 = Ounces-force (ozf; oz)
Pounds-force (lbf; lb) X 4.448 = Newtons (N) X 0.225 = Pounds-force (lbf; lb)
Newtons (N) X 0.1 = Kilograms-force (kgf; kg) X 9.81 = Newtons (N)

Pressure
Pounds-force per square inch X 0.070 = Kilograms-force per square X 14.223 = Pounds-force per square inch
(psi; lbf/in^2; lb/in^2) centimetre (kgf/cm^2; kg/cm^2) (psi; lbf/in^2; lb/in^2)
Pounds-force per square inch X 0.068 = Atmospheres (atm) X 14.696 = Pounds-force per square inch
(psi; lbf/in^2; lb/in^2) (psi; lbf/in^2; lb/in^2)
Pounds-force per square inch X 0.069 = Bars X 14.5 = Pounds-force per square inch
(psi; lbf/in^2; lb/in^2) (psi; lbf/in^2; lb/in^2)
Pounds-force per square inch X 6.895 = Kilopascals (kPa) X 0.145 = Pounds-force per square inch
(psi; lbf/in^2; lb/in^2) (psi; lbf/in^2; lb/in^2)
Kilopascals (kPa) X 0.01 = Kilograms-force per square X 98.1 = Kilopascals (kPa)
centimetre (kgf/cm^2; kg/cm^2)

Torque (moment of force)
Pounds-force inches X 1.152 = Kilograms-force centimetre X 0.868 = Pounds-force inches
(lbf in; lb in) (kgf cm; kg cm) (lbf in; lb in)
Pounds-force inches X 0.113 = Newton metres (Nm) X 8.85 = Pounds-force inches
(lbf in; lb in) (lbf in; lb in)
Pounds-force inches X 0.083 = Pounds-force feet (lbf ft; lb ft) X 12 = Pounds-force inches
(lbf in; lb in) (lbf in; lb in)
Pounds-force feet (lbf ft; lb ft) X 0.138 = Kilograms-force metres X 7.233 = Pounds-force feet (lbf ft; lb ft)
(kgf m; kg m)
Pounds-force feet (lbf ft; lb ft) X 1.356 = Newton metres (Nm) X 0.738 = Pounds-force feet (lbf ft; lb ft)
Newton metres (Nm) X 0.102 = Kilograms-force metres X 9.804 = Newton metres (Nm)
(kgf m; kg m)

Vacuum
Inches mercury (in. Hg) X 3.377 = Kilopascals (kPa) X 0.2961 = Inches mercury
Inches mercury (in. Hg) X 25.4 = Millimeters mercury (mm Hg) X 0.0394 = Inches mercury

Power
Horsepower (hp) X 745.7 = Watts (W) X 0.0013 = Horsepower (hp)

Velocity (speed)
Miles per hour (miles/hr; mph) X 1.609 = Kilometres per hour (km/hr; kph) X 0.621 = Miles per hour (miles/hr; mph)

Fuel consumption*
Miles per gallon, Imperial (mpg) X 0.354 = Kilometres per litre (km/l) X 2.825 = Miles per gallon, Imperial (mpg)
Miles per gallon, US (mpg) X 0.425 = Kilometres per litre (km/l) X 2.352 = Miles per gallon, US (mpg)

Temperature
Degrees Fahrenheit = (°C x 1.8) + 32   Degrees Celsius (Degrees Centigrade; °C) = (°F - 32) x 0.56

*It is common practice to convert from miles per gallon (mpg) to litres/100 kilometres (l/100km),
where mpg (Imperial) x l/100 km = 282 and mpg (US) x l/100 km = 235

Safety first!

Regardless of how enthusiastic you may be about getting on with the job at hand, take the time to ensure that your safety is not jeopardized. A moment's lack of attention can result in an accident, as can failure to observe certain simple safety precautions. The possibility of an accident will always exist, and the following points should not be considered a comprehensive list of all dangers. Rather, they are intended to make you aware of the risks and to encourage a safety conscious approach to all work you carry out on your vehicle.

Essential DOs and DON'Ts

DON'T rely on a jack when working under the vehicle. Always use approved jackstands to support the weight of the vehicle and place them under the recommended lift or support points.

DON'T attempt to loosen extremely tight fasteners (i.e. wheel lug nuts) while the vehicle is on a jack - it may fall.

DON'T start the engine without first making sure that the transmission is in Neutral (or Park where applicable) and the parking brake is set.

DON'T remove the radiator cap from a hot cooling system - let it cool or cover it with a cloth and release the pressure gradually.

DON'T attempt to drain the engine oil until you are sure it has cooled to the point that it will not burn you.

DON'T touch any part of the engine or exhaust system until it has cooled sufficiently to avoid burns.

DON'T siphon toxic liquids such as gasoline, antifreeze and brake fluid by mouth, or allow them to remain on your skin.

DON'T inhale brake lining dust - it is potentially hazardous (see *Asbestos* below).

DON'T allow spilled oil or grease to remain on the floor - wipe it up before someone slips on it.

DON'T use loose fitting wrenches or other tools which may slip and cause injury.

DON'T push on wrenches when loosening or tightening nuts or bolts. Always try to pull the wrench toward you. If the situation calls for pushing the wrench away, push with an open hand to avoid scraped knuckles if the wrench should slip.

DON'T attempt to lift a heavy component alone - get someone to help you.

DON'T rush or take unsafe shortcuts to finish a job.

DON'T allow children or animals in or around the vehicle while you are working on it.

DO wear eye protection when using power tools such as a drill, sander, bench grinder, etc. and when working under a vehicle.

DO keep loose clothing and long hair well out of the way of moving parts.

DO make sure that any hoist used has a safe working load rating adequate for the job.

DO get someone to check on you periodically when working alone on a vehicle.

DO carry out work in a logical sequence and make sure that everything is correctly assembled and tightened.

DO keep chemicals and fluids tightly capped and out of the reach of children and pets.

DO remember that your vehicle's safety affects that of yourself and others. If in doubt on any point, get professional advice.

Asbestos

Certain friction, insulating, sealing, and other products - such as brake linings, brake bands, clutch linings, torque converters, gaskets, etc. - may contain asbestos. Extreme care must be taken to avoid inhalation of dust from such products, since it is hazardous to health. If in doubt, assume that they do contain asbestos.

Fire

Remember at all times that gasoline is highly flammable. Never smoke or have any kind of open flame around when working on a vehicle. But the risk does not end there. A spark caused by an electrical short circuit, by two metal surfaces contacting each other, or even by static electricity built up in your body under certain conditions, can ignite gasoline vapors, which in a confined space are highly explosive. Do not, under any circumstances, use gasoline for cleaning parts. Use an approved safety solvent.

Always disconnect the battery ground (-) cable at the battery before working on any part of the fuel system or electrical system. Never risk spilling fuel on a hot engine or exhaust component. It is strongly recommended that a fire extinguisher suitable for use on fuel and electrical fires be kept handy in the garage or workshop at all times. Never try to extinguish a fuel or electrical fire with water.

Fumes

Certain fumes are highly toxic and can quickly cause unconsciousness and even death if inhaled to any extent. Gasoline vapor falls into this category, as do the vapors from some cleaning solvents. Any draining or pouring of such volatile fluids should be done in a well ventilated area.

When using cleaning fluids and solvents, read the instructions on the container carefully. Never use materials from unmarked containers.

Never run the engine in an enclosed space, such as a garage. Exhaust fumes contain carbon monoxide, which is extremely poisonous. If you need to run the engine, always do so in the open air, or at least have the rear of the vehicle outside the work area.

If you are fortunate enough to have the use of an inspection pit, never drain or pour gasoline and never run the engine while the vehicle is over the pit. The fumes, being heavier than air, will concentrate in the pit with possibly lethal results.

The battery

Never create a spark or allow a bare light bulb near a battery. They normally give off a certain amount of hydrogen gas, which is highly explosive.

Always disconnect the battery ground (-) cable at the battery before working on the fuel or electrical systems.

If possible, loosen the filler caps or cover when charging the battery from an external source (this does not apply to sealed or maintenance-free batteries). Do not charge at an excessive rate or the battery may burst.

Take care when adding water to a non maintenance-free battery and when carrying a battery. The electrolyte, even when diluted, is very corrosive and should not be allowed to contact clothing or skin.

Always wear eye protection when cleaning the battery to prevent the caustic deposits from entering your eyes.

Household current

When using an electric power tool, inspection light, etc., which operates on household current, always make sure that the tool is correctly connected to its plug and that, where necessary, it is properly grounded. Do not use such items in damp conditions and, again, do not create a spark or apply excessive heat in the vicinity of fuel or fuel vapor.

Secondary ignition system voltage

A severe electric shock can result from touching certain parts of the ignition system (such as the spark plug wires) when the engine is running or being cranked, particularly if components are damp or the insulation is defective. In the case of an electronic ignition system, the secondary system voltage is much higher and could prove fatal.

Troubleshooting

Contents

This section provides an easy reference guide to the more common problems which may occur during the operation of your vehicle. These problems and their possible causes are grouped under headings denoting various components or systems, such as Engine, Cooling system, etc. They also refer you to the chapter and/or section which deals with the problem.

Remember that successful troubleshooting is not a mysterious "black art" practiced only by professional mechanics. It is simply the result of the right knowledge combined with an intelligent, systematic approach to the problem. Always work by process of elimination, starting with the simplest solution and working through to the most complex - and never overlook the obvious. Anyone can run the gas tank dry or leave the lights on overnight, so don't assume that you are exempt from such oversights.

Finally, always establish a clear idea of why a problem has occurred and take steps to ensure that it doesn't happen again. If the electrical system fails because of a poor connection, check the other connections in the system to make sure that they don't fail as well. If a particular fuse continues to blow, find out why - don't just replace one fuse after another. Remember, failure of a small component can often be indicative of potential failure or incorrect functioning of a more important component or system.

Engine and performance

1 Engine will not rotate when attempting to start

1 Battery terminal connections loose or corroded. Check the cable terminals at the battery; tighten cable clamp and/or clean off corrosion as necessary (see Chapter 1).
2 Battery discharged or faulty. If the cable ends are clean and tight on the battery posts, turn the key to the On position and switch on the headlights or windshield wipers. If they won't run, the battery is discharged.
3 Automatic transmission not engaged in park (P) or Neutral (N).
4 Broken, loose or disconnected wires in the starting circuit. Inspect all wires and connectors at the battery, starter solenoid and ignition switch (on steering column).
5 Starter motor pinion jammed in flywheel ring gear. If manual transmission, place transmission in gear and rock the vehicle to manually turn the engine. Remove starter (Chapter 5) and inspect pinion and flywheel (Chapter 2) at earliest convenience.
6 Starter solenoid faulty (Chapter 5).
7 Starter motor faulty (Chapter 5).
8 Ignition switch faulty (Chapter 12).
9 Engine seized. Try to turn the crankshaft with a large socket and breaker bar on the pulley bolt.

2 Engine rotates but will not start

1 Fuel tank empty.
2 Battery discharged (engine rotates slowly). Check the operation of electrical components as described in previous Section.
3 Battery terminal connections loose or corroded. See previous Section.
4 Fuel not reaching fuel injector. Check for clogged fuel filter or lines and defective fuel pump. Also make sure the tank vent lines aren't clogged (Chapter 4).
5 Cold start injector and thermal time switch not operating (1993 and 1994 3.0L engines only) (Chapter 4)
6 Faulty distributor components. Check the cap and rotor (Chapter 1).
7 Low cylinder compression. Check as described in Chapter 2.
8 Valve clearances not properly adjusted (Chapter 1).
9 Water in fuel. Drain tank and fill with new fuel.
10 Defective ignition coil (Chapter 5).
11 Dirty fuel injector(s) (Chapter 4).
12 Wet or damaged ignition components (Chapters 1 and 5).
13 Worn, faulty or incorrectly gapped spark plugs (Chapter 1).
14 Broken, loose or disconnected wires in the starting circuit (see previous Section).
15 Loose distributor (changing ignition timing). Turn the distributor body as necessary to start the engine, then adjust the ignition timing as soon as possible (Chapter 1).
16 Broken, loose or disconnected wires at the ignition coil or faulty coil (Chapter 5).
17 Timing chain or gear failure or wear affecting valve timing (Chapter 2A).
18 Timing belt broken (Chapter 2B).

3 Starter motor operates without turning engine

1 Starter pinion sticking. Remove the starter (Chapter 5) and inspect.
2 Starter pinion or flywheel/driveplate teeth worn or broken. Remove the inspection cover and inspect.

4 Engine hard to start when cold

1 Battery discharged or low. Check as described in Chapter 1.
2 Fuel not reaching the fuel injectors. Check the fuel filter, lines and fuel pump (Chapters 1 and 4).
3 Defective spark plugs (Chapter 1).
4 Fault with the fuel injection or engine management system (Chapter 4 or 6).

5 Engine hard to start when hot

1 Air filter dirty (Chapter 1).

2 Fuel not reaching fuel injectors (see Chapter 4). Check for a vapor lock situation, brought about by clogged fuel tank vent lines.
3 Bad engine ground connection.
4 Defective pick-up coil in distributor (Chapter 5).
5 Fault with the fuel injection or engine management system (Chapter 4 or 6).

6 Starter motor noisy or engages roughly

1 Pinion or flywheel/driveplate teeth worn or broken. Remove the inspection cover on the left side of the engine and inspect.
2 Starter motor mounting bolts loose or missing.

7 Engine starts but stops immediately

1 Loose or damaged wire harness connections at distributor, coil or alternator.
2 Intake manifold vacuum leaks. Make sure all mounting bolts/nuts are tight and all vacuum hoses connected to the manifold are attached properly and in good condition (Chapters 2A, 2B and 4).
3 Insufficient fuel flow to fuel injectors (Chapters 4).
4 Idle speed incorrect (Chapter 1).

8 Engine 'lopes' while idling or idles erratically

1 Vacuum leaks. Check mounting bolts at the intake manifold for tightness. Make sure that all vacuum hoses are connected and in good condition. Use a stethoscope or a length of fuel hose held against your ear to listen for vacuum leaks while the engine is running. A hissing sound will be heard. A soapy water solution will also detect leaks. Check the intake manifold gasket surfaces.
2 Leaking EGR valve or plugged PCV valve (see Chapters 1 and 6).
3 Air filter clogged (Chapter 1).
4 Fuel pump not delivering sufficient fuel (Chapter 4).
5 Leaking head gasket. Perform a cylinder compression check (Chapter 2).
6 Timing chain worn (Chapter 2C).
7 Camshaft lobes worn (Chapter 2).
8 Valve clearance out of adjustment (Chapter 1).
9 Valves burned or otherwise leaking (Chapter 2).
10 Ignition timing out of adjustment (Chapter 1).
11 Ignition system not operating properly (Chapters 1 and 5).
12 Thermostatic air cleaner not operating properly (Chapter 1).

13 Cold start injector and thermal time switch not operating properly (3.0L engines only) (Chapter 4).
14 Dirty or clogged injector(s). (Chapter 4).
15 Idle speed out of adjustment (Chapter 1).

9 Engine misses at idle speed

1 Spark plugs faulty or not gapped properly (Chapter 1).
2 Faulty spark plug wires (Chapter 1).
3 Wet or damaged distributor components (Chapter 1).
4 Short circuits in ignition, coil or spark plug wires.
5 Sticking or faulty emissions systems (see Chapter 6).
6 Clogged fuel filter and/or foreign matter in fuel. Remove the fuel filter (Chapter 1) and inspect.
7 Vacuum leaks at intake manifold or hose connections. Check as described in Section 8.
8 Incorrect idle speed (Chapter 1) or idle mixture (Chapter 4).
9 Incorrect ignition timing (Chapter 1).
10 Low or uneven cylinder compression. Check as described in Chapter 2.
11 Cold start injector and thermal time switch not operating properly (3.0L engines only) (Chapter 4).
12 Clogged or dirty fuel injectors (Chapter 4).

10 Excessively high idle speed

1 Sticking throttle linkage (Chapter 4).
2 Idle speed incorrectly adjusted (Chapter 1).
3 Intake air leak (Chapters 2 and 4).
4 Malfunction in the engine management system (Chapter 6).

11 Battery will not hold a charge

1 Alternator drivebelt defective or not adjusted properly (Chapter 1).
2 Battery cables loose or corroded (Chapter 1).
3 Alternator not charging properly (Chapter 5).
4 Loose, broken or faulty wires in the charging circuit (Chapter 5).
5 Short circuit causing a continuous drain on the battery.
6 Battery defective internally.

12 Alternator light stays on

1 Fault in alternator or charging circuit (Chapter 5).
2 Alternator drivebelt defective or not properly adjusted (Chapter 1).

13 Alternator light fails to come on when key is turned on

1 Faulty bulb (Chapter 12).
2 Defective alternator (Chapter 5).
3 Fault in the printed circuit, dash wiring or bulb holder (Chapter 12).

14 Engine misses throughout driving speed range

1 Fuel filter clogged and/or impurities in the fuel system. Check fuel filter (Chapter 1) or clean system (Chapter 4).
2 Faulty or incorrectly gapped spark plugs (Chapter 1).
3 Incorrect ignition timing (Chapter 1).
4 Cracked distributor cap, disconnected distributor wires or damaged distributor components (Chapter 1).
5 Defective spark plug wires (Chapter 1).
6 Emissions system components faulty (Chapter 6).
7 Low or uneven cylinder compression pressures. Check as described in Chapter 2.
8 Weak or faulty ignition coil (Chapter 5).
9 Weak or faulty ignition system (Chapter 5).
10 Vacuum leaks at intake manifold or vacuum hoses (see Section 8).
11 Dirty or clogged fuel injector (Chapter 4).
12 Leaky EGR valve (Chapter 6).
13 Idle speed out of adjustment (Chapter 1).

15 Hesitation or stumble during acceleration

1 Ignition timing incorrect (Chapter 1).
2 Ignition system not operating properly (Chapter 5).
3 Dirty or clogged fuel injector (Chapter 4).
4 Low fuel pressure. Check for proper operation of the fuel pump and for restrictions in the fuel filter and lines (Chapter 4A).
5 Fault with the fuel injection or engine management system (Chapter 4 or 6).

16 Engine stalls

1 Idle speed incorrect (Chapter 1).
2 Fuel filter clogged and/or water and impurities in the fuel system (Chapter 1).
3 Damaged or wet distributor cap and wires.
4 Emissions system components faulty (Chapter 6).
5 Faulty or incorrectly gapped spark plugs (Chapter 1). Also check the spark plug wires (Chapter 1).
6 Vacuum leak at the throttle body, the intake manifold or vacuum hoses. Check as described in Section 8.

7 Valve clearances incorrect (Chapter 1).
8 Fault with the fuel injection or engine management system (Chapter 4 or 6).

17 Engine lacks power

1 Incorrect ignition timing (Chapter 1).
2 Excessive play in distributor shaft. At the same time check for faulty distributor cap, wires, etc. (Chapter 1).
3 Faulty or incorrectly gapped spark plugs (Chapter 1).
4 Air filter dirty (Chapter 1).
5 Faulty ignition coil (Chapter 5).
6 Brakes binding (Chapters 1 and 10).
7 Automatic transmission fluid level incorrect, causing slippage (Chapter 1).
8 Clutch slipping (Chapter 8).
9 Fuel filter clogged and/or impurities in the fuel system (Chapters 1 and 4).
10 EGR system not functioning properly (Chapter 6).
11 Use of sub-standard fuel. Fill tank with proper octane fuel.
12 Low or uneven cylinder compression pressures. Check as described in Chapter 2D.
13 Air leak at intake manifold (check as described in Section 8).
14 Fault with the fuel injection or engine management system (Chapter 4 or 6).

18 Engine backfires

1 EGR system not functioning properly (Chapter 6).
2 Ignition timing incorrect (Chapter 1).
3 Thermostatic air cleaner system not operating properly (Chapter 6).
4 Vacuum leak (refer to Section 8).
5 Valve clearances incorrect (Chapter 1).
6 Damaged valve springs or sticking valves (Chapter 2).
7 Intake air leak (see Section 8).

19 Engine surges while holding accelerator steady

1 Intake air leak (see Section 8).
2 Fuel pump not working properly (Chapter 4).
3 Fault with the fuel injection or engine management system (Chapter 4 or 6).

20 Pinging or knocking engine sounds when engine is under load

1 Incorrect grade of fuel. Fill tank with fuel of the proper octane rating.
2 Ignition timing incorrect (Chapter 1).
3 Carbon build-up in combustion chambers. Remove cylinder heads and clean com-

bustion chambers (Chapter 2).
4   Incorrect spark plugs (Chapter 1).

21   Engine diesels (continues to run) after being turned off

1   Idle speed too high (Chapter 1).
2   Ignition timing incorrect (Chapter 1).
3   Incorrect spark plug heat range (Chapter 1).
4   Intake air leak (see Section 8).
5   Carbon build-up in combustion chambers. Remove the cylinder heads and clean the combustion chambers (Chapter 2).
6   Valves sticking (Chapter 2).
7   Valve clearances incorrect (Chapter 1).
8   EGR system not operating properly (Chapter 6).
9   Fuel shut-off system not operating properly (Chapter 6).
10   Check for causes of overheating (Section 27).

22   Low oil pressure

1   Improper grade of oil.
2   Oil pump worn or damaged (Chapter 2).
3   Engine overheating (refer to Section 27).
4   Clogged oil filter (Chapter 1).
5   Clogged oil strainer (Chapter 2).
6   Oil pressure gauge not working properly (Chapter 2C).

23   Excessive oil consumption

1   Loose oil drain plug.
2   Loose bolts or damaged oil pan gasket (Chapter 2).
3   Loose bolts or damaged front cover gasket (Chapter 2).
4   Front or rear crankshaft oil seal leaking (Chapter 2).
5   Loose bolts or damaged rocker arm cover gasket (Chapter 2).
6   Loose oil filter (Chapter 1).
7   Loose or damaged oil pressure switch (Chapter 2).
8   Pistons and cylinders excessively worn (Chapter 2).
9   Piston rings not installed correctly on pistons (Chapter 2).
10   Worn or damaged piston rings (Chapter 2).
11   Intake and/or exhaust valve oil seals worn or damaged (Chapter 2).
12   Worn valve stems.
13   Worn or damaged valves/guides (Chapter 2).

24   Excessive fuel consumption

1   Dirty or clogged air filter element (Chapter 1).
2   Incorrect ignition timing (Chapter 1).

3   Incorrect idle speed (Chapter 1).
4   Low tire pressure or incorrect tire size (Chapter 11).
5   Fuel leakage. Check all connections, lines and components in the fuel system (Chapter 4A).
6   Dirty or clogged fuel injectors (Chapter 4).
7   Fault with the fuel injection or engine management system (Chapter 4 or 6).

25   Fuel odor

1   Fuel leakage. Check all connections, lines and components in the fuel system (Chapter 4).
2   Fuel tank overfilled. Fill only to automatic shut-off.
3   Charcoal canister filter in Evaporative Emissions Control system clogged (Chapter 1).
4   Vapor leaks from Evaporative Emissions Control system lines (Chapter 6).

26   Miscellaneous engine noises

1   A strong dull noise that becomes more rapid as the engine accelerates indicates worn or damaged crankshaft bearings or an unevenly worn crankshaft. To pinpoint the trouble spot, remove the spark plug wire from one plug at a time and crank the engine over. If the noise stops, the cylinder with the removed plug wire indicates the problem area. Replace the bearing and/or service or replace the crankshaft (Chapter 2).
2   A similar (yet slightly higher pitched) noise to the crankshaft knocking described in the previous paragraph, that becomes more rapid as the engine accelerates, indicates worn or damaged connecting rod bearings (Chapter 2). The procedure for locating the problem cylinder is the same as described in Paragraph 1.
3   An overlapping metallic noise that increases in intensity as the engine speed increases, yet diminishes as the engine warms up indicates abnormal piston and cylinder wear (Chapter 2). To locate the problem cylinder, use the procedure described in Paragraph 1.
4   A rapid clicking noise that becomes faster as the engine accelerates indicates a worn piston pin or piston pin hole. This sound will happen each time the piston hits the highest and lowest points in the stroke (Chapter 2). The procedure for locating the problem piston is described in Paragraph 1.
5   A metallic clicking noise coming from the water pump indicates worn or damaged water pump bearings or pump. Replace the water pump with a new one (Chapter 3).
6   A rapid tapping sound or clicking sound that becomes faster as the engine speed increases indicates "valve tapping" or improperly adjusted valve clearances. This can be identified by holding one end of a sec-

tion of hose to your ear and placing the other end at different spots along the rocker arm cover. The point where the sound is loudest indicates the problem valve. Adjust the valve clearance (Chapter 1). If the problem persists, you likely have a collapsed valve lifter or other damaged valve train component. Changing the engine oil and adding a high viscosity oil treatment will sometimes cure a stuck lifter problem. If the problem still persists, the lifters, pushrods and rocker arms must be removed for inspection (see Chapter 2).
7   A steady metallic rattling or rapping sound coming from the area of the timing chain cover indicates a worn, damaged or out-of-adjustment timing chain. Service or replace the chain and related components (Chapter 2).

Cooling system

27   Overheating

1   Insufficient coolant in system (Chapter 1).
2   Drivebelt defective or not adjusted properly (Chapter 1).
3   Radiator core blocked or radiator grille dirty or restricted (Chapter 3).
4   Thermostat faulty (Chapter 3).
5   Fan not functioning properly (Chapter 3).
6   Radiator cap not maintaining proper pressure. Have cap pressure tested by gas station or repair shop.
7   Ignition timing incorrect (Chapter 1).
8   Defective water pump (Chapter 3).
9   Improper grade of engine oil.
10   Inaccurate temperature gauge (Chapter 12).

28   Overcooling

1   Thermostat faulty (Chapter 3).
2   Inaccurate temperature gauge (Chapter 12).

29   External coolant leakage

1   Deteriorated or damaged hoses. Loose clamps at hose connections (Chapter 1).
2   Water pump seals defective. If this is the case, water will drip from the weep hole in the water pump body (Chapter 3).
3   Leakage from radiator core or header tank. This will require the radiator to be professionally repaired (see Chapter 3 for removal procedures).
4   Engine drain plugs or water jacket freeze plugs leaking (see Chapters 1 and 2).
5   Leak from coolant temperature switch (Chapter 3).
6   Leak from damaged gaskets or small

cracks (Chapter 2).
7   Damaged head gasket. This can be verified by checking the condition of the engine oil as noted in Section 30.

30 Internal coolant leakage

Note: *Internal coolant leaks can usually be detected by examining the oil. Check the dipstick and inside the rocker arm cover for water deposits and an oil consistency like that of a milkshake.*

1   Leaking cylinder head gasket. Have the system pressure tested or remove the cylinder head (Chapter 2) and inspect.
2   Cracked cylinder bore or cylinder head. Dismantle engine and inspect (Chapter 2).
3   Loose cylinder head bolts (tighten as described in Chapter 2).

31 Abnormal coolant loss

1   Overfilling system (Chapter 1).
2   Coolant boiling away due to overheating (see causes in Section 27).
3   Internal or external leakage (see Sections 29 and 30).
4   Faulty radiator cap. Have the cap pressure tested.
5   Cooling system being pressurized by engine compression. This could be due to a cracked head or block or leaking head gaskets.

32 Poor coolant circulation

1   Inoperative water pump. A quick test is to pinch the top radiator hose closed with your hand while the engine is idling, then release it. You should feel a surge of coolant if the pump is working properly (Chapter 3).
2   Restriction in cooling system. Drain, flush and refill the system (Chapter 1). If necessary, remove the radiator (Chapter 3) and have it reverse flushed or professionally cleaned.
3   Loose water pump drivebelt (Chapter 1).
4   Thermostat sticking (Chapter 3).
5   Insufficient coolant (Chapter 1).

33 Corrosion

1   Excessive impurities in the water. Soft, clean water is recommended. Distilled or rainwater is satisfactory.
2   Insufficient antifreeze solution (refer to Chapter 1 for the proper ratio of water to antifreeze).
3   Infrequent flushing and draining of system. Regular flushing of the cooling system should be carried out at the specified intervals as described in (Chapter 1).

Clutch

Note: *All clutch related service information is located in Chapter 8, unless otherwise noted.*

34 Fails to release (pedal pressed to the floor - shift lever does not move freely in and out of Reverse)

1   Freeplay incorrectly adjusted.
2   Clutch contaminated with oil. Remove clutch plate and inspect.
3   Clutch plate warped, distorted or otherwise damaged.
4   Diaphragm spring fatigued. Remove clutch cover/pressure plate assembly and inspect.
5   Leakage of fluid from clutch hydraulic system. Inspect master cylinder, operating cylinder and connecting lines.
6   Air in clutch hydraulic system. Bleed the system.
7   Insufficient pedal stroke. Check and adjust as necessary.
8   Piston seal in master or release cylinder deformed or damaged.
9   Lack of grease on pilot bearing.

35 Clutch slips (engine speed increases with no increase in vehicle speed)

1   Worn or oil-soaked clutch plate.
2   Clutch plate not broken in. It may take 30 or 40 normal starts for a new clutch to seat.
3   Diaphragm spring weak or damaged. Remove clutch cover/pressure plate assembly and inspect.
4   Debris in master cylinder preventing the piston from returning to its normal position.
5   Clutch hydraulic line damaged internally (not allowing fluid to return to the clutch master cylinder).
6   Binding in the release mechanism.

36 Grabbing (chattering) as clutch is engaged

1   Oil on clutch plate. Remove and inspect. Repair any leaks.
2   Worn or loose engine or transmission mounts. They may move slightly when clutch is released. Inspect mounts and bolts.
3   Worn splines on transmission input shaft. Remove clutch components and inspect.
4   Warped pressure plate or flywheel. Remove clutch components and inspect.
5   Diaphragm spring fatigued. Remove clutch cover/pressure plate assembly and inspect.
6   Clutch linings hardened or warped.
7   Clutch lining rivets loose.

37 Squeal or rumble with clutch engaged (pedal released)

1   Improper pedal adjustment. Adjust pedal freeplay.
2   Release bearing binding on transmission shaft. Remove clutch components and check bearing. Remove any burrs or nicks, clean and relubricate before reinstallation.
3   Pilot bearing worn or damaged.
4   Clutch rivets loose.
5   Clutch plate cracked.
6   Fatigued clutch plate torsion springs. Replace clutch plate.

38 Squeal or rumble with clutch disengaged (pedal depressed)

1   Worn or damaged release bearing.
2   Worn or broken pressure plate diaphragm fingers.

39 Clutch pedal stays on floor when disengaged

Binding linkage or release bearing. Inspect linkage or remove clutch components as necessary.

Manual transmission

Note: *All manual transmission service information is located in Chapter 7A, unless otherwise noted.*

40 Noisy in Neutral with engine running

1   Input shaft bearing worn.
2   Damaged main drive gear bearing.
3   Insufficient transmission oil (Chapter 1).
4   Transmission oil in poor condition. Drain and fill with proper grade oil. Check old oil for water and debris (Chapter 1).
5   Noise can be caused by variations in engine torque. Change the idle speed and see if noise disappears.

41 Noisy in all gears

1   Any of the above causes, and/or:
2   Worn or damaged output gear bearings or shaft.

42 Noisy in one particular gear

1   Worn, damaged or chipped gear teeth.
2   Worn or damaged synchronizer.

43 Slips out of gear

1 Stiff shift lever seal.
2 Shift linkage binding.
3 Broken or loose input gear bearing retainer.
4 Dirt between clutch lever and engine housing.
5 Worn linkage.
6 Damaged or worn check balls, fork rod ball grooves or check springs.
7 Worn mainshaft or countershaft bearings.
8 Loose engine mounts (Chapter 2).
9 Excessive gear end play.
10 Worn synchronizers.

44 Oil leaks

1 Excessive amount of lubricant in transmission (see Chapter 1 for correct checking procedures). Drain lubricant as required.
2 Rear oil seal or speedometer oil seal damaged.
3 To pinpoint a leak, first remove all built-up dirt and grime from the transmission. Degreasing agents and/or steam cleaning will achieve this. With the underside clean, drive the vehicle at low speeds so the air flow will not blow the leak far from its source. Raise the vehicle and determine where the leak is located.

45 Difficulty engaging gears

1 Clutch not releasing completely.
2 Loose or damaged shift linkage. Make a thorough inspection, replacing parts as necessary.
3 Insufficient transmission oil (Chapter 1).
4 Transmission oil in poor condition. Drain and fill with proper grade oil. Check oil for water and debris (Chapter 1).
5 Worn or damaged striking rod.
6 Sticking or jamming gears.

46 Noise occurs while shifting gears

1 Check for proper operation of the clutch (Chapter 8).
2 Faulty synchronizer assemblies.

Automatic transmission

Note: *Due to the complexity of the automatic transmission, it's difficult for the home mechanic to properly diagnose and service. For problems other than the following, the vehicle should be taken to a reputable mechanic.*

47 Fluid leakage

1 Automatic transmission fluid is a deep red color, and fluid leaks should not be confused with engine oil which can easily be blown by air flow to the transmission.
2 To pinpoint a leak, first remove all built-up dirt and grime from the transmission. Degreasing agents and/or steam cleaning will achieve this. With the underside clean, drive the vehicle at low speeds so the air flow will not blow the leak far from its source. Raise the vehicle and determine where the leak is located. Common areas of leakage are:
a) **Fluid pan:** *tighten mounting bolts and/or replace pan gasket as necessary (Chapter 1).*
b) **Rear extension:** *tighten bolts and/or replace oil seal as necessary.*
c) **Filler pipe:** *replace the rubber oil seal where pipe enters transmission case.*
d) **Transmission oil lines:** *tighten fittings where lines enter transmission case and/or replace lines.*
e) **Vent pipe:** *transmission overfilled and/or water in fluid (see checking procedures, Chapter 1).*
f) **Speedometer connector:** *replace the O-ring where speedometer cable enters transmission case.*

48 General shift mechanism problems

Chapter 7B deals with checking and adjusting the shift linkage on automatic transmissions. Common problems which may be caused by out of adjustment linkage are:
a) *Engine starting in gears other than P (park) or N (Neutral).*
b) *Indicator pointing to a gear other than the one actually engaged.*
c) *Vehicle moves with transmission in P (Park) position.*

49 Transmission will not downshift with the accelerator pedal pressed to the floor

Chapter 7B deals with adjusting the throttle valve cable to enable the transmission to downshift properly.

50 Engine will start in gears other than Park or Neutral

Chapter 7B deals with adjusting the Neutral start switch installed on automatic transmissions.

51 Transmission slips, shifts rough, is noisy or has no drive in forward or Reverse gears

1 There are many probable causes for the above problems, but the home mechanic should concern himself only with one possibility: fluid level.
2 Before taking the vehicle to a shop, check the fluid level and condition as described in Chapter 1. Add fluid, if necessary, or change the fluid and filter if needed. If problems persist, have a professional diagnose the transmission.

Driveshaft

Note: *Refer to Chapter 8, unless otherwise specified, for service information.*

52 Leaks at front of driveshaft

Defective transmission rear seal. See Chapter 7 for replacement procedure. As this is done, check the splined yoke for burrs or roughness that could damage the new seal. Remove burrs with a fine file or whetstone.

53 Knock or clunk when transmission is under initial load (just after transmission is put into gear)

1 Loose or disconnected rear suspension components. Check all mounting bolts and bushings (Chapters 7 and 10).
2 Loose driveshaft bolts. Inspect all bolts and nuts and tighten them securely.
3 Worn or damaged universal joint bearings. Inspect the universal joints (Chapter 8).
4 Worn sleeve yoke and mainshaft spline.

54 Metallic grating sound consistent with vehicle speed

Pronounced wear in the universal joint bearings. Replace U-joints or driveshafts, as necessary.

55 Vibration

Note: *Before blaming the driveshaft, make sure the tires are perfectly balanced and perform the following test.*
1 Install a tachometer inside the vehicle to monitor engine speed as the vehicle is driven. Drive the vehicle and note the engine speed at which the vibration (roughness) is most pronounced. Now shift the transmission to a different gear and bring the engine speed to the same point.
2 If the vibration occurs at the same engine speed (rpm) regardless of which gear the transmission is in, the driveshaft is NOT at fault since the driveshaft speed varies.
3 If the vibration decreases or is eliminated when the transmission is in a different

gear at the same engine speed, refer to the following probable causes.

4 Bent or dented driveshaft. Inspect and replace as necessary.

5 Undercoating or built-up dirt, etc. on the driveshaft. Clean the shaft thoroughly.

6 Worn universal joint bearings. Replace the U-joints or driveshaft as necessary.

7 Driveshaft and/or companion flange out of balance. Check for missing weights on the shaft. Remove driveshaft and reinstall 180-degrees from original position, then recheck. Have the driveshaft balanced if problem persists.

8 Loose driveshaft mounting bolts/nuts.

9 Defective center bearing, if so equipped.

10 Worn transmission rear bushing (Chapter 7).

56 Scraping noise

Make sure the dust cover on the sleeve yoke isn't rubbing on the transmission extension housing.

57 Whining or whistling noise

Defective center bearing, if so equipped.

Rear axle and differential

Note: *For differential servicing information, refer to Chapter 8, unless otherwise specified.*

58 Noise - same when in drive as when vehicle is coasting

1 Road noise. No corrective action available.

2 Tire noise. Inspect tires and check tire pressures (Chapter 1).

3 Front wheel bearings loose, worn or damaged (Chapters 1 and 10).

4 Insufficient differential oil (Chapter 1).

5 Defective differential.

59 Knocking sound when starting or shifting gears

Defective or incorrectly adjusted differential.

60 Noise when turning

Defective differential.

61 Vibration

See probable causes under Driveshaft.

Proceed under the guidelines listed for the driveshaft. If the problem persists, check the rear wheel bearings by raising the rear of the vehicle and spinning the wheels by hand. Listen for evidence of rough (noisy) bearings. Remove and inspect (Chapter 8).

62 Oil leaks

1 Pinion oil seal damaged (Chapter 8).

2 Axleshaft oil seals damaged (Chapter 8).

3 Differential cover leaking. Tighten mounting bolts or replace the gasket as required.

4 Loose filler or drain plug on differential (Chapter 1).

5 Clogged or damaged breather on differential.

Transfer case

Note: *Unless otherwise specified, refer to Chapter 7C for service and repair information.*

63 Gear jumping out of mesh

1 Incorrect control lever freeplay

2 Interference between the control lever and the console.

3 Play or fatigue in the transfer case mounts.

4 Internal wear or incorrect adjustments.

64 Difficult shifting

1 Lack of oil.

2 Internal wear, damage or incorrect adjustment.

65 Noise

1 Lack of oil in transfer case.

2 Noise in 4H and 4L, but not in 2H indicates cause is in the front differential or front axle.

3 Noise in 2H, 4H and 4L indicates cause is in rear differential or rear axle.

4 Noise in 2H and 4H but not in 4L, or in 4L only, indicates internal wear or damage in transfer case.

Brakes

Note: *Before assuming a brake problem exists, make sure the tires are in good condition and inflated properly, the front end alignment is correct and the vehicle is not loaded with weight in an unequal manner. All service procedures for the brakes are included in Chapter 9, unless otherwise noted.*

66 Vehicle pulls to one side during braking

1 Defective, damaged or oil contaminated brake pad on one side. Inspect as described in Chapter 1. Refer to Chapter 10 if replacement is required.

2 Excessive wear of brake pad material or disc on one side. Inspect and repair as necessary (Chapter 9).

3 Loose or disconnected front suspension components. Inspect and tighten all bolts securely (Chapters 1 and 11).

4 Defective caliper assembly. Remove caliper and inspect for stuck piston or damage.

5 Scored or out of round rotor (Chapter 9).

6 Loose caliper mounting bolts (Chapter 9).

7 Incorrect wheel bearing adjustment (Chapter 1).

67 Noise (high-pitched squeal)

1 Front brake pads worn out. This noise comes from the wear sensor rubbing against the disc. Replace pads with new ones immediately!

2 Glazed or contaminated pads.

3 Dirty or scored disc.

4 Bent support plate.

68 Excessive brake pedal travel

1 Partial brake system failure. Inspect entire system (Chapter 1) and correct as required.

2 Insufficient fluid in master cylinder. Check (Chapter 1) and add fluid - bleed system if necessary.

3 Air in system. Bleed system.

4 Brakes out of adjustment. Check the operation of the automatic adjusters.

5 Defective proportioning valve. Replace valve and bleed system.

69 Brake pedal feels spongy when depressed

1 Air in brake lines. Bleed the brake system.

2 Deteriorated rubber brake hoses. Inspect all system hoses and lines. Replace parts as necessary.

3 Master cylinder mounting nuts loose. Inspect master cylinder bolts (nuts) and tighten them securely.

4 Master cylinder faulty.

5 Incorrect shoe or pad clearance.

6 Defective check valve. Replace valve and bleed system.

7 Clogged reservoir cap vent hole.

8 Deformed rubber brake lines.

9 Soft or swollen caliper seals.

10 Poor quality brake fluid. Bleed entire system and fill with new approved fluid.

70 Excessive effort required to stop vehicle

1 Power brake booster not operating properly.
2 Excessively worn linings or pads. Check and replace if necessary.
3 One or more caliper pistons seized or sticking. Inspect and rebuild as required.
4 Brake pads or linings contaminated with oil or grease. Inspect and replace as required.
5 New pads or linings installed and not yet seated. It'll take a while for the new material to seat against the disc or drum.
6 Worn or damaged master cylinder or caliper assemblies. Check particularly for frozen pistons.
7 Also see causes listed under Section 69.

71 Pedal travels to the floor with little resistance

Little or no fluid in the master cylinder reservoir caused by leaking caliper piston(s) or loose, damaged or disconnected brake lines. Inspect entire system and repair as necessary.

72 Brake pedal pulsates during brake application

1 Wheel bearings damaged, worn or out of adjustment (Chapter 1).
2 Caliper not sliding properly due to improper installation or obstructions. Remove and inspect.
3 Disc not within specifications. Remove the disc and check for excessive lateral runout and parallelism. Have the discs resurfaced or replace them with new ones. Also make sure that all discs are the same thickness.
4 Out-of-round rear brake drums. Remove the drums and have them resurfaced or replace them with new ones.

73 Brakes drag (indicated by sluggish engine performance or wheels being very hot after driving)

1 Output rod adjustment incorrect at the brake pedal.
2 Obstructed master cylinder fill port.
3 Master cylinder piston seized in bore.
4 Caliper sticking.
5 Brake pads or shoes worn out.
6 Piston cups in master cylinder or caliper assembly deformed.

7 Parking brake assembly will not release.
8 Clogged brake lines.
9 Wheel bearings out of adjustment (Chapter 1).
10 Brake pedal height improperly adjusted.
11 Wheel cylinder sticking.
12 Improper shoe-to-drum clearance. Adjust as necessary.

74 Rear brakes lock up under light brake application

1 Tire pressures too high.
2 Tires excessively worn (Chapter 1).

75 Rear brakes lock up under heavy brake application

1 Tire pressures too high.
2 Tires excessively worn (Chapter 1).
3 Front brake pads contaminated with oil, mud or water. Clean or replace the pads.
4 Front brake pads excessively worn.
5 Defective master cylinder or caliper assembly.

Suspension and steering

Note: *All service procedures for the suspension and steering systems are included in Chapter 10, unless otherwise noted.*

76 Vehicle pulls to one side

1 Tire pressures uneven (Chapter 1).
2 Defective tire (Chapter 1).
3 Excessive wear in suspension or steering components (Chapter 1).
4 Wheel alignment incorrect.
5 Front brakes dragging. Inspect as described in Section 73.
6 Wheel bearings improperly adjusted (Chapter 1 or 8).
7 Wheel lug nuts loose.

77 Shimmy, shake or vibration

1 Tire or wheel out of balance or out of round. Have them balanced on the vehicle.
2 Loose, worn or out of adjustment wheel bearings (Chapter 1 or 8).
3 Shock absorbers and/or suspension components worn or damaged. Check for worn bushings in the upper and lower links.
4 Wheel lug nuts loose.
5 Incorrect tire pressures.
6 Excessively worn or damaged tire.
7 Loosely mounted steering gear housing.
8 Steering gear improperly adjusted.
9 Loose, worn or damaged steering components.
10 Damaged idler arm.
11 Worn balljoint.

78 Excessive pitching and/or rolling around corners or during braking

1 Defective shock absorbers. Replace as a set.
2 Broken or weak leaf springs and/or suspension components.
3 Worn or damaged stabilizer bar or bushings.

79 Wandering or general instability

1 Improper tire pressures.
2 Worn or damaged upper and lower link or tension rod bushings.
3 Incorrect front end alignment.
4 Worn or damaged steering linkage or suspension components.
5 Improperly adjusted steering gear.
6 Out-of-balance wheels.
7 Loose wheel lug nuts.
8 Worn rear shock absorbers.
9 Fatigued or damaged rear leaf springs.

80 Excessively stiff steering

1 Lack of lubricant in power steering fluid reservoir, where appropriate (Chapter 1).
2 Incorrect tire pressures (Chapter 1).
3 Lack of lubrication at balljoints (Chapter 1).
4 Front end out of alignment.
5 Steering gear out of adjustment or lacking lubrication.
6 Improperly adjusted wheel bearings.
7 Worn or damaged steering gear.
8 Interference of steering column with turn signal switch.
9 Low tire pressures.
10 Worn or damaged balljoints.
11 Worn or damaged steering linkage.
12 See also Section 79.

81 Excessive play in steering

1 Loose wheel bearings (Chapter 1 or 8).
2 Excessive wear in suspension bushings (Chapter 1).
3 Steering gear improperly adjusted.
4 Incorrect wheel alignment.
5 Steering gear mounting bolts loose.
6 Worn steering linkage.

82 Lack of power assistance

1 Steering pump drivebelt faulty or not adjusted properly (Chapter 1).
2 Fluid level low (Chapter 1).
3 Hoses or pipes restricting the flow. Inspect and replace parts as necessary.
4 Air in power steering system. Bleed system.
5 Defective power steering pump.

83 Steering wheel fails to return to straight-ahead position

1 Incorrect front end alignment.
2 Tire pressures low.
3 Steering gear worn or damaged.
4 Steering column out of alignment.
5 Worn or damaged balljoint.
6 Worn or damaged steering linkage.
7 Steering linkage in need of lubrication.
8 Insufficient oil in steering gear.
9 Lack of fluid in power steering pump.

84 Steering effort not the same in both directions (power system)

1 Leaks in steering gear.
2 Clogged fluid passage in steering gear.

85 Noisy power steering pump

1 Insufficient oil in pump.
2 Clogged hoses or oil filter in pump.
3 Loose pulley.
4 Improperly adjusted drivebelt (Chapter 1).
5 Defective pump.

86 Miscellaneous noises

1 Improper tire pressures.
2 Insufficiently lubricated balljoint or steering linkage.
3 Loose or worn steering gear, steering linkage or suspension components.
4 Defective shock absorber.
5 Defective wheel bearing.
6 Worn or damaged suspension bushings.
7 Damaged leaf spring.
8 Loose wheel lug nuts.
9 Worn or damaged rear axleshaft spline.
10 Worn or damaged rear shock absorber mounting bushing.
11 Excessive rear axle end play.
12 See also causes of noises at the rear axle and driveshaft.

87 Excessive tire wear (not specific to one area)

1 Incorrect tire pressures.
2 Tires out of balance. Have them balanced on the vehicle.
3 Wheels damaged. Inspect and replace as necessary.
4 Suspension or steering components worn (Chapter 1).

88 Excessive tire wear on outside edge

1 Incorrect tire pressure.
2 Excessive speed in turns.
3 Front end alignment incorrect (excessive toe-in).

89 Excessive tire wear on inside edge

1 Incorrect tire pressure.
2 Front end alignment incorrect (toe-out).
3 Loose or damaged steering components (Chapter 1).

90 Tire tread worn in one place

1 Tires out of balance. Have them balanced on the vehicle.
2 Damaged or buckled wheel. Inspect and replace if necessary.
3 Defective tire.

Chapter 1
Tune-up and routine maintenance

Contents

Specifications

Recommended lubricants and fluids

Engine oil
Type... API "certified for gasoline engines"
Viscosity .... See accompanying chart

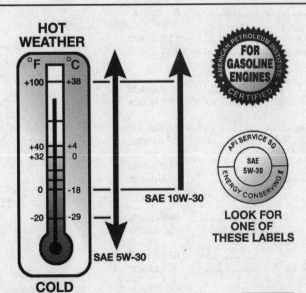

Engine oil viscosity chart - for best fuel economy and cold starting, select the lowest SAE viscosity grade for the expected temperature range

LOOK FOR ONE OF THESE LABELS

1-a3 HAYNES

Recommended lubricants and fluids (continued)

Coolant	
2000 and earlier..	Ethylene glycol based anti-freeze
2001 and later	"Toyota Long-life Coolant" or equivalent
Brake fluid...	DOT 3 brake fluid
Clutch fluid..	DOT 3 brake fluid
Power steering fluid	DEXRON II automatic transmission fluid
Automatic transmission fluid	
All models except 2003 and later 3RZFE and 5VZ engine.................	DEXRON II automatic transmission fluid
2003 and later 3RZFE and 5VZ engine	Toyota T-IV Type ATF
Manual transmission lubricant..	API GL-4 or GL-5 SAE 75W-90 gear oil
Transfer case lubricant	API GL-4 or GL-5 SAE 75W-90 gear oil
Differential lubricant	
Front	API GL-5 SAE 75W-90 hypoid gear oil
Rear	
Above 0 degrees F..	API GL-5 SAE 90 hypoid gear oil
Below 0 degrees F...	API GL-5 SAE 80W-90 hypoid gear oil
Chassis grease	NLGI No. 2 lithium base chassis grease

Capacities*

Engine oil (with filter change)	
Four cylinder engines	
2WD...	5.8 quarts
4WD	
T100...	5.0 quarts
Tacoma and 4Runner	5.7 quarts
3.0L V6 engine (1993 and 1994 T100 only)	
2WD...	5.6 quarts
4WD...	4.8 quarts
3.4L V6 engine	
2WD	
T100...	5.5 quarts
Tacoma	5.7 quarts
4WD	
T100...	5.0 quarts
Tacoma and 4Runner	5.5 quarts
Cooling system	
Four cylinder engines	
2WD	
T100	
Manual transmission	9.2 quarts
Automatic transmission......................................	10.5 quarts
Tacoma	
Manual transmission	8.5 quarts
Automatic transmission......................................	8.2 quarts
4Runner	
With rear heater	11.6 quarts
Without rear heater	10.6 quarts
4WD	
T100	
Manual transmission	10.6 quarts
Automatic transmission......................................	10.8 quarts
Tacoma	
Manual transmission	8.8 quarts
Automatic transmission......................................	8.7 quarts
4Runner	
With rear heater	11.6 quarts
Without rear heater	10.6 quarts
3.0L V6 engine (1993 and 1994 T100 only)	
2WD	
Manual transmission	10.6 quarts
Automatic transmission..	10.5 quarts
4WD	
Manual transmission	10.6 quarts
Automatic transmission..	10.8 quarts

3.4L V6 engine
  2WD
    T100
      Manual transmission .... 10.6 quarts
      Automatic transmission .... 10.5 quarts
    Tacoma
      Manual transmission .... 10.7 quarts
      Automatic transmission .... 10.5 quarts
    4Runner
      With rear heater .... 9.5 quarts
      Without rear heater .... 8.5 quarts
  4WD
    T100
      Manual transmission .... 10.6 quarts
      Automatic transmission .... 10.8 quarts
    Tacoma
      Manual transmission .... 10.7 quarts
      Automatic transmission .... 10.5 quarts
    4Runner
      With rear heater .... 9.5 quarts
      Without rear heater .... 8.5 quarts

Automatic transmission (drain and refill)
  2WD
    1996 Tacoma .... 2.5 quarts
    All others .... 1.7 quarts
  4WD .... 2.1 quarts

Manual transmission (drain and refill)
  Four cylinder engines .... 2.7 quarts
  3.0L V6 engine .... 3.2 quarts
  3.4L V6 engine
    2WD .... 2.7 quarts
    4WD .... 2.3 quarts

Transfer case (drain and refill) .... 1.2 quarts

Differential
  1993 and 1994 T100 models
    Front axle
      4WD
        Auto Differential Disconnect (ADD) .... 2.0 quarts
        Manual Locking Hubs .... 1.7 quarts
    Rear axle
      2WD .... 2.2 quarts
      4WD .... 2.2 quarts
  1995 T100 models
    Front axle
      4WD
        Auto Differential Disconnect (ADD) .... 2.0 quarts
        Manual Locking Hubs .... 1.7 quarts
    Rear axle
      2WD .... 2.5 quarts
      4WD .... 2.2 quarts
  1996 T100 models
    Front axle
      4WD
        Auto Differential Disconnect (ADD) .... 2.0 quarts
        Manual Locking Hubs .... 1.7 quarts
    Rear axle
      2WD .... 2.5 quarts
      4WD .... 2.5 quarts
  1997 and later T100 models
    Front axle .... 2.0 quarts
    Rear axle
      2WD .... 2.9 quarts
      4WD .... 3.1 quarts
  Tacoma models
    Front axle
      4WD
        Auto Differential Disconnect (ADD) .... 1.2 quarts
        Manual Locking Hubs .... 1.2 quarts

Capacities* (continued)

Rear axle
  2WD
    Four-cylinder engines .... 1.4 quarts
    3.4L V6 engines .... 2.7 quarts
  4WD
    Short wheel base
      With rear differential lock system .... 2.8 quarts
      Without rear differential lock system .... 2.7 quarts
    Long wheel base
      With rear differential lock system .... 3.1 quarts
      Without rear differential lock system .... 2.2 quarts
4Runner models
  Front axle
    4WD
      Auto Differential Disconnect (ADD)................................... 1.2 quarts
      Manual Locking Hubs.. 1.2 quarts
  Rear axle
    2WD... 2.9 quarts
    4WD
      With rear differential lock system .... 2.9 quarts
      Without rear differential lock system .... 2.6 quarts

All capacities approximate. Add as necessary to bring to appropriate level.

Spark plug and gap

Four-cylinder and 3.0L V6 2000 and earlier engines
  Type 1.. Nippondenso K16R-U or equivalent @ 0.031 inch
  Type 2.. NGK BKR5EYA or equivalent @ 0.031 inch
2001 and later
  Type 1.. Denso K16R-U or equivalent @ 0.043 inch
  Type 2.. NGK BKR5EYA1 or equivalent @ 0.043 inch
3.4L V6 engine
  Type 1.. Nippondenso K16TR11 or equivalent @ 0.043 inch
  Type 2.. NGK BKR5EKB-11 or equivalent @ 0.043 inch

Idle speed

Four cylinder engines .... 650 to 750 rpm
3.0L V6 engine .... 750 to 850 rpm
3.4L V6 engine .... 650 to 750 rpm

Note 1: *Use the information printed on the Vehicle Emissions Control Information label, if different than the Specifications listed here.*
Note 2: *Refer to Chapter 5 for the ignition timing specifications*

Firing order and distributor rotation

Four cylinder engines
  Firing order 1-3-4-2
  Distributor rotation .... Counterclockwise

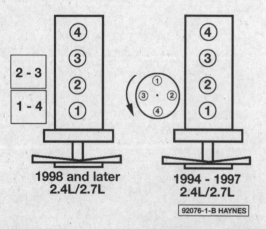

**Cylinder location and distributor rotation diagram -
Four cylinder engines**

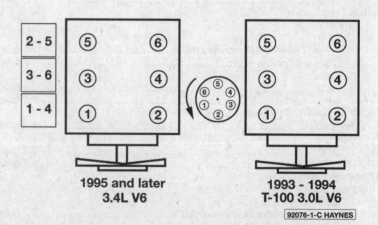

Cylinder location and distributor rotation diagram - V6 engines

3.0L V6 engine
   Firing order 1-2-3-4-5-6
   Distributor rotation .... Counterclockwise
3.4L V6 engine (distributorless ignition system)
   Firing order 1-2-3-4-5-6

Valve clearance

Four cylinder engines (engine cold)
   Intake valve .... 0.007 to 0.009 inch
   Exhaust valve .... 0.010 to 0.013 inch
3.0L V6 engine (engine cold)
   Intake valve .... 0.007 to 0.011 inch
   Exhaust valve .... 0.009 to 0.013 inch
3.4L V6 engine (engine cold)
   Intake valve .... 0.006 to 0.009 inch
   Exhaust valve .... 0.011 to 0.014 inch

Clutch pedal

Height
   T100 models
      1993 and 1994 models .... 5.98 to 6.37 inches
      1995 and later models
         Extra Cab .... 5.91 to 6.30 inches
         All other models .... 6.03 to 6.42 inches
   Tacoma models
      1996 models .... 6.77 to 7.17 inches
      1997 and later models .... 6.57 to 6.97 inches
   4Runner models .... 6.77 to 7.17 inches
Freeplay .... 0.20 to 0.60 inch

Brakes

Disc brake pad lining thickness (minimum) 1/16-inch
Drum brake shoe lining thickness (minimum) 1/16-inch
Brake pedal
   Height
      T100 models
         1993 and 1994 models
            STD .... 6.06 inches
            SR5 .... 5.91 inches
         1995 and later models
            Extra Cab 4WD .... 5.78 to 6.20 inches
            All others .... 5.89 to 6.29 inches
      Tacoma models
         1996 and 1997 models .... 6.28 to 6.68 inches
         1998 models .... 6.09 to 6.48 inches
      4Runner models
         1996 models .... 6.22 to 6.62 inches
         1997 and later models .... 6.34 to 6.74 inches
   Freeplay .... 0.12 to 0.24 inch
Parking brake adjustment
   T100 models .... 11 to 17 clicks
   Tacoma models
      2002 and earlier .... 12 to 18 clicks
      2003 and later .... 16 to 30 clicks
   4Runner models .... 7 to 9 clicks

Suspension and steering

Steering wheel freeplay limit .... 1.58 inches
Balljoint allowable movement .... 0.0 inch

Torque specifications   **Ft-lbs** (unless otherwise indicated)

Automatic transmission pan bolts .... 60 in-lbs
Automatic transmission drain plug 20
Transfer case fill/drain plug 25
Differential fill/drain plug
   Front 20
   Rear 36
Spark plugs 15
Engine oil drain plug 20
Wheel lug nuts 83

Engine compartment component locations - typical four-cylinder engine

1	PCV valve	5	Coolant reservoir	8	Power steering fluid	11 Engine oil filler cap
2	Brake fluid reservoir	6	Battery		reservoir	12 Windshield washer fluid
3	Clutch fluid reservoir	7	Radiator cap	9	Engine oil dipstick	reservoir
4	Fuse box			10	Ignition coil packs	13 Air cleaner housing

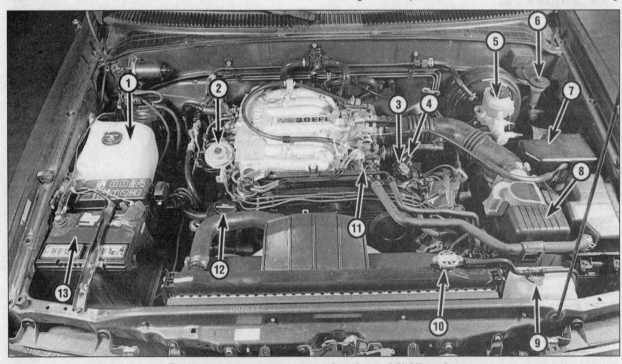

Engine compartment component locations - 3.0L V6 engine

1	Windshield washer	4	Oil level dipstick	8	Air cleaner assembly	12 Power steering fluid
	reservoir	5	Brake fluid reservoir	9	Coolant reservoir	reservoir
2	EGR valve	6	Clutch fluid reservoir	10	Radiator cap	13 Battery
3	Oil filler cap	7	Fuse box assembly	11	Distributor	

Engine compartment component locations - 3.4L engine

1	PCV valve	5	Fuse box	9	Oil level dipstick	12	Windshield washer fluid
2	EGR valve	6	Battery	10	Radiator cap		reservoir
3	Brake fluid reservoir	7	Coolant reservoir	11	Power steering fluid	13	Air cleaner housing
4	Clutch fluid reservoir	8	Oil filler cap		reservoir		

Typical engine compartment underside component locations - 2WD

1	Stabilizer bar	3	Shock absorber	5	Strut rod	6	Steering gear
2	Oil drain plug	4	Coil spring assembly				

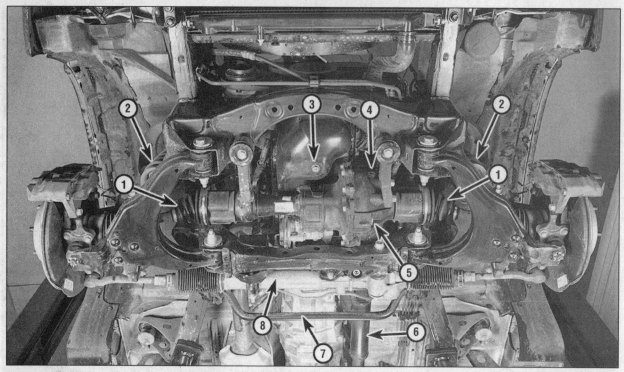

Typical engine compartment underside component locations - 4WD

1	Front driveaxle	3	Oil drain plug	5	Front differential drain plug	7	Stabilizer bar
2	Coil spring	4	Front differential fill plug	6	Front driveshaft	8	Steering gear

Typical rear underside component locations - 2WD

1	Rear brake drum	3	Rear differential fill plug	5	Leaf spring	7	Muffler
2	Rear shock absorber	4	Tail pipe	6	Rear differential drain plug		

1 Toyota T100, Tacoma and 4Runner Maintenance schedule

Every 250 miles or weekly, whichever comes first

Check the engine oil level (Section 4)
Check the engine coolant level (Section 4)
Check the windshield washer fluid level (Section 4)
Check the brake and clutch fluid level (Section 4)
Check the tires and tire pressures (Section 5)

Every 3000 miles or 3 months, whichever comes first

All items listed above, plus . . .
Check the automatic transmission fluid level (Section 6)
Check the power steering fluid level (Section 7)
Change the engine oil and filter (Section 8)

Every 7500 miles or 6 months, whichever comes first

Check and service the battery (Section 9)
Check the cooling system (Section 10)
Inspect and replace, if necessary, all underhood hoses (Section 11)
Inspect and replace, if necessary, the windshield wiper blades (Section 12)
Rotate the tires (Section 13)
Inspect the suspension and steering components (Section 14)
Lubricate the chassis components (Section 15)*
Inspect the exhaust system (Section 16)
Check the manual transmission lubricant (Section 17)
Check the transfer case lubricant level (Section 18)
Check the differential lubricant level (Section 19)
Check the seat belts (Section 20)
Check the idle speed (Section 21)

Every 15,000 miles or 12 months, whichever comes first

All items listed above, plus . . .
Check the driveaxle boots (Section 22)
Check the Positive Crankcase Ventilation (PCV) system (Section 23)
Replace the air filter (Section 24)*
Check the engine drivebelts (Section 25)
Inspect the fuel system (Section 26)
Check the brakes (Section 27)*
Check the clutch pedal for proper height and freeplay (Section 28)

Every 30,000 miles or 24 months, whichever comes first

All items listed above, plus . . .
Replace the spark plugs (Section 29)
Check and adjust if necessary, the valve clearance (Section 30)
Inspect the spark plug wires, distributor cap and rotor (Section 32)
Service the cooling system (drain, flush and refill) (Section 33)
Inspect and repack the front wheel bearings (Section 34)
Change the automatic transmission fluid and filter (Section 35)**
Change the manual transmission lubricant (Section 36)
Change the transfer case lubricant (Section 37)
Change the differential lubricant (Section 38)

Every 60,000 miles or 48 months, whichever comes first

Replace the fuel filter (Section 31)
Inspect the evaporative emissions control system (Section 39)
Check the EGR valve (Section 40)
Replace timing belt (3.0L and 3.4L V6 engines) (Chapter 2B)

Every 80,000 miles

Replace the oxygen sensor (see Chapter 6)

*This item is affected by "severe" operating conditions, as described below. If the vehicle is operated under severe conditions, perform all maintenance indicated with an asterisk (*) at 7500 mile/six-month intervals. Severe conditions exist if you mainly operate the vehicle . . .
in dusty areas
towing a trailer
idling for extended periods and/or driving at low speeds
when outside temperatures remain below freezing and most trips are less than four miles long

**If operated under one or more of the following conditions, change the automatic transmission fluid every 15,000 miles:
in heavy city traffic where the outside temperature regularly reaches 90-degrees F or higher
in hilly or mountainous terrain
frequent trailer pulling

2 Introduction

This Chapter is designed to help the home mechanic maintain the Toyota T100, Tacoma and 4Runner for peak performance, economy, safety and long life.

On the following pages is a master maintenance schedule, followed by Sections dealing specifically with each item on the schedule. Visual checks, adjustments, component replacement and other helpful items are included. Refer to the **accompanying illustrations** of the engine compartment and the underside of the vehicle for the location of various components.

Servicing your T100, Tacoma or 4Runner in accordance with the mileage/time maintenance schedule and the following Sections will provide it with a planned maintenance program that should result in a long and reliable service life. This is a comprehensive plan, so maintaining some items but not others at the specified service intervals will not produce the same results.

As you service your vehicle, you will discover that many of the procedures can, and should, be grouped together because of the nature of the particular procedure you're performing or because of the close proximity of two otherwise unrelated components to one another.

For example, if the vehicle is raised for any reason, you should inspect the exhaust, suspension, steering and fuel systems while you're under the vehicle. When you're rotating the tires, it makes good sense to check the brakes and wheel bearings since the wheels are already removed.

Finally, let's suppose you have to borrow or rent a torque wrench. Even if you only need to tighten the spark plugs, you might as well check the torque of as many critical fasteners as time allows.

The first step of this maintenance program is to prepare yourself before the actual work begins. Read through all Sections pertinent to the procedures you're planning to do, then make a list of and gather together all the parts and tools you will need to do the job. If it looks as if you might run into problems during a particular segment of some procedure, seek advice from your local parts man or dealer service department.

3 Tune-up general information

The term tune-up is used in this manual to represent a combination of individual operations rather than one specific procedure.

If, from the time the vehicle is new, the routine maintenance schedule is followed closely and frequent checks are made of fluid levels and high wear items, as suggested throughout this manual, the engine will be kept in relatively good running condition and the need for additional work will be minimized.

More likely than not, however, there will be times when the engine is running poorly due to lack of regular maintenance. This is even more likely if a used vehicle, which has not received regular and frequent maintenance checks, is purchased. In such cases, an engine tune-up will be needed outside of the regular routine maintenance intervals.

The first step in any tune-up or diagnostic procedure to help correct a poor running engine is a cylinder compression check. A compression check (see Chapter 2, Part C) will help determine the condition of internal engine components and should be used as a guide for tune-up and repair procedures. If, for instance, the compression check indicates serious internal engine wear, a conventional tune-up won't improve the performance of the engine and would be a waste of time and money. Because of its importance, the compression check should be done by someone with the right equipment and the knowledge to use it properly.

The following procedures are those most often needed to bring a generally poor running engine back into a proper state of tune.

Minor tune-up

Check all engine related fluids (Section 4)
Clean, inspect and test the battery (Section 9)
Check the cooling system (Section 10)
Check all underhood hoses (Section 11)
Check the PCV valve (Section 23)
Check the air filter (Section 24)
Replace the spark plugs (Section 29)
Inspect the spark plug wires, distributor cap and rotor (Section 32)
Check and adjust the valve clearances (Section 30)
Check and adjust the idle speed (Section 21)
Check and adjust the ignition timing (Chapter 5)
Check and adjust the drivebelts (Section 25)

Major tune-up

All items listed under Minor tune-up, plus . . .
Check the EGR system (Section 40)
Replace the PCV valve (Section 23)
Replace the air filter (Section 24)
Check the fuel system (Section 26)
Replace the fuel filter (Section 31)
Replace the distributor cap, rotor and spark plug wires (Section 32)
Check the ignition system (Chapter 5)
Check the charging system (Chapter 5)

4 Fluid level checks (every 250 miles or weekly)

Note: *The following are fluid level checks to be done on a 250 mile or weekly basis. Additional fluid level checks can be found in specific maintenance procedures which follow. Regardless of intervals, be alert to fluid leaks under the vehicle which would indicate a fault to be corrected immediately.*

4.2a The engine oil dipstick (arrow) on four cylinder engines is located at the front of the engine

1   Fluids are an essential part of the lubrication, cooling, brake and windshield washer systems. Because the fluids gradually become depleted and/or contaminated during normal operation of the vehicle, they must be periodically replenished. See *Recommended lubricants and fluids* at the beginning of this Chapter before adding fluid to any of the following components. **Note:** *The vehicle must be on level ground when fluid levels are checked.*

Engine oil

Refer to illustrations 4.2a, 4.2b, 4.4 and 4.6
2   The engine oil level is checked with a dipstick that extends through a tube and into the oil pan at the bottom of the engine **(see illustrations)**.
3   The oil level should be checked before the vehicle has been driven, or about 15 minutes after the engine has been shut off. If the oil is checked immediately after driving the vehicle, some of the oil will remain in the upper engine components, resulting in an inaccurate reading on the dipstick.
4   Pull the dipstick out of the tube and wipe all the oil from the end with a clean rag or paper towel. Insert the clean dipstick all

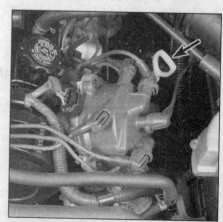

4.2b On 3.0L V6 engines, the oil dipstick (arrow) is located on the left side of the engine

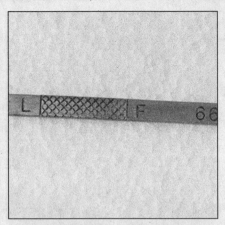

4.4 The oil level must be maintained between the marks at all times - it takes one quart of oil to raise the level from the LOW mark to the FULL mark

4.6 Oil is added to the engine after removing the twist-off cap (arrow) located on the valve cover

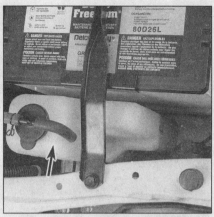

4.8 Check the coolant level in the reservoir (arrow) with the engine hot - it should be visible through the translucent reservoir

the way back into the tube, then pull it out again. Note the oil at the end of the dipstick. Add oil as necessary to keep the level between the ADD and FULL marks on the dipstick **(see illustration)**.

5   Do not overfill the engine by adding too much oil since this may result in oil-fouled spark plugs, oil leaks or oil seal failures.

6   Oil is added to the engine after removing the threaded cap from the valve cover **(see illustration)**. A funnel may help to reduce spills.

7   Checking the oil level is an important preventive maintenance step. A consistently low oil level indicates oil leakage through damaged seals, defective gaskets or past worn rings or valve guides. If the oil looks milky or has water droplets in it, the cylinder head gasket(s) may be blown or the head(s) or block may be cracked. The engine should be checked immediately. The condition of the oil should also be checked. Whenever you check the oil level, slide your thumb and index finger up the dipstick before wiping off the oil. If you see small dirt or metal particles clinging to the dipstick, the oil should be changed (see Section 8).

Engine coolant

Refer to illustration 4.8

Warning: *Do not allow antifreeze to come in contact with your skin or painted surfaces of the vehicle. Flush contaminated areas immediately with plenty of water. Don't store new coolant or leave old coolant lying around where it's accessible to children or pets – they're attracted by its sweet smell. Ingestion of even a small amount of coolant can be fatal! Wipe up garage floor and drip pan spills immediately. Keep antifreeze containers covered and repair cooling system leaks as soon as they're noticed.*

8   All vehicles covered by this manual are equipped with a pressurized coolant recovery system. A coolant reservoir which is located next to the radiator in the engine compartment is connected by a hose to the base of the coolant filler cap **(see illustration)**. Refer

to the underhood photographs at the beginning of this chapter for the exact location. If the coolant gets too hot during engine operation, coolant can escape through a pressurized filler cap, then through a connecting hose into the reservoir. As the engine cools, the coolant is automatically drawn back into the cooling system to maintain the correct level.

9   The coolant level should be checked regularly. It must be between the FULL and LOW lines on the tank. The level will vary with the temperature of the engine. When the engine is cold, the coolant level should be at or slightly above the LOW mark on the tank. Once the engine has warmed up, the level should be at or near the FULL mark. If it isn't, allow the fluid in the tank to cool, then remove the cap from the reservoir and add coolant to bring the level up to the FULL line. Use only ethylene/glycol type coolant and water in the mixture ratio recommended by your owner's manual. Do not use supplemental inhibitor additives. If only a small amount of coolant is required to bring the system up to the proper level, water can be used. However, repeated additions of water will dilute the recommended antifreeze and water solution. In order to maintain the proper ratio of antifreeze and water, it is advisable to top up the coolant level with the correct mixture. Refer to your owner's manual for the recommended ratio.

10   If the coolant level drops within a short time after replenishment, there may be a leak in the system. Inspect the radiator, hoses, engine coolant filler cap, drain plugs and water pump. If no leak is evident, have the radiator cap pressure tested by your dealer.

Warning: *Never remove the radiator cap or the coolant recovery reservoir cap when the engine is running or has just been shut down, because the cooling system is hot. Escaping steam and scalding liquid could cause serious injury.*

11   If it is necessary to open the radiator cap, wait until the system has cooled completely, then wrap a thick cloth around the

cap and turn it to the first stop. If any steam escapes, wait until the system has cooled further, then remove the cap.

12   When checking the coolant level, always note its condition. It should be relatively clear. If it is brown or rust colored, the system should be drained, flushed and refilled. Even if the coolant appears to be normal, the corrosion inhibitors wear out with use, so it must be replaced at the specified intervals.

13   Do not allow antifreeze to come in contact with your skin or painted surfaces of the vehicle. Flush contacted areas immediately with plenty of water.

Windshield washer fluid

Refer to illustration 4.14

14   Fluid for the windshield washer system is located on the right (passenger) side of the engine compartment **(see illustration)**. 4Runners are equipped with a rear window washer system built into the front washer system located near the radiator. Refer to the underhood photographs at the beginning of this chapter for the exact location. In milder climates, plain water can be used to top up the reservoir, but the reservoir should be kept

4.14 The windshield washer fluid reservoir (arrow) is located at the front of the engine compartment

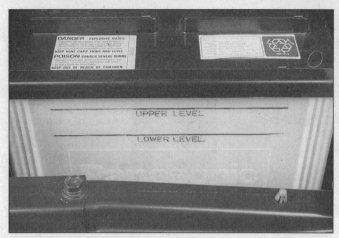

4.15 On some models the battery electrolyte level can be visually checked through the translucent battery case - if the level is to low, there is a problem with the charging system (overcharging) or the battery needs to be replaced

4.17a The fluid level inside the brake reservoir can easily be checked by observing the level from the outside - fluid can be added to the reservoir after the cover is removed by prying up on the cap (later model shown)

no more than two-thirds full to allow for expansion should the water freeze. In colder climates, the use of a specially designed windshield washer fluid, available at your dealer and any auto parts store, will help lower the freezing point of the fluid. Mix the solution with water in accordance with the manufacturer's directions on the container. Do not use regular antifreeze. It will damage the vehicle's paint.

Battery electrolyte

Refer to illustrations 4.15

15   On some batteries, you can check the electrolyte level **(see illustration)** of all six battery cells. It must be between the upper and lower levels. If the level is low, there is a problem with the charging system (overcharging) or the battery needs to be replaced.

Brake and clutch fluid

Refer to illustrations 4.17a and 4.17b

16   The brake master cylinder is mounted

on the front of the power booster unit in the engine compartment. The hydraulic clutch master cylinder used on manual transmission vehicles is located next to the brake master cylinder.

17   To check the fluid level of the brake and clutch master cylinders, simply look at the MAX and MIN marks on the reservoir **(see illustrations)**. The level should be 1/4 inch below the maximum fill line.

18   If the level is low, wipe the top of the reservoir cover with a clean rag to prevent contamination of the brake system before lifting the cover.

19   Add only the specified brake fluid to the brake and clutch reservoirs (refer to *Recommended lubricants and fluids* at the front of this Chapter or to your owner's manual). Mixing different types of brake fluid can damage the system. **Warning:** *Use caution when filling either reservoir - brake fluid can harm your eyes and damage painted surfaces. Do not use brake fluid that has been opened for more than one year or has been left open.*

Brake fluid absorbs moisture from the air. Excess moisture can cause a dangerous loss of braking.

20   While the reservoir cap is removed, inspect the master cylinder reservoir for contamination. If deposits, dirt particles or water droplets are present, the system should be drained and refilled.

21   After filling the reservoir to the proper level, make sure the lid is properly seated to prevent fluid leakage and/or system pressure loss.

22   The fluid in the brake master cylinder will drop slightly as the brake pads at each wheel wear down during normal operation. If either master cylinder requires repeated replenishing to keep it at the proper level, this is an indication of leakage in the brake or clutch system, which should be corrected immediately. If the brake system shows an indication of leakage check all brake lines and connections, along with the calipers, wheel cylinders and booster (see Section 33 for more information). If the hydraulic clutch

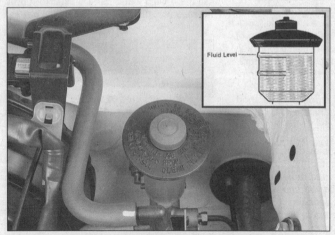

4.17b The fluid level inside the clutch reservoir can easily be checked by observing the level from the outside - fluid can be added to the reservoir after the cover is removed by prying up on the cap (early model shown)

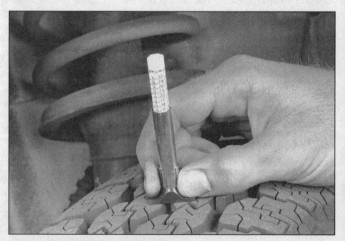

5.2 Use a tire tread depth gauge to monitor tire wear - they are available at auto parts stores and service stations and cost very little

UNDERINFLATION

CUPPING

Cupping may be caused by:
- Underinflation and/or mechanical irregularities such as out-of-balance condition of wheel and/or tire, and bent or damaged wheel.
- Loose or worn steering tie-rod or steering idler arm.
- Loose, damaged or worn front suspension parts.

OVERINFLATION

**INCORRECT TOE-IN
OR EXTREME CAMBER**

**FEATHERING DUE
TO MISALIGNMENT**

**5.3 This chart will help you determine the condition of the tires, the probable cause(s) of abnormal wear
and the corrective action necessary**

system shows an indication of leakage check all clutch lines and connections, along with the clutch release cylinder (see Chapter 8 for more information).

23 If, upon checking the brake or clutch master cylinder fluid level, you discover one or both reservoirs empty or nearly empty, the systems should be bled (see Chapter 9).

5   Tire and tire pressure checks (every 250 miles or weekly)

Refer to illustrations 5.2, 5.3, 5.4a, 5.4b and 5.8

1   Periodic inspection of the tires may spare you the inconvenience of being stranded with a flat tire. It can also provide you with vital information regarding possible problems in the steering and suspension systems before major damage occurs.

2   The original tires on this vehicle are equipped with 1/2-inch wear bands that will appear when tread depth reaches 1/16-inch. Tread wear can be monitored with a simple, inexpensive device known as a tread depth gauge **(see illustration)**.

3   Note any abnormal tread wear **(see illustration)**. Tread pattern irregularities such as cupping, flat spots and more wear on one side than the other are indications of front end alignment and/or balance problems. If any of these conditions are noted, take the

vehicle to a tire shop or service station to correct the problem.

4   Look closely for cuts, punctures and embedded nails or tacks. Sometimes a tire will hold air pressure for a short time or leak down very slowly after a nail has embedded itself in the tread. If a slow leak persists, check the valve stem core to make sure it's tight **(see illustration)**. Examine the tread for an object that may have embedded itself in the tire or for a "plug" that may have begun to

leak (radial tire punctures are repaired with a rubber plug that's installed in the hole). If a puncture is suspected, it can be easily verified by spraying a solution of soapy water onto the puncture area **(see illustration)**. The soapy solution will bubble if there's a leak. Unless the puncture is unusually large, a tire shop or service station can usually repair the tire.

5   Carefully inspect the inner sidewall of each tire for evidence of brake fluid leakage. If

5.4a If a tire loses air on a steady basis, check the valve core first to make sure it's snug (special inexpensive wrenches are commonly available at auto parts stores)

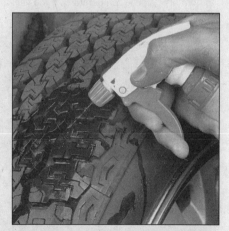

5.4b If the valve core is tight, raise the corner of the vehicle with the low tire and spray a soapy water solution onto the tread as the tire is turned slowly - leaks will cause small bubbles to appear

you see any, inspect the brakes immediately.

6   Correct air pressure adds miles to the lifespan of the tires, improves mileage and enhances overall ride quality. Tire pressure cannot be accurately estimated by looking at a tire, especially if it's a radial. A tire pressure gauge is essential. Keep an accurate gauge in the vehicle. The pressure gauges attached to the nozzles of air hoses at gas stations are often inaccurate.

7   Always check tire pressure when the tires are cold. Cold, in this case, means the vehicle has not been driven over a mile in the three hours preceding a tire pressure check. A pressure rise of four to eight pounds is not uncommon once the tires are warm.

8   Unscrew the valve cap protruding from the wheel or hubcap and push the gauge firmly onto the valve stem (see illustration). Note the reading on the gauge and compare the figure to the recommended tire pressure shown on the placard on the driver's side door pillar. Be sure to reinstall the valve cap to keep dirt and moisture out of the valve stem mechanism. Check all four tires and, if necessary, add enough air to bring them up to the recommended pressure.

9   Don't forget to keep the spare tire inflated to the specified pressure (consult your owner's manual). Note that the air pressure specified for the compact spare is significantly higher than the pressure of the regular tires.

---

6   Automatic transmission fluid level check (every 3000 miles or 3 months)

Refer to illustrations 6.4 and 6.6

1   The level of the automatic transmission fluid should be carefully maintained. Low fluid level can lead to slipping or loss of drive, while overfilling can cause foaming, loss of fluid and transmission damage.

2   The transmission fluid level should only be checked when the transmission is hot (at its normal operating temperature). If the vehi-

cle has just been driven over 10 miles (15 miles in a frigid climate), and the fluid temperature is 160 to 175-degrees F, the transmission is hot. **Caution:** *If the vehicle has just been driven for a long time at high speed or in city traffic in hot weather, or if it has been pulling a trailer, an accurate fluid level reading cannot be obtained. Allow the fluid to cool down for about 30 minutes.*

3   If the vehicle has not been driven, park the vehicle on level ground, set the parking brake, then start the engine and bring it to operating temperature. While the engine is idling, depress the brake pedal and move the selector lever through all the gear ranges, beginning and ending in Park.

4   With the engine still idling, remove the dipstick from its tube (see illustration). Check the level of the fluid on the dipstick and note its condition. Refer to the underhood photographs at the beginning of this chapter for the exact location of the automatic transmission dipstick.

5   Wipe the fluid from the dipstick with a clean rag and reinsert it back into the filler tube until the cap seats.

6   Pull the dipstick out again and note the fluid level (see illustration). If the transmission is cold, the level should be in the COLD or COOL range on the dipstick. If it is hot, the fluid level should be in the HOT range. If the level is at the low side of either range, add the specified automatic transmission fluid through the dipstick tube with a funnel.

7   Add just enough of the recommended fluid to fill the transmission to the proper level. It takes about one pint to raise the level from the low mark to the high mark when the fluid is hot, so add the fluid a little at a time and keep checking the level until it is correct.

8   The condition of the fluid should also be checked along with the level. If the fluid at the end of the dipstick is black or a dark reddish brown color, or if it emits a burned smell, the fluid should be changed (see Section 35). If you are in doubt about the condition of the fluid, purchase some new fluid and compare the two for color and smell.

5.8 To extend the life of the tires, check the air pressure at least once a week with an accurate gauge (don't forget the spare)

---

7   Power steering fluid level check (every 3000 miles or 3 months)

Refer to illustrations 7.2 and 7.6

1   Unlike manual steering, the power steering system relies on fluid which may, over a period of time, require replenishing.

2   The fluid reservoir for the power steering pump on most models is located on the pump body at the front of the engine. Later models are equipped with a remote fluid reservoir which is mounted on the right side of the engine (see illustration).

3   For the check, the front wheels should be pointed straight ahead and the engine should be off.

4   Use a clean rag to wipe off the reservoir cap and the area around the cap. This will help prevent any foreign matter from entering the reservoir during the check.

5   Twist off the cap and determine the temperature of the fluid at the end of the dipstick with your finger.

6   Wipe off the fluid with a clean rag, reinsert the dipstick, then withdraw it and read the fluid level. The fluid should be at the proper level, depending on whether it was

6.4 The automatic transmission fluid dipstick is located at the rear of the engine compartment

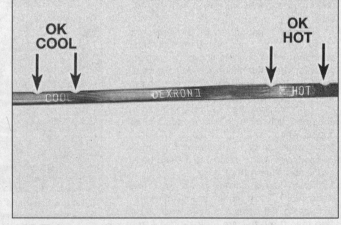

6.6 The automatic transmission fluid level must be maintained between the notches at the indicated operating temperature

7.2 The power steering fluid dipstick is located in the power steering pump reservoir - turn the cap (arrow) counterclockwise to remove it

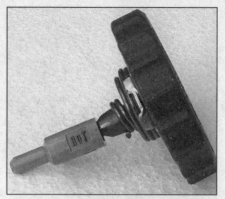

7.6 The marks on the dipstick indicate the safe fluid range

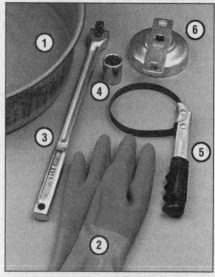

8.2 These tools are required when changing the engine oil and filter

checked hot or cold **(see illustration)**. Never allow the fluid level to drop below the lower mark on the dipstick.

7   If additional fluid is required, pour the specified type directly into the reservoir, using a funnel to prevent spills.

8   If the reservoir requires frequent fluid additions, all power steering hoses, hose connections and the power steering pump should be carefully checked for leaks.

8   Engine oil and filter change (every 3000 miles or 3 months)

Refer to illustrations 8.2, 8.7, 8.13 and 8.15

1   Frequent oil changes are the best preventive maintenance the home mechanic can give the engine, because aging oil becomes diluted and contaminated, which leads to premature engine wear.

2   Make sure that you have all the necessary tools before you begin this procedure **(see illustration)**. You should also have plenty of rags or newspapers handy for mopping up any spills.

3   Access to the underside of the vehicle is greatly improved if the vehicle can be lifted on a hoist, driven onto ramps or supported by jackstands.

4   If this is your first oil change, get under the vehicle and familiarize yourself with the location of the oil drain plug. The engine and exhaust components will be warm during the actual work, so try to anticipate any potential problems before the engine and accessories are hot.

5   Park the vehicle on a level spot. Start the engine and allow it to reach its normal operating temperature (the needle on the temperature gauge should be at least above the bottom mark). Warm oil and contaminates will flow out more easily. Turn off the engine when it's warmed up. Remove the filler cap in the valve cover.

6   Raise the vehicle and support it on jackstands. **Warning:** *To avoid personal injury, never get beneath the vehicle when it is supported by only by a jack. The jack provided with your vehicle is designed solely for raising*

the vehicle to remove and replace the wheels. Always use jackstands to support the vehicle when it becomes necessary to place your body underneath the vehicle.

7   Being careful not to touch the hot exhaust components, place the drain pan under the drain plug in the bottom of the pan and remove the plug **(see illustration)**. You may want to wear gloves while unscrewing the plug the final few turns if the engine is really hot.

8   Allow the old oil to drain into the pan. It may be necessary to move the pan farther under the engine as the oil flow slows to a trickle. Inspect the old oil for the presence of metal shavings and chips.

9   After all the oil has drained, wipe off the drain plug with a clean rag. Even minute metal particles clinging to the plug would immediately contaminate the new oil.

10   Clean the area around the drain plug opening, reinstall the plug and tighten it securely, but do not strip the threads.

11   Move the drain pan into position under the oil filter.

12   Remove all tools, rags, etc. from under the vehicle, being careful not to spill the oil in the drain pan, then lower the vehicle.

13   Loosen the oil filter by turning it counterclockwise with the filter wrench **(see illustra-**

1   Drain pan - It should be fairly shallow in depth, but wide to prevent spills

2   Rubber gloves - When removing the drain plug and filter, you will get oil on your hands (the gloves will prevent burns)

3   Breaker bar - Sometimes the oil drain plug is tight, and a long breaker bar is needed to loosen it

4   Socket - To be used with the breaker bar or a ratchet (must be the correct size to fit the drain plug)

5   Filter wrench - This is a metal band-type wrench, which requires clearance around the filter to be effective

6   Filter wrench - This type fits on the bottom of the filter and can be turned with a ratchet or breaker bar (different size wrenches are available for different types of filters)

tion). Any standard filter wrench should work. Once the filter is loose, use your hands to unscrew it from the block. Just as the filter is detached from the block, immediately tilt the open end up to prevent the oil inside the filter

8.7 The engine oil drain plug is located on the bottom of the oil pan - it is usually very tight, so use the proper size box end wrench or socket to avoid rounding it off

8.13 The oil filter is usually on very tight and will require a special wrench for removal - DO NOT use the wrench to tighten the new filter!

from spilling out. **Warning:** *The engine exhaust manifold may still be hot, so be careful.*

14   With a clean rag, wipe off the mounting surface on the block. If a residue of old oil is allowed to remain, it will smoke when the block is heated up. It will also prevent the new filter from seating properly. Also make sure that the none of the old gasket remains stuck to the mounting surface. It can be removed with a scraper if necessary.

15   Compare the old filter with the new one to make sure they are the same type. Smear some engine oil on the rubber gasket of the new filter and screw it into place **(see illustration)**. Because over-tightening the filter will damage the gasket, do not use a filter wrench to tighten the filter. Tighten it by hand until the gasket contacts the seating surface. Then seat the filter by giving it an additional 3/4-turn.

16   Add new oil to the engine through the oil filler cap in the valve cover. Use a spout or funnel to prevent oil from spilling onto the top of the engine. Pour three quarts of fresh oil into the engine. Wait a few minutes to allow the oil to drain into the pan, then check the level on the oil dipstick (see Section 4 if necessary). If the oil level is at or near the H mark, install the filler cap hand tight, start the engine and allow the new oil to circulate.

17   Allow the engine to run for about a minute. While the engine is running, look under the vehicle and check for leaks at the oil pan drain plug and around the oil filter. If either is leaking, stop the engine and tighten the plug or filter slightly.

18   Wait a few minutes to allow the oil to trickle down into the pan, then recheck the level on the dipstick and, if necessary, add enough oil to bring the level to the H mark.

19   During the first few trips after an oil change, make it a point to check frequently for leaks and proper oil level.

20   The old oil drained from the engine cannot be reused in its present state and should be discarded. Oil reclamation centers, auto repair shops and gas stations will normally accept the oil, which can be recycled. After the oil has cooled, it can be drained into a suitable container (capped plastic jugs, topped bottles, milk cartons, etc.) for transport to one of these disposal sites.

9   Battery check, maintenance and charging (every 7500 miles or 6 months)

Refer to illustrations 9.1, 9.6a, 9.6b, 9.7a and 9.7b

Warning: *Certain precautions must be followed when checking and servicing the battery. Hydrogen gas, which is highly flammable, is always present in the battery cells, so keep lighted tobacco and all other open flames and sparks away from the battery. The electrolyte inside the battery is actually dilute sulfuric acid, which will cause injury if splashed on your skin or in your eyes. It will*

8.15 Lubricate the oil filter gasket with clean engine oil before installing the filter on the engine

also ruin clothes and painted surfaces. When removing the battery cables, always detach the negative cable first and hook it up last!

Caution: *If the stereo in your vehicle is equipped with an anti-theft system, make sure you have the correct activation code before disconnecting the battery.*

Maintenance

1   A routine preventive maintenance program for the battery in your vehicle is the only way to ensure quick and reliable starts. But before performing any battery maintenance, make sure that you have the proper equipment necessary to work safely around the battery **(see illustration)**.

2   There are also several precautions that should be taken whenever battery maintenance is performed. Before servicing the battery, always turn the engine and all accessories off and disconnect the cable from the negative terminal of the battery.

3   The battery produces hydrogen gas, which is both flammable and explosive. Never create a spark, smoke or light a match around the battery. Always charge the battery in a ventilated area.

4   Electrolyte contains poisonous and corrosive sulfuric acid. Do not allow it to get in your eyes, on your skin on your clothes. Never ingest it. Wear protective safety glasses when working near the battery. Keep children away from the battery.

5   Note the external condition of the battery. If the positive terminal and cable clamp on your vehicle's battery is equipped with a rubber protector, make sure that it's not torn or damaged. It should completely cover the terminal. Look for any corroded or loose connections, cracks in the case or cover or loose hold-down clamps. Also check the entire length of each cable for cracks and frayed conductors.

6   If corrosion, which looks like white, fluffy deposits **(see illustration)** is evident, particularly around the terminals, the battery should be removed for cleaning. Loosen the cable clamp bolts with a wrench, being careful to remove the ground cable first, and slide them

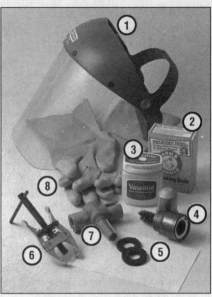

9.1 Tools and materials required for battery maintenance

1   *Face shield/safety goggles - When removing corrosion with a brush, the acidic particles can easily fly up into your eyes*

2   *Baking soda - A solution of baking soda and water can be used to neutralize corrosion*

3   *Petroleum jelly - A layer of this on the battery posts will help prevent corrosion*

4   *Battery post/cable cleaner - This wire brush cleaning tool will remove all traces of corrosion from the battery posts and cable clamps*

5   *Treated felt washers - Placing one of these on each post, directly under the cable clamps, will help prevent corrosion*

6   *Puller - Sometimes the cable clamps are very difficult to pull off the posts, even after the nut/bolt has been completely loosened. This tool pulls the clamp straight up and off the post without damage*

7   *Battery post/cable cleaner - Here is another cleaning tool which is a slightly different version of Number 4 above, but it does the same thing*

8   *Rubber gloves - Another safety item to consider when servicing the battery; remember that's acid inside the battery!*

off the terminals **(see illustration)**. Then disconnect the hold-down clamp bolt and nut, remove the clamp and lift the battery from the engine compartment.

7   Clean the cable clamps thoroughly with a battery brush or a terminal cleaner and a solution of warm water and baking soda **(see illustration)**. Wash the terminals and the top of the battery case with the same solution but make sure that the solution doesn't get into the battery. When cleaning the cables, terminals and battery top, wear safety goggles and

9.6a Battery terminal corrosion usually appears as light, fluffy powder

9.6b Removing the cable from a battery post with a wrench - sometimes special battery pliers are required for this procedure if corrosion has caused deterioration of the nut hex (always remove the ground cable first and hook it up last!)

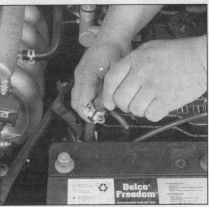

9.7a When cleaning the cable clamps, all corrosion must be removed (the inside of the clamp is tapered to match the taper on the post, so don't remove too much material)

9.7b Regardless of the type of tool used on the battery posts, a clean, shiny surface should be the end result

rubber gloves to prevent any solution from coming in contact with your eyes or hands. Wear old clothes too - even diluted, sulfuric acid splashed onto clothes will burn holes in them. If the terminals have been extensively corroded, clean them up with a terminal cleaner **(see illustration)**. Thoroughly wash all cleaned areas with plain water.

8   Make sure that the battery tray is in good condition and the hold-down clamp bolts are tight. If the battery is removed from the tray, make sure no parts remain in the bottom of the tray when the battery is reinstalled. When reinstalling the hold-down clamp bolts, do not overtighten them.

9   Any metal parts of the vehicle damaged by corrosion should be covered with a zinc-based primer, then painted.

10   Information on removing and installing the battery can be found in Chapter 5. Information on jump starting can be found at the front of this manual. For more detailed battery checking procedures, refer to the *Haynes Automotive Electrical Manual*.

Charging

Warning: *When batteries are being charged, hydrogen gas, which is very explosive and flammable, is produced. Do not smoke or allow open flames near a battery. Wear eye protection when near the battery during*

charging. Also, make sure the charger is unplugged before connecting or disconnecting the battery from the charger.

Note: *The manufacturer recommends the battery be removed from the vehicle for charging because the gas that escapes during this procedure can damage the paint. Fast charging with the battery cables connected can result in damage to the electrical system.*

11   Slow-rate charging is the best way to restore a battery that's discharged to the point where it will not start the engine. It's also a good way to maintain the battery charge in a vehicle that's only driven a few miles between starts. Maintaining the battery charge is particularly important in the winter when the battery must work harder to start the engine and electrical accessories that drain the battery are in greater use.

12   It's best to use a one or two-amp battery charger (sometimes called a "trickle" charger). They are the safest and put the least strain on the battery. They are also the least expensive. For a faster charge, you can use a higher amperage charger, but don't use one rated more than 1/10th the amp/hour rating of the battery. Rapid boost charges that claim to restore the power of the battery in one to two hours are hardest on the battery and can damage batteries not in good condition. This type of charging should only be used in emergency situations.

13   The average time necessary to charge a battery should be listed in the instructions that come with the charger. As a general rule, a trickle charger will charge a battery in 12 to 16 hours.

14   Remove all the cell caps (if equipped) and cover the holes with a clean cloth to prevent spattering electrolyte. Disconnect the negative battery cable and hook the battery charger cable clamps up to the battery posts (positive to positive, negative to negative), then plug in the charger. Make sure it is set at 12-volts if it has a selector switch.

15   If you're using a charger with a rate higher than two amps, check the battery regularly during charging to make sure it doesn't overheat. If you're using a trickle charger, you can safely let the battery charge overnight after you've checked it regularly for the first couple of hours.

16   If the battery has removable cell caps, measure the specific gravity with a hydrometer every hour during the last few hours of the charging cycle. Hydrometers are available inexpensively from auto parts stores - follow the instructions that come with the hydrometer. Consider the battery charged when there's no change in the specific gravity reading for two hours and the electrolyte in the cells is gassing (bubbling) freely. The specific gravity reading from each cell should be very close to the others. If not, the battery probably has a bad cell(s).

17   Some batteries with sealed tops have built-in hydrometers on the top that indicate the state of charge by the color displayed in the hydrometer window. Normally, a bright-colored hydrometer indicates a full charge and a dark hydrometer indicates the battery still needs charging.

18   If the battery has a sealed top and no built-in hydrometer, you can hook up a voltmeter across the battery terminals to check the charge. A fully charged battery should read 12.6 volts or higher after the surface charge has been removed.

19   Further information on the battery and jump starting can be found in Chapter 5 and at the front of this manual.

10   Cooling system check (every 7500 miles or 6 months)

Refer to illustration 10.4

1   Many major engine failures can be attributed to a faulty cooling system. If the vehicle is equipped with an automatic transmission, the cooling system also cools the transmission fluid and thus plays an important role in prolonging transmission life.

2   The cooling system should be checked with the engine cold. Do this before the vehicle is driven for the day or after it has been shut off for at least three hours.

3   Remove the radiator cap by turning it to the left until it reaches a stop. If you hear a hissing sound (indicating there is still pressure in the system), wait until this stops. Now press down on the cap with the palm of your hand and continue turning to the left until the cap can be removed. Thoroughly clean the cap, inside and out, with clean water. Also clean the filler neck on the radiator. All traces of corrosion should be removed. The coolant inside the radiator should be relatively transparent. If it is rust colored, the system should be drained and refilled (see Section 33). If the coolant level is not up to the top, add additional antifreeze/coolant mixture (see Section 4).

4   Carefully check the large upper and lower radiator hoses along with the smaller diameter heater hoses which run from the engine to the firewall. Inspect each hose along its entire length, replacing any hose which is cracked, swollen or shows signs of deterioration. Cracks may become more apparent if the hose is squeezed **(see illustration)**. Regardless of condition, it's a good idea to replace hoses with new ones every two years.

5   Make sure all hose connections are tight. A leak in the cooling system will usually show up as white or rust colored deposits on the areas adjoining the leak. If wire-type clamps are used at the ends of the hoses, it may be a good idea to replace them with more secure screw-type clamps.

6   Use compressed air or a soft brush to remove bugs, leaves, etc. from the front of the radiator or air conditioning condenser. Be careful not to damage the delicate cooling fins or cut yourself on them.

7   Every other inspection, or at the first indication of cooling system problems, have the cap and system pressure tested. If you don't have a pressure tester, most gas stations and repair shops will do this for a minimal charge.

11   Underhood hose check and replacement (every 7500 miles or 6 months)

General

1   **Warning:** *Replacement of air conditioning hoses must be left to a dealer service department or air conditioning shop that has the equipment to depressurize the system safely. Never remove air conditioning components or hoses until the system has been depressurized.*

2   High temperatures in the engine compartment can cause the deterioration of the rubber and plastic hoses used for engine, accessory and emission systems operation. Periodic inspection should be made for cracks, loose clamps, material hardening and leaks. Information specific to the cooling system hoses can be found in Section 10.

3   Some, but not all, hoses are secured to the fittings with clamps. Where clamps are used, check to be sure they haven't lost their tension, allowing the hose to leak. If clamps aren't used, make sure the hose has not expanded and/or hardened where it slips over the fitting, allowing it to leak.

Vacuum hoses

4   It's quite common for vacuum hoses, especially those in the emissions system, to be color coded or identified by colored stripes molded into them. Various systems require hoses with different wall thickness, collapse resistance and temperature resistance. When replacing hoses, be sure the new ones are made of the same material.

5   Often the only effective way to check a hose is to remove it completely from the vehicle. If more than one hose is removed, be sure to label the hoses and fittings to ensure correct installation.

6   When checking vacuum hoses, be sure to include any plastic T-fittings in the check. Inspect the fittings for cracks and the hose where it fits over the fitting for distortion, which could cause leakage.

7   A small piece of vacuum hose (1/4-inch inside diameter) can be used as a stethoscope to detect vacuum leaks. Hold one end of the hose to your ear and probe around vacuum hoses and fittings, listening for the "hissing" sound characteristic of a vacuum leak. **Warning:** *When probing with the vacuum hose stethoscope, be very careful not to come into contact with moving engine components such as the drivebelt, cooling fan, etc.*

Fuel hose

Warning: *There are certain precautions which must be taken when inspecting or servicing fuel system components. Work in a well ventilated area and do not allow open flames (cigarettes, appliance pilot lights, etc.) or bare light bulbs near the work area. Mop up any spills immediately and do not store fuel soaked rags where they could ignite.*

8   Check all rubber fuel lines for deterioration and chafing. Check especially for cracks in areas where the hose bends and just before fittings, such as where a hose attaches to the fuel filter.

9   Only high quality fuel line should be used for fuel line replacement. Never, under any circumstances, use unreinforced vacuum line, clear plastic tubing or water hose for fuel lines.

10   Spring-type clamps are commonly used on fuel lines. These clamps often lose their tension over a period of time, and can be "sprung" during removal. Replace all spring-type clamps with screw clamps whenever a hose is replaced.

Metal lines

11   Sections of metal line are often used in the fuel system. Check carefully to be sure the line has not been bent or crimped and that cracks have not started in the line.

12   If a section of metal fuel line must be replaced, only seamless steel tubing should be used, since copper and aluminum tubing

Check for a chafed area that could fail prematurely.

Check for a soft area indicating the hose has deteriorated inside.

Overtightening the clamp on a hardened hose will damage the hose and cause a leak.

Check each hose for swelling and oil-soaked ends. Cracks and breaks can be located by squeezing the hose.

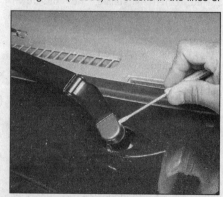

10.4 Hoses, like drivebelts, have a habit of failing at the worst possible time - to prevent the inconvenience of a blown radiator or heater hose, inspect them carefully as shown here

don't have the strength necessary to withstand normal engine vibration.

13   Check the metal brake lines where they enter the master cylinder and brake proportioning unit (if used) for cracks in the lines or

12.3 Pry open the trim cap and check the tightness of the wiper arm retaining nut

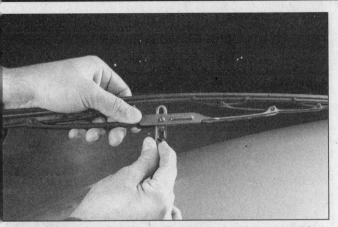

12.5 Press on the release tab, then push the blade assembly down and out of the hook in the arm

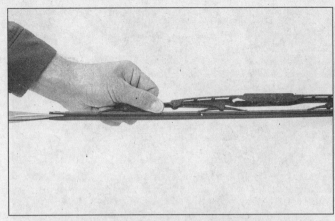

12.6 Use needle-nose pliers to compress the rubber element, then slide the element out - slide the new element in and lock the blade assembly fingers into the notches of the wiper element

loose fittings. Any sign of brake fluid leakage calls for an immediate thorough inspection of the brake system.

12 Wiper blade inspection and replacement (every 7500 miles or 6 months)

Refer to illustrations 12.3, 12.5 and 12.6

1   The windshield wiper and blade assembly should be inspected periodically for damage, loose components and cracked or worn blade elements.

2   Road film can build up on the wiper blades and affect their efficiency, so they should be washed regularly with a mild detergent solution.

3   The action of the wiping mechanism can loosen bolts, nuts and fasteners, so they should be checked and tightened, as necessary **(see illustration)**, at the same time the wiper blades are checked.

4   If the wiper blade elements are cracked, worn or warped, or no longer clean adequately, they should be replaced with new ones.

5   Lift the arm assembly away from the glass for clearance, press on the release lever, then slide the wiper blade assembly out of the hook in the end of the arm **(see illustration)**.

6   Use needle-nose pliers to compress the blade element, then slide the element out of the frame and discard it **(see illustration)**.

7   Installation is the reverse of removal.

13 Tire rotation (every 7500 miles or 6 months)

Refer to illustration 13.2

1   The tires should be rotated at the specified intervals and whenever uneven wear is noticed. Since the vehicle will be raised and the tires removed anyway, check the brakes (see Section 27) at this time.

2   Radial tires must be rotated in a specific pattern **(see illustration)**.

3   Refer to the information in *Jacking and towing* at the front of this manual for the proper procedures to follow when raising the vehicle and changing a tire. If the brakes are to be checked, do not apply the parking brake as stated. Make sure the tires are blocked to prevent the vehicle from rolling.

4   Preferably, the entire vehicle should be raised at the same time. This can be done on a hoist or by jacking up each corner and then lowering the vehicle onto jackstands placed under the frame rails. Always use four jackstands and make sure the vehicle is firmly supported.

5   After rotation, check and adjust the tire pressures as necessary and be sure to check the lug nut tightness.

6   For further information on the wheels and tires, refer to Chapter 10.

14 Suspension and steering check (every 7500 miles or 6 months)

Refer to illustrations 14.1, 14.6a, 14.6b and 14.7

Note: *For detailed illustrations of the steering and suspension components, refer to Chapter 10.*

With the wheels on the ground

1   With the vehicle stopped and the front wheels pointed straight ahead, rock the steering wheel gently back and forth. If freeplay **(see illustration)** is excessive, a

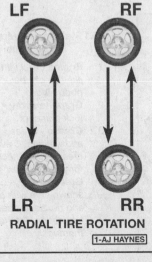

13.2 Tire rotation diagram for radial tires

RADIAL TIRE ROTATION

14.1 Steering wheel freeplay is the amount of travel between an initial steering input and the point at which the front wheels begin to turn (indicated by a slight resistance)

14.6a Inspect the suspension for deteriorated rubber bushings and torn grease seals (arrow)

14.6b Check the stabilizer bar bushings for deterioration at the front and the rear of the vehicle

front wheel bearing, main shaft yoke, intermediate shaft yoke, steering knuckle bearing (4WD) or tie rod end is worn or the steering gear is out of adjustment or broken. Refer to Chapter 10 for the appropriate repair procedure.

2   Other symptoms, such as excessive vehicle body movement over rough roads, swaying (leaning) around corners and binding as the steering wheel is turned, may indicate faulty steering and/or suspension components.

3   Check the shock absorbers by pushing down and releasing the vehicle several times at each corner. If the vehicle does not come back to a level position within one or two bounces, the shocks/struts are worn and must be replaced. When bouncing the vehicle up and down, listen for squeaks and noises from the suspension components.

Under the vehicle

4   Raise the vehicle with a floor jack and support it securely on jackstands. See *Jacking and towing* at the front of this book for proper jacking points.

5   Check the tires for irregular wear patterns and proper inflation. See Section 5 in this Chapter for information regarding tire wear.

6   Inspect the universal joint between the steering shaft and the steering rack. Check the steering rack and driveaxle boots for grease leakage. Check the steering linkage for looseness or damage. Check the tie-rod ends for excessive play. Look for loose bolts, broken or disconnected parts and deteriorated rubber bushings on all suspension and steering components **(see illustrations)**. While an assistant turns the steering wheel from side to side, check the steering components for free movement, chafing and binding. If the steering components do not seem to be reacting with the movement of the steering wheel, try to determine where the slack is located.

7   Check the wheel bearings. Do this by spinning the front wheels. Listen for any abnormal noises and watch to make sure the wheel spins true (doesn't wobble). Grab the top and bottom of the tire and pull in-and-out on it. Notice any movement which would indicate a loose wheel bearing assembly **(see illustration)**. If the bearings are suspect, they should be checked and repacked. Refer to

Section 34 for more information. Refer to Chapter 10 for additional information on the 4WD hub and bearing systems.

8   Check the steering knuckle, moving the knuckle up and down with a pry bar to ensure that knuckle bearings have no play. If the bearings are suspect, they should be checked and repacked. Refer to Chapter 10 for more information.

9   Inspect the driveshafts for worn U-joints and for excessive play in the slip yoke and spline area (see Chapter 8).

10   Check the transfer case and differentials for evidence of fluid leakage.

15   Chassis lubrication (every 7500 miles or 6 months)

Refer to illustrations 15.1, 15.8, 15.9 and 15.11

1   Refer to *Recommended lubricants and fluids* at the front of this Chapter to obtain the necessary grease, etc. You will also need a grease gun **(see illustration)**. Occasionally plugs will be installed rather than grease fittings. If so, grease fittings will have to be purchased and installed.

14.7 Grasp the tire as shown and check for endplay at the wheel bearings - if endplay is found the wheel bearings must be repacked and adjusted

15.1 Materials required for chassis and body lubrication

1   *Engine oil - Light engine oil in a can like this can be used for door and hood hinges*

2   *Graphite spray - Used to lubricate lock cylinders*

3   *Grease - Grease, in a variety of types and weights, is available for use in a grease gun. Check the Specifications for your requirements*

4   *Grease gun - A common grease gun, shown here with a detachable hose and nozzle, is needed for chassis lubrication. After use, clean it thoroughly*

15.8 The slip joint grease fitting is located on the yoke - pump grease into it until it comes out of the slip joint seal

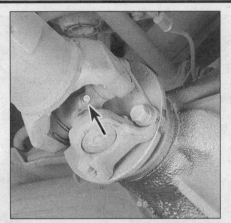

15.9 Pump grease into the universal joints until it can be seen coming out of the contact surfaces

15.11 Use lithium base grease to lubricate the contact points on the steering knuckle stop and adjustment bolt if equipped

2   Look under the vehicle for grease fittings or plugs on the steering, suspension, and driveline components. They are normally found on the tie-rod ends and universal joints. If there are plugs, remove them and install grease fittings, which will thread into the component. An automotive parts store will be able to supply the correct fittings. Straight, as well as angled, fittings are available.

3   For easier access under the vehicle, raise it with a jack and place jackstands under the frame. Make sure it is safely supported by the stands. If the wheels are to be removed at this interval for tire rotation or brake inspection, loosen the lug nuts slightly while the vehicle is still on the ground.

4   Before beginning, force a little grease out of the nozzle to remove any dirt from the end of the gun. Wipe the nozzle clean with a rag.

5   With the grease gun and plenty of clean rags, crawl under the vehicle and begin lubricating the components.

6   Wipe the area around the grease fitting free of dirt, then squeeze the trigger on the grease gun to force grease into the component. Continue pumping grease into the fitting until it oozes out of the joint between the two components. If it escapes around the grease gun nozzle, the fitting is clogged or

the nozzle is not completely seated on the fitting. Resecure the gun nozzle to the fitting and try again. If necessary, replace the fitting with a new one.

7   Wipe the excess grease from the components and the grease fitting. Repeat the procedure for the remaining fittings.

8   Lubricate the driveshaft slip yoke by pumping grease into the fitting until it can be seen coming out of the slip yoke seal **(see illustration)**.

9   Lubricate conventional universal joints until grease can be seen coming out of the contact points **(see illustration)**.

10   While you are under the vehicle, clean and lubricate the parking brake cable along with the cable guides and levers. This can be done by smearing some chassis grease onto the cable and its related parts with your fingers.

11   Lubricate the contact points on the steering knuckle stop and adjustment bolt if equipped **(see illustration)**.

12   Open the hood and smear a little chassis grease on the hood latch mechanism. Have an assistant pull the hood release lever from inside the vehicle as you lubricate the cable at the latch.

13   Lubricate all the hinges (door, hood,

etc.) with engine oil to keep them in proper working order.

14   The key lock cylinders can be lubricated with spray-on graphite or silicone lubricant, which is available at auto parts stores.

15   Lubricate the door weatherstripping with silicone spray. This will reduce chafing and retard wear.

16   Exhaust system check (every 7500 miles or 6 months)

Refer to illustrations 16.2a and 16.2b

1   With the engine cold (at least three hours after the vehicle has been driven), check the complete exhaust system from the manifold to the end of the tailpipe. Be careful around the catalytic converter (if equipped), which may be hot even after three hours. The inspection should be done with the vehicle on a hoist to permit unrestricted access. If a hoist isn't available, raise the vehicle and support it securely on jackstands.

2   Check the exhaust pipes and connections for signs of leakage and/or corrosion indicating a potential failure. Make sure that all brackets and hangers are in good condition and tight **(see illustrations)**.

16.2a Check the exhaust pipes and connections (arrow) for signs of leakage and corrosion

16.2b Check the exhaust system rubber hangers for cracks and damage

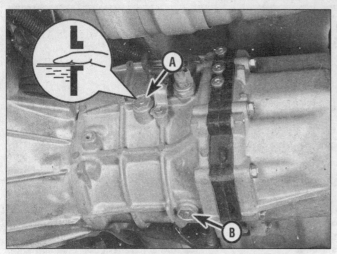

17.2 The manual transmission fill plug (A) and drain plug (B) are located on the side of the transmission case - use your finger as a dipstick to check the lubricant level

18.2 The transfer case fill plug (A) and drain plug (B) are located in the middle of the transfer case housing - use your finger as a dipstick to check the lubricant level

3   Inspect the underside of the body for holes, corrosion, open seams, etc. which may allow exhaust gasses to enter the passenger compartment. Seal all body openings with silicone sealant or body putty.

4   Rattles and other noises can often be traced to the exhaust system, especially the hangers, mounts and heat shields. Try to move the pipes, mufflers and catalytic converter. If the components can come in contact with the body or suspension parts, secure the exhaust system with new brackets and hangers.

17   Manual transmission lubricant level check (every 7500 miles or 6 months)

Refer to illustration 17.2

1   The manual transmission has a filler plug which must be removed to check the lubricant level. If the vehicle is raised to gain access to the plug, be sure to support it safely on jackstands - DO NOT crawl under a

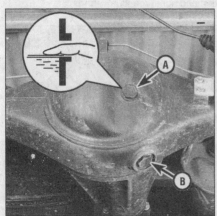

19.2 The differential fill plug (A) and drain plug (B) are located on the axle housing - use your finger as a dipstick to check the lubricant level

vehicle which is supported only by a jack! Be sure the vehicle is level or the check may be inaccurate.

2   Using a wrench, unscrew the fill plug from the transmission **(see illustration)** and use a finger to reach inside the housing to determine the lubricant level. The level should be at or near the bottom of the plug hole.

3   If it isn't, add the recommended lubricant through the plug hole with a pump or squeeze bottle.

4   Install and tighten the plug and check for leaks after the first few miles of driving.

18   Transfer case lubricant level check (4WD models only) (every 7500 miles or 6 months)

Refer to illustration 18.2

1   The transfer case lubricant level is checked by removing the upper plug located in the back of the case.

2   Use a finger to reach inside the housing to determine the lubricant level. The lubricant level should be just at the bottom of the hole **(see illustration)**. If not, add the appropriate lubricant through the opening.

3   Install and tighten the plug and check for leaks after the first few miles of driving.

19   Differential lubricant level check (every 7500 miles or 6 months)

Refer to illustration 19.2

Note: *4WD models covered by this manual have two differentials, be sure to check the lubricant level in both differentials.*

1   The differential has a check/fill plug which must be removed to check the lubricant level. If the vehicle must be raised to gain access to the plug, be sure to support it safely on jackstands - DO NOT crawl under the vehicle when it's supported only by the jack.

2   Remove the oil check/fill plug from the back of the rear differential or the front of the front differential **(see illustration)**. On some models a tag is located in the area of the plug which gives information regarding lubricant type, particularly on models equipped with a limited-slip differential.

3   Use a finger to reach inside the housing to determine the lubricant level. The oil level should be at the bottom of the plug opening. If it isn't, use a hand pump (available at auto parts stores) to add the specified lubricant until it just starts to run out of the opening.

4   Install the plug and tighten it securely.

20   Seat belt check (every 7500 miles or 6 months)

1   Check the seat belts, buckles, latch plates and guide loops for any obvious damage or signs of wear.

2   Make sure the seat belt reminder light comes on when the key is turned on.

3   The seat belts are designed to lock up during a sudden stop or impact, yet allow free movement during normal driving. The retractors should hold the belt against your chest while driving and rewind the belt when the buckle is unlatched.

4   If any of the above checks reveal problems with the seat belt system, replace parts as necessary.

21   Idle speed check and adjustment (every 7,500 miles or 6 months)

Refer to illustration 21.8

1   Engine idle speed is the speed at which the engine operates when no accelerator pedal pressure is applied. The idle speed is critical to the performance of the engine as well as many engine sub-systems.

2   Make sure the air cleaner and all the

21.8 The idle speed can only be adjusted on OBD I engines (1993 and 1994 3.0L V6 engines). All other vehicles will require the IAC valve assembly to be checked

vacuum lines are installed correctly and there are no obvious intake leaks that could affect the idle speed.

3 Make sure the parking brake is firmly set and the wheels blocked to prevent the vehicle from rolling. Make sure all the accessories are OFF and the ignition timing is set correctly (see Chapter 5).

4 A hand-held tachometer must be used when adjusting idle speed to get an accurate reading. The exact hook-up for these meters varies with the manufacturer, so follow the particular directions included with the instrument.

5 The engine must be completely warmed-up to operating temperature, which will automatically render the fast idle inoperative.

6 Place the transmission in Neutral.

7 Raise the engine rpm to 2,500 and hold for approximately 1 to 3 minutes. Release the throttle and allow the engine to return to idle speed. Now set the idle speed to the Specifications listed in the beginning of this Chapter.

8 For most applications, the idle speed is set by turning an adjustment screw which is

23.2 The PCV valve is located in the valve cover - with the engine running, put your finger over the end of the PCV valve - you should feel vacuum

22.2 Check the condition of the driveaxle boot for signs of cracks and grease leaks

located next to the throttle body **(see illustration)**. Once you have located the idle screw, experiment with different length screwdrivers until the adjustment can be easily made without coming into contact with hot or moving engine components. **Note:** *On engines equipped with the OBD II system, if the idle speed is out of specification, check the operation of the IAC valve (see Chapter 4). These systems rely specifically on the IAC valve for adjustment of the idle speed.*

9 Most models have a tune-up decal or Vehicle Emission Control Information (VECI) label located in the engine compartment with instructions for setting idle speed. If no VECI label is found refer to the Specifications Section at the beginning of this Chapter.

22 Driveaxle boot check (every 15,000 miles or 12 months)

Refer to illustration 22.2

1 The driveaxle boots are important because they prevent dirt, water and foreign material from entering and damaging the constant velocity joints (CV). Oil and grease can cause the boot material to deteriorate

24.4 The first step in removing the air filter is detaching the clips on the housing

prematurely, so it's a good idea to wash the boots with soap and water.

2 Inspect the boots for tears and cracks as well as loose clamps **(see illustration)**. If there is any evidence of cracks or leaking grease, they must be replaced as described in Chapter 8.

23 Positive Crankcase Ventilation (PCV) valve check and replacement (every 15,000 miles or 12 months)

Refer to illustration 23.2

1 The PCV valve is usually located in the valve cover.

2 With the engine idling at normal operating temperature, pull the valve (with hose attached) from the valve cover or intake manifold **(see illustration)**.

3 Place your finger over the valve opening or hose. If there's no vacuum, check for a plugged hose, manifold port, or the valve itself. Replace any plugged or deteriorated hoses.

4 Turn off the engine and shake the PCV valve, listening for a rattle. If the valve doesn't rattle, replace it with a new one.

5 To replace the valve, pull it from the end of the hose, noting its installed position.

6 When purchasing a replacement PCV valve, make sure it's for your particular vehicle and engine size. Compare the old valve with the new one to make sure they're the same.

7 Push the valve into the end of the hose until it's seated.

8 Inspect all rubber hoses and grommets for damage and hardening. Replace them, if necessary.

9 Press the PCV valve and hose securely into position.

24 Air filter check and replacement (every 15,000 miles or 12 months)

Refer to illustrations 24.4 and 24.5

1 At the specified intervals, the air filter should be replaced with a new one. A thorough preventive maintenance schedule would also require the filter to be inspected between filter changes.

2 On four cylinder and 3.4L V6 engines, the air filter housing is mounted on right side of the the engine compartment.

3 On 3.0L V6 engines, the air filter housing is located at the left side of the engine compartment.

4 Remove the cover retaining clips **(see illustration)**. Then detach all hoses that would interfere with the removal of the air cleaner cover from the air cleaner housing. While the top cover is off, be careful not to drop anything down into the air cleaner assembly.

5   Lift the air filter element out of the housing **(see illustration)** and wipe out the inside of the air cleaner housing with a clean rag.

6   Inspect the outer surface of the filter element. If it is dirty, replace it. If it is only moderately dusty, it can be reused by blowing it clean from the back to the front surface with compressed air. Because it is a pleated paper type filter, it cannot be washed or oiled. If it cannot be cleaned satisfactorily with compressed air, discard and replace it. **Caution:** *Never drive the vehicle with the air cleaner removed. Excessive engine wear could result and backfiring could even cause a fire under the hood.*

7   Place the new filter in the air cleaner housing, making sure it seats properly.

8   Installation of the cover is the reverse of removal.

---

25   Drivebelt check, adjustment and replacement (every 15,000 miles or 12 months)

Check

Refer to illustrations 25.3a, 25.3b and 25.4

1   The drivebelts, or V-belts as they are sometimes called, are located at the front of the engine and play an important role in the overall operation of the vehicle and its components. Due to their function and material make-up, the belts are prone to failure after a period of time and should be inspected and adjusted periodically to prevent major engine damage.

2   The number of belts used on a particular vehicle depends on the accessories installed. Drivebelts are used to turn the alternator, power steering pump, water pump and air conditioning compressor. Depending on the pulley arrangement, more than one of these components may be driven by a single belt.

3   With the engine off, open the hood and locate the various belts at the front of the

24.5 After setting the top cover aside, the filter element can be lifted out of the housing

engine. Using your fingers (and a flashlight, if necessary), move along the belts checking for cracks and separation of the belt plies. Also check for fraying and glazing, which gives the belt a shiny appearance **(see illustrations)**. Both sides of each belt should be inspected, which means you will have to twist the belt to check the underside.

4   The tension of each belt is checked by pushing on the belt at a distance halfway between the pulleys. Push firmly with your thumb and see how much the belt moves (deflects) **(see illustration)**. As rule of thumb, if the distance from pulley center-to-pulley center is between 7 and 11 inches, the belt should deflect 1/4-inch. If the belt travels between pulleys spaced 12 to 16 inches apart, the belt should deflect 1/2-inch for a V-belt or 1/4-inch for a multi-ribbed belt.

Adjustment

Refer to illustration 25.6

5   If it is necessary to adjust the belt tension, either to make the belt tighter or looser, it is done by moving the belt-driven accessory on the bracket.

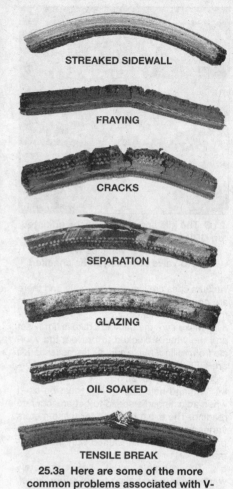

25.3a Here are some of the more common problems associated with V-drivebelts (check the belts very carefully to prevent an untimely breakdown)

6   For each belt on the engine there will be one component with an adjusting bolt and a pivot bolt. These bolts must be loosened slightly to enable you to move the component **(see illustration)**.

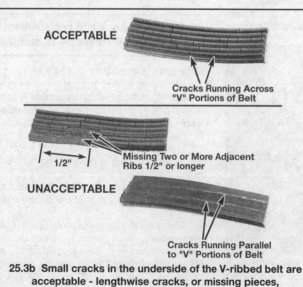

25.3b Small cracks in the underside of the V-ribbed belt are acceptable - lengthwise cracks, or missing pieces, are cause for replacement

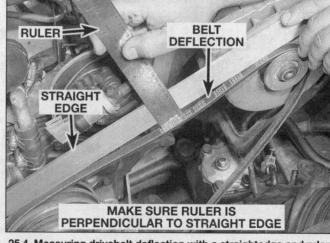

25.4 Measuring drivebelt deflection with a straightedge and ruler

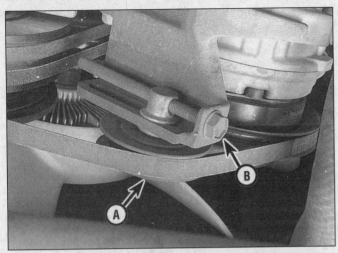

25.6 Loosen the lock bolt (A) on the front of the pulley and turn the adjustment bolt (B) in the desired direction to adjust the drive belt

27.5 With the wheels removed, the brake pad lining (arrow) can be inspected

7   After the two bolts have been loosened, move the component away from the engine to tighten the belt or toward the engine to loosen the belt. Hold the accessory in position and check the belt tension. If it is correct, tighten the two bolts until just snug, then recheck the tension. If the tension is all right, tighten the bolts.

8   On earlier models it will be necessary to use some sort of prybar to move the accessory while the belt is adjusted. If this must be done to gain the proper leverage, be very careful not to damage the component being moved or the part being pried against.

Replacement

9   To replace a belt, follow the above procedures for drivebelt adjustment but slip the belt off the pulleys and remove it. Since belts tend to wear out more or less at the same time, it's a good idea to replace all of them at the same time. Mark each belt and the corresponding pulley grooves so the replacement belts can be installed properly.

10 Take the old belts with you when purchasing new ones in order to make a direct comparison for length, width and design.

11 Adjust the belts as described earlier in this Section.

26 Fuel system check (every 15,000 miles or 12 months)

Warning: *Gasoline is extremely flammable, so take extra precautions when you work on any part of the fuel system. Don't smoke or allow open flames or bare light bulbs near the work area, and don't work in a garage where a natural gas-type appliance (such as a water heater or clothes dryer) with a pilot light is present. Since gasoline is carcinogenic, wear latex gloves when there's a possibility of being exposed to fuel, and, if you spill any fuel on your skin, rinse it off immediately with*

soap and water. Mop up any spills immediately and do not store fuel-soaked rags where they could ignite. The fuel system is under constant pressure, so, if any fuel lines are to be disconnected, the fuel pressure in the system must be relieved first (see Chapter 4 for more information). When you perform any kind of work on the fuel system, wear safety glasses and have a Class B type fire extinguisher on hand.

1   The fuel system is most easily checked with the vehicle raised on a hoist so the components underneath the vehicle are readily visible and accessible.

2   If the smell of gasoline is noticed while driving or after the vehicle has been in the sun, the system should be thoroughly inspected immediately.

3   Remove the gas tank cap and check for damage, corrosion and an unbroken sealing imprint on the gasket. Replace the cap with a new one if necessary.

4   With the vehicle raised and safely supported, inspect the gas tank and filler neck for punctures, cracks and other damage. The connection between the filler neck and the tank is particularly critical. Sometimes a rubber filler neck will leak because of loose clamps or deteriorated rubber. These are problems a home mechanic can usually rectify. **Warning:** *Do not, under any circumstances, try to repair a fuel tank (except rubber components). A welding torch or any open flame can easily cause fuel vapors inside the tank to explode.*

5   Carefully check all rubber hoses and metal lines leading away from the fuel tank. Check for loose connections, deteriorated hoses, crimped lines and other damage. Follow the lines to the front of the vehicle, carefully inspecting them all the way to the carburetor or fuel injection system. Repair or replace damaged sections as necessary.

6   If a fuel odor is still evident after the inspection, refer to Chapter 6 and check the EVAP system.

27 Brake check (every 15,000 miles or 12 months)

Warning: *The dust created by the brake system may contain asbestos, which is harmful to your health. Never blow it out with compressed air and don't inhale any of it. An approved filtering mask should be worn when working on the brakes. Do not, under any circumstances, use petroleum-based solvents to clean brake parts. Use brake system cleaner only! Try to use non-asbestos replacement parts whenever possible.*
Note: *For detailed photographs of the brake system, refer to Chapter 9.*

1   In addition to the specified intervals, the brakes should be inspected every time the wheels are removed or whenever a defect is suspected. Any of the following symptoms could indicate a potential brake system defect: The vehicle pulls to one side when the brake pedal is depressed; the brakes make squealing or dragging noises when applied; brake pedal travel is excessive; the pedal pulsates; brake fluid leaks, usually onto the inside of the tire or wheel.

2   Loosen the wheel lug nuts.

3   Raise the vehicle and place it securely on jackstands.

4   Remove the wheels (see *Jacking and towing* at the front of this book, or your owner's manual, if necessary).

Disc brakes

Refer to illustrations 27.5 and 27.10

5   There are two pads (an outer and an inner) in each caliper. The pads are visible after the wheels are removed **(see illustration)**.

6   Measure the pad thickness. If the lining material is less than the thickness listed in this Chapter's Specifications, replace the pads. **Note:** *Keep in mind that the lining material is riveted or bonded to a metal backing plate and the metal portion is not included in this measurement.*

7   If it is difficult to determine the exact thickness of the remaining pad material by the above method, or if you are at all concerned about the condition of the pads, remove the caliper(s), then remove the pads from the calipers for further inspection (refer to Chapter 9).

8   Once the pads are removed from the calipers, clean them with brake cleaner and re-measure them with a ruler or a vernier caliper.

9   Measure the disc thickness with a micrometer to make sure that it still has service life remaining. If any disc is thinner than the specified minimum thickness, replace it (refer to Chapter 9). Even if the disc has service life remaining, check its condition. Look for scoring, gouging and burned spots. If these conditions exist, remove the disc and have it resurfaced (see Chapter 9).

10   Before installing the wheels, check all brake lines and hoses for damage, wear, deformation, cracks, corrosion, leakage, bends and twists, particularly in the vicinity of the rubber hoses at the calipers **(see illustration)**. Check the clamps for tightness and the connections for leakage. Make sure that all hoses and lines are clear of sharp edges, moving parts and the exhaust system. If any of the above conditions are noted, repair, reroute or replace the lines and/or fittings as necessary (see Chapter 9).

Drum brakes

Refer to illustrations 27.12 and 27.14

11   Refer to Chapter 9 and remove the brake drums.

12   Note the thickness of the lining material on the brake shoes **(see illustration)** and look for signs of contamination by brake fluid and grease. If the lining material is within 1/16-inch of the recessed rivets or metal shoes, replace the brake shoes with new ones. The shoes should also be replaced if they are cracked, glazed (shiny lining sur-

faces) or contaminated with brake fluid or grease. See Chapter 9 for the replacement procedure.

13   Check the shoe return and hold-down springs and the adjusting mechanism to make sure they're installed correctly and in good condition (see Chapter 9). Deteriorated or distorted springs, if not replaced, could allow the linings to drag and wear prematurely.

14   Check the wheel cylinders for leakage by carefully peeling back the rubber boots **(see illustration)**. If brake fluid is noted behind the boots, the wheel cylinders must be replaced (see Chapter 9).

15   Check the drums for cracks, score marks, deep scratches and hard spots, which will appear as small discolored areas. If imperfections cannot be removed with emery cloth, the drums must be resurfaced by an automotive machine shop (see Chapter 9 for more detailed information).

16   Refer to Chapter 9 and install the brake drums.

17   Install the wheels and snug the wheel lug nuts finger tight.

18   Remove the jackstands and lower the vehicle.

19   Tighten the wheel lug nuts to the torque listed in this Chapter's Specifications.

Brake booster check

20   Sit in the driver's seat and perform the following sequence of tests.

21   With the engine stopped, depress the brake pedal several times - the travel distance should not change.

22   With the brake fully depressed, start the engine - the pedal should move down a little when the engine starts.

23   Depress the brake, stop the engine and hold the pedal in for about 30 seconds - the pedal should neither sink nor rise.

24   Restart the engine, run it for about a minute and turn it off. Then firmly depress the

27.10 Check for any sign of brake fluid leakage at the brake line fittings and the brake hoses (arrow)

brake several times - the pedal travel should decrease with each application.

25   If your brakes do not operate as described above when the preceding tests are performed, the brake booster is either in need of repair or has failed. Refer to Chapter 9 for the removal procedure.

Parking brake

26   Slowly pull up on the parking brake and count the number of clicks you hear until the handle is up as far as it will go. The adjustment should be within the specified number of clicks listed in this Chapter's Specifications. If you hear more or fewer clicks, it's time to adjust the parking brake (refer to Chapter 9).

27   An alternative method of checking the parking brake is to park the vehicle on a steep hill with the parking brake set and the transmission in Neutral (be sure to stay in the vehicle during this check!). If the parking brake cannot prevent the vehicle from rolling, it is in need of adjustment (see Chapter 9).

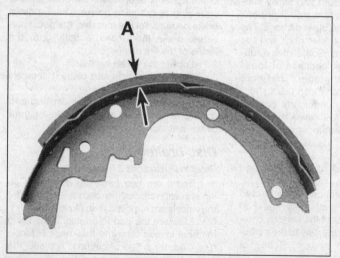

27.12 If the lining is bonded to the brake shoe, measure the lining thickness from the outer surface to the metal shoe, as shown here; if the lining is riveted to the shoe, measure from the lining outer surface to the rivet head

27.14 Check for fluid leakage at both ends of the wheel cylinder dust covers (arrow)

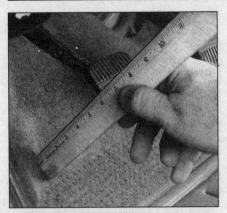

28.1 Pedal height is the distance between the pedal pad and the floor

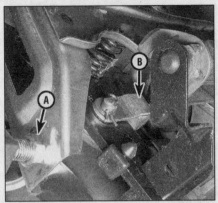

28.2 Back the stopper bolt or switch (A) out for clearance, then loosen the locknut on the pushrod (B). Turn the pushrod to adjust the pedal height

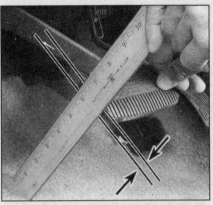

28.5 Pedal freeplay is the distance from the natural resting point of the pedal to the point at which resistance is felt

28 Clutch/brake pedal height and freeplay adjustment (every 15,000 miles or 12 months)

Pedal height

Refer to illustrations 28.1 and 28.2

1   The height of the clutch and brake pedal is the distance the pedal sits off the floor **(see illustration)**. If the pedal height is not within the specified range, it must be adjusted.

2   To adjust the clutch pedal, loosen the locknut and back the stopper bolt or switch out for clearance, then loosen the locknut on the clutch pushrod. Turn the pushrod to adjust the pedal height in the middle of the specified range, then retighten the locknut **(see illustration)**.

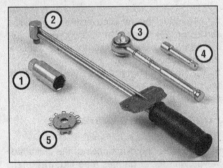

29.1 Tools required for changing spark plugs

1   **Spark plug socket** - This will have special padding inside to protect the spark plug's porcelain insulator
2   **Torque wrench** - Although not mandatory, using this tool is the best way to ensure the plugs are tightened properly
3   **Ratchet** - Standard hand tool to fit the spark plug socket
4   **Extension** - Depending on model and accessories, you may need special extensions and universal joints to reach one or more of the plugs
5   **Spark plug gap gauge** - This gauge for checking the gap comes in a variety of styles. Make sure the gap for your engine is included

3   Before measuring the brake pedal height make sure the pedal is in the fully returned position, then start the engine and depress the accelerator several times to activate the brake power booster. Measure the pedal height and adjust if necessary. To adjust the pedal height loosen the locknut and back the stopper bolt or switch but for clearance, then loosen the locknut on the brake pushrod. Turn the pushrod to adjust the pedal height in the middle of the specified range, then retighten the locknut.

4   Adjust the pedal switch or stopper bolt by turning it clockwise until the switch body or stopper bolt just contacts the pedal arm.

Pedal freeplay

Refer to illustration 28.5

5   The freeplay is the pedal slack, or the distance the pedal can be depressed before it begins to have any effect on the clutch or brake system **(see illustration)**. If the pedal freeplay is not within the specified range, it must be adjusted.

6   To adjust the clutch pedal freeplay loosen the locknut on the clutch pushrod. Then back off the pushrod to adjust the pedal

29.4a Spark plug manufacturers recommend using a wire type gauge when checking the gap - if the wire does not slide between the electrodes with a slight drag, adjustment is required

freeplay to the specified range and retighten the locknut.

7   Before measuring the brake pedal freeplay turn off the engine and depress the brake pedal a half dozen times. Measure the pedal freeplay and adjust if necessary. Loosen the locknut on the brake pushrod, then back off the pushrod to adjust the pedal freeplay to the specified range and retighten the locknut.

29 Spark plug replacement (every 30,000 miles or 24 months)

Refer to illustrations 29.1, 29.4a and 29.4b

1   Spark plug replacement requires a spark plug socket which fits onto a ratchet wrench. This socket is lined with a rubber grommet to protect the porcelain insulator of the spark plug and to hold the plug while you insert it into the spark plug hole. You will also need a wire-type feeler gauge to check and adjust the spark plug gap and a torque wrench to tighten the new plugs to the specified torque **(see illustration)**.

2   If you are replacing the plugs, purchase the new plugs, adjust them to the proper gap and then replace each plug one at a time. **Note:** *When buying new spark plugs, it's essential that you obtain the correct plugs for your specific vehicle. This information can be found in the Specifications Section at the beginning of this Chapter, on the Vehicle Emissions Control Information (VECI) label located on the underside of the hood or in the owner's manual. If these sources specify different plugs, purchase the spark plug type specified on the VECI label because that information is provided specifically for your engine.*

3   Inspect each of the new plugs for defects. If there are any signs of cracks in the porcelain insulator of a plug, don't use it.

4   Check the electrode gaps of the new plugs. Check the gap by inserting the wire gauge of the proper thickness between the electrodes at the tip of the plug **(see illustration)**. The gap between the electrodes should be identical to that listed in this Chapter's

29.4b To change the gap, bend the side electrode only, as indicated by the arrows, and be very careful not to crack or chip the porcelain insulator surrounding the center electrode

29.6 When removing the spark plug wires, pull only on the boot and use a twisting, pulling motion

29.8 Use a socket wrench with a long extension to unscrew the spark plugs

Specifications or on the VECI label. If the gap is incorrect, use the notched adjuster on the feeler gauge body to bend the curved side electrode slightly **(see illustration)**.

5   If the side electrode is not exactly over the center electrode, use the notched adjuster to align them.

Removal

Refer to illustrations 29.6 and 29.8

6   To prevent the possibility of mixing up spark plug wires, work on one spark plug at a time. Remove the wire and boot from one spark plug. Grasp the boot - not the cable - as shown, give it a half twisting motion and pull straight up **(see illustration)**. Note: *On models with the coil over plug ignition system, remove the entire assembly from the valve cover to access the spark plug. Refer to Chapter 5 for additional information and illustrations.*

7   If compressed air is available, blow any dirt or foreign material away from the spark plug area before proceeding (a common bicycle pump will also work).

8   Remove the spark plug **(see illustration)**.

9   Whether you are replacing the plugs at this time or intend to reuse the old plugs, compare each old spark plug with the chart shown on the inside back cover of this manual to determine the overall running condition of the engine.

Installation

Refer to illustrations 29.10a and 29.10b

10   Prior to installation, apply a coat of anti-seize compound to the plug threads. It's often difficult to insert spark plugs into their holes without cross-threading them. To avoid this possibility, fit a short piece of rubber hose over the end of the spark plug **(see illustrations)**. The flexible hose acts as a universal joint to help align the plug with the plug hole. Should the plug begin to cross-thread, the hose will slip on the spark plug, preventing thread damage. Tighten the plug to the torque listed in this Chapter's Specifications.

29.10a Apply a thin coat of anti-seize compound to the spark plug threads

11   Attach the plug wire to the new spark plug, again using a twisting motion on the boot until it is firmly seated on the end of the spark plug.

12   Follow the above procedure for the remaining spark plugs, replacing them one at a time to prevent mixing up the spark plug wires.

---

30   Valve clearance check and adjustment (every 30,000 miles or 24 months)

Note: *This procedure requires the use of special valve lifter tools. The tools are available from the dealer, specialty tool manufacturers and auto parts stores. It is impossible to perform this task without them.*

1   Disconnect the negative cable from the battery. **Caution:** *If the stereo in your vehicle is equipped with an anti-theft system, make sure you have the correct activation code before disconnecting the battery.*

2   Disconnect the spark plug wires and remove any other components that will interfere with valve cover removal.

3   Blow out the recessed area around the spark plug openings with compressed air, if available, to remove any debris that might fall into the cylinders, then remove the spark plugs (see Section 29).

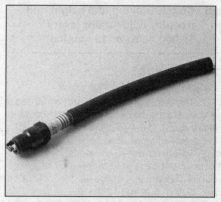

29.10b A length of rubber hose will save time and prevent damaged threads when installing the spark plugs

4   Remove the valve cover (refer to Chapter 2A or 2B). Note: *On V6 engines, the air intake plenum must be removed to access the valve covers.*

5   Refer to Chapter 2A or 2B and position the number 1 piston at TDC on the compression stroke.

Four cylinder engines

Refer to illustrations 30.6a, 30.6b and 30.7

6   Measure the clearances of the indicated valves with feeler gauges **(see illustrations)**. Record the measurements which are out of

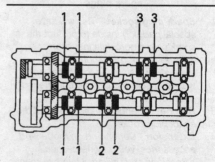

30.6a With the No. 1 piston at TDC on the compression stroke, check the number 1 intake and exhaust valves, the number 3 exhaust valves and the number 2 intake valves (four cylinder engines)

30.6b Check the clearance for each valve with a feeler gauge of the specified thickness - if the clearance is correct, you should feel a slight drag on the gauge as you pull it out (all engines)

specification. They will be used later to determine the required replacement shims.

7   Turn the crankshaft one complete revolution (360 degrees) and realign the timing marks. Measure the remaining valves **(see illustration)**.

3.0L V6 engine

Refer to illustrations 30.8, 30.9a, 30.9b, 30.9c, 30.9d and 30.9e

8   With the engine at TDC for number 1, measure the clearances of the indicated valves with feeler gauges **(see illustration)**. Record the measurements which are out of specification. They will be used later to determine the required replacement shims.

9   Turn the crankshaft 1/3 revolution (120 degrees) and adjust the number 1 INTAKE valve and the number 3 EXHAUST valve **(see illustration)**. Turn the crankshaft 1/3 revolution again and set the next group of valves **(see illustration)**. Measure the remaining valves **(see illustrations)**. Make notes of the cylinder number and the valve type (intake or exhaust) that need to be adjusted.

3.4L V6 engine

Refer to illustrations 30.10, 30.11a and 30.11b

10   Measure the clearances of the indicated valves with feeler gauges **(see illustration)**. Record the measurements which are out of

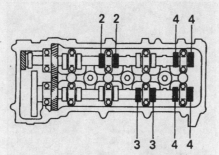

30.7 Rotate the crankshaft 360-degrees from No. 1 TDC, then check and adjust the clearance of the indicated valves (four cylinder engines)

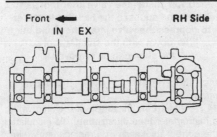

30.9a Rotate the crankshaft 1/3 turn (120 degrees) and check the number 1 intake valve and the number 3 exhaust valve (3.0L V6 engine)

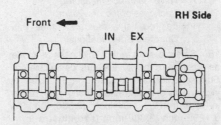

30.9c Rotate the crankshaft 1/3 turn (120 degrees) and check the number 3 intake valve and the number 5 exhaust valve (3.0L V6 engine)

specification. They will be used later to determine the required replacement shims.

11   Turn the crankshaft 2/3 revolution (240 degrees) and adjust the indicated valves **(see illustration)**. Turn the crankshaft 2/3 revolu-

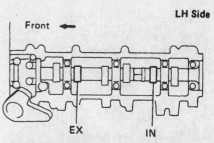

30.8 With the No. 1 piston at TDC on the compression stroke, check the number 2 exhaust valve and the number 6 intake valve (3.0L V6 engine)

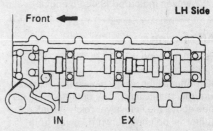

30.9b Rotate the crankshaft 1/3 turn (120 degrees) and check the number 2 intake valve and the number 4 exhaust valve (3.0L V6 engine)

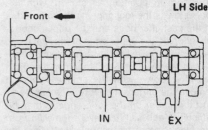

30.9d Rotate the crankshaft 1/3 turn (120 degrees) and check the number 4 intake valve and the number 6 exhaust valve (3.0L V6 engine)

tion again and set the next group of valves **(see illustration)**. Measure the remaining valves **(see illustration)**. Make notes of the cylinder number and the valve type (intake or exhaust) that need to be adjusted.

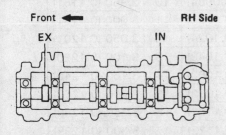

30.9e Rotate the crankshaft 1/3 turn (120 degrees) and check the number 5 intake valve and the number 1 exhaust valve (3.0L V6 engine)

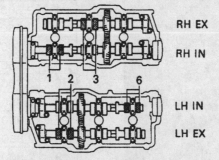

30.10 With the No. 1 piston at TDC on the compression stroke, check the indicated valves (3.4L V6 engine)

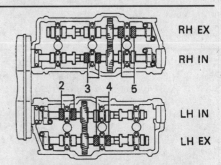

30.11a Rotate the crankshaft 2/3 turn (240 degrees) and check the indicated valves (3.4L V6 engine)

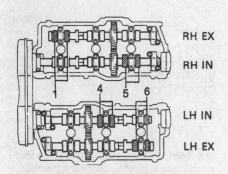

30.11b Rotate the crankshaft 2/3 turn (240 degrees) and check the remaining valves indicated (3.4L V6 engine)

30.13a Install the valve lifter tool as shown and squeeze the handles together to depress the valve lifter, then hold the lifter down with the smaller tool so the shim can be removed

30.13b Keep pressure on the lifter with the smaller tool and remove the shim with a small screwdriver . . .

30.13c . . . a pair of tweezers or a magnet as shown here

All engines

Refer to illustrations 30.13a, 30.13b, 30.13c, 30.14 and 30.15

12   After all the valves have been measured, turn the crankshaft pulley until the camshaft lobe above the first valve which you intend to adjust is pointing upward, away from the shim.

13   Position the notch in the valve lifter toward the spark plug. Then depress the valve lifter with the special valve lifter tools **(see illustrations)**. Place the special valve lifter tool in position as shown, with the longer jaw of the tool gripping the lower edge of the cast lifter boss and the upper, shorter jaw gripping the upper edge of the lifter itself. Depress the valve lifter by squeezing the handles of the valve lifter tool together, then hold the lifter down with the smaller tool and remove the larger one. **Note:** *The number 1 and 6 cylinder on the 3.4L engines may be difficult to access. To prevent the shim from pinching the tool, tilt the tool slightly from the intake side.* Remove the adjusting shim with a small screwdriver or a pair of tweezers **(see illustrations)**. Note that the wire hook on the end of some valve lifter tool handles can be used to clamp both handles together to keep

the lifter depressed while the shim is removed.

14   Measure the thickness of the shim with a micrometer **(see illustration)**. To calculate the correct thickness of a replacement shim that will place the valve clearance within the specified value, use the following formula:

$$N = T + (A - V)$$

T = thickness of the old shim
A = valve clearance measured
N = thickness of the new shim
V = desired valve clearance (see this Chapters Specifications)

15   Select a shim with a thickness as close as possible to the valve clearance calculated. Shims, which are available in 17 sizes in increments of 0.0020-inch (0.050 mm), range in size from 0.0984-inch (2.500 mm) to 0.1299-inch (3.300 mm) **(see illustration)**. **Note:** *Through careful analysis of the shim sizes needed to bring the out-of-specification valve clearance within specification, it is often possible to simply move a shim that has to come out anyway to another valve lifter requiring a shim of that particular size,*

thereby reducing the number of new shims that must be purchased.

16   Place the special valve lifter tool in position as shown in **illustration 30.13a**, with the longer jaw of the tool gripping the lower edge of the cast lifter boss and the upper, shorter jaw gripping the upper edge of the lifter itself,

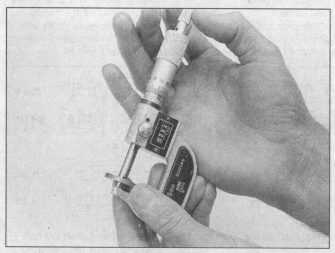

30.14 Measure the shim thickness with a micrometer

Shim No.	Thickness	Shim No.	Thickness
1	2.500 (0.0984)	10	2.950 (0.1161)
2	2.550 (0.1004)	11	3.000 (0.1181)
3	2.600 (0.1024)	12	3.050 (0.1201)
4	2.650 (0.1043)	13	3.100 (0.1220)
5	2.700 (0.1063)	14	3.150 (0.1240)
6	2.750 (0.1083)	15	3.200 (0.1260)
7	2.800 (0.1102)	16	3.250 (0.1280)
8	2.850 (0.1122)	17	3.300 (0.1299)
9	2.900 (0.1142)		

New shim thickness   mm (in.)

30.15 Valve adjusting shim thickness chart

31.2 Remove the banjo fittings (arrows) from the fuel filter (1998 four-cylinder Tacoma shown, others similar)

32.11a Remove the distributor cap retaining screws - pull the cap out and up to access the rotor

press down the valve lifter by squeezing the handles of the valve lifter tool together and install the new adjusting shim (note that the wire hook on the end of one valve lifter tool handle can be used to clamp the handles together to keep the lifter depressed while the shim is inserted. Measure the clearance with a feeler gauge to make sure that your calculations are correct.

17   Repeat this procedure until all the valves which are out of clearance have been corrected.

18   Installation of the spark plugs, valve cover, spark plug wires and boots, etc. is the reverse of removal.

31   Fuel filter replacement (every 60,000 miles or 48 months)

Refer to illustration 31.2

Warning 1: *Gasoline is extremely flammable, so take extra precautions when you work on any part of the fuel system. Don't smoke or allow open flames or bare light bulbs near the work area, and don't work in a garage where a natural gas-type appliance (such as a water heater or clothes dryer) with a pilot light is present. Since gasoline is carcinogenic, wear latex gloves when there's a possibility of being exposed to fuel, and, if you spill any fuel on your skin, rinse it off immediately with soap and water. Mop up any spills immediately and do not store fuel-soaked rags where they could ignite. When you perform any kind of work on the fuel system, wear safety glasses and have a Class B Type fire extinguisher on hand.*

Warning 2: *Refer to* Chapter 4 *and depressurize the fuel system before removing the filter!*

1   This job should be done with the engine cold (after sitting at least three hours). Place a metal container, rags or newspapers under the filter to catch spilled fuel. Relieve the fuel system pressure (see Chapter 4).

2   Unscrew the banjo bolts on both ends of the fuel filter **(see illustration)**. Disconnect both lines. **Note:** *The fuel filter on Tacoma and 4Runners is located under the chassis.*

3   Remove both bracket bolts and detach the old filter and the filter support bracket.

4   Remove the filter clamp bolt and separate the old filter from the bracket. Note that the inlet and outlet lines are clearly labeled and that the flanged end of the filter faces down.

5   Install the new filter and bracket assembly and tighten the bracket bolts securely. Make sure that the new filter is installed flanged end down.

6   Using the new sealing washers - two per banjo fitting - provided by the filter manufacturer, install the inlet and outlet banjo bolts and tighten them to the specified torque.

7   The remainder of installation is the reverse of the removal.

32   Spark plug wire, distributor cap and rotor check and replacement (every 30,000 miles or 24 months)

Refer to illustrations 32.11a, 32.11b and 32.12

1   The spark plug wires should be checked whenever new spark plugs are installed.

2   Begin this procedure by making a visual check of the spark plug wires while the engine is running. In a darkened garage (make sure there is adequate ventilation) start the engine and observe each plug wire. Be careful not to come into contact with any moving engine parts. If there is a break in the wire, you will see arcing or a small spark at the damaged area. If arcing is noticed, make a note to obtain new wires, then allow the engine to cool and check the distributor cap and rotor.

3   The spark plug wires should be inspected one at a time to prevent mixing up the order, which is essential for proper engine

operation. Each original plug wire should be numbered to help identify its location. If the number is illegible, a piece of tape can be marked with the correct number and wrapped around the plug wire.

4   Disconnect the plug wire from the spark plug. A removal tool can be used for this purpose or you can grasp the rubber boot, twist the boot half a turn and pull the boot free. Do not pull on the wire itself. **Note:** *Later models require removing a cover on the top of the valve cover to access the spark plugs.*

5   Check inside the boot for corrosion, which will look like a white crusty powder.

6   Push the wire and boot back onto the end of the spark plug. It should fit tightly onto the end of the plug. If it doesn't, remove the wire and use pliers to carefully crimp the metal connector inside the wire boot until the fit is snug.

7   Using a clean rag, wipe the entire length of the wire to remove built-up dirt and grease. Once the wire is clean, check for burns, cracks and other damage. Do not bend the wire sharply, because the conductor might break.

8   Remove the rubber boot (if equipped) and disconnect the wire from the distributor. Again, pull only on the rubber boot. Check for corrosion and a tight fit. Replace the wire in the distributor.

9   Inspect the remaining spark plug wires, making sure that each one is securely fastened at the distributor and spark plug when the check is complete.

10   If new spark plug wires are required, purchase a set for your specific engine model. Remove and replace the wires one at a time to avoid mix-ups in the firing order.

11   Detach the distributor cap (if equipped) by loosening the cap retaining screws. Look inside it for cracks, carbon tracks and worn, burned or loose contacts **(see illustrations)**. **Note:** *Some engines are equipped with a Coil Over plug (COP) type ignition systems. Refer to Chapter 5 for the inspection procedures on COP type ignition systems.*

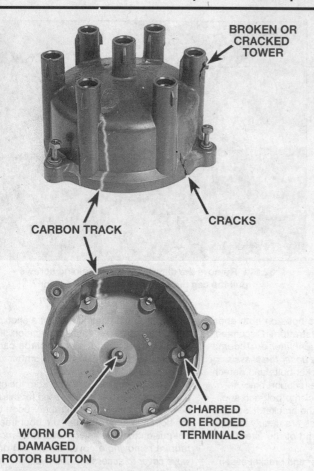

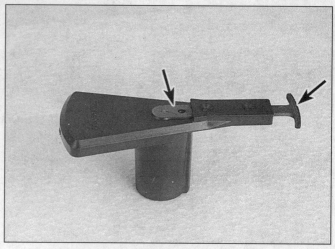

32.12 The ignition rotor should be checked for wear and corrosion as indicated here (if in doubt about its condition, install a new one)

32.11b Shown here are some of the common defects to look for when inspecting the distributor cap (if in doubt about its condition, install a new one)

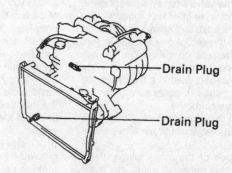

33.3a Drain plug locations on four cylinder engines

12   Pull the rotor off the distributor shaft and examine it for cracks and carbon tracks **(see illustration)**. Replace the cap and rotor if any damage or defects are noted.

13   It is common practice to install a new cap and rotor whenever new spark plug wires are installed, but if you wish to continue using the old cap, check the resistance between the spark plug wires and the cap first. If the indicated resistance is more than the maximum value listed in this Chapter's Specifications, replace the cap and/or wires.

14   When installing a new cap, remove the wires from the old cap one at a time and attach them to the new cap in the exact same location **Note:** *If an accidental mix-up occurs, refer to the firing order Specifications at the beginning of this Chapter.*

33 Cooling system servicing (draining, flushing and refilling) (every 30,000 miles or 24 months)

Refer to illustrations 33.3a, 33.3b and 33.3c
Warning: *Do not allow antifreeze to come in contact with your skin or painted surfaces of the vehicle. Rinse off spills immediately with plenty of water. Antifreeze is highly toxic if ingested. Never leave antifreeze lying around*

in an open container or in puddles on the floor; children and pets are attracted by it's sweet smell and may drink it. Check with local authorities about disposing of used antifreeze. Many communities have collection centers which will see that antifreeze is disposed of safely.

1   Periodically, the cooling system should be drained, flushed and refilled to replenish the antifreeze mixture and prevent formation of rust and corrosion, which can impair the performance of the cooling system and cause engine damage. When the cooling system is serviced, all hoses and the radiator cap should

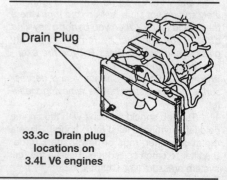

33.3b Drain plug locations on 3.0L V6 engines

be checked and replaced if necessary.

2   Apply the parking brake and block the wheels. **Warning:** *If the vehicle has just been driven, wait several hours to allow the engine to cool down before beginning this procedure.*

3   Move a large container under the radiator drain to catch the coolant. The radiator drain plug is located on the side of the lower tank of the radiator **(see illustrations)**. Attach a 3/8-inch diameter hose to the drain fitting (if possible) to direct the coolant into the container, then open the drain fitting (a pair of pliers may be required to turn it).

4   Remove the radiator cap and allow the radiator to drain, then, move the container under the drivers side of the engine block.

33.3c Drain plug locations on 3.4L V6 engines

Remove the engine block drain plug and allow the coolant in the block to drain (see illustration 33.3a). Note: *Frequently, the coolant will not drain from the block after the plug is removed. This is due to a rust layer that has built up behind the plug. Insert a Phillips screwdriver into the hole to break the rust barrier.*

5   While the coolant is draining, check the condition of the radiator hoses, heater hoses and clamps (refer to Section 10 if necessary).

6   Replace any damaged clamps or hoses.

7   Once the system is completely drained, flush the radiator with fresh water from a garden hose until it runs clear at the drain. The flushing action of the water will remove sediments from the radiator but will not remove rust and scale from the engine and cooling tube surfaces.

8   These deposits can be removed with a chemical cleaner. Follow the procedure outlined in the manufacturer's instructions. If the radiator is severely corroded, damaged or leaking, it should be removed (see Chapter 3) and taken to a radiator repair shop.

9   Remove the overflow hose from the coolant reservoir and flush the reservoir with clean water, then reconnect the hose.

10   Close and tighten the radiator drain fitting. Install and tighten the block drain plug.

11   Place the heater temperature control in the maximum heat position.

12   Slowly add new coolant (a 50/50 mixture of water and antifreeze) to the radiator until it's full. Add coolant to the reservoir up to the lower mark.

13   Leave the radiator cap off and run the engine in a well-ventilated area until the thermostat opens (coolant will begin flowing through the radiator and the upper radiator hose will become hot).

14   Turn the engine off and let it cool. Add more coolant mixture to bring the level back up to the lip on the radiator filler neck.

15   Squeeze the upper radiator hose to expel air, then add more coolant mixture if necessary. Replace the radiator cap.

16   Start the engine, allow it to reach normal operating temperature and check for leaks.

34   Front hub and wheel bearing check, repack and adjustment (every 30,000 miles or 24 months)

Note: *This procedure applies to Tacoma and T100 models only. 4Runner and 1996 and later 4WD Tacoma models use a front wheel bearing that is permanently sealed and can not be lubricated.*

Check and repack

Refer to illustrations 34.1, 34.7a, 34.7b, 34.7c, 34.8a, 34.8b, 34.8c, 34.9, 34.10, 34.11, 34.15 and 34.19

1   In most cases the front wheel bearings will not need servicing until the brake shoes or pads are changed. However, the bearings should be checked whenever the front of the vehicle is raised for any reason. Several items, including a torque wrench and special grease, are required for this procedure (see illustration).

2   With the vehicle securely supported on jackstands, spin each wheel and check for noise, rolling resistance and endplay.

3   Grasp the top of each tire with one hand and the bottom with the other. Move the wheel in and out on the spindle. If there's any noticeable movement, the bearings should be checked and then repacked with grease, or replaced if necessary.

4   Remove the wheel.

5   Remove the disc brake caliper (see Chapter 9) and hang it out of the way on a piece of wire.

6   On 4WD vehicles, remove the freewheel hub (see Chapter 8).

7   On 2WD vehicles, use a small chisel and hammer to remove the dust cover (see illustration). Remove the cotter pin from the spindle using a pair of needle nose pliers or cutting pliers to grip the slippery surface (see illustration). Remove the nut-lock, spindle nut and thrust washer from the spindle (see illustration).

8   On 4WD vehicles, use a small chisel and hammer to bend back the tabs on the lock washer which is located between the inner and outer locknuts. Remove the outer

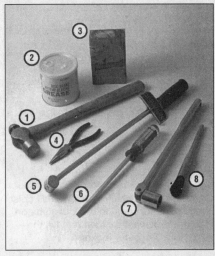

34.1 Tools and materials needed for front wheel bearing maintenance

1   *Hammer - A common hammer will do just fine*

2   *Grease - High-temperature grease that is formulated specially for front wheel bearings should be used*

3   *Wood block - If you have a scrap piece of 2x4, it can be used to drive the new seal into the hub*

4   *Needle-nose pliers - Used to straighten and remove the cotter pin in the spindle*

5   *Torque wrench - This is very important in this procedure; if the bearing is too tight, the wheel won't turn freely - if it's too loose, the wheel will "wobble" on the spindle. Either way, it could mean extensive damage*

6   *Screwdriver - Used to remove the seal from the hub (a long screwdriver is preferred)*

7   *Socket/breaker bar - Needed to loosen the nut on the spindle if it's extremely tight*

8   *Brush - Together with some clean solvent, this will be used to remove old grease from the hub and spindle*

34.7a On 2WD vehicles, use a small chisel and hammer to remove the dust cover from the front hub . . .

34.7b . . . then, remove the cotter pin, the nut-lock . . .

34.7c . . . the spindle nut and the thrust washer from the spindle

34.8a On 4WD vehicles, use a small chisel and hammer to bend back the tabs on the lock washer, then remove the outer locknut

34.8b Remove the lock washer, the inner locknut . . .

34.8c . . . and the thrust washer

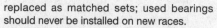

34.9 Pull the hub assembly out slightly, then push it back in to disengage the outer wheel bearing

34.10 Remove the brake disc and bearing assembly from the spindle

locknut, lock washer, inner locknut and the thrust washer **(see illustrations)**.

9   Pull the hub assembly out slightly, then push it back in. This should force the outer bearing and cup off the spindle so it can be removed **(see illustration)**.

10   Pull the hub assembly off the spindle **(see illustration)**.

11   Use a screwdriver or a seal puller tool to pry the seal out of the rear of the hub assembly **(see illustration)**. Note how the seal is installed.

12   Remove the inner wheel bearing from the hub assembly.

13   Use solvent to remove all traces of the old grease from the bearings, hub and spindle. A small brush may prove helpful; however make sure no bristles from the brush embed themselves inside the bearing rollers. Allow the parts to air dry.

14   Carefully inspect the bearings for cracks, heat discoloration, worn rollers, etc. Check the bearing races inside the hub for wear and damage. If the bearing races are defective, drive the bearing race out of the hub using a brass drift. Drive the new race into the hub using the appropriate size bearing driver (inexpensive bearing driver sets are available at most automotive parts stores). Note that the bearings and races are

replaced as matched sets; used bearings should never be installed on new races.

15   Use only high-temperature front wheel bearing grease to pack the bearings. Inexpensive bearing packing tools are available at automotive parts stores, but not entirely necessary **(see illustration)**. If one is not available, pack the grease by hand completely into the bearings, forcing it between the rollers, cone and cage from the back side.

16   Apply a thin coat of grease to the spindle at the outer bearing seat, inner bearing seat, shoulder and seal seat.

17   Place a small quantity of grease inboard of each bearing race inside the hub. Using your finger, form a dam at these points to provide extra grease availability and to keep thinned grease from flowing out of the bearing.

18   Place the grease-packed inner bearing into the rear of the hub and put a little more grease outboard of the bearing.

19   Place a new seal over the inner bearing and tap the seal evenly into place with a hammer and block of wood until it's flush with the hub **(see illustration)**.

34.11 Use a screwdriver or seal removal tool to pry out the grease seal

34.15 If available, insert the bearing into the wheel bearing packing tool and pump the grease into the fitting located in the center of the tool

34.19 A block of wood and a hammer can be used to reinstall the new grease seal

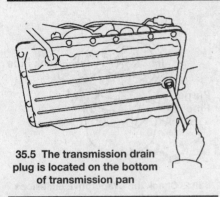

35.5 The transmission drain plug is located on the bottom of transmission pan

35.7 Using a rubber mallet, carefully tap on the pan to break the gasket seal between the pan and the transmission case

35.9 Remove the filter bolts (arrows) (typical filter shown)

Adjustment

20   Carefully place the hub assembly onto the spindle and push the grease-packed outer bearing into position.

21   On 2WD vehicles, install the washer and spindle nut. Tighten the nut only slightly (no more than 12 ft-lbs of torque). Spin the hub in a forward direction while tightening the spindle nut to approximately 20 ft-lbs to seat the bearings and remove any grease or burrs which could cause excessive bearing play later. Loosen the spindle nut 1/4 turn, then using your hand (not a wrench of any kind), tighten the nut until it is snug. Install the nut lock and a new cotter pin through the hole in the spindle and the slots in the nut-lock. If the nut lock slots do not line up, remove the nut lock and turn it slightly until they do. Bend the ends of the cotter pin until they are flattened against the nut. Cut off any extra length that could interfere with the dust cover. Install the dust cover, tapping it into place with a hammer.

22   On 4WD vehicles, install the thrust washer and the inner locknut on to the spindle. Then tighten the inner locknut to 43 ft-lbs while rotating the hub to seat the bearings. Back off the inner locknut until it can be loosened by hand. Tighten the inner locknut to 18 ft-lbs while rotating the hub assembly. Verify that the hub assembly rotates smoothly and no endplay is present. Install the lock washer and tighten outer locknut to a 35 ft-lbs. Recheck the bearing preload. If there's any noticeable endplay readjust the inner locknut. Bend one lock washer tab towards the inner

locknut and another lock washer tab towards the outer locknut.

23   The remainder of the installation is the reverse of removal. **Note:** *Lightly grease the internal components of the manual locking hub assembly with chassis grease. DO NOT pack the hubs full of grease or poor operation may occur.*

35   Automatic transmission fluid and filter change (every 30,000 miles or 24 months)

Refer to illustrations 35.5, 35.7, 35.9, 35.11 and 35.12

1   At the specified intervals, the transmission fluid should be drained and replaced. Since the fluid will remain hot long after driving, perform this procedure only after the engine has cooled down completely.

2   Before beginning work, purchase the specified transmission fluid (see *Recommended lubricants and fluids* at the front of this Chapter) and a new filter.

3   Other tools necessary for this job include a floor jack, jackstands to support the vehicle in a raised position, a drain pan capable of holding at least eight quarts, newspapers and clean rags.

4   Raise the vehicle and support it securely on jackstands.

5   Place the drain pan underneath the transmission pan and remove the drain plug. Allow the fluid to completely drain from the transmission **(see illustration),** then reinstall the drain plug.

6   Detach the transmission pan rock shield (if equipped) and remove the pan mounting bolts from the outer edges of the pan.

7   Using a rubber mallet, carefully tap on the pan to break the layer of gasket sealer between the pan and the transmission case **(see illustration). Note:** *Prying between the pan and the transmission case with a screwdriver or similar tool may result in damage to the sealing surface on the transmission case.*

8   Lower the pan from the vehicle and drain the remaining transmission fluid from

the pan.

9   Remove the filter retaining screws from the valve body and remove the filter **(see illustration).**

10   Thoroughly inspect the bottom of the pan, the filter and the fluid. Although normally bright red, transmission fluid may turn dark red or brown during normal use. If you find the fluid very dark colored, or if it smells burned, it usually indicates the transmission has been overheated. If you find small pieces of metal or clutch material in the pan or filter, it indicates wear or damage have occurred to the internal parts or clutches. If you have any concerns about the condition of your transmission based on what you find in the fluid, pan and filter, it's a good idea to take your vehicle to your dealer or a transmission shop for further evaluation.

11   Clean the pan with solvent and dry it with compressed air if available. Use a gasket scraper to remove any traces of old gasket material remaining on the transmission case or valve body. **Note:** *Be very careful not to gouge the delicate aluminum gasket surface on the valve body.* Install a new filter and gasket **(see illustration).**

12   Make sure the gasket surface on the transmission pan is clean, then install a bead of RTV sealant to the pan **(see illustration).**

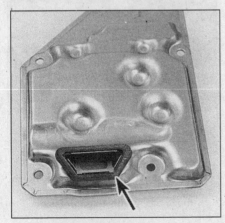

35.11 Make sure to install a new gasket (arrow) on the filter

35.12 Place a bead of RTV sealant all the way around the pan mating surface, inboard of the bolt holes

Reinsert the filler tube onto the dipstick tube and place the pan against the transmission case. Working around the pan, tighten each bolt a little at a time to the torque listed in this Chapter's Specifications.

13　Lower the vehicle and add approximately three quarts of the specified type of automatic transmission fluid through the filler tube (see Section 6).

14　With the transmission in Park and the parking brake set, start the engine.

15　Move the gear selector through each range and back to Park. Check the fluid level and add fluid, if necessary, until the level is within the correct range on the dipstick.

16　Check under the vehicle for leaks during the first few trips. Check the fluid level again when the transmission is hot (see Section 6).

36　Manual transmission lubricant change (every 30,000 miles or 24 months)

1　Raise the vehicle and support it securely on jackstands.

2　Move a drain pan, rags, newspapers and wrenches under the transmission.

3　Remove the transmission drain plug at the bottom of the case and allow the lubricant to drain into the pan **(see illustration 17.2)**.

4　After the lubricant has drained completely, reinstall the plug and tighten it securely.

5　Remove the fill plug from the side of the transmission case. Using a hand pump, syringe or funnel, fill the transmission with the specified lubricant until it is level with the lower edge of the filler hole. Reinstall the fill plug and tighten it securely.

6　Lower the vehicle.

7　Drive the vehicle for a short distance, then check the drain and fill plugs for leakage.

37　Transfer case lubricant change (4WD models only)(every 30,000 miles or 24 months)

1　Drive the vehicle for at least 15 minutes to warm the lubricant in the case. Perform this warm-up procedure with 4WD engaged, if possible. Use all gears, including Reverse, to ensure the lubricant is sufficiently warm to drain completely.

2　Raise the vehicle and support it securely on jackstands.

3　Remove the drain plug from the lower part of the case and allow the old lubricant to drain completely **(see illustrations 18.2)**.

4　After the lubricant has drained completely, reinstall the plug and tighten it securely.

5　Remove the filler plug from the case.

6　Fill the case with the specified lubricant until it is level with the lower edge of the filler hole.

7　Install the filler plug and tighten it securely.

8　Drive the vehicle for a short distance and recheck the lubricant level. In some instances a small amount of additional lubricant will have to be added.

38　Differential lubricant change (every 30,000 miles or 24 months)

Note: *The following procedure is used for the rear differential as well as the front differential.*

1　Drive the vehicle for several miles to warm up the differential oil, then raise the vehicle and support it securely on jackstands.

2　Move a drain pan, rags, newspapers and the proper tools under the vehicle.

3　With the drain pan under the differential, use a socket and ratchet to loosen the drain plug. It's the lower of the two plugs **(see illustration 19.2)**.

4　Once loosened, carefully unscrew it with your fingers until you can remove it from the case.

5　Allow all of the oil to drain into the pan, then replace the drain plug and tighten it securely.

6　Feel with your hands along the bottom of the drain pan for any metal bits that may have come out with the oil. If there are any, it's a sign of excessive wear, indicating that the internal components should be carefully inspected in the near future.

7　Remove the differential check/fill plug (see Section 19). Using a hand pump, syringe or funnel, fill the differential with the correct amount and grade of oil (see the Specifications) until the level is just at the bottom of the plug hole.

8　Reinstall the plug and tighten it securely.

9　Lower the vehicle. Check for leaks at the drain plug after the first few miles of driving.

39　Evaporative emissions control system check (every 60,000 miles or 48 months)

Refer to illustration 39.2

1　The function of the evaporative emissions control system is to draw fuel vapors from the gas tank and fuel system, store them in a charcoal canister and route them to the intake manifold during normal engine operation.

2　The most common symptom of a fault in the evaporative emissions system is a strong fuel odor in the engine compartment. If a fuel odor is detected, inspect the charcoal canister, located in the front of the engine compartment **(see illustration)**. Check the

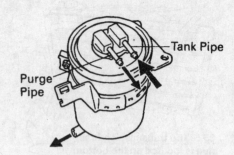

39.2　Check the evaporative emissions control canister and the hose connections for cracks and damage

canister and all hoses for damage and deterioration.

3　The evaporative emissions control system is explained in more detail in Chapter 6.

40　Exhaust Gas Recirculation (EGR) system check (every 60,000 miles or 48 months)

Refer to illustration 40.2

1　The EGR valve is usually located on the intake manifold. Most of the time when a problem develops in this emissions system, it's due to a stuck or defective EGR valve.

2　With the engine cold, to prevent burns, push on the EGR valve diaphragm. Using moderate pressure, you should be able to push the diaphragm up into the housing **(see illustration)**.

3　If the diaphragm doesn't move or is hard to move, replace the EGR valve with a new one. If in doubt about the condition of the valve, compare the free movement of your EGR valve with a new valve.

4　Refer to Chapter 6 for more information on the EGR system.

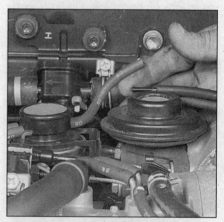

40.2　The diaphragm in the EGR valve (which can be reached through the holes in the underside of the valve) should move easily with finger pressure

Chapter 2 Part A
Four-cylinder engines

Contents

Specifications

General

Engine designation	
2.4L	2RZ-FE
2.7L	3RZ-FE
Displacement	
2RZ-FE	2.4 liters (146.4 cu.in.)
3RZ-FE	2.7 liters (164.7 cu.in.)
Cylinder numbers (drivebelt end-to-transmission end)	1-2-3-4
Firing order	1-3-4-2

Camshaft

Journal diameter	1.0614 to 1.0620 inches (26.959 to 26.975 mm)
Journal-to-bearing (oil) clearance	
Standard	0.0010 to 0.0024 inch (0.025 to 0.062 mm)
Limit	0.0031 inch (0.08 mm)
Journal out-of-round limit	0.0024 inch (0.06 mm)
Lobe height	
Intake	1.7839 to 1.7878 inches (45.31 to 45.41 mm)
Exhaust	1.7740 to 1.7779 inches (45.06 to 45.16 mm)

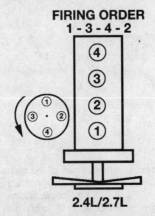

FIRING ORDER
1 - 3 - 4 - 2

2.4L/2.7L

Cylinder location and distributor rotation diagram -
1994 through 1997 models

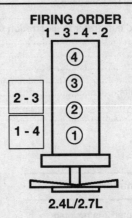

FIRING ORDER
1 - 3 - 4 - 2

2.4L/2.7L

Cylinder location and coil terminal identification diagram -
1998 and later models

Camshaft (continued)

Thrust clearance (endplay)
    Standard... 0.0016 to 0.0037 inch (0.040 to 0.095 mm)
    Limit .... 0.0047 inch (0.12 mm)
Camshaft gear backlash
    Standard... 0.0008 to 0.0079 inch (0.020 to 0.200 mm)
    Limit .... 0.0188 inch (0.30 mm)
Camshaft gear spring free length .... 0.886 to 0.902 inch (22.5 to 22.9 mm)

Oil pump

Rotor-to-body clearance
    Standard... 0.0039 to 0.0069 inch (0.100 to 0.175 mm)
    Service limit... 0.0118 inch (0.30 mm)
Rotor tip clearance
    Standard... 0.0043 to 0.0094 inch (0.011 to 0.240 mm)
    Service limit... 0.0098 inch (0.25 mm)
Rotor-to-cover clearance
    Standard... 0.0012 to 0.0035 inch (0.030 to 0.090 mm)
    Service limit... 0.0059 inch (0.15 mm)

Torque specifications

	Ft-lbs (unless otherwise indicated)
Air intake plenum	15
Distributor gear	34
Intake manifold bolts	22
Exhaust manifold nuts	36
Exhaust pipe-to-exhaust manifold	46
Heat insulator-to-exhaust manifold	48 in-lbs
Air pipe (PAIR system)	
Bolt	14
Nut	15
Crankshaft pulley-to-crankshaft bolt	193
Flywheel bolts (manual transmission)	
Step 1	19
Step 2	Tighten an additional 90-degrees
Driveplate bolts (automatic transmission)	54
Heater inlet pipe and hose bolt	15
Idler pulley bolts	27
Cylinder head bolts	
Step 1	29
Step 2	Tighten an additional 90-degrees
Step 3	Tighten an additional 90-degrees
Cylinder head-to-timing cover bolts	15
Camshaft bearing cap bolts	12
Camshaft sprocket bolt	54
Oil pump bolts	12
Oil pick-up tubestrainer assembly nuts	13
Oil jet	13
Oil pan bolts	9
Oil relief valve	36
Rear crankshaft oil seal retainer bolts	15
Stiffener plate bolts	27
Timing cover bolts and nuts **(refer to illustration 9.23)**	
Bolt A	14
Bolt B	18
Bolt C	32
Nut D	14
Backside cover bolts	13
Timing chain tensioner nuts	15
Valve cover bolts	15

1 General information

This Part of Chapter 2 is devoted to in-vehicle repair procedures for the 2.4L and 2.7L DOHC four-cylinder engines. All information concerning engine removal and installation and engine block and cylinder head overhaul can be found in Part C of this Chapter.

The following repair procedures are based on the assumption that the engine is installed in the vehicle. If the engine has been removed from the vehicle and mounted on a stand, many of the steps outlined in this Part of Chapter 2 will not apply.

The Specifications included in this Part of Chapter 2 apply only to the procedures contained in this Part. Part C of Chapter 2 contains the Specifications necessary for cylinder head and engine block rebuilding.

Both of these engines are equipped with overhead camshafts, driven by a timing chain. Each cylinder is equipped with two intake valves and two exhaust valves. The left camshaft (driver's side) operates the intake valves while the right camshaft (passenger's side) operates the exhaust valves. The 2.7L engine is equipped with balance shafts that are driven by another chain and sprocket.

The 2.4L engine produces 143 horsepower while the 2.7L produces 150 horsepower.

2   Repair operations possible with the engine in the vehicle

Many major repair operations can be accomplished without removing the engine from the vehicle.

Clean the engine compartment and the exterior of the engine with some type of degreaser before any work is done. It will make the job easier and help keep dirt out of the internal areas of the engine.

Depending on the components involved, it may be helpful to remove the hood to improve access to the engine as repairs are performed (refer to Chapter 11 if necessary). Cover the fenders to prevent damage to the paint. Special pads are available, but an old bedspread or blanket will also work.

If vacuum, exhaust, oil or coolant leaks develop, indicating a need for gasket or seal replacement, the repairs can generally be made with the engine in the vehicle. The intake and exhaust manifold gaskets, oil pan gasket, crankshaft oil seals and cylinder head gasket are all accessible with the engine in place. On balance shaft engines, remove the engine before replacing the balance shaft assembly.

Exterior engine components, such as the intake and exhaust manifolds, the oil pan, the oil pump, the water pump, the starter motor, the alternator, the distributor and the fuel system components can be removed for repair with the engine in place.

Since the cylinder head can be removed without pulling the engine, camshaft and valve component servicing can also be accomplished with the engine in the vehicle. Replacement of the timing chain and pulleys is also possible with the engine in the vehicle.

In extreme cases caused by a lack of necessary equipment, repair or replacement of piston rings, pistons, connecting rods and rod bearings is possible with the engine in the vehicle. However, this practice is not recommended because of the cleaning and preparation work that must be done to the components involved.

3   Top Dead Center (TDC) for number one piston - locating

Note: *The following procedure is based on the assumption that the distributor is correctly installed. If you are trying to locate TDC to install the distributor correctly, piston posi-*

3.8 The timing mark on the pulley should align with the 0-degree mark on the timing cover

tion must be determined by feeling for compression at the number one spark plug hole, then aligning the ignition timing marks as described in step 8.

1   Top Dead Center (TDC) is the highest point in the cylinder that each piston reaches as it travels up the cylinder bore. Each piston reaches TDC on the compression stroke and again on the exhaust stroke, but TDC generally refers to piston position on the compression stroke.

2   Positioning the piston(s) at TDC is an essential part of many procedures such as valve timing, camshaft and timing belt/pulley removal and distributor removal.

3   Before beginning this procedure, be sure to place the transmission in Neutral (manual transmission) or Park (automatic transmission) and apply the parking brake or block the rear wheels. Also, disable the ignition system by detaching the primary (low voltage) wires from the coil(s). Remove the spark plugs (see Chapter 1).

4   In order to bring any piston to TDC, the crankshaft must be turned using one of the methods outlined below. When looking at the front of the engine, normal crankshaft rotation is clockwise.

a)   *The preferred method is to turn the crankshaft with a socket and ratchet attached to the bolt threaded into the front of the crankshaft. Apply pressure on the bolt in a clockwise direction only. Never turn the bolt counterclockwise.*

b)   *A remote starter switch, which may save some time, can also be used. Follow the instructions included with the switch. Once the piston is close to TDC, use a socket and ratchet as described in the previous paragraph.*

c)   *If an assistant is available to turn the ignition switch to the Start position in short bursts, you can get the piston close to TDC without a remote starter switch. Make sure your assistant is out of the vehicle, away from the ignition switch, then use a socket and ratchet as described in Paragraph (a) to complete the procedure.*

3.11 Rotate the distributor until the rotor is aligned with the number one terminal on the distributor cap and mark this position on the distributor body

Distributor ignition system

Refer to illustrations 3.8 and 3.11

5   Note the position of the terminal for the number one spark plug wire on the distributor cap. Refer to the Specifications diagram. If the terminal isn't marked, follow the plug wire from the number one cylinder spark plug to the cap.

6   Use a felt-tip pen or chalk to make a mark on the distributor body directly under the terminal.

7   Detach the cap from the distributor and set it aside (see Chapter 1 if necessary).

8   Turn the crankshaft (see Step 4) until the notch in the crankshaft pulley is aligned with the 0 on the timing scale (located at the front of the engine) **(see illustration)**.

9   Look at the distributor rotor - it should be pointing directly at the mark you made on the distributor body.

10   If the rotor is 180-degrees off, the number one piston is at TDC on the exhaust stroke.

11   To get the piston to TDC on the compression stroke, turn the crankshaft one complete turn (360-degrees) clockwise. The rotor should now be pointing at the mark on the distributor **(see illustration)**. When the rotor is pointing at the number one spark plug wire terminal in the distributor cap and the ignition timing marks are aligned, the number one piston is at TDC on the compression stroke.

12   After the number one piston has been positioned at TDC on the compression stroke, TDC for any of the remaining pistons can be located by turning the crankshaft and following the firing order. Mark the remaining spark plug wire terminal locations on the distributor body just like you did for the number one terminal, then number the marks to correspond with the cylinder numbers. As you turn the crankshaft, the rotor will also turn. When it's pointing directly at one of the marks on the distributor, the piston for that particular cylinder is at TDC on the compression stroke.

4.5 Remove the bolts around the perimeter of the valve cover

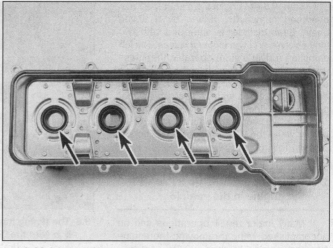

4.6 Make sure the spark plug tube seals (arrows) are in place before installing the valve cover

Distributorless ignition system

13   1998 and later models do not have a distributor, but rather two coil packs, fired in sequence by signals from the computer. To find TDC on the compression stroke for the number one cylinder, remove the spark plug from cylinder number one.

14   Install a compression gauge in the number one spark plug hole (refer to Chapter 2C). It should be a gauge with a screw-in fitting and a hose at least six inches long.

15   Rotate the crankshaft using one of the methods described in Step 4 while observing the compression gauge. When the compression stroke of the number one cylinder is reached, compression pressure will show on the gauge as the marks are beginning to line up. If you go past the marks, release the gauge pressure and rotate the crankshaft around two more revolutions. **Note:** *The most positive method for finding TDC on engines equipped with the distributorless ignition system is to examine the crankshaft timing marks and camshaft sprocket timing marks (see Section 7).*

4   Valve cover - removal and installation

Removal

Refer to illustration 4.5

1   Disconnect the negative cable from the battery. **Caution:** *If the stereo in your vehicle is equipped with an anti-theft system, make sure you have the correct activation code before disconnecting the battery.*

2   Remove the air intake duct (see Chapter 4). Detach the PCV hoses from the valve cover.

3   Remove the spark plug wire covers. Remove the spark plug wires from the spark plugs, handling them by the boots, not

pulling on the wires.

4   Disconnect the accelerator and cruise control cables from the throttle body and position them out of the way (see Chapter 4). If equipped, remove the number one engine hanger located on the front section of the intake manifold.

5   Remove the valve cover mounting bolts, then detach the valve cover and gasket from the cylinder head **(see illustration)**. If the valve cover is stuck to the cylinder head, bump the end with a wood block and a hammer to jar it loose. If that doesn't work, try to slip a flexible putty knife between the cylinder head and valve cover to break the seal. **Caution:** *Don't pry at the valve cover-to-cylinder head joint or damage to the sealing surfaces may occur, leading to oil leaks after the valve cover is reinstalled.*

Installation

Refer to illustrations 4.6 and 4.7

6   The mating surfaces of the cylinder head and valve cover must be clean when the valve cover is installed. The rubber sealing gasket can be reused unless the rubber has hardened or cracked. If necessary, pull out the rubber gasket and clean the mating surfaces with lacquer thinner or acetone. Install a new rubber gasket, pressing it evenly into the groove around the underside of the valve cover. If there's residue or oil on the mating surfaces when the valve cover is installed, oil leaks may develop. **Note:** *Make sure the spark plug tube gaskets are in place on the underside of the valve cover before reinstalling it* **(see illustration).**

7   Apply RTV sealant to the semi-circular rubber plugs and install them onto the cylinder head **(see illustration).**

8   Install the valve cover and bolts, tightening the bolts securely.

9   Reinstall the remaining components, run the engine and check for oil leaks.

5   Intake manifold - removal and installation

Removal

Refer to illustration 5.7

Note: *If the intake manifold is to be removed only for removal of the cylinder head, then the intake manifold can simply be unbolted from the cylinder head and pushed away from the cylinder head, without disconnecting any hoses, wires or linkage. The following procedure is for complete removal of the manifold from the vehicle.*

1   Disconnect the negative cable from the battery. **Caution:** *If the stereo in your vehicle is equipped with an anti-theft system, make sure you have the correct activation code before disconnecting the battery.*

2   Refer to Chapter 4 and relieve the fuel system pressure.

3   Label and detach the PCV and vacuum hoses connected to the intake manifold, including those from the brake booster and the air conditioning idle-up valve.

4   Remove the throttle body and air intake plenum (see Chapter 4).

5   Remove the fuel rail and injectors as an assembly from the intake manifold (see Chapter 4).

6   Disconnect the vacuum hoses from the EGR valve and vacuum modulator (if equipped), label them correctly and unbolt the EGR pipe from the intake manifold (see Chapter 4). Set the EGR assembly aside.

7   Remove the ground strap and mounting nuts/bolts, then detach the manifold from the engine **(see illustration)**. **Note:** *Be sure to remove the fuel return line from the lower section of the cylinder head before removing the intake manifold (see Chapter 4).*

Installation

8   Clean the mating surfaces of the intake manifold and the cylinder head mounting sur-

4.7 Apply sealant to the rubber plugs before installing the valve cover

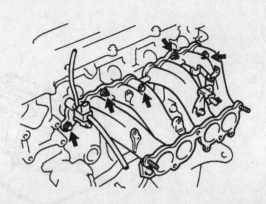

5.7 Remove the intake manifold bolts/nuts (arrows) and remove the intake manifold

6.3 Remove the bolts that retain the heat insulator to the exhaust manifold (arrows)

6.5 Remove the nuts (arrows) and remove the exhaust manifold

face with lacquer thinner or acetone. If the gasket shows signs of leaking, have the manifold checked for warpage at an automotive machine shop and resurfaced if necessary.

9   Install a new gasket, then position the manifold on the cylinder head and install the nuts/bolts.

10   Tighten the nuts/bolts in three equal steps to the torque listed in this Chapter's Specifications. Work from the center out towards the ends to avoid warping the manifold.

11   Install the remaining parts in the reverse order of removal.

12   Before starting the engine, check the throttle linkage for smooth operation.

13   Run the engine and check for coolant and vacuum leaks.

14   Road test the vehicle and check for proper operation of all accessories, including the cruise control system, if equipped.

6   Exhaust manifold - removal and installation

Warning: *The engine must be completely cool before beginning this procedure.*

Removal

Refer to illustrations 6.3 and 6.5

1   Disconnect the negative cable from the battery. **Caution:** *If the stereo in your vehicle is equipped with an anti-theft system, make sure you have the correct activation code before disconnecting the battery.*

2   If the engine is equipped with the Pulse Air Injection (PAIR) system, remove the pipes and valve assembly from the cylinder head and exhaust manifold area (see Chapter 6).

3   Remove the upper heat insulator (if equipped) from the manifold **(see illustration).**

4   Apply penetrating oil to the exhaust manifold mounting nuts, and the nuts retaining the exhaust pipe to the manifold. After the nuts have soaked, remove the nuts retaining the exhaust pipe to the manifold (see Chapter 4).

5   Remove the nuts and detach the manifold and gasket **(see illustration).**

Installation

6   Use a scraper to remove all traces of old gasket material and carbon deposits from the manifold and the cylinder head mating sur-

face. If the gasket was leaking, have the manifold checked for warpage at an automotive machine shop and resurfaced if necessary.

7   Position a new gasket over the cylinder head studs. **Note:** *The marks on the gasket should face out (away from the cylinder head). Consult the parts representative concerning the position of the gasket if in doubt.*

8   Install the manifold and thread the mounting nuts into place.

9   Working from the center out, tighten the nuts to the torque listed in this Chapter's Specifications in three or four equal steps.

10   Reinstall the remaining parts in the reverse order of removal.

11   Run the engine and check for exhaust leaks.

7   Camshafts and valve lifters - removal, inspection and installation

Note: *Before beginning this procedure, obtain two 6 x 1.0 mm bolts, 16 to 20 mm long. They will be referred to as service bolts in the text.*

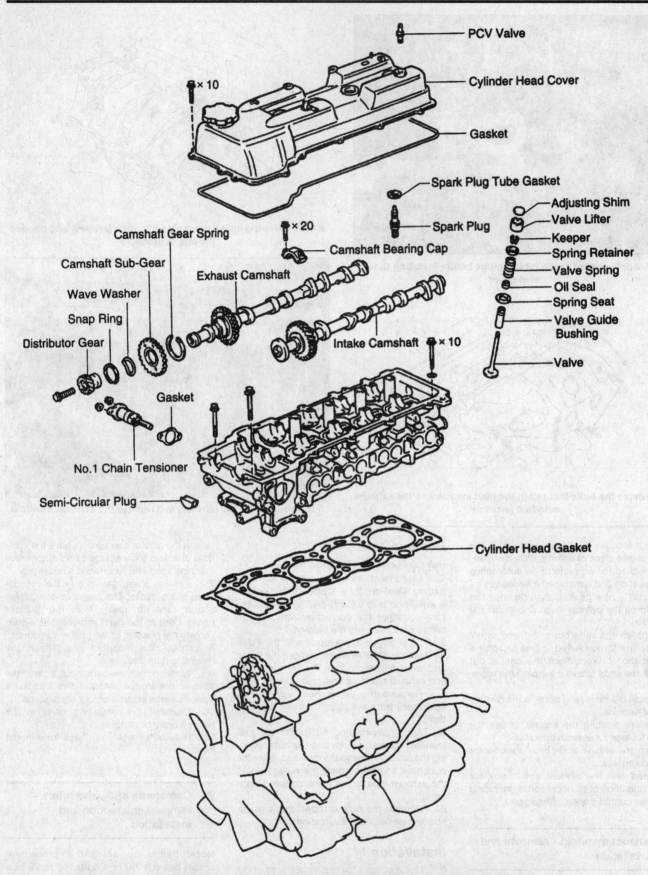

7.1 Exploded view of the cylinder head assembly (2.4L and 2.7L engines)

7.2 With the No. 1 piston at TDC on the compression stroke, the two dots on the exhaust camshaft gear align with the single dot on the intake camshaft

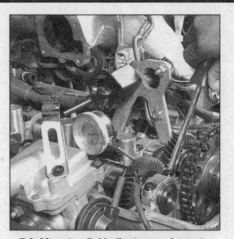

7.3 Mount a dial indicator as shown to measure camshaft endplay - pry the camshaft to the rear, then zero the dial and pry the camshaft forward to read the endplay

7.5a Remove the timing chain tensioner cover bolts (arrows) . . .

7.5b . . . and withdraw the tensioner from the timing cover

7.6a Apply a paint mark on the timing chain link aligned with the camshaft sprocket timing mark

7.6b Use a wrench placed on the hex provided to hold the camshaft while removing the camshaft sprocket bolt

Removal

Refer to illustrations 7.1, 7.2, 7.3, 7.5a, 7.5b, 7.6a, 7.6b, 7.6c, 7.8, 7.9, 7.10, 7.15a and 7.15b

1   Remove the valve cover as described in Section 4 **(see illustration)**.
2   Refer to Section 3 and place the engine on TDC for number 1 cylinder. Make sure the alignment marks (dots) of the camshaft drive and driven gears are in a straight line in relation to the cylinder head/valve cover mating surface **(see illustration)**. If not, double-check the TDC mark on the crankshaft pulley and rotate the engine 360-degrees to obtain the correct setting.
3   Measure the camshaft thrust clearance (endplay) with a dial indicator **(see illustration)**. If the clearance is greater than the service limit, replace the camshaft and/or the cylinder head.
4   Remove the distributor, if equipped (see Chapter 5).

5   Remove the timing chain tensioner **(see illustrations)**.
6   Apply a paint mark on the timing chain link aligned with the timing mark on the camshaft sprocket. Hold the intake camshaft with a wrench and remove the camshaft sprocket bolt. Remove the distributor drive gear. Carefully remove the camshaft sprocket and chain from the camshaft and rest it on the chain guides **(see illustrations)**.

Exhaust camshaft

7   First, remove the exhaust camshaft. Before it is removed, however, the spring-loaded sub-gear must be retained as follows. **Caution:** *The camshafts must be removed from the cylinder head in sequence and kept horizontal to the plane of the cylinder head when loosened to avoid damaging the portion of the cylinder head that regulates the thrust clearance of the camshafts.*
8   Rotate the camshaft until the service bolt hole of the camshaft sub-gear is facing

7.6c Remove the camshaft sprocket and chain from the intake camshaft - lower the sprocket onto the chain guides

7.8 Install a service bolt through the sub-gear and thread it into the main gear (arrow)

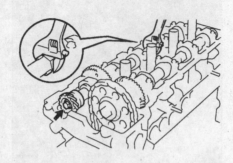

7.9 On engines equipped with a distributor, use a wrench to prevent the camshaft from rotating and remove the distributor drive gear retaining bolt

7.10 Removal sequence for the camshaft bearing caps. These numbers do not designate the bearing cap numbers, but indicate the proper order for removal

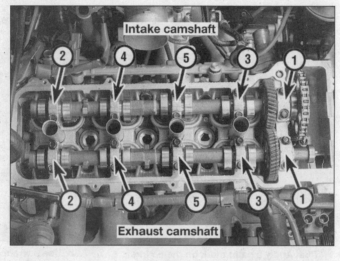

the number 1 bearing cap bolts by alternately loosening the bolts a little at a time (see illustration).

11   Loosen and remove the bearing cap bolts in several passes, alternately loosening the right and left bolts uniformly. Watch to make sure the camshaft rises evenly in a horizontal plane to the cylinder head. If the camshaft does not come up evenly, reinstall the number 3 bearing cap bolts (third from front) and tighten the two bearing cap bolts back down and slowly loosen them while keeping the camshaft gear level.

Intake camshaft

12   Next, remove the intake camshaft. Lightly push the camshaft toward the front of the engine and loosen the number 1 bearing cap bolts by alternately loosening the bolts a little at a time (see illustration 7.10).

13   Loosen and remove the bearing cap bolts in several passes, alternately loosening the right and left bolts uniformly. Watch to make sure the camshaft rises evenly in a horizontal plane to the cylinder head. If the camshaft does not come up evenly, reinstall the number 3 bearing cap bolts (third from front) and tighten the two bearing cap bolts back down and slowly loosen them while keeping the camshaft gear level.

14   Remove the intake camshaft.

15   Clean the oil from the valve lifter shims, mark them with a felt-tip marker and remove the lifters, keeping the shims with their respective lifters (see illustration). Store the camshaft bearing caps, lifters and shims so they can be reinstalled in their original locations (see illustration).

Inspection

Refer to illustrations 7.16, 7.17a, 7.17b, 7.18, 7.19, 7.20, 7.21, 7.22a, 7.22b and 7.23

16   Position the exhaust camshaft in a vise, clamping it on the hex portion. Using a two-pin spanner, rotate the sub-gear clockwise and remove the service bolt from the threaded hole, then allow the sub-gear to rotate back until all tension is relieved (see illustration).

up (see illustration). Secure the sub-gear to the main gear with a service bolt (6 mm thread diameter, 1 mm thread pitch and 16 to 20 mm long).

9   On distributor-equipped engines, hold the exhaust camshaft with a wrench and remove the bolt and distributor gear (see illustration).

10   Lightly push the camshafts toward the rear of the engine compartment and loosen

7.15a Mark the lifters/shims (I for intake, E for exhaust, and number their location) and remove them with a magnetic retrieval tool

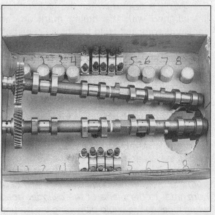

7.15b Mark up a cardboard box to store the lifters/shims and bearing caps

7.16 With the hex portion of the exhaust camshaft clamped in a vise, use a spanner to relieve the tension on the service bolt, remove the bolt, then release the tension on the sub-gear

7.17a Remove the snap-ring with a pair of snap-ring pliers

7.17b Remove the wave washer (1), the camshaft sub-gear (2) and the gear spring (3)

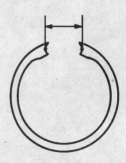

7.18 Measure the distance between the ends of the camshaft gear spring

7.19 Inspect each lifter for wear and scuffing

7.20 Measure the lobe heights on each camshaft - if any lobe height is less than the specified allowable minimum, replace that camshaft

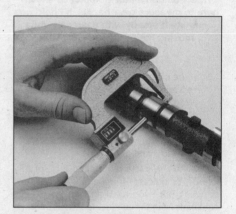

7.21 Measure each journal diameter with a micrometer (if any journal measures less than the specified limit, replace the camshaft)

17   Remove the sub-gear snap-ring. The wave washer, sub-gear and camshaft gear spring can now be removed from the camshaft **(see illustrations)**.

18   Measure the free length (distance between the ends) of the camshaft gear spring **(see illustration)** and compare it to this Chapter's Specifications. If not as specified, replace the spring.

.19   Inspect each lifter for scuffing and score marks **(see illustration)**.

20   Visually examine the cam lobes and bearing journals for score marks, pitting, galling and evidence of overheating (blue, discolored areas). Look for flaking away of the hardened surface layer of each lobe. Using a micrometer, measure the height of each camshaft lobe **(see illustration)**. Compare your measurements with this Chapter's Specifications. If the height for any one lobe is less than the specified minimum, replace the camshaft.

21   Using a micrometer, measure the diameter of each journal at several points **(see illustration)**. Compare your measurements with this Chapter's Specifications. If the diameter of any one journal is less than specified, replace the camshaft.

22   Check the oil clearance for each camshaft journal as follows:

a)   Clean the bearing caps and the camshaft journals with lacquer thinner or acetone.

7.22a The camshaft bearing caps are numbered with an arrow facing the front of the engine

b)   Carefully lay the camshaft(s) in place in the cylinder head. Don't install the lifters or intake camshaft sub-gear and don't use any lubrication.

c)   Lay a strip of Plastigage on each journal.

d)   Install the bearing caps with the arrows pointing toward the front (timing chain end) of the engine **(see illustration)**.

7.22b Compare the width of the crushed Plastigage to the scale on the envelope to determine the oil clearance

e)   Tighten the bolts to the torque listed in this Chapter's Specifications in 1/4-turn increments. **Note:** Don't turn the camshaft while the Plastigage is in place.

f)   Remove the bolts and detach the caps.

g)   Compare the width of the crushed Plastigage (at its widest point) to the scale on the Plastigage envelope **(see illustration)**.

7.23 Position a dial indicator as shown here to measure gear backlash - hold one camshaft steady with a wrench while moving the other camshaft with another wrench

h) If the clearance is greater than specified, replace the camshaft and/or cylinder head.
i) Scrape off the Plastigage with your fingernail or the edge of a credit card - don't scratch or nick the journals or bearing caps.

23 With the caps reinstalled temporarily, use a dial indicator to measure the backlash between the two camshaft gears. Hold one camshaft from turning (using a wrench on the hex portion) while measuring the movement in the other camshaft gear, and compare the results to Specifications **(see illustration)**. If the backlash is beyond Specifications, replace both camshafts.

Installation

Refer to illustrations 7.26, 7.28, 7.33, 7.36, 7.42a, 7.42b, 7.42c and 7.42d

Intake camshaft

24 Apply camshaft installation lube to the lifters, then install them in their original locations. Make sure the valve adjustment shims are in place on the lifters.
25 Apply camshaft installation lube to the camshaft lobes and bearing journals. Also,

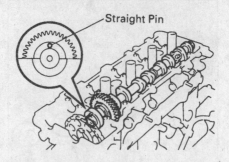

7.26 Gently place the intake camshaft into position with the straight pin facing up

apply lubrication to the thrust portion of the intake camshaft.
26 Position the intake camshaft in the cylinder head with the pin on the front end of the shaft facing up **(see illustration)**.
27 Lightly push the camshaft toward the front of the engine and install the bearing caps in the proper location. The bearing caps are numbered 1 through 5 with number 1 toward the front of the engine. Make sure the arrows are pointing toward the front of the engine.
28 Temporarily tighten the bolts uniformly and in sequence **(see illustration)**.
29 After the intake camshaft is secured, tighten all the intake bearing cap bolts to the torque listed in this Chapter's Specifications in several stages.

Exhaust camshaft

30 Reassemble the exhaust camshaft subgear. Install the camshaft gear spring, subgear and wave washer. Install the snap-ring **(see illustrations 7.17a and 7.17b)**. Align the hole in the sub-gear with the hole in the camshaft gear and install the service bolt.
31 Apply camshaft installation lube to the lifters, then install them in their original locations. Make sure the valve adjustment shims are in place on the lifters.
32 Apply camshaft installation lube to the camshaft lobes and bearing journals.
33 Align the intake camshaft gear with the exhaust camshaft gear by matching up the two dot alignment marks on the gears **(see**

illustration). The straight pin on the front of the exhaust camshaft must be pointed up. This is a non-interference engine and the camshafts must be tightened at this position and later rotated back into the TDC position to allow the thrust surface area to mate evenly without the hindrance of the spring pressure upon certain lobes. Follow the instructions carefully.
34 Roll the exhaust camshaft down into position. Turn the exhaust camshaft back and forth a little until the exhaust camshaft sits in the bearings evenly.
35 Lightly push the camshaft toward the front of the engine and install the bearing caps in the proper location. The bearing caps are numbered 1 through 5 with number 1 toward the front of the engine. Make sure the arrows are pointing toward the front of the engine.
36 Temporarily tighten the bolts uniformly and in sequence **(see illustration)**.
37 Tighten all the exhaust bearing cap bolts to the torque listed in this Chapter's Specifications in several stages.
38 Rotate the camshafts until the service bolt is pointing up, then remove the service bolt. Make sure the camshafts rotate smoothly.
39 Position the camshafts with the timing marks aligned at TDC **(see illustration 7.2)**. Make sure the crankshaft pulley is still aligned at TDC.
40 Install the camshaft sprocket and chain. Make sure the alignment marks made in Step 6 are aligned. Install the bolt and tighten it to the torque listed in this Chapter's Specifications.
41 Install the distributor gear, if equipped. Install the bolt and tighten it to the torque listed in this Chapter's Specifications.
42 Depress the the plunger of the chain tensioner and lock it in place with the pawl, then install the tensioner (using a new gasket), tightening the nuts to the torque listed in this Chapter's Specifications **(see illustrations)**. Rotate the crankshaft slightly counterclockwise to release the tensioner **(see illustrations)**, then rotate it back clockwise to realign the timing marks and position the engine at TDC for cylinder number one.

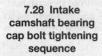

7.28 Intake camshaft bearing cap bolt tightening sequence

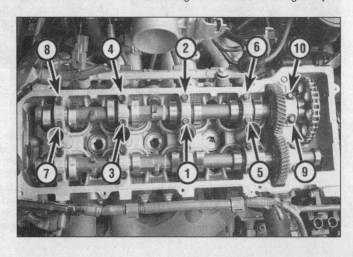

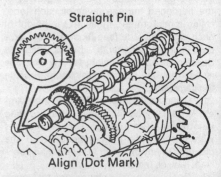

7.33 Align the camshaft gears as shown here using the alignment dots on the gears and the straight pin mark

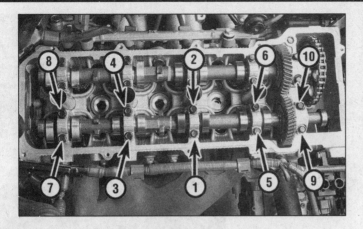

7.36 Exhaust camshaft bearing cap bolt tightening sequence

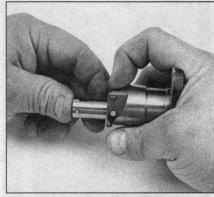

7.42a Release the ratchet pawl with the index finger and push in the plunger

7.42b Swing the hook into position to retain the plunger

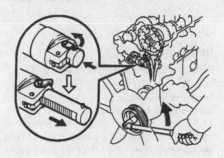

7.42c To set the chain tensioner, turn the crankshaft to the left so the hook of the chain tensioner is released from the pin on the plunger

7.42d If the plunger does not spring out, press the tensioner shoe into the chain tensioner until the hook releases the plunger

43 The remainder of installation is the reverse of the removal procedure. Check and adjust the valve clearance (see Chapter 1), if necessary, and the ignition timing (see Chapter 5).

8 Cylinder head - removal and installation

Warning: *The engine must be completely cool before beginning this procedure.*

Removal

Refer to illustrations 8.11, 8.12, 8.13a, 8.13b and 8.14

1 Disconnect the negative cable from the battery. **Caution:** *If the stereo in your vehicle is equipped with an anti-theft system, make sure you have the correct activation code before disconnecting the battery.*

2 Drain the coolant from the engine block and radiator (see Chapter 1).

3 Drain the engine oil and remove the oil filter (see Chapter 1).

4 Remove the throttle body, air intake plenum, fuel injectors and fuel rail (see Chapter 4).

5 Remove the intake manifold (see Section 5).

6 Remove the exhaust manifold (see Section 6). **Note:** *It is possible to leave the intake and exhaust manifolds attached to the cylin-*

8.11 Remove the ground strap bolt from the cylinder head (arrow)

der head, to be removed along with the cylinder head for disassembly on the bench (but this assembly will weigh considerably more than the cylinder head alone).

7 Remove the alternator and distributor (see Chapter 5).

8 Remove the camshaft sprocket from the intake camshaft and rest it on the timing chain guides (see Section 7).

9 Remove the camshafts and valve lifters (see Section 7).

8.12 Remove the dipstick tube mounting bolt from the cylinder head (arrow)

10 Unbolt the upper bracket of the power steering pump and set the pump aside without disconnecting the hoses.

11 Label and remove any remaining items, such as coolant fittings, brackets, tubes, cables and hoses **(see illustration)**. Disconnect the wiring harness connectors from the various sensors.

12 Remove the dipstick tube bolt and separate it from the cylinder head **(see illustration)**.

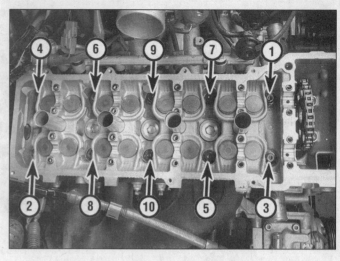

8.13b   Cylinder head bolt LOOSENING sequence

8.13a   Remove the two cylinder head-to-timing cover bolts (arrows)

13   Remove the two cylinder head-to-timing cover bolts **(see illustration)**. Using a socket bit and a breaker bar, loosen the cylinder head bolts in 1/4-turn increments until they can be removed by hand. Loosen the cylinder head bolts using the proper sequence to avoid warping or cracking the cylinder head **(see illustration)**. **Caution:** *Because cylinder head bolts are often damaged by stretching, thread collapsing or stripping, have each head bolt examined by a qualified machinist. If in doubt about the integrity of the cylinder head bolts, replace them with new ones.*
14   Lift the cylinder head off the engine block. If it's stuck, very carefully pry up underneath the power steering pump bracket, beyond the gasket surface of the engine block **(see illustration)**.
15   Remove all external components from the cylinder head to allow for thorough cleaning and inspection. See Chapter 2, Part C, for cylinder head servicing procedures.

Installation

Refer to illustrations 8.17, 8.22 and 8.25

16   The mating surfaces of the cylinder head and block must be perfectly clean when the cylinder head is installed.
17   Use a gasket scraper to remove all traces of carbon and old gasket material **(see illustration)**, then clean the mating surfaces with lacquer thinner or acetone. If there's oil on the mating surfaces when the cylinder head is installed, the gasket may not seal correctly and leaks could develop. When working on the block, stuff the cylinders with clean shop rags to keep out debris. Use a vacuum cleaner to remove material that falls into the cylinders.
18   Check the block and cylinder head mating surfaces for nicks, deep scratches and other damage. If damage is slight, it can be removed with a file; if it's excessive, machining may be the only alternative.
19   Use a tap of the correct size to chase

the threads in the cylinder head bolt holes, then clean the holes with compressed air - make sure that nothing remains in the holes. **Warning:** *Wear eye protection when using compressed air!*
20   Mount each bolt in a vise and run a die down the threads to remove corrosion and restore the threads. Dirt, corrosion, sealant and damaged threads will affect torque readings.
21   Install the components that were removed from the cylinder head.
22   Position the new gasket over the dowel pins in the block **(see illustration)**.
23   Carefully set the cylinder head on the block without disturbing the gasket.
24   Before installing the cylinder head bolts, apply a small amount of clean engine oil to the threads and under the bolt heads.
25   Install the bolts in their original locations and tighten them finger tight. Install the shorter bolts along the intake side of the cylinder head and the longer bolts along the

8.14   Use a large screwdriver or prybar and pry the cylinder head off the engine block using the power steering pump bracket for leverage to avoid damaging the soft aluminum material of the cylinder head

8.17   Remove all traces of old gasket material - the cylinder head and block mating surfaces must be perfectly clean to ensure a good gasket seal

8.22   Place the cylinder head gasket over the dowel pins, making sure it is installed with the correct side up

exhaust side. Following the recommended sequence, tighten the bolts in three steps to the torque listed in this Chapter's Specifications **(see illustration)**. Steps 2 and 3 of the tightening sequence each require the bolts to be tightened an additional 90-degrees (1/4-turn). If you don't have an angle-torque attachment for your torque wrench, simply apply a paint mark at one edge of each cylinder head bolt and tighten the bolt until that mark is 90-degrees from where you started. After Step 3, the marks will be 180-degrees from where they started. Install the two cylinder head-to-timing cover bolts and tighten them to the torque listed in this Chapter's Specifications.

26   The remaining installation steps are the reverse of removal, refer to the appropriate Sections for component installation.

27   Check and adjust the valves (see Chapter 1).

28   Refill the cooling system, install a new oil filter and add oil to the engine (see Chapter 1).

29   Run the engine and check for leaks. Adjust the ignition timing (see Chapter 5) and road test the vehicle.

9   Timing cover and chain - removal, inspection and installation

Warning: *The engine must be completely cool before beginning this procedure.*

Removal

> **** CAUTION ****
>
> The timing system is complex. Severe engine damage will occur if you make any mistakes. Do not attempt this procedure unless you are highly experienced with this type of repair. If you are at all unsure of your abilities, consult an expert. Double-check all your work and be sure everything is correct before you attempt to start the engine.

Refer to illustrations 9.7, 9.8, 9.14a, 9.14b, 9.15a, 9.15b, 9.15c and 9.16

1   Disconnect the negative cable from the battery. **Caution:** *If the stereo in your vehicle is equipped with an anti-theft system, make sure you have the correct activation code before disconnecting the battery.*

2   Block the rear wheels and apply the parking brake. Drain the engine coolant and the engine oil (see Chapter 1).

3   Raise the front of the vehicle and support it securely on jackstands.

4   If equipped, remove the protective cover under the front of the engine compartment.

5   Remove the coolant expansion tank (see Chapter 3).

6   Remove the spark plugs and drivebelts (see Chapter 1).

7   Detach the air conditioning compressor, without disconnecting the refrigerant lines,

8.25 Cylinder head bolt TIGHTENING sequence

and position the compressor aside (see Chapter 3). Remove the compressor mounting bracket **(see illustration)**.

8   Remove the alternator, the alternator bracket assembly, the drivebelt idler pulley and the adjustment bracket from the engine **(see illustration)**.

9   Unbolt the cruise control actuator (if equipped) and set it aside.

10   Detach and lower the radiator hose from the inlet and remove the two nuts from the bracket. Remove the water pump (see

Chapter 3).

11   Position the number one piston at TDC on the compression stroke (see Section 3).

12   Remove the cylinder head (see Section 8).

13   Remove the oil pan (see Section 11) and oil strainer.

14   Loosen the crankshaft pulley bolt, using a chain wrench or strap wrench **(see illustration)**. The crankshaft pulley should slide off the crankshaft. If necessary, use a bolt-type puller to pull it off **(see illustration)**.

9.8 Remove the bolts (arrows) that retain the lower alternator bracket to the timing cover

9.7 Remove the bolts (arrows) that retain the air conditioning compressor bracket to the timing cover and the engine block

9.14a Install a strap or chain wrench over the crankshaft pulley (be sure to wrap an old drivebelt or thick rag under the chain links to prevent damage to the pulley), then loosen the pulley bolt

9.14b Remove the crankshaft pulley with a puller that bolts to the threaded holes in the pulley

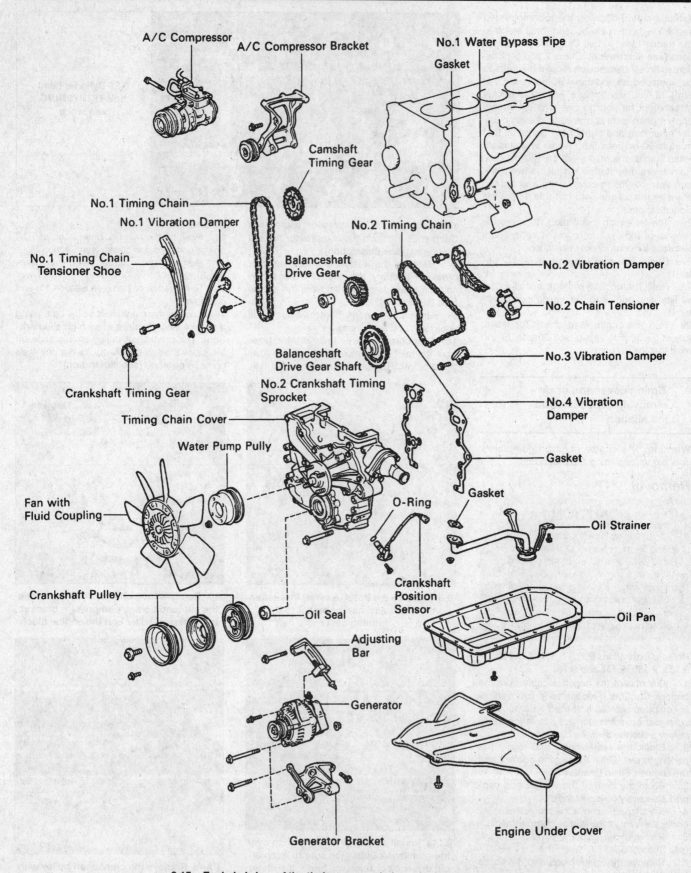

9.15a Exploded view of the timing cover, chain and related components

9.15b Remove the two bolts (arrows) from the backside of the timing cover

9.15c Carefully pry the timing chain cover off the front of the engine block with a dull screwdriver

Installation

15   Remove the timing chain cover bolts and nuts **(see illustrations)**. Carefully pry the timing chain cover off with a dull screwdriver being careful not to nick or gouge the aluminum **(see illustration)**.

16   Remove the timing chain and camshaft sprocket **(see illustration)**. **Note:** *Refer to Chapter 2C for the timing chain guide removal and the balance shaft assembly removal procedures.*

Inspection

Refer to illustrations 9.18a and 9.18b

17   Inspect the individual sprocket teeth and keyways for wear and damage. Check the chain for cracked plates, pitted or worn rollers, Check the chain guides for wear or

damage. Replace any worn or excessively worn or defective parts with new ones. **Caution:** *If excessive plastic material is missing from the chain guides, the oil pan should be removed and cleaned of all debris. Check the oil pick-up tube and screen. Replace the assembly if it is clogged.*

18   Check the timing chain tensioner for proper operation:

a) *Check that the plunger moves smoothly when the ratchet pawl is raised with your finger* **(see illustration)**.

b) *Release the ratchet pawl and make sure the plunger is locked in place by the ratchet pawl and does not move when pushed with your finger* **(see illustration)**.

19   Remove the oil jet and inspect the orifice for restrictions.

Refer to illustrations 9.20, 9.21a, 9.21b and 9.23

20   Remove all dirt, oil and grease from the timing chain area at the front of the engine and the timing chain cover. Clean the sealing surface of the cover and install two new O-rings. Install the oil jet and make sure it is directed toward the timing gear **(see illustration)**.

21   Install the timing chain over the camshaft sprocket, aligning the timing mark on the sprocket with the bright link on the chain. Place the timing chain/camshaft sprocket assembly into position on the engine, looping the chain around the crankshaft gear and aligning the other bright link with the mark on the crankshaft sprocket. Tie the timing chain guides together to retain the chain in position **(see illustrations)**.

22   Apply a 3 mm bead of RTV sealant to the timing cover sealing surface. Make sure the O-rings are in place and install the timing chain cover onto the engine block, engaging the splined shaft of the oil pump drive rotor

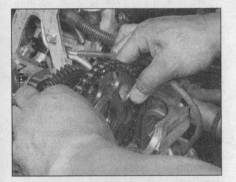

9.16 Remove the camshaft sprocket and chain from the intake camshaft

9.18a The tensioner plunger must move freely in the bore of the housing

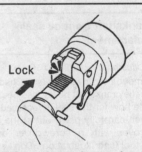

9.18b Release the ratchet pawl and make sure the plunger locks in place

9.20 Install the oil jet and make sure it is pointing toward the timing gear

9.21a Align the mark on the camshaft sprocket with the bright link on the chain - use a tie strap, rubber band or a piece of cord to secure the timing chain in position

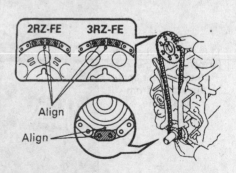

9.21b Align the mark on the crankshaft sprocket with the other bright link

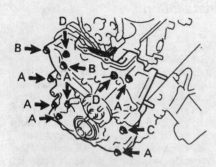

9.23 Bolt size designation for the timing chain cover (see this Chapter's Specifications for the torque values)

10.2 Use a seal puller to remove the crankshaft front oil seal from the oil pump housing - do not nick or scratch the crankshaft or the oil pump housing in the process

10.4 Use a large socket with a slightly smaller diameter than the seal bore and carefully and evenly drive the seal into the oil pump housing

with the oil pump drive gear. **Note:** *Installation must be completed within five minutes of applying the sealant.*

23   Install the timing cover bolts and tighten them to the torque listed in this Chapter's Specifications **(see illustration)**. Remove the cord securing the timing chain and guides.

24   Reinstall the remaining parts in the reverse order of removal, referring to the appropriate sections for component installation. **Caution:** *DO NOT start the engine until you're absolutely certain that the timing chain is installed correctly. Serious and costly engine damage could occur if the chain is installed incorrectly.*

25   Add engine oil and coolant (see Chapter 1).

26   Start the engine and set the ignition timing (see Chapter 5). Check for leaks and proper operation.

10   Crankshaft front oil seal - replacement

Refer to illustrations 10.2 and 10.4

1   Remove the drivebelts (see Chapter 1). Remove the crankshaft pulley (see Section 9).

2   Note how far the seal is recessed in the bore, then carefully pry it out of the timing chain cover with a screwdriver or seal removal tool **(see illustration)**. Don't scratch the cover bore or damage the crankshaft in

the process (if the crankshaft is damaged, the new seal will end up leaking).

3   Clean the bore in the cover and coat the outer edge and the lip of the new seal with engine oil or multi-purpose grease.

4   Using a socket with an outside diameter slightly smaller than the outside diameter of the seal, carefully drive the new seal into place with a seal driver or large socket **(see illustration)**. Make sure it's installed squarely and driven in to the same depth as the original. If a socket isn't available, a short section of large diameter pipe will also work. Check the seal after installation to make sure the spring didn't pop out of place.

5   Reinstall the crankshaft pulley and drivebelts.

6   Run the engine and check for oil leaks at the front seal.

11   Oil pan - removal and installation

Removal

Refer to illustrations 11.8, 11.12, 11.13, 11.15 and 11.16

1   Disconnect the negative cable from the battery. **Caution:** *If the stereo in your vehicle*

is equipped with an anti-theft system, make sure you have the correct activation code before disconnecting the battery.

2   Set the parking brake and block the rear wheels.

3   Raise the front of the vehicle and support it securely on jackstands.

4   If equipped, remove the engine protector plate under the engine **(see illustration 9.15a)**.

5   Drain the engine oil and remove the oil filter (see Chapter 1). Remove the oil dipstick.

6   Remove the front stabilizer bar (see Chapter 10).

7   Remove the two nuts retaining the front exhaust pipe to the exhaust manifold, then the two bolts/nuts connecting the pipe to the rear of the exhaust system (see Chapter 4). Remove the exhaust assembly.

8   Remove the front crossmember **(see illustration)**.

9   Remove the A/C compressor and bracket from the engine (see Chapter 3).

10   Remove the alternator and bracket assembly from the engine (see Chapter 5).

11   Remove the crankshaft position sensor from the timing cover (see Chapter 6).

12   Remove the right and left stiffener plates **(see illustration)**.

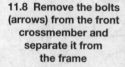

11.8 Remove the bolts (arrows) from the front crossmember and separate it from the frame

11.12 Remove the stiffener plate bolts (arrows) and separate the left and right side plates from the engine and transmission

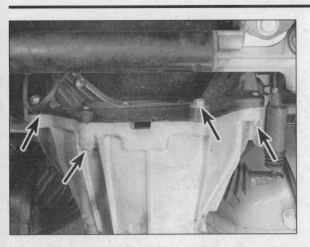

**11.13 Remove the
transmission
brace bolts**

**11.15 Remove the oil pan from the engine
block by angling it down and away from
the front suspension**

13   Remove the transmission brace from the engine block **(see illustration)**.
14   Remove the bolts around the perimeter of the oil pan, then carefully pry between the engine block and the oil pan to loosen the oil pan. Be careful not to gouge the engine block or distort the flange of the steel pan.
15   Angle the oil pan down and away from the front stabilizer bar **(see illustration)**.
16   Unbolt the pick-up tube/oil strainer assembly and remove it for cleaning **(see illustrations)**.

Installation

Refer to illustration 11.21

17   Use a scraper to remove all traces of old gasket material and sealant from the block and oil pan. Clean the mating surfaces with lacquer thinner or acetone.
18   Make sure the threaded bolt holes in the block are clean.
19   Check the oil pan flange for distortion, particularly around the bolt holes. If necessary, place the oil pan on a wood block and use a hammer to flatten and restore the gasket surface.
20   Inspect the oil pump pick-up tube assembly for cracks and a blocked strainer. Install the oil pick-up tube.
21   Install a new oil pick-up tube gasket **(see illustration)**.

22   Apply a 3 mm wide bead of RTV sealant to the oil pan flange. The bead of sealant must travel inboard of the bolt holes. **Note:** *Installation must be completed within 5 minutes of applying the sealer.*
23   Carefully position the oil pan on the engine block and install the bolts. Working from the center out, tighten the bolts to the torque listed in this Chapter's Specifications in three or four steps.
24   The remainder of installation is the reverse of removal. Be sure to add oil and install a new oil filter. Use new gasket/seals on the front exhaust pipe.
25   Run the engine and check for oil pressure and leaks.

---

12   Oil pump - removal, inspection and installation

Removal

Refer to illustrations 12.4 and 12.6

1   Remove the drivebelts and the idler pulley from the front of the engine.
2   Remove the oil pan (see Section 11). **Note:** *This step is only necessary if the pressure relief valve is to be removed.*
3   Remove the crankshaft pulley and, if the pressure relief valve is to be removed, the

**11.16 Remove the oil pick-up tube
mounting nuts (arrows)**

timing chain cover (see Section 8).
4   Remove the nine screws and detach the oil pump body from the timing cover **(see illustration)**.
5   Clean off all traces of sealant and old gasket material from the pump body and timing cover, then clean the mating surfaces with lacquer thinner or acetone.

11.21 Install a new oil pick-up tube gasket

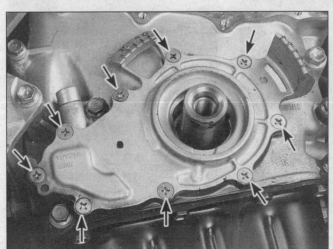

**12.4 Remove the
screws and separate
the oil pump
assembly from the
front cover**

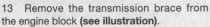

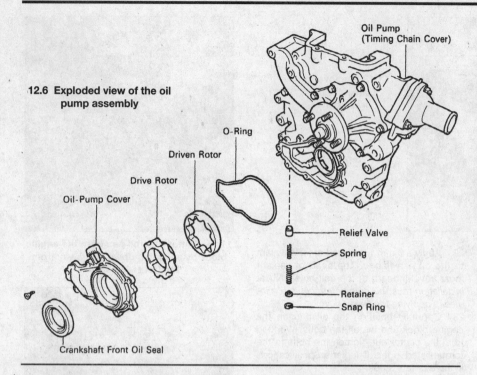

12.6 Exploded view of the oil pump assembly

Oil Pump (Timing Chain Cover)

O-Ring

Driven Rotor

Drive Rotor

Oil-Pump Cover

Relief Valve

Spring

Retainer

Snap Ring

Crankshaft Front Oil Seal

12.10a Measure the driven rotor-to-body clearance with a feeler gauge

6   Lift out the drive and driven rotors **(see illustration)**.

7   Remove the oil pressure relief valve snap-ring retainer, spring and piston located on the side of the cover **(see illustration 12.6)**. **Warning:** *The spring is tightly compressed - be careful and wear eye protection.*

Inspection

Refer to illustrations 12.10a, 12.10b and 12.10c

8   Clean all components with solvent, inspect them for wear and damage.

9   Check the oil pressure relief valve piston sliding surface and valve spring. If either the spring or the valve is damaged, they must be replaced as a set.

10   Check the driven rotor-to-body clearance, rotor-to-cover clearance and drive rotor tip clearance with a feeler gauge **(see illustrations)** and compare the results to this Chapter's Specifications. If any clearance is excessive, replace the rotors as a set. If necessary, replace the oil pump body (timing cover).

Installation

Refer to illustration 12.12

11   Lubricate the drive and driven rotors with clean engine oil and place them in the pump body.

12   Pack the pump cavities with petroleum jelly - this will help prime the pump when the engine is first started. Install a new O-ring in the groove in the timing cover **(see illustration)** and attach the pump, tightening the screws to the torque listed in this Chapter's Specifications.

13   Lubricate the oil pressure relief valve piston with clean engine oil and reinstall the valve components in the pump body.

14   If the timing cover was removed, place a new gasket on the engine block (the dowel pins should hold it in place).

15   Install the timing cover onto the engine block, engaging the oil pump drive gear with the oil pump gear on the crankshaft (see Section 9).

16   Reinstall the remaining parts in the reverse order of removal, referring to the appropriate Sections for component installation.

17   Add oil (and coolant, if the timing cover was removed), start the engine and check for oil pressure and leaks.

13 Flywheel/driveplate - removal and installation

Removal

1   Disconnect the negative cable from the battery. **Caution:** *If the stereo in your vehicle is equipped with an anti-theft system, make*

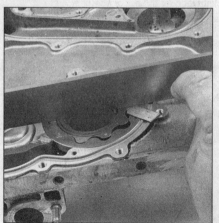

12.10b Using a straightedge and feeler gauge, measure the rotor-to-cover clearance

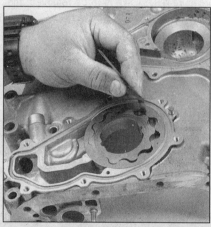

12.10c Measure the rotor tip clearance with a feeler gauge - install the rotors with the marks facing out, against the cover

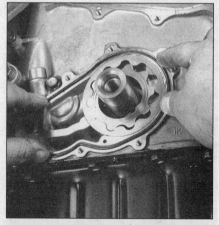

12.12 Install a new O-ring seal into the front cover before installing the pump cover

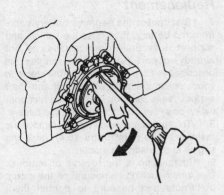

14.2 The rear main oil seal may be pried out with a screwdriver - when installing, lubricate the crankshaft journal and the lip of the new seal with multi-purpose grease and press the new seal into place - the seal lip is very stiff and can be easily damaged during installation if you're not careful

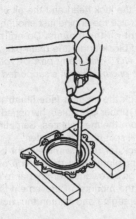

14.5 After removing the retainer assembly from the engine block, support it between two wooden blocks and drive out the old seal with a screwdriver and hammer

14.6 Drive the new seal into the retainer with a wood block or a section of pipe - make sure that you don't cock the seal in the retainer bore

sure you have the correct activation code before disconnecting the battery. Raise the vehicle and support it securely on jackstands, then refer to Chapter 7 and remove the transmission.

2   If equipped, remove the pressure plate and clutch disc (see Chapter 8) (manual transmission equipped vehicles).

3   Make alignment marks on the flywheel/driveplate and crankshaft to ensure correct alignment during reinstallation.

4   Remove the bolts securing the flywheel/driveplate to the crankshaft. If the crankshaft turns, wedge a screwdriver in the ring gear teeth to hold the flywheel/driveplate.

5   Remove the flywheel/driveplate from the crankshaft. Since the flywheel is fairly heavy, be sure to support it while removing the last bolt. Automatic transmission equipped vehicles have spacers on both sides of the driveplate. Keep them with the driveplate. **Warning:** *The ring-gear teeth may be sharp, wear gloves to protect your hands.*

Installation

6   Clean the flywheel/driveplate to remove grease and oil. Inspect the surface for cracks, rivet grooves, burned areas and score marks. Light scoring can be removed with emery cloth. Check for cracked or broken ring gear teeth. Lay the flywheel/driveplate on a flat surface and use a straightedge to check for warpage.

7   Clean and inspect the mating surfaces of the flywheel/driveplate and the crankshaft. If the crankshaft rear seal is leaking, replace it before reinstalling the flywheel/driveplate (see Section 14).

8   Position the flywheel/driveplate against the crankshaft. Be sure to align the marks made during removal. Note that some engines have an alignment dowel or stag-

gered bolt holes to ensure correct installation. Before installing the bolts, apply threadlocking compound to the threads.

9   Wedge a screwdriver in the ring gear teeth to keep the flywheel/driveplate from turning and tighten the bolts to the torque listed in this Chapter's Specifications. Follow a criss-cross pattern and work up to the final torque in three or four steps.

10   The remainder of installation is the reverse of the removal procedure.

14   Rear main oil seal - replacement

Refer to illustrations 14.2, 14.5 and 14.6

1   Remove the transmission (see Chapter 7). Remove the rear end plate.

2   The seal can be replaced without removing the oil pan or seal retainer. However, this method is not recommended because the lip of the seal is quite stiff and it's possible to cock the seal in the retainer bore or damage it during installation. If you want to take the chance, pry out the old seal with a screwdriver **(see illustration)**. Apply multi-purpose grease to the crankshaft seal journal and the lip of the new seal and carefully press the new seal into place. The lip is stiff so carefully work it onto the seal journal of the crankshaft with a smooth object like the end of an extension as you tap the seal into place. Don't rush it or you may damage the seal.

3   The following method is recommended but requires removing the seal retainer and resealing the rear of the oil pan (see Section 11).

4   After removing the two rearmost oil pan-to-seal retainer bolts, break the seal between the rear of the oil pan and the bottom of the seal retainer with a putty knife. Remove the retainer-to-engine block bolts, detach the seal retainer and remove all the old gasket material. remove the sealant from the top of the oil pan flange. **Note:** *Cover the open area*

of the oil pan with clean rags to keep debris out while bracing the pan flange.

5   Position the seal and retainer assembly between two wood blocks on a workbench and drive the old seal out from the back side with a screwdriver **(see illustration)**.

6   Drive the new seal into the retainer with a wood block **(see illustration)** or a section of pipe slightly smaller in diameter than the outside diameter of the seal.

7   Lubricate the crankshaft seal journal and the lip of the new seal with multi-purpose grease. Position a new gasket on the engine block. Apply a bead of RTV sealant to the exposed portion of oil pan flange and particularly at the pan-to-block mating surface.

8   Slowly and carefully push the seal and retainer onto the crankshaft. The seal lip is stiff, so work it onto the crankshaft with a smooth object such as the end of an extension as you push the retainer against the block.

9   Install and tighten the retainer bolts to the torque listed in this Chapter's Specifications.

10   The remainder of installation is the reverse of removal.

15   Engine mounts - check and replacement

1   Engine mounts seldom require attention, but broken or deteriorated mounts should be replaced immediately or the added strain placed on the driveline components may cause damage or wear.

Check

Refer to illustration 15.4

2   During the check, the engine must be raised slightly to remove the weight from the mounts.

3   Raise the vehicle and support it securely on jackstands, then position a jack under the engine oil pan. Place a large wood block

15.4 Location of the left and right engine mounts

between the jack head and the oil pan, then carefully raise the engine just enough to take the weight off the mounts. Do not position the wood block under the drain plug. **Warning:** *DO NOT place any part of your body under the engine when it's supported only by a jack!*

4   Check the mounts **(see illustration)** to see if the rubber is cracked, hardened or separated from the metal plates. Sometimes the rubber will split down the center.

5   Check for relative movement between the mount plates and the engine or frame (use a large screwdriver or pry bar to attempt to move the mounts). If movement is noted, lower the engine and tighten the mount fasteners.

6   Rubber preservative should be applied to the mounts to slow deterioration.

Replacement

7   Disconnect the negative battery cable from the battery, then raise the vehicle and support it securely on jackstands (if not already done). Support the engine as described in Step 3. **Caution:** *If the stereo in your vehicle is equipped with an anti-theft system, make sure you have the correct activation code before disconnecting the battery.*

8   To remove an engine mount, remove the fasteners **(see illustration 15.4)**, raise the engine and detach the mount.

9   Installation is the reverse of removal. Use thread locking compound on the mount bolts/nuts and be sure to tighten them securely.

10   See Chapter 7 for transmission mount replacement.

Chapter 2 Part B
V6 engines

Contents

Specifications

3.0L engines (1993 and 1994)

General

Engine designation	3VZ-E
Displacement	3.0 liters
Cylinder numbers (timing belt end-to-transmission end)	
Right (passenger's) side	1-3-5
Left (driver's) side	2-4-6
Firing order	1-2-3-4-5-6

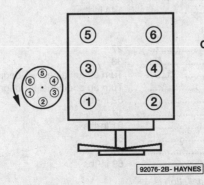

**Cylinder numbering and terminal
locations - 3.0L engines**

92076-2B- HAYNES

3.0L engines (1993 and 1994) (continued)

Warpage limits

Cylinder head	0.0039 inch (0.10 mm)
Intake manifold	0.0039 inch (0.10 mm)
Exhaust manifolds	0.0276 inch (0.70 mm)

Camshaft and related components

Valve clearance (engine cold)	
Intake	0.007 to 0.011 inch (0.18 to 0.28 mm)
Exhaust	0.009 to 0.013 inch (0.22 to 0.32 mm)
Bearing journal diameter	1.3370 to 1.3376 inches (33.959 to 33.975 mm)
Bearing oil clearance	
Standard	0.0010 to 0.0026 inch (0.025 to 0.066 mm)
Service limit	0.0039 inch (0.10 mm)
Lobe height (intake and exhaust lobes)	
Standard	1.8830 to 1.8870 inches (47.830 to 47.930 mm)
Service Limit	1.8701 inches (47.50 mm)
Thrust clearance (endplay)	
Standard	0.0031 to 0.0075 inch (0.08 to 0.19 mm)
Service limit	0.0098 inch (0.25 mm)
Runout limit (total indicator reading)	0.0024 inch (0.06 mm)
Timing belt tensioner protrusion	0.394 to 0.425 inch (10.0 to 10.8 mm)
Lifters	
Outside diameter	1.4930 to 1.4934 inch (37.922 to 37.932 mm)
Bore diameter	1.4945 to 1.4951 inch (37.960 to 37.975 mm)
Lifter-to-bore (oil) clearance	
Standard	0.0011 to 0.0021 inch (0.028 to 0.053 mm)
Service limit	0.004 inch (0.10 mm)

Oil pump

Driven rotor-to-pump body clearance	
Standard	0.0039 to 0.0051 inch (0.10 to 0.13 mm)
Service limit	0.0118 inch (0.30 mm)
Rotor tip clearance	
Standard	0.0043 to 0.0094 inch (0.11 to 0.93 mm)
Service limit	0.0138 inch (0.35 mm)
Rotor side clearance	
Standard	0.0012 to 0.0035 inch (0.03 to 0.09 mm)
Service limit	0.0059 inch (0.15 mm)

Torque specifications

	Ft-lbs (unless otherwise indicated)
Intake manifold bolts/nuts	13
Exhaust manifold nuts	29
Exhaust crossover pipe	33
Crankshaft pulley bolt	181
Timing belt cover bolts (no. 3)	74 in-lbs
Idler pulley bolts*	
No. 1	25
No. 2	13
Timing belt tensioner bolts	20
Valve cover nuts	52 in-lbs
Camshaft pulley bolts	80
Camshaft bearing cap bolts	144 in-lbs
Cylinder head bolts	
Step 1	
10 mm bolt	27
All other bolts	33
Step 2	Turn an additional 90-degrees (1/4-turn)
Step 3	Turn an additional 90-degrees (1/4-turn)
Oil pan bolts	52 in-lbs
Oil pump mounting bolts	14
Oil pick-up tube mounting bolts	61 in-lbs
Flywheel bolts*	65
Driveplate bolts*	61
Rear crankshaft oil seal retainer mounting bolts	69 in-lbs

Apply thread locking compound to the threads prior to installation

3.4L engines (1995 and later)

General

Engine designation	5VZ-FE
Displacement	3.4 liters
Cylinder numbers (timing belt end-to-transmission end)	
Right (passenger) side...	1-3-5
Left (driver) side..	2-4-6
Firing order	1-2-3-4-5-6

Warpage limits

Cylinder head..	0.0039 inch (0.10 mm)
Intake manifold	0.0039 inch (0.10 mm)
Exhaust manifolds	0.0394 inch (1.00 mm)

```
┌───────────┬──────────────────┐
│  2 - 5    │   ⑤        ⑥     │
│           │                  │
│  3 - 6    │   ③        ④     │
│           │                  │
│  1 - 4    │   ①        ②     │
└───────────┴──────────────────┘
          92076-2B- HAYNES
```

Cylinder numbering and terminal locations - 3.4L engines

Camshaft and related components

Valve clearance (engine cold)	
Intake..	0.006 to 0.009 inch (0.13 to 0.23 mm)
Exhaust...	0.011 to 0.014 inch (0.27 to 0.37 mm)
Bearing journal diameter..	1.0610 to 1.0616 inches (26.949 to 26.965 mm)
Bearing oil clearance	
Standard	0.0014 to 0.0028 inch (0.035 to 0.072 mm)
Service limit	0.0039 inch (0.10 mm)
Lobe height	
Intake	
Standard	1.6657 to 1.6697 inches (42.31 to 42.41 mm)
Service Limit	1.6598 inches (42.16 mm)
Exhaust	
Standard	1.6520 to 1.6559 inches (41.96 to 42.06 mm)
Service Limit	1.6461 inches (41.81 mm)
Thrust clearance (endplay)	
Standard	0.0013 to 0.0031 inch (0.033 to 0.080 mm)
Service limit	0.0047 inch (0.12 mm)
Runout limit (total indicator reading)................................	0.0024 inch (0.06 mm)
Camshaft gear backlash	
Standard	0.0008 to 0.0079 inch (0.020 to 0.200 mm)
Service limit	0.0188 inch (0.30 mm)
Camshaft gear spring free length	0.712 to 0.740 inch (18.2 to 18.8 mm)
Timing belt tensioner protrusion.......................................	0.394 to 0.425 inch (10.0 to 10.8 mm)
Lifters	
Outside diameter..	1.2191 to 1.2195 inch (30.966 to 30.976 mm)
Bore diameter..	1.2205 to 1.2212 inch (31.960 to 31.018 mm)
Lifter-to-bore (oil) clearance	
Standard	0.0009 to 0.0020 inch (0.024 to 0.052 mm)
Service limit	0.003 inch (0.08 mm)

Oil pump

Driven rotor-to-pump body clearance	
Standard	0.0039 to 0.0069 inch (0.10 to 0.18 mm)
Service limit	0.0118 inch (0.30 mm)
Rotor tip clearance	
Standard	0.0043 to 0.0094 inch (0.11 to 0.94 mm)
Service limit	0.0138 inch (0.35 mm)
Rotor side clearance	
Standard	0.0012 to 0.0035 inch (0.03 to 0.09 mm)
Service limit	0.0059 inch (0.15 mm)

Torque specifications

	Ft-lbs (unless otherwise indicated)
Intake manifold bolts/nuts	13
Exhaust manifold nuts	30
Exhaust crossover pipe	33
Crankshaft pulley bolt...	184
Timing belt cover bolts (no. 3)	74 in-lbs
Idler pulley bolts*	
No. 1	26
No. 2	30
Timing belt tensioner bolts	20
Valve cover nuts	53 in-lbs

3.4L engines (1995 and later) (continued)

Camshaft pulley bolts	81
Camshaft bearing cap bolts	12
Cylinder head bolts	
12-point head	
Step 1	25
Step 2	Turn an additional 90-degrees (1/4-turn)
Step 3	Turn an additional 90-degrees (1/4-turn)
Recessed head bolts**	13
Oil pan bolts	52 in-lbs
Oil pump mounting bolts	
A	14
B	31
Oil pick-up tube mounting bolts	66 in-lbs
Flywheel/driveplate bolts*	61
Rear crankshaft oil seal retainer mounting bolts	69 in-lbs

Apply thread locking compound to the threads prior to installation
** *Recessed head bolts are torqued once and are NOT torqued again at a 90-degree turn like the 12-point head bolts*

1　General information

The models covered by this manual are equipped with either one of two V6 engines; the 3.0L (3VZ-E) used in 1993 and 1994 models, and the 3.4L (5VZ-FE) used in 1995 and later models. The 3.0L V6 engine is designed with overhead camshafts, one on each cylinder head. Each camshaft opens and closes an exhaust valve and intake valve (12 total) for each cylinder. The 3.4L V6 engine is designed with a Double-OverHead-Cam (DOHC) arrangement with four valves per cylinder (24 in all).

This Part of Chapter 2 is devoted to in-vehicle engine repair procedures for the V6 engines. All information concerning engine removal and installation and engine block and cylinder head overhaul can be found in Part C of this Chapter.

The following repair procedures are based on the assumption that the engine is installed in the vehicle. If the engine has been removed from the vehicle and mounted on a stand, many of the steps outlined in this Part of Chapter 2 will not apply.

The Specifications included in this Part of Chapter 2 apply only to the procedures contained in this Part. Part C of Chapter 2 contains the Specifications necessary for cylinder head and engine block rebuilding.

2　Repair operations possible with the engine in the vehicle

1　Many major repair operations can be accomplished without removing the engine from the vehicle. Clean the engine compartment and the exterior of the engine with some type of degreaser before any work is done. It will make the job easier and help keep dirt out of the internal areas of the engine.

2　Depending on the components involved, it may be helpful to remove the hood to improve access to the engine as repairs are performed (refer to Chapter 11 if necessary). Cover the fenders to prevent damage to the paint. Special pads are available, but an old bedspread or blanket will also work.

3　If vacuum, exhaust, oil or coolant leaks develop, indicating a need for gasket or seal replacement, the repairs can generally be made with the engine in the vehicle. The intake and exhaust manifold gaskets, oil pan gasket, crankshaft oil seals and cylinder head gaskets are all accessible with the engine in place.

4　Exterior engine components, such as the intake and exhaust manifolds, the oil pan, the oil pump, the water pump, the starter motor, the alternator and the fuel system components can be removed for repair with the engine in place.

5　Since the cylinder heads can be removed without pulling the engine, valve component servicing can also be accomplished with the engine in the vehicle. Replacement of the camshafts, timing belt and pulleys is also possible with the engine in the vehicle.

6　In extreme cases caused by a lack of necessary equipment, repair or replacement of piston rings, pistons, connecting rods and rod bearings is possible with the engine in the vehicle. However, this practice is not recommended because of the cleaning and preparation work that must be done to the components involved.

3　Top Dead Center (TDC) for number one piston - locating

Refer to illustrations 3.5 and 3.8
Note: *The following procedure is based on the assumption that the distributor is correctly installed (3.0L engine only). If you are trying to locate TDC to install the distributor correctly, piston position must be determined by feeling for compression at the number one spark plug hole, then aligning the ignition timing marks as described in Step 8.*

1　Top Dead Center (TDC) is the highest point in the cylinder that each piston reaches as it travels up the cylinder bore. Each piston reaches TDC on the compression stroke and again on the exhaust stroke, but TDC generally refers to piston position on the compression stroke.

2　Positioning the piston(s) at TDC is an essential part of many procedures such as valve timing, camshaft and timing belt/pulley removal and distributor removal.

3　Before beginning this procedure, remove the Number One spark plug (see Chapter 1, if necessary). Also, be sure to place the transmission in Neutral and apply the parking brake or block the rear wheels. Disable the ignition system in one of the following ways:

a) *On 3.0L engines, detach the coil wire from the center terminal of the distributor cap and ground it on the block with a jumper wire.*

b) *On 3.4L engines, disconnect the primary (small-diameter wires) electrical connector from each of the three ignition coil packs.*

4　In order to bring any piston to TDC, the crankshaft must be turned using one of the methods outlined below. When looking at the front of the engine, normal crankshaft rotation is clockwise.

a) *The preferred method is to turn the crankshaft with a socket and ratchet attached to the bolt threaded into the front of the crankshaft. Apply pressure on the bolt in a clockwise direction only. Never turn the bolt counterclockwise.*

b) *A remote starter switch, which may save some time, can also be used. Follow the instructions included with the switch. Once the piston is close to TDC, use a socket and ratchet as described in the previous paragraph.*

c) *If an assistant is available to turn the ignition switch to the Start position in short bursts, you can get the piston*

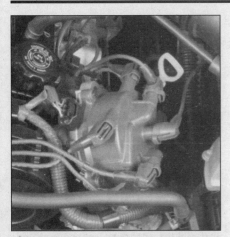

3.5 Make a mark on the distributor body, directly below the no. 1 spark plug wire terminal

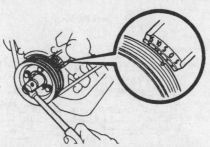

3.8 Turn the crankshaft until the notch in the pulley (arrow) aligns with the zero (0) on the timing plate

close to TDC without a remote starter switch. Make sure your assistant is out of the vehicle, away from the ignition switch, then use a socket and ratchet as described in Paragraph (a) to complete the procedure.

3.0L engine

5   Note the position of the terminal for the number one spark plug wire on the distributor cap **(see illustration)**. If the terminal isn't marked, follow the plug wire from the number one cylinder spark plug to the cap.

6   Use a felt-tip pen or chalk to make a mark on the distributor body directly under the terminal.

7   Detach the cap from the distributor and set it aside (see Chapter 1 if necessary).

8   Turn the crankshaft (see Paragraph 3 above) until the notch in the crankshaft pulley is aligned with the 0 on the timing plate (located at the front of the engine) **(see illustration)**.

9   Look at the distributor rotor - it should be pointing directly at the mark you made on the distributor body.

10   If the rotor is 180-degrees off, the number one piston is at TDC on the exhaust stroke.

11   To get the piston to TDC on the com-

pression stroke, turn the crankshaft one complete turn (360-degrees) clockwise. The rotor should now be pointing at the mark on the distributor. When the rotor is pointing at the number one spark plug wire terminal in the distributor cap and the ignition timing marks are aligned, the number one piston is at TDC on the compression stroke.

12   After the number one piston has been positioned at TDC on the compression stroke, TDC for any of the remaining pistons can be located by turning the crankshaft and following the firing order. Mark the remaining spark plug wire terminal locations on the distributor body just like you did for the number one terminal, then number the marks to correspond with the cylinder numbers. As you turn the crankshaft, the rotor will also turn. When it's pointing directly at one of the marks on the distributor, the piston for that particular cylinder is at TDC on the compression stroke.

3.4L engine

13   The 3.4L engine does not have a distributor, but rather a separate coil for each pair of companion cylinders and the spark plugs, fired in sequence by signals from the computer. If not already done, disconnect the primary wires from the coil packs and remove the Number One spark plug (see Chapter 1).

14   Mount a compression pressure gauge in the number one spark plug hole (refer to Chapter 2C). It should be a gauge with a screw-in fitting and a hose at least six inches long.

15   Rotate the crankshaft using one of the methods described above while observing the compression gauge. When TDC for the compression stroke of number one cylinder is reached, compression pressure will show on the gauge as the marks are beginning to line up. If you go past the marks, release the gauge pressure and rotate the crankshaft around two more revolutions. **Note:** *The most positive method for finding TDC on the 3.4L engine is to examine the crankshaft timing marks and camshaft sprocket timing marks (see Section 7).*

4   Valve covers - removal and installation

Removal

Refer to illustration 4.5a and 4.5b

1   Disconnect the negative cable from the battery. **Caution:** *If the stereo in your vehicle is equipped with an anti-theft system, make sure you have the correct activation code before disconnecting the battery.*

2   Remove the air intake plenum from the intake manifold (see Chapter 4). This will require a large amount of disassembly so read the procedure carefully and mark any harness connectors or vacuum lines with tape to insure proper installation.

3   Remove the spark plug connectors and wires from the spark plugs. Be sure to mark each spark plug wire using tape or other marking device to insure proper reassembly. See Chapter 5 for additional details.

4   Disconnect any vacuum lines or wires that may interfere with the removal process: Mark them carefully to insure proper reassembly.

5   Remove the retaining bolts **(see illustrations)**, then detach the cover(s). If the cover is stuck to the head, bump the end with a wood block and a hammer to jar it loose. If that doesn't work, try to slip a flexible putty knife between the head and cover to break the seal. **Caution:** *Don't pry at the cover-to-head joint or damage to the sealing surfaces may occur, leading to oil leaks after the cover is reinstalled.*

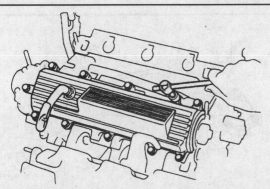

4.5a On 3.0L engines, each valve cover is secured by 11 bolts

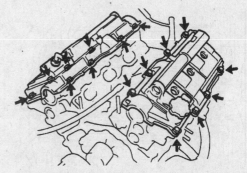

4.5b Valve cover bolt locations on the 3.4L engine

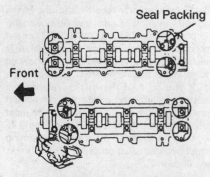

4.7a Apply RTV sealant to the shaded areas before installing the gasket and valve cover (3.0L engine)

Installation

Refer to illustration 4.7a and 4.7b

6   The mating surfaces of the cylinder head and cover must be clean when the cover is installed. Use a gasket scraper to remove all traces of sealant and old gasket material, then clean the mating surfaces with lacquer thinner or acetone. If there's residue or oil on the mating surfaces when the cover is installed, oil leaks may develop.

7   Position the semi-circular seals in the cylinder head cutouts, sealing them with RTV sealant, then apply a thin, uniform layer of RTV sealant to the gasket/seal joints **(see illustrations)**.

8   Position a new gasket on the valve cover, then install the cover, sealing washers and nuts. **Note:** *On 3.4L engines, install new tube seals into the valve cover.*

9   Tighten the nuts to the torque listed in this Chapter's Specifications in three or four equal steps.

10   Reinstall the remaining parts, run the engine and check for oil leaks.

5   Intake manifold - removal and installation

Removal

Refer to illustrations 5.5a and 5.5b

1   Disconnect the negative cable from the battery. **Caution:** *If the stereo in your vehicle*

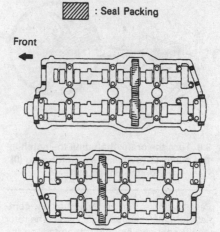

4.7b On 3.4L engines, be sure to use RTV sealant at the shaded areas

is equipped with an anti-theft system, make sure you have the correct activation code before disconnecting the battery.

2   Drain the coolant into a clean container (see Chapter 1).

3   Remove the air cleaner assembly, throttle body, fuel injectors and air intake plenum (see Chapter 4).

4   Clearly label, then detach all remaining wires, hoses and brackets still attached to the intake manifold and coolant outlets.

5   Remove the mounting nuts/bolts, then detach the intake manifold from the engine **(see illustrations)**. Start with the outer bolts first and work your way to the inner bolts on the manifold. Make several passes to insure that the manifold is separated from the cylinder heads evenly to avoid damage to the cylinder head and manifold surfaces. If it's stuck, don't pry between the gasket mating surfaces or damage may result.

Installation

6   Use a scraper to remove all traces of old gasket material and sealant from the manifold and cylinder heads, then clean the mating surfaces with lacquer thinner or acetone.

7   Install new gaskets, then position the manifold on the engine. Make sure the gas-

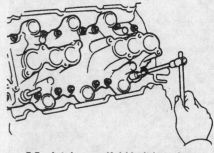

5.5a Intake manifold bolt locations (3.0L engines)

kets haven't shifted and install the nuts/bolts. Start with the inner bolts first and work your way to the outer bolts on the manifold. Make several passes to insure that the manifold is mated to the cylinder heads evenly to avoid damage to the cylinder head and manifold surfaces.

8   Tighten the nuts/bolts, in three or four equal steps, to the torque listed in this Chapter's Specifications. Work from the center out towards the ends to avoid warping the manifold.

9   Install the remaining parts in the reverse order of removal.

10   Refill the cooling system. Run the engine and check for fuel, vacuum and coolant leaks.

6   Exhaust manifolds - removal and installation

Refer to illustrations 6.3a, 6.3b and 6.5

Warning: *The engine must be completely cool before beginning this procedure.*

1   Disconnect the negative cable from the battery. **Caution:** *If the stereo in your vehicle is equipped with an anti-theft system, make sure you have the correct activation code before disconnecting the battery.*

2   Spray penetrating oil on the exhaust manifold fasteners and allow it to soak in.

3   Remove the exhaust crossover pipe from the back of the cylinder heads **(see illustrations)**.

4   Remove the EGR pipe from the exhaust

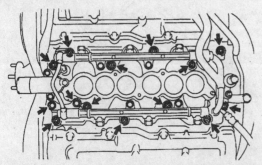

5.5b Intake manifold bolt locations (3.4L engines)

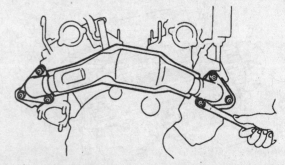

6.3a Exhaust crossover pipe installation details (3.0L engine)

6.3b Exhaust crossover pipe installation details (3.4L engine)

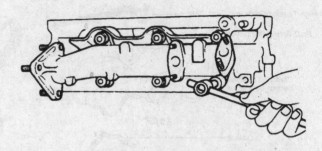

6.5 Exhaust manifold installation details (3.0L engine shown, 3.4L similar)

manifold (see Chapter 6).

5   Unbolt the exhaust manifolds from the cylinder heads **(see illustration)**.

6   Carefully inspect the manifolds and fasteners for cracks and damage.

7   Use a scraper to remove all traces of old gasket material and carbon deposits from the manifolds and cylinder head mating surfaces. If the gasket was leaking, have the manifolds checked for warpage at an automotive machine shop and resurfaced if necessary.

8   Position new gaskets over the cylinder head studs.

9   Install the manifolds and thread the mounting nuts into place.

10   Working from the center out, tighten the nuts to the torque listed in this Chapter's Specifications in three or four equal steps.

11   Reinstall the remaining parts in the reverse order of removal. Use new gaskets when connecting the exhaust pipes.

12   Run the engine and check for exhaust leaks.

7   Timing belt and sprockets - removal, inspection and installation

Removal

> **** CAUTION ****
>
> The timing system is complex. Severe engine damage will occur if you make any mistakes. Do not attempt this procedure unless you are highly experienced with this type of repair. If you are at all unsure of your abilities, consult an expert. Double-check all your work and be sure everything is correct before you attempt to start the engine.

Refer to illustrations 7.8, 7.12a, 7.12b, 7.15a, 7.15b, 7.16a, 7.16b, 7.21, 7.23 and 7.28

1   Disconnect the negative cable from the battery. **Caution:** *If the stereo in your vehicle is equipped with an anti-theft system, make sure you have the correct activation code before disconnecting the battery.*

2   Remove the engine protection cover from below the engine compartment.

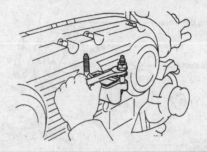

7.8 Remove the studs from the water outlet on 3.0L engines

3   Remove the fan shroud and the fan assembly (see Chapter 3).

4   Drain the coolant and remove the radiator from the engine compartment (see Chapter 3).

5   Remove the drivebelts from the alternator and power steering pump (see Chapter 1).

6   Remove the spark plug wires (see Chapter 1).

7   Raise the front of the vehicle and support it securely on jackstands. Apply the parking brake and block the rear wheels.

8   On 3.0L engines, remove the studs from the water outlet **(see illustration)**.

9   On 3.4L engines, remove the power steering pump without disconnecting the hoses and secure it aside (see Chapter 10).

10   Remove the A/C compressor and the bracket from the engine (see Chapter 3).

11   Remove the spark plugs (see Chapter 1).

12   Remove the upper (no. 2) timing belt cover and gasket **(see illustration)**. On 3.4L engines, also unbolt and remove the fan hub

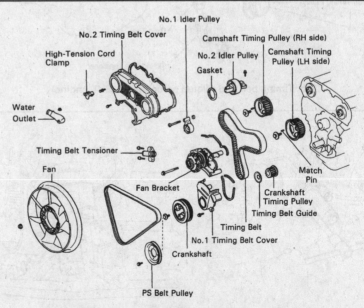

No.1 Idler Pulley
No.2 Timing Belt Cover
High-Tension Cord Clamp
Camshaft Timing Pulley (RH side)
No.2 Idler Pulley
Camshaft Timing Pulley (LH side)
Gasket
Water Outlet
Timing Belt Tensioner
Fan
Match Pin
Fan Bracket
Crankshaft Timing Pulley
Timing Belt Guide
Timing Belt
No.1 Timing Belt Cover
Crankshaft
PS Belt Pulley

7.12a Timing belt and related components (3.0L engine)

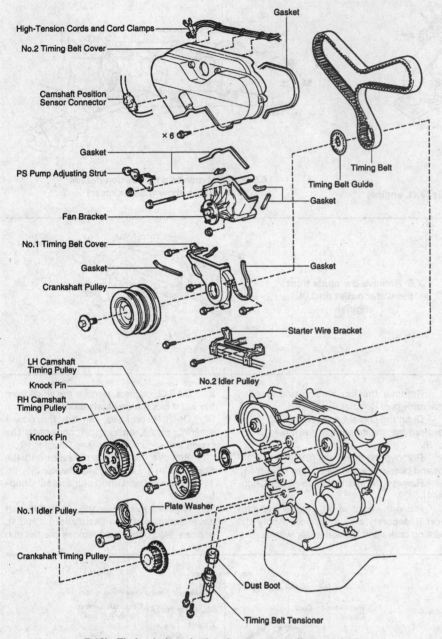

High-Tension Cords and Cord Clamps

No.2 Timing Belt Cover

Camshaft Position Sensor Connector

× 6

Gasket

PS Pump Adjusting Strut

Fan Bracket

No.1 Timing Belt Cover

Gasket

Crankshaft Pulley

Gasket

Timing Belt

Timing Belt Guide

Gasket

Gasket

Starter Wire Bracket

LH Camshaft Timing Pulley

Knock Pin

RH Camshaft Timing Pulley

Knock Pin

No.1 Idler Pulley

No.2 Idler Pulley

Plate Washer

Crankshaft Timing Pulley

Dust Boot

Timing Belt Tensioner

7.12b Timing belt and related components (3.4L engine)

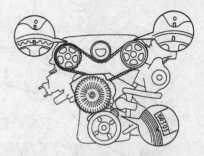

7.15a Timing marks on the 3.0L engine

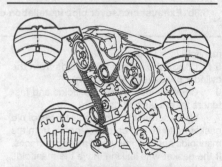

7.15b Timing marks on the 3.4L engine

and bracket.

13   Position the number one piston at TDC (see Section 3).

14   Check to see if there are installation marks on the timing belt - If you intend to re-use the belt and the marks have been obscured, make new ones.

15   Make sure the camshaft pulley timing marks are properly aligned **(see illustrations)**.

16   Remove the timing belt tensioner **(see illustrations)**. Be sure to remove the rubber boot as well; it may stick in the tensioner recess.

17   If you plan to re-use the timing belt and the marks were worn off, place a new mark on the belt at the exact location of each timing mark on each sprocket. This will allow easy and accurate timing belt alignment when the old timing belt is reused.

18   Remove the timing belt from the camshaft sprockets.

19   The camshaft sprockets can be removed at this point, if they are worn or damaged. Remove the valve cover(s) (see Section 4) and hold the camshaft with a wrench on the cast-in hex while loosening the sprocket bolt. Remove the bolt and detach the sprocket.

20   Remove the number 2 idler pulley **(see illustration 7.12a and 7.12b)**.

21   Remove the crankshaft (drivebelt) pulley bolt. Wedge a large screwdriver into the flywheel/driveplate ring gear teeth or against a converter bolt to keep the engine from turning. Use a breaker bar and socket to loosen the pulley bolt **(see illustration)**.

22   When the crankshaft pulley bolt is loosened, the TDC position of the crankshaft may

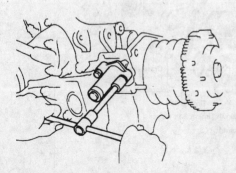

7.16a Tensioner location on the 3.0L engine

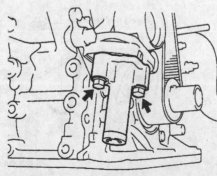

7.16b Tensioner location on the 3.4L engine

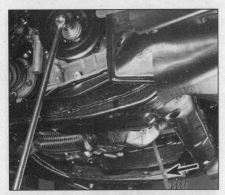

7.21 Remove the flywheel/driveplate cover and use a prybar (arrow) wedged against the ring gear teeth or a converter bolt to hold the crankshaft while loosening the pulley bolt with a breaker bar - the bolt is very tight, so use the appropriate tools

7.23 A puller should not be necessary to remove the crankshaft pulley - if it is stuck, use two prybars behind it

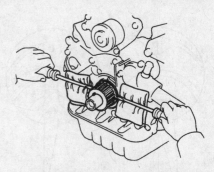

7.28 Pad the front of the engine when prying off the crankshaft sprocket

7.31 Check the tensioner for signs of leakage and test for leakdown by forcing it against an immovable object

be disturbed. Check and align again, if necessary.

23 The crankshaft pulley should come off with strong hand pressure **(see illustration)**; if not, use two prybars behind it to lever it off. Do not use a jaw-type puller.

24 Remove the lower (no. 1) timing belt cover and gasket. **Note:** *Remove the fan bracket assembly from the engine block before removing the lower (no. 1) timing belt cover on 3.4L engines.*

25 Slip the timing belt guide off the crankshaft.

26 Remove the number 1 idler pulley from the engine block.

27 If you're re-using the belt, check for a mark on the belt adjacent to the drilled mark on the crankshaft sprocket. If the original mark is gone, make a new one, then slip the belt off the sprocket.

28 If it's worn or damaged, or if you're replacing the crankshaft front oil seal, the crankshaft sprocket can now be removed. If it won't come off by hand, lever it off with two screwdrivers **(see illustration)**. A steering wheel type puller may be needed to remove the sprocket. Be careful not to damage the crankshaft sensor portion of the sprocket during the removal process. If necessary, remove the lower sprocket retainer.

Inspection

Refer to illustrations 7.31 and 7.32

29 Inspect the timing belt for cracks, tears, torn belt strands, cut edges or broken belt teeth. Replace the timing belt if there are any signs of damage or prolonged wear (high mileage).

30 Check the belt tensioner for visible oil leakage. If there's only a faint trace of oil on the pushrod side, the tensioner seal is in satisfactory condition.

31 Hold the tensioner in both hands and push it forcefully against an immovable object **(see illustration)**. If the pushrod moves, replace the tensioner.

32 Measure the protrusion of the pushrod

from the housing end **(see illustration)**. Compare your measurement to this Chapter's Specifications. If the protrusion is not as specified, replace the tensioner.

33 Check that the idler pulleys turn smoothly.

** CAUTION **

Before starting the engine, carefully rotate the crankshaft by hand through at least two full revolutions (use a socket and breaker bar on the crankshaft pulley center bolt). If you feel any resistance, STOP! There is something wrong - most likely, valves are contacting the pistons. You must find the problem before proceeding. Check your work and see if any updated repair information is available.

Installation

Refer to illustrations 7.35a, 7.35b, 7.44a, 7.44b and 7.50f

34 Remove all dirt, oil and grease from the timing belt area at the front of the engine.

35 Align the crankshaft timing sprocket keyway with the crankshaft key and install the sprocket with the flange side up against the engine. On 3.4L engines, be careful not to damage the crankshaft sensor portion of the crankshaft sprocket. Check the alignment of

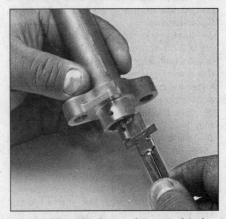

7.32 Measure the tensioner pushrod protrusion and compare it to the Specifications

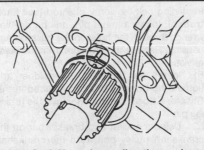

7.35a On 3.0L engines, align the marks on the crankshaft timing sprocket with the marks on the oil pump case (circled in drawing)

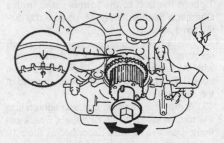

7.35b Timing gear marks on the 3.4L engine

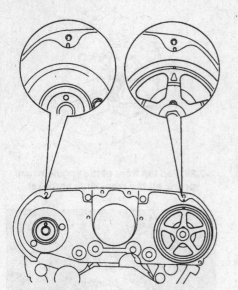

7.44a Alignment marks on the 3.0L engine

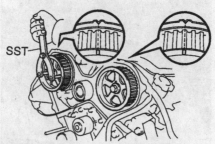

7.44b Alignment marks on the 3.4L engine

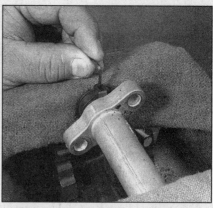

7.50 Restrain the tensioner pushrod by compressing the unit in a vise and inserting a pin approximately 0.050-inch (1.27 mm) in diameter - make sure the rubber boot is in place

the TDC marks on the sprocket and the oil pump housing, then reinstall the retainer and bolt **(see illustrations)**.

36   Apply thread locking compound to the first two or three threads on the number 1 idler pulley bolt, then position the idler pulley and washer and install the bolt. Tighten the bolt to the torque listed in this Chapter's Specifications.

37   Install the timing belt, starting at the crankshaft sprocket. If you're re-using the original belt, align the marks on the belt with the marks on the sprockets and covers. Install the belt over the lower number 1 idler and water pump pulleys.

38   Slip the belt guide over the crankshaft with the cupped side facing out.

39   Install the lower (no. 1) timing belt cover and gasket **(see illustrations 7.12a and 7.12b)**.

40   Slip the crankshaft (drivebelt) sprocket onto the crankshaft, aligning the pulley keyway with the crankshaft key. Install the bolt and tighten it to the torque listed in this Chapter's Specifications. Use the method described in Step 21 to keep the crankshaft from turning.

41   Install the upper (no. 2) idler pulley. Tighten the bolt to the torque listed in this Chapter's Specifications. Make sure the pulley turns smoothly.

42   Install the front (left-hand) camshaft sprocket (if it was removed) on the camshaft with the flange side facing OUT. Align the pin hole in the sprocket with the pin in the end of the camshaft.

43   Install the retaining bolt and tighten it to the torque listed in this Chapter's Specifications. Use the method described in Step 19 to keep the camshaft from turning.

44   Recheck the timing marks to be sure the crankshaft hasn't turned **(see illustrations 7.15a and 7.15b)**. If you're re-using the original belt, the installation mark should line

up as it did in Step 18. If not, change the position of the timing belt on the crankshaft sprocket. The mark on the front (left-hand) camshaft sprocket should be at the top (12 o'clock position), aligned with the mark on the rear (no. 3) timing cover **(see illustrations)**.

45   The rear (right-hand) camshaft knock pin hole should be at the top (12 o'clock position). If necessary, remove the valve cover and turn the camshaft slightly with a wrench to align the sprocket with the mark on the rear (no. 3) cover.

46   Turn the front (left-hand) camshaft sprocket clockwise slightly (about one tooth) with a pin spanner. If the special tool isn't available, grip the hex on the camshaft with a wrench and turn it. If you're re-using the original belt, align the installation mark with the camshaft timing mark. Slip the belt onto the sprocket, then turn the camshaft counterclockwise, back to its original position. There should now be slight tension on the belt.

47   Install the rear (right-hand) camshaft sprocket (if it was removed) on the camshaft with the flange side facing IN. Align the pin hole in the sprocket with the knock pin in the end of the camshaft.

48   Install the retaining bolt and tighten it to the torque listed in this Chapter's Specifications. Use the method described in Step 19 to keep the camshaft from turning. Be sure the timing mark is still aligned with the rear (no. 3) cover.

49   Slip the belt onto the sprocket. If you're re-using the original belt, align the installation marks.

50   Using a press or vise, slowly compress the timing belt tensioner pushrod **(see illustration)**. Insert a metal pin, drill bit or Allen wrench through the holes in the pushrod and housing. Release the pressure from the press or vise.

51   Install the timing belt tensioner and tighten the bolts to the torque listed in this Chapter's Specifications. Remove the retaining pin.

52   Using a socket and breaker bar on the crankshaft pulley bolt, turn the crankshaft slowly through two complete revolutions (720-degrees). Recheck the timing marks. **Caution:** *If the timing marks are not aligned exactly as shown, repeat the timing*

belt installation procedure. DO NOT start the engine until you're absolutely certain that the timing belt is installed correctly. Serious and costly engine damage could occur if the belt is installed wrong.

53   Install the upper (no. 2) timing belt cover and gasket.

54   Reinstall the remaining parts in the reverse order of removal.

8   Crankshaft front oil seal - replacement

Refer to illustrations 8.3 and 8.5

1   Remove the timing belt and crankshaft timing belt sprocket (see Section 7).

2   Note how far the seal is recessed in the bore, then cut away the seal lip with a razor knife.

3   Carefully pry the seal out of the engine with a screwdriver or seal removal tool **(see illustration)**. If you use a screwdriver, wrap tape around the tip - don't scratch the housing bore or damage the crankshaft (if the crankshaft is damaged, the new seal will end up leaking).

4   Clean the bore in the engine and coat the outer edge of the new seal with engine oil or multi-purpose grease. Apply the same

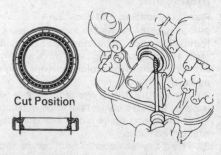

8.3 Cut away the crankshaft seal lip, wrap a screwdriver tip with tape and pry out the seal

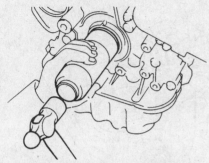

8.5 Lubricate the seal lip and drive the new crankshaft seal into place with a large socket or piece of pipe and a hammer

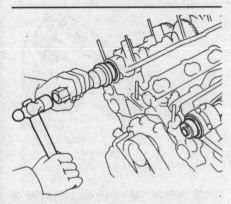

9.5 Lubricate the seal lip and tap the new camshaft seal into place with a large socket or piece of pipe and a hammer

grease to the seal lip.

5   Using a socket with an outside diameter slightly smaller than the outside diameter of the seal, carefully drive the new seal into place with a hammer **(see illustration)**. Make sure it's installed squarely and driven in to the same depth as the original. If a socket isn't available, a short section of large diameter pipe will also work. Check the seal after installation to make sure the spring didn't pop out of place.

6   Reinstall the crankshaft timing sprocket and timing belt (see Section 7). On 1MZ-FE engines, be careful not to scratch the crankshaft sensor portion of the sprocket.

7   Run the engine and check for oil leaks at the front seal.

9   Camshaft oil seals - replacement

Refer to illustration 9.5

1   Remove the timing belt and camshaft sprocket(s) (see Section 7).

2   Remove the bolts and detach the rear (no. 3) timing belt cover.

3   Note how far the seal is seated in the bore, then carefully pry it out with a straight-slot screwdriver. Wrap the screwdriver tip with tape - don't scratch the bore or damage the camshaft (if the camshaft is damaged, the new seal will end up leaking).

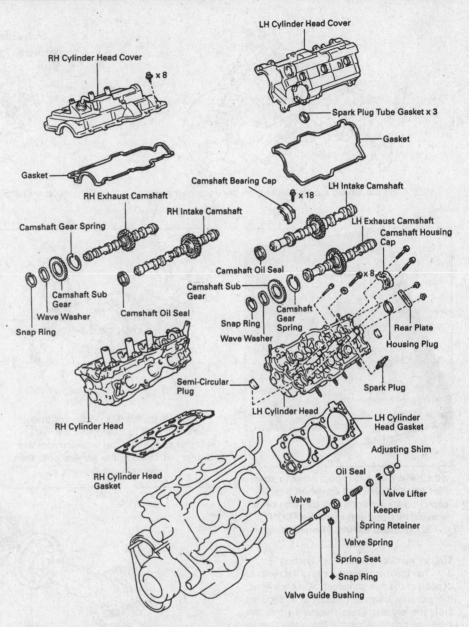

10.1 Exploded view of the camshafts and components on the 3.4L engine

4   Clean the bore and coat the outer edge of the new seal with engine oil or multi-purpose grease. Apply multi-purpose grease to the seal lip.

5   Using a socket with an outside diameter slightly smaller than the outside diameter of the seal, carefully drive the new seal into place with a hammer. Make sure it's installed squarely and driven in to the same depth as the original. If a socket isn't available, a short section of pipe will also work **(see illustration)**.

6   Reinstall the rear timing belt cover and tighten the bolts.

7   Reinstall the camshaft sprocket(s) and timing belt (see Section 7).

8   Run the engine and check for oil leaks at the camshaft seal.

10 Camshafts and lifters - removal, inspection and installation

3.4L engine

Note: *Before beginning this procedure, obtain two 6 x 1.0 mm bolts 16 to 20 mm long. They will be referred to as service bolts in the text.*

Removal

Refer to illustrations 10.1, 10.3, 10.4, 10.10, 10.12, 10.13 and 10.14

1   Remove the valve covers (see Section 4) and the timing belt (see Section 7) **(see illustration)**.

2   Make sure the engine is positioned on

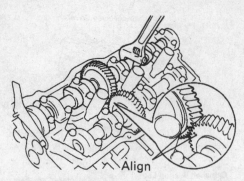

10.3 Align the timing marks (circled) on the camshaft gears

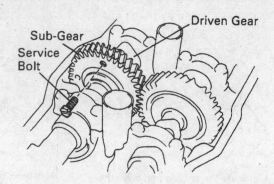

10.4 Install a service bolt through the sub-gear into the driven gear

10.10 Mark up a cardboard box to store the lifters/shims and camshaft bearing caps - use a separate box for each set to avoid mix-ups and mark the FRONT, INTAKE and EXHAUST orientation

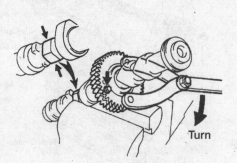

10.12 With the hex portion of the camshaft held in a vise, use a two-pin spanner to remove the tension from the subgear and remove the service bolt, then release the subgear

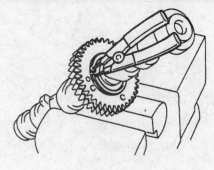

10.13 Remove the snap-ring with a pair of snap-ring pliers

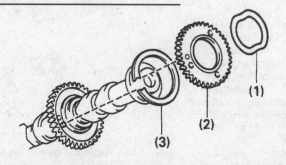

10.14 Remove the wave washer (1), the camshaft subgear (2) and the gear spring (3)

TDC for number 1 piston (see Section 3).

3   The following steps apply to the removal of each of the four camshafts. On each head, the exhaust camshaft subgear is secured first, the exhaust cam removed, then the intake camshaft. Align the cam timing marks on the drive and driven gears **(see illustration)**. Turn the camshaft with a wrench if necessary. **Note:** *For reference purposes, the outside camshafts are the exhaust camshafts while the inner camshafts are the intake camshafts. The right side cylinder head (passenger's side) is called the right bank while the left side cylinder head (driver's side) is called the left bank.*

4   Secure the exhaust camshaft sub-gear to the driven gear with a service bolt installed in the threaded hole **(see illustration)**. **Caution:** *Since the camshaft thrust clearance is minimal, the camshafts must be held level as they are being removed. If they aren't, the portion of the cylinder head next to the cam gears may crack or be damaged by the gear leverage. Before lifting a camshaft out of the head, make certain that the torsional spring force of the sub-gear has been eliminated by the service bolt.*

5   Loosen the camshaft bearing cap bolts in 1/4-turn increments until they can be removed by hand. Follow the reverse of the recommended tightening sequence **(see illustration 10.29)**.

6   Remove the bearing caps and gently lift out the exhaust camshaft. Be sure to keep it level.

7   Loosen the intake camshaft bearing cap bolts in 1/4-turn increments until they can be removed by hand. Follow the reverse of the recommended tightening sequence **(see illustration 10.24)**.

8   Remove the intake bearing caps and oil seal and gently lift out the intake camshaft. Be sure to keep it level.

9   Repeat the steps for the left-hand (front) cylinder head.

10   Store the bearing caps in the correct order. **Note:** *If necessary, the valve lifters and shims can now be removed with a magnetic tool. Be sure to store them separately so they can be reinstalled in their original locations* **(see illustration)**.

11   To disassemble an exhaust camshaft gear, mount the cam in a vise with the jaws gripping the large hex on the shaft.

12   Install a second service bolt in the unthreaded hole in the camshaft sub-gear. Using a screwdriver positioned against the service bolt just installed, rotate the sub-gear clockwise and remove the first service bolt. The second bolt isn't needed if you have a two-pin spanner **(see illustration)**.

13   Remove the sub-gear snap-ring **(see illustration)**.

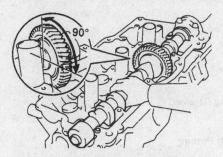

10.21 Set the right cylinder head intake camshaft into place with the two dots at the 3 o'clock position (facing the exhaust camshaft)

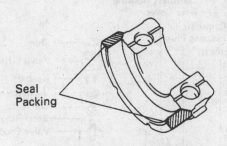

Seal Packing

10.22 Apply RTV sealant to the shaded areas on the bearing cap

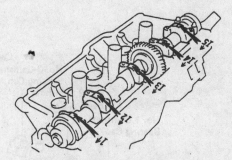

10.23 Install the intake camshaft bearing caps as shown with the arrows pointing toward the timing belt end of the engine

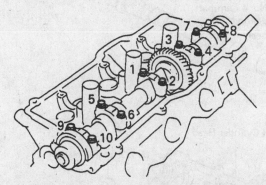

10.24 Tightening sequence for the intake camshaft bearing caps

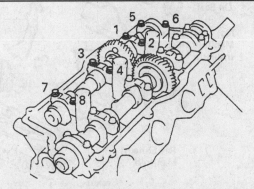

10.29 Tightening sequence for the exhaust camshaft bearing caps

14   The wave washer, sub-gear and camshaft gear spring can now be removed from the camshaft **(see illustration)**. Be sure to keep the parts from the left side camshaft separate from the right side.

Inspection

15   Refer to Chapter 2, Part A for camshaft, lifter and related component inspection procedures. Be sure to use the Specifications in this Part of Chapter 2.

Installation

Refer to illustrations 10.21, 10.22, 10.23, 10.24 and 10.29

16   Reassemble the exhaust camshaft gear(s) by installing the camshaft gear spring, sub-gear, wave washer and snap-ring.

17   Mount the camshaft in a padded vise.

18   Insert a service bolt into the unthreaded hole in the camshaft subgear. Using a screwdriver, align the holes of the camshaft driven gear and sub-gear by turning the camshaft sub-gear clockwise. Install a second service bolt in the threaded hole, tightening it to clamp the gears together. Remove the service bolt from the unthreaded hole. Repeat the procedure for the other camshaft.

19   Apply moly-base grease or engine assembly lube to the lifters, then install them in their original locations in the cylinder heads. Make sure the valve adjustment shims are in place in the lifters, and that all lifters are installed in their original bores.

Intake camshaft head

Note: *For reference purposes, the outside camshafts are the exhaust camshafts while the inner camshafts are the intake camshafts. The right side cylinder head (passenger) is called the right bank while the left side cylinder head (driver) is called the left bank.*

20   Apply moly-base grease or engine assembly lube to the camshaft lobes, bearing journals and gear thrust faces.

21   Set the intake camshaft in place in the right cylinder head with the timing marks (two dots) facing the exhaust camshaft side of the head **(see illustration)**.

22   Apply a thin coat of RTV sealant to the outer edges of the front bearing cap cylinder head mating surfaces **(see illustration)**.

23   Install the bearing caps in numerical order with the arrows pointing toward the front (timing belt end) of the engine **(see illustration)**.

24   Tighten the bearing cap bolts in 1/4-turn increments to the torque listed in this Chapter's Specifications. Follow the recommended sequence **(see illustration)**.

25   Refer to Section 9 and install a new camshaft oil seal.

Exhaust camshaft

26   Apply moly-base grease or engine assembly lube to the camshaft lobes, bearing journals and gear thrust faces.

27   Set the exhaust camshaft in place in the

right cylinder head with the timing marks (two dots) aligned with the intake camshaft timing marks **(see illustration 10.3)**.

28   Install the bearing caps in numerical order with the arrows pointing toward the front (timing-belt end) of the engine.

29   Tighten the bearing cap bolts in 1/4-turn increments to the torque listed in this Chapter's Specifications. Follow the recommended sequence **(see illustration)**.

30   Remove the service bolt.

31   Repeat steps 16 through 30 for the camshafts on the left-bank cylinder head.

32   Reinstall the timing belt (see Section 7).

33   Reinstall the remaining components in the reverse order of removal.

34   Before reinstalling the valve covers, use RTV sealant in the areas indicated **(see illustrations 4.7a and 4.7b)**. Clean the rubber half-circle plugs for the back of the heads and reinstall them with RTV sealant.

35   The remainder of installation is the reverse of removal.

36   Run the engine, then check for leaks and proper operation.

3.0L engine

Removal

Refer to illustrations 10.38, 10.39, 10.40, 10.42, 10.44, 10.48 and 10.49

37   Remove the valve covers (see Section 4) and the timing belt (see Section 7).

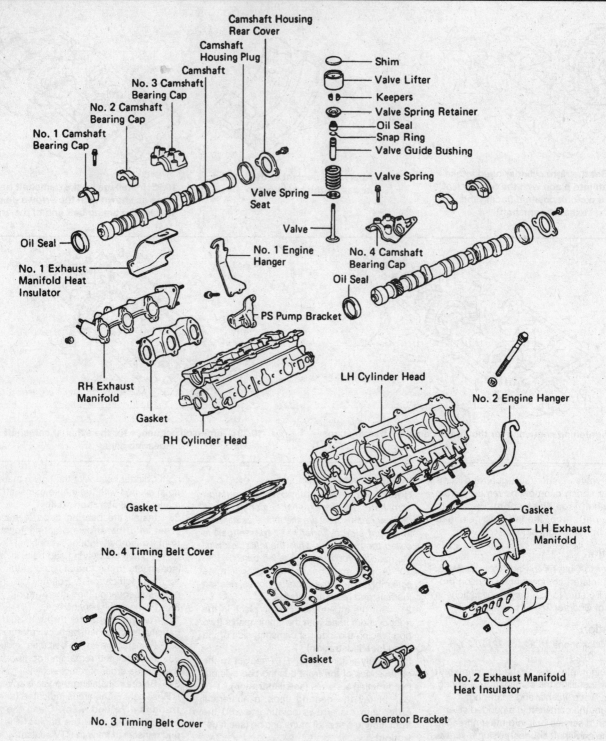

10.38 Exploded view of the 3.0L engine camshafts and components

38   Remove the number 3 timing belt cover **(see illustration)**.

39   Remove the camshaft housing rear cover on the right bank camshaft **(see illustration)**. **Note:** *For reference purposes, the right side cylinder head (passenger) is called the right bank while the left side cylinder head (driver) is called the left bank.*

40   Working on the right bank camshaft,

loosen the camshaft bearing cap bolts in 1/4-turn increments until they can be removed by hand **(see illustration)**.

41   Remove the bearing caps and gently lift out the camshaft. Be sure to keep it level.

42   Loosen the left bank camshaft bearing cap bolts in 1/4-turn increments until they can be removed by hand **(see illustration)**.

43   Remove the left bank bearing caps and

oil seal and gently lift out the camshaft. Be sure to keep it level.

44   Store the bearing caps in the correct order. **Note:** *If necessary, the valve lifters and shims can now be removed with a magnetic tool. Be sure to store them separately so they can be reinstalled in their original locations* **(see illustration)**.

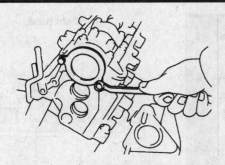

10.39 Working on the backside of the cylinder head, remove the retaining plate bolts

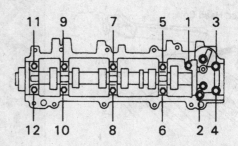

10.40 The camshaft bearing cap loosening sequence for the right bank cylinder head

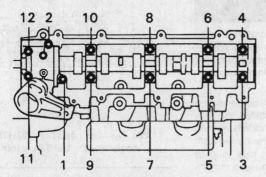

10.42 The camshaft bearing cap loosening sequence for the left bank cylinder head

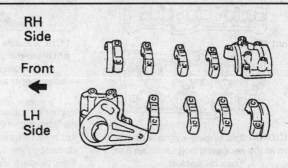

10.44 Mark up a cardboard box to store the lifters/shims and camshaft bearing caps - use a separate box for each set to avoid mix-ups and mark their orientation

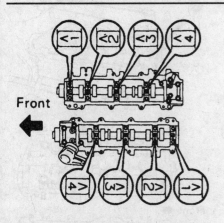

10.48 Install the camshaft bearing caps as shown with the arrows pointing toward the timing belt end of the engine

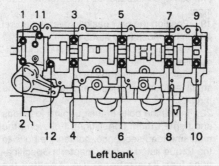

10.49 Camshaft bearing cap tightening sequence

Inspection

45 Refer to Chapter 2, Part A for camshaft, lifter and related component inspection procedures. Be sure to use the Specifications in this Part of Chapter 2 for the V6 engines.

Installation

Refer to illustrations 10.48 and 10.49

46 Apply moly-base grease or engine assembly lube to the lifters, then install them in their original locations in the cylinder heads. Make sure the valve adjustment shims are in place in the lifters, and that all lifters are installed in their original bores.

47 Apply moly-base grease or engine assembly lube to the camshaft lobes, bearing journals and gear thrust faces.

48 Set the camshafts in place in the cylinder heads with the bearing caps on each journal pointing forward **(see illustration)**.

49 Apply a thin coat of RTV sealant to the outer edges of the numbers 1 and 4 (left bank) or 1 and 3 (right bank) bearing cap cylinder head mating surfaces **(see illustration)**.

50 Tighten the bearing cap bolts in 1/4-turn increments to the torque listed in this Chapter's Specifications. Follow the recommended sequence.

51 Refer to Section 9 and install a new camshaft oil seal.

52 Reinstall the remaining components in the reverse order of removal.

53 Before reinstalling the valve covers, use RTV sealant in the areas indicated **(see illustrations 4.9a)**. Clean the rubber half-circle plugs for the back of the heads and reinstall with new RTV sealant.

54 The remainder of the installation is the reverse of the disassembly sequence.

55 Run the engine, then check for leaks and proper operation.

11 Cylinder heads - removal and installation

Removal

Refer to illustration 11.10

1 Disconnect the negative cable from the battery. **Caution:** *If the stereo in your vehicle is equipped with an anti-theft system, make sure you have the correct activation code before disconnecting the battery.*

2 Drain the cooling system, including the block (see Chapter 1).

3 Remove the air intake plenum, fuel delivery pipes and injectors (see Chapter 4).

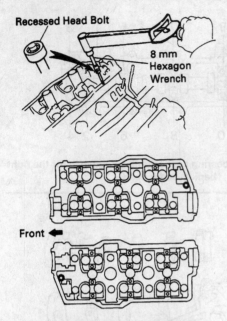

11.10 On 3.4L engine cylinder heads, remove the recessed bolts with an 8 mm hex bit socket

11.19 Be sure the new head gaskets are positioned right side up (check all holes and coolant passages for correct alignment) and over the block dowels

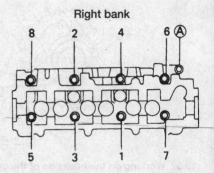

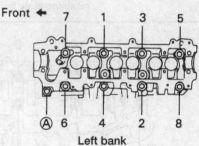

11.22a Cylinder head bolt TIGHTENING sequence for the 3.0L engine

4   Remove the exhaust manifold(s) (see Section 6).

5   Remove the alternator and, if equipped, the distributor (see Chapter 5).

6   Remove the intake manifold (see Section 5).

7   Remove the timing belt, camshaft sprockets and upper idler pulley (see Section 7).

8   Remove the upper timing belt cover 3.

9   Remove the camshaft(s) from the head(s) you intend to remove (see Section 10).

10   On 3.4L engines, using an 8 mm hex bit or Allen wrench, remove the recessed head bolts (one in each head) **(see illustration)**.

11   Using a 12-point socket, loosen the cylinder head bolts in 1/4-turn increments until they can be removed by hand. Follow the reverse order of the factory recommended tightening sequence **(see illustration 11.22a and 11.22b)**.

12   Lift the cylinder head off the engine block. If the head is stuck, place a wood block against it and strike the wood with a hammer. **Caution:** *Don't pry between the head and block. The gasket surfaces may be damaged and leaks could result.*

13   Repeat the procedure for the other head.

Installation

Refer to illustrations 11.19, 11.22a and 11.22b

14   The mating surfaces of the cylinder heads and block must be perfectly clean when the heads are installed.

15   Use a gasket scraper to remove all traces of carbon and old gasket material, then clean the mating surfaces with lacquer

thinner or acetone. If there's oil on the mating surfaces when the head is installed, the gasket may not seal correctly and leaks could develop. When working on the block, stuff the cylinders with clean shop rags to keep out debris. Use a vacuum cleaner to remove material that falls into the cylinders.

16   Check the block and head mating surfaces for nicks, deep scratches and other damage. If damage is slight, it can be removed with a file; if it's excessive, machining may be the only alternative.

17   Use a tap of the correct size to chase the threads in the cylinder head bolt holes, then clean the holes with compressed air - make sure that nothing remains in the holes. **Warning:** *Wear eye protection when using compressed air!*

18   Mount each bolt in a vise and run a die down the threads to remove corrosion and restore the threads. Dirt, corrosion, sealant and damaged threads will affect torque readings.

19   Position the new gaskets over the dowel pins in the block **(see illustration)**.

20   Carefully set the head on the block without disturbing the gasket.

21   Before installing the head bolts, apply a small amount of clean engine oil to the threads.

22   Install the bolts in their original locations and tighten them finger tight. Following the recommended sequence, tighten the bolts to the torque listed in this Chapter's Specifications **(see illustrations)**. Don't tighten the recessed bolt at this time.

23   Mark the front of each bolt head with paint. You can also mark the socket you are using. Place the socket over the 12-point bolt so that you can observe the mark, and reference Step 24.

24   Following the same sequence, tighten each bolt an additional 1/4-turn (90-degrees).

25   Tighten each bolt yet another 1/4-turn (90-degrees) following the same sequence. The paint marks should now all be 180-degrees from the starting point.

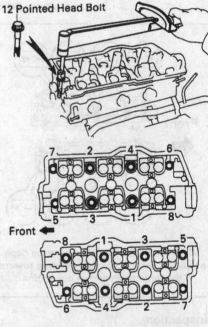

11.22b Cylinder head bolt TIGHTENING sequence for the 3.4L engine

26   On 3.4L engines, tighten the recessed bolt to the torque listed in this Chapter's Specifications.

27   Repeat the entire procedure to install the other cylinder head.

28   The remaining installation steps are the reverse of removal.

29   Refill the cooling system, change the oil and filter (see Chapter 1), run the engine and check for leaks.

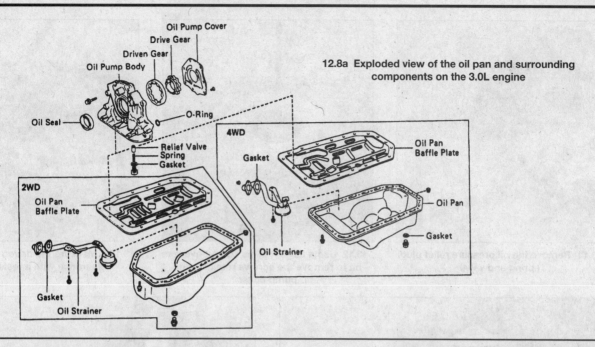

12.8a Exploded view of the oil pan and surrounding components on the 3.0L engine

12   Oil pan - removal and installation

Note: *Removing the oil pan on 4WD models will require removal of the front drive shafts and front differential assembly. Therefore, it will often be easier to remove the engine when removing the oil pan on 4WD models.*

Removal

Refer to illustrations 12.8a and 12.8b

1   Remove the protective cover from under the engine compartment.

2   Disconnect the negative cable from the battery. **Caution:** *If the stereo in your vehicle is equipped with an anti-theft system, make sure you have the correct activation code before disconnecting the battery.*

3   Raise the vehicle and support it securely on jackstands.

4   On 4WD models, remove the front differential and drive axles (see Chapter 8).

5   Drain the engine oil and remove the oil filter.

6   Remove the timing belt and the crankshaft pulley (see Section 7).

7   Remove the flywheel housing cover.

8   Remove the bolts and nuts securing the oil pan and detach the pan **(see illustrations)**. If it's stuck, pry it loose very carefully with a small screwdriver or putty knife. Don't damage the mating surfaces of the pan or oil leaks could develop.

9   Remove the oil pump strainer/pickup.

10   Remove the baffle plate from the bottom of the engine.

Installation

11   Use a scraper to remove all traces of old sealant from the block and oil pan. Clean the mating surfaces with lacquer thinner or acetone.

12   Make sure the threaded bolt holes in the block are clean.

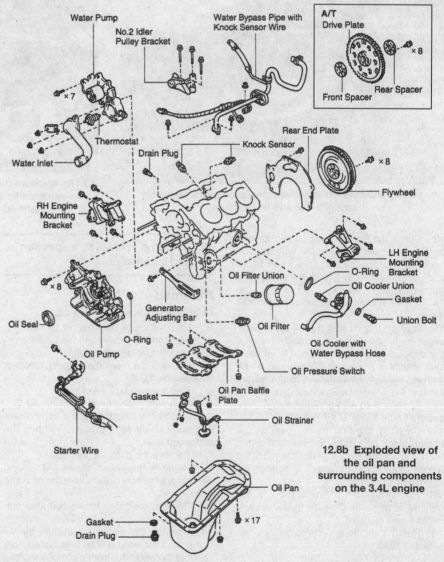

12.8b Exploded view of the oil pan and surrounding components on the 3.4L engine

13.11 Remove the oil pressure relief plug, spring and valve

13.12 Use a large Phillips screwdriver or bit to remove the screws retaining the pump cover

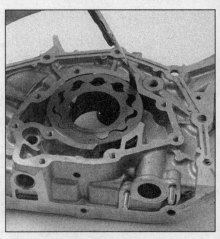

13.17a Measure the driven rotor-to-body clearance with a feeler gauge

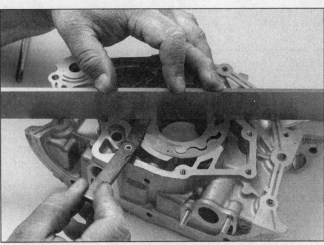

13.17b Measure the rotor side clearance with a precision straightedge and feeler gauge

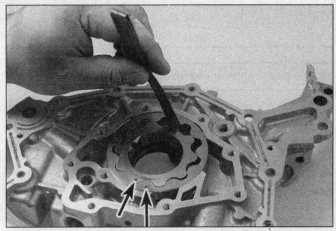

13.17c Measure the rotor tip clearance with a feeler gauge - note the rotor marks are facing out (when the pump body cover is installed, the marks will be against the cover)

13 Check the flange of the oil pan for distortion, particularly around the bolt holes. If necessary, place the pan on a wood block and use a hammer to flatten and restore the gasket surface.

14 If the baffle has been removed, reinstall it now.

15 Inspect the oil pump pick-up/strainer assembly for cracks and a blocked strainer. If the pick-up was removed, clean it with solvent or thinner and install it now, using a new gasket. Tighten the fasteners to the torque listed in this Chapter's Specifications.

16 Apply a 3 to 4 mm wide bead of RTV sealant to the flange of the oil pan.

17 Carefully position the oil pan on the engine block and install the bolts. Working from the center out, tighten them to the torque listed in this Chapter's Specifications in three or four steps.

18 The remainder of installation is the reverse of removal. Be sure to add oil and install a new oil filter.

19 Run the engine and check for oil pressure and leaks.

13   Oil pump - removal, inspection and installation

Removal

Refer to illustrations 13.11 and 13.12

1   Remove the oil pan (see Section 12).

2   Remove the timing belt (see Section 7) and lower timing belt idler pulley.

3   Remove the crankshaft timing sprocket (see Section 7).

4   Remove the oil pick-up tube.

5   Remove the alternator (see Chapter 5).

6   Unbolt the air conditioning compressor and set it aside without disconnecting the refrigerant lines.

7   Remove the compressor bracket.

8   Remove the power steering adjusting bar and pry the pump away from the oil pump body.

9   Remove the lower timing belt idler pulley.

10   Remove the bolts and detach the oil pump from the engine. You may have to pry carefully between the front main bearing cap

and the pump body with a screwdriver.

11   Remove the O-ring. Remove the oil pressure relief valve snap-ring, retainer, spring and valve **(see illustration)**. **Warning:** *The spring is tightly compressed - be careful and wear eye protection.*

12   Use a large Phillips screwdriver to remove the eight screws retaining the body cover to the rear of the oil pump **(see illustration)**.

13   Lift the cover off and remove the pump rotors.

14   Use a scraper to remove all traces of sealant and old gasket material from the pump body and engine block, then clean the mating surfaces with lacquer thinner or acetone.

Inspection

Refer to illustrations 13.17a, 13.17b and 13.17c

15   Clean all components with solvent, then inspect them for wear and damage.

16   Check the oil pressure relief valve sliding surface and valve spring. If either the spring or the valve is damaged, they must be

13.26 Be sure to align the drive rotor and the crankshaft as the oil pump is installed, and install a new O-ring (arrow) on the block

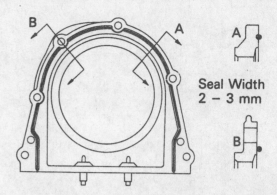

Seal Width
2 – 3 mm

15.1 On 3.4L engines, apply RTV sealant to the oil seal retainer-to-block mating surface

replaced as a set.

17 Check the clearance of the following components with a feeler gauge and compare the measurements to this Chapter's Specifications **(see illustrations)**:

a) *Driven rotor-to-oil pump body*
b) *Rotor side clearance*
c) *Rotor tip clearance*

Installation

Refer to illustration 13.26

18 Pry the old crankshaft seal out with a screwdriver.

19 Apply multi-purpose grease or engine oil to the outer edge of the new seal and carefully drive it into place with a deep socket and a hammer. Also apply multi-purpose grease to the seal lip.

20 Place the drive and driven rotors into the pump body with the marks facing out **(see illustration 13.17c)**.

21 Pack the pump cavity with petroleum jelly and install the cover. Tighten the screws securely following a criss-cross pattern.

22 Lubricate the oil pressure relief valve with engine oil and install the valve components in the pump body.

23 Use acetone or lacquer thinner and a clean rag to remove all traces of oil from the gasket surfaces.

24 Apply a 2 to 3 mm wide bead of RTV sealant to the oil pump. Avoid using an excessive amount of sealer, especially around oil passages and bolt holes. Assembly must be completed within five minutes of sealant application, otherwise the material must be removed and reapplied.

25 Position a new O-ring on the block.

26 Engage the spline teeth on the oil pump drive rotor with the large teeth on the crankshaft and slide the pump into place **(see illustration)**.

27 Install the oil pump mounting bolts in their original locations and tighten them to the torque listed in this Chapter's Specifications in a criss-cross pattern.

28 Using a new gasket, install the oil pick-up tube and tighten the fasteners to the torque listed in this Chapter's Specifications.

29 Reinstall the remaining parts in the reverse order of removal.

30 Add oil, start the engine and check for oil leaks.

31 Recheck the engine oil level.

14 Flywheel/driveplate - removal and installation

Refer to Chapter 2, Part A for this proce-

dure, but be sure to use the torque specifications in this Part of Chapter 2 for the V6 engine.

15 Rear main oil seal - replacement

Refer to illustration 15.1

Refer to Chapter 2, Part A for this procedure, but note that the V6 engine doesn't have a gasket between the seal retainer and the engine block. Instead, apply a 2 to 3 mm wide bead of RTV sealant to the retainer flange **(see illustration)** before attaching the retainer to the block. Also, be sure to use the torque specifications in this Part of Chapter 2 for the V6 engine.

16 Engine mounts - check and replacement

Refer to illustrations 16.1a and 16.1b

Refer to Chapter 2, Part A, but note that the V6 engine mounts are slightly different in ways that don't significantly affect the check and replacement procedures **(see illustrations)**.

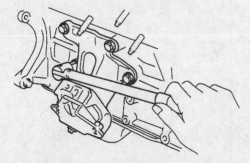

16.1a Removing an engine mount on a 3.0L engine

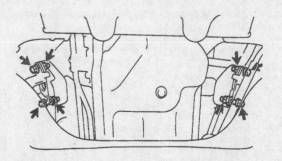

16.1b Engine mount bolt locations on a 3.4L engine

Notes

Chapter 2 Part C
General engine overhaul procedures

Contents

Specifications

Four-cylinder engines

General

Displacement	
2.4L engine	148 cubic inches (2.4 liters)
2.7L engine	164 cubic inches (2.7 liters)
Cylinder compression pressure at 250 rpm	
Standard	178 psi
Minimum	127 psi
Maximum variation between cylinders	30 psi
Oil pressure	
At idle (600 rpm)	4.3 psi minimum
Above 3000 rpm	36 to 71 psi

Engine block

Maximum warpage	0.0020 inch (0.05 mm)
Cylinder bore diameter (standard)	3.7400 to 3.7403 inches (94.990 to 95.003 mm)
Cylinder bore maximum diameter	3.7425 (95.06 mm)
Maximum taper and out-of-round	0.001 inch (0.025 mm)

Cylinder head and valves

Warpage limit	0.002 inch (0.05 mm)
Valve margin (standard)	
Intake	0.039 inch (1.0 mm)
Exhaust	0.039 inch (1.0 mm)
Valve margin (limit)	
Intake	0.020 inch (0.5 mm)
Exhaust	0.020 inch (0.5 mm)
Valve stem diameter	
Intake	0.2350 to 0.2356 inch (5.970 to 5.985 mm)
Exhaust	0.2348 to 0.2354 inch (5.965 to 5.980 mm)
Valve stem-to-guide clearance	
Standard	
Intake	0.0010 to 0.0024 inch (0.025 to 0.060 mm)
Exhaust	0.0012 to 0.0026 inch (0.030 to 0.065 mm)
Limit	
Intake	0.0031 inch (0.08 mm)
Exhaust	0.0039 inch (0.10 mm)
Valve spring free length	1.7299 to 1.7740 inches (43.94 to 45.06 mm)
Valve spring installed height	1.406 inches (37.5 mm)

Crankshaft and connecting rods

Connecting rod journal	
Diameter	2.0861 to 2.0866 inches (52.987 to 53.000 mm)
Bearing oil clearance	0.0012 to 0.0022 inch (0.030 to 0.055 mm)
Connecting rod side clearance (endplay)	
Standard	0.0063 to 0.0123 inch (0.160 to 0.312 mm)
Limit	0.0138 inch (0.35 mm)
Main bearing journal (also see Fig. 20.10a)	
Journals 1, 2, 4 and 5	
Diameter	2.3617 to 2.3622 inches (59.987 to 60.000 mm)
Bearing oil clearance	0.0009 to 0.0019 inch (0.024 to 0.049 mm)
Journal 3	
Diameter	2.2615 to 2.3620 inches (59.981 to 59.994 mm)
Bearing oil clearance	0.0012 to 0.0022 inch (0.030 to 0.055 mm)
Crankshaft endplay	
Standard	0.0008 to 0.0087 inch (0.020 to 0.022 mm)
Limit	0.0118 inch (0.30 mm)
Maximum taper and out-of-round	0.0002 inch (0.005 mm)

Pistons and rings

Piston diameter (standard)	
2.4L engine	3.7371 to 3.7375 inches (94.923 to 94.933 mm)
2.7L engine	3.7354 to 3.7379 inches (94.933 to 94.943 mm)
Piston-to-bore clearance	
2.4L engine	0.0022 to 0.0031 inch (0.057 to 0.080 mm)
2.7L engine	0.0019 to 0.0028 inch (0.047 to 0.070 mm)
Piston ring end gap	
Number 1 (top) compression ring	
Standard	0.0118 to 0.0157 inch (0.300 to 0.400 mm)
Service limit	0.0157 inch (0.40 mm)
Number 2 (second) compression ring	
Standard	
Mark "T"	0.0157 to 0.0197 inch (0.400 to 0.500 mm)
Mark "N"	0.0157 to 0.0194 inch (0.400 to 0.500 mm)
Service limit	0.0196 inch (0.50 mm)
Piston side clearance	
Number 1 (top) compression ring	
Standard	0.0008 to 0.0028 inch (0.020 to 0.070 mm)
Limit	0.0028 inch (0.070 mm)
Number 2 (second) compression ring	
Standard	0.0012 to 0.0028 inch (0.030 to 0.070 mm)
Limit	0.0028 inch (0.070 mm)

Balance shafts

Balance shaft thrust clearance	
Standard	0.0027 to 0.0051 inches (0.07 to 0.13 mm)
Maximum	0.0079 inch (0.2 mm)

Torque specifications *	Ft-lbs
Crankshaft oil nozzles	12
Balance shaft retainer bolts	13
Balance shaft drive gear bolt	18
Balance shaft tensioner nut	13
Number 3 damper bolts	13
Number 2 damper bolt	20
Main bearing cap bolts	
Step 1	29
Step 2	Tighten an additional 90-degrees
Connecting rod cap nuts	
Step 1	33
Step 2	Tighten an additional 90-degrees

* Note: *Refer to Part A for additional torque specifications.*

3.0L V6 engine

General

Displacement	180 cubic inches (3.0 liters)
Cylinder compression pressure at 250 rpm	
Standard	171 psi
Minimum	142 psi
Oil pressure (engine hot)	
At 3000 rpm	36 to 75 psi
At idle	4.3 psi minimum

Cylinder head

Warpage limit	0.0039 inch (0.10 mm)

Valves and related components

Valve margin width	
Standard	0.059 inch (1.5 mm)
Minimum	0.051 inch (1.3 mm)
Valve stem diameter	
Intake	0.3138 to 0.3144 inch (7.970 to 7.985 mm)
Exhaust	0.3136 to 0.3142 inch (7.965 to 7.980 mm)
Valve stem-to-guide clearance	
Intake	
Standard	0.0010 to 0.0024 inch (0.025 to 0.060 mm)
Service limit	0.0031 inch (0.08 mm)
Exhaust	
Standard	0.0012 to 0.0026 inch (0.030 to 0.065 mm)
Service limit	0.0039 inch (0.10 mm)
Valve spring	
Out-of-square limit	0.0484 inch (1.23 mm)
Free length	1.8508 inches (47.01 mm)
Installed height	1.575 inches (40.0 mm)
Valve lifter	
Outside diameter	1.4930 to 1.4934 inches (37.922 to 37.932 mm)
Bore diameter	1.4945 to 1.4951 inches (37.960 to 37.975 mm)
Lifter-to-bore (oil) clearance	
Standard	0.0011 to 0.0021 inch (0.028 to 0.053 mm)
Service limit	0.004 inch (0.10 mm)

Crankshaft and connecting rods

Connecting rod journal	
Diameter	2.1648 to 2.1654 inches (54.987 to 55.000 mm)
Taper and out-of-round limits	0.0008 inch (0.02 mm)
Bearing oil clearance	
Standard	0.0009 to 0.0021 inch (0.024 to 0.053 mm)
Service limit	0.0031 inch (0.08 mm)
Connecting rod side clearance (endplay)	
Standard	0.0059 to 0.0130 inch (0.15 to 0.33 mm)
Service limit	0.0150 inch (0.38 mm)
Main bearing journal (also see Fig. 20.10b)	
Diameter	2.5195 to 2.5197 inches (63.996 to 64.000 mm)
Taper and out-of-round limits	0.0008 inch (0.02 mm)
Bearing oil clearance	
Standard	0.0009 to 0.0017 inch (0.0024 to 0.0042 mm)
Service limit	0.0031 inch (0.80 mm)

Crankshaft and connecting rods (continued)

Crankshaft endplay
    Standard.. 0.0008 to 0.0098 inch (2.44 to 2.49 mm)
    Service limit .... 0.0118 inch (0.30 mm)
    Thrust washer thickness .... 0.0961 to 0.0980 inch (2.44 to 2.49 mm)

Engine block

Deck warpage limit .... 0.0020 inch (0.05 mm)
Cylinder bore diameter
    Standard
        Mark 1 .... 3.4449 to 3.4453 inches (87.500 to 87.510 mm)
        Mark 2 .... 3.4453 to 3.4457 inches (87.511 to 87.520 mm)
        Mark 3 .... 3.4457 to 3.4461 inches (87.521 to 87.530 mm)

Pistons and rings

Piston diameter (standard)
    Mark 1 .... 3.4394 to 3.4398 inches (87.360 to 87.370 mm)
    Mark 2 .... 3.4398 to 3.4402 inches (87.370 to 87.380 mm)
    Mark 3 .... 3.4402 to 3.4406 inches (87.380 to 87.390 mm)
Piston-to-bore clearance
    Standard.. 0.0051 to 0.0059 inch (0.13 to 0.15 mm)
    Service limit .... 0.0067 inch (0.017 mm)
Piston ring end gap
    No. 1 (top) compression ring
        Standard .... 0.0091 to 0.0130 inch (0.23 to 0.33 mm)
        Service limit.. 0.0327 inch (0.83 mm)
    No. 2 (middle) compression ring
        Standard .... 0.0150 to 0.0189 inch (0.38 to 0.48 mm)
        Service limit.. 0.0366 inch (0.93 mm)
    Oil ring
        Standard .... 0.0059 to 0.0157 inch (0.15 to 0.40 mm)
        Service limit.. 0.0354 inch (0.90 mm)
Piston ring groove clearance
    1993 engines
        Standard .... 0.0012 to 0.0028 inch (0.03 to 0.07 mm)
        Service limit.. 0.0079 inch (0.20 mm)
    1994 engines
        No. 1 (top) compression ring .... 0.0008 to 0.0024 inch (0.02 to 0.06 mm)
        No. 2 (middle) compression ring................................ 0.0012 to 0.0028 inch (0.030 to 0.070 mm)
        Service limit (both rings) .... 0.0079 inch (0.20 mm)

Torque specifications*

Ft-lbs (unless otherwise indicated)

Main bearing cap assembly bolts
    Step 1 45
    Step 2 .... Turn an additional 90-degrees (1/4-turn)
Connecting rod cap nuts
    Step 1 18
    Step 2 .... Turn an additional 90-degrees (1/4-turn)

* **Note:** *Refer to Part B for additional torque specifications.*

3.4L V6 engine

General

Displacement... 206 cubic inches (3.4 liters)
Cylinder compression pressure at 250 rpm
    Standard.. 218 psi
    Minimum.. 145 psi
Oil pressure (engine hot)
    At 3000 rpm.. 36 to 75 psi
    At idle .... 4.3 psi minimum

Cylinder head

Warpage limit.. 0.0039 inch (0.10 mm)

Valves and related components

Valve margin width
    Standard.. 0.039 inch (1.0 mm)
    Minimum.. 0.020 inch (0.5 mm)
Valve stem diameter
    Intake.. 0.2350 to 0.2356 inch (5.970 to 5.985 mm)
    Exhaust... 0.2348 to 0.2354 inch (5.965 to 5.980 mm)

Valve stem-to-guide clearance
  Intake
    Standard .... 0.0010 to 0.0024 inch (0.025 to 0.060 mm)
    Service limit.. 0.0031 inch (0.08 mm)
  Exhaust
    Standard .... 0.0012 to 0.0026 inch (0.030 to 0.065 mm)
  Service limit... 0.0039 inch (0.10 mm)
Valve spring
  Out-of-square limit .... 0.079 inch (2.0 mm)
  Free length .... 1.7630 inches (44.78 mm)
  Installed height .... 1.311 inches (33.3 mm)
Valve lifter
  Outside diameter... 1.2191 to 1.2195 inch (30.966 to 30.976 mm)
  Bore diameter... 1.2205 to 1.2212 inch (31.960 to 31.018 mm)
  Lifter-to-bore (oil) clearance
    Standard .... 0.0009 to 0.0020 inch (0.024 to 0.052 mm)
    Service limit.. 0.003 inch (0.08 mm)

Crankshaft and connecting rods

Connecting rod journal
  Diameter... 2.1648 to 2.1654 inches (54.987 to 55.000 mm)
  Taper and out-of-round limits .... 0.0008 inch (0.02 mm)
  Bearing oil clearance
    Standard .... 0.0008 to 0.0015 inch (0.020 to 0.038 mm)
    Service limit.. 0.0031 inch (0.08 mm)
Connecting rod side clearance (endplay)
  Standard.. 0.0059 to 0.0130 inch (0.150 to 0.330 mm)
  Service limit.. 0.0150 inch (0.380 mm)

Main bearing journal (also see Fig. 20.10c)

Diameter... 2.5191 to 2.5197 inches (63.985 to 64.000 mm)
Taper and out-of-round limits .... 0.0008 inch (0.02 mm)
Bearing oil clearance
  Number 1 journal
    Standard .... 0.0008 to 0.0015 inch (0.020 to 0.038 mm)
    Service limit .... 0.0031 inch (0.08 mm)
  All other journals
    Standard .... 0.0009 to 0.0017 inch (0.024 to 0.042 mm)
    Service limit .... 0.0031 inch (0.08 mm)
Crankshaft endplay
  Standard.. 0.0008 to 0.0087 inch (0.020 to 0.220 mm)
  Service limit .... 0.0118 inch (0.30 mm)
  Thrust washer thickness .... 0.0961 to 0.0980 inch (0.020 to 0.038 mm)

Engine block

Deck warpage limit .... 0.0020 inch (0.05 mm)
Cylinder bore diameter
  Standard
    Mark 1 .... 3.6811 to 3.6815 inches (93.500 to 93.510 mm)
    Mark 2 .... 3.6815 to 3.6819 inches (93.510 to 93.520 mm)
    Mark 3 .... 3.6819 to 3.6823 inches (93.520 to 93.530 mm)
  Service limit.. 0.008 inches (0.2 mm)

Pistons and rings

Piston diameter (standard)
  Mark 1 .... 3.6754 to 3.6758 inches (93.356 to 93.366 mm)
  Mark 2 .... 3.6759 to 3.6762 inches (93.367 to 93.376 mm)
  Mark 3 .... 3.6763 to 3.6766 inches (93.377 to 93.386 mm)
Piston-to-bore clearance
  Standard.. 0.0053 to 0.0060 inch (0.134 to 0.154 mm)
  Service limit.. 0.0069 inch (0.174 mm)
Piston ring end gap
  No. 1 (top) compression ring
    Standard .... 0.0118 to 0.0197 inch (0.30 to 0.50 mm)
    Service limit.. 0.0433 inch (1.10 mm)
  No. 2 (middle) compression ring
    Standard .... 0.0157 to 0.0236 inch (0.40 to 0.60 mm)
    Service limit.. 0.0472 inch (1.20 mm)
  Oil ring
    Standard .... 0.0059 to 0.0217 inch (0.15 to 0.55 mm)
    Service limit.. 0.0453 inch (1.15 mm)

Pistons and rings (continued)

Piston ring groove clearance
    No. 1 (top) compression ring.. 0.0016 to 0.0031 inch (0.04 to 0.08 mm)
    No. 2 (middle) compression ring .... 0.0012 to 0.0028 inch (0.030 to 0.070 mm)
    Service limit.. 0.0079 inch (0.20 mm)

Torque specifications*   **Ft-lbs** (unless otherwise indicated)

Main bearing cap assembly bolts
    Step 1... 45
    Step 2... Turn an additional 90-degrees (1/4-turn)
Connecting rod cap nuts
    Step 1... 18
    Step 2 .... Turn an additional 90-degrees (1/4-turn)

Note: *Refer to Part B for additional torque specifications*

1   General information

Included in this portion of Chapter 2 are the general overhaul procedures for the cylinder head and internal engine components.

The information ranges from advice concerning preparation for an overhaul and the purchase of replacement parts to detailed, step-by-step procedures covering removal and installation of internal engine components and the inspection of parts.

The following Sections have been written based on the assumption that the engine has been removed from the vehicle. For information concerning in-vehicle engine repair, as well as removal and installation of the external components necessary for the overhaul, see Chapter 2A (2.4L and 2.7L) or 2B (3.0L and 3.4L) and Section 8 of this Chapter. The Specifications included in this Part are only those necessary for the inspection and overhaul procedures which follow. Refer to Chapter 2, Part A or Part B for additional Specifications.

It's not always easy to determine when, or if, an engine should be completely overhauled, as a number of factors must be considered.

High mileage is not necessarily an indication that an overhaul is needed, while low mileage doesn't preclude the need for an overhaul. Frequency of servicing is probably the most important consideration. An engine that's had regular and frequent oil and filter changes, as well as other required maintenance, will most likely give many thousands of miles of reliable service. Conversely, a neglected engine may require an overhaul very early in its life.

Excessive oil consumption is an indication that piston rings, valve seals and/or valve guides are in need of attention. Make sure that oil leaks aren't responsible before deciding that the rings and/or guides are bad. Perform a cylinder compression check to determine the extent of the work required (see Section 3). Also check the vacuum readings under various conditions (see Section 4).

Loss of power, rough running, knocking or metallic engine noises, excessive valve train noise and high fuel consumption rates may also point to the need for an overhaul, especially if they're all present at the same time. If a complete tune-up doesn't remedy the situation, major mechanical work is the only solution.

An engine overhaul involves restoring the internal parts to the specifications of a new engine. During an overhaul, the piston rings are replaced and the cylinder walls are reconditioned (re-bored and/or honed). If a re-bore is done by an automotive machine shop, new oversize pistons will also be installed. The main bearings, connecting rod bearings and camshaft bearings are generally replaced with new ones and, if necessary, the crankshaft may be reground to restore the journals. Generally, the valves are serviced as well, since they're usually in less-than-perfect condition at this point. While the engine is being overhauled, other components, such as the distributor, starter and alternator, can be rebuilt as well. The end result should be a like new engine that will give many trouble free miles. **Note:** *Critical cooling system components such as the hoses, drivebelts, thermostat and water pump should be replaced with new parts when an engine is overhauled. The radiator should be checked carefully to ensure that it isn't clogged or leaking (see Chapter 3). If you purchase a rebuilt engine or short block, some rebuilders will not warranty their engines unless the radiator has been professionally flushed. Also, we don't recommend overhauling the oil pump - always install a new one when an engine is rebuilt.*

Before beginning the engine overhaul, read through the entire procedure to familiarize yourself with the scope and requirements of the job. Overhauling an engine isn't difficult, but it is time-consuming. Plan on the vehicle being tied up for a minimum of two weeks, especially if parts must be taken to an automotive machine shop for repair or reconditioning. Check on availability of parts and make sure that any necessary special tools and equipment are obtained in advance.

Most work can be done with typical hand tools, although a number of precision measuring tools are required for inspecting parts to determine if they must be replaced. Often an automotive machine shop will handle the inspection of parts and offer advice concerning reconditioning and replacement. **Note:** *Always wait until the engine has been completely disassembled and all components, especially the engine block, have been inspected before deciding what service and repair operations must be performed by an automotive machine shop.* Since the block's condition will be the major factor to consider when determining whether to overhaul the original engine or buy a rebuilt one, never purchase parts or have machine work done on other components until the block has been thoroughly inspected. As a general rule, time is the primary cost of an overhaul, so it doesn't pay to install worn or substandard parts.

As a final note, to ensure maximum life and minimum trouble from a rebuilt engine, everything must be assembled with care in a spotlessly-clean environment.

2   Oil pressure check

Refer to illustrations 2.2a, 2.2b and 2.2c

1   Low engine oil pressure can be a sign of an engine in need of rebuilding. A "low oil pressure" indicator (often called an "idiot light") is not a test of the oiling system. Such indicators only come on when the oil pressure is dangerously low. Even a factory oil pressure gauge in the instrument panel is only a relative indication, although much better for driver information than a warning light. A better test is with a mechanical (not electrical) oil pressure gauge. When used in conjunction with an accurate tachometer, an engine's oil pressure performance can be compared to factory Specifications for that year and model.

2   Find the oil pressure sending unit **(see illustrations)**.

3   Remove the oil pressure sending unit and install a fitting which will allow you to

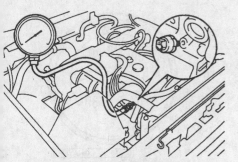

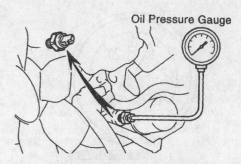

2.2a Oil pressure sending unit and pressure gauge mounting details - four-cylinder engines

2.2b Oil pressure sending unit and pressure gauge mounting details - 3.0L V6 engines

2.2c Oil pressure sending unit and pressure gauge mounting details - 3.4L V6 engines

directly connect your hand-held, mechanical oil pressure gauge. Use Teflon tape or sealant on the threads of the adapter and the fitting on the end of your gauge's hose.

4   Connect an accurate tachometer to the engine, according to the tachometer manufacturer's instructions.

5   Check the oil pressure with the engine running (full operating temperature) at the specified engine speed, and compare it to this Chapter's Specifications. If it's extremely low, the bearings and/or oil pump are probably worn out.

3   Cylinder compression check

Refer to illustration 3.6

1   A compression check will tell you what mechanical condition the upper end (pistons, rings, valves, head gaskets) of the engine is in. Specifically, it can tell you if the compression is down due to leakage caused by worn piston rings, defective valves and seats or a blown head gasket. **Note:** *The engine must be at normal operating temperature and the battery must be fully charged for this check.*

2   Begin by cleaning the area around the spark plugs before you remove them. Com-

3.6 A compression gauge with a threaded fitting for the spark plug hole is preferred over the type that requires hand pressure to maintain the seal - be sure to open the throttle valve as far as possible during the compression check

pressed air should be used, if available, otherwise a small brush or even a bicycle tire pump will work. The idea is to prevent dirt from getting into the cylinders as the compression check is being done.

3   Remove all of the spark plugs from the engine (see Chapter 1).

4   Block the throttle wide open.

5   Disable the ignition systems by removing the IGN fuse from the fuse box (see Chapter 5) and disable the fuel pump by disconnecting the fuel pump harness connector at the fuel pump (see Chapter 4).

6   Install the compression gauge in the number one spark plug hole **(see illustration)**.

7   Crank the engine over at least seven compression strokes and watch the gauge. The compression should build up quickly in a healthy engine. Low compression on the first stroke, followed by gradually increasing pressure on successive strokes, indicates worn piston rings. A low compression reading on the first stroke, which doesn't build up during successive strokes, indicates leaking valves or a blown head gasket (a cracked head could also be the cause). Deposits on the undersides of the valve heads can also cause low compression. Record the highest gauge reading obtained.

8   Repeat the procedure for the remaining cylinders, turning the engine over for the same length of time for each cylinder, and compare the results to this Chapter's Specifications.

9   If the readings are below normal, add some engine oil (about three squirts from a plunger-type oil can) to each cylinder, through the spark plug hole, and repeat the test.

10   If the compression increases after the oil is added, the piston rings are definitely worn. If the compression doesn't increase significantly, the leakage is occurring at the valves or head gasket. Leakage past the valves may be caused by burned valve seats and/or faces or warped, cracked or bent valves.

11   If two adjacent cylinders have equally low compression, there's a strong possibility the head gasket between them is blown. The appearance of coolant in the combustion chambers or the crankcase would verify this condition.

12   If one cylinder is about 20-percent lower than the others, and the engine has a slightly rough idle, a worn exhaust lobe on the camshaft could be the cause.

13   If the compression is unusually high, the combustion chambers are probably coated with carbon deposits. If that's the case, the cylinder heads should be removed and decarbonized.

14   If compression is way down or varies greatly between cylinders, it would be a good idea to have a leak-down test performed by an automotive repair shop. This test will pinpoint exactly where the leakage is occurring and how severe it is.

15   Install the fuses and drive the vehicle to restore the "block learn" memory.

4   Vacuum gauge diagnostic checks

Refer to illustrations 4.1, 4.7, 4.8, 4.9, 4.10, 4.11, 4.12 and 4.13

1   A vacuum gauge provides valuable information about what is going on in the engine at a low cost **(see illustration)**. You can check for worn rings or cylinder walls, leaking head or intake manifold gaskets, incorrect carburetor adjustments, restricted exhaust, stuck or burned valves, weak valve springs, improper ignition or valve timing and ignition problems.

4.1 Install the vacuum gauge to obtain manifold vacuum

4.7 Low, steady reading

4.8 Low, fluctuating needle

4.9 Regular drops

4.10 Irregular drops

4.11 Rapid vibration

4.13 Large fluctuation

2   Unfortunately, vacuum gauge readings are easy to misinterpret, so they should be used in conjunction with other tests to confirm the diagnosis.

3   Both the gauge readings and the rate of needle movement are important for accurate interpretation. Most gauges measure vacuum in inches of mercury (in-Hg). As vacuum increases (or atmospheric pressure decreases), the reading will increase. Also, for every 1,000-foot increase in elevation above sea level, the gauge readings will decrease about one inch of mercury.

4   Connect the vacuum gauge directly to intake manifold vacuum, not to ported (before throttle plate) vacuum. Be sure no hoses are left disconnected during the test or false readings will result.

5   Before you begin the test, allow the engine to warm up completely. Block the wheels and set the parking brake. With the transmission in Park, start the engine and allow it to run at normal idle speed.

6   Read the vacuum gauge; an average, healthy engine should normally produce about 17 to 22 inches of vacuum with a fairly steady needle. Refer to the following vacuum gauge readings and what they indicate about the engine's condition:

7   A low, steady reading usually indicates a leaking gasket between the intake manifold and carburetor or throttle body, a leaky vacuum hose, late ignition timing or incorrect camshaft timing **(see illustration)**. Eliminate all other possible causes, utilizing the tests provided in this Chapter before you remove the timing chain cover to check the timing marks.

8   If the reading is three to eight inches below normal and it fluctuates at that low reading, suspect an intake manifold gasket leak at an intake port **(see illustration)**.

9   If the needle has regular drops of about two to four inches at a steady rate, the valves are probably leaking. Perform a compression or leak-down test to confirm this **(see illustration)**.

10   An irregular drop or down-flick of the needle can be caused by a sticking valve or an ignition misfire. Perform a compression or leak-down test and read the spark plugs **(see illustration)**.

11   A rapid vibration of about four inches-Hg vibration at idle combined with exhaust smoke indicates worn valve guides **(see illustration)**. Perform a leak-down test to confirm this. If the rapid vibration occurs with an increase in engine speed, check for a leaking intake manifold gasket or head gasket, weak valve springs, burned valves or ignition misfire.

12   A slight fluctuation, say one inch up and down, may mean ignition problems. Check all the usual tune-up items and, if necessary, run the engine on an ignition analyzer.

13   If there is a large fluctuation, perform a compression or leak-down test to look for a weak or dead cylinder or a blown head gasket **(see illustration)**.

14   If the needle moves slowly through a wide range, check for a clogged PCV system, incorrect idle fuel mixture, throttle body or intake manifold gasket leaks.

15   Check for a slow return after revving the engine by quickly snapping the throttle open until the engine reaches about 2,500 rpm and

4.15 Slow return after revving

let it shut **(see illustration)**. Normally the reading should drop to near zero, rise above normal idle reading (about 5 in-Hg over) and then return to the previous idle reading. If the vacuum returns slowly and doesn't peak when the throttle is snapped shut, the rings may be worn. If there is a long delay, look for a restricted exhaust system (often the muffler or catalytic converter). An easy way to check this is to temporarily disconnect the exhaust ahead of the suspected part and re-test.

5   Engine removal - methods and precautions

1   If you've decided that an engine must be removed for overhaul or major repair work, several preliminary steps should be taken.

2   Locating a suitable place to work is extremely important. Adequate work space, along with storage space for the vehicle, will

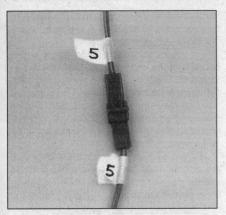

6.7 Label both ends of each wire and hose before disconnecting it

be needed. If a shop or garage isn't available, at the very least a flat, level, clean work surface made of concrete or asphalt is required.

3 Cleaning the engine compartment and engine before beginning the removal procedure will help keep tools clean and organized.

4 An engine hoist or A-frame will also be necessary. Make sure the equipment is rated in excess of the combined weight of the engine and transmission. Safety is of primary importance, considering the potential hazards involved in lifting the engine out of the vehicle.

5 If the engine is being removed by a novice, a helper should be available. Advice and aid from someone more experienced would also be helpful. There are many instances when one person cannot simultaneously perform all of the operations required when lifting the engine out of the vehicle.

6 Plan the operation ahead of time. Arrange for or obtain all of the tools and equipment you'll need prior to beginning the job. Some of the equipment necessary to perform engine removal and installation safely and with relative ease are (in addition to an engine hoist) a heavy duty floor jack, complete sets of wrenches and sockets as described in the front of this manual, wooden blocks and plenty of rags and cleaning solvent for mopping up spilled oil, coolant and gasoline. If the hoist must be rented, make sure that you arrange for it in advance and perform all of the operations possible without it beforehand. This will save you money and time.

7 Plan for the vehicle to be out of use for quite a while. A machine shop will be required to perform some of the work which the do-it-yourselfer can't accomplish without special equipment. These shops often have a busy schedule, so it would be a good idea to consult them before removing the engine in order to accurately estimate the amount of time required to rebuild or repair components that may need work.

8 Always be extremely careful when removing and installing the engine. Serious injury can result from careless actions. Plan ahead, take your time and a job of this nature, although major, can be accomplished successfully.

6 Engine - removal and installation

Note: *Read through the entire Section before beginning this procedure. The factory recommends removing the engine and transmission from the top as a unit, then separating the engine from the transmission on the shop floor. If the transmission is not being serviced, it is possible to leave the transmission in the vehicle and remove the engine from the top by itself, by removing the front crank pulley and tilting up the timing belt end of the engine for clearance.*

Removal

Refer to illustration 6.7

Warning: *These models are equipped with airbags. The airbag is armed and can deploy (inflate) anytime the battery is connected. To prevent accidental deployment (and possible injury), turn the ignition key to LOCK and disconnect the negative battery cable whenever working near airbag components. After the battery is disconnected, wait at least 90 seconds before beginning work (the system has a back-up capacitor that fully discharge). For more information see Chapter 12.*

Note: *The airbag system will be disabled if the battery is disconnected for more than a brief period. If the airbag light comes on and stays on after the battery is reconnected, the vehicle must be taken to a dealer to have the system reset with a special tool.*

1 Relieve the fuel system pressure (see Chapter 4).

2 Disconnect the negative cable from the battery. **Caution:** *If the stereo in your vehicle is equipped with an anti-theft system, make sure you have the correct activation code before disconnecting the battery.*

3 Remove the battery and battery tray.

4 Place protective covers on the fenders and cowl and remove the hood (see Chapter 11).

5 Remove the air cleaner assembly (see Chapter 4).

6 Raise the vehicle and support it securely on jackstands. Drain the cooling system and engine oil and remove the drivebelts (see Chapter 1).

7 Clearly label, then disconnect all vacuum lines, coolant and emissions hoses, wiring harness connectors **(see illustration)**, ground straps and fuel lines. Masking tape and/or a touch up paint applicator work well for marking items. Take instant photos or sketch the locations of components and brackets.

8 Remove the windshield washer tank and coolant reservoir tank.

9 Remove the cooling fan, shroud and radiator (see Chapter 3).

10 Disconnect the heater hoses.

11 Release the residual fuel pressure in the tank by removing the gas cap, then undo the fuel lines connecting the engine to the chassis (see Chapter 4). Plug or cap all open fittings.

12 Disconnect the accelerator cable, transmission Throttle Valve (TV) cable and cruise control cable, if equipped, from the engine (see Chapter 4).

13 Remove the front grill and radiator support brace from the front of the vehicle (see Chapter 11).

14 Disconnect the wire harness clips at the transmission end of the engine and pull back the wiring on all sides to clear the engine.

15 On power steering equipped vehicles, unbolt the power steering pump. If clearance allows, tie the pump aside without disconnecting the hoses. If necessary, remove the pump (see Chapter 10).

16 On air-conditioned models, unbolt the compressor and set it aside. Do not disconnect the refrigerant hoses.

17 Detach the exhaust pipe(s) from the manifold(s) (see Chapter 4).

18 On models equipped with an oil cooler (see Chapter 3), remove the hoses connected to the cooler, and the oil cooler.

19 Attach a lifting sling to the engine. Position a hoist and connect the sling to it. Take up the slack until there is slight tension on the hoist.

20 Remove the driveline (see Chapter 8).

21 Remove the bolts securing the engine mounts to the frame (see Chapter 2A or 2B).

22 On automatic transmission equipped models, detach the torque converter dust shield from the lower bellhousing. Remove the torque converter-to-driveplate fasteners (see Chapter 7B) and push the converter back slightly into the bellhousing.

23 Remove the engine-to-transmission bolts and separate the engine from the transmission. The torque converter should remain in the transmission. **Note:** *If the transmission is to be removed at the same time, disconnect the ECM harness connectors (see Chapter 6).*

24 Recheck to be sure nothing except the mounts are still connecting the engine to the vehicle or to the transmission. Disconnect and label anything still remaining.

25 Support the transmission with a floor jack. Place a block of wood on the jack head to prevent damage to the transmission. Remove the bolts from the engine mounts, leaving those attached to the transmission in place. **Warning:** *Do not place any part of your body under the engine/transmission when it's supported only by a hoist or other lifting device.*

26 Slowly lift the engine (or engine/transmission) out of the vehicle. It may be necessary to pry the mounts away from the frame brackets.

27 Move the engine away from the vehicle and carefully lower the hoist until the engine can be set on the floor; or remove the flywheel/driveplate and mount the engine on an engine stand. **Note:** *On automatic transmission-equipped models, mark the front and rear spacer plates and keep them with the driveplate.*

Installation

28   Check the engine/transmission mounts. If they're worn or damaged, replace them.

29   On manual transmission equipped models, inspect the clutch components (see Chapter 8) and on automatic models inspect the converter seal and bushing.

30   On manual transmission equipped vehicles, apply a dab of high temperature grease to the pilot bearing. On automatic transmission equipped models, apply a dab of grease to the nose of the converter.

31   Carefully guide the transmission into place, following the procedure outlined in Chapter 7B. **Caution:** *Do not use the bolts to force the engine and transmission into alignment. It may crack or damage major components.*

32   Install the engine-to-transmission bolts and tighten them securely.

33   Attach the hoist to the engine and carefully lower the engine/transmission assembly into the engine compartment. **Note:** *If the engine was removed with the transmission remaining in the car, lower the engine into the car until an assistant can help you line up the dowels pins on the block with the transmission. Some twisting and angling of the engine and/or the transmission will be necessary to secure proper alignment of the two.*

34   Install the mount bolts and tighten them securely.

35   Reinstall the remaining components and fasteners in the reverse order of removal.

36   Add coolant, oil, power steering and transmission fluids as needed (see Chapter 1).

37   Run the engine and check for proper operation and leaks. Shut off the engine and recheck the fluid levels.

7   Engine rebuilding alternatives

1   The do-it-yourselfer is faced with a number of options when performing an engine overhaul. The decision to replace the engine block, piston/connecting rod assemblies and crankshaft depends on a number of factors, with the number one consideration being the condition of the block. Other considerations are cost, access to machine shop facilities, parts availability, time required to complete the project and the extent of prior mechanical experience on the part of the do-it-yourselfer.

2   Some of the rebuilding alternatives include:

Individual parts - If the inspection procedures reveal that the engine block and most engine components are in reusable condition, purchasing individual parts may be the most economical alternative. The block, crankshaft and piston/connecting rod assemblies should all be inspected carefully. Even if the block shows little wear, the cylinder bores should be surface honed.

Short block - A short block consists of an engine block with a crankshaft and piston/connecting rod assemblies already installed. All new bearings are incorporated and all clearances will be correct. The existing camshaft, valve train components, cylinder head(s) and external parts can be bolted to the short block with little or no machine shop work necessary.

Long block - A long block consists of a short block plus an oil pump, oil pan, cylinder head(s), valve cover(s), camshaft and valve train components, timing sprockets and chain or gears and timing cover. All components are installed with new bearings, seals and gaskets incorporated throughout. The installation of manifolds and external parts is all that's necessary.

Used Engine - While rebuilding provides the best assurance of a like-new engine, used engines available from wrecking yards and importers are often a very simple and economical solution. Many used engines come with warranties, but always give any used engine a thorough diagnostic check-out before purchase. Check compression and also for signs of oil leakage. If possible, have the seller run the engine either in the vehicle or on a test stand so you can be sure it runs smoothly with no knocking or other noises.

3   Give careful thought to which alternative is best for you and discuss the situation with local automotive machine shops, auto parts dealers and experienced rebuilders before ordering or purchasing replacement parts.

8   Engine overhaul - disassembly sequence

Refer to illustrations 8.5a, 8.5b and 8.5c

1   It's much easier to disassemble and work on the engine if it's mounted on a portable engine stand. A stand can often be rented quite cheaply from an equipment rental yard. Before the engine is mounted on a stand, the flywheel/driveplate and rear oil seal retainer should be removed from the engine.

2   If a stand isn't available, it's possible to disassemble the engine with it blocked up on the floor. Be extra careful not to tip or drop the engine when working without a stand.

3   If you're going to obtain a rebuilt engine, all external components must come off first, to be transferred to the replacement engine, just as they will if you're doing a complete engine overhaul yourself. These include:

   Alternator and brackets
   Emissions control components
   Distributor, spark plug wires and spark plugs
   Thermostat and housing cover
   Water pump
   EFI components
   Intake/exhaust manifolds
   Oil filter
   Engine mounts
   Clutch and flywheel/driveplate
   Engine rear plate

Note: *When removing the external components from the engine, pay close attention to details that may be helpful or important during installation. Note the installed position of gaskets, seals, spacers, pins, brackets, washers, bolts and other small items.*

4   If you're obtaining a short block, which consists of the engine block, crankshaft, pistons and connecting rods all assembled, then the cylinder head(s), oil pan and oil pump will have to be removed as well. See *Engine rebuilding alternatives* for additional information regarding the different possibilities to be considered.

5   If you're planning a complete overhaul, the engine must be disassembled and the internal components removed in the following order **(see illustrations)**.

   Intake and exhaust manifolds
   Valve cover(s)
   Timing chain cover, timing chain and sprockets (four-cylinder engines)
   Timing belt covers, timing belt and sprockets (V6 engines)
   Cylinder head(s)
   Oil pan
   Oil pump
   Engine balance shafts and assembly (2.7L V6 engine)
   Piston/connecting rod assemblies
   Crankshaft rear oil seal retainer
   Crankshaft and main bearings

6   Before beginning the disassembly and overhaul procedures, make sure the following items are available. Also, refer to Section 22 for a list of tools and materials needed for engine reassembly.

   Common hand tools
   Small cardboard boxes or plastic bags for storing parts
   Gasket scraper
   Ridge reamer
   Vibration damper puller
   Micrometers
   Telescoping gauges
   Dial indicator set
   Valve spring compressor
   Cylinder surfacing hone
   Piston ring groove cleaning tool
   Electric drill motor
   Tap and die set
   Wire brushes
   Oil gallery brushes
   Cleaning solvent

9   Cylinder head - disassembly

Refer to illustrations 9.2, 9.3a, 9.3b and 9.4

Note: *New and rebuilt cylinder heads are commonly available for most engines at dealerships and auto parts stores. Due to the fact that some specialized tools are necessary for the disassembly and inspection procedures, and replacement parts may not be readily available, it may be more practical and economical for the home mechanic to purchase replacement head(s) rather than taking the time to disassemble, inspect and recondition the original(s).*

1   Cylinder head disassembly involves removal of the intake and exhaust valves and

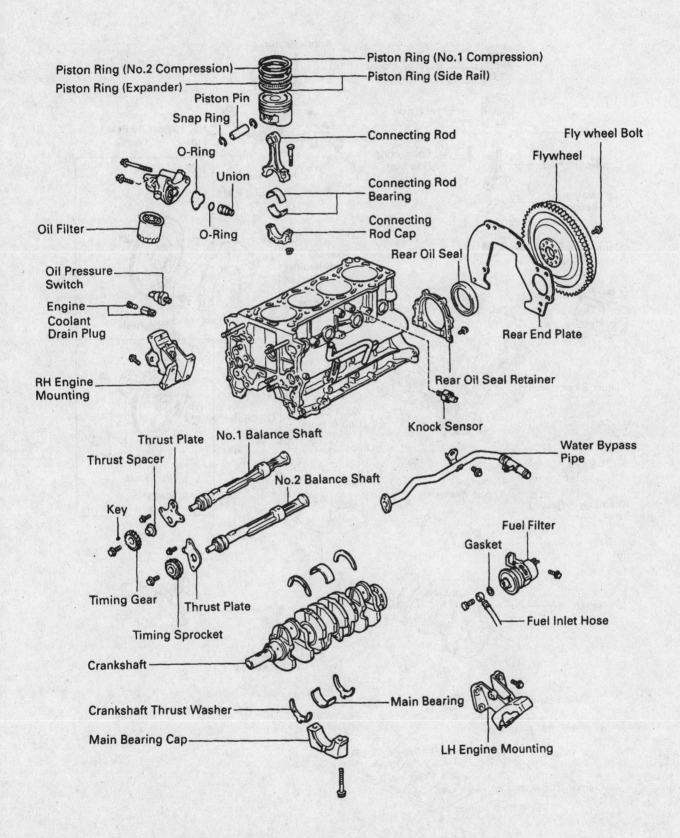

8.5a Exploded view of the four-cylinder engine block and components

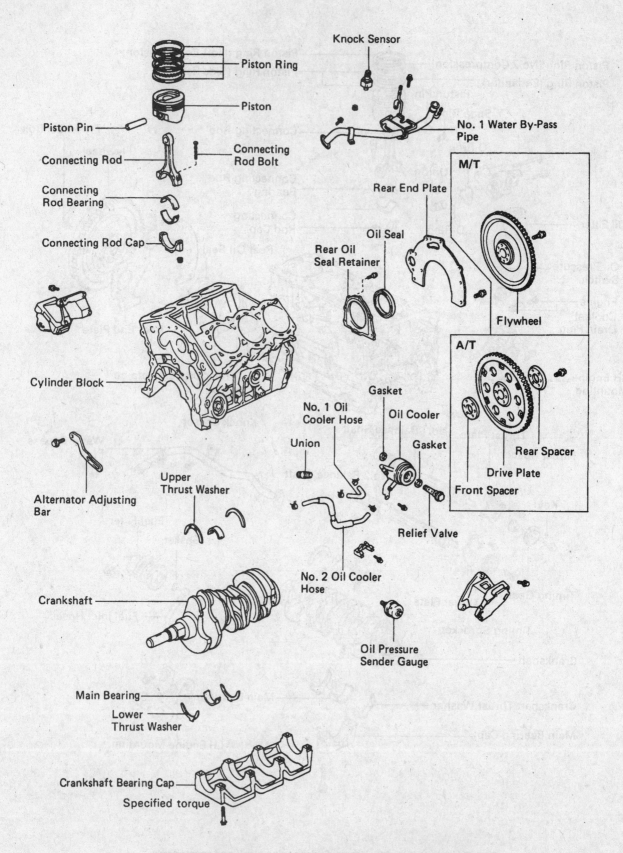

8.5b Exploded view of the 3.0L V6 engine block and components

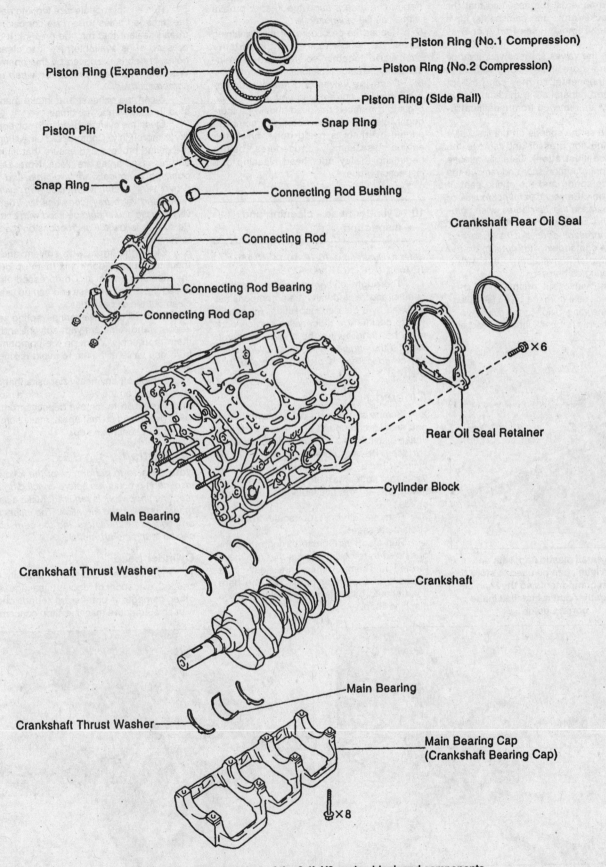

Piston Ring (No.1 Compression)

Piston Ring (Expander)

Piston Ring (No.2 Compression)

Piston Ring (Side Rail)

Piston

Piston Pin

Snap Ring

Snap Ring

Connecting Rod Bushing

Crankshaft Rear Oil Seal

Connecting Rod

Connecting Rod Bearing

Connecting Rod Cap

×6

Rear Oil Seal Retainer

Cylinder Block

Main Bearing

Crankshaft Thrust Washer

Crankshaft

Main Bearing

Crankshaft Thrust Washer

Main Bearing Cap
(Crankshaft Bearing Cap)

×8

8.5c Exploded view of the 3.4L V6 engine block and components

related components. It's assumed that the lifters or rocker arms and camshaft(s) have already been removed (see Part A or B as needed).

2   Before the valves are removed, arrange to label and store them, along with their related components, so they can be kept separate and reinstalled in the same valve guides they are removed from **(see illustration)**.

3   Compress the springs on the first valve with a spring compressor and remove the keepers **(see illustration)**. Carefully release the valve spring compressor and remove the retainer, the spring and the spring seat (if used). *Caution: Be very careful not to nick or otherwise damage the lifter bores when compressing the valve springs.* **Note:** *If your spring compressor does not have an end such as the one shown with cutouts on the side, an adapter is available to use with a standard spring compressor.*

4   Pull the valve out of the head, then remove the oil seal from the guide **(see illustration)**. If the valve binds in the guide (won't pull through), push it back into the head and

9.2 A small plastic bag, with an appropriate label, can be used to store the valve train components so they can be kept together and reinstalled in the correct guide

deburr the area around the keeper groove with a fine file or whetstone.

5   Repeat the procedure for the remaining valves. Remember to keep all the parts for each valve together so they can be reinstalled in the same locations.

6   Once the valves and related components have been removed and stored in an organized manner, the head should be thoroughly cleaned and inspected. If a complete engine overhaul is being done, finish the engine disassembly procedures before beginning the cylinder head cleaning and inspection process.

10   Cylinder head - cleaning and inspection

Refer to illustrations 10.12, 10.14, 10.15a, 10.15b, 10.16, 10.17 and 10.18

1   Thorough cleaning of the cylinder head(s) and related valve train components, followed by a detailed inspection, will enable you to decide how much valve service work must be done during the engine overhaul. **Note:** *If the engine was severely overheated, the cylinder head is probably warped (see Step 12).*

Cleaning

2   Scrape all traces of old gasket material and sealing compound off the head gasket, intake manifold and exhaust manifold sealing surfaces. Be very careful not to gouge the cylinder head. Special gasket removal solvents that soften gaskets and make removal much easier are available at auto parts stores.

3   Remove all built up scale from the coolant passages.

4   Run a stiff wire brush through the various holes to remove deposits that may have formed in them. If there are heavy rust deposits in the water passages, the bare head should be professionally cleaned at a machine shop.

5   Run an appropriate size tap into each of the threaded holes to remove corrosion and thread sealant that may be present. If compressed air is available, use it to clear the holes of debris produced by this operation. **Warning:** *Wear eye protection when using compressed air!*

6   Clean the exhaust and intake manifold stud threads with a wire brush.

7   Clean the cylinder head with solvent and dry it thoroughly. Compressed air will speed the drying process and ensure that all holes and recessed areas are clean. **Note:** *Decarbonizing chemicals are available and may prove very useful when cleaning cylinder heads and valve train components. They are very caustic and should be used with caution. Be sure to follow the instructions on the container.*

8   Clean the lifters with solvent and dry them thoroughly (don't mix them up during the cleaning process). Compressed air will speed the drying process and can be used to clean out the oil passages.

9   Clean all the valve springs, spring seats, keepers and retainers with solvent and dry them thoroughly. Work on the components from one valve at a time to avoid mixing up the parts.

10   Scrape off any heavy deposits that may have formed on the valves, then use a motorized wire brush to remove deposits from the valve heads and stems. Again, make sure the valves don't get mixed up.

Inspection

Note: *Be sure to perform all of the following inspection procedures before concluding that machine shop work is required. Make a list of the items that need attention. The inspection procedures for the lifters and the camshafts, can be found in Part A or B.*

Cylinder head

11   Inspect the head very carefully for cracks, evidence of coolant leakage and other damage. If cracks are found, check with an automotive machine shop concerning

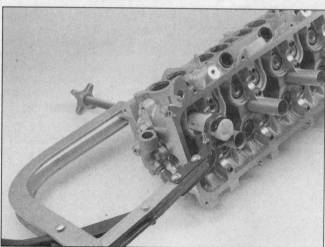

9.3a Compress the spring until the keepers can be removed with a small magnetic screwdriver or needle-nose pliers

9.3b Remove the keepers through the slot in the side of the tool

9.4 Remove the valve stem seal from the tip of the valve guide using a pair of needle-nose pliers

10.12 Check the cylinder head gasket surfaces for warpage by trying to slip a feeler gauge under the precision straightedge (see the Specifications for the maximum warpage allowed and use a feeler gauge of that thickness)

10.14 A dial indicator can be used to determine the valve stem-to-guide clearance (move the valve stem as indicated by the arrows)

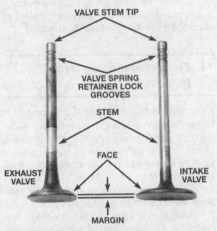

10.15a Check for valve wear at the points shown here

repair. If repair isn't possible, a new cylinder head should be obtained.

12   Using a straightedge and feeler gauge, check the head gasket mating surface for warpage **(see illustration)**. If the warpage exceeds the limit found in this Chapter's Specifications, it can be resurfaced at an automotive machine shop. **Note:** *If the V6 engine heads are resurfaced, the intake manifold flanges may also require machining. Have the intake manifold checked by a qualified automotive machine shop.*

13   Examine the valve seats in each of the combustion chambers. If they're pitted, cracked or burned, the head will require valve service that's beyond the scope of the home mechanic.

14   Check the valve stem-to-guide clearance with a small hole gauge and micrometer. Also, check the valve stem deflection with a dial indicator attached securely to the head **(see illustration)**. The valve must be in the guide and approximately 1/16-inch off the seat. The total valve stem movement indicated by the gauge needle must be noted, then divided by two to obtain the actual clearance value. If it exceeds the stem-to-guide clearance limit found in this Chapter's Specifications, the valve guides should be replaced. After this is done, if there's still some doubt regarding the condition of the valve guides they should be checked by an automotive machine shop (the cost should be minimal).

Valves

15   Carefully inspect each valve face for uneven wear, deformation, cracks, pits and burned areas. Check the valve stem for scuffing and galling and the neck for cracks. Rotate the valve and check for any obvious indication that it's bent. Look for pits and excessive wear on the end of the stem. The presence of any of these conditions indicates the need for valve service by an automotive machine shop **(see illustrations)**.

16   Measure the margin width on each valve **(see illustration)**. Any valve with a margin narrower than that listed in this Chapter's Specifications will have to be replaced with a new one.

Valve components

17   Check each valve spring for wear (on the ends) and pits. Measure the free length and compare it to this Chapter's Specifications **(see illustration)**. Any springs that are shorter than specified have sagged and should not be re-used. The tension of all springs should be pressure checked with a special fixture before deciding that they're suitable for use in a rebuilt engine (take the springs to an automotive machine shop for this check).

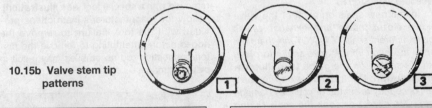

10.15b Valve stem tip patterns

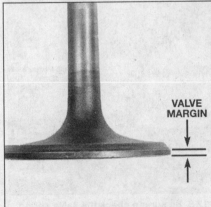

10.16 The margin width on each valve must be as specified (if no margin exists, the valve cannot be re-used)

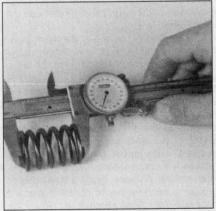

10.17 Measure the free length of each valve spring with a dial or vernier caliper

**10.18 Check each valve spring
for squareness**

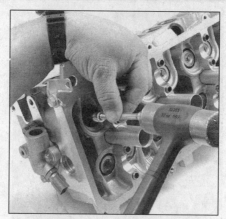

**12.3 Gently tap the valve seals into place
with a deep socket and hammer**

**12.6 The small valve stem keepers are
easier to position when coated
with grease**

18   Stand each spring on a flat surface and check it for squareness **(see illustration)**. If any of the springs are distorted or sagged, replace all of them with new parts.

19   Check the spring retainers and keepers for obvious wear and cracks. Any questionable parts should be replaced with new ones, as extensive damage will occur if they fail during engine operation.

20   Any damaged or excessively worn parts must be replaced with new ones.

21   If the inspection process indicates that the valve components are in generally poor condition and worn beyond the limits specified, which is usually the case in an engine that's being overhauled, reassemble the valves in the cylinder head and refer to Section 11 for valve servicing recommendations.

11 Valves - servicing

1   Because of the complex nature of the job and the special tools and equipment needed, servicing of the valves, the valve seats and the valve guides, commonly known as a valve job, should be done by a professional.

2   The home mechanic can remove and disassemble the head(s), do the initial cleaning and inspection, then reassemble and deliver them to a dealer service department or an automotive machine shop for the actual service work. Doing the inspection will enable you to see what condition the head(s) and valvetrain components are in and will ensure that you know what work and new parts are required when dealing with an automotive machine shop.

3   The dealer service department, or automotive machine shop, will remove the valves and springs, recondition or replace the valves and valve seats, recondition the valve guides, check and replace the valve springs, spring retainers and keepers (as necessary), replace the valve seals with new ones, reassemble the valve components and make sure the installed spring height is correct. The cylinder head gasket surface will also be resurfaced if it's warped.

4   After the valve job has been performed by a professional, the head(s) will be in like new condition. When the heads are returned, be sure to clean them again before installation on the engine to remove any metal particles and abrasive grit that may still be present from the valve service or head resurfacing operations. Use compressed air, if available, to blow out all the oil holes and passages.

12 Cylinder head - reassembly

Refer to illustrations 12.3, 12.6 and 12.8

1   Regardless of whether or not the head was sent to an automotive machine shop for valve servicing, make sure it's clean before beginning reassembly.

2   If the head was sent out for valve servicing, the valves and related components will already be in place. Begin the reassembly procedure with Step 8.

3   Install new seals on each of the valve guides. **Note:** *Intake and exhaust valves require different seals - DO NOT mix them up! Gently tap each intake valve seal into place until it's seated on the guide* **(see illustration)**. **Caution:** *Don't hammer on the valve seals once they're seated or you may damage them. Don't twist or cock the seals during installation or they won't seat properly on the valve stems.*

4   Beginning at one end of the head, lubricate and install the first valve. Apply moly-base grease or clean engine oil to the valve stem.

5   Drop the spring seat or shim(s) over the valve guide and set the valve spring and retainer in place.

6   Compress the springs with a valve spring compressor and carefully install the keepers in the upper groove, then slowly release the compressor and make sure the keepers seat properly. Apply a small dab of grease to each keeper to hold it in place if necessary **(see illustration)**.

7   Repeat the procedure for the remaining valves. Be sure to return the components to their original locations - don't mix them up!

8   Check the valve spring installed height - a dial or vernier caliper provides the most accurate measurement **(see illustration)**.

13 Pistons/connecting rods - removal

Refer to illustrations 13.2, 13.4, 13.5 and 13.7
Note: *Prior to removing the piston/connecting rod assemblies, remove the cylinder head(s), the oil pan and the oil pump pick-up tube by referring to the appropriate Sections in Chapter 2A or 2B.*

1   On 2.7L engines only, remove the balance shaft assembly (see Section 21).

2   Use your fingernail to feel if a ridge has formed at the upper limit of ring travel (about 1/4-inch down from the top of each cylinder). If carbon deposits or cylinder wear have produced ridges, they must be completely removed with a special tool **(see illustration)**. Follow the manufacturer's instructions provided with the tool. Failure to remove the ridges before attempting to remove the piston/connecting rod assemblies may result in piston damage.

**12.8 Be sure to check the valve spring
installed height (the distance from the top
of the seat/shims to the top of the shield
or the bottom of the retainer)**

13.2 A ridge reamer is required to remove the ridge from the top of each cylinder - do this before removing the pistons!

13.4 Check the connecting rod side clearance with a feeler gauge as shown here

13.5 The connecting rods and caps should be marked to indicate which cylinder they're installed in - if they aren't, mark them with a center punch to avoid confusion during reassembly - do not confuse the markings shown here with rod numbers; these are bearing size identifications

3   After the cylinder ridges have been removed, turn the engine upside-down so the crankshaft is facing up.

4   Before the connecting rods are removed, check the endplay with feeler gauges. Slide them between the first connecting rod and the crankshaft throw until the play is removed **(see illustration)**. The endplay is equal to the thickness of the feeler gauge(s). If the endplay exceeds the specified service limit, new connecting rods will be required. If new rods (or a new crankshaft) are installed, the endplay may fall under the service limit (if it does, the rods will have to be machined to restore it - consult an automotive machine shop for advice if necessary). Repeat the procedure for the remaining connecting rods.

5   Check the connecting rods and caps for identification marks. If they aren't plainly marked, use a small center punch to make the appropriate number of indentations on each rod and cap (1, 2, 3, etc., depending on the engine type and cylinder they're associated with) **(see illustration)**.

6   Loosen each of the connecting rod cap nuts 1/2-turn at a time until they can be

removed by hand. Remove the number one connecting rod cap and bearing insert. Don't drop the bearing insert out of the cap.

7   Slip a short length of plastic or rubber hose over each connecting rod cap bolt to protect the crankshaft journal and cylinder wall as the piston is removed **(see illustration)**.

8   Remove the bearing insert and push the connecting rod/piston assembly out through the top of the engine. Use a wooden hammer handle to push on the upper bearing surface in the connecting rod. If resistance is felt, double-check to make sure that all of the ridge was removed from the cylinder.

9   Repeat the procedure for the remaining cylinders. **Note:** *Turn the crankshaft as needed to put the rod to be removed close to parallel with the cylinder bore, i.e. don't try to drive it out while at a large angle to the bore.*

10   After removal, reassemble the connecting rod caps and bearing inserts in their respective connecting rods and install the cap nuts finger tight. Leaving the old bearing inserts in place until reassembly will help prevent the connecting rod bearing surfaces from being accidentally nicked or gouged.

11   Don't separate the pistons from the connecting rods (see Section 18 for additional information).

14   Crankshaft - removal

Refer to illustrations 14.1, 14.3, 14.4a, 14.4b, 14.4c and 14.4d

Note: *The crankshaft can be removed only after the engine has been removed from the vehicle. It's assumed that the flywheel or driveplate, vibration damper, timing belt, oil pan, oil pick-up tube, oil pump and piston/connecting rod assemblies have already been removed. The rear main oil seal and retainer must be removed from the block before proceeding with crankshaft removal.*

1   Before the crankshaft is removed, check the endplay. Mount a dial indicator with the stem in line with the crankshaft and just touching one of the crank throws **(see illustration)**.

13.7 To prevent damage to the crankshaft journals and cylinder walls, slip sections of hose over the rod bolts before removing the pistons

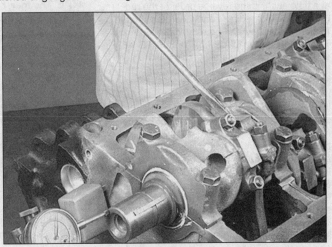

14.1 Checking crankshaft endplay with a dial indicator

14.3 Checking crankshaft endplay with a feeler gauge

14.4a The crankshaft main bearing journal is designated with a stamped number (arrow) for each cap

14.4b Use a center-punch or number stamping dies to mark the main bearing caps to ensure installation in their original locations on the block (make the punch marks near one of the bolt heads)

2   Push the crankshaft all the way to the rear and zero the dial indicator. Next, pry the crankshaft to the front as far as possible and check the reading on the dial indicator. The distance that it moves is the endplay. If it's greater than specified, check the crankshaft thrust surfaces for wear. If no wear is evident, new thrust washers should correct the end-play.

3   If a dial indicator isn't available, feeler gauges can be used. Gently pry or push the crankshaft all the way to the front of the engine. Slip feeler gauges between the crankshaft and the front face of the thrust main bearing to determine the clearance **(see illustration)**. The thrust bearing on four-cylinder engines is the number three (center) bearing, while on the V6 engines it's the number two journal.

4   Check the main bearing caps to see if they're marked to indicate their locations. They should be numbered consecutively from the front of the engine to the rear. If they aren't, mark them with number stamping dies or a center punch **(see illustrations)**. Main bearing caps generally have a cast-in arrow, which points to the front of the engine. Loosen the main bearing cap bolts 1/4-turn at a time each, in the reverse order of the rec-ommended tightening sequence **(see illus-tration)**, until they can be removed by hand. The main bearing caps on the 3VZ-FE V6 engine are a one-piece assembly which may have to be carefully pried away from the block. Note if any stud bolts are used and make sure they're returned to their original locations when the crankshaft is reinstalled.

5   Gently tap the caps with a soft-face hammer, then separate them from the engine block. If necessary, use the bolts as levers to remove the caps. Try not to drop the bearing inserts if they come out with the caps.

6   Carefully lift the crankshaft out of the engine. It may be a good idea to have an assistant available, since the crankshaft is quite heavy. With the bearing inserts in place in the engine block and main bearing caps or cap assembly, return the caps to their respective locations on the engine block and tighten the bolts finger tight.

15   Engine block - cleaning

Refer to illustrations 15.1a, 15.1b, 15.8 and 15.10.

Caution: *The core plugs (also known as freeze or soft plugs) may be difficult or impos-sible to retrieve if they're driven completely into the block coolant passages.*

1   Using the blunt end of a punch, tap in on the outer edge of the core plug to turn the plug sideways in the bore. Then using pliers, pull the core plug from the engine block **(see**

illustrations)**.

2   Using a gasket scraper, remove all traces of gasket material from the engine block. Be very careful not to nick or gouge the gasket sealing surfaces.

3   Remove the main bearing caps or cap assembly and separate the bearing inserts from the caps and the engine block. Tag the bearings, indicating which cylinder they were removed from and whether they were in the cap or the block, then set them aside.

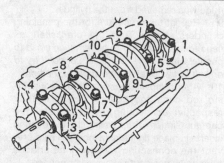

14.4c The four-cylinder engine main bearing cap loosening sequence

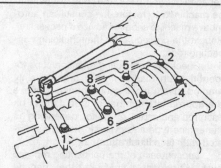

14.4d The V6 engine main bearing cap loosening sequence

15.1a A hammer and a large punch can be used to knock the core plugs sideways in their bores

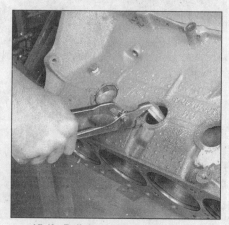

15.1b Pull the core plugs from the block with pliers

15.8 All bolt holes in the block - particularly the main bearing cap and head bolt holes - should be cleaned and restored with a tap (be sure to remove debris from the holes after this is done)

15.10 A large socket on an extension can be used to drive the new core plugs into the bores

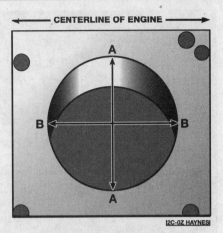

16.4a Measure the diameter of each cylinder just under the wear ridge (A), at the center (B) and at the bottom (C)

4   Remove all of the threaded oil gallery plugs from the block. The plugs are usually very tight - they may have to be drilled out and the holes retapped. Use new plugs when the engine is reassembled.

5   If the engine is extremely dirty, it should be taken to an automotive machine shop to be steam cleaned or hot tanked.

6   After the block is returned, clean all oil holes and oil galleries one more time. Brushes specifically designed for this purpose are available at most auto parts stores. Flush the passages with warm water until the water runs clear, dry the block thoroughly and wipe all machined surfaces with a light, rust preventive oil. If you have access to compressed air, use it to speed the drying process and to blow out all the oil holes and galleries. **Warning:** *Wear eye protection when using compressed air!*

7   If the block isn't extremely dirty or sludged up, you can do an adequate cleaning job with hot soapy water and a stiff brush. Take plenty of time and do a thorough job. Regardless of the cleaning method used, be sure to clean all oil holes and galleries very thoroughly, dry the block completely and coat all machined surfaces with light oil.

8   The threaded holes in the block must be clean to ensure accurate torque readings during reassembly. Run the proper size tap into each of the holes to remove rust, corrosion, thread sealant or sludge and restore damaged threads **(see illustration)**. If possible, use compressed air to clear the holes of debris produced by this operation. Now is a good time to clean the threads on the head bolts and the main bearing cap bolts as well.

9   Reinstall the main bearing caps and tighten the bolts finger tight.

10   After coating the sealing surfaces of the new core plugs with Permatex no. 2 sealant, install them in the engine block **(see illustration)**. Make sure they're driven in straight and seated properly or leakage could result. Special tools are available for this purpose, but a large socket, with an outside diameter that

will just slip into the core plug, a 1/2-inch drive extension and a hammer will work just as well.

11   Apply non-hardening sealant (such as Permatex no. 2 or Teflon pipe sealant) to the new oil gallery plugs and thread them into the holes in the block. Make sure they're tightened securely.

12   If the engine isn't going to be reassembled right away, cover it with a large plastic trash bag to keep it clean.

16 Engine block - inspection

Refer to illustrations 16.4a, 16.4b, 16.4c and 16.12

1   Before the block is inspected, it should be cleaned as described in Section 15.

2   Visually check the block for cracks, rust and corrosion. Look for stripped threads in the threaded holes. It's also a good idea to have the block checked for hidden cracks by an automotive machine shop that has the special equipment to do this type of work, especially if the vehicle had a history of overheating or using coolant. If defects are found, have the block repaired, if possible, or replaced.

3   Check the cylinder bores for scuffing and scoring.

4   Measure the diameter of each cylinder at the top (just under the ridge area), center and bottom of the cylinder bore, parallel to the crankshaft axis **(see illustrations)**.

5   Next, measure each cylinder's diameter at the same three locations across the crankshaft axis. Compare the results to this Chapter's Specifications.

6   If the required precision measuring tools aren't available and there isn't a tool rental facility nearby, the piston-to-cylinder clearances can be obtained, though not quite as accurately, using feeler gauge stock. Feeler gauge stock comes in 12-inch lengths and various thickness and is generally available at auto parts stores.

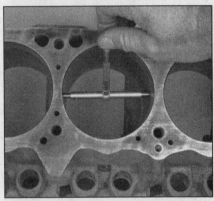

16.4b The ability to "feel" when the telescoping gauge is at the correct point will be developed over time, so work slowly and repeat the check until you're satisfied that the bore measurement is accurate

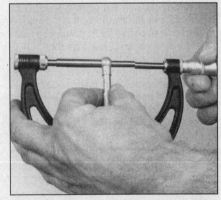

16.4c The gauge is then measured with a micrometer to determine the bore size

7   To check the clearance with feeler stock, select a feeler gauge and slip it into the cylinder along with the matching piston. The piston must be positioned exactly as it normally would be. The feeler gauge must be between the piston and cylinder on one of the thrust faces (90-degrees to the piston pin bore).

16.12 Check the block deck (both banks on a V6 engine) for distortion with a precision straightedge and feeler gauges

17.3a A "bottle brush" hone will produce better results for home mechanics with little engine honing experience

8   The piston should slip through the cylinder (with the feeler gauge in place) with moderate pressure.

9   If it falls through or slides through easily, the clearance is excessive and a new piston will be required. If the piston binds at the lower end of the cylinder and is loose toward the top, the cylinder is tapered. If tight spots are encountered as the piston/feeler gauge is rotated in the cylinder, the cylinder is out-of-round.

10   Repeat the procedure for the remaining pistons and cylinders.

11   If the cylinder walls are badly scuffed or scored, or if they're out-of-round or tapered beyond the limits given in this Chapter's Specifications, have the engine block rebored and honed at an automotive machine shop. If a rebore is done, oversize pistons and rings will be required.

12   Using a precision straightedge and feeler gauge, check the block deck (the surface that mates with the cylinder head[s]) for distortion **(see illustration)**. If it's distorted beyond the specified limit, it can be resurfaced by an automotive machine shop.

13   If the cylinders are in reasonably good condition and not worn to the outside of the limits, and if the piston-to-cylinder clearances can be maintained properly, then they don't have to be rebored. Honing is all that's necessary (refer to Section 17).

17 Cylinder honing

Refer to illustrations 17.3a and 17.3b

1   Prior to engine reassembly, the cylinder bores must be honed so the new piston rings will seat correctly and provide the best possible combustion chamber seal. **Note:** *If you don't have the tools or don't want to tackle the honing operation, most automotive machine shops will do it for a reasonable fee.*

2   Before honing the cylinders, install the main bearing caps or cap assembly (without bearing inserts) and tighten the bolts to the

specified torque.

3   Two types of cylinder hones are commonly available - the flex hone or "bottle brush" type and the more traditional surfacing hone with spring-loaded stones. Both will do the job, but for the less experienced mechanic the "bottle brush" hone will probably be easier to use. You'll also need some kerosene or honing oil, rags and an electric drill motor. The drill motor should be operated at a steady, slow speed. Use a large 1/2-inch drill or a 3/8-inch variable-speed drill. Proceed as follows:

a) *Mount the hone in the drill motor, compress the stones and slip it into the first cylinder* **(see illustration)**. **Warning:** *Be sure to wear safety goggles or a face shield!*

b) *Lubricate the cylinder with plenty of honing oil, turn on the drill and move the hone up-and-down in the cylinder at a pace that will produce a fine crosshatch pattern on the cylinder walls. Ideally, the crosshatch lines should intersect at approximately a 60-degree angle* **(see illustration)**. *Be sure to use plenty of lubricant and don't take off any more material than is absolutely necessary to produce the desired finish.* **Note:** *Piston ring manufacturers may specify a smaller crosshatch angle than the traditional 60-degrees - read and follow any instructions included with the new rings.*

c) *Don't withdraw the hone from the cylinder while it's running. Instead, shut off the drill and continue moving the hone up-and-down in the cylinder until it comes to a complete stop, then compress the stones and withdraw the hone. If you're using a "bottle brush" type hone, stop the drill motor, then turn the chuck in the normal direction of rotation while withdrawing the hone from the cylinder.*

d) *Wipe the oil out of the cylinder and repeat the procedure for the remaining cylinders.*

4   After the honing job is complete, chamfer the top edges of the cylinder bores with a small file so the rings won't catch when the pistons are installed. Be very careful not to nick the cylinder walls with the end of the file.

5   The entire engine block must be washed again very thoroughly with warm, soapy water to remove all traces of the abrasive grit produced during the honing operation. **Note:** *The bores can be considered clean when a lint-free white cloth - dampened with clean engine oil - used to wipe them out doesn't pick up any more honing residue, which will show up as gray areas on the cloth. Be sure to run a brush through all oil holes and galleries and flush them with running water.*

6   After rinsing, dry the block and apply a coat of light rust preventive oil to all machined surfaces. Wrap the block in a plastic trash bag to keep it clean and set it aside until reassembly.

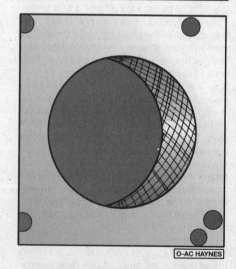

17.3b The cylinder hone should leave a smooth, crosshatch pattern with the lines intersecting at approximately a 60-degree angle

18.4a The piston ring grooves can be cleaned with a special tool, as shown here . . .

18.4b . . . or a section of a broken ring

18 Pistons/connecting rods - inspection

Refer to illustrations 18.4a, 18.4b, 18.10 and 18.11

1 Before the inspection process can be carried out, the piston/connecting rod assemblies must be cleaned and the original piston rings removed from the pistons. **Note:** *Always use new piston rings when the engine is reassembled.*

2 Using a piston ring installation tool, carefully remove the rings from the pistons. Be careful not to nick or gouge the pistons in the process.

3 Scrape all traces of carbon from the top of the piston. A hand-held wire brush or a piece of fine emery cloth can be used once the majority of the deposits have been scraped away. Do not, under any circumstances, use a wire brush mounted in a drill motor to remove deposits from the pistons. The piston material is soft and may be eroded away by the wire brush.

4 Use a piston ring groove-cleaning tool to remove carbon deposits from the ring grooves. If a tool isn't available, a piece broken off the old ring will do the job. Be very careful to remove only the carbon deposits - don't remove any metal and do not nick or scratch the sides of the ring grooves **(see illustrations)**.

5 Once the deposits have been removed, clean the piston/rod assemblies with solvent and dry them with compressed air (if available). Make sure the oil return holes in the back sides of the ring grooves and the oil hole in the lower end of each rod are clear.

6 If the pistons and cylinder walls aren't damaged or worn excessively, and if the engine block is not rebored, new pistons won't be necessary. Normal piston wear appears as even vertical wear on the piston thrust surfaces and slight looseness of the top ring in its groove. New piston rings, however, should always be used when an engine is rebuilt.

7 Carefully inspect each piston for cracks around the skirt, at the pin bosses and at the ring lands.

8 Look for scoring and scuffing on the thrust faces of the skirt, holes in the piston crown and burned areas at the edge of the crown. If the skirt is scored or scuffed, the engine may have been suffering from over-heating and/or abnormal combustion, which caused excessively high operating temperatures. The cooling and lubrication systems should be checked thoroughly. A hole in the piston crown is an indication that abnormal combustion (preignition) was occurring. Burned areas at the edge of the piston crown are usually evidence of spark knock (detonation). If any of the above problems exist, the causes must be corrected or the damage will occur again. The causes may include intake air leaks, incorrect air/fuel mixture, incorrect ignition timing and EGR system malfunctions.

9 Corrosion of the piston, in the form of small pits, indicates that coolant is leaking into the combustion chamber and/or the crankcase. Again, the cause must be corrected or the problem may persist in the rebuilt engine.

10 Measure the piston ring groove clearance by laying a new piston ring in each ring groove and slipping a feeler gauge in beside it **(see illustration)**. Check the clearance at three or four locations around each groove. Be sure to use the correct ring for each groove - they are different. If the clearance is greater than that listed in this Chapter's Specifications, new pistons will have to be used.

11 Check the piston-to-bore clearance by measuring the bore (see Section 16) and the piston diameter. Make sure the pistons and bores are correctly matched. Measure the piston across the skirt, at a 90-degree angle to the piston pin **(see illustration)**. Subtract the piston diameter from the bore diameter to obtain the clearance. If it's greater than specified, the block will have to be rebored and new pistons and rings installed.

12 Check the piston-to-rod clearance by twisting the piston and rod in opposite directions. Any noticeable play indicates excessive wear, which must be corrected.

13 If the pistons must be removed from the connecting rods for any reason, the rods

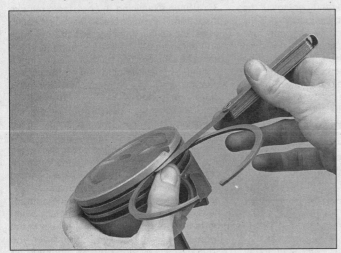

18.10 Check the ring groove clearance with a feeler gauge at several points around the groove

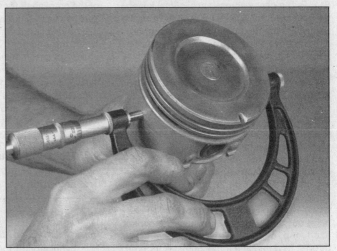

18.11 Measure the piston diameter at a 90-degree angle to the piston pin, at the bottom of the piston pin area - a precision caliper may be used if a micrometer isn't available

19.6 Measure the diameter of each crankshaft journal at several points to detect taper and out-of-round conditions

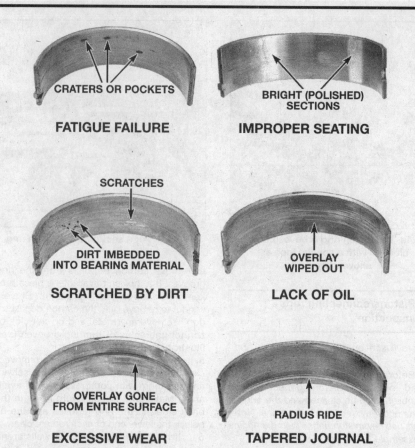

20.1 When inspecting the main and connecting rod bearings, look for these problems

should be taken to an automotive machine shop, to be checked for bend and twist, since automotive machine shops have special equipment for this purpose.

14   Check the connecting rods for cracks and other damage. Temporarily remove the rod caps, lift out the old bearing inserts, wipe the rod and cap bearing surfaces clean and inspect them for nicks, gouges and scratches. After checking the rods, replace the old bearings, slip the caps into place and tighten the nuts finger tight. **Note:** *If the engine is being rebuilt because of a connecting rod knock, be sure to install new rods.*

19   Crankshaft - inspection

Refer to illustration 19.6

1   Clean the crankshaft with solvent and dry it with compressed air (if available). Be sure to clean the oil holes with a stiff brush and flush them with solvent.
2   Check the main and connecting rod bearing journals for uneven wear, scoring, pits and cracks.
3   Rub a penny across each journal several times. If a journal picks up copper from the penny, it's too rough and must be reground.
4   Remove all burrs from the crankshaft oil holes with a stone, file or scraper.
5   Check the rest of the crankshaft for cracks and other damage. It should be magnafluxed to reveal hidden cracks - an automotive machine shop will handle the procedure.
6   Using a micrometer, measure the diameter of the main and connecting rod journals and compare the results to this Chapter's Specifications **(see illustration)**. By measuring the diameter at a number of points around each journal's circumference, you'll be able to determine whether or not the journal is out-of-round. Take the measurement at each end of the journal, near the crank throws, to determine if the journal is tapered. Crankshaft runout should be checked also, but large V-blocks and a dial indicator are

needed to do it correctly. If you don't have the equipment, have a machine shop check the runout.
7   If the crankshaft journals are damaged, tapered, out-of-round or worn beyond the limits given in the Specifications, have the crankshaft reground by an automotive machine shop. Be sure to use the correct size bearing inserts if the crankshaft is reconditioned.
8   Check the oil seal journals at each end of the crankshaft for wear and damage. If the seal has worn a groove in the journal, or if it's nicked or scratched, the new seal may leak when the engine is reassembled. In some cases, an automotive machine shop may be able to repair the journal by pressing on a thin sleeve. If repair isn't feasible, a new or different crankshaft should be installed.
9   Refer to Section 20 and examine the main and rod bearing inserts.

20   Main and connecting rod bearings - inspection and selection

Inspection

Refer to illustration 20.1

1   Even though the main and connecting rod bearings should be replaced with new ones during the engine overhaul, the old

bearings should be retained for close examination, as they may reveal valuable information about the condition of the engine **(see illustration)**.
2   Bearing failure occurs because of lack of lubrication, the presence of dirt or other foreign particles, overloading the engine and corrosion. Regardless of the cause of bearing failure, it must be corrected before the engine is reassembled to prevent it from happening again.
3   When examining the bearings, remove them from the engine block, the main bearing caps, the connecting rods and the rod caps and lay them out on a clean surface in the same general position as their location in the engine. This will enable you to match any bearing problems with the corresponding crankshaft journal.
4   Dirt and other foreign particles get into the engine in a variety of ways. It may be left in the engine during assembly, or it may pass through filters or the PCV system. It may get into the oil, and from there into the bearings. Metal chips from machining operations and normal engine wear are often present. Abrasives are sometimes left in engine components after reconditioning, especially when parts are not thoroughly cleaned using the proper cleaning methods. Whatever the source, these foreign objects often end up embedded in the soft bearing material and are easily recognized. Large particles will not

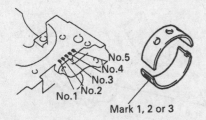

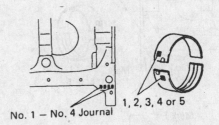

Cylinder block main journal bore diameter:

STD Mark "1"	64.004 – 64.010 mm (2.5198 – 2.5201 in.)
STD Mark "2"	64.011 – 64.016 mm (2.5201 – 2.5203 in.)
STD Mark "3"	64.017 – 64.022 mm (2.5203 – 2.5205 in.)
U/S 0.25	64.000 – 64.024 mm (2.5197 – 2.5206 in.)

Crankshaft Journal diameter:

STD No.3	59.981 – 59.994 mm (2.2615 – 2.3620 in.)
STD Others	59.987 – 60.000 mm (2.3617 – 2.3622 in.)
U/S 0.25 No.3	59.740 – 59.750 mm (2.3520 – 2.3524 in.)
U/S 0.25 Others	59.745 – 59.755 mm (2.3522 – 2.3526 in.)

Bearing center wall thickness:

STD Mark "1"	1.987 – 1.990 mm (0.0782 – 0.0783 in.)
STD Mark "2"	1.991 – 1.993 mm (0.0784 – 0.0785 in.)
STD Mark "3"	1.994 – 1.996 mm (0.0785 – 0.0786 in.)
U/S 0.25	2.106 – 2.112 mm (0.0829 – 0.0831 in.)

20.10a On four-cylinder engines, when using standard-size bearings, make sure the number on the engine block matches the mark on the main bearing. Use the chart with the various specifications to doublecheck for the correct sizes

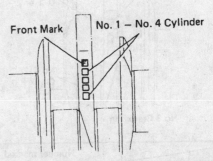

Cylinder Block No.	1	2	1	3	2	1	3	2	3
Crankshaft No.	0	0	1	0	1	2	1	2	2
Bearing No.	1	2	2	3	3	3	4	4	5

20.10b On 3.0L V6 engines, match the journal number stamped onto the engine block with the number stamped onto the crankshaft for the correct standard main bearing size

embed in the bearing and will score or gouge the bearing and journal. The best prevention for this cause of bearing failure is to clean all parts thoroughly and keep everything spotlessly clean during engine assembly. Frequent and regular engine oil and filter changes are also recommended.

5   Lack of lubrication (or lubrication breakdown) has a number of interrelated causes. Excessive heat (which thins the oil), overloading (which squeezes the oil from the bearing face) and oil leakage or throw off (from excessive bearing clearances, worn oil pump or high engine speeds) all contribute to lubrication breakdown. Blocked oil passages, which usually are the result of misaligned oil holes in a bearing shell, will also oil starve a bearing and destroy it. When lack of lubrication is the cause of bearing failure, the bearing material is wiped or extruded from the steel backing of the bearing. Temperatures may increase to the point where the steel backing turns blue from overheating.

6   Driving habits can have a definite effect on bearing life. Driving habits can have a definite effect on bearing life. Low speed operation in too high a gear (lugging the engine) puts very high loads on bearings, which tends to squeeze out the oil film. These loads cause the bearings to flex, which produces fine cracks in the bearing face (fatigue failure).

Eventually the bearing material will loosen in pieces and tear away from the steel backing. Short trip driving leads to corrosion of bearings because insufficient engine heat is produced to drive off the condensed water and corrosive gases. These products collect in the engine oil, forming acid and sludge. As the oil is carried to the engine bearings, the acid attacks and corrodes the bearing material.

7   Incorrect bearing installation during engine assembly will lead to bearing failure as well. Tight-fitting bearings leave insufficient bearing oil clearance and will result in oil starvation. Dirt or foreign particles trapped behind a bearing insert result in high spots on the bearing which lead to failure.

Selection

Refer to illustrations 20.10a, 20.10b and 20.10c

8   If the original bearings are worn or damaged, or if the oil clearances are incorrect (see Sections 24 or 26), the following procedures should be used to select the correct new bearings for engine reassembly. However, if the crankshaft has been reground, new undersize bearings must be installed - the following procedure should not be used if undersize bearings are required! The automotive machine shop that reconditions the crankshaft will provide or help you select the

correct size bearings. Regardless of how the bearing sizes are determined, use the oil clearance, measured with Plastigage, as a guide to ensure the bearings are the right size.

Main bearings

9   If you need to use a STANDARD size main bearing, install one that has the same number as the original bearing **(see illustrations 20.10a, 20.10b and 20.10c for the bearing number locations)**. There are five sizes of main bearings.

10   If the number on the original main bearing has been obscured, locate the main journal grade numbers stamped into the oil pan mating surface on the engine block and the crankshaft counterweights **(see illustrations)**.

11   Match the block number to the crank number for a particular journal will give the recommended bearing size. Use the accompanying chart to determine the correct bearings.

Connecting rod bearings

Refer to illustration 20.12

12   If you need to use a STANDARD size rod bearing, install one that has the same number as the number stamped into the connecting rod cap **(see illustration)**.

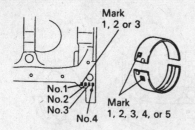

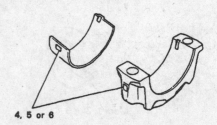

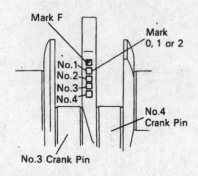

STD Mark "4"	56.000 – 56.006 mm (2.2047 – 2.2050 in.)
STD Mark "5"	56.006 – 56.012 mm (2.2050 – 2.2052 in.)
STD Mark "6"	56.012 – 56.018 mm (2.2052 – 2.2054 in.)
U/S 0.25	56.000 – 56.018 mm (2.2047 – 2.2054 in.)

Crankshaft crank pin diameter:

STD	52.987 – 53.000 mm (2.0861 – 2.0866 in.)
U/S 0.25	52.745 – 52.755 mm (2.0766 – 2.0770 in.)

Standard sized bearing center wall thickness:

STD Mark "4"	1.482 – 1.485 mm (0.0583 – 0.0585 in.)
STD Mark "5"	1.485 – 1.488 mm (0.0585 – 0.0586 in.)
STD Mark "6"	1.488 – 1.491 mm (0.0586 – 0.0587 in.)
U/S 0.25	1.601 – 1.607 mm (0.0630 – 0.0633 in.)

	Number marked								
Cylinder block	1			2			3		
Crankshaft	0	1	2	0	1	2	0	1	2
Use bearing	1	2	3	2	3	4	3	4	5

EXAMPLE: Cylinder block "2" + Crankshaft "1"
= Total number 3 (Use bearing "3")

20.10c On 3.4L V6 engines, match the journal number stamped onto the engine block with the number stamped onto the crankshaft for the correct standard main bearing size

20.12 Typical connecting rod bearing marks and chart

All bearings

13   Remember, the oil clearance is the final judge when selecting new bearing sizes. If you have any questions or are unsure which bearings to use, get help from a Toyota dealer parts or service department.

---

21 Balance shafts (2.7L four-cylinder engine) - removal, inspection and installation

Removal

Refer to illustrations 21.3, 21.4, 21.5, 21.6, 21.7 and 21.8

1   The engine balance shafts are built into the engine block on the right and left side of the engine block assembly. The two balance shafts are driven by a separate timing chain connected to the crankshaft. Refer to Section 5 for an exploded view drawing of the balance shaft assembly.

2   Remove the number one timing chain tensioner, tensioner slipper or guide, the number 1 sprocket and timing chain (see Chapter 2A).

3   Install a pin into the number 2 tensioner and lock the plunger in place **(see illustration)**.

4   Remove the bolt and the number 2 timing chain damper **(see illustration)**.

5   Remove the bolts and the number 3 damper **(see illustration)**.

6   Remove the nut and the balance shaft chain tensioner **(see illustration)**.

7   First, remove the balance shaft drive gear bolt (top balance shaft) and then remove the balance shaft drive gear with the shaft **(see illustration)**.

8   Remove the number 4 vibration damper bolts **(see illustration)** and lift the damper from the engine block.

9   Inspect the balance shaft chain, balance shafts and tensioner.

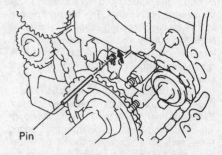

21.3 Lock the balance shaft chain tensioner using a long pin

21.4 Remove the number 2 damper bolt from the engine block

21.5 Remove the bolts and the number 3 damper from the engine block

Inspection

Timing chain and sprockets

10　Timing chains and sprockets should be replaced in sets. If you intend to install a new balance shaft timing chain, remove the crankshaft sprocket with a puller and install a new one. Be sure to align the key in the crankshaft with the keyway in the sprocket during installation.

11　Clean the timing chain and sprockets with solvent and dry them with compressed air (if available). **Warning:** *Wear eye protection when using compressed air.*

12　Inspect the components for wear and damage. Look for teeth that are deformed, chipped, pitted and cracked. Inspect the balance shaft tensioner. Refer to Chapter 2A for the complete inspection and cleaning procedure. This tensioner is basically the same as the number 1 timing chain tensioner.

13　The balance shaft timing chain should be replaced with a new one if the engine has high mileage, the chain has visible damage, or total freeplay (without the tensioner) midway between the sprockets exceeds one inch. Failure to replace a worn timing chain may result in erratic engine performance, loss of power and decreased fuel mileage. Loose chains can "jump" timing and could result in severe engine vibration.

Balance shafts

Refer to illustrations 21.14, 21.15 and 21.19

14　Check the thrust clearance of the balance shafts **(see illustration)**. Using a dial indicator, measure the thrust clearance while moving the balance shaft back and forth. Refer to the Specifications listed in this Chapter for the correct tolerance range.

15　Remove the balance shafts from the engine block **(see illustration)**.

16　Have the balance shafts inspected by a qualified machine shop specialist if you suspect balance shaft damage or wear.

Installation

Note: *Prior to installation, the crankshaft must be installed (see Sections 23 through 26). Assure the No. 1 piston is at TDC and that the weights of the Number 1 and Num-*

21.6 Remove the balance shaft tensioner nut

ber 2 balance shafts are on the bottom side.

17　Install the balance shafts and tighten the retainers to the torque listed in this Chapter's Specifications.

18　Install the number 4 vibration damper with the two bolts **(see illustration 21.8)**.

19　Install the Number 2 timing chain by matching its mark links with the timing marks on the Number 2 crankshaft timing sprocket and balance shaft timing sprocket **(see illustration)**. Position the other mark link of the number 2 timing chain on the sprocket behind the large timing mark of the balance shaft drive gear. Insert the balance shaft drive gear shaft through the balance shaft drive gear so that it fits into the thrust plate hole. Align the small timing mark of the balance shaft drive gear with the timing mark of the balance shaft timing gear.

20　Install the bolt to the balance shaft drive gear and torque the bolt to the Specification listed in this Chapter.

21　Install the vibration dampers and the chain tensioner **(see illustration 21.6)**. Torque the chain tensioner nut to the Specifications listed in this Chapter.

22　Install the number 3 damper and torque the bolt to the Specifications listed in this Chapter.

23　Install the number 2 damper and torque the bolt to the Specifications listed in this Chapter.

24　Remove the pin from the chain tensioner and free the plunger.

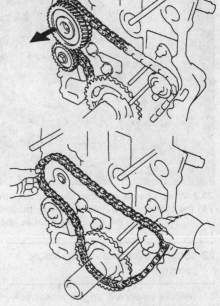

21.7 Remove the balance-shaft drive gear and take the chain off the sprocket assemblies

21.8 Remove the number 4 vibration damper bolts

21.14 Check the thrust clearance of the two balance shafts using a dial indicator mounted to the engine block with a magnet stand

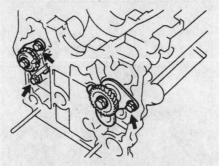

21.15 Remove the balance shaft assembly bolts (arrows) and pull the balance shafts straight out of the engine block

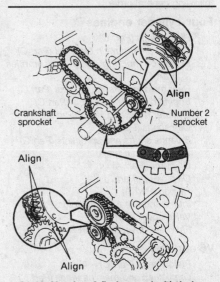

Align

Crankshaft sprocket

Number 2 sprocket

Align

Align

21.19 Number 2 (balance shaft) timing chain alignment marks

23.3 When checking piston ring end gap, the ring must be square in the cylinder bore (this is done by pushing the ring down with the top of a piston as shown)

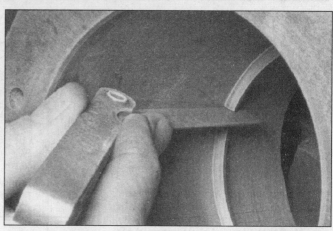

23.4 With the ring square in the cylinder, measure the end gap with a feeler gauge

22 Engine overhaul - reassembly sequence

1 Before beginning engine reassembly, make sure you have all the necessary new parts, gaskets and seals as well as the following items on hand:

Common hand tools
A 1/2-inch drive torque wrench
Piston ring installation tool
Piston ring compressor
Short lengths of rubber or plastic hose to fit over connecting rod bolts
Plastigage
Feeler gauges
A fine-tooth file
New engine oil
Engine assembly lube or moly-base grease
Gasket sealer
Thread locking compound

2 In order to save time and avoid problems, engine reassembly must be done in the following general order:

Four-cylinder engines

Piston rings (Part C)
Crankshaft and main bearings (Part C)
Piston/connecting rod assemblies (Part C)
Rear main (crankshaft) oil seal (Part C)
Engine balancer assembly (Part C)
Cylinder head and lifters (Part A)
Camshafts (Part A)
Balance shafts and sprockets (Part C)
Timing chain (Part A)
Oil pump (Part A)
Oil pick-up (Part A)
Oil pan (Part A)
Intake and exhaust manifolds (Part A)
Valve cover (Part A)
Flywheel/driveplate (Part A)

V6 engines

Piston rings (Part C)
Crankshaft and main bearings (Part C)
Piston/connecting rod assemblies (Part C)

Rear main oil seal/retainer (Part C)
Oil pump (Part B)
Oil pan (Part B)
Cylinder heads (Part B)
Camshafts and lifters (Part B)
Timing belt and sprockets (Part B)
Timing belt covers (Part B)
Valve covers (Part B)
Intake and exhaust manifolds (Part B)
Flywheel/driveplate (Part B)

23 Piston rings - installation

Refer to illustrations 23.3, 23.4, 23.9a, 23.9b and 23.12

1 Before installing the new piston rings, the ring end gaps must be checked. It's assumed that the piston ring groove clearance has been checked and verified correct (see Section 18).

2 Lay out the piston/connecting rod assemblies and the new ring sets so the ring sets will be matched with the same piston and cylinder during the end gap measurement and engine assembly.

3 Insert the top (number one) ring into the first cylinder and square it up with the cylinder walls by pushing it in with the top of the piston **(see illustration)**. The ring should be near the bottom of the cylinder, at the lower

limit of ring travel.

4 To measure the end gap, slip feeler gauges between the ends of the ring until a gauge equal to the gap width is found **(see illustration)**. The feeler gauge should slide between the ring ends with a slight amount of drag. Compare the measurement to that found in this Chapter's Specifications. If the gap is larger or smaller than specified, double-check to make sure you have the correct rings before proceeding.

5 If the gap is too small, replace the rings - DO NOT file the ends to increase the clearance.

6 Excess end gap isn't critical unless it's greater than 0.040-inch. Again, double-check to make sure you have the correct rings for your engine.

7 Repeat the procedure for each ring that will be installed in the first cylinder and for each ring in the remaining cylinders. Remember to keep rings, pistons and cylinders matched up.

8 Once the ring end gaps have been checked/corrected, the rings can be installed on the pistons.

9 The oil control ring (lowest one on the piston) is usually installed first. It's composed of three separate components. Slip the spacer/expander into the groove **(see illustration)**. If an anti-rotation tang is used, make

23.9a Install the spacer/expander in the oil control ring groove

23.9b DO NOT use a piston ring installation tool when installing the oil ring side rails

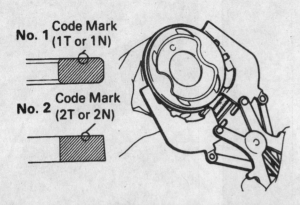

23.12 Install the compression rings with a ring expander - the marks on the rings must face up (four-cylinder engine shown - on V6 engines, the top rings are marked 1R or T, second rings are marked 2R or T2)

24.10 Lay the Plastigage strips on the main bearing journals, parallel to the crankshaft centerline

sure it's inserted into the drilled hole in the ring groove. Next, install the lower side rail. Don't use a piston ring installation tool on the oil ring side rails, as they may be damaged. Instead, place one end of the side rail into the groove between the spacer/expander and the ring land, hold it firmly in place and slide a finger around the piston while pushing the rail into the groove (see illustration). Next, install the upper side rail in the same manner.

10   After the three oil ring components have been installed, check to make sure that both the upper and lower side rails can be turned smoothly in the ring groove.

11   The number two (middle) ring is installed next. It's usually stamped with a mark which must face up, toward the top of the piston. **Note:** *Always follow the instructions printed on the ring package or box - different manufacturers may require different approaches. Do not mix up the top and middle rings, as they have different cross sections.*

12   Use a piston ring installation tool and make sure the ring's identification mark is facing the top of the piston, then slip the ring into the middle groove on the piston (see illustration). Don't expand the ring any more than necessary to slide it over the piston.

13   Install the number one (top) ring in the same manner. Make sure the mark is facing up. Be careful not to confuse the number one and number two rings.

14   Repeat the procedure for the remaining pistons and rings.

24 Crankshaft - installation and main bearing oil clearance check

Refer to illustrations 24.10, 24.12a, 24.12b, 24.12c, 24.14, 24.19a and 24.19b

1   Crankshaft installation is the first major step in engine reassembly. It's assumed at this point that the engine block and crankshaft have been cleaned, inspected and repaired or reconditioned.

2   Position the engine with the bottom facing up.

3   Remove the main bearing cap bolts and lift out the caps or cap assembly. Lay the caps out in the proper.

4   If they're still in place, remove the old bearing inserts from the block and the main bearing caps. Wipe the main bearing surfaces of the block and caps with a clean, lint free cloth. They must be kept spotlessly clean!

Main bearing oil clearance check

5   Clean the back sides of the new main bearing inserts and lay the bearing half with the oil groove in each main bearing saddle in the block. Lay the other bearing half from each bearing set in the corresponding main bearing cap. Make sure the tab on each bearing insert fits into the recess in the block or cap. Also, the oil holes in the block must line up with the oil holes in the bearing insert. **Caution:** *Do not hammer the bearings into place and don't nick or gouge the bearing faces. No lubrication should be used at this time.*

6   If you're working on a V6 engine, the thrust bearings (washers) must be installed in the number two cap and saddle. On four-cylinder engines, the thrust bearings (washers) must be installed in the number three (center) cap.

7   Clean the faces of the bearings in the block and the crankshaft main bearing journals with a clean, lint free cloth. Check or clean the oil holes in the crankshaft, as any dirt here can go only one way - straight through the new bearings.

8   Once you're certain the crankshaft is clean, carefully lay it in position in the main bearings.

9   Before the crankshaft can be permanently installed, the main bearing oil clearance must be checked.

10   Trim several pieces of the appropriate size Plastigage (they must be slightly shorter than the width of the main bearings) and place one piece on each crankshaft main bearing journal, parallel with the journal axis (see illustration).

11   Clean the faces of the bearings in the caps and install the caps in their respective positions (don't mix them up) with the arrows pointing toward the front of the engine. If you're working on a 3VZ-FE engine, carefully lay the main bearing cap assembly in place. Don't disturb the Plastigage. Apply a light coat of oil to the bolt threads and the undersides of the bolt heads, then install them.

12   Following the recommended sequence (see illustrations), tighten the main bearing cap bolts, in three steps, to the torque listed in this Chapter's Specifications. Don't rotate the crankshaft at any time during this operation! **Note:** *On V6 engines only, after reaching*

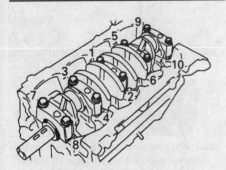

24.12a Main bearing cap bolt tightening sequence - four-cylinder engines

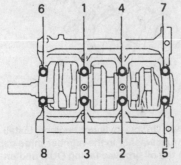

24.12b Main bearing cap bolt tightening sequence - V6 engines

24.12c After reaching the specified torque, mark the front side of each bolt with paint as shown here, plus a paint mark on the socket, then turn the bolts an additional 1/4-turn - the paint marks should now be 90-degrees from their original position

24.14 Compare the width of the crushed Plastigage to the scale on the envelope to determine the main bearing oil clearance (always take the measurement at the widest point of the Plastigage) - be sure to use the correct scale; standard and metric scales are included

24.19a Rotate the thrust washer into position with the oil grooves facing OUT

the specified torque on all of the bolts, tighten each bolt in sequence an additional 90-degrees (except the six-point bolts on the 1MZ-FE engine) **(see illustration)**.

13   Remove the bolts and carefully lift off the main bearing caps or cap assembly. Keep them in order. Don't disturb the Plastigage or rotate the crankshaft. If any of the main bearing caps are difficult to remove, tap them gently from side-to-side with a soft-face hammer to loosen them.

14   Compare the width of the crushed Plastigage on each journal to the scale printed on the Plastigage envelope to obtain the main bearing oil clearance **(see illustration)**. Check the Specifications to make sure it's correct.

15   If the clearance is not as specified, the bearing inserts may be the wrong size (which means different ones will be required - see Section 20). Before deciding that different inserts are needed, make sure that no dirt or oil was between the bearing inserts and the caps or block when the clearance was measured. If the Plastigage is noticeably wider at one end than the other, the journal may be tapered (see Section 19).

16   Carefully scrape all traces of the Plastigage material off the main bearing journals and/or the bearing faces. Don't nick or scratch the bearing faces.

Final crankshaft installation

17   Carefully lift the crankshaft out of the engine. Clean the bearing faces in the block, then apply a thin, uniform layer of clean moly-base grease or engine assembly lube to each of the bearing surfaces. Coat the thrust washers as well.

18   Lubricate the crankshaft surfaces that contact the oil seals with moly-base grease, engine assembly lube or clean engine oil.

19   Make sure the crankshaft journals are clean, then lay the crankshaft back in place in the block. Clean the faces of the bearings in the caps or cap assembly, then apply lubri-

cant to them. Install the caps in their respective positions with the arrows pointing toward the front of the engine. **Note:** *Be sure to install the thrust washers. On four-cylinder engines, the thrust washers go with the number 3 main journal, and the number 2 main journal on V6 engines.* The upper (block side) thrust washers can be rotated into position around the crank with the crank in the block, with the thrust washer grooves facing OUT. The tanged lower thrust washers should be placed on the caps with their grooves OUT and the tangs fitting into the cap slots **(see illustrations)**.

20   Apply a light coat of oil to the bolt threads and the under sides of the bolt heads, then install them. Tighten all main bearing cap bolts to the torque listed in this Chapter's Specifications, following the recommended sequence.

21   On manual transmission equipped models, install a new pilot bearing in the end of the crankshaft.

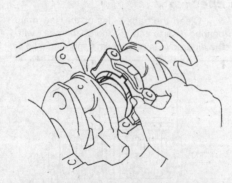

24.19b On four-cylinder engines, install the thrust washer in the number three cap with the oil grooves facing OUT, and on V6 engines, the tangs should fit into the slots on the caps

22   Rotate the crankshaft a number of times by hand to check for any obvious binding.

23   Check the crankshaft endplay with a feeler gauge or a dial indicator as described in Section 14. The endplay should be correct if the crankshaft thrust faces aren't worn or damaged and new thrust washers have been installed.

24   Install a new rear main oil seal, then bolt the retainer to the block (see Section 25).

25   Rear main oil seal installation

Refer to illustration 25.3

1   The crankshaft must be installed first and the main bearing caps or cap assembly bolted in place, then the new seal should be installed in the retainer and the retainer bolted to the block.

2   Check the seal contact surface on the crankshaft very carefully for scratches and nicks that could damage the new seal lip and cause oil leaks. If the crankshaft is damaged, the only alternative is a new or different crankshaft.

3   The old seal can be removed from the retainer by driving it out from the back side

25.3 After removing the retainer from the block, support it on a couple of wood blocks and drive out the old seal with a punch or screwdriver and hammer

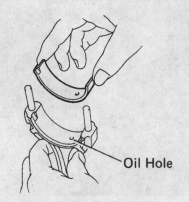

26.3 Align the oil hole in the bearing with the oil hole in the connecting rod

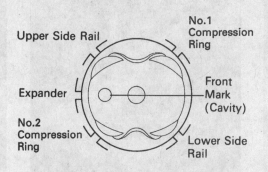

26.5 Stagger the ring end gaps around the piston, as shown, before installing the pistons. The Front mark or dot must face the front of the engine

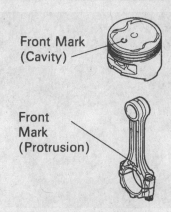

26.9 Check to be sure both the mark on the piston and the mark on the connecting rod are aligned as shown

with a hammer and punch **(see illustration)**. Be sure to note how far it's recessed into the bore before removing it; the new seal will have to be recessed an equal amount. Be very careful not to scratch or otherwise damage the bore in the retainer or oil leaks could develop.

4   Make sure the retainer is clean, then apply a thin coat of engine oil to the outer edge of the new seal. The seal must be pressed squarely into the bore, so hammering it into place isn't recommended. If you don't have access to a press, sandwich the housing and seal between two smooth pieces of wood and press the seal into place with the jaws of a large vise. The pieces of wood must be thick enough to distribute the force evenly around the entire circumference of the seal. Work slowly and make sure the seal enters the bore squarely.

5   As a last resort, the seal can be tapped into the retainer with a hammer. Use a block of wood to distribute the force evenly and make sure the seal is driven in squarely.

6   The seal lips must be lubricated with clean engine oil or moly-based grease before the seal/retainer is slipped over the crankshaft and bolted to the block. On

26.11 The piston can be driven gently into the cylinder bore with the end of a wooden or plastic hammer handle

four-cylinder engines, use a new gasket - and sealant- and make sure the dowel pins are in place before installing the retainer. On V6 engines, no gasket is required. Instead, apply a 2 mm wide bead of RTV sealant to the retainer-to-block surface.

7   Tighten the bolts a little at a time to the torque listed in Chapter 2A or 2B Specifications.

26 Pistons/connecting rods - installation and rod bearing oil clearance check

Refer to illustrations 26.3, 26.5, 26.9, 26.11, 26.13, 26.15 and 26.17

1   Before installing the piston/connecting rod assemblies, the cylinder walls must be perfectly clean, the top edge of each cylinder must be chamfered, and the crankshaft must be in place.

2   Remove the cap from the end of the number one connecting rod (refer to the marks made during removal). Remove the original bearing inserts and wipe the bearing surfaces of the connecting rod and cap with a clean, lint-free cloth. They must be kept spotlessly clean.

Connecting rod bearing oil clearance check

3   Clean the back side of the new upper bearing insert, then lay it in place in the connecting rod. Make sure the tab on the bearing fits into the recess in the rod so the oil holes line up **(see illustration)**. Don't hammer the bearing insert into place and be very careful not to nick or gouge the bearing face. Don't lubricate the bearing at this time.

4   Clean the back side of the other bearing insert and install it in the rod cap. Again, make sure the tab on the bearing fits into the recess in the cap, and don't apply any lubricant. It's critically important that the mating surfaces of the bearing and connecting rod are perfectly clean and oil free when they're

assembled.

5   Position the piston ring gaps at staggered intervals around the piston **(see illustration)**.

6   Slip a section of plastic or rubber hose over each connecting rod cap bolt.

7   Lubricate the piston and rings with clean engine oil and attach a piston ring compressor to the piston. Leave the skirt protruding about 1/4-inch to guide the piston into the cylinder. The rings must be compressed until they're flush with the piston.

8   Rotate the crankshaft until the number one connecting rod journal is at BDC (bottom dead center) and apply a coat of engine oil to the cylinder wall.

9   With the mark on top of the piston **(see illustration)** facing the front of the engine, gently insert the piston/connecting rod assembly into the number one cylinder bore and rest the bottom edge of the ring compressor on the engine block.

10   Tap the top edge of the ring compressor to make sure it's contacting the block around its entire circumference.

11   Gently tap on the top of the piston with the end of a wooden hammer handle **(see illustration)** while guiding the end of the connecting rod into place on the crankshaft journal. The piston rings may try to pop out of the ring compressor just before entering the cylinder bore, so keep some downward pressure on the ring compressor. Work slowly, and if any resistance is felt as the piston enters the cylinder, stop immediately. Find out what's hanging up and fix it before proceeding. **Caution:** *Do not, for any reason, force the piston into the cylinder - you might break a ring and/or the piston.*

12   Once the piston/connecting rod assembly is installed, the connecting rod bearing oil clearance must be checked before the rod cap is permanently bolted in place.

13   Cut a piece of the appropriate size Plastigage slightly shorter than the width of the connecting rod bearing and lay it in place on the number one connecting rod journal, parallel with the journal axis **(see illustration)**.

26.13 Lay the Plastigage strips on each rod bearing journal, parallel to the crankshaft centerline

26.15 Install the connecting rod caps with the front mark (arrow) facing the timing belt end of the engine, and torque to Specifications - for the 90-degree second step, use an angle gauge as shown, or paint reference marks on the rod nuts and the socket

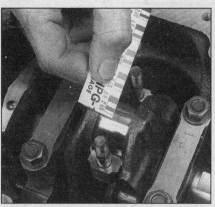

26.17 Measure the width of the crushed Plastigage to determine the rod bearing oil clearance (be sure to use the correct scale - standard and metric scales are included)

14   Clean the connecting rod cap bearing face, remove the protective hoses from the connecting rod bolts and install the rod cap. Make sure the mating mark on the cap is on the same side as the mark on the connecting rod. Check the cap to make sure the front mark is facing the timing belt end of the engine.

15   Apply a light coat of oil to the under sides of the nuts, then install and tighten them to the torque listed in this Chapter's Specifications, working up to it in three steps. Use a thin-wall socket to avoid erroneous torque readings that can result if the socket is wedged between the rod cap and nut. If the socket tends to wedge itself between the nut and the cap, lift up on it slightly until it no longer contacts the cap. Do not rotate the crankshaft at any time during this operation. **Note:** *After reaching the specified torque, tighten each nut an additional 90-degrees (1/4-turn)* **(see illustration).**

16   Remove the nuts and detach the rod cap, being very careful not to disturb the Plastigage.

17   Compare the width of the crushed Plastigage to the scale printed on the Plastigage envelope to obtain the oil clearance **(see illustration).** Compare it to this Chapter's Specifications to make sure the clearance is correct.

18   If the clearance is not as specified, the bearing inserts may be the wrong size (which means different ones will be required). Before deciding that different inserts are needed, make sure that no dirt or oil was between the bearing inserts and the connecting rod or cap when the clearance was measured. Also, recheck the journal diameter. If the Plastigage was wider at one end than the other, the journal may be tapered (refer to Section 19).

Final connecting rod installation

19   Carefully scrape all traces of the Plastigage material off the rod journal and/or bearing face. Be very careful not to scratch the bearing, use your fingernail or the edge of a credit card to remove the Plastigage.

20   Make sure the bearing faces are perfectly clean, then apply a uniform layer of clean moly-base grease or engine assembly lube to both of them. You'll have to push the piston higher into the cylinder to expose the face of the bearing insert in the connecting rod, be sure to slip the protective hoses over the rod bolts first.

21   Slide the connecting rod back into place on the journal, remove the protective hoses from the rod cap bolts, install the rod cap and tighten the nuts to the torque listed in this Chapter's Specifications. Again, work up to the torque in three steps.

22   Repeat the entire procedure for the remaining pistons/connecting rods.

23   The important points to remember are:

a) Keep the back sides of the bearing inserts and the insides of the connecting rods and caps perfectly clean when assembling them.

b) Make sure you have the correct piston/rod assembly for each cylinder.

c) The dimple on the piston must face the front of the engine.

d) Lubricate the cylinder walls with clean oil.

e) Lubricate the bearing faces when installing the rod caps after the oil clearance has been checked.

24   After all the piston/connecting rod assemblies have been properly installed, rotate the crankshaft a number of times by hand to check for any obvious binding.

25   As a final step, the connecting rod endplay must be checked. Refer to Section 13 for this procedure.

26   Compare the measured endplay to this Chapter's Specifications to make sure it's correct. If it was correct before disassembly and the original crankshaft and rods were reinstalled, it should still be right. If new rods or a new crankshaft were installed, the endplay may be inadequate. If so, the rods will have to be removed and taken to an automotive machine shop for resizing.

27   Initial start-up and break-in after overhaul

Warning: *Have a fire extinguisher handy when starting the engine for the first time.*

1   Once the engine has been installed in the vehicle, double-check the engine oil and coolant levels.

2   With the spark plugs out of the engine and both the ignition system and fuel pump disabled (see Section 3), crank the engine until oil pressure registers on the gauge or the light goes out.

3   Install the spark plugs, hook up the plug wires and restore the ignition system and fuel pump functions (see Section 3).

4   Start the engine. It may take a few moments for the fuel system to build up pressure, but the engine should start without a great deal of effort.

5   After the engine starts, it should be allowed to warm up to normal operating temperature. While the engine is warming up, make a thorough check for fuel, oil and coolant leaks.

6   Shut the engine off and recheck the engine oil and coolant levels.

7   Drive the vehicle to an area with minimum traffic, accelerate from 30 to 50 mph, then allow the vehicle to slow to 30 mph with the throttle closed. Repeat the procedure 10 or 12 times. This will load the piston rings and cause them to seat properly against the cylinder walls. Check again for oil and coolant leaks.

8   Drive the vehicle gently for the first 500 miles (no sustained high speeds) and keep a constant check on the oil level. It is not unusual for an engine to use oil during the break-in period.

9   At approximately 500 to 600 miles, change the oil and filter.

10   For the next few hundred miles, drive the vehicle normally. Do not pamper it or abuse it.

11   After 2000 miles, change the oil and filter again and consider the engine broken in.

Chapter 3
Cooling, heating and air conditioning systems

Contents

Specifications

General

Radiator cap pressure rating	8.5 to 14.9 psi
Thermostat rating	
Four-cylinder engines	176 to 183-degrees F
3.0L V6 engine	180 to 203-degrees F
3.4L V6 engine	176 to 183-degrees F
Refrigerant type	R-134a
Refrigerant capacity	
T100 models	21 to 25 ounces
Tacoma models	20 to 23 ounces
4Runner models	21 to 25 ounces

Torque specifications

	Ft-lbs (unless otherwise indicated)
Oil cooler relief valve	43
Oil cooler mounting bolt	29
Radiator mounting bolts	23
Thermostat housing bolts	
Four-cylinder engines	15
V6 engines	168 in-lbs
Water pump-to-block bolts	
Four-cylinder engines	
12 mm head	78 in-lbs
14 mm head	18
3.0L V6 engine (refer to illustration 8.17)	
Short bolts (A)	156 in-lbs
Long bolts (B)	168 in-lbs
3.4L V6 engine	168 in-lbs

1 General information

Engine cooling system

All vehicles covered by this manual employ a pressurized engine cooling system with thermostatically controlled coolant circulation. An impeller type water pump mounted on the front of the block pumps coolant through the engine. The coolant flows around each cylinder and toward the rear of the engine. Cast-in coolant passages direct coolant around the intake and exhaust ports, near the spark plug areas and in proximity to the exhaust valve guides. The four-cylinder engines are designed with the water pump mounted directly on the timing cover while the V6 engines are mounted on the block and require timing belt cover and timing belt removal.

A wax-pellet type thermostat is located in the thermostat housing at the radiator end of the engine. During warm up, the closed thermostat prevents coolant from circulating through the radiator. When the engine reaches normal operating temperature, the thermostat opens and allows hot coolant to travel through the radiator, where it is cooled before returning to the engine.

The cooling system is sealed by a pressure-type radiator cap. This raises the boiling point of the coolant, and the higher boiling point of the coolant increases the cooling efficiency of the radiator. If the system pressure exceeds the cap pressure-relief value, the excess pressure in the system forces the spring-loaded valve inside the cap off its seat and allows the coolant to escape through the overflow tube into a coolant reservoir. When the system cools, the excess coolant is automatically drawn from the reservoir back into the radiator.

The coolant reservoir serves as both the point at which fresh coolant is added to the cooling system to maintain the proper fluid level and as a holding tank for overheated coolant.

This type of cooling system is known as a closed design because coolant that escapes past the pressure cap is saved and reused.

Heating system

The heating system consists of a blower fan and heater core located within the heater box under the dashboard, the inlet and outlet hoses connecting the heater core to the engine cooling system and the heater/air conditioning control head on the dashboard. Hot engine coolant is circulated through the heater core. When the heater mode is activated, a flap opens to expose the heater box to the passenger compartment. A fan switch on the control head activates the blower motor, which forces air through the core, heating the air.

Air conditioning system

The air conditioning system consists of a condenser mounted in front of the radiator,

2.4 An inexpensive hydrometer can be used to test the condition of your coolant

an evaporator mounted adjacent to the heater core, a compressor mounted on the engine, a filter-drier which contains a high pressure relief valve and the plumbing connecting all of the above.

A blower fan forces the warmer air of the passenger compartment through the evaporator core (sort of a radiator-in-reverse), transferring the heat from the air to the refrigerant. The liquid refrigerant boils off into low pressure vapor, taking the heat with it when it leaves the evaporator. The compressor keeps refrigerant circulating through the system, pumping the warmed coolant through the condenser where it is cooled and then circulated back to the evaporator.

2 Antifreeze - general information

Refer to illustration 2.4
Warning: *Do not allow antifreeze to come in contact with your skin or painted surfaces of the vehicle. Rinse off spills immediately with plenty of water. Antifreeze is highly toxic if ingested. Never leave antifreeze lying around in an open container or in puddles on the floor; children and pets are attracted by it's sweet smell and may drink it. Check with local authorities about disposing of used antifreeze. Many communities have collection centers which will see that antifreeze is disposed of safely. Never dump used antifreeze on the ground or into drains.*
Note: *Non-toxic antifreeze is now manufactured and available at local auto parts stores, but even these types should be disposed of properly.*

The cooling system should be filled with a water/ethylene-glycol based antifreeze solution, which will prevent freezing down to at least -20 degrees F, or lower if local climate requires it. It also provides protection against corrosion and increases the coolant boiling point.

The cooling system should be drained, flushed and refilled every 30,000 miles or every two years (see Chapter 1). The use of antifreeze solutions for periods of longer than two years is likely to cause damage and

encourage the formation of rust and scale in the system. If your tap water is "hard", i.e. contains a lot of dissolved minerals, use distilled water with the antifreeze.

Before adding antifreeze to the system, check all hose connections, because antifreeze tends to leak through very minute openings. Engines do not normally consume coolant. Therefore, if the level goes down, find the cause and correct it.

The exact mixture of antifreeze-to-water you should use depends on the relative weather conditions. The mixture should contain at least 50-percent antifreeze, but should never contain more than 70-percent antifreeze. Consult the mixture ratio chart on the antifreeze container before adding coolant. Hydrometers are available at most auto parts stores to test the ratio of antifreeze to water **(see illustration)**. Use antifreeze which meets the vehicle manufacturer's specifications.

3 Thermostat - check and replacement

Warning: *Do not remove the radiator cap, coolant or thermostat until the engine has cooled completely.*

Check

1   Before assuming the thermostat is responsible for a cooling system problem, check the coolant level (Chapter 1), drivebelt tension (Chapter 1) and temperature gauge (or light) operation.
2   If the engine takes a long time to warm up (as indicated by the temperature gauge or heater operation), the thermostat is probably stuck open. Replace the thermostat with a new one.
3   If the engine runs hot, use your hand to check the temperature of the lower radiator hose. If the hose is not hot, but the engine is, the thermostat is probably stuck in the closed position, preventing the coolant inside the engine from traveling through the radiator. Replace the thermostat. **Caution:** *On models equipped with fuel injection, do not drive the vehicle without a thermostat. The computer may stay in open loop and emissions and fuel economy will suffer.*
4   If the lower radiator hose is hot, it means that the coolant is flowing and the thermostat is open. Consult the *Troubleshooting* section at the front of this manual for further diagnosis.

Replacement

Refer to illustrations 3.8a, 3.8b, 3.9, 3.10 and 3.11
5   Disconnect the negative cable from the battery. **Caution:** *If the stereo in your vehicle is equipped with an anti-theft system, make sure you have the correct activation code before disconnecting the battery.*
6   Drain the cooling system (see Chapter 1).
7   If equipped, disconnect the vacuum hoses on the thermostat housing.
8   Detach the housing from the engine

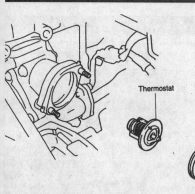

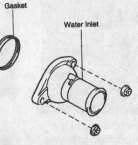

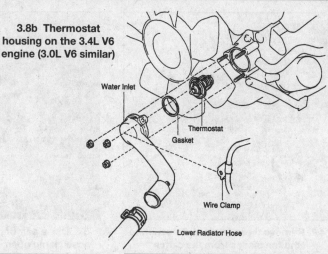

3.8b Thermostat housing on the 3.4L V6 engine (3.0L V6 similar)

3.8a Thermostat housing on the four-cylinder engines

3.9 The thermostat is installed with the spring end towards the cylinder head

3.10 The thermostat gasket, which is actually a grooved sealing ring, fits around the edge of the thermostat

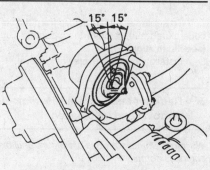

3.11 The jiggle valve must be within 15-degrees of the 12 o'clock position when installed

(see illustrations). Be prepared for some coolant to spill as the gasket seal is broken. The radiator hose can be left attached to the housing, unless the housing itself is to be replaced.
9   Remove the thermostat, noting the direction in which it was installed in the housing, and thoroughly clean the sealing surfaces (see illustration).
10   Install a new gasket onto the thermostat or housing (see illustration). Make sure it is evenly fitted all the way around.
11   Install the thermostat and housing, positioning the jiggle pin, if equipped, at the highest point (see illustration).
12   Tighten the housing fasteners to the torque listed in this Chapter's Specifications and reinstall the remaining components in the reverse order of removal.
13   Refill the cooling system (see Chapter 1), run the engine and check for leaks and proper operation.

4   Engine cooling fan/clutch assembly - check, removal and installation

Check

1   Check the fan carefully for cracks, especially around the base of each blade. If any

cracks are evident, replace the fan.
2   Check the fan clutch for fluid leakage. If it's leaking, replace it.
3   Try to move the fan blades in a front-to-rear direction. If they wobble, replace the fan clutch.
4   Spin the fan by hand. It should resist spinning (more resistance when the engine is hot). If it spins freely, or won't spin at all, replace the fan clutch.

4.6a Unscrew the four nuts (arrows) that retain the fan to the water pump, detach the fan/clutch assembly . . .

Removal

Refer to illustrations 4.6a, 4.6b and 4.7
5   Remove the fan shroud mounting bolts.
Note: *It will be necessary to remove the lower fan shroud (number 2) first, before removing the main fan shroud (see illustration 5.10).*
6   Remove the fan clutch-to-water pump mounting nuts (see illustration) and separate the fan from the water pump. Lift the fan and shroud from the engine compartment (see illustration).

4.6b . . . and remove the fan shroud and fan at the same time

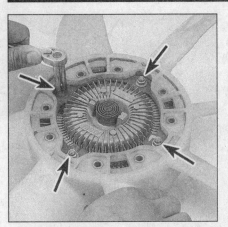

4.7 Remove these four nuts to separate the fan blades from the clutch

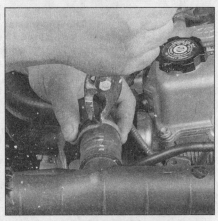

5.3 Use a pair of pliers to squeeze the hose clamp open, then slide the clamp back on the hose

5.10a Remove the radiator mounting bolts (arrows)

7   To separate the fan blades from the viscous clutch hub, remove the mounting nuts **(see illustration)**.

8   Installation is the reverse of removal.

5   Radiator and coolant reservoir - removal and installation

Warning: *Do not start this procedure until the engine is completely cool.*

Radiator

Refer to illustrations 5.3, 5.10a and 5.10b

1   Disconnect the negative battery cable. **Caution:** *If the stereo in your vehicle is*

equipped with an anti-theft system, make sure you have the correct activation code before disconnecting the battery.

2   Drain the coolant into a container (see Chapter 1).

3   Detach the upper and lower radiator hoses from the radiator **(see illustration)**. If the hoses stick, twist them with a pair of large pliers to break the bond, but be careful not to damage the fittings on the radiator.

4   Disconnect the reservoir hose from the radiator filler neck.

5   Disconnect the air pipe from the top of the radiator.

6   Remove the cooling fan and fan shroud (see Section 4).

7   If equipped with an automatic transmission, disconnect the cooler lines from the radiator. Place a drip pan to catch the fluid and cap the fittings.

8   Remove the battery and the battery tray if it will interfere with removal of the radiator (see Chapter 5). **Note:** *This isn't necessary on all models.*

9   Remove the radiator grille (see Chapter 11).

10   Remove the radiator mounting bolts **(see illustrations)**.

11   Lift out the radiator. Be aware of dripping fluids and the sharp fins.

12   With the radiator removed, it can be inspected for leaks, damage and internal blockage. If in need of repairs, have a radiator shop or dealer service department perform

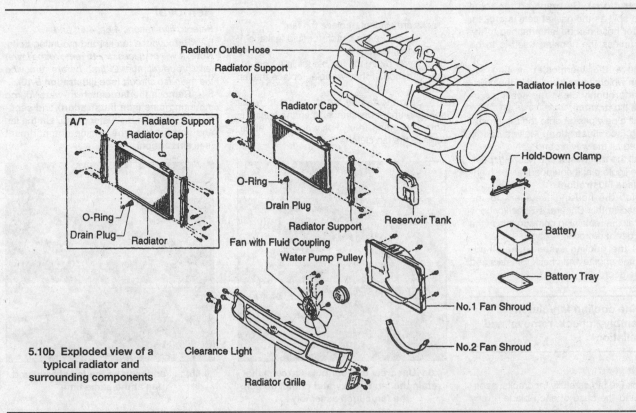

5.10b Exploded view of a typical radiator and surrounding components

Radiator Outlet Hose
Radiator Support
Radiator Cap
Radiator Inlet Hose
A/T
Radiator Support
Radiator Cap
O-Ring
Drain Plug
Radiator
O-Ring
Drain Plug
Radiator Support
Reservoir Tank
Hold-Down Clamp
Battery
Battery Tray
Fan with Fluid Coupling
Water Pump Pulley
No.1 Fan Shroud
No.2 Fan Shroud
Clearance Light
Radiator Grille

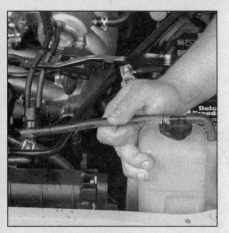

5.18 Detach the coolant reservoir hose, then pull the reservoir bottle out of its bracket

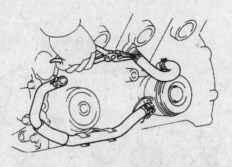

6.8 Disconnect the coolant hoses from the oil cooler

6.9 Remove the oil cooler mounting bolt with a breaker bar and socket

the work as special techniques are required.
13   Bugs and dirt can be cleaned from the radiator with compressed air and a soft brush. Don't bend the cooling fins as this is done. **Warning:** *Wear eye protection when using compressed air.*
14   Installation is the reverse of the removal procedure.
15   After installation, fill the cooling system with the proper mixture of antifreeze and water. Refer to Chapter 1 if necessary.
16   Start the engine and check for leaks. Allow the engine to reach normal operating temperature, indicated by both radiator hoses becoming hot. Recheck the coolant level and add more if required.
17   On automatic transmission equipped models, check and add fluid as needed.

Coolant reservoir

Refer to illustration 5.18
18   On most models, the coolant reservoir simply pulls up and out of the bracket next to the battery **(see illustration)**.
19   Pour the coolant into a container. Wash out and inspect the reservoir for cracks and

chafing. Replace it if damaged.
20   Installation is the reverse of removal.

---

6   Oil cooler - removal and installation

Refer to illustrations 6.8, 6.9 and 6.10
Warning: *Wait until the engine is completely cool before beginning this procedure.*
1   Disconnect the negative battery cable.
Caution: *If the stereo in your vehicle is equipped with an anti-theft system, make sure you have the correct activation code before disconnecting the battery.*
2   Drain the coolant into a container (see Chapter 1).
3   Remove the air cleaner assembly (see Chapter 4).
4   Remove the front exhaust pipe assembly from the vehicle.
5   If equipped with the PAIR emission system, remove the air pipe (see Chapter 6).
6   Remove the exhaust manifold (see Chapter 2A or 2B).

7   Remove the oil pressure switch (see Chapter 2C).
8   Remove the oil cooler hoses **(see illustration)**.
9   Remove the oil cooler mounting bolt **(see illustration)**.
10   Installation is the reverse of removal. Be sure to use a new gasket under the relief valve and a new O-ring between the oil cooler and the engine block **(see illustration)**. If equipped, make sure the alignment tab engages with the projection on the engine block. Tighten the relief valve to the torque listed in this Chapter's Specifications.

---

7   Water pump - check

Refer to illustration 7.3
1   A failure in the water pump can cause serious engine damage due to overheating.
2   With the engine running and warmed to normal operating temperature, squeeze the upper radiator hose. If the water pump is working properly, a pressure surge should be felt as the hose is released. **Warning:** *Keep hands away from fan blades!*
3   Water pumps are equipped with weep or vent holes **(see illustration)**. If a failure

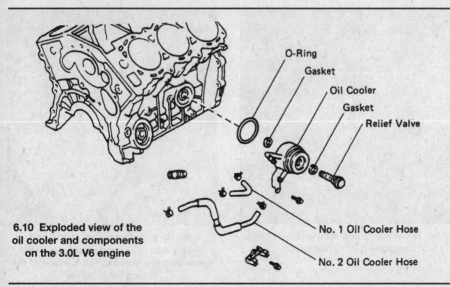

6.10 Exploded view of the oil cooler and components on the 3.0L V6 engine

O-Ring
Gasket
Oil Cooler
Gasket
Relief Valve
No. 1 Oil Cooler Hose
No. 2 Oil Cooler Hose

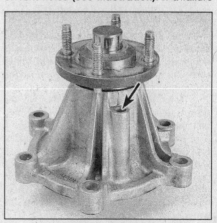

7.3 Typical weep hole on a water pump (arrow)

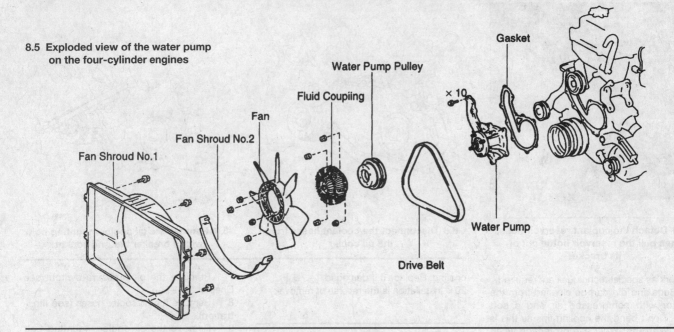

8.5 Exploded view of the water pump on the four-cylinder engines

occurs in the pump seal, coolant will leak from this hole. In most cases it will be necessary to use a flashlight to find the hole on the water pump by looking through the space behind the pulley just below the water pump shaft.

4   If the water pump shaft bearings fail there may be a howling sound at the front of the engine while it is running. Bearing wear can be felt if the water pump pulley is rocked up and down. Do not mistake drivebelt slippage, which causes a squealing sound, for water pump failure. Spray automotive drivebelt dressing on the belts to eliminate the belt as a possible cause of the noise.

8   Water pump - removal and installation

Warning: *Do not start this procedure until the engine is completely cool.*

Four-cylinder engines

Refer to illustrations 8.5, 8.6a and 8.6b
1   Disconnect the negative battery cable and drain the cooling system (see Chapter 1). **Caution:** *If the stereo in your vehicle is equipped with an anti-theft system, make sure you have the correct activation code before disconnecting the battery.*
2   Refer to Chapter 1 and remove the power steering belt, alternator/water pump belt and air conditioning belt.
3   Remove the fan shroud from the radiator (see Section 4). **Note:** *On Tacoma models, it will be necessary to remove the oil dipstick guide and the air pipe that runs across the top of the fan shroud.*
4   Remove the fan assembly from the water pump (see Section 4).
5   Remove the water pump pulley from the water pump **(see illustration)**. Disconnect

the radiator inlet hose and the bypass hose.
6   Remove the bolts retaining the water pump to the engine block and remove the water pump **(see illustrations)**.
7   Thoroughly clean the gasket sealing surface on the timing chain cover.
8   Installation is the reverse of removal. Be sure to use a new gasket and tighten the water pump bolts to the torque listed in this Chapter's Specifications.
9   Refill the cooling system (see Chapter 1), run the engine and check for leaks.

V6 engines

Refer to illustrations 8.14a, 8.14b and 8.17
10   Disconnect the negative battery cable and drain the cooling system (see Chapter 1). **Caution:** *If the stereo in your vehicle is equipped with an anti-theft system, make sure you have the correct activation code before disconnecting the battery.*

11   Remove the timing belt (see Chapter 2B).
12   Remove the alternator adjuster bracket and bolt assembly and remove the thermostat housing and thermostat from the water pump (see Section 3).
13   If the engine is equipped with an oil cooler, disconnect the number 2 oil cooler hose from the water pump.
14   Remove the water pump bolts and separate the pump from the engine **(see illustrations)**. Disconnect the radiator inlet hose and the bypass hose.
15   Thoroughly clean the gasket mating surfaces, removing all traces of oil with acetone or lacquer thinner and a clean rag.
16   Apply a 3 mm bead of RTV sealant to the water pump. Be sure to install the water pump within five minutes of sealant application.
17   Installation is the reverse of removal. Tighten the water pump bolts to the torque

8.6a The water pump on the four-cylinder engines has 10 bolts total

8.6b Be sure to remove all the bolts evenly and in several passes to avoid damaging the pump or the surface of the timing chain cover

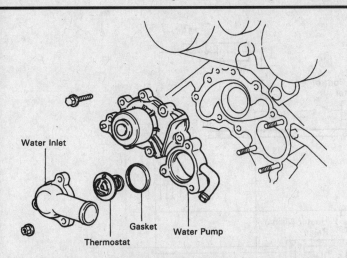

8.14a Exploded view of the water pump and components on the 3.0L V6 engine

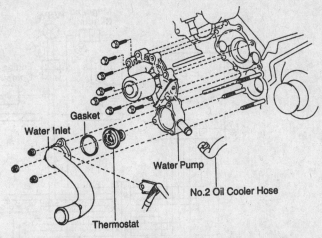

8.14b Exploded view of the water pump and components on the 3.4L V6 engine

listed in this Chapter's Specifications. **Note:** *The 3.0L V6 engine is equipped with two different size water pump bolts* **(see illustration).** *Be sure to apply the correct amount of torque for each bolt. Refer to this Chapter's Specifications for the correct torque values.*

18 Refill the cooling system (see Chapter 1), run the engine and check for leaks.

9 Coolant temperature sending unit - check and replacement

Warning: *Do not start this procedure until the engine is completely cool.*

Check

Refer to illustrations 9.3a, 9.3b and 9.3c

1 If the coolant temperature gauge is inoperative, check the fuses first (see Chapter 12).

2 If the temperature gauge indicates excessive temperature after running awhile, see the *Troubleshooting* section in the front of the manual.

3 If the temperature gauge indicates HOT as soon as the engine is started cold, disconnect the wire at the coolant temperature sender **(see illustrations).** If the gauge reading drops, replace the sending unit. If the reading remains high, the wire to the gauge may be shorted to ground or the gauge is faulty.

4 If the coolant temperature gauge fails to show any indication after the engine has been warmed up, (approximately 10 minutes) and the fuses checked out OK, shut off the engine. Disconnect the wire at the sending unit and, using a jumper wire, connect the wire to a clean ground on the engine. Briefly turn on the ignition without starting the engine. If the gauge now indicates Hot, replace the sending unit. **Caution:** *Don't leave the jumper wire connected any longer than necessary.*

5 If the gauge fails to respond, the circuit may be open or the gauge may be faulty - see Chapter 12 for additional information.

Replacement

6 Disconnect the electrical connector from the sending unit.

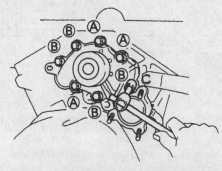

8.17 Install the long and short bolts into the correct locations before torquing the water pump (3.0L V6 engine)

7 Using a deep socket or a wrench, remove the sending unit. Be prepared for coolant spillage.

8 Install the new unit and tighten it securely.

9 Reconnect the electrical connector, refill the cooling system and check for coolant leakage and proper gauge function.

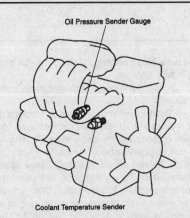

9.3a Location of the coolant temperature sending unit on the four-cylinder engines

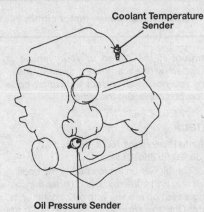

9.3b Location of the coolant temperature sending unit on the 3.0L V6 engine

9.3c Location of the coolant temperature sending unit on the 3.4L V6 engine

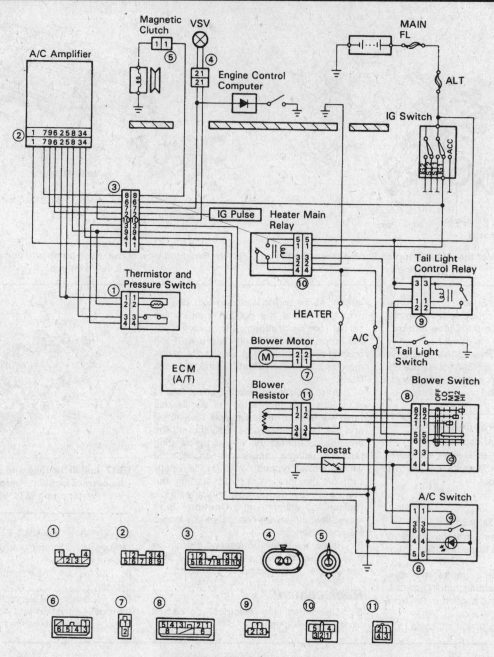

10.1a Typical blower motor circuit

10 Blower motor and circuit - check and component replacement

Warning: *Some models covered by this manual are equipped with airbags. The airbag is armed and can deploy (inflate) anytime the battery is connected. To prevent accidental deployment (and possible injury), turn the ignition key to LOCK and disconnect the negative battery cable whenever working near airbag components. After the battery is disconnected, wait at least two minutes before beginning work (the system has a back-up capacitor that must fully discharge). For more information see Chapter 12.*

Caution: *If the stereo in your vehicle is equipped with an anti-theft system, make sure you have the correct activation code before disconnecting the battery.*

Check

Refer to illustrations 10.1a, 10.1b, 10.3, 10.5a, 10.5b and 10.5c

1   The blower unit is located in the cooling assembly under the dash, and under the passenger seat on models with rear heater units. **Note:** *Only the 4Runner is equipped with the rear-mounted heater option.* If the blower doesn't work, check the fuse and all connections in the circuit for looseness and corro-

sion **(see illustrations)**. Make sure the battery is fully charged.

2   Locate the blower unit electrical connector.

3   If the blower motor does not operate, disconnect the electrical connector at the blower motor, turn the ignition key On (engine not running) and check for battery voltage with the blower speed switch ON **(see illustration)**. If battery voltage is not present, there is a problem in the ignition feed circuit, the blower switch, the heater main relay or in the circuit from the blower switch to the motor.

4   If battery voltage is present, reconnect the terminal to the blower motor and back-

10.1b The instrument panel has been removed to show the location of the blower motor (arrow)

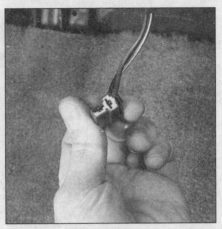

10.3 Unplug the electrical connector and check for battery voltage to the blower motor with the ignition key and the blower switch ON (engine not running)

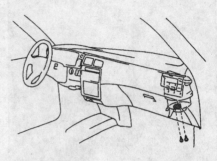

10.5a Location of the blower motor resistor (typical)

10.5b To check the resistor, check for continuity across terminals 1-2, 1-3 and 1-4. Continuity should exist

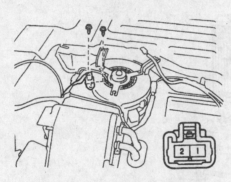

10.5c On 4Runner models, check the resistor continuity for the rear blower motor

10.6a Remove the blower motor mounting bolts (arrows)

probe the correct terminal (terminal 2) with a jumper wire connected to ground. If the motor still does not operate, the motor is probably faulty. Apply fused power and ground connections to the blower motor terminals, if the motor does not operate, replace it.

5   If the motor is good but doesn't operate, the blower resistor **(see illustrations)** or the heater/air conditioning control switch is probably faulty. Remove the control assembly (see Section 12) and check for continuity through the switch in each position. Remove the resistor and check for continuity across each of the terminals.

Replacement

Refer to illustration 10.6a and 10.6b

6   If the blower motor must be replaced, remove the bracket retaining the wiring connector to the blower, then remove the three mounting screws and lower the blower assembly from the housing **(see illustrations)**. The fan can be removed and reused on the new blower motor. For access to the

rear blower motor on 4Runner models, the passenger seat will have to be removed (see Chapter 11).

7   Installation is the reverse of removal. Check for proper operation.

11 Heater core - removal and installation

Refer to illustrations 11.3, 11.4, 11.11a and 11.11b

Warning: *Some models covered by this manual are equipped with airbags. The airbag is armed and can deploy (inflate) anytime the battery is connected. To prevent accidental deployment (and possible injury), turn the ignition key to LOCK and disconnect the negative battery cable whenever working near airbag components. After the battery is disconnected, wait at least two minutes before beginning work (the system has a back-up capacitor that must fully discharge). For more information see Chapter 12.*

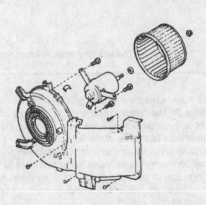

10.6b Rear blower motor details on a 4Runner

Note 1: *The following procedure details removing the heater core assembly by itself, but it is much easier to remove the heater core housing if the evaporator (cooling) assembly is removed first, although this necessitates having the refrigerant discharged and recovered before work begins. See Section 17 for evaporator removal, and*

11.3 Disconnect the heater hoses at the firewall

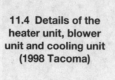

11.4 Details of the heater unit, blower unit and cooling unit (1998 Tacoma)

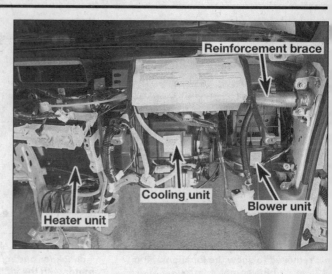

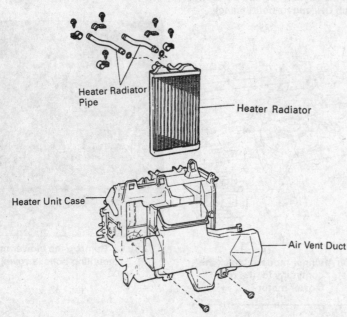

11.11a Details of a typical front mounted heater unit case and heater core

8   Unbolt and remove the center ventilation duct.

9   Unbolt and remove the lower center duct.

10   Loosen the screws that retain the heater tubes to the housing.

11   Pull the heater core out of the housing **(see illustration)**. Keep plenty of towels or rags on the carpeting to catch any coolant that may drip. **Caution:** *Work slowly and carefully to avoid breaking any plastic components during removal. The assembly must be pulled out (toward the rear of the vehicle) far enough for the plastic tabs to clear anything that might inhibit removal.*

12   Installation is the reverse order of removal.

13   Refill the cooling system, reconnect the battery and run the engine. Check for leaks and proper system operation.

---

12   Heater and air conditioning control assembly - check, removal and installation

Warning: *Some models covered by this manual are equipped with airbags. The airbag is armed and can deploy (inflate) anytime the battery is connected. To prevent accidental deployment (and possible injury), turn the ignition key to LOCK and disconnect the negative battery cable whenever working near airbag components. After the battery is disconnected, wait at least two minutes before beginning work (the system has a back-up capacitor that must fully discharge). For more information see Chapter 12.*

Removal and installation

Refer to illustrations 12.3a and 12.3b

1   Disconnect the negative cable from the battery. **Caution:** *If the stereo in your vehicle is equipped with an anti-theft system, make sure you have the correct activation code before disconnecting the battery.*

2   Remove the center cluster trim panels (see Chapter 11).

be sure to read the **Warning** in Section 12.

Note 2: *The factory recommends removal of the entire instrument panel and lowering the steering column to remove the heater core. This involves disconnecting numerous electrical connectors and there is the potential for breakage of delicate plastic tabs on various components. This is a difficult job for the average home mechanic.*

Note 3: *The heater core for the rear A/C and heating systems on 4Runners is accessible by removing both front seats.*

1   Disconnect the negative cable from the battery. **Caution:** *If the stereo in your vehicle is equipped with an anti-theft system, make sure you have the correct activation code before disconnecting the battery.*

2   Wait until the engine is completely cool, then drain the cooling system (see Chapter 1).

3   Working in the engine compartment,

disconnect the heater hoses at the firewall **(see illustration)**. Push the rubber seal around the hoses toward the inside of the vehicle, releasing it from the sheetmetal. Plug the heater core tubes to prevent leakage when it is removed.

4   Refer to Chapters 11 and 12 and remove the center console, glove compartment, glove compartment liner, ashtray, radio and center dash bezels and instrument panel **(see illustration)**. Also, remove the instrument panel reinforcement brace.

5   Refer to Section 12 of this Chapter to remove the heater/air conditioning controls from the panel on the dash.

6   Refer to Chapter 6 and remove the ECM without disconnecting the connectors. Set the ECM aside to allow room under the heater core housing.

7   Disconnect the control cables from the heater unit.

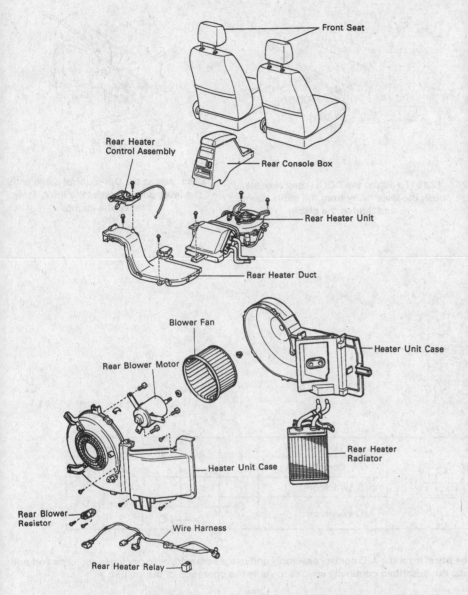

12.3a Pull the selector knob straight off

**12.3b Pull the knobs off the
rotary switches**

11.11b Details of the 4Runner rear mounted heater unit case and heater core

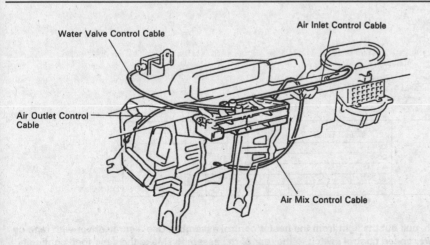

12.8 Control cable layout (1997 T100 shown)

3   Pull off the control knobs **(see illustrations).**

4   Remove the mounting screws located on the front of the control assembly (see Chapter 12).

5   Pull the control out slightly. If equipped with cables, twist the flags on the control cable mounts and remove the cables from the control. Disconnect the electrical connectors.

6   Installation is the reverse of the removal procedure.

7   Run the engine and check for proper functioning of the heater (and air conditioning, if equipped).

Cable adjustment

Refer to illustrations 12.8, 12.9, 12.10 and 12.11

8   With the cables attached at the control end and the control assembly installed in the dash, adjust the cables at their ends. The controls should be set to: RECIRC, COOL, and DEF **(see illustration).**

9   To adjust the air inlet damper control cable set the damper lever to FRESH, install

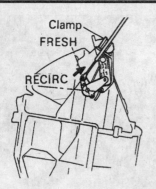

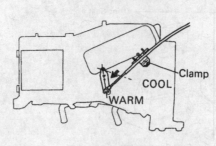

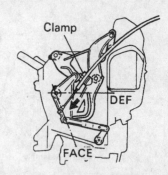

12.9 To adjust the FRESH door cable, move the arm up and tighten the clamp. Some models may have a slightly different location of the lever and cable but the adjustment procedure is the same

12.10 To adjust the COOL control cable, push the lever away from the cable clamp and tighten the clamp

12.11 Adjust the DEF control cable with the lever pulled toward the front, then tighten the clamp

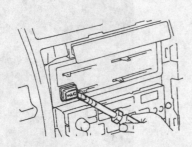

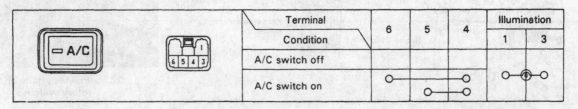

Terminal / Condition	6	5	4	Illumination 1	Illumination 3
A/C switch off					
A/C switch on	○———		———○	○———|———○	
		○———	———○		

12.12 To remove the A/C switch, remove the bezel from the A/C control assembly and use a screwdriver to pry loose the clips and pull out the A/C switch. Make the described continuity checks to verify the operation of the switch

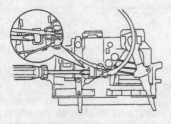

Terminal / Switch position	1	2	5	6	8	Illumination 3	Illumination 4
OFF							
LO			○	○			
○ (M1)	○		○	○		○———|———○	
○ (M2)		○	○	○			
H1			○	○	○		

12.13a To access the blower speed control switch, pull out the light from the heater control assembly. Use a screwdriver with tape on the tip to pry the clip loose and push out the blower speed control switch to the rear of the assembly. Make the described continuity checks to verify the operation of the switch

the cable and clamp it in place **(see illustration)**.

10   To adjust the air mix control cable, set the air mix damper to COOL, install the cable and lock the clamp while applying slight pressure on the outer cable **(see illustration)**.

11   To adjust the mode damper control cable, set the mode damper to the DEF mode, hook the cable end on and tighten the clamp **(see illustration)**.

Electrical checks

Refer to illustrations 12.12, 12.13a and 12.13b

12   Check the air conditioning switch following the accompanying tables **(see illustrations)**.

13   Check the heater control switch following the accompanying tables **(see illustrations)**. If the switch fails any of the tests, replace the control assembly.

---

13   Air conditioning and heating system - check and maintenance

Air conditioning system

Refer to illustration 13.1a, 13.1b and 13.1c
Warning: *The air conditioning system is under high pressure. Do not loosen any hose fittings or remove any components until the system has been discharged. Air conditioning refrigerant should be properly discharged into an EPA-approved recovery/recycling unit by a dealer service department or an automotive air conditioning repair facility. Always wear eye protection when disconnecting air conditioning system fittings.*

1   The following maintenance checks should be performed on a regular basis to ensure that the air conditioner continues to operate at peak efficiency **(see illustrations)**.

  a) *Inspect the condition of the compressor drivebelt. If it is worn or deteriorated, replace it (see Chapter 1).*
  b) *Check the drivebelt tension and, if necessary, adjust it (see Chapter 1).*
  c) *Inspect the system hoses. Look for cracks, bubbles, hardening and deterioration. Inspect the hoses and all fittings for oil bubbles or seepage. If there is any evidence of wear, damage or leakage, replace the hose(s).*
  d) *Inspect the condenser fins for leaves, bugs and any other foreign material that may have embedded itself in the fins. Use a "fin comb" or compressed air to remove debris from the condenser.*
  e) *Make sure the system has the correct refrigerant charge.*

2   It's a good idea to operate the system for about ten minutes at least once a month. This is particularly important during the winter months because long term non-use can cause hardening, and subsequent failure, of the seals.

3   Leaks in the air conditioning system are best spotted when the system is brought up

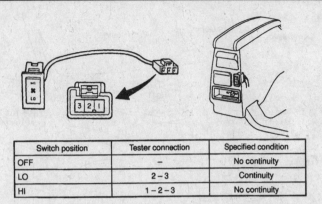

Switch position	Tester connection	Specified condition
OFF	–	No continuity
LO	2 – 3	Continuity
HI	1 – 2 – 3	No continuity

12.13b Check the operation of the rear blower motor switch on 4Runner models

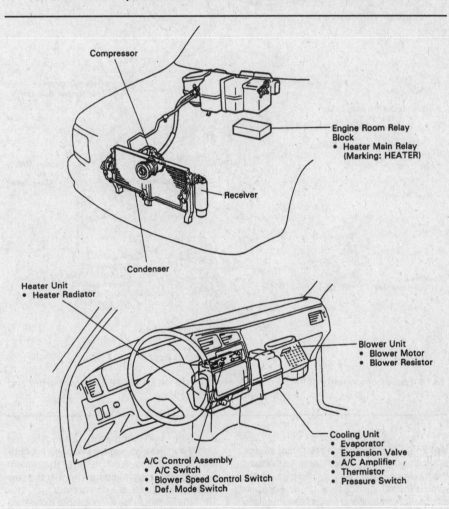

13.1a Basic components of the air conditioning system on a 1997 T100 model

to operating temperature and pressure, by running the engine with the air conditioning ON for five minutes. Shut the engine off and inspect the air conditioning hoses and connections. Traces of oil usually indicate refrigerant leaks.

4   Because of the complexity of the air conditioning system and the special equipment required to effectively work on it, accurate troubleshooting of the system should be left to a professional technician.

5   If the air conditioning system doesn't operate at all, check the fuse panel and the air conditioning relay, located in the fuse/relay box in the engine compartment. Refer to Sections 10 and 11 for electrical checks of heating/air conditioning system components.

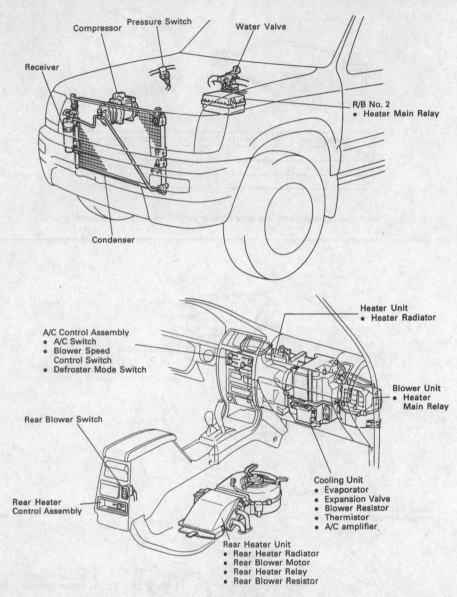

13.1b Basic components of the air conditioning system on a 1996 4Runner with front and rear heating and A/C systems

6   The most common cause of poor cooling is simply a low system refrigerant charge. If a noticeable drop in cool air output occurs, the following quick check will help you determine if the refrigerant level is low. For more information on air conditioning systems, refer to the *Haynes Automotive Heating and Air Conditioning Manual*.

Checking the refrigerant charge

Refer to illustrations 13.10 and 13.11

7   Warm the engine up to normal operating temperature.

8   Place the air conditioning temperature selector at the coldest setting and put the blower at the highest setting. Open the doors (to make sure the air conditioning system doesn't cycle off as soon as it cools the passenger compartment).

9   With the compressor engaged, the clutch will make an audible click and the center of the clutch will rotate. After the system reaches operating temperature, feel the two pipes connected to the compressor.

10   There should be a noticeable difference in temperature between the two pipes. If not, the system probably needs a charge. Insert a thermometer in the center air distribution duct while operating the air conditioning system **(see illustration)** - the temperature of the output air should be 35 to 40-degrees F below the ambient air temperature (down to approximately 40-degrees F). If the ambient (outside) air temperature is very high, say 110 degrees F, the duct air temperature may be as high as 60-degrees F, but generally the air conditioning is 35 to 40-degrees F cooler than the ambient air. If the air isn't as cold as

it used to be, the system probably needs a charge. Further inspection or testing of the system is beyond the scope of the home mechanic and should be left to a professional.

11   Inspect the sight glass If the refrigerant looks foamy when running, it's low **(see illustration)**. When ambient temperatures are very hot, bubbles may show in the sight glass even with the proper amount of refrigerant. With the proper amount of refrigerant, when the air conditioning is turned off, the sight glass should show refrigerant that foams, then clears.

Adding refrigerant

Refer to illustrations 13.12 and 13.15

Caution: *Refrigerant has changed from the use of R-12 to the "environmentally friendly" R-134a used in 1994 and later models. The two refrigerants are NOT compatible. Even after purging and evacuating an R-12 system, there is enough residual oil and refrigerant in the hoses and components that simply filling the system with R-134a cannot be done. Special fittings and manifold gauge sets are used on the different refrigerant types so that an accidental hook-up of the two systems cannot be made. When replacing entire components, additional refrigerant oil should be added equal to the amount that is removed with the component being replaced. Refrigerant oils, just like refrigerant R-12 vs. R-134a, are not compatible. Be sure to read the can before adding any oil to the system, to make sure it is compatible with the type of system being repaired.*

Note: *Because of Federal regulations, R-12 refrigerant is not available for home-mechanic use, however, cans of R-134 refrigerant are commonly available in auto parts stores. Models with R-12 systems will have to be serviced at a dealership or air conditioning shop.*

12   Buy an automotive charging kit at an auto parts store. A charging kit includes a 14-ounce can of R-134a refrigerant, a tap valve and a short section of hose that can be attached between the tap valve and the system low side service valve **(see illustration)**. Because one can of refrigerant may not be sufficient to bring the system charge up to the proper level, it's a good idea to buy a couple of additional cans. Try to find at least one can that contains red refrigerant dye. If the system is leaking, the red dye will leak out with the refrigerant and help you pinpoint the location of the leak.

13   Connect the charging kit by following the manufacturer's instructions.

14   Back off the valve handle on the charging kit and screw the kit onto the refrigerant can, making sure first that the O-ring or rubber seal inside the threaded portion of the kit is in place. **Warning:** *Wear protective eye wear when dealing with pressurized refrigerant cans.*

15   Remove the dust cap from the low-side charging port and attach the quick-connect fitting on the kit hose **(see illustration)**. **Warning:** *DO NOT hook the charging kit hose*

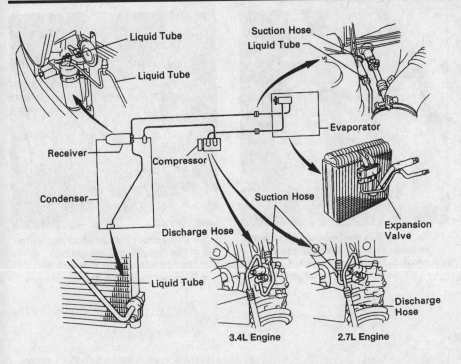

13.10 Check the temperature of the output air in the center register with a thermometer - it should be approximately 35 to 40-degrees F below the ambient air temperature

13.1c Basic components of the typical air conditioning system

to the system high side! The fittings on the charging kit are designed to fit only on the low side of the system.

16   Warm the engine to normal operating temperature and turn on the air conditioner. Keep the charging kit hose away from the fan and other moving parts.

17   Turn the valve handle on the kit until the stem pierces the can, then back the handle out to release the refrigerant. You should be able to hear the rush of gas. Add refrigerant to the low side of the system until both the outlet and the evaporator inlet pipe feel about the same temperature. Allow stabilization time between each addition. **Warning:** *Never add more than two cans of refrigerant to the*

system. **Note:** *The can may tend to frost up, slowing the procedure. Wrap a shop towel wet with hot water around the bottom of the can to keep it from frosting.*

18   If you have an accurate thermometer, you can place it in the center air conditioning duct inside the vehicle to monitor the air temperature. A charged system that is working properly, should output air down to approximately 40-degrees F.

19   When the can is empty, turn the valve handle to the closed position and release the connection from the low-side port. Replace the dust cap.

20   Remove the charging kit from the can and store the kit for future use with the pierc-

ing valve in the UP position, to prevent inadvertently piercing the can on the next use.

Heating systems

21   If the air coming out of the heater vents isn't hot, the problem could stem from any of the following causes:

a) *The thermostat is stuck open, preventing the engine coolant from warming up enough to carry heat to the heater core. Replace the thermostat (see Section 3).*

b) *A heater hose is blocked, preventing the flow of coolant through the heater core. Feel both heater hoses at the firewall. They should be hot. If one of them is cold, there is an obstruction in one of the hoses or in the heater core, or the heater control valve is shut. Detach the hoses and back flush the heater core with a water hose. If the heater core is clear but circulation is impeded, remove the two hoses and flush them out with a water hose.*

13.11 The sight glass (arrow) is located on the receiver/drier

13.12 A basic charging kit is available at most auto parts stores - it must say R-134a and so must the cans of refrigerant you buy

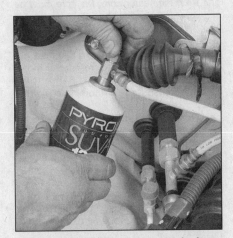

13.15 Add R-134a refrigerant to the low-side port only - the procedure will go faster if you wrap the can with a warm, wet towel to prevent icing

14.3a After the system has been discharged, detach the refrigerant lines from the top of the receiver/drier and cap them

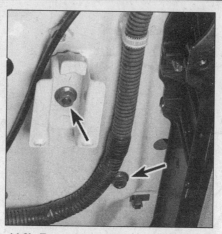

14.3b To access the back-up nuts on the receiver drier, remove the coolant reservoir and locate the bracket with the mounting nuts (arrows)

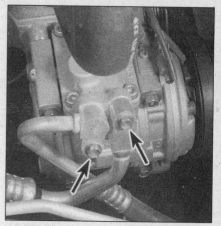

15.4 Disconnect the electrical connector at the compressor, then unbolt the flanges (arrows) and detach the refrigerant lines from the compressor

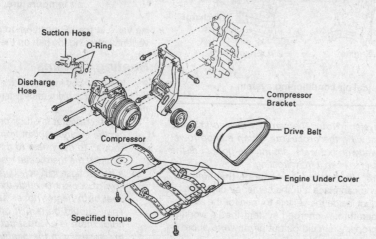

Suction Hose
O-Ring
Discharge Hose
Compressor
Specified torque
Compressor Bracket
Drive Belt
Engine Under Cover

15.5a Remove the compressor mounting bolts (arrows indicate the two bottom bolts, two more are near the top of the compressor) and remove the compressor (four-cylinder engines)

c) *If flushing fails to remove the blockage from the heater core, the core must be replaced (see Section 11).*

22   If the blower motor speed does not correspond to the setting selected on the blower switch, the problem could be a bad fuse, circuit, switch, blower motor resistor or motor (see Section 10).

23   If there isn't any air coming out of the vents:

a) *Turn the ignition ON and activate the fan control. Place your ear at the heating/air conditioning register (vent) and listen. Most motors are audible. Can you hear the motor running?*

b) *If you can't (and have already verified that the blower switch and the blower motor resistor are good), the blower motor itself is probably bad (see Section 9).*

24   If the carpet under the heater core is damp, or if antifreeze vapor or steam is coming through the vents, the heater core is leaking. Remove it (see Section 11) and install a new unit (most radiator shops will not repair a leaking heater core).

25   Inspect the drain hose from the heater/air conditioning assembly, make sure it is not clogged.

14   Air conditioning receiver/drier - removal and installation

Refer to illustrations 14.3a and 14.3b
Warning: *The air conditioning system is under high pressure. Do not loosen any hose fittings or remove any components until the system has been discharged. Air conditioning refrigerant should be properly discharged into an EPA-approved recovery/recycling unit by a dealer service department or an automotive air conditioning repair facility. Always wear eye protection when disconnecting air conditioning system fittings.*

1   Have the refrigerant discharged and recovered by an air conditioning technician.

2   Refer to Chapter 11 and remove the grille.
3   Disconnect the refrigerant lines from the receiver/drier and cap the open fittings to prevent entry of moisture **(see illustrations)**.
4   Loosen the pinch bolt (or bracket mounting bolts, whichever is easier to get a wrench on) and remove the receiver/drier.
5   Installation is the reverse of removal.
6   Have the system evacuated, charged and leak tested by the shop that discharged it. If the receiver was replaced, have them add about 0.34 ounces of refrigerant oil to the system. Use only the refrigerant oil compatible with the refrigerant of your system (R-134a).

15   Air conditioning compressor - removal and installation

Refer to illustrations 15.4, 15.5a and 15.5b
Warning: *The air conditioning system is under high pressure. Do not loosen any hose fittings or remove any components until the system has been discharged. Air conditioning refrigerant should be properly discharged into an EPA-approved recovery/recycling unit by a dealer service department or an automotive air conditioning repair facility. Always wear eye protection when disconnecting air conditioning system fittings.*

1   Have the refrigerant discharged by an automotive air conditioning technician.
2   Disconnect the negative cable from the battery. **Caution:** *If the stereo in your vehicle is equipped with an anti-theft system, make sure you have the correct activation code before disconnecting the battery.*
3   Remove the drivebelt from the compressor (see Chapter 1).
4   Detach the electrical connector and disconnect the refrigerant lines **(see illustration)**.
5   Unbolt the compressor and lift it from the vehicle **(see illustrations)**.

6   If a new or rebuilt compressor is being installed, follow the directions supplied with the compressor regarding the proper level of oil prior to installation.

7   Installation is the reverse of removal. Replace any O-rings with new ones specifically made for the type of refrigerant in your system and lubricate them with refrigerant oil, also designed specifically for your system (R-134a).

8   Have the system evacuated, recharged and leak tested by the shop that discharged it.

16 Air conditioning condenser - removal and installation

Refer to illustrations 16.2 and 16.3

Warning: *The air conditioning system is under high pressure. Do not loosen any hose fittings or remove any components until the system has been discharged. Air conditioning refrigerant should be properly discharged into an EPA-approved recovery/recycling unit by a dealer service department or an automotive air conditioning repair facility. Always wear eye protection when disconnecting air conditioning system fittings.*
Note: *If the condenser is to be replaced with a new unit, add 1.4 to 1.7 fluid ounces of compressor oil to the system.*

1   Have the refrigerant discharged by an air conditioning technician.

2   Remove the front grille, the hood lock brace and center support brace for access (see Chapter 11). Disconnect the condenser inlet and outlet fittings **(see illustration)**. Cap the open fittings immediately to keep moisture and contamination out of the system.
Note: *The left-side fitting is connected to the receiver/drier (see Section 14).*

3   Remove the condenser mounting bolts, pull the condenser forward and lift it out **(see illustration)**.

4   Install the condenser, brackets and bolts, making sure the rubber cushions fit on

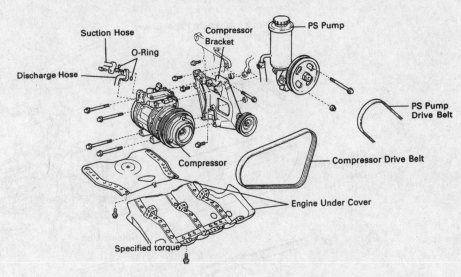

15.5b Mounting details of the air conditioning compressor on a 3.4L V6 engine

the mounting points properly.

5   Reconnect the refrigerant lines, using new O-rings where needed. If a new condenser has been installed, add approximately 1.4 to 1.7 ounces (50 cc) of new refrigerant oil of the correct type (R-134a).

6   Reinstall the remaining parts in the reverse order of removal.

7   Have the system evacuated, charged and leak tested by the shop that discharged it.

17 Air conditioning evaporator and expansion valve - removal and installation

Refer to illustrations 17.2, 17.4, 17.5a and 17.5b

Warning: *The air conditioning system is under high pressure. Do not loosen any hose fittings or remove any components until the system has been discharged. Air conditioning refrigerant should be properly discharged into an EPA-approved recovery/recycling unit by a dealer service department or an automotive air conditioning repair facility. Always wear eye protection when disconnecting air conditioning system fittings.*

1   Have the air conditioning system discharged (see the **Warning** above). Disconnect the negative cable from the battery.
Caution: *If the stereo in your vehicle is equipped with an anti-theft system, make sure you have the correct activation code before disconnecting the battery.* Remove the glove compartment assembly (see Chapter 11).

2   Disconnect the air conditioning lines at the firewall **(see illustration)**. Cap the open fittings after disassembly to prevent the entry of air or dirt.

3   Remove the ECM (see Chapter 6).

16.2 When disconnecting the condenser refrigerant lines, use two wrenches to prevent twisting the lines

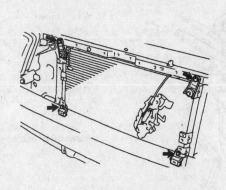

16.3 Remove the condenser mounting bolts (arrows)

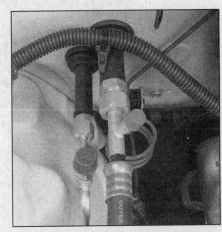

17.2 Disconnecting the air conditioning lines at the firewall

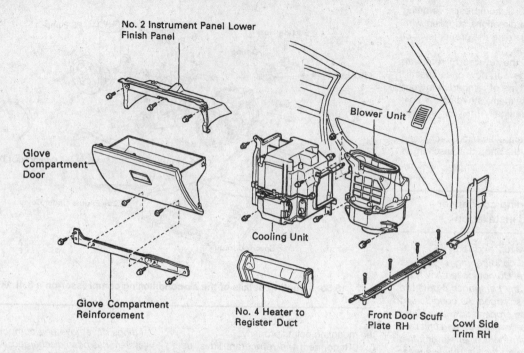

17.4 Remove the mounting bolts from the cooling unit and separate the assembly from the dash area

4   Remove nuts and screws retaining the evaporator unit to the firewall and pull the unit out of the vehicle (**see illustration**).

5   With the evaporator unit on the bench, remove the screws and clips and separate the top and bottom halves of the case and pull out the evaporator (**see illustrations**).

6   Pull the thermistor sensor probe from the evaporator core and unbolt the expansion valve and the two short refrigerant lines.

7   The evaporator core can be cleaned with a "fin comb" and blown off with compressed air. **Warning:** *Be sure to wear eye protection when using compressed air.*

8   If the evaporator core is replaced with a new unit, add 1.4 ounces of new refrigerant oil of the correct type (for R-134a systems) to the system.

9   The remainder of the installation is the reverse of the removal process. Be sure to use new O-rings, and new gaskets on the expansion valve.

10   Have the system evacuated, charged and leak tested by the shop that discharged it.

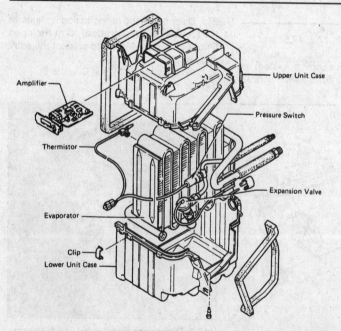

17.5a   Exploded view of the cooling unit and the evaporator on early T100 models

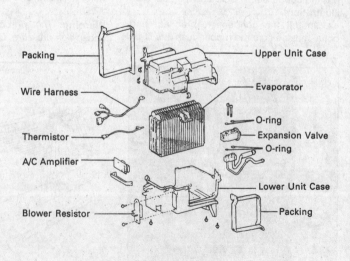

17.5b   Exploded view of the cooling unit and the evaporator on later 4Runners

Chapter 4
Fuel and exhaust systems

Contents

Specifications

Fuel system

Fuel pressure
Ignition ON, engine not running .... 38 to 46 psi
Engine idling
    Vacuum hose detached .... 38 to 44 psi
    Vacuum hose attached .... 31 to 37 psi
Fuel system hold pressure .... 21 psi
Fuel injector resistance .... 12 to 16 ohms
Idle Air Control (IAC) valve resistance
Cold (below 122-degrees F) .... 17 to 25 ohms
Hot (above 122-degrees F) .... 20 to 30 ohms
Cold start injector resistance .... 2 to 4 ohms
Idle Speed .... See Chapter 1

Torque specifications

Throttle body mounting bolts .... 144 in-lbs
Fuel rail mounting bolts .... 132 in-lbs
Fuel line banjo bolts .... 22 ft-lbs
Air intake plenum bolts/nuts .... 156 in-lbs

1 General information

The fuel system consists of a fuel tank, an electric fuel pump (located in the fuel tank), an EFI main relay, fuel injectors, a fuel pressure regulator, an air cleaner assembly and a throttle body unit. Early models are equipped with a Vacuum Switching Valve (VSV) that regulates the vacuum to the fuel pressure regulator according to engine drive-ability conditions. All OBD II fuel injection and emissions systems are equipped with the Mass Airflow Sensor instead of the Vane air-flow sensor or meter. Refer to Chapter 6 for additional information on the MAF and Vane type airflow detection sensors.

Electronic Fuel Injection (EFI) system

Electronic fuel injection uses timed impulses to inject the fuel directly into the intake port of each cylinder. The injectors are controlled by the Electronic Control Module (ECM). The ECM monitors various engine parameters and delivers the exact amount of fuel, in the correct sequence, into the intake ports. The throttle body serves only to control the amount of air passing into the system. Because each cylinder is equipped with an injector mounted immediately adjacent to the intake valve, much better control of the air/fuel mixture ratio is possible.

Early EFI models are equipped with a Vacuum Switching Valve (VSV) for fuel pres-sure control. This valve switches vacuum to the fuel pressure regulator during warm start-up if the computer detects high coolant temperatures. This allows for less fuel pressure and a leaner air/fuel mixture. This system uses the computer to activate the vacuum valve using data sent by the information sensors of the fuel injection and emission control systems (see Chapter 6).

Fuel pump and lines

Fuel is circulated from the fuel tank to the fuel injection system, and back to the fuel tank, through a pair of metal lines running along the underside of the vehicle. An electric fuel pump is attached to the fuel sending unit inside the fuel tank. A vapor return system routes all vapors and hot fuel back to the fuel tank through a separate return line.

The fuel pump will operate as long as the engine is cranking or running and the ECM is receiving ignition reference pulses from the electronic ignition system (see Chapter 5). If there are no reference pulses, the fuel pump will shut off after 2 or 3 seconds.

Exhaust system

The exhaust system includes an exhaust manifold fitted with an exhaust oxygen sensor, a catalytic converter, an exhaust pipe, and a muffler.

The catalytic converter is an emission control device added to the exhaust system to reduce pollutants. A single-bed converter is used in combination with a three-way (reduction) catalyst. Refer to Chapter 6 for more information regarding the catalytic converter.

---

2   Fuel pressure relief

Warning: *Gasoline is extremely flammable, so take extra precautions when you work on any part of the fuel system. Don't smoke or allow open flames or bare light bulbs near the work area, and don't work in a garage where a natural gas-type appliance (such as a water heater or a clothes dryer) with a pilot light is present. Since gasoline is carcinogenic, wear latex gloves when there's a possibility of being exposed to fuel, and, if you spill any fuel on your skin, rinse it off immediately with soap and water. Mop up any spills immediately and do not store fuel-soaked rags where they could ignite. The fuel system is under constant pressure, so, if any fuel lines are to be disconnected, the fuel pressure in the system must be relieved first. When you perform any kind of work on the fuel system, wear safety glasses and have a Class B type fire extinguisher on hand.*

1   Before servicing any fuel system component, you must relieve the fuel pressure to minimize the risk of fire or personal injury.
2   Remove the fuel filler cap - this will relieve any pressure built up in the tank.
3   There are two methods for relieving the fuel pressure on these models; disconnecting the fuel pump harness connector or removing the Circuit Opening Relay. Check both locations on your model to determine which will

be easier. To disconnect the fuel pump harness connector, refer to Section 7; disconnect the harness directly at the fuel tank. To disable the fuel pump circuit, locate the circuit opening relay and unplug it. Refer to **illustrations 3.6a through 3.6d** for the location of the circuit opening relay.
4   Start the engine and wait for the engine to stall, then turn the ignition key to Off.
5   The fuel system is now depressurized.
Note: *Place a rag around the fuel line before removing any hose clamp or fitting to absorb any fuel that spills out.*
6   Before working on the fuel system, disconnect the cable from the negative terminal of the battery. **Caution:** *If the stereo in your vehicle is equipped with an anti-theft system, make sure you have the correct activation code before disconnecting the battery.*

---

3   Fuel pump/fuel pressure - check

Warning: *Gasoline is extremely flammable, so take extra precautions when you work on any part of the fuel system. Don't smoke or allow open flames or bare light bulbs near the work area, and don't work in a garage where a natural gas-type appliance (such as a water heater or a clothes dryer) with a pilot light is present. Since gasoline is carcinogenic, wear latex gloves when there's a possibility of being exposed to fuel, and, if you spill any fuel on your skin, rinse it off immediately with soap and water. Mop up any spills immediately and do not store fuel-soaked rags where*

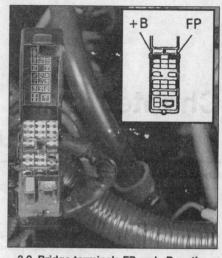

3.2 Bridge terminals FP and +B on the test connector using a jumper wire or paper clip

they could ignite. The fuel system is under constant pressure, so, if any fuel lines are to be disconnected, the fuel pressure in the system must be relieved first. When you perform any kind of work on the fuel system, wear safety glasses and have a Class B type fire extinguisher on hand.
Note: *1993 and 1994 V6 engines are equipped with the OBD I system. This earlier system has certain testing features and self diagnostic capabilities that all the other models do not. After 1995, these models are*

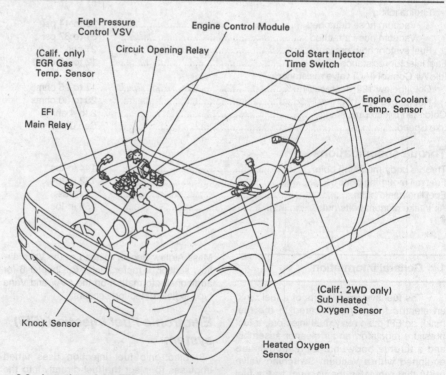

3.6a Location of the EFI main relay, the circuit opening relay and other fuel system components on 1993 and 1994 V6 T100 models

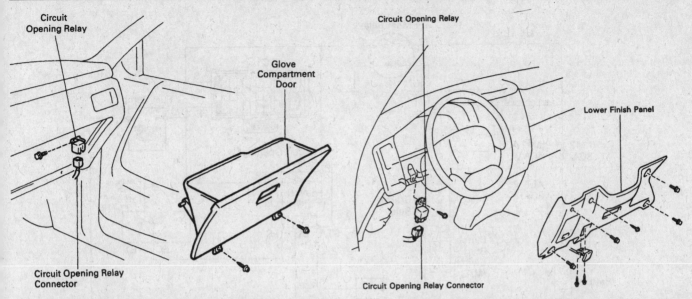

3.6b Location of the circuit opening relay on 1994 four-cylinder and 1995 and later T100 models

3.6c Location of the circuit opening relay on Tacoma models

equipped with the OBD II self diagnosis system. Refer to Chapter 6 for additional information on these updated fuel and emissions systems. For fuel system testing purposes, 1994 2.4L and 2.7L engines are considered an OBD I system. Because 1994 was a "changeover" year, these models are equipped with the OBD I fuel system design but have the later "updated" codes and self diagnostic capabilities.

Fuel pump operation check

Refer to illustrations 3.2, 3.6a, 3.6b, 3.6c, 3.6d, 3.6e and 3.6f

1   Turn ON the ignition switch (but do not start the engine).

2   Activate the fuel pump. On 1994 2.4L and 2.7L engines and 1993 and 1994 3.0L V6 engines (OBD I systems), bridge terminals +B and FP of the test connector with a jumper wire **(see illustration)**. On all other models (OBD II systems), use the ignition key to activate the fuel pump. **Note:** *On OBD II models, it is not possible to power the fuel pump using the test connector. On these models, start the engine to obtain fuel pressure readings.*

3   The fuel pump is now activated. Listen for fuel pump noise from the fuel tank.

4   Remove the jumper wire. Close the cap on the test connector.

5   Turn the ignition switch OFF.

6   If the fuel pump did not operate, inspect the following electrical components: the EFI 15-amp fuse and the ignition switch 30-amp fuse (AM2) (see Chapter 12) and/or the EFI main relay and the circuit opening relay, as described later in this section, battery voltage to the fuel pump, and the wiring and electrical connectors **(see illustrations)**.

Fuel pressure check

Refer to illustrations 3.11

Note: *The fuel pressure checks will require a special fuel pressure gauge and fittings that will adapt to the Toyota fuel line connectors.*

3.6d Location of the circuit opening relay on 4Runner models

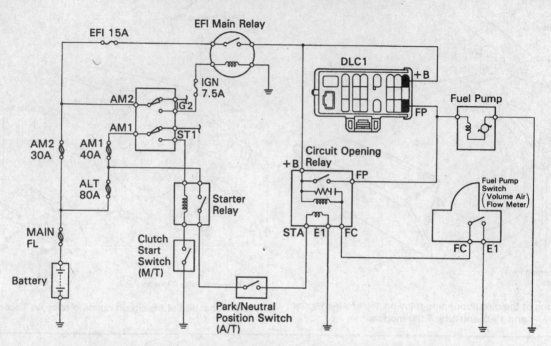

3.6e Typical wiring diagram of the fuel pump circuit on 1993 and 1994 V6 models

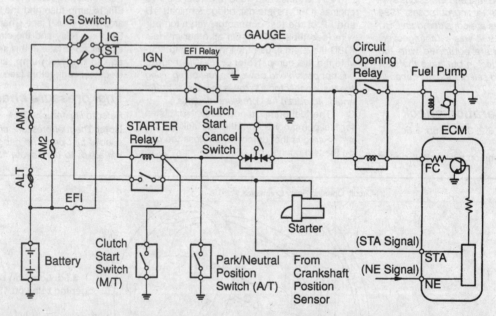

3.6f Typical wiring diagram of the fuel pump circuit on all models except 1993 and 1994 with V6 engines

Purchase the special fuel pressure gauge test kit at an automotive tool distributor or other automotive parts department that handles specialized automotive testing equipment.

7   A fuel pressure gauge, capable of measuring at least 60-psi, equipped with a banjo fitting on the end of the hose is required for the following procedure (available at an automotive parts store).

8   Remove the fuel tank cap to relieve any pressure that has built up in the tank.

9   Verify that the battery voltage is 12 volts or more (see Chapter 5).

10   Relieve the fuel pressure (see Section 2).

11   There are several different locations to install the fuel pressure gauge depending upon the model and engine type **(see illustration)**.

12   To attach the fuel pressure gauge, use the special banjo fitting on the fuel rail to attach the fuel pressure gauge to the fuel rail. Be sure to use sealing washers on both sides of the banjo fitting.

13   Wipe off any gasoline that has leaked

out of the fuel rail (or filter).

14   Place the transmission in Neutral (manual) or Park (automatic) and apply the parking brake.

15   On OBD I models, bridge terminals +B and FP of the test connector **(see illustration 3.2)**.

16   On all other models (OBD II), turn the ignition to ON (engine not running). Measure the fuel pressure and compare it to the fuel pressure listed in this Chapter's Specifications.

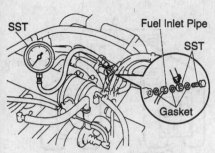

2.4L and 2.7L engines

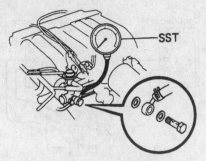

3.0L engines

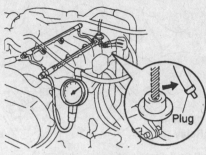

3.4L engines

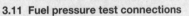

3.11 Fuel pressure test connections

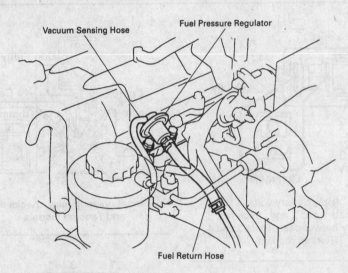

3.20a Location of the fuel pressure regulator on four-cylinder engines

a) If the pressure is high, check for a restricted fuel return line. If the line is clear, replace the pressure regulator.

b) If the pressure is low, pinch the fuel return line. If the pressure goes up, replace the fuel pressure regulator. If the pressure does not increase, check the fuel feed line, the fuel pump and the fuel filter.

17   On OBD I models, remove the jumper wire from the service electrical connector or fuel pump connector. **Note:** On OBD II models, it is not possible to power the fuel pump using the test connector. On these models, start the engine to obtain fuel pressure readings.

18   Start the engine.

a) Measure the fuel pressure at idle and compare your reading to the fuel pressure listed in this Chapter's Specifications.

b) If the pressure is not as specified, check the vacuum sensing hose and fuel pressure regulator (see Steps 20 through 24).

19   Stop the engine and verify that the fuel pressure remains at 21 psi or more for five minutes after the engine is turned off. If the pressure bleeds down, the fuel pressure regulator, the fuel pump or a fuel injector may be leaking.

Fuel pressure regulator check

Refer to illustrations 3.20a, 3.20b and 3.22

20   Disconnect and plug the vacuum hose from the fuel pressure regulator and connect a hand-held vacuum pump to the regulator. Start the engine and read the fuel pressure gauge without vacuum applied to the fuel pressure regulator. Apply vacuum to the regulator and check the fuel pressure again **(see illustrations)**. The fuel pressure should decrease as vacuum increases. Compare your readings with the values listed in this Chapter's Specifications. **Note:** *Refer to illustration 3.11 for the location of the fuel pressure regulator on the 3.4L engine.*

21   Reconnect the vacuum hose to the regulator and check the fuel pressure at idle, comparing your reading with the value listed in this Chapter's Specifications. Disconnect the hose and watch the gauge - the pressure should rise as soon as the hose is disconnected. If the pressure at idle was too high (with the hose disconnected), connect a vacuum gauge to the hose and check for vacuum. If there is no reading on the gauge, check the hose, the air intake plenum and intake manifold for a vacuum leak.

22   Some models are equipped with a Vacuum Switching Valve (VSV) for fuel pressure control **(see illustration)**. This valve switches vacuum to the fuel pressure regulator during warm start-up if the computer detects high coolant temperatures. This allows for less fuel pressure and a leaner air/fuel mixture. The computer regulates the VSV from information it receives from the sensors and consequently it regulates the fuel pressure. The VSV should allow air to pass through when it is energized (connected to battery voltage), but should not allow air to pass through when not energized. The resistance across the terminals of the VSV should be approxi-

3.20b Location of the fuel pressure regulator on 3.0L engines

3.22 Location of the VSV for fuel pressure control (used on 1993 and 1994 V6 models)

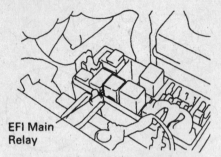

3.31 Locate and remove the EFI main relay and check for battery voltage to the relay with the ignition key ON (1994 T100 model shown)

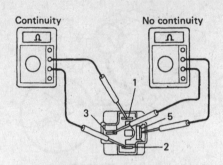

3.34a EFI main relay checks on the T100 and Tacoma models

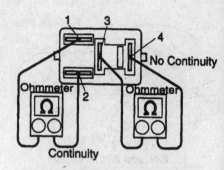

3.34b EFI main relay checks on the 4Runner models

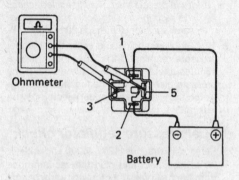

3.35a Apply battery voltage to terminals 1 and 2 and check for continuity between terminals 3 and 5 (T100 and Tacoma models)

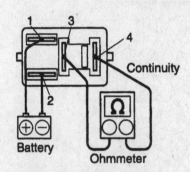

3.35b Apply battery voltage to terminals 1 and 2 and check for continuity between terminals 3 and 4 (4Runner models)

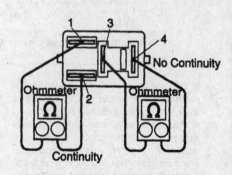

3.36a Circuit opening relay checks on T100 and Tacoma models

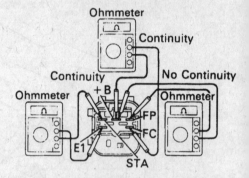

3.36b Circuit opening relay checks on 4Runner models

mately 30 to 50 ohms.

23   If the fuel pressure is LOW, pinch the fuel return line shut and watch the gauge. The pressure should rise slowly. If the pressure doesn't rise, the fuel pump is defective or there is a restriction in the fuel feed line. If the pressure rises sharply, replace the fuel pressure regulator (see Section 11).

24   If the indicated fuel pressure is too high, relieve the fuel pressure (see Section 2), disconnect the fuel return line and blow through it to check for blockage. If there is no blockage, replace the fuel pressure regulator (see Section 11).

25   If the fuel pressure does not fluctuate as described in Step 21, replace the fuel pressure regulator (see Section 11).

26   Relieve the fuel pressure and remove the fuel pressure gauge. Be sure to cover the fitting with a rag before loosening it.

27   Using new sealing washers, reattach the fuel line and banjo fitting to the fuel rail.

28   Wipe up any spilled gasoline.

29   Start the engine and check for leaks.

EFI main relay and circuit opening relay checks

Voltage checks

Refer to illustration 3.31

30   There are two relays involved in the fuel pump circuit: the EFI main relay and the circuit opening relay. The EFI main relay is located in the fuse/relay center in the engine compartment. The circuit opening relay is located under the dash in various locations depending upon the year and model of the vehicle. First, test for battery voltage to the EFI main relay and then the circuit opening relay.

31   Remove the EFI main relay from the electrical connector and, with the ignition key ON (engine not running), check for battery voltage **(see illustration)**.

32   If battery voltage is present, insert the relay back into the connector and check for battery voltage at the circuit opening relay **(see illustrations 3.6a, 3.6b, 3.6c and 3.6d)**.

33   If battery voltage is present at the relay connectors, check the relays.

EFI main relay

Refer to illustrations 3.34a, 3.34b, 3.35a and 3.35b

34   Using an ohmmeter, check for continuity across terminals 1 and 2 **(see illustrations)**. Check that there is no continuity across terminals 3 and 5 (all except 4Runner) or across terminals 3 and 4 (4Runner).

35   Connect a 12 volt battery to terminals 1 and 2 **(see illustrations)**. Using an ohmmeter, check for continuity. On all except 4Runner, there should be continuity across terminals 3 and 5. On 4Runner models, there

should be continuity between terminals 3 and 4. If the test results are incorrect, replace the relay.

Circuit opening relay

Refer to illustrations 3.36a, 3.36b, 3.37a and 3.37b

36   On all except 4Runner, check for continuity across terminals STA and E1 **(see illustration)**. Also, check for continuity across +B and FC. Check that there is no continuity across terminals +B and FP. On 4Runner models, check that there is continuity between terminals 1 and 2 but no continuity between terminals 3 and 4.

37   On all except 4Runner connect a 12-volt

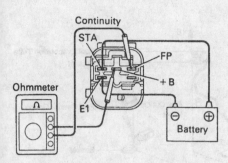

3.37a Apply battery voltage to terminals E1 and STA and check for continuity between terminals B+ and FP (T100 and Tacoma models)

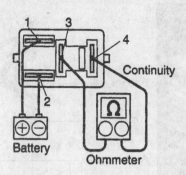

3.37b Apply battery voltage to terminals 1 and 2 and check for continuity between terminals 3 and 4 (4Runner models)

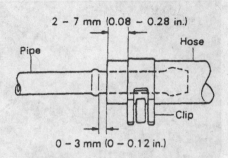

4.6 When attaching a section of rubber hose to a metal fuel line, be sure to overlap the hose as shown and secure it to the line with a new hose clamp of the proper type

battery to terminals STA and E1 **(see illustration)**. Check for continuity across terminals +B and FP. Continuity should exist. On 4Runner models check that there is continuity across terminals 3 and 4 with battery voltage applied to terminals 1 and 2. If the test results are incorrect, replace the relay.

4   Fuel lines and fittings - inspection and replacement

Warning: *Gasoline is extremely flammable, so take extra precautions when you work on any part of the fuel system. Don't smoke or allow open flames or bare light bulbs near the work area, and don't work in a garage where a natural gas-type appliance (such as a water heater or a clothes dryer) with a pilot light is present. Since gasoline is carcinogenic, wear latex gloves when there's a possibility of being exposed to fuel, and, if you spill any fuel on your skin, rinse it off immediately with soap and water. Mop up any spills immediately and do not store fuel-soaked rags where they could ignite. The fuel system is under constant pressure, so, if any fuel lines are to be disconnected, the fuel pressure in the system must be relieved first. When you perform any kind of work on the fuel system, wear safety glasses and have a Class B type fire extinguisher on hand.*

Inspection

1   Once in a while, you will have to raise the vehicle to service or replace some component (an exhaust pipe hanger, for example). Whenever you work under the vehicle, always inspect fuel lines and all fittings and connections for damage or deterioration.
2   Check all hoses and pipes for cracks, kinks, deformation or obstructions.
3   Make sure all hoses and pipe clips attach their associated hoses or pipes securely to the underside of the vehicle.
4   Verify all hose clamps attaching rubber hoses to metal fuel lines or pipes are snug enough to assure a tight fit between the hoses and pipes.

Replacement

Refer to illustration 4.6

5   If you must replace any damaged sections, use original equipment replacement hoses or pipes constructed from exactly the same material as the section you are replacing. Do not install substitutes constructed from inferior or inappropriate material or you could cause a fuel leak or a fire.
6   Always, before detaching or disassembling any part of the fuel line system, note the routing of all hoses and pipes and the orientation of all clamps and clips to assure that replacement sections are installed in exactly the same manner. When attaching hoses to metal lines, overlap them as shown **(see illustration)**.
7   Before detaching any part of the fuel system, be sure to relieve the fuel line and tank pressure (see Section 2). Cover the fitting being disconnected with a rag to absorb any fuel that may spray out.

5   Fuel tank – removal and installation

Refer to illustrations 5.5, 5.6, 5.7a and 5.7b
Warning: *Gasoline is extremely flammable, so take extra precautions when you work on any part of the fuel system. Don't smoke or allow open flames or bare light bulbs near the work area, and don't work in a garage where a natural gas-type appliance (such as a water heater or a clothes dryer) with a pilot light is present. Since gasoline is carcinogenic, wear latex gloves when there's a possibility of being exposed to fuel, and, if you spill any fuel on your skin, rinse it off immediately with soap and water. Mop up any spills immediately and do not store fuel-soaked rags where they could ignite. The fuel system is under constant pressure, so, if any fuel lines are to be disconnected, the fuel pressure in the system must be relieved first. When you perform any kind of work on the fuel system, wear safety glasses and have a Class B type fire extinguisher on hand.*
Note: *The following procedure is much easier*

to perform if the fuel tank is empty. Some tanks have a drain plug for this purpose. If the tank does not have a drain plug, drain the fuel into an approved fuel container using a commercially available siphoning kit (NEVER start the siphoning action by mouth) or wait until the fuel tank is nearly empty, if possible.
1   Remove the fuel tank filler cap to relieve fuel tank pressure.
2   Detach the cable from the negative terminal of the battery. **Caution:** *If the stereo in your vehicle is equipped with an anti-theft system, make sure you have the correct activation code before disconnecting the battery.*
3   If the tank still has fuel in it, you can drain it at the fuel filler hose after raising the vehicle. If the tank has a drain plug, remove it and allow the fuel to collect in an approved gasoline container.
4   Raise the vehicle and place it securely on jackstands.
5   Remove the screws from the top of the fuel filler neck and disconnect the fuel filler neck from the body of the vehicle **(see illustration)**. **Note:** *Some models do not have the filler neck attached near the top but instead have several bolts and nuts that attach the filler pipe to the body.*

5.5 Disconnect the bolts from the neck of the fuel tank filler pipe (arrows)

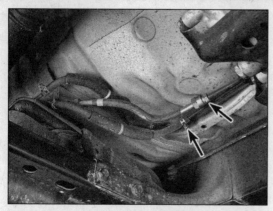

5.6 Disconnect the fuel lines (arrows) at the fuel tank. Use a back-up wrench on the stationary fitting when disconnecting threaded fuel line connections

6   Disconnect the fuel lines **(see illustration)** and the vapor return line. **Note:** *The fuel feed and return lines and the vapor return line are three different diameters, so reattachment is simplified. If you have any doubts, however, clearly label the three lines and the fittings. Be sure to plug the hoses to prevent leakage and contamination of the fuel system.*

7   Loosen the hose clamp(s) and detach the fuel filler neck from the tank **(see illustrations)**. If there is still fuel in the tank, siphon it out from the fuel feed port. Remember - NEVER start the siphoning action by mouth! Use a siphoning kit, which can be purchased at most auto parts stores.

8   If the fuel tank is equipped with a protective shield, remove the nuts and detach it from the underside of the chassis.

9   Support the fuel tank with a floor jack. Position a piece of wood between the jack head and the fuel tank to protect the tank.

10   Disconnect both fuel tank retaining straps and pivot them down until they are hanging out of the way.

11   Lower the tank enough to disconnect the wires and ground strap from the fuel pump/fuel gauge sending unit, if you have not already done so. Remove the tank from the vehicle.

12   Some models are equipped with an auxiliary fuel tank. Removal of these tanks is similar to the main fuel tank, but instead of being retained by straps, they are retained by bolts around the flange of the tank.

13   Installation is the reverse of removal.

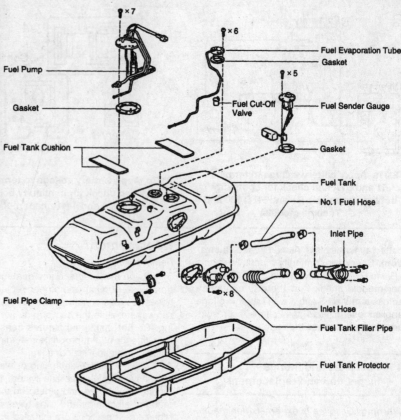

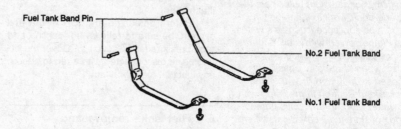

5.7a An exploded view of a typical fuel tank and surrounding components on a T100 model

6   Fuel tank cleaning and repair - general information

1   All repairs to the fuel tank or filler neck should be carried out by a professional who has experience in this critical and potentially dangerous work. Even after cleaning and flushing of the fuel system, explosive fumes can remain and ignite during repair of the tank.

2   If the fuel tank is removed from the vehicle, it should not be placed in an area where sparks or open flames could ignite the fumes coming out of the tank. Be especially careful inside garages where a natural gas-type appliance is located; because the pilot light could cause an explosion.

7   Fuel pump - removal and installation

Warning: *Gasoline is extremely flammable, so take extra precautions when you work on any part of the fuel system. Don't smoke or allow open flames or bare light bulbs near the work area, and don't work in a garage where a natural gas-type appliance (such as a water heater or a clothes dryer) with a pilot light is present. Since gasoline is carcinogenic, wear latex gloves when there's a possibility of being exposed to fuel, and, if you spill any fuel on your skin, rinse it off immediately with soap and water. Mop up any spills immediately and do not store fuel-soaked rags where they could ignite. The fuel system is under constant pressure, so, if any fuel lines are to be disconnected, the fuel pressure in the system must be relieved first. When you perform any kind of work on the fuel system, wear safety glasses and have a Class B type fire extinguisher on hand.*
Note: *T100's are equipped with a separate fuel pump and fuel level sending unit which are both mounted in the top of the fuel tank. The electrical connectors will have different configurations than the fuel level sending unit/fuel pump assemblies in other models but the tests and the replacement procedures will be the same.*

Removal

Refer to illustrations 7.6, 7.9, 7.10 and 7.13

1   Relieve the fuel system pressure (see Section 2).

2   Disconnect the cable from the negative terminal of the battery. **Caution:** *If the stereo in your vehicle is equipped with an anti-theft system, make sure you have the correct activation code before disconnecting the battery.*

3   Remove the fuel tank from the vehicle (see Section 5).

4   Disconnect the electrical connector.

5   Disconnect the fuel lines from the fuel pump assembly at the fuel tank.

6   Remove the fuel pump/sending unit retaining bolts **(see illustration)**.

7   Carefully withdraw the fuel pump/fuel level sending unit assembly from the fuel tank.

8   Pry the lower end of the fuel pump loose from the bracket.

9   Remove the rubber gasket from the fuel pump assembly cover **(see illustration)**.

10   Remove the rubber cushion and clip securing the inlet screen to the pump **(see illustration)**.

11   Remove the screen and inspect it for contamination. If it is dirty, replace it.

12   If you are only replacing the fuel pump inlet screen, install the new screen, the clip and the rubber cushion, push the lower end of the pump back into the bracket and install the pump/sending unit assembly in the fuel tank.

13   If you are replacing the fuel pump, remove the hose clamp at the upper end of the pump and disconnect the pump from the

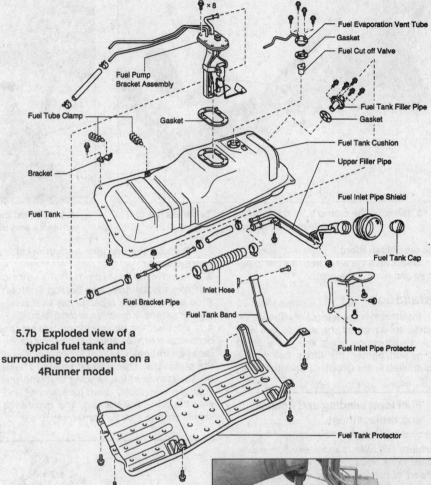

5.7b Exploded view of a typical fuel tank and surrounding components on a 4Runner model

7.9 Remove the rubber gasket and replace it with a new one to prevent leakage

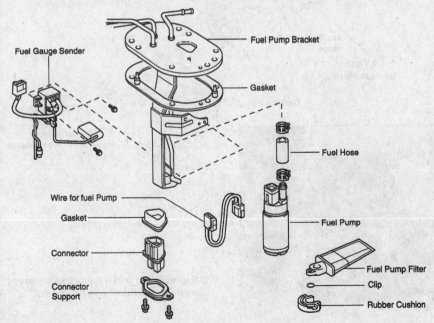

7.6 Lift the fuel pump/sending unit assembly from the fuel tank at an angle so as not to damage the inlet screen or float arm

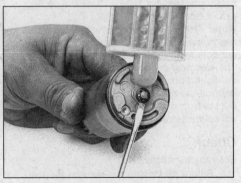

7.10 Remove the clip that retains the pump screen to the bottom of the fuel pump

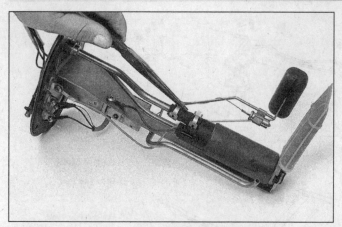

7.13 Remove the clamp from the fuel line and separate the fuel line from the fuel pump

8.4 Position the probes of the ohmmeter onto the correct terminals and observe the fuel level sending unit resistance

hose **(see illustration)**.

14   Disconnect the wires from the pump terminals and remove the pump.

Installation

15   Installation is the reverse of removal. On models so equipped, be sure to use new sealing washers on either side of the banjo fitting, and tighten the fitting bolt to the torque listed in this Chapter's Specifications.

8   Fuel level sending unit - check and replacement

Warning: *Gasoline is extremely flammable, so take extra precautions when you work on any part of the fuel system. Don't smoke or allow open flames or bare light bulbs near the work area, and don't work in a garage where a natural gas-type appliance (such as a water heater or a clothes dryer) with a pilot light is present. Since gasoline is carcinogenic, wear latex gloves when there's a possibility of being exposed to fuel, and, if you spill any fuel on your skin, rinse it off immediately with soap and water. Mop up any spills immediately and do not store fuel-soaked rags where they could ignite. The fuel system is under constant pressure, so, if any fuel lines are to be disconnected, the fuel pressure in the system must be relieved first. When you perform any kind of work on the fuel system, wear safety glasses and have a Class B type fire extinguisher on hand.*
Note: *T100's are equipped with a separate fuel pump and fuel level sending unit which are both mounted in the top of the fuel tank. The electrical connectors will have different configurations than the fuel level sending unit/fuel pump assemblies in other models but the tests and the replacement procedures will be the same.*

Check

Refer to illustrations 8.4

1   Before performing the tests on the fuel level sending unit, determine the actual fuel level in the fuel tank.

2   Remove the fuel tank from the vehicle (see Section 5).

3   Remove the fuel pump/fuel level sending unit from the fuel tank (see Section 7). **Note:** *T100 models have a separate fuel level sending unit assembly mounted in the fuel tank.*

4   Position the ohmmeter probes on the connector terminals and check for resistance **(see illustration)**. Use the 200-ohm scale on the ohmmeter. Using an ohmmeter, check the resistance of the sending unit with the float arm completely down (tank empty) and with the arm up (tank full). The resistance should change steadily from empty to full.

5   When the tank is nearly empty, the resistance of the sending unit should be approximately 110 ohms.

6   With the fuel tank completely full, the resistance should be approximately 3 ohms.

7   If the readings are incorrect, replace the sending unit.

Replacement

8   Remove the fuel pump/fuel level sending unit assembly from the fuel tank (see Section 7).

9   Carefully angle the sending unit out of the opening without damaging the fuel level

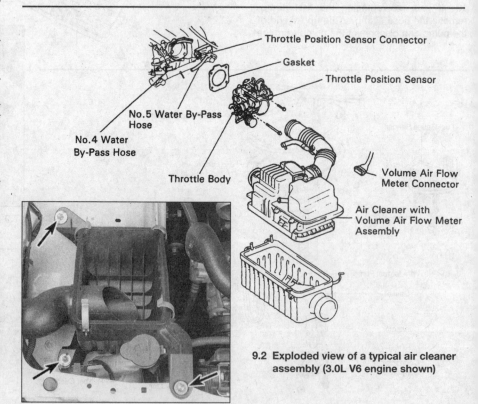

9.2 Exploded view of a typical air cleaner assembly (3.0L V6 engine shown)

9.3 Remove the bolts (arrows) that retain the air cleaner housing to the engine compartment

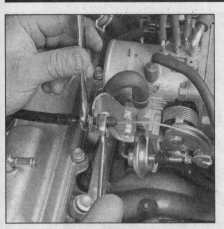

10.2 Loosen the locknut on the threaded portion of the accelerator cable

10.3 Rotate the throttle lever and remove the cable end from the slot

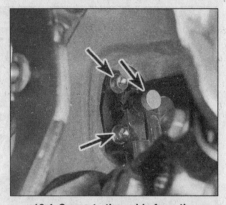

10.4 Separate the cable from the accelerator pedal and slide the cable end (center arrow) out of the slot in the housing - to free the cable casing, remove the two bolts (upper and lower arrows)

float located at the bottom of the assembly.

10   Disconnect the electrical connectors from the sending unit.

11   Remove the screw from the side of the sending unit bracket and separate the sending unit from the assembly.

12   Installation is the reverse of removal.

9   Air cleaner assembly - removal and installation

Refer to illustration 9.2 and 9.3

1   Detach the clips and remove the air filter and the filter element (see Chapter 1).

2   Disconnect the air intake hose from the assembly **(see illustration)**.

3   Remove the three bolts and remove the air cleaner assembly from the engine compartment **(see illustration)**.

4   Installation is the reverse of removal.

10   Accelerator cable - removal, installation and adjustment

Refer to illustrations 10.2, 10.3 and 10.4

Removal

1   Detach the cable from the negative terminal of the battery. **Caution:** *If the stereo in your vehicle is equipped with an anti-theft system, make sure you have the correct activation code before disconnecting the battery.*

2   Loosen the locknut on the threaded portion of the throttle cable at the throttle body **(see illustration)**.

3   Rotate the throttle lever and slip the throttle cable end out of the slot in the lever **(see illustration)**.

4   Detach the throttle cable from the accelerator pedal **(see illustration)**. Remove the two bolts securing the cable casing to the firewall.

5   From inside the engine compartment, pull the cable through the firewall.

Installation and adjustment

6   Installation is the reverse of removal. Make sure the cable casing grommet seats properly in the firewall.

7   To adjust the cable, fully depress the accelerator pedal and check that the throttle is fully opened.

8   If not fully opened, loosen the locknuts, depress accelerator pedal and adjust the cable until the throttle is fully open.

9   Tighten the locknuts and recheck the adjustment. Make sure the throttle closes fully when the pedal is released.

11   Electronic Fuel Injection (EFI) system - general information

Refer to illustrations 11.1a, 11.1b and 11.1c

1   These models are equipped with an

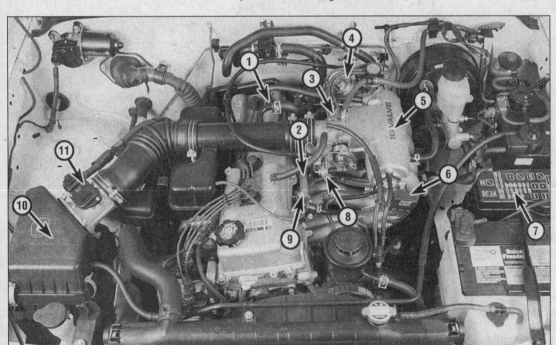

11.1a Underhood component locations for the Electronic Fuel Injection (EFI) system on four-cylinder engines (for information on the MAF, TPS and EGR, see Chapter 6)

1   *PCV valve*
2   *Fuel rail and injectors*
3   *Throttle Position Sensor (TPS)*
4   *Exhaust Gas Recirculation (EGR) valve*
5   *Air intake plenum*
6   *Test Connector*
7   *Fuse and relay box*
8   *Dashpot*
9   *Fuel pressure regulator*
10   *Air cleaner assembly*
11   *Mass airflow (MAF) sensor*

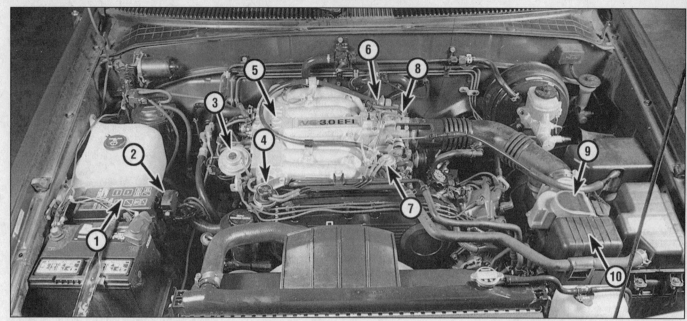

11.1b Underhood component locations for the Electronic Fuel Injection (EFI) system on 3.0L V6 engines (for information on the airflow meter, TPS and EGR, see Chapter 6)

1	Fuse box	4	EGR vacuum modulator	8	Throttle Position Sensor (TPS)
2	Test Connector	5	Air intake plenum	9	Airflow meter
3	Exhaust Gas Recirculation (EGR) valve	6	Dashpot	10	Air cleaner assembly
		7	Fuel pressure regulator		

Electronic Fuel Injection (EFI) system. The EFI system is composed of three basic subsystems: the fuel delivery system, the air induction system and the electronic control system **(see illustrations)**.

Fuel system

2   An electric fuel pump located inside the fuel tank supplies fuel under constant pressure to the fuel rail, which distributes fuel evenly to all injectors. From the fuel rail, fuel is injected into the intake ports, just above the intake valves, by fuel injectors. The amount of fuel supplied by the injectors is precisely controlled by an Electronic Control

11.1c Underhood component locations for the Electronic Fuel Injection (EFI) system on 3.4L V6 engines (for information on the MAF, TPS and EGR, see Chapter 6)

1	Air cleaner assembly	5	Air intake plenum
2	Mass airflow (MAF) sensor	6	Fuel pressure regulator (under plenum)
3	Throttle Position Sensor (TPS)	7	Test Connector
4	EGR valve (under plenum)	8	Fuse and relay box

12.6 With the engine off, use aerosol carburetor cleaner (make sure it is safe for use with catalytic converters and oxygen sensors) and a rag to clean the throttle body - open the throttle plate so you can clean behind it

12.7 Use a stethoscope or a screwdriver to determine if the injectors are working properly - they should make a steady clicking sound that rises and falls with engine speed changes

Module (ECM). A pressure regulator controls system pressure in relation to intake manifold vacuum. A fuel filter between the fuel pump and the fuel rail filters fuel to protect the components of the system.

Air induction system

3   The air induction system consists of an air filter housing, the throttle body and the duct connecting the two. An Intake Air Temperature (IAT) sensor monitors the temperature of the incoming air. This information helps the ECM determine the amount of fuel to be injected by the injectors. The throttle plate inside the throttle body is controlled by the driver. As the throttle plate opens, the speed of the incoming air increases, which lowers the temperature of the air. The IAT sends this information to the ECM and the ECM signals the injectors to increase the amount of fuel delivered to the intake ports.

Electronic control system

4   The Computer Control System controls the EFI and other systems by means of an Electronic Control Module (ECM), which employs a microcomputer. The ECM receives signals from a number of information sensors which monitor such variables as intake air temperature, throttle angle, coolant temperature, engine rpm, vehicle speed and exhaust oxygen content. These signals help the ECM determine the injection duration necessary for the optimum air/fuel ratio. Some of these sensors and their corresponding ECM-controlled relays are not contained within EFI components, but are located throughout the engine compartment. For further information regarding the ECM and its relationship to the engine electrical and ignition system, see Chapter 6.

12 Electronic Fuel Injection (EFI) system - check

Refer to illustrations 12.6, 12.7, 12.8 and 12.9
1   Check the ground wire connections for

12.8 Install the "noid" light into the fuel injector electrical connector and check to see that it blinks with the engine running

tightness. Check all wiring and electrical connectors that are related to the system. Loose electrical connectors and poor grounds can cause many problems that resemble more serious malfunctions.
2   Check to see that the battery is fully charged, as the control unit and sensors depend on an accurate supply voltage in order to properly meter the fuel.
3   Check the air filter element - a dirty or partially blocked filter will severely impede performance and economy (see Chapter 1).
4   If a blown fuse is found, replace it and see if it blows again. If it does, search for a grounded wire in the harness related to the system.
5   Check the air intake duct from the air cleaner housing to the intake manifold for leaks, which will result in an excessively lean mixture. Also check the condition of the vacuum hoses connected to the intake manifold.
6   Remove the air intake duct from the throttle body and check for carbon and residue build-up. If it's dirty, clean it with aerosol carburetor cleaner (make sure the can says it's safe for use with oxygen sensors and catalytic converters) and a shop towel **(see illustration)**.

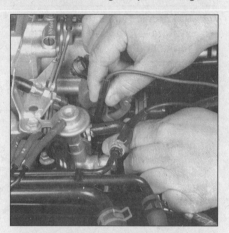

12.9 Using an ohmmeter, measure the resistance across the terminals of the injector

7   With the engine running, place a stethoscope against each injector, one at a time, and listen for a clicking sound, indicating operation **(see illustration)**. If you don't have an automotive stethoscope you can use a long screwdriver; just place the tip of the screwdriver against the injector body and press your ear against the handle.
8   If there is a problem with an injector, purchase a special injector test light ("noid" light) and install it into the injector electrical connector **(see illustration)**. Start the engine and make sure that each injector connector flashes the noid light. This will test for the proper voltage signal to the injector.
9   With the engine OFF and the fuel injector electrical connectors disconnected, measure the resistance of each injector **(see illustration)**. Each injector should measure about 12 to 16 ohms. If not, the injector is probably faulty.
10   Check the self-diagnosis system for any stored trouble codes (see Chapter 6).
11   The remainder of the system checks should be left to a dealer service department or other qualified repair shop, as there is a chance that the control unit may be damaged if not performed properly.

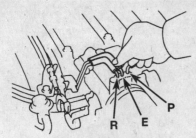

Port name	At idling	At 3,500rpm
E	No vacuum	Vacuum
R	No vacuum	Vacuum
P	No vacuum	Vacuum

13.2a Throttle body vacuum port guide and table for 1993 and 1994 models

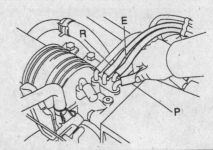

Port name	At idle	At 3,500 rpm
P	Vacuum	Vacuum
E	No vacuum	Vacuum
R	No vacuum	Vacuum

13.2b Throttle body vacuum port guide and table for 1995 and 1996 models

13 Electronic Fuel Injection (EFI) system - component check and replacement

Warning: *Gasoline is extremely flammable, so take extra precautions when you work on*

13.2c Throttle body vacuum port guide and table for 1997 and 1998 models

Port name	At idle	3,500 rpm or more
E	No vacuum	Vacuum
R	No vacuum	Vacuum

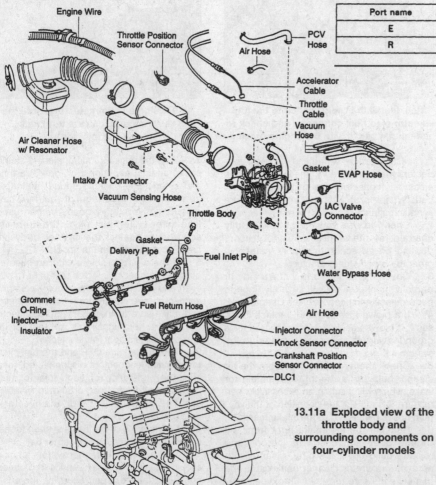

13.11a Exploded view of the throttle body and surrounding components on four-cylinder models

any part of the fuel system. Don't smoke or allow open flames or bare light bulbs near the work area, and don't work in a garage where a natural gas-type appliance (such as a water heater or a clothes dryer) with a pilot light is present. Since gasoline is carcinogenic, wear latex gloves when there's a possibility of being exposed to fuel, and, if you spill any fuel on your skin, rinse it off immediately with soap and water. Mop up any spills immediately and do not store fuel-soaked rags where they could ignite. The fuel system is under constant pressure, so, if any fuel lines are to be disconnected, the fuel pressure in the system must be relieved first. When you perform any kind of work on the fuel system, wear safety glasses and have a Class B type fire extinguisher on hand.

Caution: *If the stereo in your vehicle is equipped with an anti-theft system, make sure you have the correct activation code before disconnecting the battery.*

Throttle body

Refer to illustrations 13.2a, 13.2b, 13.2c, 13.11a and 13.11b

Check

1   Verify that the throttle linkage operates smoothly.

2   Start the engine, detach each vacuum hose and, using a vacuum gauge, check the vacuum at each port on the throttle body with the engine at idle and above idle, then com-

pare your observations with the accompanying tables **(see illustrations)**.

Replacement

Warning: *Wait until the engine is completely cool before beginning this procedure.*

3   Detach the cable from the negative terminal of the battery (see the **Caution** at the beginning of this section).

4   Loosen the hose clamps and remove the air intake duct.

5   Detach the accelerator cable from the throttle lever (see Section 8).

6   Detach the throttle cable bracket and set it aside (it's not necessary to detach the throttle cable from the bracket).

7   If your vehicle is equipped with an automatic transmission, detach the throttle valve (TV) cable from the throttle linkage (see Chapter 7B), detach the TV cable brackets from the engine and set the cable and brackets aside.

8   Clearly label, then detach, all vacuum and coolant hoses from the throttle body. Plug the coolant hoses to prevent coolant loss.

9   Disconnect the electrical connector from the throttle position sensor (TPS).

10   Remove the throttle body mounting bolts.

11   Detach the throttle body and gasket **(see illustrations)** from the intake manifold. Refer to **illustration 9.2** for an exploded view of the throttle body on the 3.0L engine.

12   Using a soft brush and aerosol carburetor cleaner, thoroughly clean the throttle body casting, then blow out all passages with compressed air. **Caution:** *Do not clean the throttle position sensor with anything. Just wipe it off carefully with a clean, soft cloth.*

13   Installation of the throttle body is the reverse of removal.

14   Be sure to tighten the throttle body mounting bolts to the torque listed in this Chapter's Specifications.

Fuel pressure regulator

Refer to illustrations 13.19a, 13.19b and 3.19c

Check

15   Refer to the fuel pump/fuel pressure check procedure (see Section 3).

Replacement

16   Relieve the fuel pressure (see Section 2) and detach the cable from the negative terminal of the battery (see the **Caution** at the beginning of this section).

17   Detach the vacuum sensing hose from the regulator.

18   Place a metal container or shop towel under the fuel return hose.

19   Squeeze the hose clamp and detach the fuel return hose from the regulator **(see illustrations)**.

20   On 2.4L, 2.7L and 3.4L engines, remove the pressure regulator mounting bolts and detach the pressure regulator from the fuel rail. On 3.0L engines, unscrew the regulator

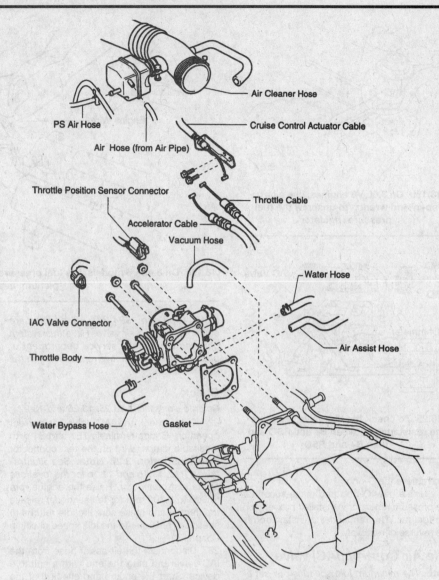

13.11b Exploded view of the throttle body and surrounding components on 3.4L V6 models

13.19a On four-cylinder engines, to remove the fuel pressure regulator from the fuel rail, detach the fuel return line, remove the two regulator bolts and separate the regulator from the fuel rail

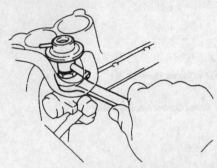

13.19b On 3.0L V6 engines, use a large open-end wrench to unscrew the fuel pressure regulator

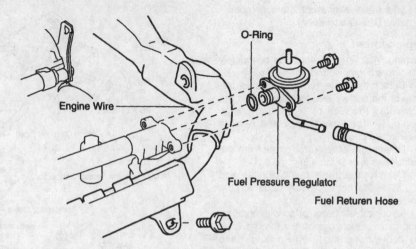

13.19c On 3.4L V6 models, the fuel pressure regulator is located on the rear of the intake plenum, near the firewall

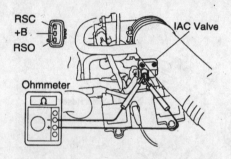

13.25 To check the IAC valve, measure the resistance between B+ and RSC and then B+ and RSO

and retrieve the O-ring.

21   Use a new O-ring and make sure that the pressure regulator is installed properly on the fuel rail. The remainder of installation is the reverse of removal.

Idle Air Control (IAC) valve

Note: *The minimum idle speed is pre-set at the factory and should not require adjustment under normal operating conditions; however if the throttle body has been replaced or you suspect the minimum idle speed has been tampered with (for example, if the idle speed screw was removed from the throttle body) have the vehicle checked by a dealer service department or other qualified automotive repair shop.*

Note: *1993 and 1994 3.0L V6 engines are equipped with an air valve. Have this system checked by a dealer service department or other qualified automotive repair facility in the event of failure.*

Check

Refer to illustrations 13.25, 13.26 and 13.27

22   First, check the IAC valve for correct operation. Bridge terminals TE1 and E1 with a suitable jumper wire on the test connector **(see illustration 3.2)**. **Note:** *See illustrations 11.1a, 11.1b and 11.1c for the locations of the test connector.* Raise the engine rpm to 900 to 1,300 rpm for ten seconds, release the throttle and make sure the idle returns to specified rpm (refer to the idle speed check in Chapter 1).

23   Disconnect the air assist hose from the IAC valve and plug the end with a suitable device. Start the engine and check that the idle speed lowers to approximately 500 rpm. The engine may stall at this time. If the engine rpm remains higher, there is most likely an air intake leak in the IAC valve, gasket or hoses that relate to the throttle body system.

24   Install the air assist hose and remove the jumper wire from the test connector.

25   Next, disconnect the IAC valve harness connector. Measure the resistance between terminals +B and RSC and then +B and RSO **(see illustration)**. Refer to the Specifications listed in this Chapter. If the resistance is incorrect, replace the IAC valve with a new one.

26   Also check the operation of the IAC valve. For this test it will be necessary to remove the IAC valve from the throttle body (see Steps 28 through 31). Use a jumper wire and connect the B+ (positive) side of the battery to terminal +B on the IAC and negative jumper lead (-) to the RSC terminal on the IAC valve. The valve should be closed **(see illustration)**.

27   Next, use a jumper wire and connect the B+ (positive) side of the battery to terminal +B on the IAC and negative jumper lead (-) to the RSO terminal on the IAC valve. The valve should be open **(see illustration)**.

Replacement

Refer to illustrations 13.29

28   If you find it difficult to access the IAC valve screws, remove the throttle body (see Steps 3 through 11).

29   Remove the mounting screws and detach the valve and gasket **(see illustration)**.

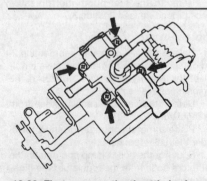

13.29 First, remove the throttle body and then remove the mounting screws (arrows) that retain the IAC valve to the throttle body

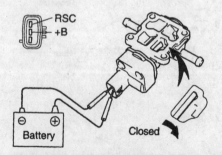

13.26 With battery voltage applied to RSC and B+, the shutter should close

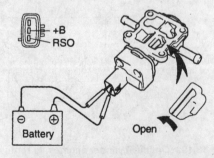

13.27 With battery voltage applied to B+ and RSO, the shutter should open

13.40 Remove the bolts (arrows) that retain the fuel rail to the intake manifold (four-cylinder engine shown)

13.41 Remove the fuel rail with the injectors attached

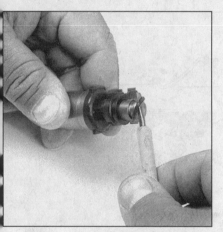

13.43a Remove the O-ring from the injector

13.43b Remove the grommet from the top of the injector

13.43c Remove the O-rings from the bores in the intake manifold

30   If you're replacing the valve, be sure to install the Temperature Vacuum Valve (TVV) from the original assembly into the new unit (if equipped).

31   Installation of the valve is the reverse of removal. Be sure to use a new gasket.

Fuel rail and fuel injectors

Refer to illustrations 13.40, 13.41, 13.43a, 13.43b and 13.43c

Check

32   Refer to the fuel injection system checking procedure (see Section 10).

Replacement

33   Relieve the fuel pressure (see Section 2).

34   Detach the cable from the negative terminal of the battery (see the **Caution** at the beginning of this Section).

35   Remove the PCV hose from the cylinder head and intake manifold.

36   Remove the air intake plenum (see Steps 70 through 79).

37   Carefully mark each injector connector with a felt pen or paint. Disconnect the fuel injector electrical connectors and set the injector wire harness aside.

38   Detach the vacuum sensing hose from

the fuel pressure regulator.

39   Disconnect the fuel lines from the fuel pressure regulator and the fuel rail.

40   Remove the fuel rail mounting bolts **(see illustration)**.

41   Remove the fuel rail with the fuel injectors attached **(see illustration)**.

42   Pull the fuel injector(s) straight out from the fuel rail.

43   If you intend to re-use the same injectors, replace the grommets and O-rings **(see illustrations)**.

44   Installation of the fuel injectors is the reverse of removal.

45   Tighten the fuel rail mounting bolts to the torque listed in this Chapter's Specifications.

Cold start injector (1993 and 1994 3.0L models)

Refer to illustrations 13.47 and 13.52

Check

46   Disconnect the electrical connector from the cold start injector.

47   Using an ohmmeter, measure the resistance between the injector terminals **(see illustration)**. Compare your measurement to

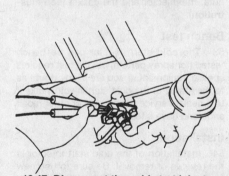

13.47 Disconnect the cold start injector and check the resistance

the resistance listed in this Chapter's Specifications.

a) *If the indicated resistance is within the specified range, the cold start injector is okay. Check the start injector time switch for correct operation (see Steps 55 through 58).*

b) *If the indicated resistance isn't within the specified range, replace the cold start injector.*

48   Connect the cold start injector electrical connector.

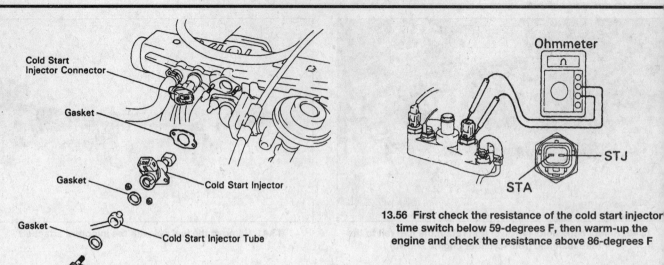

13.52 Remove the cold start injector mounting nuts or bolts

13.56 First check the resistance of the cold start injector time switch below 59-degrees F, then warm-up the engine and check the resistance above 86-degrees F

Removal

49 Relieve the fuel pressure (see Section 2). Disconnect the cable from the negative terminal of the battery (see **Caution** at the beginning of this section).

50 Disconnect the cold start injector electrical connector.

51 Place a metal container or shop towel under the banjo fitting and remove the banjo bolt and sealing washers. Discard the washers.

52 Remove the cold start injector mounting nuts, the injector and the gasket (**see illustration**).

Bench test

53 The cold start injector can be bench tested (for spray pattern) but the test requires special equipment. If you are in any doubt as to the status of the cold start injector, take it to a dealer service department or other repair shop and have it tested.

Installation

54 Installation of the cold start injector is the reverse of removal. Be sure to use new sealing washers on each side of the banjo fitting.

Cold start injector time switch (1993 and 1994 3.0L models)

Refer to illustration 13.56

Check

55 Disconnect the electrical connector from the start injector time switch and using an ohmmeter, check the resistance between each terminal. **Note:** *The cold start injector time switch is located next to the thermostat housing).*

56 First, check the resistance of the switch with the engine cold (below 59-degrees F). It

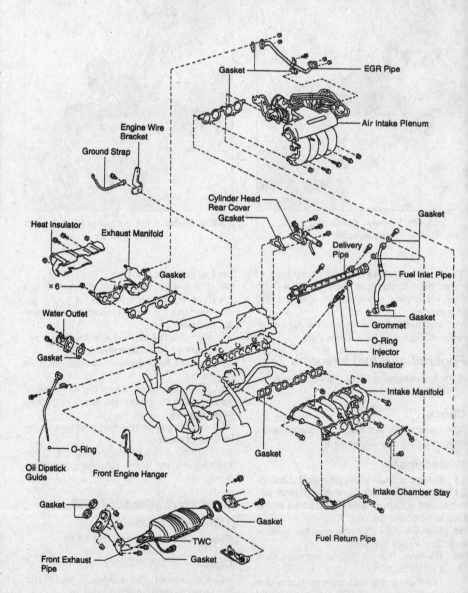

13.65a Exploded view of the air intake plenum and surrounding components on the four-cylinder engines

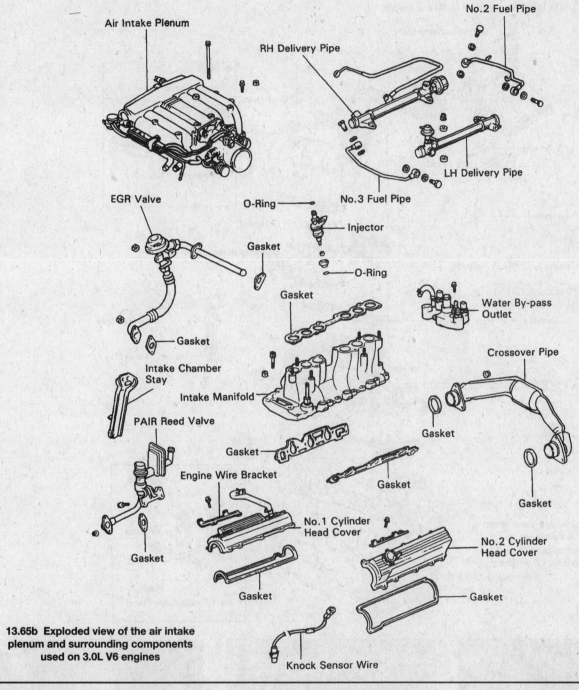

Air Intake Plenum

No.2 Fuel Pipe

RH Delivery Pipe

LH Delivery Pipe

No.3 Fuel Pipe

EGR Valve

O-Ring

Injector

Gasket

O-Ring

Gasket

Water By-pass Outlet

Gasket

Intake Chamber Stay

Crossover Pipe

Intake Manifold

Gasket

PAIR Reed Valve

Gasket

Gasket

Gasket

Gasket

Engine Wire Bracket

No.1 Cylinder Head Cover

No.2 Cylinder Head Cover

Gasket

Gasket

Gasket

Gasket

Knock Sensor Wire

13.65b Exploded view of the air intake plenum and surrounding components used on 3.0L V6 engines

should have 30 to 50 ohms resistance **(see illustration)**.

57   Next, warm up the engine (above 86-degrees F) and check the resistance of the switch. It should read 70 to 90 ohms resistance.

58   Check the resistance of terminal STA to ground. It should read 30 to 90 ohms. **Note:** *Terminal STA is the terminal which corresponds with the black/red wire on the wiring harness.*

Replacement

Warning: *Wait until the engine is completely cool before beginning this procedure.*

59   Prepare the new switch by wrapping the threads with Teflon sealing tape.

60   Use a deep socket and remove the switch from the engine.

61   Install the new switch as quickly as possible to minimize coolant loss. Tighten the switch securely. Check the coolant level and add some, if necessary.

Air intake plenum

Refer to illustrations 13.65a, 13.65b, 13.65c, 13.66, 13.68 and 13.70

Removal

Warning: *Wait until the engine is completely*

cool before beginning this procedure.

62   Detach the cable from the negative terminal of the battery (see the **Caution** at the beginning of this section).

63   Disconnect the electrical connectors at the ISC/IAC valve, throttle position sensor (TPS) and EGR/EVAP canister control solenoid.

64   Detach the accelerator cable (see Section 8) and transmission linkage (see Chapter 7) from the throttle body assembly.

65   Remove the EGR pipe from the EGR valve **(see illustrations)**.

66   Clearly label, then detach, the vacuum lines from the air intake plenum, the EGR

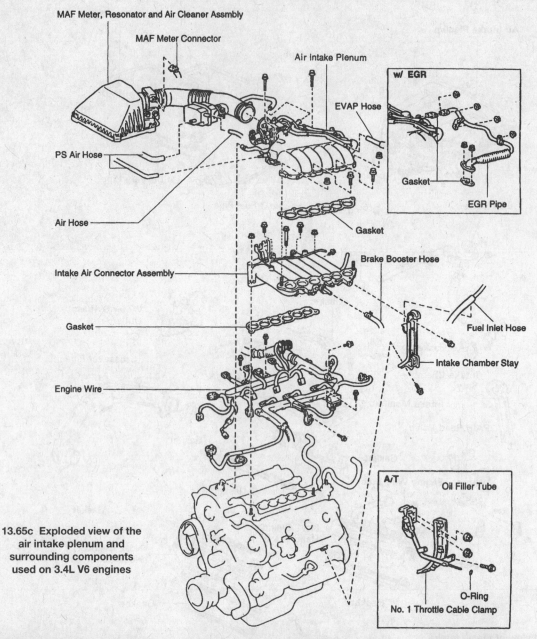

MAF Meter, Resonator and Air Cleaner Assmbly

MAF Meter Connector

Air Intake Plenum

EVAP Hose

w/ EGR

Gasket

EGR Pipe

PS Air Hose

Air Hose

Gasket

Intake Air Connector Assembly

Brake Booster Hose

Fuel Inlet Hose

Gasket

Intake Chamber Stay

Engine Wire

A/T

Oil Filler Tube

O-Ring

No. 1 Throttle Cable Clamp

13.65c Exploded view of the air intake plenum and surrounding components used on 3.4L V6 engines

13.66 Carefully label each vacuum line

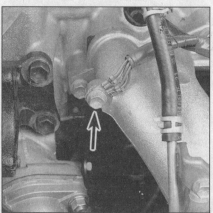

13.68 Remove the bolt (arrow) that retains the ground connectors to the intake manifold

13.70 Remove the bolts (arrows) that retain the air intake plenum to the intake manifold

14.1a Spray penetrating lubricant onto the exhaust bolts before attempting to remove them

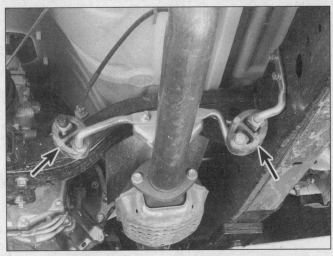

14.1b Check the condition of the rubber hangers (arrows)

valve and the fuel pressure regulator **(see illustration)**.

67   Detach the PCV system by disconnecting the hose from the fitting on the air intake plenum.

68   Remove the plenum ground cable and bolt (if equipped) **(see illustration)**.

69   Detach the coolant hoses from the throttle body and plug them.

70   Remove the air intake plenum retaining bolts and nuts **(see illustration)** and the lower (side) retaining bolts.

71   Remove the air intake plenum and throttle body as an assembly from the lower intake manifold.

Installation

72   Be sure to clean and inspect the mounting surface of the lower intake manifold and the air intake plenum before positioning the new gasket onto the lower intake mounting face. Install the air intake plenum and throttle body assembly onto the intake manifold. Ensure the gasket remains in place. Install the retaining bolts and nuts and tighten the bolts to the torque listed in this Chapter's Specifications. Installation is otherwise the reverse of removal.

14   Exhaust system servicing - general information

Warning: *The vehicle's exhaust system generates very high temperatures and must be allowed to cool down completely before any of the components are touched. Be especially careful around the catalytic converter, where the highest temperatures are generated.*

General Information

Refer to illustrations 14.1a, 14.1b, 14.1c and 14.1d

1   Replacement of exhaust system components is basically a matter of removing the

heat shields, disconnecting the component and installing a new one **(see illustrations)**. The heat shields and exhaust system hangers must be reinstalled in the original locations or damage could result. Due to the high temperatures and exposed locations of the exhaust system components, rust and corrosion can

seize parts together. Penetrating oils are available to help loosen frozen fasteners. However, in some cases it may be necessary to cut the pieces apart with a hacksaw or cutting torch. The latter method should be employed only by persons experienced in this work.

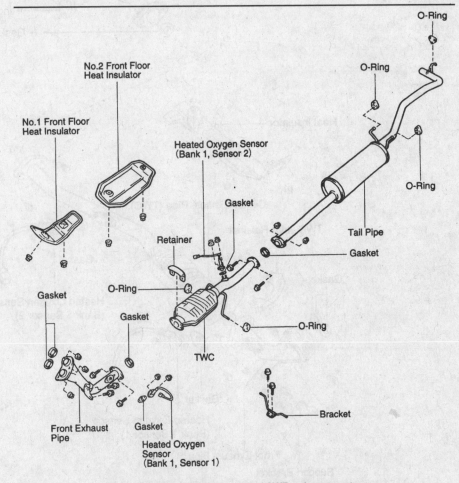

14.1c Exploded view of a typical 2WD exhaust system

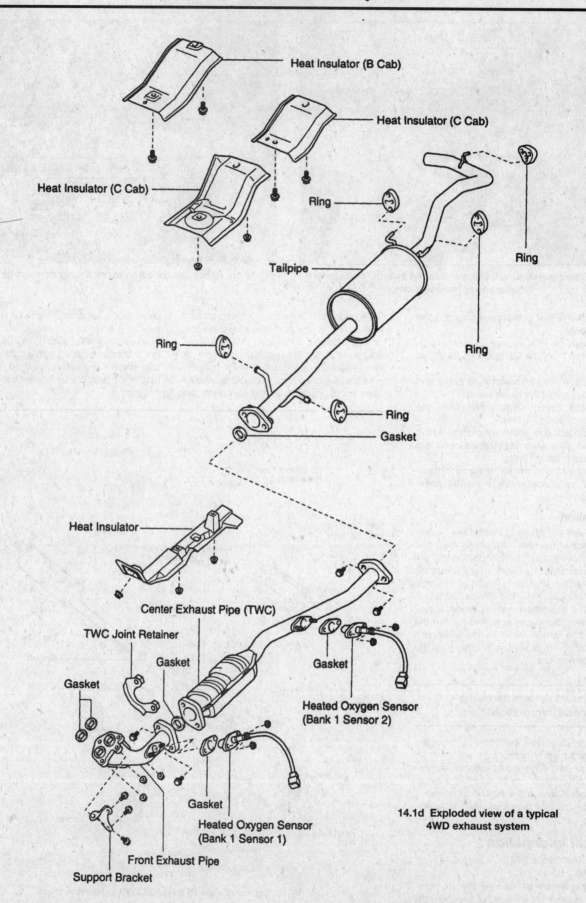

Heat Insulator (B Cab)

Heat Insulator (C Cab)

Heat Insulator (C Cab)

Ring

Ring

Tailpipe

Ring

Ring

Ring

Ring

Gasket

Heat Insulator

Center Exhaust Pipe (TWC)

TWC Joint Retainer

Gasket

Gasket

Gasket

Heated Oxygen Sensor
(Bank 1 Sensor 2)

Gasket

Heated Oxygen Sensor
(Bank 1 Sensor 1)

Front Exhaust Pipe

Support Bracket

14.1d Exploded view of a typical
4WD exhaust system

Chapter 5
Engine electrical systems

Contents

Specifications

Ignition timing

Four-cylinder engines
  1994 models
    With test terminals TE1 and E1 grounded .... 5-degrees BTDC
    Without test terminals TE1 and E1 grounded .... not available
  1995 and later models
    With test terminals TE1 and E1 grounded .... 3 to 7-degrees BTDC
    Without test terminals TE1 and E1 grounded .... 4 to 18-degrees BTDC
3.0L V6 engines
  With test terminals TE1 and E1 grounded .... 10-degrees BTDC
  Without test terminals TE1 and E1 grounded .... 8-degrees BTDC
3.4L V6 engines
  1995 through 1998 T100 models
    With test terminals TE1 and E1 grounded .... 8 to 12-degrees BTDC
    Without test terminals TE1 and E1 grounded .... 12 to 22-degrees BTDC
  1995 and 1996 Tacoma models
    With test terminals TE1 and E1 grounded .... 8 to 12-degrees BTDC
    Without test terminals TE1 and E1 grounded .... 12 to 22-degrees BTDC
  1997 and 1998 Tacoma models
    With test terminals TE1 and E1 grounded .... 8 to 12-degrees BTDC
    Without test terminals TE1 and E1 grounded .... 3 to 19-degrees BTDC
  1996 and later 4Runner models
    With test terminals TE1 and E1 grounded .... 8 to 12-degrees BTDC
    Without test terminals TE1 and E1 grounded .... 3 to 19-degrees BTDC

Ignition coil

Internal coil type distributor (1994 through 1997 four-cylinder engines)
    Primary resistance.. 0.36 to 0.55 ohms
    Secondary resistance... 9.0 to 15.4 K-ohms
External coil type distributor (1993 and 1994 3.0L V6 engines)
    Primary resistance.. 0.36 to 0.55 ohms
    Secondary resistance... 9.0 to 15.4 K-ohms
Distributorless ignition coil (1996 through 1998 3.4L V6 engine and 1998 four-cylinder engines)
    Primary resistance.. 0.67 to 1.05 ohms
    Secondary resistance... 9.3 to 16K ohms

Distributor

Air gap
    Internal coil type distributor... 0.008 to 0.016 inch
    External coil type distributor .... 0.008 to 0.020 inch
Pick-up coil resistance
    External coil type distributor
        Ne to G- terminals.. 155 to 250 ohms
        G1 to G- terminals .... 125 to 200 ohms
        G2 to G- terminals .... 125 to 200 ohms
    Internal coil type distributor
        G+ to G- terminals .... 185 to 275 ohms

Charging system

Charging voltage .... 13.9 to 15.1 volts
Standard amperage
    All lights and accessories turned off .... less than 10 amps
    Headlights (hi-beam) and heater blower motor turned on .... 30 amps or more
Alternator brush length
    Standard... 0.413 inch
    Minimum... 0.059 inch

1   General information

The engine electrical systems include all ignition, charging and starting components. Because of their engine related functions, these components are discussed separately from chassis electrical devices such as the lights, the instruments, etc. (which are included in Chapter 12).

Always observe the following precautions when working on the electrical systems:

a) *Be extremely careful when servicing engine electrical components. They are easily damaged if checked, connected or handled improperly.*

b) *Never leave the ignition switch on for long periods of time (10 minutes maximum) with the engine off.*

c) *Don't disconnect the battery cables while the engine is running.*

d) *Maintain correct polarity when connecting a battery cable from another vehicle during jump starting.*

e) *Always disconnect the negative cable first and hook it up last or the battery may be shorted by the tool being used to loosen the cable clamps.*

It's also a good idea to review the safety-related information regarding the engine electrical systems located in the *Safety first* section near the front of this manual before beginning any operation included in this Chapter.

2   Battery - emergency jump starting

Refer to the Booster battery (jump) starting procedure at the front of this manual.

3   Battery - removal and installation

Refer to illustration 3.1

1   Starting with the negative battery terminal, disconnect both cables from the battery terminals **(see illustration)**. **Caution:** *If the stereo in your vehicle is equipped with an anti-theft system, make sure you have the correct activation code before disconnecting the battery.*

2   Remove the battery hold-down clamp.

3   Lift out the battery. Be careful, it's heavy.

4   While the battery is out, inspect the carrier (tray) for corrosion.

5   If you are replacing the battery, make sure that you get one that's identical, with the same dimensions, amperage rating, cold cranking rating, etc. as the original.

6   Installation is the reverse of removal.

4   Battery cables - check and replacement

Caution: *If the stereo in your vehicle is equipped with an anti-theft system, make*

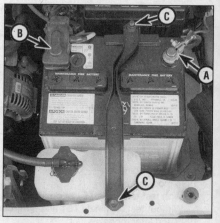

3.1 To remove the battery, detach the negative battery cable first (A), then the positive cable (B), remove the hold-down strap nuts (C) and lift the battery out

sure you have the correct activation code before disconnecting the battery.

Note: *The airbag system will be disabled if the battery is disconnected for more than a brief period. If the airbag light comes on and stays on after the battery is reconnected, the vehicle must be taken to a dealer service department to have the system reset with a special tool.*

1   Periodically inspect the entire length of each battery cable for damage, cracked or burned insulation and corrosion. Poor battery cable connections can cause starting prob-

lems and decreased engine performance.

2   Check the cable-to-terminal connections at the ends of the cables for cracks, loose wire strands and corrosion. The presence of white, fluffy deposits under the insulation at the cable terminal connection is a sign that the cable is corroded and should be replaced. Check the terminals for distortion, missing mounting bolts and corrosion.

3   When removing the cables, always disconnect the negative cable first and hook it up last or the battery may be shorted by the tool used to loosen the cable clamps. Even if only the positive cable is being replaced, be sure to disconnect the negative cable from the battery first (see Chapter 1 for further information regarding battery cable removal).

4   Disconnect the old cables from the battery, then trace each of them to their opposite ends and detach them from the starter solenoid and ground terminals. Note the routing of each cable to ensure correct installation.

5   If you are replacing either or both of the old cables, take them with you when buying new cables. It is vitally important that you replace the cables with identical parts. Cables have characteristics that make them easy to identify: positive cables are usually red, larger in cross-section and have a larger diameter battery post clamp; ground cables are usually black, smaller in cross-section and have a slightly smaller diameter clamp for the negative post.

6   Clean the threads of the solenoid or ground connection with a wire brush to remove rust and corrosion. Apply a light coat of battery terminal corrosion inhibitor, or petroleum jelly, to the threads to prevent future corrosion.

7   Attach the cable to the solenoid or ground connection and tighten the mounting nut/bolt securely.

8   Before connecting a new cable to the battery, make sure that it reaches the battery post without having to be stretched.

9   Connect the positive cable first, followed by the negative cable.

5   Ignition system - general information and precautions

Refer to illustrations 5.2a, 5.2b, 5.3a, 5.3b and 5.4

1   There are two types of ignition systems equipped on the models covered by this manual - breakerless ignition systems and distributorless ignition systems. 3.0L V6 engines are equipped with the breakerless ignition system. 1997 and earlier four-cylinder engines are also equipped with the breakerless ignition system. 1995 and later 3.4L V6 engines are equipped with the distributorless ignition system, as are four-cylinder engines as of 1998.

Breakerless ignition systems

2   The breakerless ignition system includes

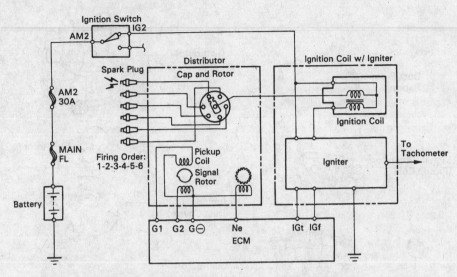

5.2a Schematic of the breakerless electronic ignition system with an internal ignition coil

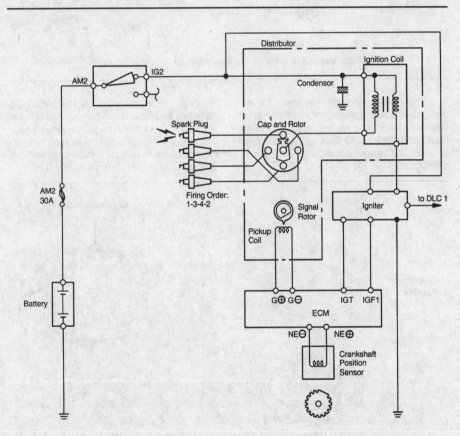

5.2b Schematic of the breakerless electronic ignition system with an external ignition coil

the ignition switch, the battery, the igniter, the pick-up coil(s), the ignition coil, the primary (low voltage) and secondary (high voltage) wiring circuits, the distributor and the spark plugs **(see illustrations)**. The ignition system is controlled by the Electronic Control Module (ECM). Using data provided by information sensors which monitor various engine functions (such as rpm, intake air volume, engine temperature, etc.), the ECM ensures a perfectly timed spark under all conditions. The igniter (module) is a separate component from the distributor and is mounted on the right side of the engine compartment under the air intake duct on four cylinder engines or in the left side of the engine compartment together with the ignition coil on 3.0L V6 engines.

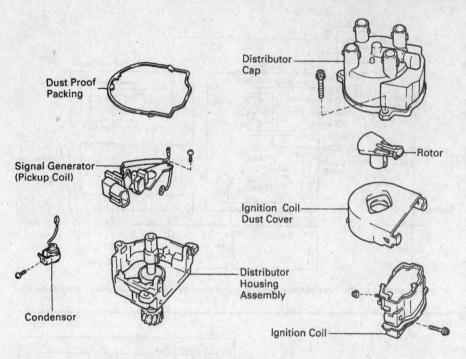

5.3a Exploded view of the internal coil type distributor

3   The breakerless ignition systems are divided into two groups; external coil type distributors and internal coil type distributors **(see illustrations)**. Ali four cylinder engines through 1997 are equipped with internal coil distributors while the 1993 and 1994 3.0L V6

engines are equipped with the externally mounted ignition coils. When replacing these units be sure to make all the necessary ignition system checks before replacing the distributor as these units are expensive and can only be replaced as a single component.

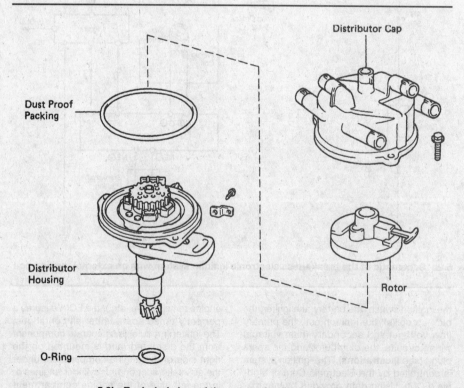

5.3b Exploded view of the external coil type distributor

Distributorless ignition system

4   The DIS system **(see illustration)** includes the camshaft position sensor, the crankshaft position sensor, individual coils (one at each cylinder) and the igniter. The ECM (computer) generates cylinder identification signals which allow the igniter to trigger the correct coil while cranking the engine. The ECM determines the correct ignition timing based on the input signals from the information sensors that are incorporated into the EFI and ignition system; the ECT, VSS, TPS, A/C switch signal, airflow meter or MAF sensor, knock sensor (refer to Chapter 6 for additional information). The igniter distributes the signal to the proper coil driver circuit and determines dwell period based on coil primary current flow.

5   The DIS system uses a waste spark method for distribution. Two cylinders are fired simultaneously by the ECM while one is on its compression stroke and the other is on its exhaust stroke. The cylinder set to fire (compression) will use the most of the voltage supplied to the two spark plugs due to the load demand on the cylinder. The companion cylinder will fire minimally, only to disperse any remaining air/fuel molecules for combustion and emission efficiency. The V6 engine is paired 1-4, 2-5, 3-6 while the four cylinder engine is paired 1-4 and 2-3.

6   When working on the ignition system, take the following precautions:

a) *Do not keep the ignition switch on for more than 10 seconds if the engine will not start.*

b) *Always connect a tachometer in accordance with the manufacturer's instructions. Some tachometers may be incompatible with this ignition system. Consult a dealer service department before buying a tachometer for use with this vehicle.*

c) *Never allow the ignition coil terminals to touch ground. Grounding the coil could result in damage to the igniter and/or the ignition coil.*

d) *Do not disconnect the battery when the engine is running.*

e) *Make sure that the igniter is properly grounded.*

6   Ignition system - check

Warning: *Because of the high voltage generated by the ignition system, extreme care should be taken whenever an operation is performed involving ignition components. This not only includes the igniter, coil, distributor and spark plug wires, but related components such as plug connectors, tachometer and other test equipment also.*

Breakerless ignition systems

Refer to illustration 6.1

1   If the engine turns over but won't start, disconnect the spark plug wire from any

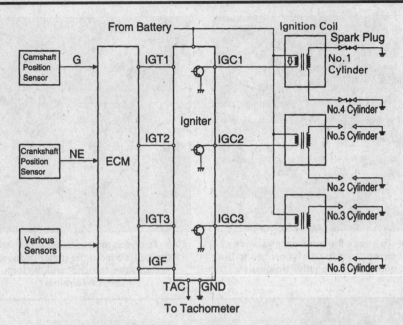

5.4 Schematic of the distributorless ignition system on the 3.4L V6 engine

6.1 To use a calibrated ignition tester (available at most auto parts stores), remove a an ignition wire from a cylinder, connect the spark plug boot to the tester and clip the tester to a good ground - if there is enough voltage to fire the plug, sparks will be clearly visible between the electrode tip and the tester body as the engine is turned over

spark plug and attach it to a calibrated tester (available at most auto parts stores). Connect the clip on the tester to a bolt or metal bracket on the engine **(see illustration)**. If you're unable to obtain a calibrated ignition tester, remove the wire from one of the spark plugs and using an insulated tool, pull back the boot and hold the end of the wire about 1/4-inch from a good ground.

2   Crank the engine and watch the end of the tester or spark plug wire to see if bright blue, well-defined sparks occur.

3   If sparks occur, sufficient voltage is reaching the plug to fire it (repeat the check at the remaining plug wires to verify that the distributor cap and rotor are OK). However, the plugs themselves may be fouled, so remove and check them as described in Chapter 1.

4   If no sparks or intermittent sparks occur, remove the distributor cap and check the cap and rotor as described in Chapter 1. If moisture is present, dry out the cap and rotor, then reinstall the cap and repeat the spark test.

5   If there's still no spark, detach the coil secondary wire from the distributor cap and hook it up to the tester (reattach the plug wire to the spark plug), then repeat the spark check. Again, if you don't have a tester, hold the end of the wire about 1/4-inch from a good ground.

6   If sparks now occur, the distributor cap, rotor or plug wire(s) may be defective.

7   If no sparks occur, check the primary wire connections at the coil to make sure they're clean and tight. Check for voltage to the coil on the primary circuit from the ignition switch. Check the ignition coil (see Section 7) and the distributor pick-up coil (see Section 11). Make any necessary repairs, then repeat the check again.

8   If there's still no spark, the coil-to-cap wire may be bad (check the resistance with an ohmmeter and compare it to the spark plug wire resistance Specifications found in Chapter 1). If a known good wire doesn't make any difference in the test results, the igniter may be defective. **Note:** *Because the igniter and ECM are expensive ignition system components, have them checked by a dealer service department or other qualified automotive repair facility before replacing them.*

Distributorless Ignition system

Refer to illustrations 6.9, 6.12 and 6.13

9   If the engine turns over but won't start, disconnect the coil wire from one of the spark plugs on the left cylinder bank and attach it to a calibrated ignition tester (available at most auto parts stores) **(see accompanying illustration and illustration 6.1)**. Make sure the tester is designed for distributorless ignition systems if a universal tester isn't available. **Note:** *On 3.4L engines, use the spark plug wires on the left bank (cylinders 2, 4 and 6) to check for spark. Because these systems use the waste spark system, the companion cylinders fire simultaneously. Therefore, each cylinder checks two cylinders at one time. This method is preferred because of the extra disassembly necessary to check the spark directly at the coil packs on the right bank (1, 3 and 5).*

10   Connect the clip on the tester to a bolt or metal bracket on the engine, crank the engine and watch the end of the tester to see if bright blue, well-defined sparks occur.

11   If sparks occur, sufficient voltage is reaching the spark plug to fire it (repeat the check at the remaining coils to verify that all the ignition coils are functioning). However, the plugs themselves may be fouled, so

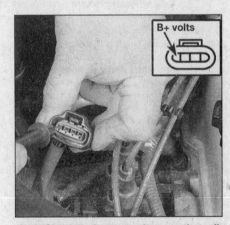

6.9 Location of the coil packs on the 3.4L V6 engine

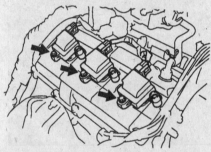

6.12 Check for battery voltage to the coil primary circuit

remove and check them as described in Chapter 1 or install new ones.

12   If no sparks or intermittent sparks occur, check for battery voltage to the ignition coil **(see illustration)**. Check the coils (see Section 7). Check the camshaft and crankshaft position sensors (see Chapter 6).

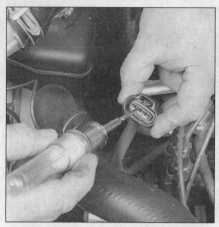

6.13 Connect an LED test light to the battery positive terminal, crank the engine over and see if the light flashes as the igniter signals the coil to fire

7.4a To check the primary resistance of the coil, connect the meter probes to the positive and negative terminals

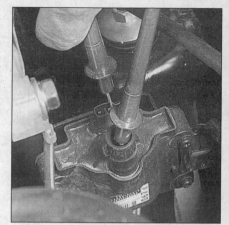

7.4b To check the secondary resistance of the coil, connect the meter probes to the positive terminal and the high tension terminal

7.8 Remove the retaining bolts (arrows) and lift the coil from the engine compartment

7.12a On internal coil type distributors, remove the screws (arrows) and . . .

7.12b . . . separate the heat shield from the coil

13   Also check for an igniter voltage signal to the coil packs. Unplug the electrical connector from each coil pack and attach a 12 volt test light to the battery positive terminal. Make sure it is an LED (Light Emitting Diode) type test light. Have an assistant crank the engine over and see if the test light blinks as the igniter provides the voltage signal to the coil pack **(see illustration)**. Make this test for each coil pack. **Note:** *Because the igniter and ECM are expensive ignition system components, have them checked by a dealer service department or other qualified automotive repair facility before replacing them.*

---

7   Ignition coil(s) - check and replacement

Breakerless ignition systems

External coil type

Check

Refer to illustrations 7.4a and 7.4b

1   Detach the cable from the negative ter-

minal of the battery. **Caution:** *If the stereo in your vehicle is equipped with an anti-theft system, make sure you have the correct activation code before disconnecting the battery.*
2   Disconnect the electrical connector and the coil wire from the coil.
3   Remove the coil mounting bolts and place the coil on the bench for testing.
4   Using an ohmmeter, check the coil:
   a) *Measure the resistance between the positive and negative terminals* **(see illustration)**. *Compare your reading with the specified coil primary resistance listed in this Chapter's Specifications.*
   b) *Measure the resistance between the positive terminal and the high tension terminal* **(see illustration)**. *Compare your reading with the specified coil secondary resistance listed in this Chapter's Specifications.*
5   If either of the above tests yield resistance values outside the specified amount, replace the coil.

Replacement

Refer to illustration 7.8

6   Detach the cable from the negative ter-

7.13 Remove the nuts from the coil terminals (arrows)

minal of the battery (see **Caution** and **Note** above).
7   If equipped, remove the heat shield from the coil.
8   Remove the coil mounting bolts **(see illustration)**.
9   Label and disconnect the wires from the

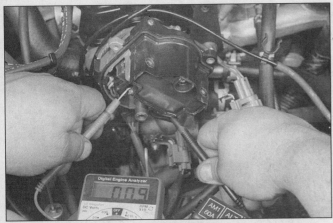

7.14a To check the primary resistance of the coil, connect the meter probes to the positive and the negative terminals

7.14b To check the secondary resistance of the coil, connect the meter probes to the positive terminal and the high tension terminal

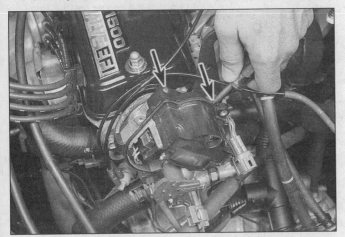

7.19a Remove the retaining screws (arrows) . . .

7.19b . . . and lift the coil from the distributor housing

coil terminals.

10   Installation is the reverse of removal.

Internal coil type

Check

Refer to illustrations 7.12a, 7.12b, 7.13, 7.14a and 7.14b

11   Detach the cable from the negative terminal of the battery (see the **Caution** in Step 1).

12   Remove the heat shield from the coil **(see illustrations)**.

13   Remove the mounting bolts from the coil electrical connectors **(see illustration)**.

14   Using an ohmmeter, check the coil:

a) *Measure the resistance between the positive and negative terminals* **(see illustration)**. *Compare your reading with the specified coil primary resistance listed in this Chapter's Specifications.*

b) *Measure the resistance between the positive terminal and the high tension terminal* **(see illustration)**. *Compare your reading with the specified coil secondary resistance listed in this Chapter's Specifications.*

15   If either of the above tests yield resistance values outside the specified amount, replace the coil.

Replacement

Refer to illustrations 7.19a and 7.19b

16   Detach the cable from the negative terminal of the battery (see the **Caution** in Step 1).

17   Remove the heat shield from the coil.

18   Label and disconnect the wires from the coil terminals.

19   Remove the coil mounting bolts **(see illustrations)**.

20   Installation is the reverse of removal.

Distributorless Ignition System

Check

Refer to illustrations 7.21 and 7.22

21   With the ignition key OFF, disconnect the electrical connector(s) from each coil. Connect an ohmmeter across the coil primary terminals **(see illustration)**. The resistance should be as listed in this Chapter's Specifications.

22   With the ignition key OFF, disconnect the electrical connector(s) from each coil.

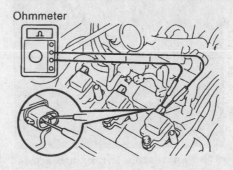

7.21 Checking the coil primary resistance on a DIS coil

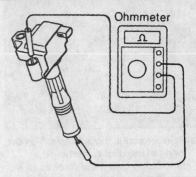

7.22 Checking the coil secondary resistance on a DIS coil

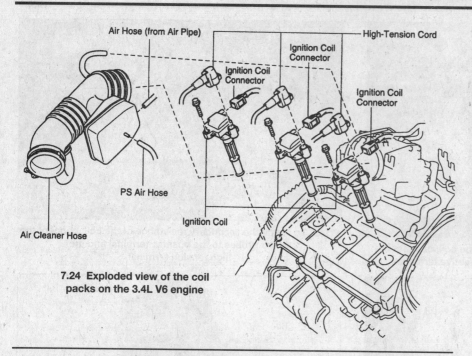

7.24 Exploded view of the coil packs on the 3.4L V6 engine

7.25 The coil packs are mounted at the right front of the engine on 1998 four-cylinder engines

Connect an ohmmeter across the coil secondary terminals (see illustration). The resistance should be as listed in this Chapter's Specifications. If not, replace the coil.

Replacement

Refer to illustrations 7.24 and 7.25

23 Disconnect the negative cable from the battery (see **Caution** and **Note** above).
24 Disconnect the ignition coil electrical connector(s) from each individual coil pack. Label each connector so they don't get mixed up (see illustration).
25 Remove the bolts securing the ignition coil to the mounting bracket on the engine and remove the coil (see illustration).
26 Installation is the reverse of the removal procedure.

8 Distributor - removal and installation

Removal

Refer to illustrations 8.5a and 8.5b

1 Detach the cable from the negative battery terminal. **Caution:** *If the stereo in your vehicle is equipped with an anti-theft system, make sure you have the correct activation code before disconnecting the battery.*
2 Disconnect the electrical connectors from the distributor.
3 Look for a raised "1" on the distributor cap. This marks the location for the number one cylinder spark plug wire terminal. If the cap does not have a mark for the number one

terminal, locate the number one spark plug and trace the wire back to the terminal on the cap. Refer to the firing order schematics in the Specifications in Chapter 1.
4 Remove the distributor cap (see Chapter 1) and turn the engine over until the rotor is pointing toward the number one spark plug terminal (see locating TDC procedure in Chapter 2A or 2B).
5 Make a mark on the edge of the distributor base directly below the rotor tip and in line with it. Also, mark the distributor base and the engine block to ensure that the distributor is installed correctly (see illustrations).
6 If equipped with collar bolts, loosen but do not remove the two bolts in the distributor collar. This will give the distributor shaft clearance.
7 Remove the distributor hold-down bolt, then pull the distributor straight out to remove it. **Caution:** *DO NOT turn the crankshaft while the distributor is out of the engine, or the alignment marks will be useless.*

8.5a Paint or scribe a mark (arrow) on the edge of the distributor housing immediately below the rotor tip to ensure that the rotor is pointing in the same direction when it is reinstalled

8.5b Paint or scribe another mark across the cylinder head and the distributor body (arrows) to ensure that the distributor is aligned correctly when it is reinstalled

8.8 If you have set the engine at TDC compression for number one cylinder, align the cut-out portion of the coupling with the groove in the distributor housing (3.0L V6 engine shown, others similar)

8.9 Install the distributor with the coupling on the distributor collar aligned with the cutout in the engine block

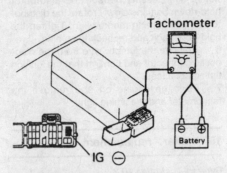

9.1 Connect the tachometer lead to the IG terminal located on the check connector

and tighten the distributor hold-down bolt securely.

9 Ignition timing - check and adjustment

Refer to illustrations 9.1, 9.2, 9.3, 9.4 and 9.5
Note: *The following ignition timing procedure should apply to most models covered by this manual. However, if the procedure specified on the VECI label of your vehicle differs from this one, use the procedure found on the VECI label.*

1   Connect a tachometer according to the manufacturer's specifications **(see illustration)**.
2   Locate the check connector and insert a jumper wire between terminals E1 and TE1 **(see illustration)**. **(For locations of all the check connectors, see illustrations 11.1a, 11.1b and 11.1c in Chapter 4)**.
3   With the ignition switch off, connect a timing light according to the tool manufacturer's instructions **(see illustration)**. Most timing lights are powered by the battery. Also, an inductive style pick-up is connected to the number one cylinder spark plug wire.
4   Locate the timing marks on the timing cover and the crankshaft pulley **(see illustration)**.

Installation

Refer to illustrations 8.8 and 8.9
Note: *If the crankshaft has been moved while the distributor is out, locate Top Dead Center (TDC) for the number one piston (see Chapter 2A or 2B) and position the distributor and the rotor accordingly.*

8   Align the cut-out portion of the coupling with the groove in the housing **(see illustration)**.
9   Insert the distributor into the engine in exactly the same relationship to the block

that it was in when removed **(see illustration)**.
10   If the distributor does not seat completely, recheck the alignment marks between the distributor base and the block to verify that the distributor is in the same position it was in before removal. Also check the rotor to see if it's aligned with the mark you made on the edge of the distributor base.
11   Loosely install the distributor hold-down bolt(s).
12   Installation is the reverse of removal.
13   Check the ignition timing (see Section 9)

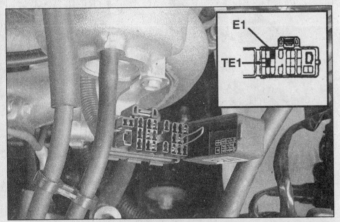

9.2 Attach a jumper wire between terminals E1 and TE1 on the check connector

9.4 The timing marks are clearly stamped onto the front timing cover

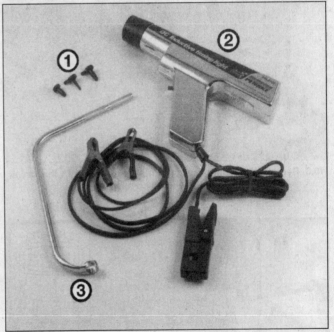

9.3 Tools needed to check and adjust the ignition timing

1   ***Vacuum plugs*** - *Vacuum hoses will, in most cases, have to be disconnected and plugged. Molded plugs in various shapes and sizes are available for this*
2   ***Inductive pick-up timing light*** - *Flashes a bright, concentrated beam of light when the number one spark plug fires. Connect the leads according to the instructions supplied with the light*
3   ***Distributor wrench*** - *On some models, the hold-down bolt for the distributor is difficult to reach and turn with conventional wrenches or sockets. A special wrench like this must be used*

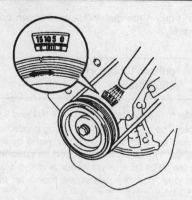

9.5 Point the timing light at the timing marks with the engine at idle

5   Start the engine and allow it to warm up to normal operating temperature (upper radiator hose hot). Verify that the engine idle is correct (see Chapter 1). Aim the timing light at the timing scale on the front engine cover **(see illustration)**. The mark on the crankshaft pulley should line up with the proper mark on the scale (refer to this Chapter's Specifica-

tions). If necessary, loosen the distributor hold-down bolt and slowly rotate the distributor until the timing marks align. Tighten the hold-down bolt and recheck the timing.
6   Remove the jumper wire from the diagnostic connector and confirm that the ignition timing advances.
7   Turn the engine off and remove the tachometer and the timing light.

10   Igniter - replacement

Refer to illustration 10.3
Note: *The igniter (module) on breakerless ignition systems is a separate component from the distributor and is mounted on the right side of the engine compartment under the air intake duct on four-cylinder engines or in the left side of the engine compartment together with the ignition coil on 3.0L V6 engines. The igniter on the distributorless ignition systems (DIS) is in integral component with the coil assembly. The igniter cannot be replaced as a separate part on these systems.*

1   Detach the cable from the negative terminal of the battery. **Caution:** *If the stereo in your vehicle is equipped with an anti-theft system, make sure you have the correct activation code before disconnecting the battery.*
2   Disconnect the electrical connector from the igniter.
3   Remove the bolts from the bracket and pull the igniter/bracket assembly out of the engine compartment **(see illustration)**.
4   Installation is the reverse of removal.

11   Pick-up coil - check

Pick-up coil check

Refer to illustrations 11.1a and 11.1b
1   Disconnect the electrical connector at the distributor and using an ohmmeter, measure the resistance between the pick-up coil terminals **(see illustrations)**.
2   Compare the measurements to those listed in this Chapter's Specifications. If the resistance is not as specified, replace the distributor.

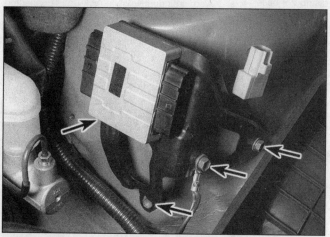

10.3   Remove the igniter bracket bolts (arrows) and lift the igniter unit from the engine compartment

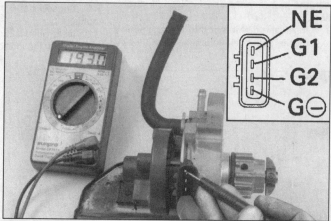

11.1a   Check the resistance between terminals NE and G- on the pick-up coil (external coil type distributor). Follow the terminal designations and the resistance values for the remaining terminals listed in this Chapter's Specifications

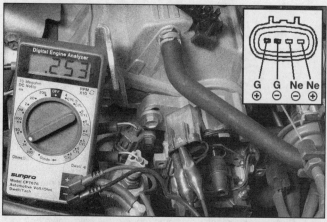

11.1b   Check resistance on terminals G+ and G- on the pick-up coil (internal coil type distributor)

11.5a   Measure the air gap between the signal rotor and the pick-up coil projection - if the gap is not within specification, replace the distributor (internal coil type distributor shown)

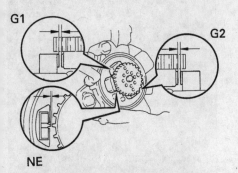

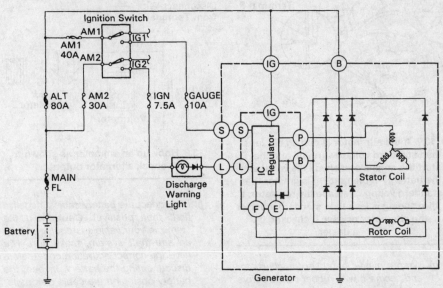

11.5b On the external coil type distributor there are three pick-up coils in the distributor housing. Because G1 and G2 are located under the rotor, it may be necessary to use a special service tool or modified feeler gauge to check the air gap

12.1 Schematic of a typical charging system

Air gap check

Refer to illustrations 11.5a and 11.5b

3   Detach the cable from the negative terminal of the battery. **Caution:** *If the stereo in your vehicle is equipped with an anti-theft system, make sure you have the correct activation code before disconnecting the battery.*
4   Remove the distributor cap.
5   Using a brass feeler gauge, measure the gap between the signal rotor and the pick-up coil projection **(see illustrations)**. Compare your measurement to the air gap listed in this Chapter's Specifications. If the air gap is not as specified, replace the distributor, as the air gap is not adjustable.

12 Charging system - general information and precautions

Refer to illustrations 12.1 and 12.3

1   The charging system includes the alternator, an internal voltage regulator, a charge indicator, the battery, fusible links and the wiring between all the components **(see illustration)**. The charging system supplies electrical power for the ignition system, the lights, the radio, etc. The alternator is driven by a drivebelt at the front of the engine.
2   The purpose of the voltage regulator is to limit the alternator's voltage to a preset value. This prevents power surges, circuit overloads, etc., during peak voltage output.
3   The fusible links on these models resemble fuses, only much larger to handle the higher current that passes through them. They are located in the underhood relay block **(see illustration)**.
4   The charging system doesn't ordinarily require periodic maintenance. However, the drivebelt, battery and wires and connections should be inspected at the intervals outlined in Chapter 1.
5   The dashboard warning light should come on when the ignition key is turned to Start, then should go off immediately. If it

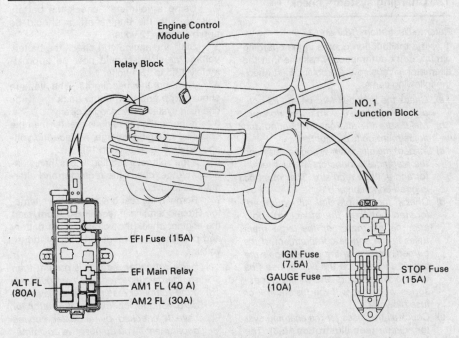

12.3 Typical charging system fuses and fusible links (3.0L shown)

remains on, there is a malfunction in the charging system. Some vehicles are also equipped with a voltage gauge. If the voltage gauge indicates abnormally high or low voltage, check the charging system (see Section 13).
6   Be very careful when making electrical circuit connections to a vehicle equipped with an alternator and note the following:

a) *When reconnecting wires to the alternator from the battery, be sure to note the polarity.*
b) *Before using arc welding equipment to repair any part of the vehicle, disconnect the wires from the alternator and the battery terminals.*
c) *Never start the engine with a battery charger connected.*
d) *Always disconnect both battery cables before using a battery charger.*
e) *The alternator is driven by an engine drivebelt which could cause serious injury if your hand, hair or clothes become entangled in it with the engine running.*
f) *Because the alternator is connected directly to the battery, it could arc or cause a fire if overloaded or shorted out.*

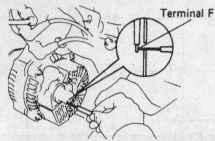

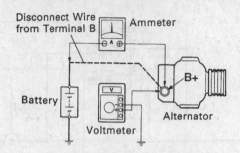

13.7 If the alternator is putting out less than standard voltage, ground terminal F, start the engine and check the voltage at the battery - if the reading is greater than standard voltage, replace the regulator; if the reading is less than standard, check the alternator or have it checked by a dealer

13.8 Hook up an ammeter as shown to check alternator output

14.3 First loosen the locking bolt (A) and then turn the adjustment bolt (B) to release the tension on the drivebelt

g) *Wrap a plastic bag over the alternator and secure it with rubber bands before steam cleaning the engine.*

13   Charging system - check

Refer to illustrations 13.7 and 13.8

1   If a malfunction occurs in the charging circuit, don't automatically assume that the alternator is causing the problem. First check the following items:

a) *Check the drivebelt tension and its condition. Replace it if worn or deteriorated.*
b) *Make sure the alternator mounting and adjustment bolts are tight.*
c) *Inspect the alternator wiring harness and the electrical connectors at the alternator and voltage regulator. They must be in good condition and tight.*
d) *Check the fusible link (if equipped) located between the starter solenoid and the alternator or the large main fuses in the engine compartment. If it's burned, determine the cause, repair the circuit and replace the link or fuse (the vehicle won't start and/or the accessories won't work if the fusible link or fuse blows).*
e) *Check all the fuses for the charging system circuit* **(see illustration 12.3)**. *The location of these fuses and fusible links may vary from year and model but the designations are the same; main fusible link (FL), ALT FL (80 amp), AM1 FL (40 amp), AM2 FL (30 amp), IG2 (7.5 amp), Gauge 10A, and ALT (7.5 amp).*
f) *Start the engine and check the alternator for abnormal noises (a shrieking or squealing sound indicates a bad bushing).*
g) *Check the specific gravity of the battery electrolyte. If it's low, charge the battery (doesn't apply to maintenance free batteries).*
h) *Make sure that the battery is fully charged (one bad cell in a battery can cause overcharging by the alternator).*

i) *Disconnect the battery cables (negative first, then positive).* **Caution:** *If the stereo in your vehicle is equipped with an anti-theft system, make sure you have the correct activation code before disconnecting the battery. Inspect the battery posts and the cable clamps for corrosion. Clean them thoroughly if necessary (see Chapter 1). Reconnect the positive cable, then the negative cable.*

2   Using a voltmeter, check the battery voltage with the engine off. It should be approximately 12 volts.
3   Start the engine and check the battery voltage again. It should now be approximately 13.5 to 15.1 volts.
4   Turn on the headlights. The voltage should drop and then come back up, if the charging system is working properly.
5   If the voltage reading is greater than the specified charging voltage, replace the voltage regulator (see Section 15).
6   If the voltmeter reading is less than standard voltage, check the regulator and alternator as follows.
7   Remove the rear cover from the alternator. Ground terminal F **(see illustration)**, start the engine, check the voltage at the battery and compare your reading to the standard voltage.

a) *If the voltmeter reading is greater than standard voltage, replace the regulator.*
b) *If the voltmeter reading is less than standard voltage, check the alternator (or have it checked by a dealer service department if you do not have an ammeter).*

8   If you have an ammeter, hook it up to the charging system as shown **(see illustration)**. If you don't have a professional ammeter, you can also use an inductive-type current indicator. This device is inexpensive, readily available at auto parts stores and accurate enough to perform simple amperage checks like the following test.
9   With the engine running at 2,000 rpm, check the reading on the ammeter with all accessories and lights off, then again with the high-beam headlights on and the heater blower switch turned to the HI position. Compare your readings to the standard amperage listed in this Chapter's Specifications.
10   If the ammeter reading is less than stan-

14.4a Location of the alternator pivot bolt (arrow) on the 2.7L four-cylinder engine (as seen from below)

dard amperage, repair or replace the alternator.

14   Alternator - removal and installation

Refer to illustrations 14.3, 14.4a, 14.4b and 14.4c

1   Detach the cable from the negative terminal of the battery. **Caution:** *If the stereo in your vehicle is equipped with an anti-theft system, make sure you have the correct activation code before disconnecting the battery.*
2   Detach the electrical connectors from the alternator.
3   Loosen the alternator locking bolt and adjustment bolt **(see illustration)** and detach the drivebelt.
4   Remove the locking bolt and pivot bolt from the alternator adjustment bracket **(see illustrations)**.
5   If you are replacing the alternator, take the old alternator with you when purchasing a replacement unit. Make sure that the new/rebuilt unit is identical to the old alterna-

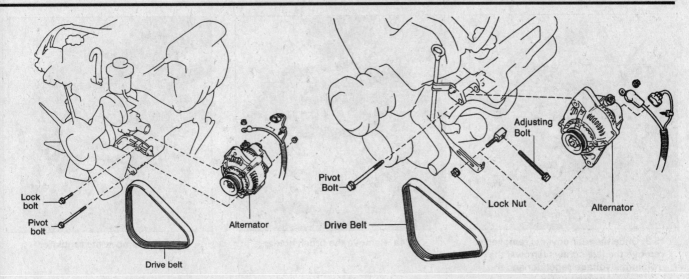

14.4b Typical alternator mounting details for the four-cylinder engines

14.4c Typical alternator mounting details for the 3.4L V6 engines (3.0L V6 engine similar)

tor. Look at the terminals - they should be the same in number, size and locations as the terminals on the old alternator. Finally, look at the identification markings - they will be stamped in the housing or printed on a tag or plaque affixed to the housing. Make sure that these numbers are the same on both alternators.

6   Many new/rebuilt alternators do not have a pulley installed, so you may have to switch the pulley from the old unit to the new/rebuilt one. When buying an alternator, find out the shop's policy regarding installation of pulleys - some shops will perform this service free of charge.

7   Installation is the reverse of removal **(see illustrations).**

8   After the alternator is installed, adjust the drivebelt tension (see Chapter 1).

9   Check the charging voltage to verify proper operation of the alternator (see Section 13).

15   Alternator components - check and replacement

Disassembly

Refer to illustrations 15.2a, 15.2b, 15.2c, 15.3, 15.4a, 15.4b, 15.5 and 15.7

1   Remove the alternator (see Section 14) and place it on a clean workbench.

2   Remove the rear cover nuts, the nut and

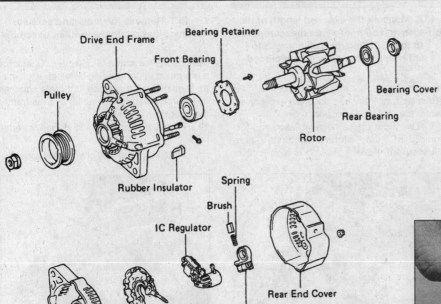

15.2a Exploded view of a typical alternator assembly

15.2b Remove the three nuts from the rear cover

15.2c Take the nut, washer and insulator off terminal B and remove the alternator end cover

15.3 Once the rear cover is removed, remove the five screws (arrows) that retain the voltage regulator and the brush holder

15.4a Remove the brush holder

15.4b Remove the regulator

terminal insulator and the rear cover **(see illustrations)**.

3   Remove the voltage regulator and brush holder mounting screws **(see illustration)**.

4   Remove the brush holder and the regulator from the rear end frame **(see illustrations)**. If you are only replacing the regulator, proceed to Step 8, install the new unit, reassemble the alternator and install it on the engine (see Section 14). If you are going to replace the brushes, proceed with the next Step.

5   Measure the exposed length of each brush **(see illustration)** and compare it to the minimum length listed in this Chapter's Specifications. If the length of either brush is less than the specified minimum, replace the brushes and brush holder assembly. **Note:** *On some models, it may be necessary to solder the new brushes in place.*

6   Make sure that each brush moves smoothly in the brush holder.

7   Remove the rectifier assembly **(see illustration)**. Remove the four rubber insulators and the seal plate.

8   Scribe or paint marks on the front and rear end frame housings of the alternator to facilitate reassembly.

9   Remove the nut retaining the pulley to the rotor shaft and remove the pulley.

10   Remove the four nuts retaining the front and rear end frames together, then separate the rear end frame assembly from the front end frame **(see illustration 15.2a)**.

11   Remove the thrust washer and remove the rotor from the front end frame.

Component checks

Refer to illustrations 15.12a, 15.12b, 15.13, 15.14a, 15.14b, 15.14c and 15.14d

12   Check for an open between the two slip rings **(see illustration)**. There should be 2 to 4 ohms resistance between the slip rings. Check for grounds between each slip ring and the rotor **(see illustration)**. There should be no continuity (infinite resistance) between

15.5 Measure the exposed length of the brushes and compare your measurements to the specified minimum length to determine if they should be replaced

the rotor and either slip ring. If the rotor fails either test, or if the slip rings are excessively worn, the rotor is defective.

13   Check for opens between each end terminal of the stator windings **(see illustration)**. If either reading is high (infinite

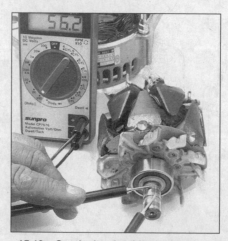

15.12a Continuity should exist between the rotor slip rings

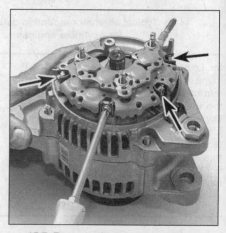

15.7 Remove the mounting screws (arrows) that retain the rectifier assembly

resistance), the stator is defective. Check for a grounded stator winding between each stator terminal and the frame. If there's continuity between any stator winding and the frame, the stator is defective.

14   Check the positive and negative rectifiers.

   a) First start the checks on the positive

15.12b Check the continuity between the rotor and the slip rings. There should be NO continuity

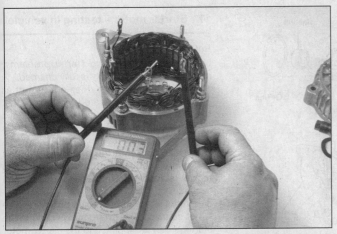

15.13 Check for continuity between the stator windings

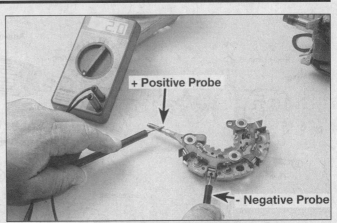

15.14a Position the positive probe of the ohmmeter onto the diode assembly positive post and the negative probe to ground. Continuity should exist

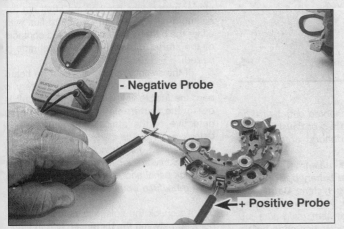

15.14b Switch the polarity of the ohmmeter probes and observe that now there is NO continuity within the diodes. Check each diode (four total) individually

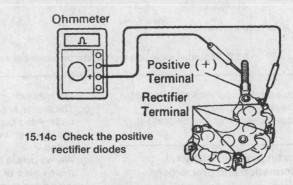

15.14c Check the positive rectifier diodes

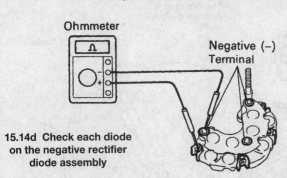

15.14d Check each diode on the negative rectifier diode assembly

15.16 To facilitate installation of the brush holder, depress each brush with a small screwdriver to clear the shaft

---

diode assembly by touching the positive probe of the ohmmeter onto the diode terminal and the negative probe onto one of the other diode terminals (see illustration). Then reverse the probes and check again (see illustration). The diode should have continuity with the ohmmeter one way and no continuity when the probes are reversed (see illustration). Check each of the terminals in this manner. If any of the diodes fail the test, the diode assembly is defective.

b) Now, check the negative diode assembly by touching the negative probe of the ohmmeter onto the NEGATIVE TERMINALS (see illustration) and the other probe onto each rectifier terminal. Reverse the polarity (reverse probes) and check to make sure there is no continuity in one position and continuity in the other position. Check each of the terminals in this manner. If any of the diodes fail the test, the diode assembly is defective.

Reassembly

Refer to illustration 15.16

15   Install the components in the reverse order of removal, noting the following:

16   Install the brush holder by depressing each brush with a small screwdriver to clear the shaft (see illustration).

17   Install the voltage regulator and brush holder screws into the rear frame.

18   Install the rear cover and tighten the three nuts securely.

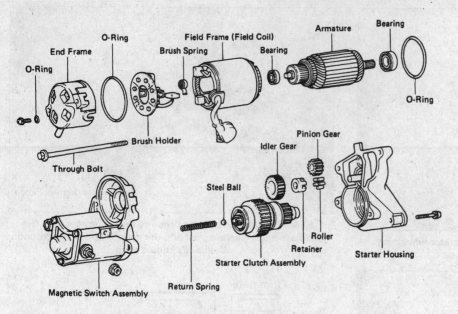

16.2 Exploded view of a typical starter/solenoid assembly

19   Install the terminal insulator and tighten it with the nut.
20   Install the alternator (see Section 14).

16 Starting system - general information and precautions

Refer to illustration 16.2

1   The sole function of the starting system is to turn over the engine quickly enough to allow it to start.
2   The starting system consists of the battery, the starter motor, the starter solenoid and the electrical circuit connecting the components. The solenoid (magnetic switch) is mounted directly on the starter motor **(see illustration)**.
3   The solenoid/starter motor assembly is installed on the rear of the engine, next to the transmission bellhousing.
4   When the ignition key is turned to the START position, the starter solenoid is actuated through the starter control circuit. The starter solenoid then connects the battery to the starter. The battery supplies the electrical energy to the starter motor, which does the actual work of cranking the engine.
5   The starter motor on a vehicle equipped with a manual transmission can be operated only when the clutch pedal is depressed; the starter on a vehicle equipped with an automatic transmission can be operated only when the transmission selector lever is in Park or Neutral.
6   Always observe the following precautions when working on the starting system:
a) *Excessive cranking of the starter motor can overheat it and cause serious damage. Never operate the starter motor for more than 15 seconds at a time without pausing to allow it to cool for at least*

two minutes.
b) *The starter is connected directly to the battery and could arc or cause a fire if mishandled, overloaded or short circuited.*
c) *Always detach the cable from the negative terminal of the battery before working on the starting system.* **Caution:** *If the stereo in your vehicle is equipped with an anti-theft system, make sure you have the correct activation code before disconnecting the battery.*

17 Starter motor - testing in vehicle

Refer to illustration 17.5
Note: *Before diagnosing starter problems, make sure that the battery is fully charged.*
1   If the starter motor does not turn at all when the switch is operated, make sure that the shift lever is in Neutral or Park (automatic transmission) or that the clutch pedal is depressed (manual transmission).
2   Make sure that the battery is charged and that all cables, both at the battery and starter solenoid terminals, are clean and secure.
3   If the starter motor spins but the engine is not cranking, the overrunning clutch in the starter motor is slipping and the starter motor must be replaced.
4   If, when the switch is actuated, the starter motor does not operate at all but the solenoid clicks, then the problem lies with either the battery, the main solenoid contacts or the starter motor itself (or the engine is seized).
5   If the solenoid plunger cannot be heard when the switch is actuated, the battery is bad, the fusible link is burned (the circuit is open), the starter relay **(see illustration)** is defective or the starter solenoid itself is defective. **Note:** *The starter relay is located in various places depending upon the year and model. Some are located behind the driver's side kick panel and others are located in the main relay/fuse box in the engine compartment.*
6   To check the solenoid, connect a jumper lead between the battery (+) and the ignition switch terminal (the small terminal) on the

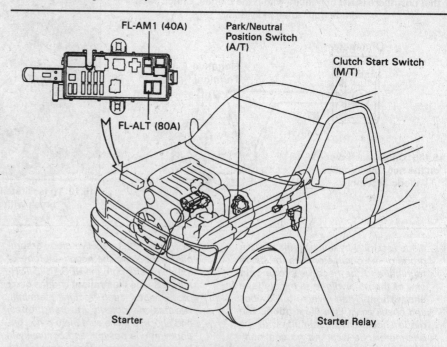

17.5 Locations of the various starting system components (T100 with 3.0L V6 engine shown)

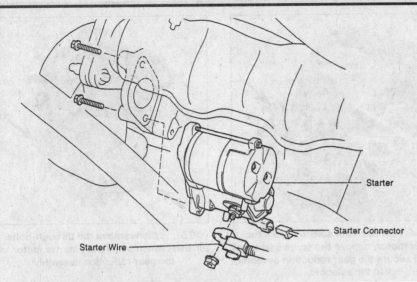

18.4b On 2WD 2.7L engines, access the starter bolts (arrows) from behind the transmission bellhousing

18.4a To remove the starter motor/solenoid assembly, detach the cable from the negative terminal of the battery, disconnect the electrical connectors and remove the mounting bolts (four cylinder engine shown)

18.4c Location of the lower starter bolt on the 4WD T100 models

18.5 On some 4WD models it will be necessary to access the starter through the wheel well

solenoid. If the starter motor now operates, the solenoid is OK and the problem is in the ignition switch, Neutral start switch or in the wiring.

7   If the starter motor still does not operate, remove the starter/solenoid assembly for disassembly, testing and repair.

8   If the starter motor cranks the engine at an abnormally slow speed, first make sure that the battery is charged and that all terminal connections are tight. If the engine is partially seized, or has the wrong viscosity oil in it, it will crank slowly.

9   Run the engine until normal operating temperature is reached, then disconnect the coil wire from the distributor cap and ground it on the engine. On models with distributorless ignition systems, detach the primary (low voltage) electrical connectors from the ignition coils.

10   Connect a voltmeter positive lead to the battery positive post and connect the negative lead to the negative post.

11   Crank the engine and take the voltmeter

readings as soon as a steady figure is indicated. Do not allow the starter motor to turn for more than 15 seconds at a time. A reading of nine volts or more, with the starter motor turning at normal cranking speed, is normal. If the reading is nine volts or more but the cranking speed is slow, the motor is faulty. If the reading is less than nine volts and the cranking speed is slow, the solenoid contacts are probably burned, the starter motor is bad, the battery is discharged or there is a bad connection.

18   Starter motor - removal and installation

Refer to illustrations 18.4a, 18.4b, 18.4c and 18.5

1   Detach the cable from the negative terminal of the battery. **Caution:** *If the stereo in your vehicle is equipped with an anti-theft*

system, make sure you have the correct activation code before disconnecting the battery.

2   Raise the front of the vehicle and support it securely on jackstands.

3   Detach the electrical connectors from the starter/solenoid assembly.

4   Remove the starter motor mounting bolts **(see illustrations)**.

5   Remove the bracket from the upper section of the starter/solenoid assembly. **Note:** *On 4WD models, it may be necessary to remove the front wheel and fender liner and access the starter motor through the opening* **(see illustration)**.

6   Installation is the reverse of removal.

19   Starter solenoid - removal and installation

Refer to illustrations 19.2, 19.3, 19.4, 19.5, 19.6a and 19.6b

1   Remove the starter motor (see Section 18).

2   Scribe or paint a mark across the starter motor and gear reduction assembly **(see illustration)**.

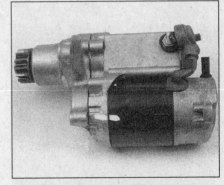

19.2 Before disassembling the starter motor, solenoid and gear reduction assembly, scribe or paint an alignment mark across the starter motor and the gear reduction assembly

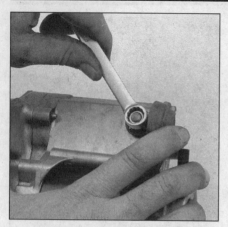

19.3 To disconnect the strap that connects the starter to the solenoid, remove this nut

19.4 To detach the solenoid from the starter motor, remove the screws (arrows) which secure the gear reduction assembly to the solenoid . . .

19.5 . . . then remove the through-bolts (arrows) which secure the starter motor to the gear reduction assembly

3   Disconnect the strap from the solenoid to the starter motor terminal **(see illustration)**.
4   Remove the screws **(see illustration)** which secure the gear reduction assembly to the solenoid.

5   Remove the through-bolts **(see illustration)** which secure the starter motor to the gear reduction assembly.
6   Separate the motor from the gear reduc-

tion and solenoid assembly then remove the solenoid from the gear reduction assembly **(see illustrations)**.
7   Installation is the reverse of removal. Be sure to align the paint or scribe mark.

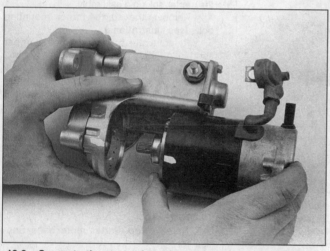

19.6a Separate the starter from the gear reduction assembly . . .

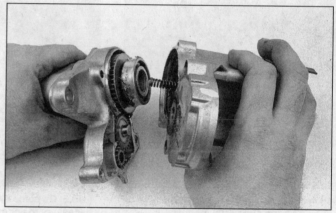

19.6b . . . then separate the solenoid from the gear reduction assembly (note the return spring protruding from the solenoid assembly - make sure that this spring is installed before reassembling the solenoid and the gear reduction assembly)

Chapter 6
Emissions and engine control systems

Contents

Specifications

Oxygen sensor heater resistance

1993 and 1994 models	5 to 7 ohms
1995 and 1996 models	
T100	
Upstream O2 sensor	5 to 7 ohms
Downstream O2 sensor	6 to 11 ohms
Tacoma	
Four-cylinder engines	
Upstream O2 sensor	5 to 7 ohms
Downstream O2 sensor	6 to 11 ohms
3.4L V6 engines	6 to 11 ohms
4Runner	11 to 16 ohms
1997 and later models	
T100 models	
Four-cylinder engines	11 to 16 ohms
3.4L V6 engines with manual transmission	
Upstream O2 sensor	5 to 7 ohms
Downstream O2 sensor	11 to 16 ohms
3.4L V6 engines with automatic transmission	11 to 16 ohms
Tacoma models	
Four-cylinder engines (1997 only)	
Upstream O2 sensor	5 to 7 ohms
Downstream O2 sensor	11 to 16 ohms
3.4L V6 and 1998 four-cylinder engines	11 to 16 ohms
4Runner models	11 to 16 ohms

EGR gas temperature sensor resistance

112-degrees F .... 69 to 89 K-ohms
212-degrees F .... 11 to 15 K-ohms
300-degrees F .... 2 to 4 K-ohms

Crankshaft position sensor

Ne+ to Ne- terminals .... 1,630 to 2,740 ohms

Camshaft position sensor (1996 and later 3.4L V6 engines)

G+ to G- terminals .... 835 to 1,400 ohms

Torque specifications

Crankshaft sensor bolt
   Four-cylinder engines.. 74 in-lbs
   3.4L V6 engines... 69 in-lbs
Camshaft sensor bolt
   Four-cylinder engines.. 48 in-lbs
   3.4L V6 engines... 69 in-lbs

1.1 The Vehicle Emission Control Information (VECI) label is a handy reference guide for tune-up information and for the types of emission devices used on your vehicle - another label (not shown) near this one provides a vacuum schematic

1   General information

Refer to illustrations 1.1, 1.3a, 1.3b and 1.3c

1   To prevent pollution of the atmosphere from burned and evaporating gases, a number of major and auxiliary emission control systems are incorporated on the vehicles covered by this manual. The combination of systems used depends on the year in which the vehicle was manufactured, the locality to which it was originally delivered and the engine type. Check the Vehicle Emissions Control Information (VECI) label **(see illustration)** in your engine compartment to determine which systems are used on your vehicle. The major systems incorporated include:

   Pulse Air Injection system
   Catalytic Converter system
   Evaporative Emission Control system
   Exhaust Gas Recirculation system
   Positive Crankcase Ventilation system
   On Board Diagnosis (OBD) system

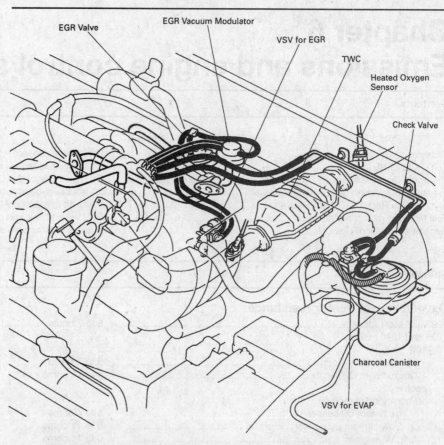

1.3a Vacuum hose routing diagram - 2.7L four-cylinder engine (2.4L similar)

Note: *To verify which emission control systems are installed on a particular vehicle, check the VECI label for a list of systems or refer to a dealer service department for additional information.*

2   The Sections in this Chapter include general descriptions, checking procedures (where possible) and component replacement procedures (where applicable) for each of the systems listed above.

3   Before assuming that an emission control system is malfunctioning, check the fuel and ignition systems carefully. In some cases, special tools and equipment, as well as specialized training, are required to accurately diagnose the causes of a rough running or difficult-to-start engine. If checking and servicing become too difficult or if a procedure is beyond the scope of the home mechanic, consult a dealer service department. This does not necessarily mean, however, that the emission control systems are

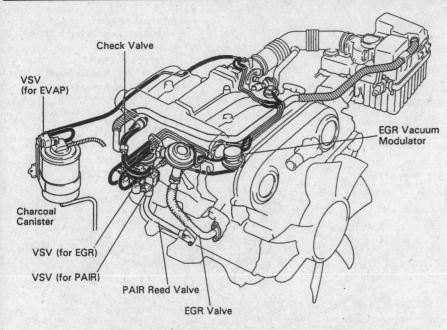

1.3b Vacuum hose routing diagram - 3.0L V6 engine

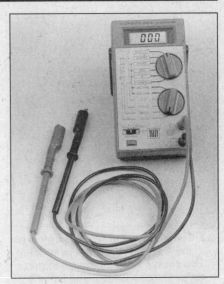

2.1 Digital multimeters can be used for testing all types of circuits; because of their high impedance, they are much more accurate than analog meters for measuring millivolts in low-voltage computer circuits

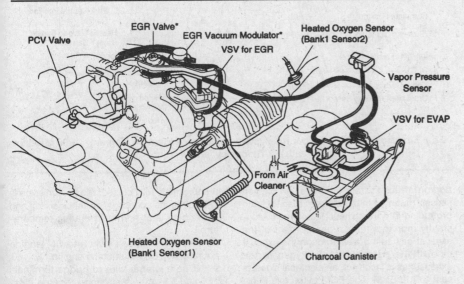

1.3c Vacuum hose routing diagram - 3.4L V6 engine

particularly difficult to maintain and repair. You can quickly and easily perform many checks and do most (if not all) of the regular maintenance at home with common tune-up and hand tools. **Note:** *The most frequent cause of emission system problems is simply a loose or broken vacuum hose or wiring connection* **(see illustrations)**. *Therefore, always check hose and wiring connections first.*

4   Pay close attention to any special precautions outlined in this Chapter (particularly those concerning the catalytic converter). It should be noted that the illustrations of the various systems may not exactly match the systems installed in your particular vehicle, due to changes made by the manufacturer during production or from year to year.

2   On Board Diagnosis (OBD) system and trouble codes

Note: *1993 and 1994 3.0L V6 engines are equipped with the OBD I self-diagnosis system, while all later models are equipped with the OBD II self diagnosis system. OBD I systems can be accessed using a jumper wire on the correct terminals of the check connector, but OBD II systems require the use of a Scan tool to access trouble codes. However, many of the information sensor checks and replacement procedures do apply to both systems. Because OBD II systems require a special SCAN tool to access the trouble codes, have*

the vehicle diagnosed by a dealer service department or other qualified automotive repair facility if the proper SCAN tool is not available. The OBD II five-digit codes indicated in the text are designed and mandated by the EPA for all 1995 and later OBD II vehicles produced by automobile manufacturers. These generic trouble codes do not include the manufacturer's specific trouble codes. Consult a dealer service department or other qualified repair shop for additional information. Refer to the troubleshooting tips in the beginning of this manual to gain some insight to the most likely causes of a problem.

Diagnostic tool information

Refer to illustrations 2.1 and 2.2

1   A digital multimeter is a necessary tool for checking fuel injection and emission related components **(see illustration)**. A digital volt-ohmmeter is preferred over an analog multimeter for several reasons. The analog multimeter cannot display the volts-ohms or amps measurement in hundredths and thousandths increments. When working with electronic circuits which are often very low voltage, this accurate reading is most important. Another good reason for using a digital multimeter is because of its high-impedance circuitry (10 million ohms). Because a voltmeter is hooked up in parallel with the circuit when testing, it is vital that none of the voltage being measured should be allowed to travel the parallel path set up by the meter itself. This dilemma does not show itself when measuring larger amounts of voltage (9 to 12 volt circuits) but if you are measuring a low voltage circuit such as the oxygen sensor signal voltage, a fraction of a volt may be a significant amount when diagnosing a problem.

2.2 Scanners like the Actron Scantool and the AutoXray XP240 are powerful diagnostic aids - programmed with comprehensive diagnostic information, they can tell you just about anything you want to know about your engine management system, but they are expensive

2   Hand-held scanners are the most powerful and versatile tools for analyzing engine management systems used on later model vehicles **(see illustration)**. Unfortunately, they are the most expensive. Early model scanners handle codes and some diagnostics for many OBD I systems. Each brand scan tool must be examined carefully to match the year, make and model of the vehicle you are working on. Often interchangeable cartridges are available to access the particular manufacturer; Toyota, Ford, GM, Chrysler, etc.). Some manufacturers will be categorized by continent; Asia, Europe, USA, etc.

3   With the arrival of the federally mandated emission control system (OBD II), a specially designed scanner is required. Ask the parts counterperson at a local auto parts store for additional information concerning these tools. **Note:** *Although OBD II codes cannot be accessed without a Scan tool, follow the simple component checks in Section 4.*

General description

Refer to illustrations 2.4a and 2.4b

4   The electronically controlled fuel and emissions system is linked with many other related engine management systems. It consists mainly of sensors, output actuators and an Electronic Control Module (ECM) **(see illustrations)**. Completing the system are various other components which respond to commands from the ECM.

5   In many ways, this system can be compared to the central nervous system in the human body. The sensors (nerve endings) constantly gather information and send this data to the ECM (brain), which processes the data and, if necessary, sends out a command for some type of vehicle change (limbs).

6   Here's a specific example of how one

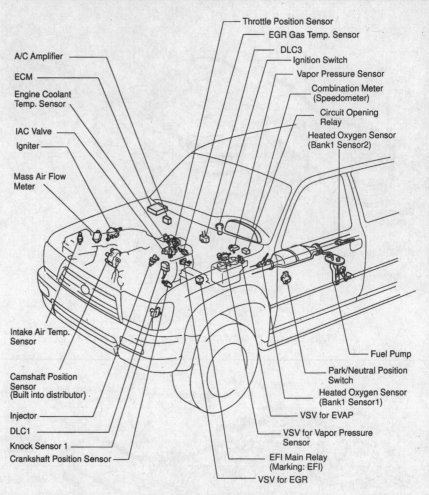

2.4a Emissions and engine control system component location diagram - 1996 4Runner with a 2.7L four-cylinder engine

portion of this system operates: An oxygen sensor, mounted in the exhaust manifold and protruding into the exhaust gas stream, constantly monitors the oxygen content of the exhaust gas as it travels through the exhaust pipe. If the percentage of oxygen in the exhaust gas is incorrect, an electrical signal is sent to the ECM. The ECM takes this information, processes it and then sends a command to the fuel injectors, telling it to change the fuel/air mixture. To be effective, all this happens in a fraction of a second, and it goes on continuously while the engine is running. The end result is a fuel/air mixture which is constantly kept at a predetermined ratio, regardless of driving conditions.

Obtaining OBD I trouble codes (1993 and 1994 3.0L V6 models)

Refer to illustrations 2.9 and 2.10

7   One might think that a system which uses exotic electrical sensors and is controlled by an on-board computer would be difficult to diagnose. This is not necessarily the case. To retrieve a diagnostic code, verify first that the battery voltage is above 11 volts,

the throttle is fully closed, the transmission is in Neutral, the accessory switches are off and the engine is at normal operating temperature.

8   Turn the ignition switch to ON (engine not running). Do not start the engine.

9   Use a jumper wire to bridge terminals TE1 and E1 of the test connector **(see illustration)**.

10   Read the diagnostic code as indicated by the number of flashes of the "CHECK ENGINE" light on the dash **(see illustration)**. Normal system operation is indicated by Code No. 1 (no malfunctions) for all models. The "CHECK ENGINE" light displays a Code No. 1 by blinking once every 0.25 seconds. Each code will be displayed by first blinking the first digit of the code, then pause, then blink the second digit of the code. **For example**; Code 24 (IAT sensor) will flash two times, pause, and then flash four times. Each flash will be the exact same length but the distinction will be the pause that separates the digits of the code. Only code 1 (normal operation) will flash continuously without a pause.

11   If there are any malfunctions in the system, their corresponding trouble codes are stored in computer memory and the light will

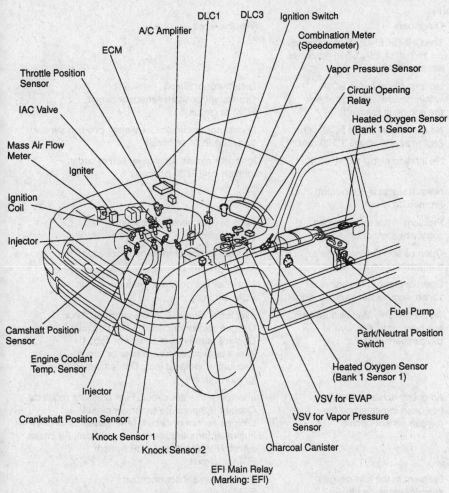

2.4b Emissions and engine control system component location diagram - 1996 4Runner with a 3.4L V6 engine

Throttle Position Sensor
A/C Amplifier
DLC1
DLC3
Ignition Switch
Combination Meter (Speedometer)
Vapor Pressure Sensor
Circuit Opening Relay
Heated Oxygen Sensor (Bank 1 Sensor 2)
ECM
IAC Valve
Mass Air Flow Meter
Igniter
Ignition Coil
Injector
Camshaft Position Sensor
Engine Coolant Temp. Sensor
Injector
Crankshaft Position Sensor
Knock Sensor 1
Knock Sensor 2
EFI Main Relay (Marking: EFI)
Charcoal Canister
VSV for Vapor Pressure Sensor
VSV for EVAP
Heated Oxygen Sensor (Bank 1 Sensor 1)
Park/Neutral Position Switch
Fuel Pump

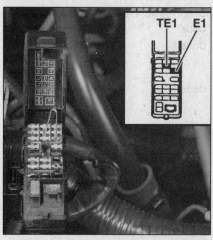

2.9 To access the self diagnosis system, locate the test connector in the engine compartment and using a jumper wire, bridge terminals TE1 and E1

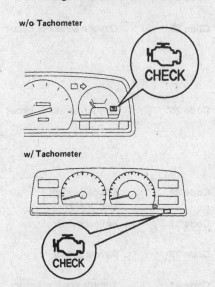

w/o Tachometer

CHECK

w/ Tachometer

CHECK

2.10 The CHECK ENGINE light is located in different locations depending on the tachometer option

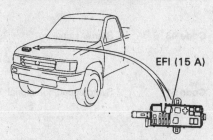

EFI (15 A)

2.13 Location of the 15A EFI fuse that cancels the diagnostic codes on OBD I models

blink the requisite number of times for the indicated trouble codes. If there's more than one trouble code in the memory, they'll be displayed in numerical order (from lowest to highest) with a pause between each one. After the code with the largest number of flashes has been displayed, there will be another pause and then the sequence will begin all over again. **Note:** *The diagnostic trouble codes 25, 26, 27 and 71 use a special diagnostic capability called "two-trip detection logic". With this system, when a malfunction is first detected, it is temporarily stored in the ECM on the first trip. The engine must be turned off and the vehicle taken on another trip to allow the malfunction to be stored permanently in the ECM. This will distinguish a true problem from a false alarm. Normally the self-diagnosis system will detect the malfunctions, but in the event you want to double-check the diagnosis by canceling the codes and rechecking, then it will be necessary to go on two test drives to confirm any malfunctions with these particular codes.*

12   To ensure correct interpretation of the flashing "CHECK ENGINE" light, watch carefully for the interval between the end of one code and the beginning of the next; otherwise, you will become confused by the apparent number of flashes and misinterpret the display (the length of this interval varies with the model year).

Canceling an OBD I diagnostic code (1993 and 1994 3.0L V6 models)

Refer to illustration 2.13

13   After the malfunctioning component has been repaired/replaced, the trouble codes stored in computer memory must be canceled. To accomplish this, simply remove the 15A EFI fuse **(see illustration)** for at least 10 seconds with the ignition switch off.

14   A stored code can also be canceled by removing the cable from the negative battery terminal, but other memory systems (such as the clock and radio presets) will also be canceled. **Caution:** *If the stereo in your vehicle is equipped with an anti-theft system, make sure you have the correct activation code before disconnecting the battery.*

15   If the diagnostic code is not canceled, it will be stored by the ECM and appear with any new codes in the event of future trouble.

16   Should it become necessary to work on engine components requiring removal of the battery terminal, always check to see if a diagnostic code has been recorded before disconnecting the battery.

Diagnostic Trouble Codes (OBD I models)

Code	Circuit or system	Diagnosis	Trouble area
Code 1	Normal	The CHECK ENGINE light flashes on and off rapidly when no codes are identified	
Code 12	RPM signal	No rpm signal to the ECM within several seconds after the engine is cranked	Distributor or circuit Crankshaft position sensor or circuit ECM or circuit
Code 13	RPM signal	No rpm signal to the ECM with engine speed above 1,500 rpm	Distributor or circuit; Crankshaft position sensor or circuit ECM or circuit
Code 14	Ignition signal	No ignition signal to the ECM	Igniter or circuit; Ignition switch or circuit Ignition coil; ECM or circuit
Code 16	A/T Control Signal	Normal signal is not output From ECM	ECM
Code 21	Oxygen sensor	Problem in the main oxygen sensor heater circuit	Main oxygen sensor or circuit ECM or circuit
Code 22	Coolant temperature	Open or short in the coolant temperature sensor circuit	Coolant temperature sensor or circuit ECM or circuit
Code 24	Intake air temperature	Open or short in the intake air sensor temperature sensor circuit	Intake air temperature sensor or circuit ECM or circuit
Code 25	Oxygen sensor or circuit	An excessively lean air/fuel ratio has been indicated by the oxygen sensor circuit	Injector or circuit; Fuel pressure regulator Oxygen sensor or circuit; ECM or circuit Coolant temperature sensor or circuit Intake air temperature sensor or circuit Vacuum or exhaust leak; Contaminated fuel Ignition system
Code 26	Oxygen sensor or circuit	An overly rich air/fuel ratio has been indicated by the oxygen sensor circuit	Injector or injector circuit; Fuel pressure regulator Coolant temperature sensor or circuit Oxygen sensor or circuit; MAP sensor or circuit Intake air temperature sensor or circuit; Air intake system EVAP system; EGR system; ECM or circuit
Code 27	Oxygen sensor Heater signal	Problem in the sub oxygen sensor heater circuit	Sub oxygen sensor or circuit ECM or circuit
Code 31	Airflow sensor	Open or short in airflow sensor circuit at idle	Airflow sensor or circuit ECM or circuit
Code 32	Airflow sensor	Open or short in airflow sensor circuit during acceleration	Airflow sensor or circuit ECM or circuit
Code 41	Throttle position sensor	Open or short in the throttle position sensor circuit	Throttle position sensor or circuit ECM or circuit
Code 42	Vehicle speed sensor	No speed signal for 8 seconds when the engine speed is between 3,000 and 5,000 rpm and the transmission is in gear	Vehicle speed sensor or circuit ECM or circuit Speedometer Instrument panel printed circuit
Code 43	Starter signal	No starter signal to the ECM until engine speed reaches 800 rpm with the vehicle not moving	Starter signal circuit Ignition switch ECM or circuit
Code 51	Switch condition signal	No TPS signal, gear selector signal or air conditioning signal to the ECM	Air conditioning switch or circuit Air conditioning amplifier Neutral/start switch or TPS ECM or circuit
Code 52	Knock sensor signal	Open or short circuit in knock sensor circuit	Knock sensor circuit ECM or circuit
Code 53	Knock sensor signal	Open or short circuit in knock sensor circuit	ECM or circuit
Code 71	EGR system	EGR temperature signal is too low	EGR system (EGR valve, hoses, etc.) EGR temperature sensor or circuit EGR vacuum switching valve; ECM or circuit

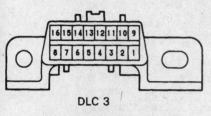

DLC 3

2.18 16-pin test connector for OBD II systems

Obtaining OBD II trouble codes

Refer to illustration 2.18

17   1994 four-cylinder engines and all 1995 and later models are equipped with the OBD II self-diagnosis system. This system is similar in operation to the OBD I system, but it monitors the engine operating parameters more precisely. It still has the capability to store trouble codes to facilitate problem diagnosis.

18   To retrieve this information from the ECM on all OBD II systems, a SCAN tool must be connected to the test connector **(see illustration)**. The SCAN tool is a hand-held digital computer that interfaces with the on-board computer. The SCAN tool is a very powerful tool; it not only reads the trouble codes but also displays the actual operating conditions of the sensors and actuators.

SCAN tools are expensive, but they are necessary to accurately diagnose a modern computerized fuel-injected engine. SCAN tools are available from automotive parts stores and specialty tool companies.

19   The self-diagnosis feature built into this system does not detect all possible faults. If you suspect a problem with the On Board Diagnostic (OBD) system, but the CHECK ENGINE light has not come on and no trouble codes have been stored, take the vehicle to a dealer service department or other qualified repair shop for diagnosis. Furthermore, when diagnosing an engine performance, fuel economy or exhaust emissions problem (which is not accompanied by a CHECK ENGINE light) do not automatically assume the fault lies in this system. Perform all standard troubleshooting procedures, as indicated at the beginning of this manual, before turning to the On Board Diagnostic (OBD) system.

20   Finally, since this is an electronic system, you should have a basic knowledge of automotive electronics before attempting any diagnosis. Damage to the ECM or related components can easily occur if care is not exercised.

Clearing OBD II trouble codes

21   To clear the codes from the ECM memory, install the SCAN tool, scroll the menu for the function that describes "CLEARING CODES" and follow the prescribed method

for that particular SCAN tool or momentarily remove the EFI fuse from the fuse box for 30 seconds. Clearing codes may also be accomplished by removing the fusible link (main power fuse) located near the battery positive terminal (see Chapter 12) or by disconnecting the cable from the positive terminal (+) of the battery. **Caution:** *On models equipped with an anti-theft audio system, be sure you have the correct activation code before disconnecting the battery cable. Also, disconnecting the battery will erase any radio preset codes that have been stored.* **Caution:** *To prevent damage to the ECM, the ignition switch must be OFF when disconnecting or connecting power to the ECM.*

Trouble Code Identification

22   Following is a list of the typical Trouble Codes which may be encountered while diagnosing the On Board Diagnostic (OBD II) system. Also included are simplified troubleshooting procedures. If the problem persists after these checks have been made, the vehicle must be diagnosed by a professional mechanic who can use specialized diagnostic tools and advanced troubleshooting methods to check the system. Procedures marked with an asterisk (*) indicate component replacements which may not cure the problem in all cases. For this reason, you may want to seek professional advice before purchasing replacement parts.

OBD II Trouble Codes

Code	Code Definition	Location
P0100	Mass Airflow (MAF) sensor error circuit	See Section 4
P0101	Mass Airflow (MAF) sensor error	See Section 4
P0110	Intake Air Temperature (IAT) sensor circuit	See Section 4
P0115	Electronic Coolant Temperature (ECT) sensor circuit low input	See Section 4
P0116	Electronic Coolant Temperature (ECT) sensor circuit high input	See Section 4
P0120	Throttle Position Sensor (TPS) circuit	See Section 4
P0121	Throttle Position Sensor (TPS) circuit or range/performance problem	See Section 4
P0125	O_2 sensor heater circuit fault	See Section 4
P0130	Upstream heated O_2 sensor circuit low voltage (Bank 1, Sensor 1)	See Section 4
P0133	Upstream heated O_2 sensor circuit high voltage (Bank 1, Sensor 1)	See Section 4
P0135	Upstream heated O_2 sensor heater circuit high voltage (Bank 1, Sensor 1)	See Section 4
P0136	Downstream heated O_2 sensor circuit low voltage (Bank 1, Sensor 2)	See Section 4
P0138	Downstream heated O_2 sensor circuit high voltage (Bank 1, Sensor 2)	See Section 4
P0141	O_2 sensor heater circuit fault (Bank 1, Sensor 2)	See Section 4
P0171	System Adaptive fuel too lean	See Chapter 4
P0172	System Adaptive fuel too rich	See Chapter 4
P0191	Injector Pressure sensor system performance	See Chapter 4
P0192	Injector Pressure sensor circuit low input	See Chapter 4

OBD II Trouble Codes (continued)

Code	Code Definition	Location
P0193	Injector Pressure sensor circuit high input	See Chapter 4
P0300	Random cylinder misfire detected	See Chapter 5
P0301	Cylinder number 1 misfire detected	See Chapter 5
P0302	Cylinder number 2 misfire detected	See Chapter 5
P0303	Cylinder number 3 misfire detected	See Chapter 5
P0304	Cylinder number 4 misfire detected	See Chapter 5
P0305	Cylinder number 5 misfire detected	See Chapter 5
P0306	Cylinder number 6 misfire detected	See Chapter 5
P0325	Knock sensor circuit 1 fault	See Section 4
P0330	Knock sensor circuit 2 fault	See Section 4
P0335	Crankshaft Position Sensor circuit fault	See Section 4
P0340	Camshaft Position sensor circuit fault	See Section 4
P0401	EGR insufficient flow detected	See Section 7
P0402	EGR excessive flow detected	See Section 7
P0420	Catalyst system efficiency below threshold (Bank 1)	See Section 10
P0421	Catalyst system efficiency below threshold (Bank 1)	See Section 10
P0430	Catalyst system efficiency below threshold (Bank 2)	See Section 10
P0431	Catalyst system efficiency below threshold (Bank 2)	See Section 10
P0440	EVAP incorrect purge flow	See Section 6
P0441	EVAP VSV circuit fault	See Section 6
P0446	EVAP vent control malfunction	See Section 6
P0450	EVAP fuel tank pressure sensor circuit	See Section 6
P0500	VSS circuit range performance	See Section 4
P0505	IAC system rpm incorrect	See Chapter 4
P0510	TPS malfunction	See Section 4

Component replacement may not cure the problem in all cases. For this reason, you may want to seek professional advice before purchasing replacement parts.

---

3   Electronic Control Module (ECM) - check and replacement

Check

1   The ECM on all models is located in the right front corner of the passenger compartment behind the glovebox. Remove the glovebox (see Chapter 11) for access to the ECM.

2   Using the tips of your fingers, tap vigorously on the side of the computer while the engine is running. If the computer is not functioning properly, the engine may stumble or stall and display glitches on the engine data stream obtained using a SCAN tool or other diagnostic equipment.

3   If the ECM fails this test, check the electrical connectors. Each connector is color coded to fit its respective slot in the computer body. If there are no obvious signs of damage, have the unit checked at a dealer service department or other qualified repair shop.

Replacement

Refer to illustrations 3.4a and 3.4b

Warning: *Some models covered by this manual are equipped with airbags. The airbag is*

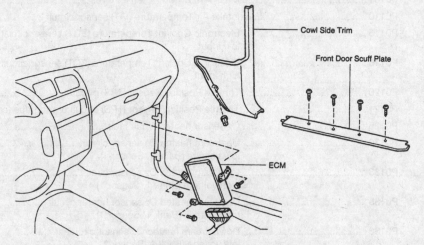

3.4a ECM location on T100 models

armed and can deploy (inflate) anytime the battery is connected. To prevent accidental deployment (and possible injury), turn the ignition key to LOCK and disconnect the negative battery cable whenever working near airbag components. After the battery is disconnected, wait at least two minutes before beginning work (the system has a back-up

capacitor that must fully discharge). For more information see Chapter 12.

Caution: *To prevent damage to the ECM, the ignition switch must be turned Off when disconnecting or connecting the ECM connectors.*

4   The ECM on T100 models is located in the right front corner of the passenger com-

3.4b The ECM (arrow) on 4Runners and Tacoma models is located behind the glove box

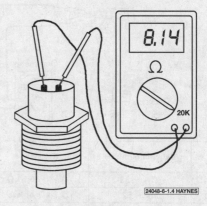

4.1a Be sure the meter probes make clean contact with the terminals of the sensor when checking the resistance (thermistor type sensor shown)

partment, behind the side trim panel **(see illustration)**. On 4Runner and Tacoma models it's located behind the glove box **(see illustration)**.

5   Disconnect the cable from the negative battery terminal. **Caution:** *On models equipped with an anti-theft audio system, be sure you have the correct activation code before disconnecting the battery cable* If you're working on a 4Runner or Tacoma, disable the airbag system (see the **Warning** above), then remove the glove box (see Chapter 11). If you're working on a T100, remove the side trim panel from the passenger's footwell area.

6   Disconnect the ECM electrical connectors. Each connector is color coded to fit its respective receptacle in the ECM. If available, ground yourself to the vehicle with special computer grounding strap (available at some auto parts stores and computer supply outlets), or be sure to touch a good vehicle ground before touching the ECM.

7   Unscrew the mounting bolts and carefully remove the ECM.

8   Installation is the reverse of removal.

4   Information sensors - general information and testing

Caution 1: *When performing the following tests, use only a high-impedance (10 mega ohms) digital multimeter to prevent damage to the ECM.*

Caution 2: *On models equipped with an anti-theft audio system, be sure you have the correct activation code before disconnecting the battery.*

Note 1: *Because OBD II systems require a special SCAN tool to access the self-diagnosis system, have the vehicle codes extracted by a dealer service department or other qualified repair facility if the SCAN tool is not available for diagnostic purposes. There are several checks the home mechanic can perform to test for a NO START condition but in the event the driveability symptoms are intermittent or varied, it will be necessary to monitor the operation of the sensor(s) with a SCAN tool.*

Temperature (degrees-F)	Resistance (ohms)
212	176
194	240
176	332
158	458
140	668
122	972
112	1182
104	1458
95	1800
86	2238
76	2795
68	3520
58	4450
50	5670
40	7280
32	9420

4.1b Coolant temperature and intake air temperature sensors approximate temperature vs. resistance relationships

Thermistor (two-wire) sensors (coolant temperature, intake air temperature, EGR temperature sensor etc.)

Refer to illustrations 4.1a and 4.1b

1   Thermistors are variable resistors that sense temperature level changes and convert them to a voltage signal. The engine coolant temperature sensor (ECT) and the intake air temperature sensor (IAT) are thermistor type sensors. As the sensor temperature DECREASES, the resistance will INCREASE. As the sensor temperature INCREASES, the resistance will DECREASE. To check thermistor type sensors, select the ohms range on the multi-meter, disconnect the electrical connector at the sensor and connect the test probes to the sensor terminals **(see illustration)**. The resistance reading (ohms) should be high when the sensor is cold, and low when the sensor is hot **(see illustration)**. Be sure the tips of the probe make clean contact with the terminals inside the sensor to insure an accurate reading.

2   After the resistance of the sensor has been checked, test the system for the proper reference voltage from the computer. Simply disconnect the harness connector at the sensor, select the voltage range on the multimeter and probe the terminals on the harness

for the voltage signal. Reference voltage should be approximately 5.0 volts. The ignition switch must be in the ON position (engine not running). If there is no reference voltage available to the sensor, then the circuit and the computer must be checked.

Potentiometer sensors (Throttle Position Sensors)

Refer to illustration 4.4a, 4.4b, 4.4c, 4.4d and 4.6

3   The potentiometer is a variable resistor that converts the voltage signal by varying the resistance according to the driving situation. The signal the potentiometer generates is used by the computer to determine position and direction of the device within the component. There are two different diagnostic methods that can be used on these type sensors. The first method checks the resistance changes of the potentiometer as it is moved through its operating range (closed to wide open throttle). The other method checks the voltage signal changes that occur during operation. The first method is used to check 4-terminal TP sensors installed on most models up to 1996. This testing method is preferred because the older style TP sensors are equipped with a switch that detects an ON/OFF signal when the accelerator is first opened in addition to the normal throttle

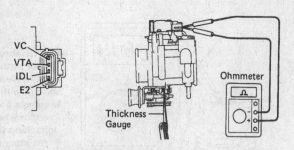

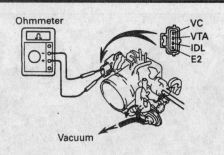

Clearance between lever and stop screw	Between terminals	Resistance
0 mm (0 in.)	VTA − E2	0.47 − 6.1 kΩ
0.50 mm (0.0197 in.)	IDL − E2	2.3 kΩ or less
0.77 mm (0.0303 in.)	IDL − E2	Infinity
Throttle valve fully open	VTA − E2	3.1 − 12.1 kΩ
−	VC − E2	3.9 − 9.0 kΩ

4.4a Throttle Position Sensor resistance table - T100 3.0L V6 models

Clearance between lever and stop screw	Between terminals	Resistance
0 mm (0 in.)	VTA − E2	0.2 − 5.7 kΩ
0.50 mm (0.020 in.)	IDL − E2	2.3 kΩ or less
0.75 mm (0.030 in.)	IDL − E2	Infinity
Throttle valve fully open	VTA − E2	2.0 − 10.2 kΩ
−	VC − E2	2.5 − 5.9 kΩ

4.4b Throttle Position Sensor resistance table - 2.4L four-cylinder engine

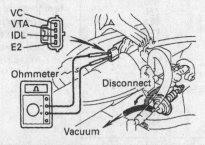

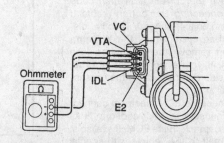

Clearance between lever and stop screw	Between terminals	Resistance
0 mm (0 in.)	VTA – E2	0.2 – 5.7 kΩ
0.57 mm (0.022 in.)	IDL – E2	2.3 kΩ or less
0.74 mm (0.029 in.)	IDL – E2	Infinity
Throttle valve fully open	VTA – E2	2.0 – 10.2 kΩ
−	VC – E2	2.5 – 5.9 kΩ

4.4c Throttle Position Sensor resistance table - 2.7L four-cylinder engine

Clearance between lever and stop screw	Between terminals	Resistance
0 mm (0 in.)	VTA – E2	0.28 – 6.4 kΩ
0.32 mm (0.013 in.)	IDL – E2	0.5 kΩ or less
0.54 mm (0.021 in.)	IDL – E2	Infinity
Throttle valve fully open	VTA – E2	2.0 – 11.6 kΩ
−	VC – E2	2.7 – 7.7 kΩ

4.4d Throttle Position Sensor resistance table - 3.4L V6 engine

detection capabilities. This circuit is referred to as IDL - E2 in the accompanying illustrations.

4 Disconnect the electrical connector from the throttle position sensor (TPS). If equipped with a throttle positioner, remove the vacuum line and apply vacuum to the throttle positioner. Insert a feeler gauge of the specified thickness between the throttle stop screw and the throttle lever. Using an ohmmeter, measure the resistance between the indicated terminal pairs (see illustrations).

5 If the resistance is not as specified, insert a feeler gauge between the throttle stop screw and lever, and connect the ohmmeter to terminals IDL and E2. Use a size approximately halfway between the two IDL - E2 specifications shown in illustrations 4.4a

through d; for example, a 0.025 in. (0.60 mm) feeler gauge on 3.0L V6 models. Loosen the TPS mounting screws and slowly rotate the sensor clockwise until the ohmmeter needle (or readout) just deflects, then stop. **Note:** *Follow the specifications on the charts listed in Step 4.* Tighten the mounting screws, and using the proper feeler gauge, recheck the continuity between the specified terminals.

6 The second method monitors the voltage changes through the operating range of the sensor with voltage applied. This method requires the TPS harness to be backprobed with long pins to link the voltmeter probes to the circuit. These later style TP sensors are 3-terminal harness connectors. Select the DC volts function on the multi-meter, carefully backprobe the harness connector using

straight pins inserted into the correct terminals and connect the meter probes to the pins (see illustration). Connect the negative probe (-) to the ground terminal and the positive probe to the SIGNAL terminal. It will be necessary to refer to the wiring diagrams at the end of this manual for the correct terminals. Observe the meter as the signal arm is moved through its complete range (sweep). The voltage should vary as the arm is moved from closed to wide-open-throttle.

7 After the signal voltage has been checked, test the system for the proper reference voltage from the computer. Simply disconnect the harness connector at the sensor, select the voltage range on the rotary switch on the volt/ohmmeter and probe the correct terminals on the harness for the voltage sig-

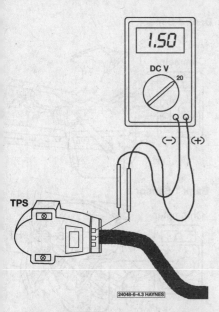

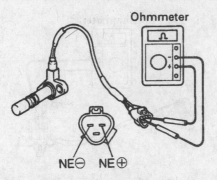

4.8a Testing the crankshaft sensor on the four-cylinder engine

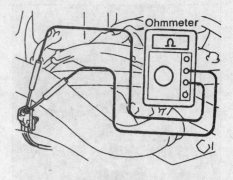

4.8b Testing the camshaft sensor on the 3.4L V6 engine

4.6 Carefully backprobe the GROUND (-) and the SIGNAL (+) terminals using sewing pins to make contact without disconnecting the harness connector (potentiometer type sensor shown)

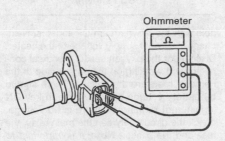

4.8c Testing the crankshaft sensor on the 3.4L V6 engine

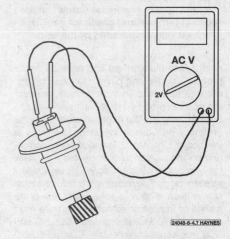

4.8d Connect the probes of the voltmeter directly to the VSS and observe A/C voltage fluctuations as the drive gear is slowly rotated

nal. Reference voltage should be approximately 5.0 volts. The ignition switch must be in the ON position (engine not running). If there is no reference voltage available to the sensor, then the circuit and the computer must be checked.

Magnetic reluctance (two-wire) sensors (crankshaft, camshaft, vehicle speed sensor, etc.)

Refer to illustrations 4.8a, 4.8b, 4.8c and 4.8d

8   Magnetic reluctance type sensors consist of a permanent magnet with a wire coil wound around the assembly. Crankshaft sensors and vehicle speed sensors are common applications of this type sensor. A steel disk mounted on a gear (crankshaft, input shaft, etc.) has tabs that pass between the pole pieces of the magnet causing a break in the magnetic field when passed near the sensor. This break in the field causes a magnetic flux producing reluctance (resistance) thereby changing the voltage signal. This voltage signal is used to determine crankshaft position, vehicle speed, etc. There are two methods for testing these types of sensors. The first test checks the resistance across the sensor leads **(see illustrations)**. This test checks the circuit within the sensor. If the sensor indicates the incorrect resistance, replace it with a new part.

The second test checks the operating condition of the sensor. Because magnetic energy is a free-standing source of energy and does not require battery power to pro-

duce voltage, this type of sensor must be checked by observing voltage fluctuations with an AC volt meter. Simply switch the voltmeter to the AC scale and connect the probes to the sensor. On vehicle speed sensors it will be necessary to place the transmission in neutral, then with the help of an assistant, hold one tire still while spinning the other tire (approximately 2 MPH or faster) and, observe the voltage fluctuations. This test can also be performed with the sensor removed from the vehicle, by turning the sensor's drive gear **(see illustration)**. **Note:** *Some vehicle speed sensors don't have a drive gear - this type of sensor will have to be checked in place.* On crankshaft position sensors it will be necessary to have an assistant crank the engine over in short bursts at the ignition key while you observe the voltage fluctuations. The meter should register slight voltage fluctuations that are constant and relatively the same range. These small voltage fluctuations indicate that the magnetic portion of the sensor is producing a magnetic field and "sensing" engine parameters for the computer.

Oxygen (O2) sensors

Refer to illustration 4.10, 4.12a and 4.12b

9   The oxygen sensor(s) monitors the oxygen content of the exhaust gas stream. The oxygen content in the exhaust reacts with the oxygen sensor to produce a voltage output which varies from 0.1-volt (high oxygen, lean mixture) to 0.9-volts (low oxygen, rich mix-

ture). The ECM constantly monitors this variable voltage output to determine the ratio of oxygen to fuel in the mixture. The ECM alters the air/fuel mixture ratio by controlling the pulse width (open time) of the fuel injectors. The ECM and the oxygen sensor(s) attempt to maintain a mixture ratio of 14.7 parts air to 1 part of fuel at all times. The oxygen sensor produces no voltage when it is below its normal operating temperature of about 600-degrees F. During this initial period before warm-up, the ECM operates in OPEN LOOP mode. When checking the oxygen sensor system, it will be necessary to test all oxygen sensors. **Note:** *Because the oxygen sensor(s) are difficult to access, probing the harness electrical connectors for testing purposes will require patience. The exhaust manifolds and pipes are extremely hot and will melt stray electrical probes and leads that touch the surface during testing. If possible, use a SCAN tool that plugs into the DLC (diagnostic link). This tool will access the ECM data stream and indicates the millivolt changes for each individual oxygen sensor.*

10   Check the oxygen sensor millivolt signal. Locate the oxygen sensor electrical con-

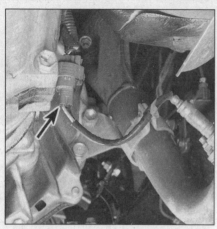

4.10 Insert a pin into the backside of the oxygen sensor connector (arrow) on the correct terminal and check for a millivolt output signal generated by the sensor

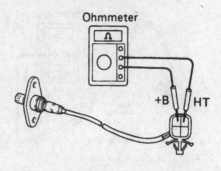

4.12a To test the oxygen sensor heater, disconnect the harness connector and check the resistance across terminals HT and +B of the oxygen sensor connector (OBD I shown)

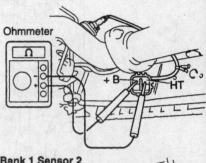

Bank 1 Sensor 1

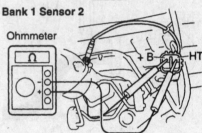

Bank 1 Sensor 2

4.12b Checking the upstream O2 sensor heater (Bank 1, Sensor 1) and the downstream O2 sensor heater (Bank 1, Sensor 2)

nector **(see illustration)** and carefully back-probe it using a long pin(s) into the appropriate wire terminals. In most models, connect the positive probe (+) of a voltmeter onto the SIGNAL wire and the negative probe (-) to the ground wire. Consult the wiring diagrams at the end of Chapter 12 for additional information on the oxygen sensor electrical connector wire color designations. **Note:** *Downstream oxygen sensors will produce much slower fluctuating voltage values to reflect the results of the catalyzed exhaust mixture from rich or lean to less presence of CO, HC and NOx molecules. Here the CO_2 and H_2O gaseous forms do not register or react with the oxygen sensors to such a large degree. Monitor the SIGNAL voltage (millivolts) as the engine goes from cold to warm.*

11   The oxygen sensor will produce a steady voltage signal of approximately 0.1 to 0.2 volts (100 to 200 millivolts) with the engine cold (open loop). After a period of approximately two minutes, the engine will reach operating temperature and the oxygen sensor will start to fluctuate between 0.1 to 0.9 volts (100 to 900 millivolts) (closed loop). If the oxygen sensor fails to reach the closed loop mode or there is a very long period of time until it does switch into closed loop mode, replace the oxygen sensor with a new part. **Note:** *Downstream oxygen sensors will not change voltage values as quickly as upstream oxygen sensors. Because the downstream oxygen sensors detect oxygen content after the exhaust has been catalyzed, voltage values should fluctuate much slower and deliberate.*

12   Also inspect the oxygen sensor heater. Disconnect the oxygen sensor electrical connector and working on the oxygen sensor side, connect an ohmmeter between the +B (+) and HT (-) terminals **(see illustrations)**. Refer to the Specifications listed in this Chapter for the correct resistance values. Some models have different values for upstream and downstream O2 sensors. Upstream O2 sensors are not interchange-

able with the downstream O2 sensors. Next, check for proper supply voltage to the heater. Disconnect the oxygen sensor electrical connector and working on the engine side of the harness, measure the voltage. There should be battery voltage with the ignition key ON (engine not running). If there is no voltage, check the circuit between the main relay, the fuse and the sensor. **Note:** *It is important to remember that supply voltage will only reach the O2 sensor with the ignition key ON (engine not running). If the oxygen sensor fails any of these tests, replace it with a new part.* **Note:** *Refer to the wiring diagrams at the end of Chapter 12 for additional information concerning the wire color codes and designations.*

Airflow sensors

Refer to illustrations 4.14a, 4.14b and 4.14c

13   The airflow sensor measures the amount of air passing through the sensor body and ultimately entering the engine through the throttle body. The ECM uses this information to control fuel delivery - the more air entering the engine (acceleration), the more fuel needed. There are two different designs incorporated into these models. 1993 and 1994 3.0L V6 models (OBD I systems), use a vane-type airflow sensor. As air enters the intake system (air cleaner), the measuring plate (vane) swings open and allows an electrical device to gather information using the position of the measuring plate. All other models use the vortex-type airflow sensor, which uses a hot-wire to measure air mass (volume and weight). This information is relayed to the computer to inject the correct amount of fuel into the combustion chamber for the volume of air (load) that is demanded. These later type airflow sensors are referred to as Mass Airflow (MAF) sensors.

14   There are three different types of airflow sensors on these models. The 7-terminal type (or vane airflow sensor) is installed on 1993 and 1994 3.0L V6 models. The 5-terminal and 3-terminal MAF sensors are installed on 1994 four-cylinder engines and all 1995 and later models (OBD II). To test a 5- or 7-

terminal airflow sensor, disconnect the electrical connector and measure the MAF sensor terminals following the designations in the charts **(see illustration)**. To check a 3-terminal airflow sensor, remove the airflow sensor from the air duct but leave the electrical connector plugged in, Turn the ignition key to the On position and connect the probes of a voltmeter to the proper terminals **(see illustration)**. Using compressed air or a hair dryer, blow through the airflow meter and watch the voltmeter - the voltage should fluctuate.

15   A SCAN tool is recommended to check the output of the MAF sensor. The SCAN tool displays the sensor output in grams per second. With the engine idling at normal operating temperature, the display should read 4 to 7 grams per second. When the engine is accelerated the values should raise and remain steady at any given RPM. A failure in the MAF sensor or circuit will also set a diagnostic trouble code.

Knock sensors

Note: *Four-cylinder engines use one knock sensor, located on the engine block, underneath the intake manifold. V6 engines use two sensors, one located on each bank of cylinders, underneath the intake manifold.*

16   Knock sensors detect abnormal vibration in the engine. The knock control system is designed to reduce spark knock during periods of heavy detonation. This allows the engine to use maximum spark advance to improve driveability. Knock sensors produce AC output voltage which increases with the severity of the knock. The signal is fed into the ECM and the timing is retarded to compensate for the severe detonation.

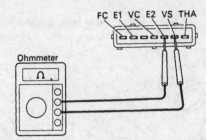

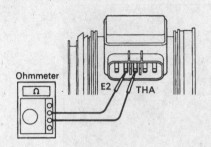

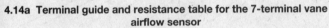

Between terminals	Resistance	Temperature
VS – E2	200 – 600 Ω	–
VC – E2	200 – 400 Ω	–
THA – E2	10 – 20 kΩ	–20°C (4°F)
THA – E2	4 – 7 kΩ	0°C (32°F)
THA – E2	2 – 3 kΩ	20°C (68°F)
THA – E2	0.9 – 1.3 kΩ	40°C (104°F)
THA – E2	0.4 – 0.7 kΩ	60°C (140°F)
FC – E1	Infinity	–

4.14a Terminal guide and resistance table for the 7-terminal vane airflow sensor

Between terminals	Resistance	Temperature
THA – E2	10 – 20 kΩ	–20°C (–4°F)
THA – E2	4 – 7 kΩ	0°C (32°F)
THA – E2	2 – 3 kΩ	20°C (68°F)
THA – E2	0.9 – 1.3 kΩ	40°C (104°F)
THA – E2	0.4 – 0.7 kΩ	60°C (140°F)
THA – E2	0.2 – 0.4 kΩ	80°C (176°F)

4.14b Terminal guide and resistance table for the 5-terminal MAF sensor

17   To check a knock sensor, disconnect the electrical connector and check for continuity between the sensor terminal and the sensor body - continuity should not exist. If it does, replace the sensor.

Neutral Start switch

18   The Neutral Start switch, located on the rear upper part of the automatic transmission, indicates to the ECM when the transmission is in Park or Neutral. This information is used for Exhaust Gas Recirculation (EGR) and Idle Air Control (IAC) valve operation. **Caution:** *The vehicle should not be driven with the Neutral Start switch disconnected because idle quality will be adversely affected.*

19   For more information regarding the Neutral Start switch, which is part of the Neutral start and back-up light switch assembly, see Chapter 7.

Air conditioning control

20   During air conditioning operation, the ECM controls the application of the air conditioning compressor clutch. The ECM controls the air conditioning clutch control relay to delay clutch engagement after the air conditioning is turned ON to allow the IAC valve to adjust the idle speed of the engine to compensate for the additional load. The ECM also controls the relay to disengage the clutch on WOT (wide open throttle) to prevent excessively high rpm on the compressor. Be sure to check the air conditioning system as detailed in Chapter 3 before attempting to diagnose the air conditioning clutch or electrical system.

Power steering pressure sensor

21   Turning the steering wheel increases power steering fluid pressure and engine load. The pressure switch will close before the load can cause an idle problem. A pressure switch that will not open or an open circuit from the ECM will cause timing to retard at idle and this will affect idle quality. A pressure switch that will not close or an open circuit may cause the engine to die when the power steering system is used heavily. Any problems with the power steering pressure switch or circuit should be repaired by a dealer service department or other qualified repair shop.

Vapor pressure sensor

22   The vapor pressure sensor is used to monitor the fuel tank pressure or vacuum during the OBD II test portion for emissions integrity. This test scans various sensors and output actuators to detect abnormal amounts of fuel vapors that may not be purging into the canister and/or the intake system for recycling. The vapor pressure helps the ECM monitor this pressure differential (pressure vs. vacuum) inside the fuel tank. If obvious problems are not found, problems with the EVAP system, the vapor pressure sensor or circuit should be repaired by a dealer service department or other qualified repair shop.

---

5   Information sensors - replacement

Engine Coolant Temperature (ECT) sensor

Refer to illustrations 5.1 and 5.2
Warning: *Wait until the engine is completely cool before beginning this procedure.*

1   The coolant temperature sensor on four-cylinder engines is located on the rear of the cylinder head **(see illustration)**. On the 3.0L

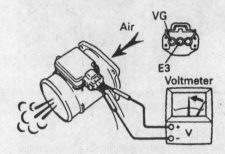

4.14c To check a 3-Terminal MAF sensor, remove the sensor (leave the electrical connector plugged in), connect the probes of a voltmeter to terminals VG and E3 and, with the ignition On, voltage should fluctuate as air is blown through the sensor

5.1 Location of the coolant temperature sensor (arrow) on the 2.7L four-cylinder engine

5.2 To prevent coolant leakage, be sure to wrap the coolant temperature sensor threads with Teflon tape before installation

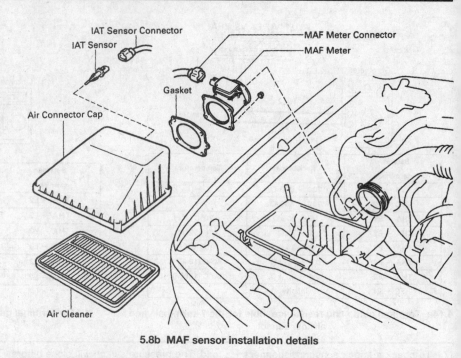

5.8b MAF sensor installation details

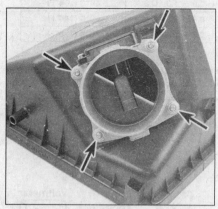

5.8a MAF sensor mounting nuts (arrows)

V6 engine, the ECT is located on the intake manifold beneath the air intake plenum at the rear of the engine (near the firewall). On the 3.4L V6 engine, the ECT is located behind the timing belt cover on the top of the intake manifold. The coolant temperature sensor is a thermistor (a resistor which varies the value of its resistance in accordance with temperature changes). Refer to Section 4 for the checking procedures.

2   Before installing the new sensor, wrap the threads with Teflon sealing tape to prevent leakage and thread corrosion **(see illustration)**.

3   To remove the sensor, release the locking tab, unplug the electrical connector, then carefully unscrew the sensor. **Caution:** *Handle the coolant sensor with care. Damage to this sensor will affect the operation of the entire fuel injection system.*

4   Install the new sensor as quickly as possible to minimize coolant loss. When you're done, check the coolant level and add some, if necessary (see Chapter 1).

Airflow sensor

MAF sensor (1994 four-cylinder engines and all 1995 and later models)

Refer to illustrations 5.8a and 5.8b

5   The Mass Airflow Sensor (MAF) is located on the air intake duct on all applica-ble models **(see illustration 2.4a and 2.4b)**. The MAF sensor is a hot-wire type sensor and is used to measure the amount (mass) of air entering the engine. Refer to Section 4 for the checking procedures.

6   Disconnect the electrical connector from the MAF sensor.

7   Remove the air cleaner assembly from the air intake duct (see Chapter 4).

8   Remove the nuts and lift the MAF sensor assembly from the air cleaner **(see illustrations)**.

9   Installation is the reverse of removal.

Vane airflow sensor (1993 and 1994 3.0L V6 engines)

Refer to illustration 5.10

10   The vane airflow sensor, also known as the Volume Air Flow (VAF) meter is located on the air intake duct on all applicable models **(see illustration)**. The VAF sensor is a vane trap-door type sensor and is used to measure the amount (volume) of air entering the engine. Refer to Section 4 for the checking procedures.

11   Disconnect the electrical connector, the two vacuum hoses and A/C idle-up VSV connector from the VAF sensor.

12   Remove the air cleaner assembly from the air intake duct (see Chapter 4).

13   Remove the nuts and lift the MAF sensor assembly from the air cleaner **(see illustration)**.

14   Installation is the reverse of removal.

Intake Air Temperature (IAT) sensor

Refer to illustration 5.15

15   The Intake Air Temperature (IAT) sensor is located inside the air cleaner housing on all models **(see illustration)**. Also refer to **illustrations 2.4a and 2.4b** if necessary. The IAT sensor is a thermistor (a resistor which varies the value of its resistance in accordance with temperature changes). Refer to Section 4 for the checking procedures.

16   To remove an IAT sensor, unplug the electrical connector and remove the sensor from the air intake duct. Carefully twist the sensor to release it from the rubber boot.

17   Installation is the reverse of removal.

Oxygen (O₂) sensor(s)

Refer to illustration 5.18

Note: *Because it is installed in the exhaust manifold or pipe, which contracts when cool, the oxygen sensor may be very difficult to loosen when the engine is cold. Rather than risk damage to the sensor (assuming you are planning to reuse it in another manifold or pipe) or the threads which it screws into, start and run the engine for a minute or two, then shut it off. Be careful not to burn yourself during the following procedure.*

Note: *OBD I 3.0L V6 engines are equipped with a single oxygen sensor except for California models which have the upstream and downstream O2 sensors.*

18   1993 and 1994 3.0L V6 models are equipped with a single heated oxygen sensor located in the rear exhaust manifold, while 1994 four-cylinder and all 1995 and later models are equipped with an upstream O2 sensor (before the catalytic converter in the rear exhaust manifold) and a downstream O2 sensor (after the catalytic converter) **(see illustration)**. The oxygen sensor(s) monitors the oxygen content of the exhaust gas stream. Oxygen content in the exhaust reacts with the oxygen sensor to produce a voltage output which allows the ECM to change the

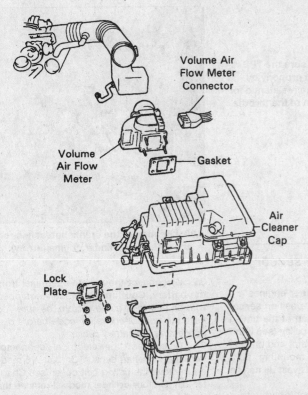

Volume Air Flow Meter Connector

Volume Air Flow Meter

Gasket

Air Cleaner Cap

Lock Plate

5.10 Exploded view of the vane airflow sensor and components

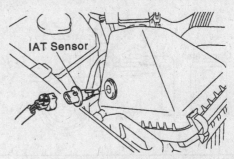

IAT Sensor

5.15 Location of the IAT sensor

Upstream O₂ Sensor

Downstream O₂ Sensor

5.18 Oxygen sensor locations on a 1998 four-cylinder model

air fuel ratio in the engine. Refer to Section 4 for the checking procedures.

19   The following is a list of special precautions which must be taken whenever the sensor is serviced.

a) *The oxygen sensor has a permanently attached pigtail and electrical connector which should not be removed from the sensor. Damage or removal of the pigtail or electrical connector can adversely affect operation of the sensor.*

b) *Grease, dirt and other contaminants should be kept away from the electrical connector and the louvered end of the sensor.*

c) *Do not use cleaning solvents of any kind on the oxygen sensor.*

d) *Do not drop or roughly handle the sensor.*

e) *The silicone boot must be installed in the correct position to prevent the boot from being melted and to allow the sensor to operate properly.*

f) *The sensor is designed to allow air circulation to the internal portion of the sensor. Whenever the sensor is removed and installed or replaced, make sure the air passages are not restricted.*

20   Disconnect the cable from the negative terminal of the battery. **Caution:** *On models equipped with an anti-theft audio system, be sure you have the correct activation code before disconnecting the battery cable.*

21   Raise the vehicle and place it securely on jackstands.

5.28 TPS location (arrow)

22   Remove any exhaust heat shields which would interfere with the removal of the oxygen sensor(s), then disconnect the electrical connector from the sensor.

23   Carefully remove the O2 sensor bolts from the exhaust manifold or the exhaust pipe.

24   Anti-seize compound must be used on the threads of the sensor to facilitate future removal. The threads of new sensors will already be coated with this compound, but if an old sensor is removed and reinstalled, recoat the threads.

25   Install the sensor and tighten it securely.

26   Reconnect the electrical connector of the pigtail lead to the main engine wiring harness.

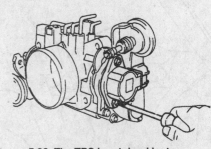

5.30 The TPS is retained by two mounting screws

27   Lower the vehicle, take it on a test drive and check to see that no trouble codes set.

Throttle Position Sensor (TPS)

Refer to illustrations 5.28, 5.30 and 5.31

28   The Throttle Position Sensor (TPS) is located on the end of the throttle shaft on the throttle body **(see illustration)**. The TPS is a potentiometer type sensor and is used to measure the throttle valve position and angle. Refer to Section 4 for the checking procedures.

29   Disconnect the electrical connector from the TPS. **Note:** *It may be necessary to remove the air inlet tube (air duct) to access the sensor connector.*

30   Remove the mounting screws from the TPS **(see illustration)** and remove the TPS from the throttle body.

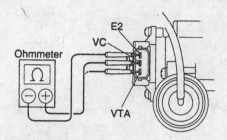

5.31 Make sure the TPS is adjusted properly by matching the resistance for the position of the throttle

Throttle valve condition	Between terminals	Resistance
Fully closed	VTA — E2	0.2 — 5.7 kΩ
Fully open	VTA — E2	2.0 — 10.2 kΩ
—	VC — E2	2.5 — 5.9 kΩ

5.33 Location of the crankshaft sensor on the 2.4L four-cylinder engine (arrow)

31   When installing the TPS, be sure to align the socket locating tangs on the TPS with the throttle shaft in the throttle body. **Note:** *Refer to Section 4 for the adjustment procedure on a 4-wire TPS. On a 3-wire TPS, there are no specific feeler gauge settings but instead, connect the ohmmeter probes to the correct terminals and observe that the specifications are correct when the throttle is completely closed. Slowly rotate the throttle and monitor the resistance changes. If the resistance readings are incorrect, replace the TPS* **(see illustration).**

32   Installation is the reverse of removal.

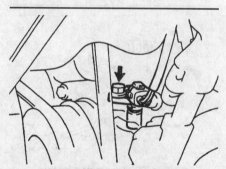

5.34 Location of the crankshaft sensor on the 3.4L V6 engine (arrow)

5.35a Location of the camshaft sensor on the 1998 2.4L four-cylinder engine (arrow)

Crankshaft position sensor

Refer to illustrations 5.33 and 5.34

33   Models with four-cylinder engines are equipped with a crankshaft position sensor mounted in the lower section of the timing cover behind the crankshaft pulley **(see illustrations).** Remove the alternator and bracket assembly to access the mounting bolt. Remove the sensor slowly to avoid damaging the component.

34   3.4L V6 models are equipped with a crankshaft position sensor mounted on the upper left side of the oil pump **(see illustration).** Remove the timing belt cover (see Chapter 2B) to access the crankshaft sensor.

Camshaft position sensor

Refer to illustrations 5.35a and 5.35b

35   The camshaft sensor on 1998 four-cylinder models is mounted in the middle of the cylinder head above the intake manifold runner **(see illustration).** The camshaft sensor on 3.4L V6 models is behind the timing belt cover **(see illustration).**

36   Disconnect the negative terminal from the battery. **Caution:** *On models equipped with an anti-theft audio system, be sure you have the correct activation code before disconnecting the battery cable.*

37   Disconnect the electrical connector from the camshaft sensor. On 3.4L V6 models, remove the timing belt cover (see Chapter 2B). On four-cylinder models, remove the throttle body assembly from the air intake plenum (see Chapter 4).

38   Remove the bolt from the camshaft sensor and remove the sensor.

39   Installation is the reverse of removal. Tighten the bolts to the torque listed in this Chapter's Specifications.

Knock sensors

Refer to illustration 5.40

Warning: *Wait for the engine to cool completely before performing this procedure.*

Note: *On 3.0L and 3.4L engines, it will be*

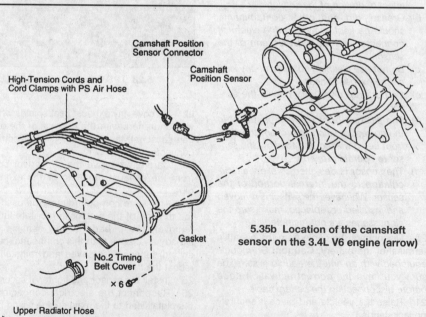

High-Tension Cords and Cord Clamps with PS Air Hose

Camshaft Position Sensor Connector

Camshaft Position Sensor

Gasket

No.2 Timing Belt Cover

× 6

Upper Radiator Hose

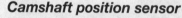

5.35b Location of the camshaft sensor on the 3.4L V6 engine (arrow)

5.40 Location of the knock sensor on the 2.4L four-cylinder engine (arrow)

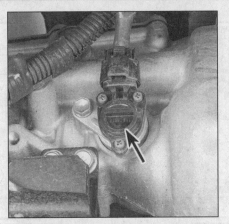

5.42 Location of the VSS (arrow)

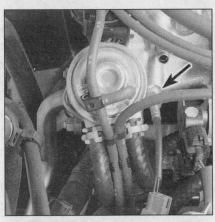

5.45 Location of the EGR temperature sensor (arrow)

necessary to remove the air intake plenum and the intake manifold to access the knock sensors. Refer to Chapters 2B and 4 for the removal procedures.

40 The knock sensor on four-cylinder engines is located on the engine block below the intake manifold,1 above the fuel filter **(see illustration)**. The knock sensors on V6 engines are located on each cylinder bank below the intake manifold. This sensor is used to control spark knock by retarding ignition timing during periods of heavy detonation. Refer to Section 4 for the checking procedures.

41 The knock sensor is threaded into the engine block coolant passage; when it is removed, the coolant will drain from the engine block. Drain the cooling system (see Chapter 1). If you're working on a four-cylinder engine, unbolt the fuel filter from the engine block for access to the sensor. Place a drain pan under the sensor, disconnect the electrical connector and remove the knock sensor. A new sensor is pre-coated with thread sealant - do not apply any additional sealant or the operation of the sensor may be affected. Install the knock sensor and tighten it securely (approximately 14 ft-lbs). Don't overtighten the sensor or damage may occur. Plug in the electrical connector, refill the cooling system and check for leaks.

Vehicle speed sensor (VSS)

Refer to illustration 5.42

42 The Vehicle Speed Sensor (VSS) is located at the rear the transmission housing **(see illustration)**. This sensor is a magnetic reluctance type sensor which sends a pulsing voltage signal to the ECM, which the ECM converts to miles per hour. Refer to Section 4 for the checking procedures.

43 To replace the VSS, detach the sensor retaining bolt(s) and or bracket, unplug the sensor and remove it from the transmission.

44 Installation is the reverse of removal.

EGR gas temperature sensor

Refer to illustration 5.45

45 The EGR temperature sensor is

mounted near the EGR valve **(see illustration)**. This sensor detects the temperature of the exhaust as it moves through the EGR valve. The information is sent to the ECM and in turn, the EGR on/off time is regulated precisely and more efficiently.

45 Disconnect the harness connector for the EGR temperature sensor and using an open-end wrench, remove the sensor from the intake manifold. Installation is the reverse of removal.

6 Evaporative Emission Control (EVAP) system

General description

Refer to illustration 6.1

1 This system is designed to trap and store fuel that evaporates from the fuel tank, throttle body and intake manifold that would normally enter the atmosphere in the form of

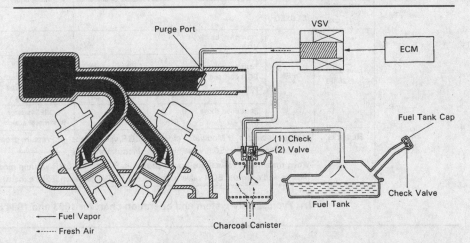

To reduce HC emission, evaporated fuel from the fuel tank is routed through the charcoal canister to the intake manifold for combustion in the cylinders.

Engine Coolant Temp.	VSV	Throttle Valve Opening	Check Valve in Charcoal Canister (1)	Check Valve in Charcoal Canister (2)	Check Valve in Cap	Evaporated Fuel (HC)
Below 45°C (113°F)	CLOSED	–	–	–	–	HC from tank is absorbed in the canister.
		Idling	–	–	–	
Above 50°C (122°F)	OPEN	Positioned below purge port	–	–	–	
		Positioned above purge port	–	–	–	HC from canister is led into air intake manifold.
High pressure in tank	–	–	OPEN	CLOSED	CLOSED	HC from tank is absorbed in the canister.
High vacuum in tank	–	–	CLOSED	OPEN	OPEN	(Air is led into the fuel tank.)

6.1 Typical EVAP system and operation chart (1993 and 1994 3.0L V6 model shown, others similar)

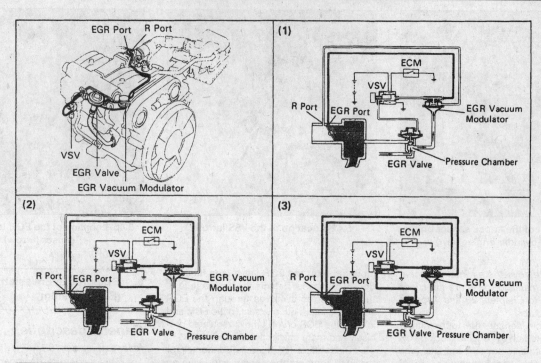

To reduce NOx emissions, part of the exhaust gases are recirculated through the EGR valve to the intake manifold to lower the maximum combustion temperature.

Engine Coolant Temp.	VSV	Throttle Valve Opening Angle	Pressure in the EGR Valve Pressure Chamber		EGR Vacuum Modulator	EGR Valve	Exhaust Gas
Below 48°C (118°F)	CLOSED	–	–		–	CLOSED	Not recirculated
Above 52°C (126°F)	OPEN	Positioned below EGR port	–		–	CLOSED	Not recirculated
		Positioned between EGR port and R port	(1) LOW	*Pressure constantly alternating between low and high	OPENS passage to atmosphere	CLOSED	Not recirculated
			(2) HIGH		CLOSES passage to atmosphere	OPEN	Recirculated
		Positioned above R port	(3) HIGH	**	CLOSES passage to atmosphere	OPEN	Recirculated (increase)

Remarks: *Pressure increases → Modulator closes → EGR valve opens → Pressure drops
EGR valve closes ← Modulator opens ←

**When the throttle valve is positioned above the R port, the EGR vacuum modulator will close the atmosphere passage and open the EGR valve to increase the EGR gas, even if the exhaust pressure is insufficiently low.

7.1 Typical EGR system and operation chart for 1993 and 1994 3.0L V6 models

hydrocarbon (HC) emissions **(see illustrations)**. The systems varied from year to year with fuel system changes and stricter emissions laws.

2   Early Evaporative Emission Control (EVAP) system consists of a charcoal-filled canister, the lines connecting the canister to the fuel tank, the coolant temperature sensor (ECT), the Vacuum Switching Valve (VSV), the ECM and a check valve mounted on the charcoal canister. Later EVAP systems are equipped with a vapor pressure sensor that is mounted on the firewall in the engine compartment. Refer to illustrations 2.4a and 2.4b for locations. On 2003 and later 3.4L V6 models, the evaporative system charcoal canister is mounted under the vehicle on a bracket at the rear of the fuel tank. The vapor pressure sensor senses pressure changes from leaks within the EVAP system ranging from the fuel tank, all the vacuum lines to the charcoal canister and throttle body. This system is incorporated into the OBD II system (refer to Sections 2 and 4). Checking these later systems will require a special OBD II Scan tool. **Note:** *The EVAP systems varied slightly from year to year and also with the various engine options. Refer to the vacuum schematic for the correct vacuum hose arrangement and the location of the various EVAP system components.*

3   Fuel vapors are transferred from the fuel tank and throttle body to a canister where they're stored when the engine isn't running. When the engine is running, the fuel vapors are purged from the canister by intake airflow and consumed in the normal combustion process.

4   The charcoal canister is equipped with a check valve that incorporates two check balls. Depending upon the running conditions and the pressure in the fuel tank, the check balls open and close the passageways to the TVV (consequently the throttle body) and fuel tank.

Check

5   Poor idle, stalling and poor driveability can be caused by an inoperative check valve, a damaged canister, split or cracked hoses or hoses connected to the wrong fittings. Check the fuel filler cap for a damaged or deformed gasket (see Chapter 1).

6   Evidence of fuel loss or fuel odor can be caused by liquid fuel leaking from fuel lines, a cracked or damaged canister, an inoperative check valve, disconnected, misrouted, kinked, deteriorated or damaged vapor or control hoses.

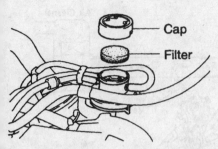

7.6 Remove the cap and filter to clean the EGR vacuum modulator

7   Inspect each hose attached to the canister for kinks, leaks and cracks along its entire length. Repair or replace as necessary.
8   Look for fuel leaking from the bottom of the canister. If fuel is leaking, replace the canister and check the hoses and hose routing.
9   Inspect the canister. If it's cracked or damaged, replace it.
10   Check for a clogged filter or a stuck check valve. Using low pressure compressed air, blow into the canister tank pipe. Air should flow freely from the other pipes. If a problem is found, replace the canister.
11   Check the operation of the VSV. With the engine completely cold, use a hand-held pump and direct air into the VSV from the manifold side. Air should not pass through the VSV. Now warm the engine to operating temperature (above 122-degrees F) and observe that air passes through the VSV. Apply battery voltage to the VSV using jumper wires to simulate warm running conditions. Air should pass through the VSV. Replace the valve if the test results are incorrect.

Charcoal canister replacement

12   Clearly label, then detach the vacuum hoses from the canister.
13   Remove the mounting clamp bolts, lower the canister with the bracket, disconnect the hoses from the check valve and remove it from the vehicle.
14   Installation is the reverse of removal.

7   Exhaust Gas Recirculation (EGR) system

General description

Refer to illustration 7.1
1   To reduce NOx emissions, part of the exhaust gases are recirculated through the EGR valve into the intake manifold to lower the combustion chamber temperatures **(see illustration)**.
2   The main component of the system is the EGR valve. It operates in conjunction with a wide variety of devices, such as the EGR vacuum modulator, the Vacuum Switching Valve (VSV) and the Vacuum Transmitting Valve (VTV), although not all components are incorporated on all models.
3   At low engine temperatures, the VSV and EGR valves are shut and the exhaust gas is not being recirculated. At higher engine temperatures, the VSV opens. When the throttle valve is pivoted open enough to expose the EGR port, and the pressure in the EGR valve is low, the pressure increases, closing the modulator and causing the EGR valve to open. The pressure then drops, reopening the modulator and closing the EGR valve, cutting off exhaust gas recirculation. The VSV(s) and VTV, where incorporated, serve the EGR system in various capacities, depending on coolant tempera-

ture, exhaust gas pressure, and ignition switch position.

Check

Refer to illustration 7.6
4   If the engine runs roughly at idle, hesitates under acceleration, accelerates poorly or gets poor mileage, the EGR system is probably not shutting off.
5   Before checking the EGR valve, always inspect the condition of all vacuum hoses in the system. Make sure they're all properly attached and are in good condition. If any of the hoses are cracked or otherwise damaged, replace them.
6   Also inspect the EGR vacuum modulator filter for contamination or damage **(see illustration)**. If it's dirty, clean it with compressed air.
7   Disconnect the vacuum hose from the EGR valve and connect a vacuum pump to it.
8   Apply vacuum directly to the EGR valve. The engine should run roughly or stall. If it doesn't, replace the EGR valve.

Replacement

Refer to illustrations 7.9a, 7.9b and 7.9c
9   Disconnect the vacuum hose, remove the retaining bolts and the valve **(see illustration)**, replace the faulty valve with a new one, using a new gasket, then install the bolts and reconnect the vacuum hoses.

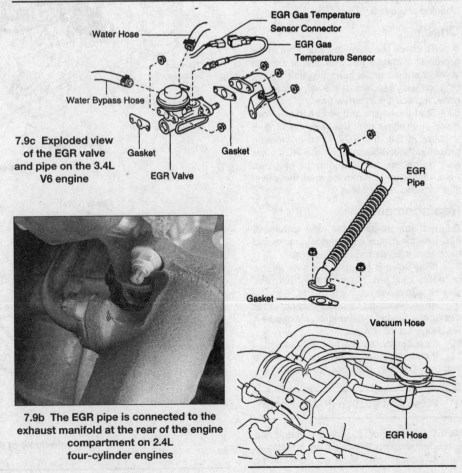

7.9c Exploded view of the EGR valve and pipe on the 3.4L V6 engine

7.9a EGR valve mounting bolts (arrows) on the 2.4L four-cylinder engine

7.9b The EGR pipe is connected to the exhaust manifold at the rear of the engine compartment on 2.4L four-cylinder engines

8   Positive Crankcase Ventilation (PCV) system

General information

Refer to illustration 8.1

1   The Positive Crankcase Ventilation (PCV) system reduces hydrocarbon emissions by scavenging crankcase vapors. It does this by circulating fresh air from the air cleaner through the crankcase, where it mixes with blow-by gases and is then rerouted through a PCV valve to the intake manifold **(see illustration)**.

2   The main components of the PCV system are the PCV valve, a fresh air intake and the vacuum hoses connecting these components to the engine.

3   To maintain idle quality, the PCV valve restricts the flow when the intake manifold vacuum is high. If abnormal operating conditions (such as piston ring problems) arise, the system is designed to allow excessive amounts of blow-by gases to flow back through the crankcase vent tube into the air cleaner to be consumed by normal combustion.

4   This system directs the blow-by into the throttle body which, over time, can cause an oily residue build up in the area near the throttle plate. Consequently, it's a good idea to periodically clean this residue from the throttle body. Refer to Chapter 4 for this cleaning procedure.

Check

5   To check the valve, first pull it out of the grommet in the valve cover and shake the valve. It should rattle, indicating that it's not clogged with deposits. If the valve does not rattle, replace it with a new one.

6   Start the engine and allow it to idle, then place your finger over the valve opening. If vacuum is felt, the PCV valve is working properly. If no vacuum is felt, the PCV valve may be bad or the hose may be plugged. Also, check for vacuum leaks at the valve, filler cap and all the hoses.

Replacement

7   Pull straight up on the valve to remove it. Check the rubber grommet for cracks and distortion. If it's damaged, replace it.

8   If the valve is clogged, the hose is also probably plugged. Remove the hose and clean it with solvent.

9   After cleaning the hose, inspect it for damage, wear and deterioration. Make sure it fits snugly on the fittings.

10   If necessary, install a new PCV valve.

11   Install the clean PCV hose. Make sure that the PCV valve and hose are secure.

9   Pulse Air Injection (PAIR) system

Note: *Because of a federally mandated extended warranty which covers emissions-related components such as the catalytic*

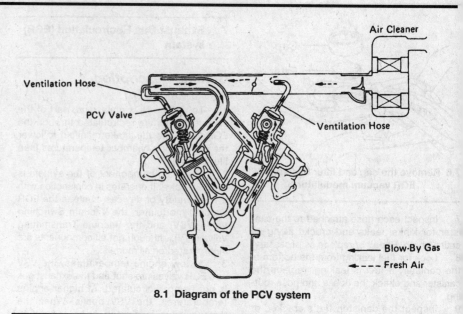

8.1 Diagram of the PCV system

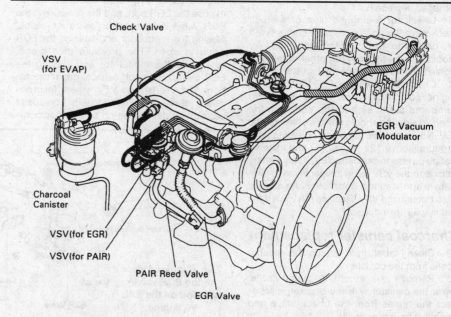

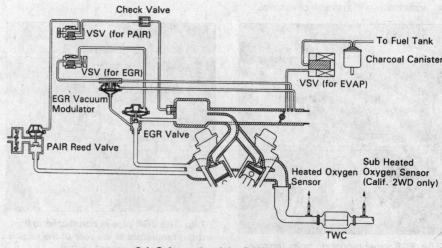

9.1 Schematic of the PAIR system

converter, check with a dealer service department before replacing any of the components of the PAIR system at your own expense.

General description

Refer to illustration 9.1

1 To reduce hydrocarbon and carbon monoxide emissions, the PAIR system draws fresh air into the exhaust ports to increase oxidation and reduction. The fresh air is drawn into the exhaust manifold by vacuum generated by the exhaust pulsation from the combustion process **(see illustration)**.

2 With the engine coolant temperature below 95 degrees F and under normal driving situations, the VSV will switch the PAIR system ON when the engine rpm is below 3,150 and then OFF above 3,150 rpm. Under deceleration and with the engine warmed to operating temperature, the VSV will switch the PAIR system OFF below 1,200 rpm or ON if the rpm is above 1,400.

Check

Refer to illustrations 9.5 and 9.8

3 Periodically inspect the hoses for cracks, damage or loose fittings. Make sure that there are no loose bolts and no leaks.

4 With the engine coolant temperature below 77-degrees F (25-degrees C), disconnect the number 2 air hose from the PAIR reed valve, start the engine and check that a bubbling noise is heard from the air pipe when the engine is idling.

5 Warm the engine to operating temperature and perform the same test. The PAIR reed valve should be quiet **(see illustration)**.

6 Raise the engine rpm and quickly close the throttle. There should be no noise from the reed valve.

7 If the test results are incorrect, replace the PAIR reed valve.

8 Also, check the VSV for the correct operation **(see illustration)**.

Replacement

9 Remove the bolts and nuts that retain the air pipe to the PAIR reed valve.

10 Remove the bolts from the PAIR reed valve and separate the assembly from the engine.

11 Installation is the reverse of removal.

---

10 Catalytic converter

Refer to illustration 10.1

Note: *Because of a federally mandated extended warranty which covers emissions-related components such as the catalytic converter, check with a dealer service department before replacing the converter at your own expense.*

General description

1 To reduce hydrocarbon, carbon monoxide and oxides of nitrogen emissions, all vehicles are equipped with a three-way catalyst system which oxidizes and reduces these chemicals, converting them into harmless nitrogen, carbon dioxide and water **(see illustration)**.

2 The catalytic converter is mounted in the exhaust system much like a muffler.

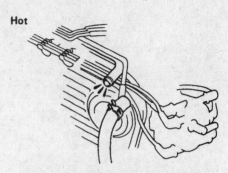

9.5 With the engine at operating temperature, the reed valve should be quiet

Check

3 Periodically inspect the catalytic converter-to-exhaust pipe mating flanges and bolts. Make sure that there are no loose bolts and no leaks between the flanges.

4 Look for dents in or damage to the catalytic converter protector. If any part of the protector is damaged or dented enough to touch the converter, repair or replace it.

5 Inspect the heat insulator for damage. Make sure that there is adequate clearance between the heat insulator and the catalytic converter.

Replacement

6 To replace the catalytic converter, refer to Chapter 4.

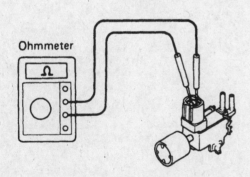

9.8 Check the resistance of the VSV. It should be 30 to 50 ohms

10.1 The catalytic converter

Notes

Chapter 7 Part A
Manual transmission

Contents

Specifications

Torque specifications

Ft-lbs (unless otherwise indicated)

Clutch cover bolts	13
Stiffener plate bolts	27
Transmission crossmember bolts	43
Transmission mount bolts	13
Transmission-to-engine bolts	53

1   General information

Vehicles covered by this manual are equipped with either a five-speed manual or a four-speed automatic transmission. Information on the manual transmission is included in this Part of Chapter 7. Information on the automatic transmission can be found in Part B of this Chapter. You'll also find certain procedures common to both transmissions - such as oil seal replacement - in this chapter. Information on the transfer case used on 4WD models is in Part C.

The W59 transmission is used on vehicles with a four-cylinder engine. The R150 and R150F transmissions are used on models with V6 engines.

Depending on the expense involved in having a transmission overhauled, it might be a better idea to consider replacing it with either a new or rebuilt unit. Your local dealer or transmission shop should be able to supply information concerning cost, availability and exchange policy. Regardless of how you decide to remedy a transmission problem, you can still save a lot of money by removing and installing the unit yourself.

2   Rear output shaft oil seal (2WD) - replacement

Refer to illustrations 2.5 and 2.7
Note: *This procedure applies to both manual and automatic transmissions.*
1   Oil leaks frequently occur due to wear of the extension housing oil seal and bushing (if equipped), and/or the speedometer drive gear oil seal and O-ring. Replacement of these seals is relatively easy, since the repairs can usually be performed without removing the transmission from the vehicle.
2   The extension housing oil seal is located at the extreme rear of the transmission, where the driveshaft is attached. Raise the vehicle and support it securely on jackstands. If the seal is leaking, transmission lubricant will be built up on the front of the driveshaft and may be dripping from the rear of the transmission.
3   Remove the driveshaft (see Chapter 8).
4   If the dust shield for the extension housing seal is in the way, use a soft-face hammer to carefully tap the shield off the extension housing. Be careful not to distort it.
5   Using a screwdriver or seal removal

tool, carefully pry the oil seal out of the rear of the transmission **(see illustration)**. Do not damage the splines on the transmission output shaft.

2.5 Pry out the old extension housing seal with a seal removal tool or a large screwdriver

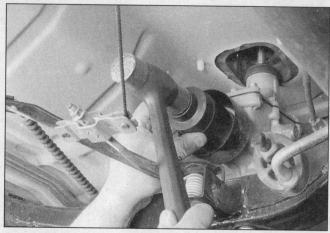

2.7 To install a new extension housing seal, tap it into place with a large socket and hammer

3.1 To check the transmission mount, insert a prybar or large screwdriver between the mount rubber and the mount bracket, then try to pry the transmission up off its mount; if the transmission moves significantly, replace the mount

6   If the oil seal cannot be removed with a screwdriver or pry bar, a special oil seal removal tool (available at auto parts stores) will be required.

7   Using a large section of pipe or a very large deep socket as a drift, install the new oil seal **(see illustration)**. Drive it into the bore squarely and make sure it's completely seated.

8   If you removed the dust shield for the extension housing, carefully tap it into place.

9   Lubricate the splines of the transmission output shaft and the outside of the driveshaft slip yoke with light-weight grease, then install the driveshaft. Be careful not to damage the lip of the new seal.

3   Transmission mount - check and replacement

Check

Refer to illustration 3.1

1   Insert a large screwdriver or pry bar into the space between the transmission and the crossmember and try to pry the transmission

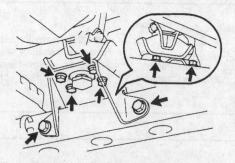

3.3a Transmission mount retaining bolts (arrows) (2WD T100 models)

up slightly **(see illustration)**.

2   The transmission should not move away from the insulator much. If there is any separation of the rubber, the mount is worn out.

Replacement

Refer to illustrations 3.3a, 3.3b, 3.3c and 3.3d

3   To replace the mount, support the transmission and remove the nuts and bolts

3.3b Transmission mount retaining bolts (arrows) (4WD T100 models)

attaching the mount to the crossmember and to the transmission **(see illustrations)**.

4   Raise the transmission slightly with the jack and remove the insulator.

5   Installation is the reverse of the removal procedure. Be sure to tighten the nuts and bolts securely.

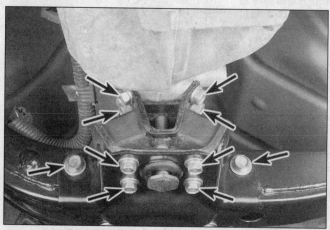

3.3c Transmission mount retaining bolts (arrows) (2WD Tacoma model shown; 2WD 4Runner similar)

3.3d Transmission mount retaining bolts (arrows) (4WD Tacoma and 4Runner models); to detach the crossmember from the frame, remove the nuts and-bolts (outer arrows) from both ends

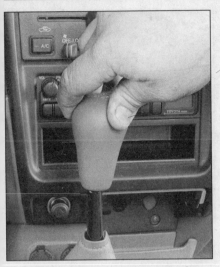

4.2a Unscrew the shift lever knob

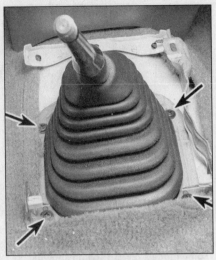

4.2b Remove the shift lever boot retaining screws (arrows), then remove the shift lever boot and the retainer (2WD model shown, others similar)

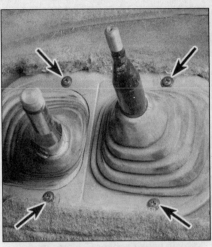

4.2c On some 4WD models, the transmission and transfer shift lever boots use a one-piece boot retainer - remove the shift lever boot retaining screws (arrows), then remove the shift lever boot and the retainer

4 Shift lever - removal and installation

Refer to illustrations 4.2a, 4.2b, 4.2c, 4.4a, 4.4b, 4.4c and 4.5

1   Remove the center console (see Chapter 11).

2   Unscrew the shift lever knob **(see illustration)**. Remove the four shift lever boot retaining screws **(see illustrations)** and remove the boot and retainer.

3   Cover the shift lever cap with a shop rag.

4   Remove the small dust boot from the shift lever cap **(see illustration)**. On some units, press down on the shift lever cap and rotate it counterclockwise to remove the shift lever **(see illustrations)**.

5   Installation is the reverse of removal. Before installing the shift lever, lubricate the friction surfaces with multipurpose grease **(see illustration)**.

4.4a Remove the dust cover from the shift lever cap

4.4b Push down on the shift lever cap and rotate it counterclockwise . . .

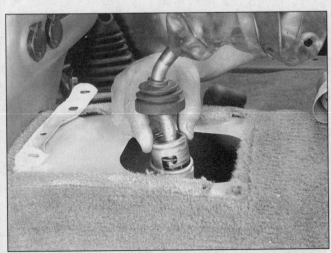

4.4c . . . then remove the shift lever (Tacoma 2WD model shown, others similar)

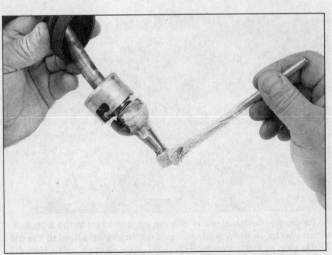

4.5 Lubricate the friction surfaces of the shift lever with multipurpose grease before installing the shift lever

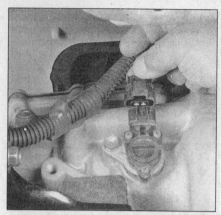

5.9a Disconnect the speedometer cable or unplug the electrical connector for the vehicle speed sensor (Tacoma model shown; speed sensor is located on right side of extension housing on all models)

5.9b The back-up light switch is located on the left side of the transmission on some models (2WD Tacoma shown) . . .

5.9c . . . or on the right side (arrow) on other models (4WD T100 shown)

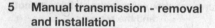

5   Manual transmission - removal and installation

Removal

Refer to illustrations 5.9a, 5.9b, 5.9c, 5.9d, 5.9e, 5.12, 5.13, 5.15, 5.19a and 5.19b

1   Disconnect the cable from the negative terminal of the battery. **Caution:** *On models equipped with an anti-theft audio system, be sure the lockout feature is turned off before performing any procedure which requires disconnecting the battery.*

2   Remove the shift lever (see Section 4).

3   On 4WD models with a manually-operated transfer case, remove the transfer shift lever (see Chapter 7C).

4   Raise the vehicle and support it securely on jackstands.

5   On T100 models, remove the stabilizer bar (see Chapter 10).

6   On 2WD 4Runner models, remove the No. 2 engine under cover. On 4WD 4Runner models, remove the No. 1 and the No. 2

engine under covers (see Chapter 2).

7   Disconnect the driveshaft(s) (see Chapter 8).

8   Remove the front exhaust pipe(s) (see Chapter 4).

9   Disconnect the speedometer cable or unplug the electrical connector for the vehicle speed sensor **(see illustration)**. Unplug the electrical connector from the back-up light switch **(see illustrations)**. Detach all wire harnesses, such as the oxygen sensor harness **(see illustrations)** from the transmission.

10   On 4WD models, unplug the electrical connectors from the transfer case.

11   Disconnect the clutch release cylinder (see Chapter 8). **Caution:** *Do not depress the clutch pedal while the transmission is out of the vehicle.*

12   On vehicles which use stiffener plates between the the engine and transmission (4WD T100 and 2WD Tacoma models, for example), unbolt the left and right stiffener plates from the transmission bellhousing **(see illustration)**.

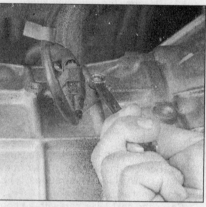

5.9d Electrical harnesses, such as this oxygen sensor harness are attached to the transmission with small brackets - remove the bracket retaining bolt(s) and detach the harness from the transmission

13   Remove the clutch cover **(see illustration)**. The accompanying table summarizes the number and type of fasteners used to secure the clutch covers on various applications.

5.9e Some electrical leads may not appear to be in the way, but when you trace them, you will find that they're attached to the top or the side of the transmission - make sure all such harnesses are unplugged and detached from the transmission, then securely fasten them aside

5.12 On vehicles which use stiffener plates between the engine and transmission, unbolt the plates from the transmission bellhousing (2WD Tacoma shown) - it's not necessary to unbolt the plates from the block

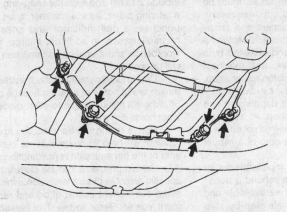

5.13 Remove the clutch cover nuts and/or bolts (arrows) (T100 shown, other models similar)

5.16 Remove the rear crossmember bolts (arrows) (4WD T100 model shown) - the rear crossmember used on 4WD Tacoma and 4Runner models is shown in illustration 3.3d

	W59 (2WD)	W59 (4WD)	R150/R150F (2WD)	R150/R150F (4WD)
T100	4 bolts and 2 nuts		4 bolts and 2 nuts	4 bolts plus 4 stiffener bolts
Tacoma	4 bolts plus 4 stiffener bolts	4 bolts and 2 nuts	4 bolts	4 bolts
4Runner	4 bolts and 2 nuts	4 bolts and 2 nuts		4 bolts

14 Jack up the transmission slightly.
15 Support the engine and transmission assembly by placing a floor jack and a block of wood under the engine oil pan.
16 On 2WD truck models, remove the transmission mount support bracket **(see Illustration 3.3c)**. On 4WD truck and all 4Runner models, remove the rear cross-member **(see illustration)**. The crossmembers on T100 models have eight bolts; the crossmembers on Tacomas and 4Runners use four through-bolts and four nuts **(see illustration 3.3d)**.
17 Unbolt the transmission mount from the transmission (see Section 3 if necessary).
18 Remove the starter (see Chapter 5).
19 Remove the six transmission-to-engine bolts on R150/R150F models or three transmission-to-engine bolts on W59 models **(see illustrations)**.
20 Make a final check that all wires have been disconnected from the transmission, then move the transmission and jack toward the rear of the vehicle until the transmission input shaft is clear of the clutch or clutch housing. On 2WD models, it will be necessary to rotate the transmission clockwise about 90 degrees, move it to the rear again and, once the input shaft is clear, lower the transmission and remove it from under the vehicle. On 4WD models, pull out the transmission and transfer case down and toward the rear.
21 On 4WD models, remove the transmission mount from the transmission.
22 On 4WD models, separate the transfer case from the transmission (see Chapter 7C).
23 Inspect the clutch components. It's a good idea to install new clutch components

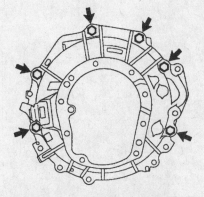

5.19a On R150/R150F model transmissions, there are six transmission-to-engine bolts

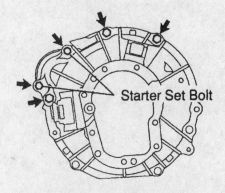

5.19b On W59 model transmissions, there are three transmission-to-engine bolts (arrows)

whenever the transmission is removed (see Chapter 8).

Installation

24 Install the clutch components, if they were removed (see Chapter 8).
25 On 4WD models, bolt the transfer case (if it was removed) to the transmission (see Chapter 7C). Also, install the transmission mount on the transmission, if it was removed (see Section 3).
26 With the transmission secured to the jack, raise it into position behind the engine, and then carefully slide it forward, engaging the input shaft with the clutch plate hub. Do not use excessive force to install the transmission - if the input shaft won't slide into place, readjust the angle of the transmission

so that it's level and/or turn the input shaft so the splines engage properly with the clutch.
27 Once the transmission is fully seated against the engine, install the transmission-to-engine bolts. Tighten the bolts to the torque listed in this Chapter's Specifications.
28 On 4WD models, install the crossmember. Tighten all nuts and bolts securely.
29 Bolt the transmission mount to the crossmember.
30 Remove the jacks supporting the transmission and the engine.
31 Install the various components removed previously. Refer to Chapter 8 for driveshaft installation and clutch hydraulic line connection procedures. Refer to Chapter 4 for help with reconnecting the exhaust system components. Refer to Chapter 10 if you need help

installing the stabilizer bar on T100 models.

32   Make a final check to verify all wires and hoses have been reconnected and the transmission has been filled with lubricant to the proper level (see Chapter 1). Lower the vehicle.

33   Install the shift lever and boot (see Section 4).

34   Connect the negative cable to the negative terminal of the battery. Road test the vehicle and check for leaks.

6   Manual transmission overhaul - general information

Overhauling a manual transmission is a difficult job for the do-it-yourselfer. It involves the disassembly and reassembly of many small parts. Numerous clearances must be precisely measured and, if necessary, changed with select fit spacers and snaprings. As a result, if transmission problems arise, it can be removed and installed by a competent do-it-yourselfer, but overhaul should be left to a transmission repair shop. Rebuilt transmissions may be available - check with your dealer parts department or a local transmission repair shop. At any rate, the time and money involved in an overhaul is almost sure to exceed the cost of a rebuilt unit.

Nevertheless, it's not impossible for an inexperienced mechanic to rebuild a transmission if the special tools are available and the job is done in a deliberate step-by-step manner so nothing is overlooked.

The tools necessary for an overhaul include internal and external snap-ring pliers, a bearing puller, a slide hammer, a set of pin punches, a dial indicator and possibly a hydraulic press. In addition, a large, sturdy workbench and a vise or transmission stand will be required.

During disassembly of the transmission, make careful notes of how each piece comes off, where it fits in relation to other pieces and what holds it in place.

Before taking the transmission apart for repair, it will help if you have some idea what area of the transmission is malfunctioning.

Certain problems can be closely tied to specific areas in the transmission, which can make component examination and replacement easier. Refer to the *Troubleshooting* Section at the front of this manual for information regarding possible sources of trouble.

Chapter 7 Part B
Automatic transmission

Contents

Specifications

General
Transmission fluid type.. See Chapter 1

Shift lock system
Shift lock solenoid resistance
    Tacoma .... 20 to 28 ohms
    4Runner .... 21 to 27 ohms
Key interlock solenoid
    Tacoma .... 12 to 17 ohms
    4Runner .... 12.5 to 16.5 ohms

Torque specifications
                                                            Ft-lbs
Cross-shaft fasteners (T100)
    A bolts (transmission side) .... 108 in-lbs
    B bolts (frame side) 21
    C nut .... 108 in-lbs
Flywheel-to-torque converter bolts (all models) 30
Park/Neutral position switch retaining bolt .... 120 in-lbs
Shift linkage-to-shift lever nut .... 120 in-lbs
Transmission-to-engine bolts (all models) 53
Valve body retaining bolts .... 84 in-lbs

1   General information

The vehicles equipped with an automatic transmission use a four-speed (three speeds plus overdrive) unit, either a model A43D, a model A340E or a model A340F, depending on the engine and drivetrain (2WD or 4WD) combination. All models are equipped with a lock-up torque converter, known as a Torque Converter Clutch (or TCC). The clutch provides a direct connection between the engine and the drive wheels for improved efficiency and fuel economy. A340E and A340F models are electronically controlled; upshifts and downshifts are initiated by a computer which controls three solenoids mounted on the valve body.

Due to the complexity of the clutches and the hydraulic control system, and because of the special tools and expertise needed to overhaul an automatic transmission, diagnosis and repair of the transmission must be handled by a dealer service department or a transmission repair shop. The procedures in this Chapter are limited to general diagnosis, routine maintenance, adjustment and transmission removal and installation. However, even though the repair work must be done by a transmission specialist, you can save money by removing and installing the transmission yourself. You can also check and adjust the shift linkage or shift cable and the throttle valve cable, replace the extension housing seal and check and replace the Park/Neutral position switch. **Caution:** *If a vehicle with an automatic transmission is disabled, do NOT tow it at speeds greater than 30 mph or distances over 50 miles.*

2   Diagnosis - general

Note: *Automatic transmission malfunctions may be caused by five general conditions: poor engine performance, improper adjustments, hydraulic malfunctions, mechanical malfunctions or malfunctions in the computer or its signal network. Diagnosis of these problems should always begin with a check of the easily repaired items: fluid level and condition (Chapter 1), shift linkage adjustment and throttle linkage adjustment. Next, perform a road test to determine if the problem has been corrected or if more diagnosis is necessary. If the problem persists after the preliminary tests and corrections are completed, additional diagnosis should be done by a dealer service department or transmission repair shop. Refer to the Troubleshooting Section at the front of this manual for information on symptoms of transmission problems.*

Preliminary checks

1   Drive the vehicle to warm the transmission to normal operating temperature.
2   Check the fluid level as described in Chapter 1:
  a) *If the fluid level is unusually low, add enough fluid to bring the level within the* designated area of the dipstick, then check for external leaks (see below).
  b) *If the fluid level is abnormally high, drain off the excess, then check the drained fluid for contamination by coolant. The presence of engine coolant in the automatic transmission fluid indicates that a failure has occurred in the internal radiator walls that separate the coolant from the transmission fluid (see Chapter 3).*
  c) *If the fluid is foaming, drain it and refill the transmission, then check for coolant in the fluid or a high fluid level.*

3   Check the engine idle speed. **Note:** *If the engine is malfunctioning, do not proceed with the preliminary checks until it has been repaired and runs normally.*
4   Inspect the shift linkage (see Section 4) or shift cable (see Section 5). Make sure it's properly adjusted and operates smoothly.

Fluid leak diagnosis

5   Most fluid leaks are easy to locate visually. Repair usually consists of replacing a seal or gasket. If a leak is difficult to find, the following procedure may help.
6   Identify the fluid. Make sure it's transmission fluid and not engine oil or brake fluid (automatic transmission fluid is a deep red color).
7   Try to pinpoint the source of the leak. Drive the vehicle several miles, then park it over a large sheet of cardboard. After a minute or two, you should be able to locate the leak by determining the source of the fluid dripping onto the cardboard.
8   Make a careful visual inspection of the suspected component and the area immediately around it. Pay particular attention to gasket mating surfaces. A mirror is often helpful for finding leaks in areas that are hard to see.
9   If the leak still cannot be found, clean the suspected area thoroughly with a degreaser or solvent, then dry it.
10   Drive the vehicle for several miles at normal operating temperature and varying speeds. After driving the vehicle, visually inspect the suspected component again.
11   Once the leak has been located, the cause must be determined before it can be properly repaired. If a gasket is replaced but the sealing flange is bent, the new gasket will not stop the leak. The bent flange must be straightened.
12   Before attempting to repair a leak, check to make sure the following conditions are corrected or they may cause another leak. **Note:** *Some of the following conditions cannot be fixed without highly specialized tools and expertise. Such problems must be referred to a transmission repair shop or a dealer service department.*

Gasket leaks

13   Check the pan periodically. Make sure the bolts are tight, no bolts are missing, the gasket is in good condition and the pan is flat (dents in the pan may indicate damage to the valve body inside).
14   If the pan gasket is leaking, the fluid level or the fluid pressure may be too high, the vent may be plugged, the pan bolts may be too tight, the pan sealing flange may be warped, the sealing surface of the transmission housing may be damaged, the gasket may be damaged or the transmission casting may be cracked or porous. If sealant instead of gasket material has been used to form a seal between the pan and the transmission housing, it may be the wrong sealant.

Seal leaks

15   If a transmission seal is leaking, the fluid level or pressure may be too high, the vent may be plugged, the seal bore may be damaged, the seal itself may be damaged or improperly installed, the surface of the shaft protruding through the seal may be damaged or a loose bearing may be causing excessive shaft movement.
16   Make sure the dipstick tube seal is in good condition and the tube is properly seated. Periodically check the area around the speedometer gear or sensor for leakage. If transmission fluid is evident, check the O-ring for damage.

Case leaks

17   If the case itself appears to be leaking, the casting is porous and will have to be repaired or replaced.
18   Make sure the oil cooler hose fittings are tight and in good condition.

Fluid comes out vent pipe or fill tube

19   If this condition occurs, the transmission is overfilled, there is coolant in the fluid, the case is porous, the dipstick is incorrect, the vent is plugged or the drain back holes are plugged.

3   Throttle valve (TV) cable - check, adjustment and replacement

Check and adjustment

Refer to illustration 3.3
Note: *2003 and later model 3.4L V6 models are not equipped with a throttle valve cable. Downshifts are controlled by an internal solenoid.*
1   Verify that the accelerator pedal is fully released and the throttle valve is fully closed.
2   Verify that the TV cable is taut (the cable itself, not the cable sheath).
3   Measure the distance between the cable sheath (the outer cable) and the stopper on the TV cable **(see illustration)**, then compare your measurement to the dimension shown.
4   If the TV cable is out of adjustment, adjust it by utilizing the adjustment nuts at the bracket.

Replacement

Refer to illustrations 3.9, 3.10a, 3.10b, 3.10c, 3.11, 3.12a, 3.12b, 3.13, 3.14a, 3.14b, 3.17a, 3.17b and 3.18
5   Disconnect the throttle cable from the throttle linkage (see Chapter 4).

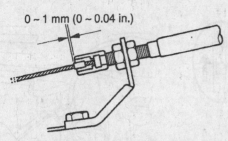

0 ~ 1 mm (0 ~ 0.04 in.)

3.3 To check the adjustment of the TV cable, measure the distance between the cable sheath and the stopper on the cable

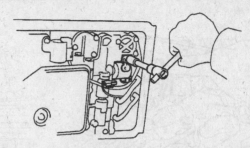

3.9 Unplug the electrical connectors from the three solenoid valves, remove the three valve mounting bolts, then remove the shift solenoid valves from the valve body

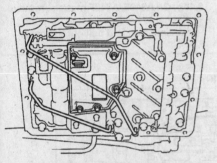

3.10a On A43D models, remove these two oil pipes by prying them out of the valve body with a screwdriver (once the ends are pried loose, they pull straight out), then remove the five oil strainer bolts

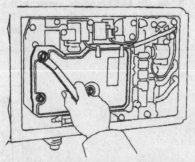

3.10b To remove the two oil pipes on A340E models, simply pry up on both ends with a screwdriver and pull them straight out

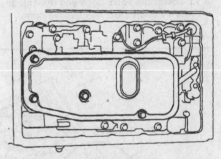

3.10c There's only one oil pipe on A340F models; it's removed the same way as the pipes on the A340E

6   Disengage the TV cable from the cable clamps in the engine compartment.
7   Remove the bolt that attaches the TV cable clamp to the torque converter housing.
8   Remove the oil pan (see Chapter 1).
9   On A340E/A340F models, remove the shift solenoid valves from the valve body **(see illustration)**.
10   Remove the oil pipes **(see illustrations)**.
11   Remove the oil strainer, if equipped **(see illustrations)**.
12   Remove the valve body **(see illustrations)**. There are 17 bolts on all valve bodies. Before removing the last bolt, support the valve body, or have an assistant support it for you, so that it doesn't fall when the last bolt is removed.

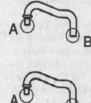

3.11 The oil strainer on A340E models has three bolts

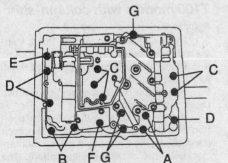

A	20 mm (0.79 inch)
B	25 mm (0.98 inch)
C	30 mm (1.18 inch)
D	35 mm (1.42 inch)
E	40 mm (1.57 inch)
F	47 mm (1.85 inch)
G	55 mm (2.17 inch)

3.12a To remove the valve body on A43D models, remove these 17 bolts; when tightening the bolts, make sure that you install a bolt of the correct length in each hole

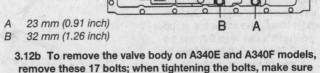

A	23 mm (0.91 inch)
B	32 mm (1.26 inch)

3.12b To remove the valve body on A340E and A340F models, remove these 17 bolts; when tightening the bolts, make sure that you install a bolt of the correct length in each hole

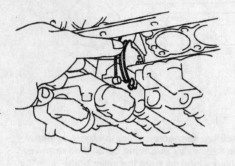

3.13 Lower the valve body and disengage the TV cable from the throttle cam

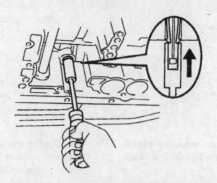

3.14a On A43D models, separate the cable from the transmission case by pushing it out with a 10mm socket

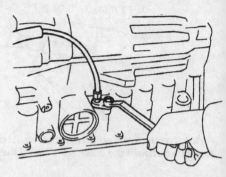

3.14b On A340E/A340F models, remove the cable hold-down bolt from the transmission and pull out the cable

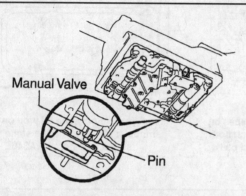

3.17a Before installing the valve body on an A43D model, make sure that the groove of the manual valve is aligned with the pin of the lever

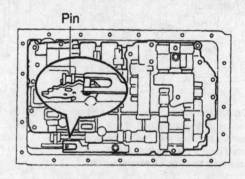

3.17b Before installing the valve body on an A340E/A340F models, make sure that the groove of the manual valve is aligned with the pin of the lever

13   Lower the valve body and disengage the TV cable from the throttle cam **(see illustration)**.

14   On A43D models, remove the TV cable from the transmission case by pushing it out of the case with a 10mm socket **(see illustration)**. On A340E/A340F models, remove the cable hold-down bolt from the transmission case **(see illustration)** and pull out the old TV cable.

15   Insert the new cable through the hole in the case and, on A340E/A340F models, install the cable hold-down bolt and tighten it securely.

16   Connect the new TV cable to the cam.

17   Before installing the valve body, make sure that the groove of the manual valve is

aligned with the pin of the lever **(see illustrations)**.

18   If the throttle cable being installed is a *new* cable, the cable stopper is not staked. First, bend the upper end of the cable to a radius of about 200 mm (7.87 inches). Pull the inner cable until you feel a slight resistance and hold it there. Stake the stopper so that it's between 0.8 and 1.5 mm (0.031 to 0.059 inch) from the end of the cable sheath **(see illustration)**.

19   The remainder of installation is the reverse of removal.

19   Fill the transmission with new ATF and check the fluid level (see Chapter 1).

20 Check and, if necessary, adjust the TV cable (see Steps 1 through 4).

4   Shift linkage - adjustment

All models

1   Move the shift lever from the Neutral position to the other gear positions and verify that the lever can be shifted smoothly and precisely to each position and that the gear position indicator points to the correct gear position. If the indicator is not correctly aligned, adjust the linkage as follows.

2   Raise the vehicle and place it securely on jackstands.

T100 models with column-shift
Refer to illustrations 4.3 and 4.6

3   Remove the nut on the No. 1 gear shifting rod **(see illustration)**.

4   Push the No. 1 gear shifting rod down (clockwise) until it stops.

5   Return the No. 1 gear shifting rod two clicks to the Neutral position.

6   Put the manual lever in the Neutral position by rotating it all the way to the right (clockwise), then moving it back (counterclockwise) two clicks **(see illustration)**. (The manual lever will produce an audible "click" as the manual shaft is rotated through each gear position.)

7   While holding the manual lever lightly

3.18 If the TV cable being installed is *new*, the cable stopper must be staked: bend the upper end of the cable to a radius of about 200 mm (7.87 inches), pull the inner cable until you feel a slight resistance, hold it there, and stake the stopper so that it's between 0.8 and 1.5 mm (0.031 to 0.059 inch) from the end of the cable sheath

200 mm (7.87 in.)

0.8 — 1.5 mm (0.031 — 0.059 in.)

No.1 Gear Shifting Rod

4.3 On T100 models with column-shift, remove the nut on the No. 1 gear shifting rod, push the rod down until it stops, then return the rod two clicks to the Neutral position

toward the Reverse position (the next gear position, just to the right of Neutral), reattach the No. 1 gear shifting rod to the manual lever and tighten the nut to the torque listed in this Chapter's Specifications.

Tacoma and 4Runner models with floor-shift

Refer to illustration 4.8

8   Loosen the nut that attaches the shift linkage to the shift lever **(see illustration)**.

9   Push the manual lever (the small lever that connects the shift linkage to the manual shaft in the transmission) all the way to the right (clockwise); you will hear and feel an audible "click" as the manual shaft moves through each gear position; keep clicking it to the right until it stops. Now return the manual lever two gear positions (two clicks) to the left (counterclockwise). The transmission is now in Neutral.

10   Place the shift lever inside the vehicle in the Neutral position.

11   While an assistant holds the shift lever inside the vehicle in the Neutral position, tighten the nut connecting the shift linkage to the lower end of the shift lever to the torque listed in this Chapter's Specifications.

All models

12   Adjust the Park/Neutral position switch (see Section 6).

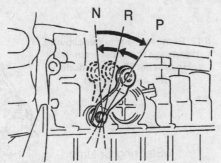

4.6 On T100 models with column-shift, put the manual lever in the Neutral position by rotating it all the way to the right (clockwise), then moving it back (counterclockwise) two clicks (the manual lever will produce an audible "click" as the manual shaft is rotated through each gear position)

13   Check the adjustment: The shift lever must go into all positions and the engine must start only in the P or N positions. If necessary, readjust the shift linkage and/or adjust the Park/Neutral position switch until your adjustment meets both these criteria.

5   Shift cable (Tacoma models with column-shift) - adjustment and replacement

Adjustment

Refer to illustration 5.3

1   Move the shift lever from the Neutral position to the other gear positions and verify that the lever can be shifted smoothly and precisely to each position and that the gear position indicator points to the correct gear position. If the indicator is not correctly aligned, adjust the linkage as follows:

2   Raise the vehicle and place it securely on jackstands.

3   Loosen the nut that attaches the shift cable to the manual lever **(see illustration)**.

4   Push the manual lever all the way forward (clockwise) until it stops (the lever will

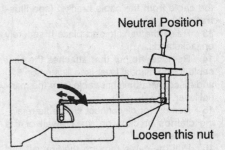

Neutral Position

Loosen this nut

4.8 To adjust the shift linkage on a floor-shift model, loosen the nut that attaches the shift linkage to the shift lever, click the manual lever on the transmission clockwise until it stops, click it back two gear positions, put the floor-shift lever in the Neutral position and tighten the nut to the torque listed in this Chapter's Specifications

produce an audible "click" as the manual shaft moves through each gear position).

5   Push the manual lever back (counterclockwise) two positions (two clicks) to the Neutral position.

6   Put the column-shift lever inside the vehicle in the Neutral position.

7   While an assistant holds the column-shift lever in the Neutral position (pushing it slightly toward the Reverse position), tighten the nut on the manual lever.

8   Adjust the Park/Neutral position switch (see Section 6).

9   Check the adjustment: The shift lever must go into all positions and the engine must start only in the P or N positions. If necessary, readjust the shift linkage and/or adjust the Park/Neutral position switch until your adjustment meets both these criteria.

Replacement

Refer to illustrations 5.11 and 5.12

10   Remove the upper and lower steering column covers and the left lower finish panel (see Chapter 11).

11   Remove the wire retaining pin **(see illustration)** and detach the upper end of the shift cable from the steering column.

Column Shift

5.3 Loosen the nut that attaches the shift cable to the manual lever, push the lever forward until it stops, push the lever back two clicks to the Neutral position, put the shift lever inside the vehicle in the Neutral position and, with an assistant holding the shift lever in the Neutral position (pushing it slightly toward the Reverse position), tighten the nut on the manual lever

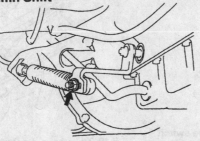

5.11 Remove the wire retaining pin and detach the upper end of the shift cable from the steering column (Tacoma models with column-shift)

12   Remove the retainer clip and disengage the cable from the cable bracket (see illustration).

13   Raise the vehicle and place it securely on jackstands.

14   Remove the nut that attaches the shift cable to the manual lever (see illustration 5.3) and disconnect the shift cable from the manual lever.

15   Remove or disconnect any cable retaining clamps or clips on the firewall or the transmission.

16   Pull the cable through the firewall and remove it.

17   Installation is the reverse of removal.

18   Adjust the shift cable (see Steps 1 through 9).

6   Park/Neutral position switch - check, adjustment and replacement

Check

Refer to illustration 6.4

1   The Park/Neutral position switch prevents the engine from starting in any gear other than Park or Neutral. If the engine starts in any position other than Park or Neutral, it's either out of adjustment or defective. First, check the switch to make sure that it's operating properly.

2   Raise the vehicle and place it securely

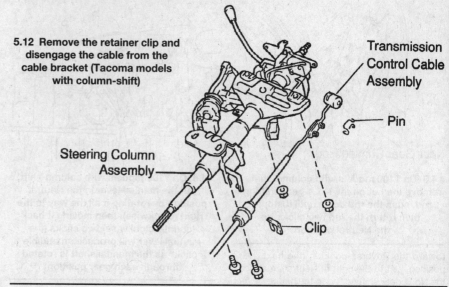

5.12 Remove the retainer clip and disengage the cable from the cable bracket (Tacoma models with column-shift)

Transmission Control Cable Assembly

Pin

Clip

Steering Column Assembly

on jackstands.

3   Unplug the electrical connector from the Park/Neutral switch.

4   Make sure the ignition key is turned to Off, then use an ohmmeter to check the continuity across the indicated terminals of the switch side of the connector (see illustration). If the switch doesn't operate as described, try adjusting it, then check it again. If it still fails to operate properly, replace it.

Adjustment

Refer to illustration 6.7

5   Place the shift lever in Neutral.

6   Raise the vehicle and place it securely on jackstands.

7   Loosen the switch retaining bolt (see illustration).

8   Align the groove and neutral basic line.

9   Holding the switch in this position, tighten the switch retaining bolt to the torque listed in this Chapter's Specifications.

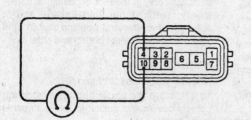

Shift Position	Terminal No. to continuity	Terminal No. to continuity
P	4 – 7	5 – 6
R	4 – 8	–
N	4 – 10	5 – 6
D	4 – 9	–
2	2 – 4	–
L	2 – 3	–

6.4 Park/Neutral position switch terminal guide and continuity table

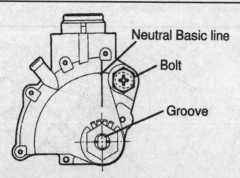

Neutral Basic line

Bolt

Groove

6.7 To adjust the Park/Neutral position switch, loosen the switch retaining bolt and align the groove and neutral basic line, hold the switch in this position, and tighten the switch retaining bolt to the torque listed in this Chapter's Specifications

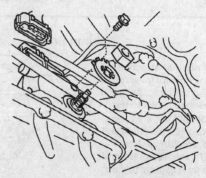

6.10 To remove the Park/Neutral position switch, pry off this lock washer and remove the nut (4Runner switch shown, other switches similar)

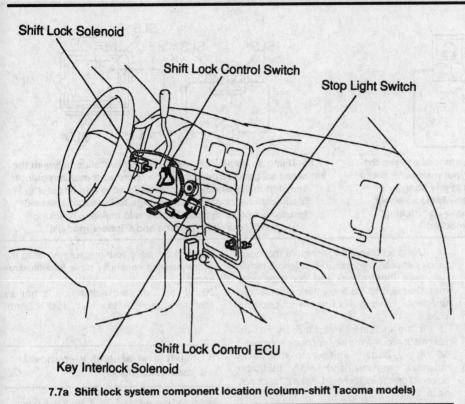

7.7a Shift lock system component location (column-shift Tacoma models)

Replacement

Refer to illustration 6.10

7   On Tacoma models, remove the exhaust pipe and heat shield (see Chapter 4).

8   On T100 and Tacoma models, detach the oil cooler pipe clamps and disconnect the oil cooler pipes.

9   Unplug the electrical connector from the Park/Neutral position switch.

10   Pry off the lock washer and remove the nut **(see illustration)**.

11   Remove the Park/Neutral position switch retaining bolt **(see illustration 6.7)**.

12   Remove the Park/Neutral position switch.

13   Installation is the reverse of removal. Be sure to adjust the switch, then check its continuity to make sure that it's properly adjusted and operating correctly.

7   Shift lock system - check and component replacement

T100 models

1   Depress the brake pedal and verify that the tip of the parking lock cable protrudes from the pedal bracket.

2   Put the shift lever in the Park position, depress the brake pedal and verify that the shift lock system is canceled. Make sure that the lock pin makes no unusual operating sound.

3   Remove the center cluster lower finish panel (see Chapter 11).

4   To check the key interlock solenoid, verify that the sliding rod protrudes when the ignition key plate is turned from the LOCK position to the ACC position. Verify that the sliding rod is released when the ignition key is turned to the LOCK position.

5   If the key interlock solenoid doesn't operate as described, replace the key lock cylinder (see Chapter 12).

Tacoma and 4Runner models

Refer to illustrations 7.7a and 7.7b

6   Remove the lower left finish panel and the steering column covers (see Chapter 11).

7   Refer to the accompanying illustrations to locate the shift lock system components **(see illustrations)**.

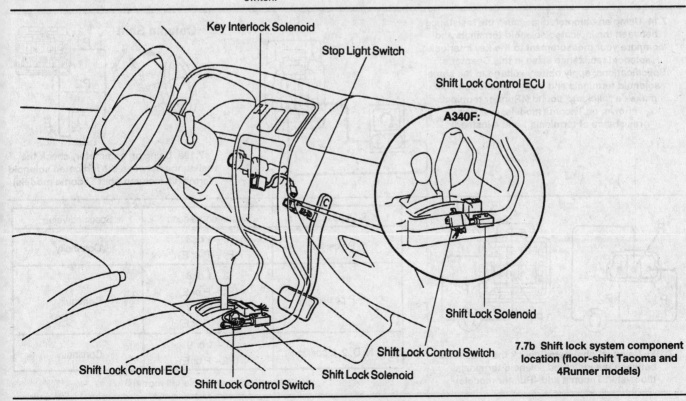

7.7b Shift lock system component location (floor-shift Tacoma and 4Runner models)

Column Shift

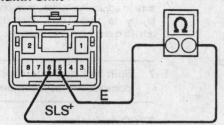

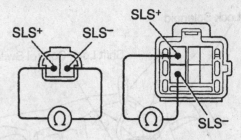

7.9a Using an ohmmeter, measure the resistance between the indicated solenoid terminals and compare your measurement to the shift lock solenoid resistance listed in this Chapter's Specifications; apply battery voltage to the same solenoid terminals and verify that the solenoid makes a "clicking" sound (column-shift Tacoma models)

7.9b Using an ohmmeter, measure the resistance between the indicated solenoid terminals and compare your measurement to the shift lock solenoid resistance listed in this Chapter's Specifications; apply battery voltage to the same solenoid terminals and verify that the solenoid makes a "clicking" sound (floor-shift Tacoma and 4Runner models)

Shift lock solenoid

Refer to illustrations 7.9a and 7.9b

8   Unplug the electrical connector from the shift lock solenoid.

9   Using an ohmmeter, measure the resistance between the indicated solenoid terminals **(see illustrations)** and compare your measurement to the shift lock solenoid resistance listed in this Chapter's Specifications.

10   If the indicated resistance is not as specified, replace the shift lock solenoid.

11   Apply battery voltage to the same solenoid terminals and verify that the solenoid operates (it should make a "clicking" sound).

12   If the solenoid doesn't operate (click) when energized, replace it.

Key interlock solenoid

Refer to illustration 7.14

13   Unplug the electrical connector from the key interlock solenoid.

14   Using an ohmmeter, measure the resistance between the indicated solenoid terminals **(see illustration)** and compare your measurement to the key interlock solenoid resistance listed in this Chapter's Specifications.

15   If the indicated resistance is not as specified, replace the key interlock solenoid.

16   Apply battery voltage to the same solenoid terminals and verify that the solenoid operates (it should make a "clicking" sound).

17   If the solenoid doesn't operate (click) when energized, replace it.

Shift lock control switch

Refer to illustrations 7.19a, 7.19b, and 7.19c

18   Unplug the electrical connector from the shift lock control switch.

19   Using an ohmmeter, check the resistance between the indicated solenoid termi-

nals and compare your measurements to the accompanying continuity table **(see illustrations)**.

20   If the indicated resistance is not as specified, replace the shift lock control switch.

8   Shift lever assembly - removal and installation

Refer to illustrations 8.3a, 8.3b, 8.4, 8.6 and 8.7

1   Remove the rear console upper panel (see Chapter 11).

2   On 4Runner models, remove the heater control knobs and pry off the heater control plate (see Chapter 3), then remove the center cluster finish panel (see Chapter 11).

3   On 4WD Tacoma models without One-

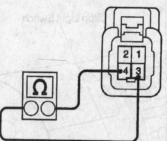

7.14 Using an ohmmeter, measure the resistance between the indicated solenoid terminals and compare your measurement to the key interlock solenoid resistance listed in this Chapter's Specifications; apply battery voltage to the same solenoid terminals and verify that the solenoid makes a "clicking" sound (4Runner terminals shown; on Tacoma models, measure resistance at terminals 1 and 4 instead)

Column Shift

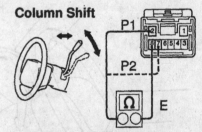

7.19a Using an ohmmeter, check the resistance between the indicated solenoid terminals (column-shift Tacoma models)

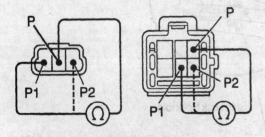

7.19b Using an ohmmeter, check the resistance between the indicated solenoid terminals (floor-shift Tacoma and 4Runner models)

Shift position	Tester connection	Specified value
*1 P position	2 – 1 or 8 (P1 – P or E)	Continuity
*2 P position	2 – 1 or 8 (P1 – P or E) 7 – 1 or 8 (P2 – P or E)	Continuity
R, N, D, 2, L position	7 – 1 or 8 (P2 – P or E)	Continuity

7.19c Continuity table (all models)

w/o One Touch 2–4 Selector

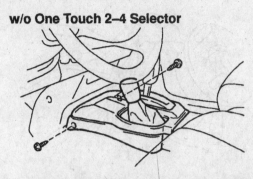

8.3a On 4WD Tacoma models without One-Touch 2-4 Selector, remove the two front console box screws, lift up the front console box with the transfer shift lever knob and unplug the electrical connectors

w/ One Touch 2–4 Selector

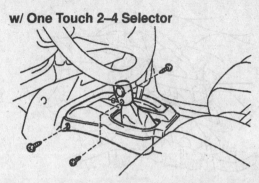

8.3b On 4WD Tacoma models with One-Touch 2-4 Selector, remove the three front console box screws and remove the front console box

Touch 2-4 Selector, remove the two front console box screws (see illustration), lift up the front console box with the transfer shift lever knob and unplug the electrical connectors. On 4WD Tacoma models with One-Touch 2-4 Selector, remove the three front console box screws (see illustration) and remove the front console box.

4   On 4WD 4Runner models without 2-4 Selector, remove the transfer shift lever knob; on 4Runner models with 2-4 Selector, remove the transfer shift lever knob screw and remove the knob (see illustration). Remove the front console upper panel (see Chapter 11). On models with 2-4 Selector, unplug the 2-4 Selector electrical connector and remove the transfer shift lever knob. Remove the two clips, the screws and the front console box.

5   Raise the vehicle and place it securely on jackstands.

6   Remove the nut and washer (see illustration) and disconnect the shift control rod from the shift lever.

7   Unplug the electrical connector, remove the shift lever base mounting bolts (see illustration) and remove the shift lever assembly.

8   Installation is the reverse of removal. Be sure to tighten the shift control rod-to-shift lever nut to the torque listed in this Chapter's Specifications.

8.4 On 4WD 4Runner models with 2-4 Selector, remove the transfer shift lever knob screw and remove the knob, remove the front console upper panel, unplug the 2-4 Selector electrical connector, remove the transfer shift lever knob, then remove the two clips, the screws and the front console box

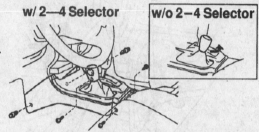

w/ 2—4 Selector   w/o 2–4 Selector

9   Automatic transmission - removal and installation

Removal

Refer to illustrations 9.14a, 9.14b, 9.16, 9.21, 9.22, 9.24, 9.25a, 9.25b, 9.27a, 9.27b, 9.28 and 9.29

1   Disconnect the negative cable from the battery.

2   Remove the dipstick.

3   Loosen the throttle valve (TV) cable adjustment nuts, disengage the TV cable from the cable bracket, and disengage the end of the cable from the throttle linkage (see Section 3). Detach all TV cable clamps.

4   On 4WD Tacoma models, remove the No. 1 fan shroud (see Chapter 3).

5   Remove the center console (see Chapter 11).

6   On floor-shift models, remove the shift lever assembly (see Section 8).

7   On 4WD models, remove the transfer shift lever (see Chapter 7C). On T100 models, remove the shift lever knob, the four boot retaining screws and the boot, and remove the snap-ring with a pair of snap-ring pliers and remove the transfer shift lever. On 4WD Tacoma and 4Runner models, the transfer shift lever should already be exposed; simply remove the snap-ring with a pair of snap-ring pliers and pull out the shift lever.

8   Raise the vehicle and support it securely on jackstands.

9   Remove any engine/transmission undercovers that are in the way (see Chapter 2).

10   Drain the transmission fluid (see Chapter 1), then reinstall the pan.

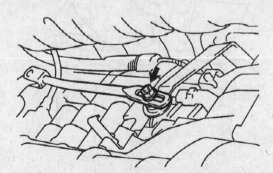

8.6 Remove the nut and washer and disconnect the shift control rod from the shift lever

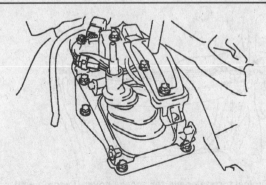

8.7 Unplug the electrical connector, remove the shift lever base mounting bolts and remove the shift lever assembly

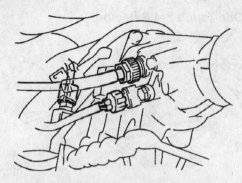

9.14a The speedometer cable is attached to the left side of the extension housing on T100 models with an A340E transmission (the electrical connector below the speedometer cable is the No. 2 vehicle speed sensor)

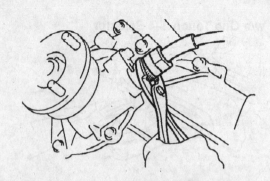

9.14b The speedometer cable is attached to the right side of the transfer case extension housing on T100 models with an A340F transmission; a pair of pliers is all you need to loosen the serrated collar that attaches the cable

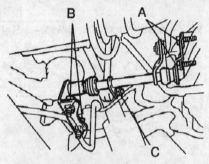

9.16 On T100 models with an A340 transmission, remove the clip, disconnect the No. 2 gear shifting rod, remove the nut, washer and four bolts, and remove the cross shaft (the letters identify the fasteners that must be tightened to the torque listed in this Chapter's Specifications when reassembling the cross shaft)

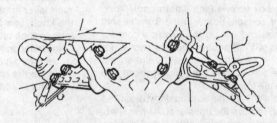

9.21 On 4WD T100 models with an A340F transmission and on Tacoma models with an A43D transmission, remove the stiffener plate bolts and remove left and right stiffener plates (T100 plates shown, Tacoma A43D plates similar)

11   Remove the dipstick tube bracket bolt(s) and remove the dipstick tube.
12   Disconnect the driveshaft(s) (see Chapter 8).
13   Remove the front exhaust pipe (see Chapter 4).
14   Loosen the serrated collar with pliers and disconnect the speedometer cable, if equipped, from the transmission (see illustrations). Don't lose the felt protector and washers.
15   Unplug the electrical connectors from

the vehicle speed sensor(s), the shift solenoids, the ATF temperature sensor, the Park/Neutral position switch and, on 4WD models, the transfer Neutral position switch, transfer L4 position switch and transfer indicator switch, then detach all wire harnesses from the transmission and set them aside.
16   On T100 models with an A340 transmission, remove the clip, disconnect the No. 2 gear shifting rod, remove the nut, washer and four bolts, and remove the cross shaft (see illustration).

17   On all floor-shift models and on column-shift models which use a shift rod instead of a shift cable, disconnect the shift rod (see Section 4). On column-shift models with a shift cable, disconnect the shift cable from the manual lever (see Section 5).
18   Remove the oil cooler pipe bracket bolts, detach all brackets and clamps and disconnect the two oil cooler pipes from the transmission.
19   Remove the starter (see Chapter 5) and set the starter wiring aside.

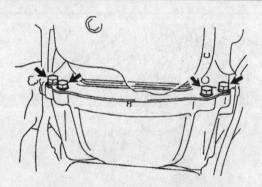

9.22 Typical torque converter access cover (Tacoma with A340E/A340F shown, others similar)

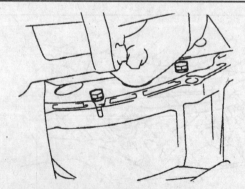

9.24 Remove the six driveplate-to-torque converter bolts by turning the crankshaft (in a clockwise direction only, viewed from the front) for access to each bolt

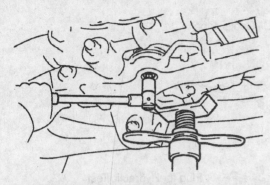

9.25a On 4WD Tacoma models, remove the nut that attaches the front differential rear mount to the front crossmember, lift up the front differential with a floor jack or transmission jack . . .

9.25b . . . and remove the two rear mount retaining bolts

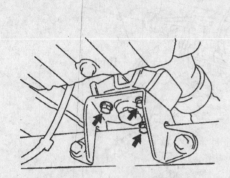

9.27a Transmission extension housing mount bolts (T100 with 3RZ-FE)

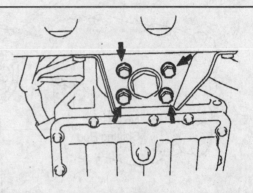

9.27b Transmission extension housing mount bolts (T100 with 5VZ-FE)

20 On all T100 models and on 4Runner models with a 5VZ-FE engine, remove the stabilizer bar (see Chapter 10).

21 On 4WD T100 models with an A340F transmission and on Tacoma models with an A43D transmission, remove the stiffener plate bolts and remove left and right stiffener plates **(see illustration)**.

22 Remove the torque converter access cover **(see illustration)**.

23 Mark the torque converter and the driveplate with a scribe or chalk so they can be installed in the same position.

24 Remove the six driveplate-to-torque converter bolts **(see illustration)**. Turn the

crankshaft (in a clockwise direction only, viewed from the front) for access to each bolt.

25 On 4WD Tacoma models, remove the nut that attaches the front differential rear mount to the front crossmember **(see illustration)**, lift up the front differential with a floor jack or transmission jack and remove the two rear mount retaining bolts **(see illustration)**.

26 Support the transmission with a jack - preferably a jack made for this purpose. Safety chains will help steady the transmission on the jack.

27 Disconnect the transmission extension

housing mount from the crossmember **(see illustrations)**.

28 On 4WD T100 models, remove the transfer under cover, remove the dynamic damper bolts and the dynamic damper, then remove the transfer-to-crossmember mounting bolts and the mount **(see illustration)**.

29 Raise the transmission enough to allow removal of the crossmember, then remove the crossmember **(see illustrations)**.

30 Support the engine with a jack. Use a block of wood under the oil pan to spread the load.

31 Remove the transmission-to-engine bolts.

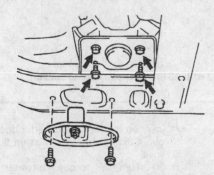

9.28 On 4WD T100 models, remove the two dynamic damper bolts and the dynamic damper, then remove the four transfer-to-crossmember mounting bolts and the mount

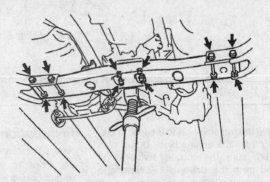

9.29 Transmission extension housing mount and crossmember bolts (Tacoma with A340F shown, 4Runner similar)

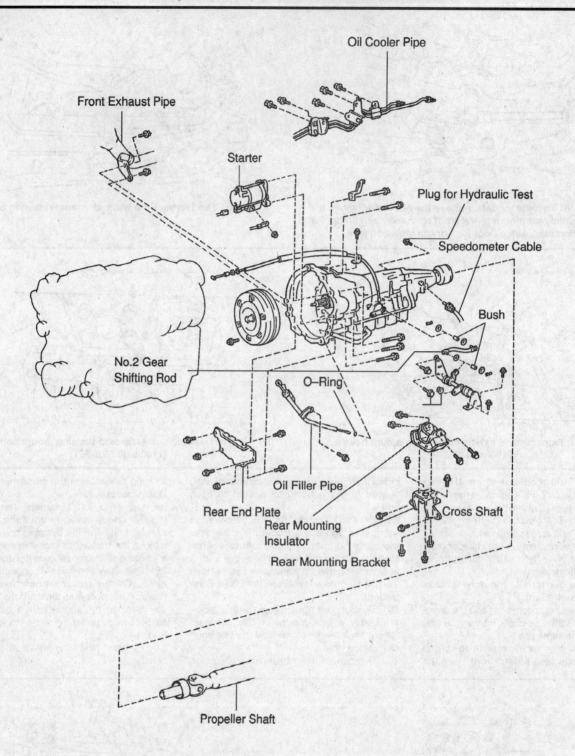

9.42a An exploded view of a typical 2WD transmission assembly (T100 with A340E shown, Tacoma similar)

32   Move the transmission to the rear to dis-engage it from the engine block dowel pins and make sure the torque converter is detached from the driveplate. Secure the torque converter to the transmission so it won't fall out during removal.

33   If the vehicle is equipped with 4WD, remove the transfer case (see Chapter 7C).

Installation
Refer to illustrations 9.42a and 9.42b

34   Prior to installation, make sure the torque converter hub is securely engaged in the pump.

35   With the transmission secured to the jack, raise it into position. Be sure to keep it

level so the torque converter doesn't slide out. Connect the transmission fluid cooler lines.

36   Turn the torque converter until the marks on the converter and driveplate are aligned.

37   Move the transmission forward carefully until the dowel pins engage with the holes in

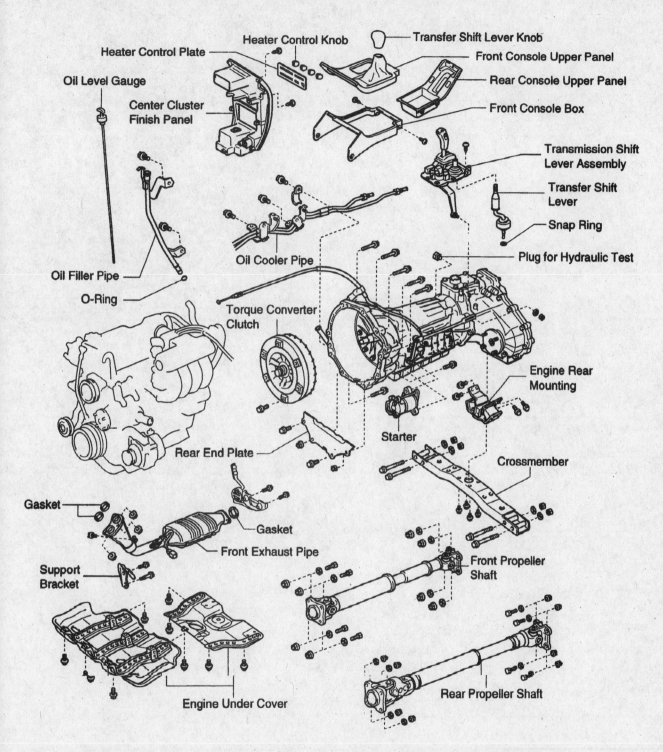

9.42b An exploded view of a typical 4WD transmission assembly (4Runner with A340F and 3RZ-FE shown, other models similar)

the bellhousing.

38 Install the transmission-to-engine bolts. Tighten them to the torque listed in this Chapter's Specifications.

39 Install the driveplate-to-torque converter bolts and tighten them to the torque listed in this Chapter's Specifications.

40 Install the crossmember and tighten the bolts and nuts securely.

41 Lower the transmission extension housing until the mount is seated on and aligned with the crossmember and tighten the nuts and bolts securely.

42 The remainder of installation is the reverse of removal **(see illustrations)**.

43 Remove all jacks supporting the transmission and engine and lower the vehicle.

43 Fill the transmission with the specified fluid (Chapter 1), run the engine and check fo fluid leaks.

Notes

Chapter 7 Part C
Transfer case

Contents

Specifications

General

Actuator resistance

Terminals 2 and 3 .... 0.3 to 100 ohms

Terminal 2 or 3 and body ground .... More than 0.5 M-ohms

Torque specifications

Ft-lbs

Companion flange nut (front and rear) 87

Transfer case output shaft yoke nut 110

Shift lever pivot bolt 75

Transmission-to-transfer case bolts

T100 27

Tacoma/4Runner 17

1 General information

Four-wheel drive (4WD) models are equipped with a transfer case mounted on the rear of the transmission. Drive is transmitted from the engine, through the transmission and the transfer case to the front and rear axles by driveshafts.

We don't recommend trying to rebuild a transfer case at home. It's difficult to overhaul without special tools, and rebuilt units are available for less than it would cost to rebuild your own. However, there are a number of components that you *can* check, adjust and/or replace - and those are the items covered in this Chapter.

2 Oil seals - replacement

Refer to illustrations 2.3a, 2.3b, 2.4, 2.5 and 2.7

Note: *This procedure applies to both the front and rear seals. Although the accompanying photos show the transfer case out of the vehicle, it's not necessary to remove the*

2.3a Unstake the companion flange retaining nut . . .

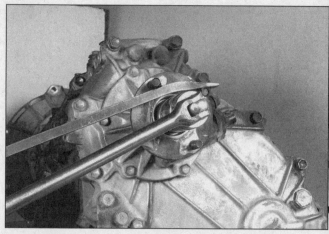

2.3b . . . then break the nut loose while holding the flange as shown

2.4 Pull the companion flange off the output shaft - it may be necessary to use a small puller

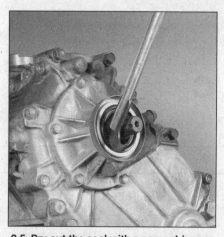

2.5 Pry out the seal with a screwdriver or a seal removal tool

2.7 Drive the seal into place with seal installer tool or a large socket

transfer case to replace a seal.

1   Raise the vehicle and support it securely on jackstands.

2   If you're replacing the front seal, remove the front driveshaft; if you're replacing the rear seal, remove the rear driveshaft (see Chapter 8).

3   Unstake and remove the companion flange retaining nut **(see illustrations)**.

4   Remove the companion flange **(see illustration)**. If the flange is difficult to remove from the output shaft, use a puller.

5   Pry out the seal with a screwdriver or a seal removal tool **(see illustration)**. Don't damage the seal bore.

6   Lubricate the new seal lips with petroleum jelly.

7   Drive the seal into place with a large socket **(see illustration)**. The outside diameter of the socket should be slightly smaller than the outside diameter of the seal.

8   There's a smaller seal inside the companion flange **(see illustration 2.4)**. If it needs to be replaced, pry it out and install a new one the same way you did the larger seal.

9   The remainder of installation is the

reverse of removal. Be sure to tighten the companion flange nut to the torque listed in this Chapter's Specifications.

---

3   Shift lever - removal and installation

T100 models

Refer to illustrations 3.3a, 3.3b and 3.3c

1   On models with a manual transmission, place the transfer case in 4-High position, remove the four front console box screws and the front console box (see Chapter 11). Then remove the four shift lever boot retainer screws and remove the shift lever boot retainer.

2   On models with an automatic transmission, remove the four shift lever boot screws and the boot.

3   Remove the small shift lever boot, remove the shift lever snap-ring and pull out the shift lever **(see illustrations)**.

4   Installation is the reverse of removal. Lubricate the lower end of the shift lever with multi-purpose grease before installing it.

3.3a To detach the transfer shift lever from the transfer case, remove the small dust cover . . .

Tacoma and 4Runner models

5   On models without the 4WD Shift Selector System, place the transfer shift lever in the 4 High position. On models with the 4WD Shift Selector System, place the transfer shift lever in the High position and turn the 2WD-4WD selector switch to the Off position.

3.3b ... remove the snap-ring with a pair of snap-ring pliers ...

3.3c ... and pull out the shift lever

6   Remove the transfer case shift lever knob retaining screw(s) and detach the shift lever knob.

7   On models equipped with a manual transmission, remove the transmission shift lever knob.

8   Remove the front and rear floor console (see Chapter 11). **Note:** *On 4Runner models with an automatic transmission it is only necessary to remove the front console upper panel for this procedure.*

9   Disconnect the electrical connector from the 4WD Shift Selector System switch if equipped.

10   On models with a manual transmission, remove the four shift lever boot retaining screws, the shift lever boot and the retainer, then remove the transfer shift lever snap-ring and pull out the lever **(see illustrations 3.3a, 3.3b and 3.3c).**

11   On models with an automatic transmission, disconnect the shift control rod from the transmission shift lever, unplug the electrical connector from the shift lever base, remove the eight shift lever assembly retaining screws and remove the shift lever assembly (see Chapter 7B). Then remove the transfer shift lever snap-ring and pull out the lever **(see illustrations 3.3a, 3.3b and 3.3c).**

12   Installation is the reverse of removal. Lubricate the lower end of the shift lever with multi-purpose grease before installing it.

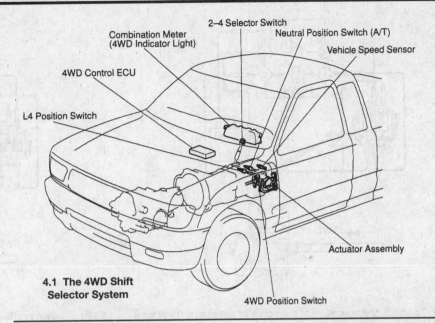

4.1 The 4WD Shift Selector System

---

4   4WD Shift Selector System - description, check and component replacement

Note: *The manufacturer refers to the 4WD Shift Selector System as the One-Touch 2-4 Selector System. Some later models are equipped with a Multi-Mode full-time 4WD system that allows shifting between 2- and 4-wheel drive while the vehicle is moving at speeds under 62 mph, by pushing the 4WD selector switch button. These vehicles use the VF3AM transfer case.*

Description

Refer to illustration 4.1

1   The 4WD Shift Selector System **(see illustration)** allows the driver to select either 2WD or 4WD with a 2-4 selector switch located in the transfer shift lever knob. Besides the switch, the system consists of the Electronic Control Unit (ECU), the actuator assembly, the 4WD position switch, the L4 (Low 4WD) switch, the Neutral position switch (automatics only), the vehicle speed sensor, and the 4WD indicator light (located

on the instrument cluster).

2   The selector switch, actuator, limit switch, No. 1 vehicle speed sensor, and 4WD indicator light can be checked and, if necessary, replaced at home. The ECU, however, should be checked by a dealer service department or other qualified repair shop.

Check and replacement

Selector switch

Refer to illustration 4.4

3   Remove the shift lever knob (see Section 3).

4   Using an ohmmeter, verify that there's no continuity between terminals 1 and 2 with the switch OFF, and that there is continuity between these terminals with the switch ON **(see illustration).**

5   If the switch doesn't operate as described, replace it.

6   Install the shift lever knob (see Section 3).

Actuator

Refer to illustration 4.9, 4.12a, 4.12b and 4.12c

7   Raise the vehicle and support it securely on jackstands.

8   Unplug the actuator electrical connector.

9   Using an ohmmeter, measure the resistance between terminals 2 and 3 **(see illustration)** and compare your measurement to the resistance listed in this Chapter's Specifications.

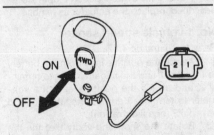

4.4 Using an ohmmeter, verify that there's no continuity between terminals 1 and 2 with the switch OFF, and that there is continuity between these terminals with the switch ON; if the selector switch doesn't operate as described, replace it

4.9 Actuator connector terminal guide (actuator side)

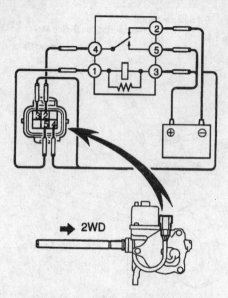

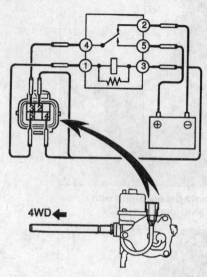

4.12a To check the operation of the actuator assembly, hook up a 12V battery and heater relay as shown and verify that the fork shaft moves to the 2WD position . . .

4.12b . . . then reattach the battery and relay leads as shown and verify that the fork shaft moves to the 4WD position

Heater Main Relay:

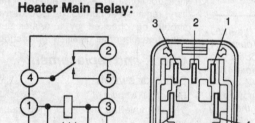

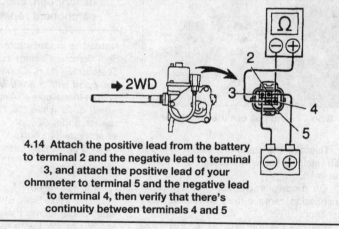

4.12c Use your own heater main relay, or obtain one just like it, for the two preceding tests

4.14 Attach the positive lead from the battery to terminal 2 and the negative lead to terminal 3, and attach the positive lead of your ohmmeter to terminal 5 and the negative lead to terminal 4, then verify that there's continuity between terminals 4 and 5

10   Measure the resistance between terminal 2 or terminal 3 and body ground and compare your measurement to the resistance listed in this Chapter's Specifications.

11   If the actuator resistance is not within the specified resistance, replace it.

12   To check the operation of the actuator assembly, hook up a 12V battery and heater relay as shown and verify that the fork shaft moves to the 2WD position, then reattach the battery and relay leads as shown and verify that the fork shaft moves to the 4WD position **(see illustrations)**.

13   If the actuator doesn't operate as described, replace it.

Limit switch

Refer to illustrations 4.14 and 4.15

14   Attach the positive lead from the battery to terminal 2 and the negative lead to terminal 3, and attach the positive lead of your ohmmeter to terminal 5 and the negative lead to terminal 4 **(see illustration)**. Verify that there's continuity between terminals 4 and 5.

15   Attach the positive lead from the battery to terminal 3 and the negative lead to terminal 2, and attach the positive lead of your ohmmeter to terminal 6 and the negative lead to terminal 4 **(see illustration)**. Verify that there's continuity between terminals 4 and 6.

16   If the limit switch doesn't operate as described, replace the actuator assembly.

No. 1 vehicle speed sensor

Refer to illustration 4.17

17   Attach the positive lead from the battery to terminal 1 and the negative lead to terminal 2, and attach the positive lead of a voltmeter to terminal 3 and the negative lead to terminal 2 **(see illustration)**.

18   Rotate the shaft and verify that the the voltage output fluctuates between zero and 11 or more volts four times per revolution.

19   If the vehicle speed sensor doesn't operate as described, replace it.

4WD indicator light

20   If the 4WD indicator light isn't working,

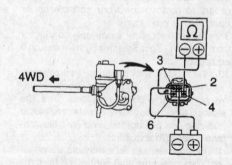

4.15 Attach the positive lead from the battery to terminal 3 and the negative lead to terminal 2, and attach the positive lead of your ohmmeter to terminal 6 and the negative lead to terminal 4, then verify that there's continuity between terminals 4 and 6

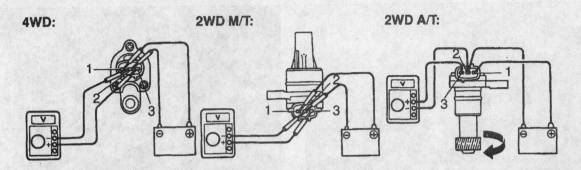

4.17 Attach the positive lead from the battery to terminal 1 and the negative lead to terminal 2, and attach the positive lead of a voltmeter to terminal 3 and the negative lead to terminal 2, rotate the shaft and verify that the the voltage output fluctuates between zero and 11 or more volts four times per revolution

5.4 To detach the skid plate, remove all retaining bolts (arrow) (T100 skid plate shown, other skid plates may vary slightly in design and number of bolts)

5.7 Unplug the electrical connector from the speed sensor, and unplug the connectors from all other electrical switches, such as the 4WD indicator switch and L4 indicator switch

check the fuse. If the fuse is OK remove the connector from the 4WD position switch and connect it to body ground, then retest. If the indicator light works now, the problem lies in the 4WD position switch. If the light still does not work, remove the instrument cluster and check the bulb and related wiring for an open circuit. (see Chapter 12).

5 Transfer case - removal and installation

Removal

Refer to illustrations 5.4, 5.7, 5.14, 5.15a, 5.15b and 5.15c

1   Remove the transfer shift lever (see Section 3).
2   Detach the breather hose from the top of the transfer case.
3   Raise the vehicle and support it securely on jackstands.
4   Remove the skid plate **(see illustration)**.
5   Drain the transfer case lubricant (see Chapter 1).
6   Remove the front and rear driveshafts (see Chapter 8).

7   Detach all vacuum and vent lines, unplug the electrical connector from the vehicle speed sensor **(see illustration)**, unplug all other electrical connectors, such as the 4WD indicator switch and the L4 indicator switch, and detach all wiring harnesses from the transfer case.
8   Support the transmission with a jack or jackstand. The transmission should remain supported at all times while the transfer case is out of the vehicle.
9   Unbolt the transfer mount from the crossmember **(see illustration 3.3b in Chapter 7A)**.
10   Remove the crossmember(s) **(see illustration 5.16 in Chapter 7A)**.
11   Support the transfer case with a jack - preferably a special jack made for this purpose. Safety chains will help steady the transfer case on the jack.
12   Remove the nuts and bolts securing the transfer case to the transmission. There are nine bolts on T100 models and eight on Tacomas and 4Runners.
13   Make a final check that all wires and hoses have been disconnected from the transfer case, then move the transfer case and jack toward the rear of the vehicle until

the transfer case is clear of the transmission. Keep the transfer case level as this is done. Once the input shaft is clear, lower the transfer case and remove it from under the vehicle.
14   If you're replacing the transfer case on a model so equipped, remove the dynamic damper **(see illustration)** from the transfer case and install it on the new or rebuilt unit.
15   If you're replacing the transfer case

5.14 If you're replacing the transfer case that has a dynamic damper like this, remove it and install it on the new or rebuilt unit

5.15a If you're replacing the transfer case, remove the 4WD indicator switch (T100 unit shown; Tacoma and 4Runner transfers have a similar switch; models with ABS, limited slip and/or ABS are also equipped with an L4 indicator switch, at this same location, which must also be swapped to the other unit)

5.15b If you're replacing the transfer case, remove the vehicle speed sensor retaining bolt (arrow) and install it on the new transfer case

5.15c Inspect the O-rings on the vehicle speed sensor - if they're cracked or torn, replace them before installing the sensor

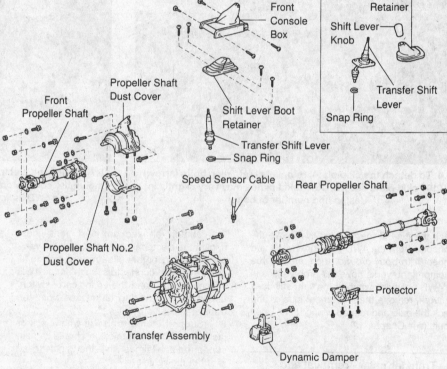

5.16a Exploded view of the T100 transfer case assembly

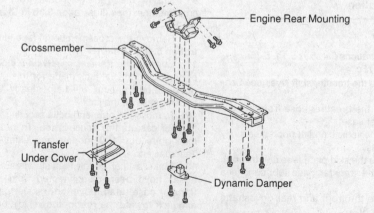

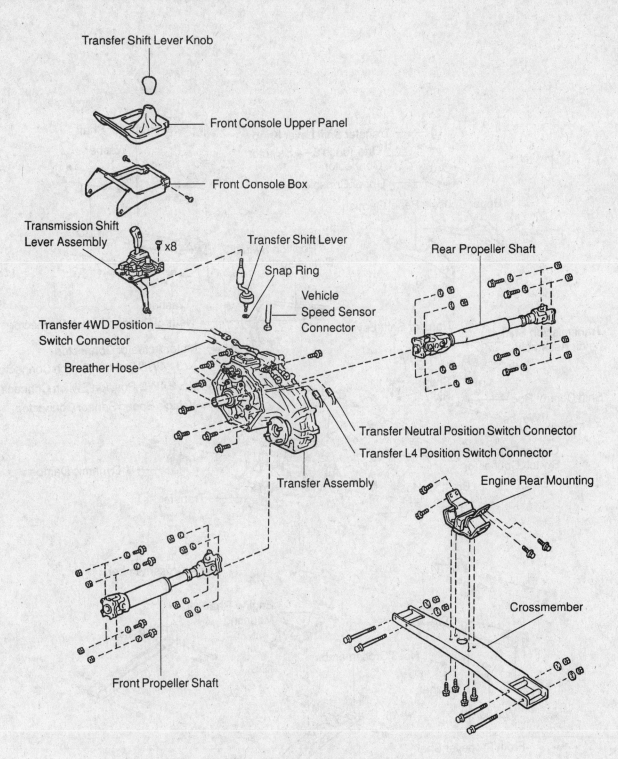

Transfer Shift Lever Knob

Front Console Upper Panel

Front Console Box

Transmission Shift Lever Assembly

x8

Transfer Shift Lever

Snap Ring

Vehicle Speed Sensor Connector

Rear Propeller Shaft

Transfer 4WD Position Switch Connector

Breather Hose

Transfer Neutral Position Switch Connector

Transfer L4 Position Switch Connector

Transfer Assembly

Engine Rear Mounting

Crossmember

Front Propeller Shaft

5.16b Exploded view of a typical Tacoma/4Runner transfer case assembly

remove the 4WD indicator switch, the L4 indicator switch (if equipped) and the vehicle speed sensor **(see illustrations)** and install them on the other unit.

Installation

Refer to illustrations 5.16a, 5.16b and 5.16c

16   Installation is the reverse of removal

(see illustrations). Be sure to tighten the transmission-to-transfer case bolts to the torque listed in this Chapter's Specifications.

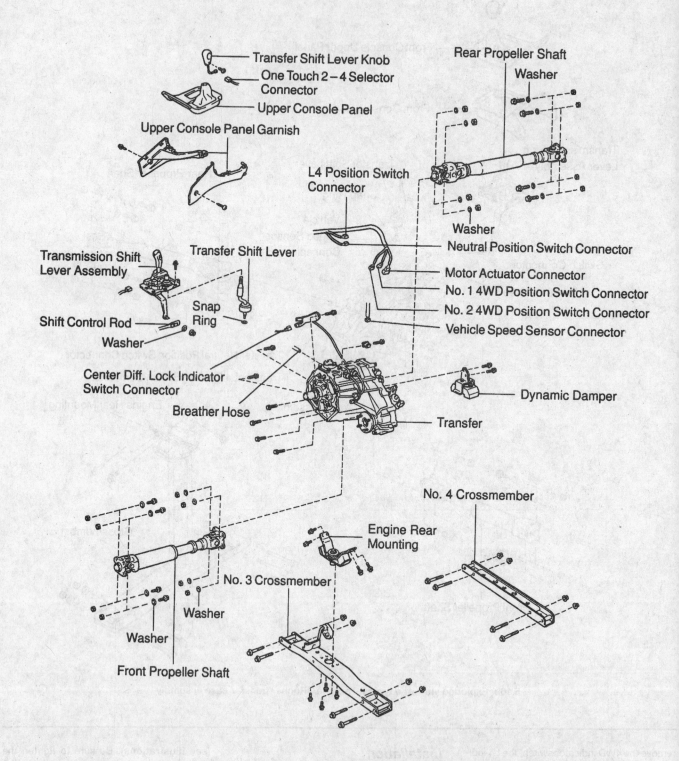

5.16c Exploded view of the Multi-Mode full-time 4WD system

Chapter 8
Clutch and driveline

Contents

Specifications

General

Clutch pedal height..	See Chapter 1
Clutch pedal freeplay..	See Chapter 1
ADD solenoid resistance	
T100 and Tacoma	37 to 44 ohms
4Runner...	37 to 47 ohms
Clutch fluid type..	See Chapter 1
Clutch disc lining minimum rivet depth	1/32-inch
Driveaxle length	
T100	18-61/64 to 19-25/64 inches
Tacoma	17-3/32 to 17-1/4 inches
4Runner..	20-45/64 to 21-3/32 inches

Torque specifications

Ft-lbs (unless otherwise indicated)

Clutch

Master cylinder nuts	108 in-lbs
Pressure plate-to-flywheel bolts...	14
Release cylinder bolts..	108 in-lbs
Release cylinder bleeder plug	96 in-lbs

Driveshaft

Flange bolts/nuts	
Front (4WD)...	54
Rear (2WD/4WD)..	54
Center bearing bolts	27
Intermediate shaft nut	
Step 1	134
Step 2	Loosen one turn
Step 3	60

Torque specifications

Ft-lbs (unless otherwise indicated)

Front driveaxle (4WD models)

Driveaxle hub nut
    Tacoma (without free-wheeling hubs) 174
    4Runner 174
CV joint-to-output shaft flange nuts (T100) 61

Rear axleshaft

Backing plate-to-axle housing nuts
    T100 51
    Tacoma 50
    4Runner 48

ADD control system

Actuator bolts 15

1   General information

The Sections in this Chapter deal with the components from the rear of the engine to the rear wheels (except for the transmission and transfer case, which are dealt with in Chapter 7) and forward to the front wheels on four-wheel drive (4WD) models. In this Chapter, the components are grouped into three categories: clutch, driveshaft(s) and axle(s). Separate Sections within this Chapter cover checks and repair procedures for components in each of these three groups.

Since nearly all these procedures involve working under the vehicle, make sure it's safely supported on sturdy jackstands or a hoist where the vehicle can be safely raised and lowered.

2   Clutch - description and check

Refer to illustration 2.1

1   All vehicles with a manual transmission have a single dry plate, diaphragm type clutch **(see illustration)**. The clutch disc has a splined hub which allows it to slide along the splines of the transmission input shaft. The clutch and pressure plate are held in contact by spring pressure exerted by the diaphragm in the pressure plate.

2   The clutch release system is operated by hydraulic pressure. The hydraulic release system consists of the clutch pedal, a master cylinder and fluid reservoir, the hydraulic line, a release (or slave) cylinder which actuates the clutch release lever and the clutch release (or throwout) bearing.

3   When pressure is applied to the clutch pedal to release the clutch, hydraulic pressure is exerted against the outer end of the clutch release lever. As the lever pivots the shaft fingers push against the release bearing. The bearing pushes against the fingers of the diaphragm spring of the pressure plate assembly, which in turn releases the clutch plate.

4   Terminology can be a problem when discussing the clutch components because common names are in some cases different from those used by the manufacturer. For example, the driven plate is also called the clutch plate or disc, the clutch release bearing is sometimes called a throwout bearing, the release cylinder is sometimes called the slave cylinder.

5   Other than to replace components with

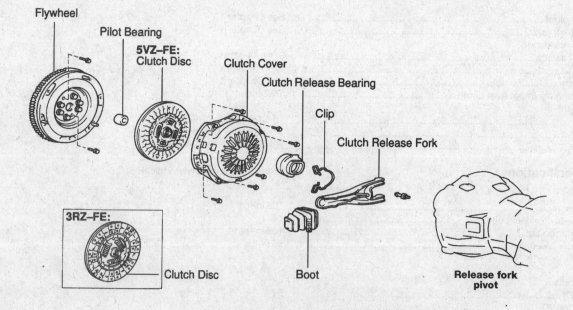

2.1 Exploded view of a typical clutch assembly (4Runner shown, other models similar)

3.2 Loosen the hydraulic line retaining nut (A) with a flare nut wrench, then remove the two mounting nuts (B) (left nut visible, right nut not visible in this photo)

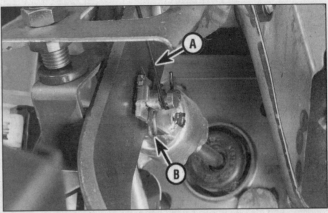

3.4 To disconnect the clutch master cylinder pushrod from the clutch pedal, pry off the return spring (A), remove the cotter pin (B) and push out the clevis pin

obvious damage, some preliminary checks should be performed to diagnose clutch problems.

a) *The first check should be of the fluid level in the clutch master cylinder. If the fluid level is low, add fluid as necessary and inspect the hydraulic system for leaks. If the master cylinder reservoir is dry, bleed the system as described in Section 8 and recheck the clutch operation.*

b) *To check "clutch spin-down time," run the engine at normal idle speed with the transmission in Neutral (clutch pedal up - engaged). Disengage the clutch (pedal down), wait several seconds and shift the transmission into Reverse. No grinding noise should be heard. A grinding noise would most likely indicate a bad pressure plate or clutch disc.*

c) *To check for complete clutch release, run the engine (with the parking brake applied to prevent vehicle movement) and hold the clutch pedal approximately 1/2-inch from the floor. Shift the transmission between 1st gear and Reverse several times. If the shift is rough, component failure is indicated. Check the release cylinder pushrod travel. With the clutch pedal depressed completely, the release cylinder pushrod should extend substantially (you may have to remove an inspection plug to see the pushrod). If it doesn't, check the fluid level in the clutch master cylinder.*

d) *Visually inspect the pivot bushing at the top of the clutch pedal to make sure there's no binding or excessive play.*

e) *Crawl under the vehicle and make sure the clutch release lever is securely attached to the ball stud.*

3 Clutch master cylinder - removal and installation

Refer to illustrations 3.2 and 3.4

1   Draw out the hydraulic fluid from the clutch master cylinder reservoir with a syringe.

2   Disconnect the clutch fluid hydraulic line **(see illustration)**; use a flare-nut wrench to protect the tube nut. Have rags handy, as some fluid will be lost as the line is removed. **Caution:** *Don't allow fluid to come into contact with the paint since it will damage the finish.* Also have a plug ready and immediately plug the line to prevent leakage and fluid contamination.

3   Working inside the passenger compartment, remove the left lower finish panel(s).

4   Disengage the return spring, remove the cotter pin and clevis pin **(see illustration)** and disconnect the clutch master cylinder pushrod from the clutch pedal.

5   Remove the master cylinder mounting nuts **(see illustration 3.2)** and detach the master cylinder from the firewall.

6   Installation is the reverse of removal. Be sure to tighten the master cylinder mounting nuts to the torque listed in this Chapter's Specifications.

7   Fill the clutch master cylinder reservoir with the fluid specified in Chapter 1 and bleed the clutch system (see Section 8).

4 Clutch release cylinder - removal and installation

Refer to illustrations 4.3 and 4.4

1   Disconnect the retainer clip from the clutch master cylinder pushrod to ensure that, if the clutch pedal is depressed, the release cylinder isn't damaged (see Section 3).

2   Raise the vehicle and support it securely on jackstands.

3   Disconnect the clutch fluid hydraulic line from the release cylinder **(see illustration)**. Use a flare-nut wrench to protect the tube nut. Have rags handy, as some fluid will be lost as the line is removed. **Caution:** *Don't allow fluid to come into contact with the paint - it will damage the finish.* Also have a plug ready and immediately plug the line to prevent leakage and fluid.

4   Remove the two release cylinder mounting bolts **(see illustration)**.

5   Detach the release cylinder.

6   Installation is the reverse of removal. Make sure the pushrod dust boot is in good

4.3 Use a flare-nut wrench to protect the tube nut, while disconnecting the clutch fluid hydraulic line from the front of the release cylinder

4.4 To detach the clutch release cylinder, remove these mounting bolts (upper arrows) (lower arrow indicates bleeder plug)

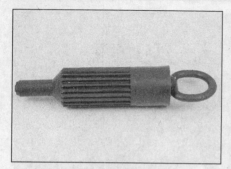

5.5a A clutch alignment tool like this one is available at most auto part stores

5.5b Insert the clutch alignment tool into the clutch disc splines prior to loosening the pressure plate bolts, or to center the clutch disc when reinstalling the pressure plate

5.6 If you're going to re-use the same pressure plate, mark its relationship to the flywheel (arrow)

condition and the pushrod is seated correctly in its pocket in the release lever. Tighten the release cylinder mounting bolts to the torque listed in this Chapter's Specifications.

7   Fill the clutch fluid reservoir with the recommended fluid (see Chapter 1).

8   Bleed the clutch hydraulic system (see Section 8).

9   Remove the jackstands and lower the vehicle.

5   Clutch components - removal, inspection and installation

Warning: *Dust produced by clutch wear and deposited on clutch components may contain asbestos, which is hazardous to your health. DO NOT blow it out with compressed air and DO NOT inhale it. DO NOT use gasoline or petroleum-based solvents to remove the dust. Brake system cleaner should be used to flush the dust into a drain pan. After the clutch components are wiped clean with a rag, dispose of the contaminated rags and cleaner in a covered, marked container.*

Removal

Refer to illustrations 5.5a, 5.5b and 5.6

Note: *The following procedure is based on the assumption that the transmission is being removed and the engine remains in place. However, anytime the transmission or engine is removed, you should inspect the clutch assembly for wear. Unless the clutch components are new or in near-perfect condition, their relatively low cost - compared to the time and trouble it takes to get to them - warrants their replacement anytime the engine or transmission is removed.*

1   Raise the vehicle and support it securely on jackstands.

2   Remove the clutch release cylinder (see Section 4).

3   Remove the transmission (see Chapter 7, Part A). Support the engine while the transmission is out. An engine hoist should be used to support it from above. If you use a jack underneath the engine instead, make sure a piece of wood is positioned between the jack and oil pan to spread the load. **Caution:** *The pick-up for the oil pump is very close to the bottom of the oil pan. If the pan is*

bent or distorted in any way, engine oil starvation could occur.

4   The clutch release lever and release bearing can remain attached to the housing for the time being.

5   To support the clutch disc during removal, install an alignment tool through the clutch disc hub **(see illustrations)**.

6   Carefully inspect the flywheel and pressure plate for indexing marks. The marks are usually an X, an O or a white letter. If they cannot be found, paint a mark so the pressure plate and the flywheel will be in the same alignment during installation **(see illustration)**.

7   Loosen the six pressure plate-to-flywheel bolts in 1/4-turn increments until they can be removed by hand. Work in a crisscross pattern until all spring pressure is relieved, then hold the pressure plate securely and completely remove the bolts, followed by the pressure plate and clutch disc.

Inspection

Refer to illustrations 5.9, 5.11 and 5.13

8   Ordinarily, when a problem occurs in the clutch, it can be attributed to wear of the clutch driven plate assembly (clutch disc). However, all components should be inspected at this time. **Note:** *If the clutch components are contaminated with oil, there will be shiny, black glazed spots on the clutch disc lining, which will cause the clutch to slip. Replacing clutch components won't completely solve the problem - be sure to check the crankshaft rear oil seal and the transmission input shaft seal for leaks. If it looks like a seal is leaking, be sure to install a new one to avoid the same problem with the new clutch.*

9   Check the flywheel for cracks, heat checking, grooves and other obvious defects **(see illustration)**. If the imperfections are slight, a machine shop can machine the surface flat and smooth, which is highly recommended regardless of the surface appear-

ance. Refer to Chapter 2, Part A, for the flywheel removal and installation procedure.

10   Inspect the pilot bearing (see Section 7).

11   Check the lining on the clutch disc. There should be at least 1/32-inch of lining above the rivet heads. Check for loose rivets, distortion, cracks, broken springs and other obvious damage **(see illustration)**. As mentioned above, ordinarily the clutch disc is routinely replaced, so if you're in doubt about its condition, replace it.

12   The release bearing should also be replaced along with the clutch disc (see Section 6).

13   Check the machined surfaces and the diaphragm spring fingers of the pressure plate **(see illustration)**. If the surface is grooved or otherwise damaged, replace the pressure plate. Also check for obvious damage, distortion, cracks, etc. Light glazing can be removed with medium-grit emery cloth. If a new pressure plate is required, new and factory-rebuilt units are available.

Installation

Refer to illustration 5.17

14   Before installation, clean the flywheel and pressure plate machined surfaces with lacquer thinner or acetone. It's important that no oil or grease is on these surfaces or the lining of the clutch disc. Handle the parts only with clean hands.

15   Position the clutch disc and pressure plate against the flywheel with the clutch held in place with an alignment tool **(see illustration 5.5b)**. Make sure it's installed properly (most replacement clutch plates will be marked "flywheel side" or something similar - if it's not marked, install the clutch disc with the damper springs toward the transmission).

16   Tighten the pressure plate-to-flywheel bolts only finger-tight, working around the pressure plate.

17   Center the clutch disc by ensuring the alignment tool extends through the splined hub and into the pilot bearing in the crankshaft. Wiggle the tool up, down or from side-to-side as needed to bottom the tool in

5.9 Inspect the surface of the flywheel for cracks, dark-colored areas (signs of overheating) and other obvious defects; resurfacing will correct minor defects (the surface of this flywheel is in fairly good condition, but resurfacing is always a good idea)

NORMAL FINGER WEAR

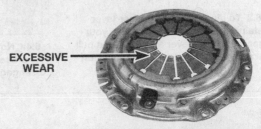

EXCESSIVE WEAR

EXCESSIVE FINGER WEAR

5.11 Inspect the clutch plate lining, springs and splines for wear

BROKEN OR BENT FINGERS

5.13 Replace the pressure plate if excessive wear or damage is noted

the pilot bearing. Tighten the pressure plate-to-flywheel bolts a little at a time, working in the order shown (see illustration), to prevent distorting the cover. After all the bolts are snug, tighten them to the torque listed in this Chapter's Specifications. Remove the alignment tool.

18 Using high-temperature grease, lubricate the inner groove of the release bearing (see Section 6). Also place grease on the release lever contact areas and the transmission input shaft bearing retainer.

19 Install the clutch release bearing (see Section 6).

20 Install the transmission, release cylinder and all components removed previously. Tighten all fasteners to the recommended torque.

6 Clutch release bearing - removal, inspection and installation

Warning: Dust produced by clutch wear and deposited on clutch components may contain asbestos, which is hazardous to your health. DO NOT blow it out with compressed

air and DO NOT inhale it. DO NOT use gasoline or petroleum-based solvents to remove the dust. Brake system cleaner should be used to flush the dust into a drain pan. After the clutch components are wiped clean with a rag, dispose of the contaminated rags and cleaner in a covered, marked container.

Removal

Refer to illustrations 6.3, 6.4a, 6.4b and 6.4c

1 Remove the release cylinder (see Section 4).

2 Remove the transmission (see Chapter 7, Part A).

3 Disengage the release lever retainer

5.17 Tighten the six pressure plate bolts in the order shown, a little at a time until they're snug, then tighten them gradually and uniformly to the torque listed in this Chapter's Specifications

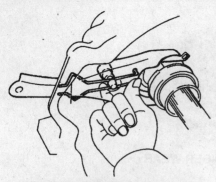

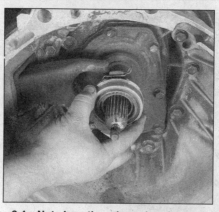

6.3 To disengage the release lever retainer from the ball stud, wrap your finger behind the lever as shown and pull toward you until the retainer "pops" off the ball stud

6.4a Note how the release bearing and the release lever fit together, then disengage them and slide off the bearing

6.4b Remove the release lever

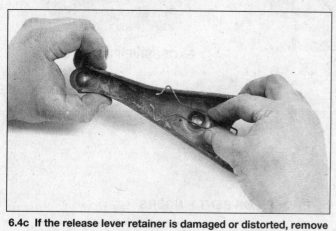

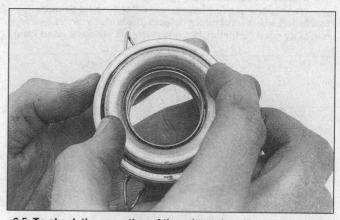

6.4c If the release lever retainer is damaged or distorted, remove and discard it - don't install the release lever with a weak or bent retainer

6.5 To check the operation of the release bearing, hold it by the outer race and rotate the inner race while applying pressure; the bearing should turn smoothly - if it doesn't, replace it

from the ball stud **(see illustration)**.

4   Note how the release lever fingers are engaged by the wire retainer on the bearing, then disengage the bearing from the lever and slide it off the input shaft **(see illustration)**. Remove the release lever **(see illustration)**. Inspect the release lever boot for cracks or tears. If it's worn or damaged, replace it. Inspect the wire retainer in the lever. If its damaged or distorted, remove it **(see illustration)** and discard it.

Inspection

Refer to illustration 6.5

5   Hold the outer portion of the bearing and rotate the center while applying pressure. If the bearing doesn't turn smoothly or if it's noisy, replace it with a new one. Wipe the bearing with a clean rag and inspect it for damage, wear and cracks. Don't immerse the bearing in solvent - it's sealed for life and to do so would ruin it.

Installation

Refer to illustrations 6.6a, 6.6b, 6.6c, 6.6d, 6.8a and 6.8b

6   Lightly lubricate the clutch release lever at the indicated spots **(see illustrations)**. If you removed the old retainer from the lever, install the new one **(see illustration)**. Also lubricate the groove around the circumference of the release bearing that's engaged by the lever, and the bearing retainer around the

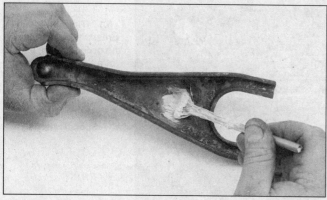

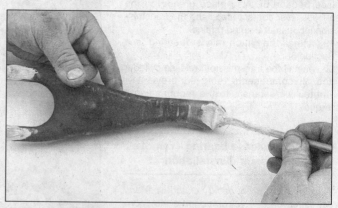

6.6a Lubricate the "pocket" for the ball stud in the backside of the release lever . . .

6.6b . . . the release lever "fingers" and the "pocket" for the release cylinder pushrod with high temperature grease

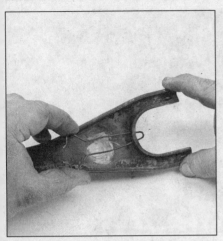

6.6c If you removed the old release lever retainer, install the new one

6.6d Lubricate the bearing retainer surrounding the input shaft with high temperature grease

6.8a Install the release lever and release bearing and push the release lever onto the ball stud (you should feel it snap into place when the ball stud pops through the wire retainer)

6.8b Slide the release bearing in and out on the retainer to verify that the release lever is locked onto the ball stud, the bearing slides freely and the two parts are properly engaged

input shaft with high-temperature grease **(see illustration)**.

7   Attach the release bearing to the release lever. Make sure the bearing is properly engaged by the retainer clip.

8   Lubricate the clutch release lever ball stud with high-temperature grease, insert the release lever through the boot, slide the release bearing onto the input shaft splines and push the lever onto the ball stud until the lever retainer "pops" onto the stud **(see illustration)**. Make sure that the release lever pivots freely and the release bearing slides freely on the input shaft splines **(see illustration)**.

9   Apply a light coat of high-temperature grease to the face of the release bearing, where it contacts the pressure plate diaphragm fingers.

10   The remainder of installation is the reverse of the removal procedure. Tighten all transmission-to-engine bolts to the torque listed in the Chapter 7A specifications.

7   Pilot bearing - inspection and replacement

Refer to illustrations 7.5, 7.9 and 7.10

1   The clutch pilot bearing is a needle roller type bearing which is pressed into the rear of the crankshaft. It's greased at the factory and does not require additional lubrication. Its primary purpose is to support the front of the transmission input shaft. The pilot bearing should be inspected whenever the clutch components are removed from the engine. Because of its inaccessibility, replace it with a new one if you have any doubt about its condition. **Note:** *If the engine has been removed from the vehicle, disregard the following Steps which don't apply.*

2   Remove the transmission (see Chapter 7A).

3   Remove the clutch components (see Section 5).

4   Using a flashlight, inspect the bearing for excessive wear, scoring, dryness, roughness and any other obvious damage. If any of these conditions are noted, replace the bearing.

5   Removal can be accomplished with a special puller **(see illustration)**, which is available at most auto parts stores, but an alternative method also works very well.

6   Find a solid steel bar or a wood dowel, or put a bolt through a socket (to make it solid).

7   Check the bar for fit - it should just slip into the bearing with very little clearance.

8   Pack the bearing and the area behind it (in the crankshaft recess) with heavy grease. Pack it tightly to eliminate as much air as possible.

9   Insert the bar into the bearing bore and strike the bar sharply with a hammer, which will force the grease to the back side of the bearing and push it out **(see illustration)**. Remove the bearing and clean all grease from the crankshaft recess.

7.5 A small slide-hammer puller is handy for removing an old pilot bearing

7.9 You can also remove the pilot bearing by packing the recess behind the bearing with heavy grease and forcing it out hydraulically with a steel rod slightly smaller than the bore in the bearing - when the hammer strikes the rod, the bearing will pop out of the crankshaft

7.10 Tap the bearing into place with a bearing installer or a socket that is slightly smaller than the outside diameter of the bearing

8.4 The setup for bleeding the clutch hydraulic system is simple: a length of rubber hose between the bleeder plug and a small container with about two inches of brake fluid it; make sure the hose is submerged in the fluid

10   To install the new bearing, lightly lubricate the outside surface with grease, then drive it into the recess with a seal installer or a socket **(see illustration)**. The bearing seal must face out.

11   Install the clutch components, transmission and all other components removed previously. Tighten all fasteners to the recommended torque.

8   Clutch hydraulic system - bleeding

Refer to illustration 8.4

1   The hydraulic system should be bled to remove all air whenever any part of the system has been removed or if the fluid level has been allowed to fall so low that air has been drawn into the master cylinder. The procedure is very similar to bleeding a brake system.

2   Fill the master cylinder with new brake fluid conforming to DOT 3 specifications. **Caution:** *Do not re-use any of the fluid coming from the system during the bleeding operation or use fluid which has been inside an open container for an extended period of time.*

3   Raise the vehicle and support it securely on jackstands to gain access to the release cylinder, which is located on the left side of the clutch housing.

4   Remove the dust cap which fits over the bleeder valve and push a length of plastic hose over the valve **(see illustration)**. Place the other end of the hose into a clear container with about two inches of brake fluid. The hose end must be in the fluid at the bottom of the container.

5   Have an assistant depress the clutch pedal and hold it. Open the bleeder valve on the release cylinder, allowing fluid to flow through the hose. Close the bleeder valve when your assistant signals the clutch pedal

is at the bottom of its travel. Once closed, have your assistant release the pedal.

6   Continue this process until all air is evacuated from the system, indicated by a solid stream of fluid being ejected from the bleeder valve each time with no air bubbles in the hose or container. Keep a close watch on the fluid level inside the clutch master cylinder reservoir - if the level drops too low, air will be sucked back into the system and the process will have to be started all over again.

7   Install the dust cap and lower the vehicle. Check carefully for proper operation before placing the vehicle in normal service.

9   Clutch pedal - check and adjustment

Refer to illustration 9.2

1   Remove any floor mats or carpeting to expose the sound deadener material.

2   With the clutch pedal at its normal (released) height, measure the distance from the floor to the pedal **(see illustration)** and compare your measurement to the pedal height listed in this Chapter's Specifications.

3   If the pedal height is incorrect, remove the lower finish panel(s) (see Chapter 11) and adjust pedal height by loosening the locknut and turning the adjustment bolt located at the top of the pedal. Once the pedal height is correct, tighten the locknut securely.

4   Depress the clutch pedal to the point at which you feel initial resistance, measure the distance from the floor to the pedal and compare your measurement to the pedal freeplay listed in this Chapter's Specifications.

5   If the pedal freeplay is incorrect, remove the lower finish panel(s) (see Chapter 11) and adjust pedal freeplay by loosening the pushrod locknut and turning the pushrod until pedal freeplay is correct. Once the pedal freeplay is correct, tighten the locknut securely.

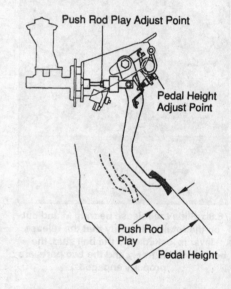

9.2 Clutch pedal adjustment details ("push rod play" is the same thing as pedal freeplay)

6   After adjusting pedal freeplay, check pedal height again and make sure that it's still within the specified range of adjustment.

7   Check and, if necessary, adjust the clutch start switch (see Section 10).

10   Clutch start switch - check, adjustment and replacement

Check

Clutch start switch

Refer to illustrations 10.1 and 10.6

1   The clutch start switch, which is mounted on a bracket near the top of the clutch pedal, prevents the engine from being

Chapter 8   Clutch and driveline

10.1 The clutch start switch (arrow) is located on a small bracket near the top of the clutch pedal; it's secured to the bracket by a pair of nuts, one above the bracket, one below, which are also used to adjust the position of the switch plunger in relation to its stopper on the pedal (Tacoma/4Runner switch shown, T100 similar)

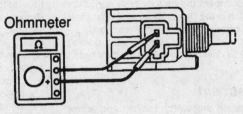

10.6 Check the continuity of the switch - when the plunger is depressed, there should be continuity; when the plunger is released (free), there should be no continuity

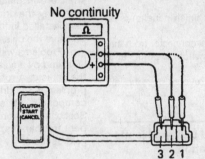

10.8a With the switch button OFF, verify that there is no continuity between any of the terminals (T100 switch shown)

started unless the clutch pedal is depressed **(see illustration)**.

2   To test the switch, verify that the engine will not start unless the clutch pedal is depressed, and that it does start when the pedal is depressed.

3   If the engine starts without depressing the clutch pedal, the switch is probably bad, but check the switch circuit first. Make sure there's voltage to the power side of the switch.

4   If there's voltage to the switch, verify that there's no voltage on the ground side of the switch unless the clutch pedal is depressed.

5   If there's a short or open in the circuit on either side of the switch, repair it and retest.

6   If the circuit is okay, check the continuity of the switch with an ohmmeter **(see illustration)**. When the plunger is depressed, there should be continuity; when the plunger is released (free), there should be no continuity. If the switch does not perform as described, replace the switch.

Clutch start cancel switch (4WD models)

Refer to illustrations 10.8a, 10.8b, 10.10a and 10.10b

7   The clutch start switch on 4WD models can be turned off by the clutch start cancel switch so that the vehicle can be driven out of difficult situations by cranking the engine with the clutch engaged (pedal not depressed). The button for the clutch start cancel switch is located on the left end of the dash; the switch itself is an integral part of the clutch start switch. The following tests will tell you whether the clutch start cancel switch is operating correctly.

8   With the switch button OFF, touch the positive lead of an ohmmeter to terminal 2 and the negative lead to terminal 1 **(see illustrations)** and verify that there is no continuity

between these two terminals.

9   With the switch button OFF, touch the positive lead of the ohmmeter to terminal 3 and the negative lead to terminal 1 **(see illustrations 10.8a and 10.8b)** and verify that there is no continuity between these two terminals, then verify that there is no continuity between terminals 2 and 3.

10   Using a pair of jumper cables, hook up the positive terminal of the battery (or a spare 12-volt battery) to terminal 3 and the negative lead to terminal 1 **(see illustrations)**, then touch the positive lead of the ohmmeter to terminal 2 and the negative lead to terminal 1 and verify that there is continuity when the clutch start cancel switch button is depressed (ON).

11   Using this same setup, verify that there is no continuity when the switch is in the OFF position.

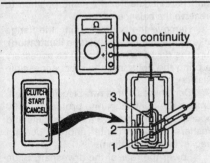

10.8b With the switch button OFF, verify that there is no continuity between any of the terminals (Tacoma and 4Runner switch shown)

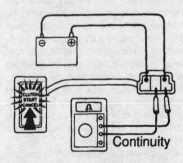

10.10a On T100 models, connect the positive terminal of the battery to terminal 3 and the negative lead to terminal 1, then touch the positive lead of the ohmmeter to terminal 2 and the negative lead to terminal 1 and verify that there is continuity with the switch in the ON position

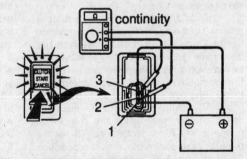

10.10b On Tacoma and 4Runner models, connect the positive terminal of the battery to terminal 3 and the negative lead to terminal 1, then touch the positive lead of the ohmmeter to terminal 2 and the negative lead to terminal 1 and verify that there is continuity with the switch in the ON position

12   Disconnect the battery leads and place the switch in the ON position, verify that there is no continuity between terminals 1 and 2.
13   If the clutch start cancel switch doesn't operate as described, replace the clutch start switch.

Adjustment

14   Loosen the switch locknut and screw the switch in or out so that the switch plunger protrudes between 0.29 and 0.33 inches (about 5/16-inch) past the locknut.

Replacement

15   Remove the lower finish panel(s) (see Chapter 11).
16   Unplug the electrical connector from the switch, remove the switch locknut and remove the switch.
17   Installation is the reverse of removal. Adjust the switch.

11   Driveshaft(s) and universal joints - general information

Refer to illustrations 14.3a through 14.3e
1   A driveshaft is a tube, or a pair of tubes, that transmits power between the transmission (or transfer case on 4WD models) and the differential. Universal joints are located at either end of the driveshaft; a third U-joint is employed just behind the center on two-piece driveshafts. The driveshaft is attached to the rear differential by a companion flange; on 4WD models, the front driveshaft is attached to the front differential the same way.
2   Driveshafts on 2WD models employ a splined yoke, known as a "slip yoke" or "sleeve yoke," at the front, which slips into the extension housing of the transmission. This arrangement allows the driveshaft to slide back-and-forth within the transmission during vehicle operation. An oil seal prevents leakage of fluid at this point and keeps dirt from entering the transmission. If leakage is evident at the front of the driveshaft, replace the oil seal (see Chapter 7, Part B).
3   On 4WD models, each driveshaft is attached to the transfer case by a companion flange. Once a front or rear driveshaft has been removed, either companion flange can be removed from the transfer case to replace the companion seal(s) (each companion flange uses two seals: one seal between the companion flange and the transfer case, the other, smaller, seal inside the companion flange itself). Refer to Chapter 7C for the transfer case seal replacement procedure. On front driveshafts, and on the one-piece rear driveshaft used on 4Runner models, the sleeve yoke is located in the driveshaft tube itself, between the two U-joints.
4   On two-piece driveshafts, center bearings support the driveline. The center bearing is a ball-type bearing mounted in a rubber cushion attached to a frame crossmember. The bearing is pre-lubricated and sealed at

the factory. On two-piece driveshafts, a sleeve yoke is employed in the rear driveshaft section.
5   The driveshaft assembly requires periodic lubrication. See Chapter 1 for the lubrication procedure and maintenance intervals.
6   Since the driveshaft is a balanced unit, it's important that no undercoating, mud, etc. be allowed to stay on it. When the vehicle is raised for service it's a good idea to clean the driveshaft and inspect it for any obvious damage. Also, make sure the small weights used to originally balance the driveshaft are in place and securely attached. Whenever the driveshaft is removed it must be reinstalled in the same relative position to preserve the balance.
7   Problems with the driveshaft are usually indicated by a noise or vibration while driving the vehicle. A road test should verify if the problem is the driveshaft or another vehicle component. Refer to the *Troubleshooting* Section at the front of this manual. If you suspect trouble, inspect the driveline (see the next Section).

12   Driveline inspection

1   Raise the rear of the vehicle and support it securely on jackstands. Block the front wheels to keep the vehicle from rolling off the stands.
2   Crawl under the vehicle and visually inspect the driveshaft. Look for any dents or cracks in the tubing. If any are found, the driveshaft must be replaced.
3   Check for oil leakage at the front and rear of the driveshaft. Leakage where the driveshaft enters the transmission or transfer case indicates a defective transmission/transfer case seal (see Chapter 7). Leakage where the driveshaft joins the differential indicates a defective pinion seal (see Section 18).
4   While under the vehicle, have an assistant rotate a rear wheel so the driveshaft will rotate. As it does, make sure the universal joints are operating properly without binding, noise or looseness. Listen for any noise from the center bearing (if equipped), indicating it's worn or damaged. Also check the rubber portion of the center bearing for cracking or separation, which will necessitate replacement.
5   The universal joint can also be checked with the driveshaft motionless, by gripping your hands on either side of the joint and attempting to twist the joint. Any movement at all in the joint is a sign of considerable wear. Lifting up on the shaft will also indicate movement in the universal joints.
6   Finally, check the driveshaft mounting bolts at the ends to make sure they're tight.
7   On 4WD models, the above driveshaft checks should be repeated on all driveshafts. In addition, check for grease leakage around the sleeve yoke, indicating failure of the yoke seal.
8   Check for leakage where the driveshafts connect to the transfer case and front differential. Leakage indicates worn oil seals.

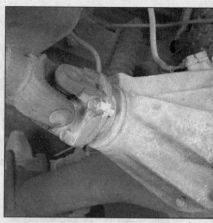

13.2 Mark the relationship of the driveshaft U-joint to the pinion flange with paint marks

9   At the same time, check for looseness in the joints of the front driveaxles. Also check for grease or oil leakage from around the driveaxles by inspecting the rubber boots and both ends of each axle. Oil leakage at the differential junction indicates a defective side oil seal. Leakage at the wheel side indicates a defective front hub seal, while leakage at the boots means a damaged rubber boot. For servicing of these components, see the appropriate Sections.

13   Driveshaft - removal and installation

1   Raise the vehicle and support it securely on jackstands. Place the transmission in Neutral with the parking brake off. Block the front wheels to prevent the vehicle from rolling.

Rear driveshaft
Removal

Refer to illustrations 13.2, 13.3, 13.4 and 13.5
2   Using a scribe, a hammer and punch, or paint, make marks on the driveshaft and the differential flange in line with each other **(see illustration)**. This is to make sure the driveshaft is reinstalled in the same position to preserve the balance.
3   Remove the bolts securing the flange yoke to the rear differential **(see illustration)**. Turn the driveshaft (or wheels) as necessary to bring the bolts into the most accessible position.
4   On vehicles with a two-piece driveshaft, remove the center bearing protector (T100 models only) and remove the bolts, nuts and washers from the center support bearing bracket **(see illustration)**.
5   Lower the rear of the driveshaft. Slide the front of the driveshaft out of the transmission or transfer case or, if equipped with a companion flange, separate the flange at the transfer case **(see illustration)**.
6   On 2WD models, wrap a plastic bag

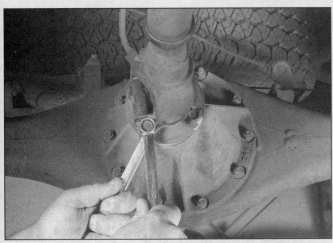

13.3 Using a backup wrench to hold each bolt, break loose all four bolts securing the flange yoke to the differential

13.4 To detach the center bearing on two-piece driveshafts, remove these four protector bolts (four lower arrows) and the protector, then remove the two center bearing bolts (upper arrows)

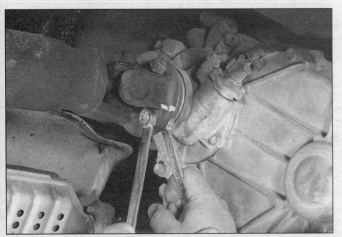

13.5 On 4WD models, mark the relationship of the driveshaft U-joint flange yoke to the companion flange, then remove the bolts securing the flange yoke to the transfer case

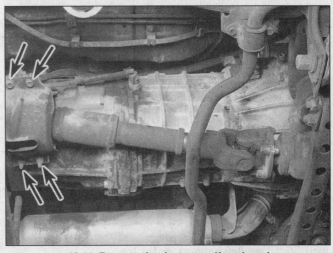

13.11 Remove the dust cover if equipped

over the transmission extension housing and hold it in place with a rubber band. This will prevent loss of fluid and protect against contamination while the driveshaft is out.

7   If you're overhauling a U-joint, refer to Section 14. If you're replacing the center bearing on a two-piece driveshaft, see Section 15. If you're replacing the pinion seal, see Section 18. If you're replacing the extension housing seal, you'll find the procedure in Chapter 7A. If you're replacing either rear seal in the transfer case on a 4WD model, go to Chapter 7C.

Installation

8   Remove the plastic bag from the transmission or transfer case and wipe the area clean. Inspect the oil seal carefully (see Chapter 7, Part A or B). Slide the front of the driveshaft into the transmission (2WD models) or bolt the U-joint flange yoke to the companion flange, installing the fasteners finger-tight (4WD models).

9   Raise the center bearing (if equipped) into place and screw the retaining bolts in a few turns. Raise the rear of the driveshaft into

position, checking to be sure the marks are in alignment. If not, turn the rear wheels to match the pinion flange and the driveshaft.

10   Tighten all nuts to the torque listed in this Chapter's Specifications. Remove the jackstands and lower the vehicle.

Front driveshaft (4WD models)

Removal

Refer to illustration 13.11

11   Remove any skid plates or under covers (if equipped). On T100 models, remove the driveshaft dust cover bolts and nuts **(see illustration)** and remove the cover.

12   Mark the relationship of the driveshaft to the front differential and the transfer case companion flanges.

13   Remove the nuts, bolts and washers from the differential and transfer companion flanges and remove the front driveshaft.

14   If you're overhauling a U-joint, refer to Section 14. If you're replacing the pinion seal in the front differential, refer to Section 18. If you're replacing either front seal in the transfer case on a 4WD model, see Chapter 7C.

Installation

15   Attach the front end of the driveshaft to the front differential companion flange and install the nuts and bolts finger-tight.

16   Extend or compress the driveshaft as necessary, attach the rear end to the transfer case flange, install the washers, nuts and bolts and tighten the nuts to the torque listed in this Chapter's Specifications.

17   Install the skid plate and/or under covers.

18   Remove the jackstands and lower the vehicle.

14 Universal joints - replacement

Note: *A press or large vise will be required for this procedure. It may be a good idea to take the driveshaft to a repair or machine shop where the U-joints can be replaced for you, usually at a reasonable charge.*
Refer to illustration 14.2, 14.3a, 14.3b, 14.3c, 14.3d, 14.3e, 14.3f, 14.4 and 14.5

1   Remove the driveshaft (see Section 13).

14.2 If either driveshaft has a U-joint (arrow) that looks like this, it's a "double-cardan" type (meaning it has two U-joints instead of one) and it can't be rebuilt; if a double-cardan U-joint is damaged or worn out, replace the driveshaft (4WD T100 rear driveshaft shown, others similar)

2   Place the driveshaft on a bench equipped with a vise. **Caution:** *Some models use driveshafts equipped with "double-cardan" type universal joints* (see illustration). *Do NOT attempt to disassemble a double-cardan U-joint. The Toyota OEM double-cardan U-joint used on vehicles covered by this manual is not rebuildable. If you determine that a double-cardan U-joint is worn out, replace the driveshaft assembly with a new or rebuilt unit.*

3   Mark the shaft and yoke for proper reassembly, then remove the snap rings from the U-joint (see illustrations). **Note:** *The driveshafts covered in this manual are equipped with u-joints that use either outer snap rings or inner snap rings to retain the bearing cap. Outer snap rings can be removed using a pair of pliers while inner snap rings require a punch and a hammer to dislodge the snap ring from the groove on the bearing cap.*

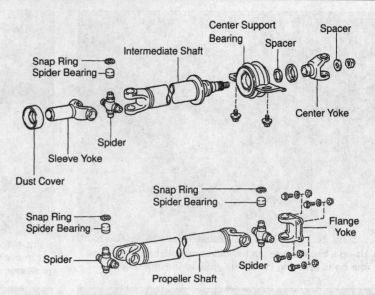

14.3a Exploded view of a driveshaft assembly (some T100 2WD models)

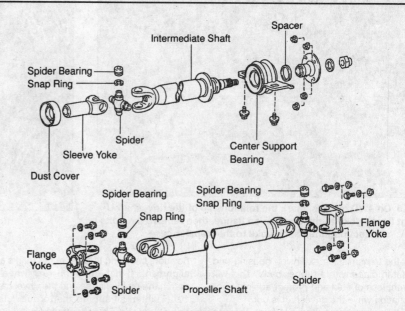

14.3b Exploded view of a typical three-joint driveshaft assembly (2WD T100 and 2WD Tacoma models)

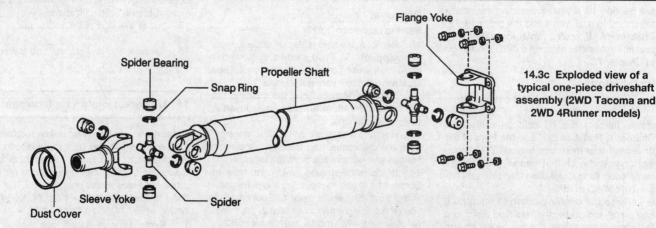

14.3c Exploded view of a typical one-piece driveshaft assembly (2WD Tacoma and 2WD 4Runner models)

Front Propeller Shaft:

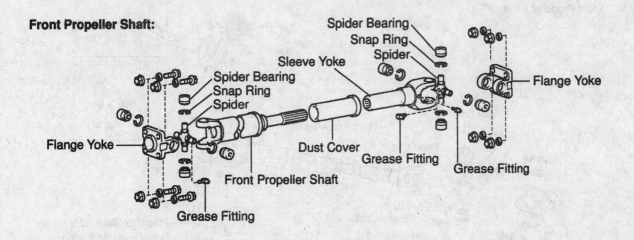

Spider Bearing
Snap Ring
Spider
Sleeve Yoke
Flange Yoke
Spider Bearing
Snap Ring
Spider
Flange Yoke
Dust Cover
Grease Fitting
Grease Fitting
Front Propeller Shaft
Grease Fitting

Rear Propeller Shaft:
2–Joint Type:

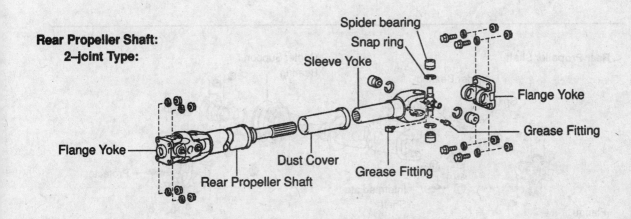

Spider bearing
Snap ring
Sleeve Yoke
Flange Yoke
Flange Yoke
Grease Fitting
Dust Cover
Rear Propeller Shaft
Grease Fitting

3–Joint Type:

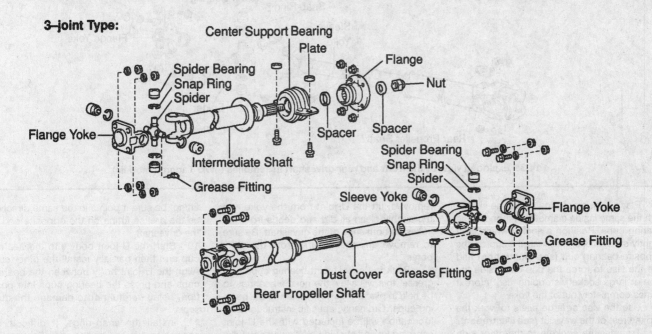

Center Support Bearing
Plate
Flange
Nut
Spider Bearing
Snap Ring
Spider
Flange Yoke
Spacer
Spacer
Intermediate Shaft
Spider Bearing
Snap Ring
Spider
Grease Fitting
Sleeve Yoke
Flange Yoke
Grease Fitting
Dust Cover
Grease Fitting
Rear Propeller Shaft

14.3d Exploded view of the front and rear driveshaft assemblies (4WD T100 and 4WD 4Runner models)

Front Propeller Shaft

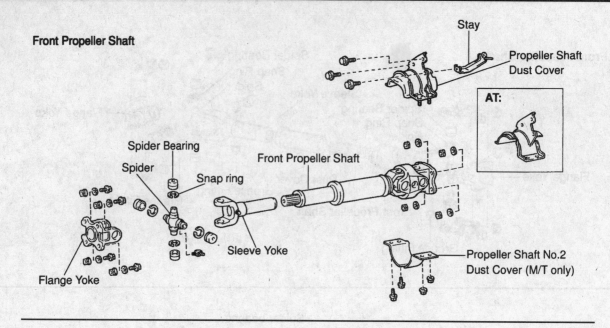

Rear Propeller Shaft

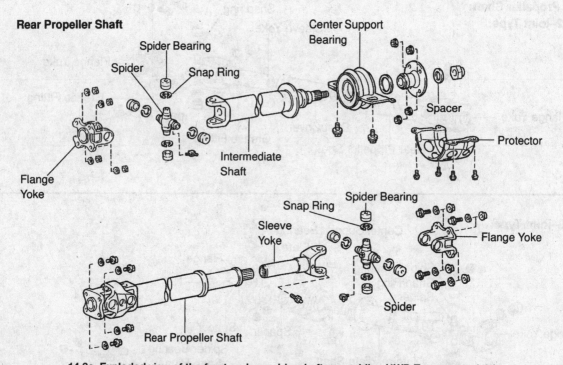

14.3e Exploded view of the front and rear driveshaft assemblies (4WD Tacoma models)

4   Place a piece of pipe or a large socket with the same inside diameter over one of the bearing cups. Position a socket which is of slightly smaller diameter than the cup on the opposite bearing cup **(see illustration)** and use the vise to force the cup out (inside the pipe or large socket), stopping just before it comes completely out of the yoke.

5   Use the vise or large pliers to work the cup the rest of the way out **(see illustration)**.

6   Transfer the sockets to the other side and press the opposite bearing cup out in the same manner.

7   After the bearing cups have been removed, lift the U-joint from the yoke and thoroughly clean all dirt and debris from the yokes on both ends of the driveshaft. Be sure to remove any metal burrs from the yoke bores.

8   Pack the new U-joint bearing cups with grease, this will allow the needle bearings to be held in place while your installing the bearing cups. Ordinarily, specific instructions for lubrication will be included with the U-joint servicing kit and should be followed carefully.

9   Position the U-joint body in the yoke and partially install one bearing cup in the yoke. If the U-joint is equipped with a grease fitting, be sure it points in the same direction as the grease fitting on the opposite end of the driveshaft.

10   Start the U-joint body into the bearing cup and then partially install the other cup. Align the U-joint body between the bearing cups and press the bearing cups into position, being careful not to damage the dust seals.

11   Install the snap-rings. If difficulty is encountered in seating the snap-rings, strike the driveshaft yoke sharply with a hammer. This will spring the yoke ears slightly and allow the snap-rings to seat in the groove.

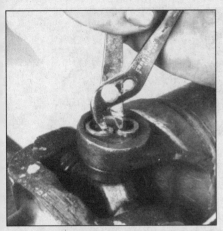

14.3f Outer type snap-rings can be removed with a small pair of pliers

14.4 To remove the U-joint from the driveshaft, use a vise as a press; the small socket will push the cross and bearing cup into the large socket

14.5 Grip the bearing cup with locking pliers and remove it from the yoke

This should also be done to center the U-joint after assembly. **Note:** *If you still have difficulty seating the snap-rings, one of the small needle bearings may have become stuck between the bearing cap and the end of the spider. Disassemble and inspect the joint.*

12   Install the driveshaft (see Section 13).

13   If the U-joint is equipped with a grease fitting, lubricate it as described in Chapter 1.

14   Remove the jackstands and lower the vehicle.

15   Center bearing - removal and installation

Refer to illustrations 15.6a, 15.6b and 15.7

1   Raise the vehicle and support it securely on jackstands.

2   Remove the driveshaft (see Section 13).

3   Clamp the driveshaft securely into a bench vise.

4   Separate the intermediate (front) part of the driveshaft from the rear part: On T100 models with a outer snap-ring type driveshaft, mark the center U-joint yoke and driveshaft, then disassemble the center U-joint (see Section 14). On all other models, mark the relationship of the center U-joint flange yoke to the flange behind the center bearing, the unbolt the center U-joint from the flange.

5   Unstake the center yoke (outer snap-ring type) or flange (inner snap ring type) retaining nut and remove it.

6   Mark the relationship of the intermediate shaft to the yoke or flange **(see illustrations)**.

7   Remove the yoke or flange from the intermediate shaft **(see illustration)**.

8   Remove the center bearing from the intermediate shaft. **Note:** *This usually requires a puller or a punch and a hammer to separate the center bearing from the intermediate shaft.*

9   Holding the center bearing assembly in one hand, turn the bearing with the other hand and verify that it operates freely and smoothly. If it's stiff or noisy, replace it.

10   Installation is the reverse of removal. Be sure to tighten the yoke or flange retaining nut to the torque listed in this Chapter's Specifications, then stake it.

16   Axles - description and check

Description

1   The rear axle assembly is a hypoid, semi-floating type (the centerline of the pinion gear is below the centerline of the ring gear). When the vehicle goes around a corner, the differential allows the outer rear tire to turn more quickly than the inner tire. The axleshafts are splined to the differential side gears, so when the vehicle goes around a corner, the inner tire, which turns more slowly than the outer tire, turns its side gear more slowly than the outer tire turns its side gear. The differential pinion gears roll around the slower side gear, driving the outer side gear - and tire - more quickly. The differential is housed within a casting with a pressed steel cover, known as the "carrier." The steel axle tubes are pressed into and welded to the carrier.

2   On 4WD models, a fully independent front axle assembly is used. This consists of a differential and a pair of driveaxles. Each driveaxle has an inner and outer constant velocity (CV) joint.

3   A locking limited-slip rear axle is used on some models. This differential allows for normal operation until one wheel loses traction. A limited-slip unit is similar in design to a conventional differential, except for the addition of a pair of clutch "cones" which slow the rotation of the differential case when one wheel is on a firm surface and the other on a slippery one. The difference in wheel rotational speed produced by this condition applies additional force to the pinion gears and through the cone, which is splined to the axleshafts, equalizes the rotation speed of the axleshaft driving the wheel with traction.

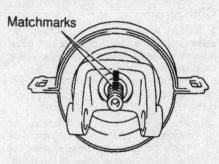

15.6a Mark the relationship of the intermediate shaft to the yoke (some 2WD T100 models) . . .

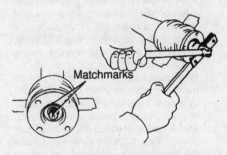

15.6b . . . or flange (all other models)

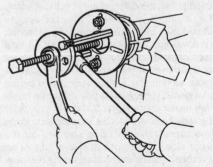

15.7 Remove the yoke or flange from the intermediate shaft with a puller

17.5 To detach the axleshaft from the rear axle housing, remove the four backing plate nuts (arrows)

17.6 Extract the axleshaft very carefully from the axle housing, especially if you don't want to replace the axleshaft seal

Check

4   Often, a suspected "axle" problem lies elsewhere. Do a thorough check of other possible causes before assuming the axle is the problem.

5   The following noises are those commonly associated with axle diagnosis procedures:

a) *Road noise is often mistaken for mechanical faults. Driving the vehicle on different surfaces will show whether the road surface is the cause of the noise. Road noise will remain the same if the vehicle is under power or coasting.*

b) *Tire noise is sometimes mistaken for mechanical problems. Tires which are worn or low on pressure are particularly susceptible to emitting vibrations and noises. Tire noise will remain about the same during varying driving situations, where axle noise will change during coasting, acceleration, etc.*

c) *Engine and transmission noise can be deceiving because it will travel along the driveline. To isolate engine and transmission noises, make a note of the engine speed at which the noise is most pronounced. Stop the vehicle and place the transmission in Neutral and run the engine to the same speed. If the noise is the same, the axle is not at fault.*

6   Because of the special tools needed, overhauling the differential isn't cost effective for a do-it-yourselfer. The procedures included in this Chapter describe axleshaft removal and installation, axleshaft oil seal replacement, axleshaft bearing replacement and removal of the entire unit for repair or replacement. Any further work should be left to a dealer service department or other qualified repair shop. **Note:** *If the rear axle must be replaced, refer to the identification code and manufacturer's code stamped on the front side of the right rear axle tube. This number contains information on the rear axle ratio, differential type, manufacturer and build date information, all of which are necessary to ensure that you get the right axle.*

17.7 Remove this O-ring from the rear axle housing; be sure to discard the old O-ring and install a new one before installing the axleshaft

17.8 Use a seal removal tool or a big screwdriver to pry out the old axleshaft seal; use a seal installer or a big socket to install the new seal

17   Axleshaft, bearing and oil seal (rear) - removal and installation

Refer to illustrations 17.5, 17.6, 17.7 and 17.8

1   Release the parking brake. Raise the rear of the vehicle, support it securely on jackstands and block the front wheels. Remove the wheel and brake drum.

2   If the vehicle is equipped with ABS, remove the ABS sensor (see Chapter 9).

3   Remove the brake assembly (see Chapter 9).

4   Disconnect the parking brake cable and the hydraulic brake line to the wheel cylinder (see Chapter 9).

5   Remove the four backing plate mounting nuts **(see illustration)**.

6   Pull the axleshaft out of the rear axle housing **(see illustration)**. Try not to damage the oil seal.

7   Remove the O-ring from the rear axle housing **(see illustration)**.

8   Remove the axleshaft oil seal from the axle housing with a seal removal tool or a big

screwdriver **(see illustration)**.

9   Further disassembly of the axleshaft assembly requires special tools and a hydraulic press. If the axleshaft, bearing or oil seal needs to be replaced, take the axleshaft assembly to an automotive machine shop.

10   Drive a new axleshaft seal into the end of the axle tube with a seal installer or a big socket. Coat the lip of the seal with clean oil or multi-purpose grease.

11   Install a new axle housing O-ring. Apply a light coat of oil to the new O-ring.

12   Make sure the axleshaft is clean and there are no burrs or metal splinters on it. Deburr any surface irregularities so the axleshaft doesn't damage the seal during installation. Lightly coat the axleshaft with clean oil, then insert it into the axle housing. Make sure the splined inner end of the axleshaft doesn't damage the lip of the new axleshaft seal.

13   Installation is the reverse of removal. Tighten the four backing plate mounting nuts to the torque listed in this Chapter's Specifications.

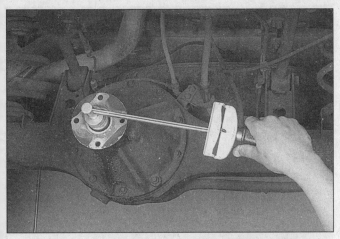

18.3 Use an inch-pound torque wrench to check the torque necessary to rotate the pinion shaft

18.4 Mark the relative positions of the pinion, nut and flange before removing the nut

18 Differential pinion seal - replacement

Refer to illustrations 18.3, 18.4, 18.6, 18.8, 18.9 and 18.10
Note: *This procedure applies to the rear pinion seal on all vehicles and the front pinion seal on 4WD models as well.*

1   Loosen the rear wheel lug nuts, raise the rear of the vehicle and support it securely on jackstands. Block the front wheels to keep the vehicle from rolling off the stands. Remove the wheels (this will allow you to obtain a more accurate pinion shaft preload reading).

2   Disconnect the driveshaft from the differential (see Section 13) and fasten it out of the way.

3   Use an inch-pound torque wrench to check the torque required to rotate the pinion **(see illustration)**. Record it for use later.

4   Scribe or punch alignment marks on the pinion shaft, nut and flange **(see illustration)**.

5   Count the number of threads visible between the end of the nut and the end of the pinion shaft and jot it down for later use.

6   A special flange-holding tool is the best way to keep the companion flange from moving while the pinion nut is loosened. If you're unable to obtain a flange-holding tool, immobilize the flange by inserting a big screwdriver through one of the U-joint bolt holes in the flange and wedge it against a bracket **(see illustration)** or reinforcement rib on the differential carrier or, if it's long enough, wedge it underneath the axle tube.

7   Remove the pinion nut.

8   Withdraw the companion flange. It may be necessary to use a puller to draw it out **(see illustration)**. Do NOT attempt to pry behind the flange or hammer on the end of the pinion shaft.

9   Pry out the old seal **(see illustration)** and discard it.

10   Lubricate the lips of the new seal with high-temperature grease and tap it evenly into position with a seal installation tool or a large socket. Make sure it enters the housing squarely and is tapped in to its full depth **(see illustration)**.

11   Align the mating marks made before

18.6 If you don't have a flange-holding tool to hold the flange while you loosen the pinion nut, lock the flange by jamming a large screwdriver through a bolt hole in the flange and wedge it underneath a bracket as shown, or under a reinforcement rib on the differential carrier, or under an axle tube

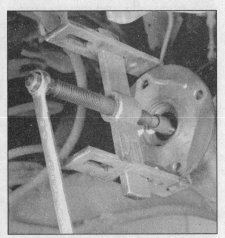

18.8 If you can't pull off the pinion flange by hand, remove it with a small puller

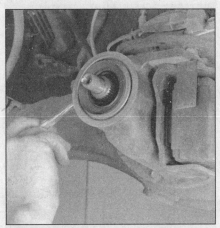

18.9 Pry out the old pinion seal with a seal removal tool or a big screwdriver or tap it out with a small punch as shown

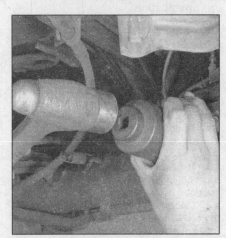

18.10 Lubricate the lips of the new pinion seal and seat it squarely in the bore, then drive it into the carrier with a seal driver or a large socket

19.5 Detach all brake hoses and lines, such as this junction block (arrow) from the axle housing; to detach the junction block, simply remove the bolt on top

20.2a Mark the relationship of the inner CV joint to the flange . . .

disassembly and install the companion flange. If necessary, tighten the pinion nut to draw the flange into place. Do not try to hammer the flange into position.

12   Apply non-hardening sealant to the ends of the splines visible in the center of the flange so oil will be sealed in.

13   Install the washer (if equipped) and pinion nut. Tighten the nut carefully, until the original number of threads are exposed.

14   Measure the torque required to rotate the pinion and tighten the nut in small increments until it matches the figure recorded in Step 3. In order to compensate for the drag of the new oil seal, the nut should be tightened more until the rotational torque of the pinion slightly exceeds what was recorded earlier, but not by more than 5 in-lbs.

15   Connect the driveshaft, install the wheels and lower the vehicle. Tighten the lug nuts to the torque listed in the Chapter 1 Specifications.

19   Axle (rear) - removal and installation

Refer to illustration 19.5

1   Loosen the rear wheel lug nuts, raise the rear of the vehicle and support it securely on jackstands placed under the frame (not under the axle). Block the front wheels to keep the vehicle from rolling off the stands. Remove the rear wheels.

2   Position a jack under the rear axle differential housing.

3   Disconnect the driveshaft from the differential (see Section 13). Fasten the driveshaft out of the way with a piece of wire from the underbody.

4   Disconnect the load sensing proportioning and bypass valve (LSP & BV) height sensing spring from the axle (see Chapter 9).

5   Detach all brake hoses and/or lines from the axle housing **(see illustration)**, then plug them to prevent fluid leakage.

6   Remove the rear brake drums and brake

assemblies (see Chapter 9).

7   Disconnect the parking brake cables from the brake assemblies and detach the cables from the rear axle housing (see Chapter 9).

8   Detach the vent hose from the axle housing and fasten it out of the way.

9   Disconnect the shock absorbers from the spring seats (T100 and Tacoma) or from the axle brackets (4Runners), then compress them to get them out of the way (see Chapter 10).

10   On T100 and Tacoma models, disconnect the leaf spring U-bolts and remove the spacers, bumpers and spring seats (see Chapter 10).

11   On 4Runner models, disconnect the stabilizer bar, lateral control rod, lateral control rod and upper and lower suspension arms (see Chapter 10).

12   Lower the jack under the differential, then remove the rear axle assembly from under the vehicle.

13   Installation is the reverse of removal. Be sure to tighten all suspension fasteners to the torque listed in the Chapter 10 Specifica-

tions. On T100 and Tacoma models, lower the vehicle weight onto the wheels before tightening the U-bolt nuts completely.

14   Bleed the brakes (see Chapter 9).

20   Driveaxle (4WD models) - removal and installation

1   Loosen the wheel lug nuts, raise the vehicle and support it securely on jackstands. Remove the wheel.

T100 models

Refer to illustrations 20.2a, 20.2b, 20.4a and 20.4b

2   Mark the relationship of the inner CV joint to the flange **(see illustration)**. Place a prybar or large screwdriver between the wheel studs to hold the driveaxle and remove the inner CV joint-to-axleshaft flange nuts **(see illustration)**.

3   Remove the freewheel hub (see Section 24).

4   Remove the driveaxle snap-ring and spacer **(see illustrations)**.

20.2b . . . and loosen the flange nuts and bolts (T100 models)

20.4a To disconnect the driveaxle assembly from the steering knuckle, remove the snap-ring . . .

20.4b . . . and the spacer (hub and bearing assembly removed for clarity) (T100 model shown)

5   Pull the inner CV joint off the axleshaft flange studs, lower the inner CV joint and pull the driveaxle assembly out of the steering knuckle.

6   Installation is the reverse of removal. Be sure to tighten the CV joint-to-axleshaft flange nuts to the torque listed in this Chapter's Specifications and the flange bolt and nuts to the torque listed in the Chapter 10 Specifications.

Tacoma and 4Runner models

7   Drain the differential (see Chapter 1).
8   On models without free-wheeling hubs, pry off the grease cap (Tacoma models only), remove the cotter pin and lock cap, place a prybar or large screwdriver between the wheel studs to hold the driveaxle and break the driveaxle hub nut loose with a large breaker bar, or have an assistant apply the brakes. Remove the nut and washer.
9   On Tacoma models with free-wheeling hubs, remove the free-wheeling hub (see Section 24), then remove the snap-ring and spacer **(see illustrations 20.4a and 20.4b)**.
10 Knock the driveaxle loose from the steering knuckle with a *brass* drift and hammer. Do NOT use a steel punch or strike the end of the driveaxle with a steel hammer; a steel punch or hammer will damage the threads or the splines on the end of the driveaxle.
11 Disconnect the lower control arm from the steering knuckle (see Chapter 10).
12 Swing the steering knuckle outward and pull the driveaxle assembly out of the steering knuckle and the differential. If the driveaxle sticks, knock it loose with a rubber mallet or brass drift.
13 Installation is the reverse of removal. Be sure to tighten the driveaxle hub nut (Tacoma models without free-wheeling hub and 4Runner models). On Tacoma models with free-wheeling hubs, use a new driveaxle snap-ring.

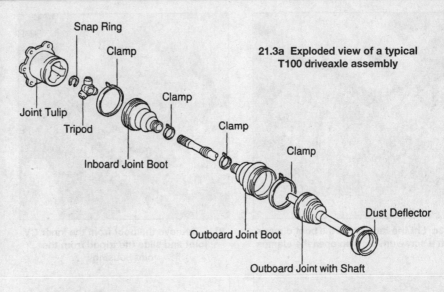

21.3a Exploded view of a typical T100 driveaxle assembly

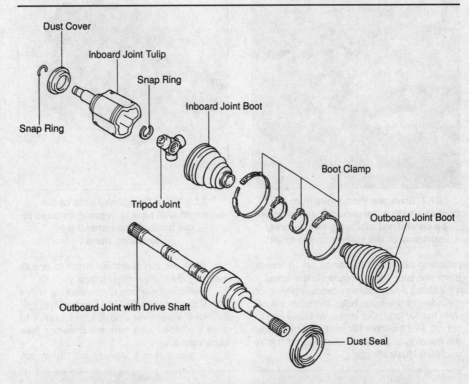

21.3b Exploded view of a typical Tacoma and 4Runner driveaxle assembly

21 Driveaxle boot replacement and CV joint overhaul

Note: *If the CV joints must be overhauled (usually due to torn boots), explore all options before beginning the job. Complete rebuilt driveaxles are available on an exchange basis, which eliminates much time and work. Whichever route you choose to take, check on the cost and availability of parts before disassembling the vehicle. Do NOT disassemble the outboard CV joint*

1   Remove the driveaxle (see Section 20).

Disassembly

Refer to illustrations 21.3a, 21.3b, 21.3c, 21.4, 21.6, 21.7 and 21.8

2   Mount the driveaxle in a vice with wood lined jaws (to prevent damage to the axleshaft). Check the CV joint for excessive play in the radial direction, which indicates worn parts. Check for smooth operation throughout the full range of motion for each CV joint. If a boot is torn, disassemble the joint, clean the components and inspect for damage due to loss of lubrication and possible contamination by foreign matter.
3   Using a small screwdriver, pry the

21.3c Lift the tabs on all the boot clamps with a screwdriver, then open the clamps

21.4 Remove the boot from the inner CV joint and slide the tripod from the joint housing

21.6 Remove the snap-ring with a pair of snap-ring pliers

21.7 Drive the tripod joint from the driveaxle with a brass punch and hammer; be careful not to damage the bearing surfaces or the splines on the shaft

21.8 Wrap the splined area of the axleshaft with tape to prevent damage to the boots when removing or installing them

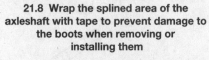
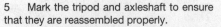

21.9 Clean the outer CV joint thoroughly with solvent and, working the joint through its entire range of motion, inspect the bearing surfaces of the balls; if they're worn or damaged, so are the bearing races

retaining tabs of the clamps up to loosen them and slide them off **(see illustrations)**.

4   Using a screwdriver, carefully pry up on the edge of the outer boot and push it away from the CV joint. Old and worn boots can be cut off. Pull the inner CV joint boot back from the housing and slide the housing off the tripod **(see illustration)**.

5   Mark the tripod and axleshaft to ensure that they are reassembled properly.
6   Remove the tripod joint snap-ring with a pair of snap-ring pliers **(see illustration)**.
7   Use a hammer and a brass punch to drive the tripod joint from the driveaxle **(see illustration)**.
8   If you haven't already cut them off,

remove both boots. Wrap the splines on the inner end the axleshaft with electrical or duct tape to protect the boots from the sharp edges of the splines **(see illustration)**. Note: *Do NOT disassemble the outboard CV joint.*

21.10a Install the boot and clamps onto the axleshaft, then install the tripod with the recessed portion of the splines facing the axleshaft

21.10b Place grease at the bottom of the CV joint housing

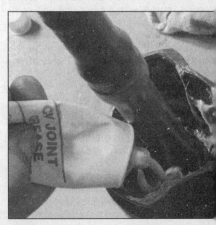

21.10c Insert the tripod into the housing, followed by the rest of the grease

21.11 Set the driveaxle length to the dimension listed in this Chapter's Specifications before the boot clamps are tightened (T100 model shown)

21.12a Equalize the pressure inside the boot by inserting a small, dull screwdriver between the boot and the outer race

Check

Refer to illustration 21.9

9 Thoroughly clean all components, including the outer CV joint assembly, with solvent until the old CV joint grease is completely removed. Inspect the bearing surfaces of the inner tripods and housings for cracks, pitting, scoring and other signs of wear. It's not possible to inspect the bearing surfaces of the inner and outer races of the outer CV joint, but you can at least check the surfaces of the ball bearings themselves **(see illustration)**. If they're in good shape, so are the races; if they're not, neither are the races. If the inner CV joint is worn, you can buy a new inner CV joint and install it on the old axleshaft; if the outer CV joint is worn, you'll have to purchase a new outer CV joint and axleshaft (they're sold preassembled).

Reassembly

Refer to illustrations 21.10a, 21.10b, 21.10c, 21.11, 21.12a, 21.12b and 21.12c

10 Slide the clamps and boot(s) onto the axleshaft, then place the tripod on the shaft. Apply grease to the tripod assembly and inside the housing. Insert the tripod into the housing and pack the remainder of the grease around the tripod. **(see illustrations)**.

11 Slide the boot into place, making sure both ends seat in their grooves. Adjust the length of the driveaxle to the dimension listed in this Chapter's Specifications **(see illustrations)**.

12 Equalize the pressure in the boot, then tighten and secure the boot clamps **(see illustrations)**.

13 Install the driveaxle assembly (see Section 20).

22 Automatic Disconnecting Differential (ADD) control system (4WD models) - description, check and component replacement

Description

Refer to illustrations 22.1a and 22.1b

1 The Automatic Disconnecting Differential (ADD) control system **(see illustrations)**

21.12b To install the new clamps, bend the tang down . . .

21.12c . . . then tap the tabs over to hold it in place

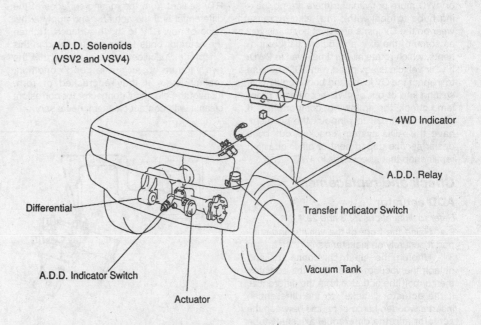

A.D.D. Solenoids (VSV2 and VSV4)

4WD Indicator

A.D.D. Relay

Transfer Indicator Switch

Differential

Vacuum Tank

A.D.D. Indicator Switch

Actuator

22.1a Automatic Disconnecting Differential (ADD) control system component location (T100 models)

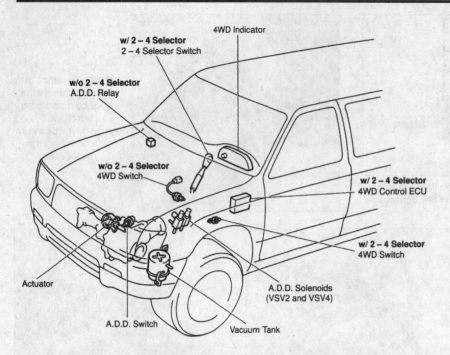

22.1b   Automatic Disconnecting Differential (ADD) control system component location (Tacoma and 4Runner models)

22.3   To detach the ADD actuator from the front differential, unplug the electrical connector and detach the vacuum hoses, then remove the four retaining bolts - If the actuator is stuck to the front differential, use a wooden hammer handle to pry it off as shown

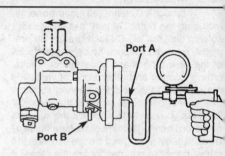

22.4   Attach a hand-operated vacuum pump to actuator port A, apply a vacuum of 20 in-Hg and verify that the sleeve fork moves to the right - Then attach the vacuum pump to actuator port B, apply a vacuum of 20 in-Hg and verify that the sleeve fork moves to the left

is optional equipment on T100 and Tacoma models and standard equipment on 4Runners. The ADD system is fairly complex, but basically it connects the power flow through the left axleshaft when 4WD mode is selected, and disconnects the power flow when 2WD mode is selected. Although ADD-equipped vehicles make selecting 2WD or 4WD more convenient (there are no locking hubs to deal with), they also increase wear on the CV joints and dust boots, as well as some of the axle and differential components, which rotate all the time, even in 2WD. If your vehicle is equipped with ADD, be sure to inspect the CV joints and boots regularly. If shifting into or out of 4WD becomes a problem, check the following components. If these checks fail to pinpoint the problem, have the ADD system checked out by a dealer service department or other qualified repair shop that specializes in 4WD.

Check and replacement

ADD actuator

Refer to illustrations 22.3 and 22.4
2   Raise the front of the vehicle and support it securely on jackstands.
3   Unplug the electrical connector and detach the vacuum hoses from the actuator, then unbolt the actuator from the differential. If the actuator "sticks" to the differential, insert a wooden hammer handle between the actuator and the differential axleshaft tube and pry it off **(see illustration)**.
4   Attach a hand-operated vacuum pump to actuator port A, apply a vacuum of 20 in-Hg and verify that the sleeve fork moves to the right **(see illustration)**.

5   Reattach the vacuum pump to port B, apply a vacuum of 20 in-Hg and verify that the sleeve fork moves to the left **(see illustration 22.4)**.
6   If the actuator doesn't operate as described, replace it.
7   Installation is the reverse of removal. Before installing the actuator, remove the old RTV sealant from the mating surfaces of the differential and the actuator and apply a thin bead of new RTV to those surfaces. Tighten the actuator bolts to the torque listed in this Chapter's Specifications. Make sure that the two vacuum hoses are in good condition; replace them if they're cracked or torn. Inspect the electrical connector for corrosion; clean it with contact cleaner if necessary.

ADD solenoids

Refer to illustrations 22.9, 22.10 and 22.11
8   Unplug the electrical connectors from the ADD solenoids.
9   Using an ohmmeter, measure the resistance of each ADD solenoid **(see illustration)** and compare your measurements to the

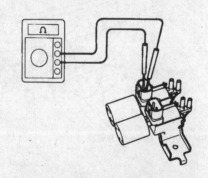

22.9   Using an ohmmeter, measure the resistance of each ADD solenoid and compare your measurements to the resistance listed in this Chapter's Specifications

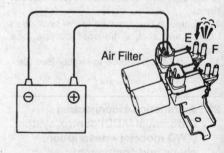

22.10   Power up each ADD solenoid and verify that air flows into port E and out port F, but not out the air filter; when battery power to each solenoid is cut, verify that air flows into port E and out the air filter, but not out port F

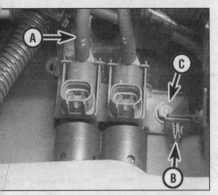

22.11 To remove the ADD solenoid, detach the vacuum lines (A), the plastic retaining clip (B) and the bracket retaining bolt (C)

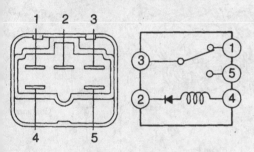

22.13 ADD relay terminal guide

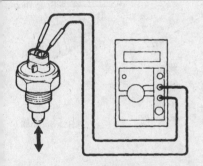

22.17 Touch the leads of an ohmmeter to the ADD switch terminals and verify that there is continuity between the terminals when the switch plunger is pushed into the switch; release the switch plunger and verify that there is no continuity between the terminals

resistance listed in this Chapter's Specifications.

10   Using jumper cables, attach the battery to one solenoid as shown **(see illustration)** and verify that air flows into port E and out port F. Also verify that air does not flow out the air filter. Disconnect the battery jumper cables from the same solenoid and verify that air flows from port E and out the air filter. Verify that air doesn't flow out port F. Check the other ADD solenoid the same way.

11   If either ADD solenoid fails any of these tests, replace the entire ADD solenoid assembly **(see illustration)**.

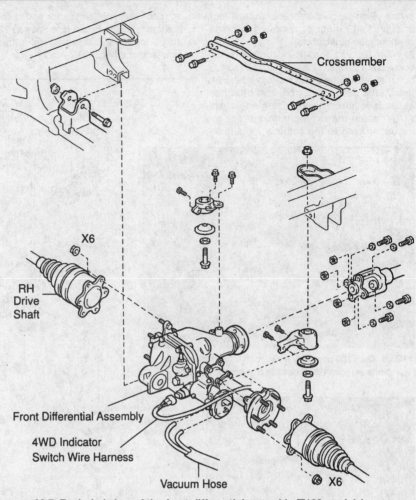

23.7 Exploded view of the front differential assembly (T100 models)

Crossmember

X6

RH
Drive
Shaft

Front Differential Assembly

4WD Indicator
Switch Wire Harness

Vacuum Hose   X6

ADD relay

Refer to illustration 22.13

12   Remove the ADD relay.
13   Using an ohmmeter, verify that there is continuity between terminals 1 and 3 and between terminals 2 and 4 **(see illustration)**.
14   Using jumper cables, connect the positive lead from the battery to terminal 4 and the negative lead to terminal 2 of the relay and verify that there is continuity between terminals 3 and 5.
15   If the relay does not operate as described, replace it.

ADD switch

Refer to illustration 22.17

16   Unplug the electrical connector and remove the ADD switch.
17   Touch the leads of an ohmmeter to the switch terminals and verify that there is continuity between the terminals when the switch plunger is pushed into the switch **(see illustration)**. Release the switch plunger and verify that there is no continuity between the terminals.
18   If the switch doesn't operate as described, replace it.

4WD selector switch

19   Refer to the 4WD Shift Selector System Section in Chapter 7 Part C.

23   Front differential (4WD models) - removal and installation

Refer to illustrations 23.7, 23.8, 23.9, 23.11a, 23.11b, 23.11c, 23.12a and 23.12b

1   Loosen the wheel lug nuts, raise the vehicle and support it securely on jackstands. Remove the wheels.
2   Remove the engine under cover.
3   Drain the lubricant from the differential (see Chapter 1).
4   Disconnect the front driveshaft from the front differential (see Section 13) and support the front end of the driveshaft with a piece of wire.
5   On T100 models, disconnect the inner CV joints from the axleshaft flanges (see Section 20) and support the inner ends of the driveaxles with wire.
6   On Tacoma and 4Runner models, remove the driveaxles (see Section 20).
7   On T100 models, disconnect the vacuum hoses and unplug the 4WD indicator

switch electrical connector **(see illustration)**.
8   On T100 models, remove the cross-member **(see illustration)**.
9   On Tacoma and 4Runner models, disconnect the breather hose, remove the single bolt that retains the metal vacuum tubing and detach the tubing assembly from the differential **(see illustration)**. On models with ADD, detach the two bolts that attach the vacuum tubing to the actuator, unplug the

actuator electrical connector and detach the actuator vacuum hoses (see Section 22).
10   Support the differential with a transmission jack or a floor jack.

11   On T100 models, remove the different front mounting bolt and nut, remove the le and rear mounting bolts **(see illustration** and lower the differential.

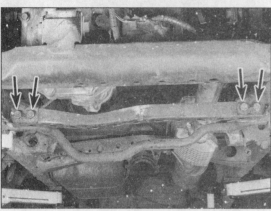

23.8 On T100 models, remove the crossmember bolts (arrows) and detach the crossmember

23.11a To detach the front differential on T100 models, remove the nut and bolt (arrows) from the front mount . . .

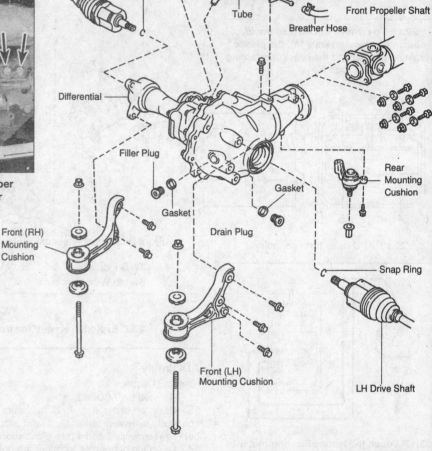

23.9 Exploded view of the front differential assembly (Tacoma and 4Runner models)

23.11b . . . remove the left bolt (arrow)

23.11c . . . and remove the rear bolt (arrow)

12 On Tacoma and 4Runner models, remove the rear mounting nut **(see illustration)**, remove the two front mounting bolts and nuts **(see illustration)** and lower the differential.

13 Installation is the reverse of removal.

24 Four-wheel drive hubs - removal and installation

Manual locking hubs

Refer to illustrations 24.2 and 24.7

1 Set the hub cover to the Free position.

2 Remove the hub cover mounting bolts and pull off the cover with the clutch assembly **(see illustration)**.

3 Remove the bolt (if equipped) from the end of the driveaxle **(see illustration 24.2)**.

4 Remove the mounting nuts from the freewheel hub body **(see illustration 24.2)**.

5 Using a brass hammer, tap on the hub body to loosen the cone washers and remove

them from the hub.

6 Pull the freewheel hub body off the driveaxle splines.

7 The freewheel hub clutch assemblies can become clogged with dirt and water which can make them inoperable. If further disassembly and inspection of the clutch assembly is required pay very close attention to the way the parts fit together when disassembling. Lay all the parts out in sequence in which they were removed. Clean the parts one at a time and lay them back out in the

same sequence. Lubricate the parts with a light coat of multi-purpose grease, then reassemble the clutch assembly in the reverse order **(see illustration)**.

8 Installation of the hub assembly on to the driveaxle is the reverse of the removal. Use new gaskets and apply multi-purpose grease to the inner hub splines. The control handle should be set to the Free position and the cover should be attached to the body with the pawl tabs aligned with the non-toothed portions of the body.

23.12a To detach the front differential on Tacoma and 4Runner models, remove the rear mounting nut (arrow) . . .

23.12b . . . and remove the front bolts and nuts (arrows) (nuts, not visible in this photo, are on top of mounting brackets)

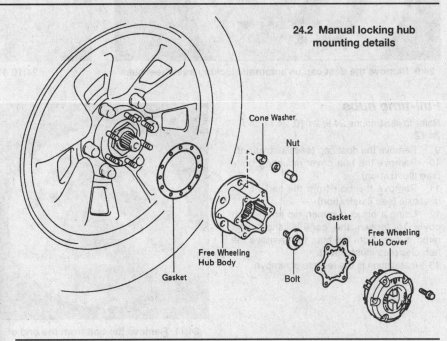

24.2 Manual locking hub mounting details

Cone Washer

Nut

Free Wheeling Hub Body

Gasket

Gasket

Bolt

Free Wheeling Hub Cover

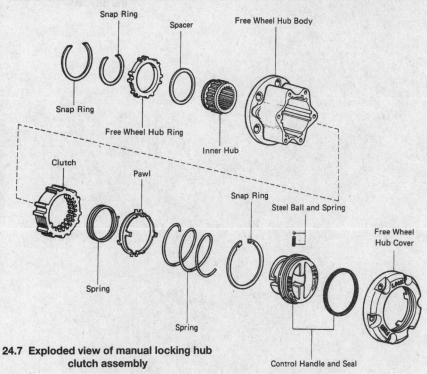

Snap Ring

Snap Ring

Spacer

Free Wheel Hub Body

Free Wheel Hub Ring

Inner Hub

Clutch

Pawl

Spring

Spring

Snap Ring

Steel Ball and Spring

Free Wheel Hub Cover

Control Handle and Seal

24.7 Exploded view of manual locking hub clutch assembly

24.9 Remove the dust cap on automatic locking freewheel hubs

24.10 Remove the hub cover mounting bolts

Full-time hubs

Refer to illustrations 24.9, 24.10, 24.11 and 24.12

9   Remove the dust cap **(see illustration)**.

10   Remove the hub cover mounting bolts **(see illustration)**.

11   Remove the bolt from the end of the driveaxle **(see illustration)**.

12   Using a brass hammer, tap on the hub cover to loosen the cone washers and remove them from the hub, then remove the hub disc **(see illustration)**.

13   Installation is the reverse of removal.

24.11 Remove the bolt from the end of the driveaxle

24.12 Use a brass hammer to dislodge the cone shaped washer

Chapter 9   Brakes

Contents

Specifications

General

Brake fluid type	See Chapter 1
Brake light switch-to-pedal stopper distance	1/64 to 3/32 inch
Brake pedal freeplay	1/8 to 1/4 inch
Brake pedal height	
T100	
All models except Extra Cab 4WD	5-57/64 to 6-9/32 inches
Extra Cab 4WD	5-49/64 to 6-5/32 inches
Tacoma	6-5/64 to 6-31/64 inches
4Runner	6-11/32 to 6-47/64 inches
Brake pedal reserve distance	
T100	
2WD 1-ton	At least 3-1/16 inches
2WD 1/2-ton	At least 2-7/8 inches
4WD Extra Cab	At least 2-3/4 inches
Tacoma and 4Runner	At least 2-53/64 inches
LSP & BV spring initial set length (4Runner)	8-3/4 inches
Parking brake cable bellcrank dimension C (T100 and 4Runner)	0.016 to 0.031 inch
Power brake booster pushrod-to-master cylinder piston clearance	0.0 inch

Disc brakes

Brake pad minimum thickness	See Chapter 1
Disc lateral runout limit	0.003 inch
Disc minimum (discard) thickness	Cast into disc

Drum brakes

Minimum brake lining thickness	See Chapter 1
Maximum drum diameter	Cast into drum

Torque specifications

	Ft-lbs (unless otherwise indicated)
Brake line-to-caliper banjo bolt	22
Caliper pins/bolts	
T100	
2WD	
1/2 ton	27
1-ton	29
4WD	90
Tacoma	
2WD	65
4WD	90
4Runner	90
Caliper torque plate bolts (2WD)	80
Brake disc-to-hub bolts	47
Load sensing proportioning valve bolts	108 in-lbs
Master cylinder mounting nuts	108 in-lbs
Vacuum booster mounting nuts	
T100 and Tacoma	108 in-lbs
4Runner	120 in-lbs
Wheel cylinder mounting bolts	84 in-lbs
Wheel lug nuts	See Chapter 1

1   General information

General

All models covered by this manual are equipped with hydraulically operated, power-assisted brake systems. All front brakes are discs, all rear brakes are drums.

All brakes are self-adjusting. The front disc brakes automatically compensate for pad wear, while the rear drum brakes incorporate an adjustment mechanism which is activated as the brakes are applied.

The hydraulic system has separate circuits for the front and rear brakes. If one circuit fails, the other circuit will remain functional and a warning indicator will light up on the dashboard when a substantial amount of brake fluid is lost, showing that a failure has occurred.

Master cylinder

The master cylinder is located under the hood, mounted to the power brake booster, and can be identified by the large fluid reservoir on top. The master cylinder has separate primary and secondary piston assemblies for the front and rear circuits.

Power brake booster

The power brake booster uses engine manifold vacuum to provide assistance to the brakes. It is mounted on the firewall in the engine compartment, directly behind the master cylinder.

Anti-lock Brake System (ABS)

An Anti-Lock Brake System (ABS) prevents wheel lockup at all four wheels. Refer to Section 2 for a description of ABS operation.

Parking brake

The parking brake mechanically operates the rear brakes only. The parking brake cables pull on a lever attached to the brake shoe assembly, causing the shoes to expand against the drum.

Precautions

There are some general precautions and warnings related to the brake system:

a) *Use only brake fluid conforming to DOT 3 specifications.*

b) *The brake pads and linings may contain asbestos fibers which are hazardous to your health if inhaled. Whenever you work on brake system components, clean all parts with brake system cleaner or denatured alcohol. Do not allow the fine dust to become airborne.*

c) *Safety should be paramount whenever any servicing of the brake components is performed. Do not use parts or fasteners which are not in perfect condition, and be sure all clearances and torque specifications are adhered to. If you are at all unsure about a certain procedure, seek professional advice. Upon completion of any brake system work, test the brakes carefully in a controlled area before driving the vehicle in traffic. If a problem is suspected in the brake system, don't drive the vehicle until it's fixed.*

2   Anti-lock Brake System (ABS) - general information

Description

Refer to illustration 2.1a, 2.1b and 2.1c

The Anti-lock Brake System (ABS) **(see illustrations)** is designed to maintain vehicle maneuverability, directional stability and optimum deceleration under severe braking conditions on most road surfaces. It does so by monitoring the rotational speed of the wheels

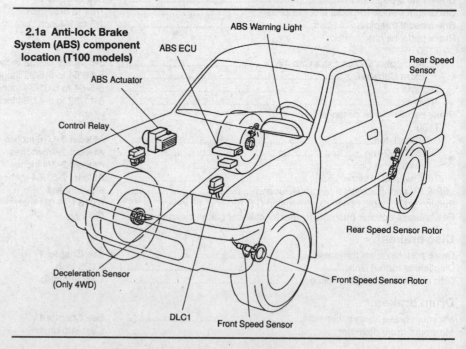

2.1a Anti-lock Brake System (ABS) component location (T100 models)

ABS Warning Light
ABS ECU
ABS Actuator
Rear Speed Sensor
Control Relay
Rear Speed Sensor Rotor
Deceleration Sensor (Only 4WD)
Front Speed Sensor Rotor
DLC1
Front Speed Sensor

nd controlling the brake line pressure during braking. This prevents the wheels from locking up.

Electronic control unit (ECU)

The electronic control unit (ECU) for the anti-lock Brake System is mounted inside the center of the dash on T100 models, is an integral part of the ABS actuator in the engine compartment on Tacoma models, and is mounted in the right kick panel on 4Runners.

The ECU monitors the rotation of each wheel with four wheel speed sensors, processes this information and avoids wheel lockup by controlling the hydraulic line pressure accordingly. Here's how it works: When the brakes are applied too firmly during a "panic stop," hydraulic line pressure inside the brake lines builds to such a high level that it "locks up" the wheels, causing the vehicle to skid out of control. On a vehicle equipped with ABS, the ECU prevents the hydraulic pressure from reaching this dangerously high level by monitoring the rotational speed of the wheels. When a wheel begins to slow down, i.e. "lock up," in relation to the other wheels, the ECU energizes the solenoid (inside the actuator) controlling the hydraulic brake fluid circuit to that wheel. The energized solenoid opens the circuit, allowing some of the brake fluid into a reservoir, thereby lowering the pressure and preventing the wheel from locking up. As soon as the rotation speed of the wheel equals that of the other wheels, the solenoid closes and pressure begins to build again. This cycle of opening and closing the circuit occurs many times a second at each wheel. The ECU can regulate the pressure to a single wheel, or to two, three or all four wheels, simultaneously.

The ECU also monitors the ABS system for malfunctions. If the ECU detects a problem, the ABS warning light on the instrument cluster lights up and a diagnostic code is stored which, when retrieved by a service technician, will indicate the problem area or component. When the engine is started, the ABS warning light glows for about three seconds (indicating that the ECU is monitoring the system for faults), then goes out; if the ABS light remains on, there's a problem in the ABS system. Take the vehicle to a dealer service department or an authorized service facility.

Actuator

The actuator assembly, which is mounted inside the engine compartment on all models, houses the solenoids which regulate brake fluid pressure in response to signals from the ECU. On Tacoma models, the ECU is an integral part of the actuator.

Speed sensors

Each wheel has its own speed sensor. The speed sensor is a small variable reluctance sensor (pick-up coil) which sends a variable voltage signal (actually, an alternating current sine wave output) to the ECU. The ECU converts this analog signal into a digital code which it compares to its "map" (pro-

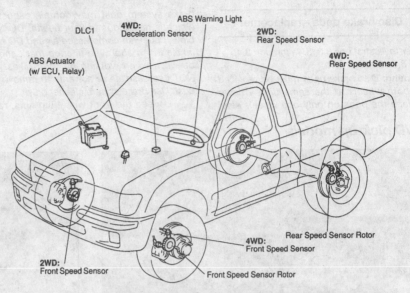

2.1b Anti-lock Brake System (ABS) component location (Tacoma models)

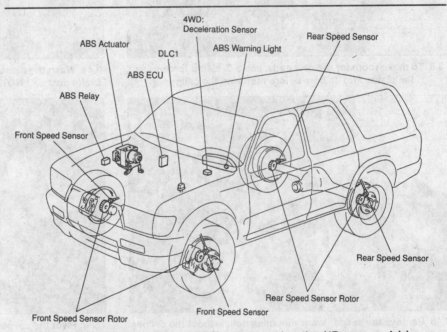

2.1c Anti-lock Brake System (ABS) component location (4Runner models)

gram), then either ignores it (if the wheel is rotating at the same speed as the other wheels) or executes a command to open a solenoid for the circuit to that wheel (if the wheel is starting to slow down in relation to the other wheels).

Brake light switch

The brake light switch signals the control unit when the driver steps on the brake pedal. Without this signal the anti-lock system won't activate.

Diagnosis and repair

If the ABS warning light on the instrument cluster comes on and stays on, make sure the parking brake is released and there's no problem with the brake hydraulic system. If neither of these is the cause, the anti-lock

system is probably malfunctioning. Although special test procedures are necessary to properly diagnose the system, the home mechanic can perform a few preliminary checks before taking the vehicle to a dealer service department.

a) *Make sure the brakes, calipers and wheel cylinders are in good condition.*
b) *Inspect the electrical connectors at the ECU. Make sure they're clean and tight.*
c) *Check the fuses.*
d) *Follow the wiring harness to the speed sensor(s) and brake light switch and make sure all connections are clean and tight and the wiring isn't damaged.*

If the above preliminary checks don't rectify the problem, the vehicle should be diagnosed by a dealer service department.

3   Disc brake pads - replacement

Refer to illustrations 3.3, 3.4a through 3.4p and 3.5a through 3.5h

Warning: *Disc brake pads must be replaced on both wheels at the same time - never replace the pads on only one wheel. Also, brake system dust may contain asbestos, which is hazardous to your health. DO NOT blow it out with compressed air and DO NOT inhale it. An approved filtering mask should be worn when working on the brakes. DO NOT use gasoline or solvents to remove the dust. Use brake system cleaner only!*

1   Loosen the front wheel lug nuts, raise the front of the vehicle and support it securely on jackstands. Apply the parking brake. Remove the wheels.

2   Remove about two-thirds of the fluid from the master cylinder reservoir and discard it; as the pistons are pushed in for clearance to allow the pads to be removed, the fluid will be forced back into the reservoir.

2WD pick-up models

3.3 To make room for the new pads, use a C-clamp to depress the piston into its bore before removing the caliper

3.4a Wash the disc and brake pads with brake cleaner to remove brake dust; DO NOT blow off the brake dust with compressed air

3.4b Remove the caliper lower mounting bolt; inspect the caliper bolt threads for damage and replace it if necessary

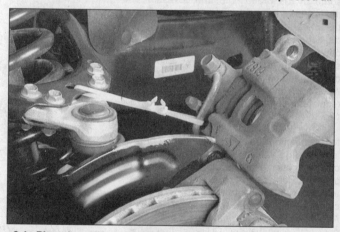

3.4c Pivot the caliper upward and support it with a piece of wire or string attached to the upper control arm

3.4d Remove the outer brake pad and shims; detach and clean the shims

3.4e Remove the inner brake pad and shims; remove and clean the inner and outer shims and the pad wear indicator plate

3.4f Remove the outer brake pad support plates and check them for damage (arrow indicates lower plate)

3.4g Remove the inner brake pad support plates (upper plate not visible in this photo)

3.4h Install the outer brake pad support plates in the torque plate; make sure they're fully seated

3.4i Install the inner brake pad support plates (left arrows) in the torque plate; make sure they're fully seated; those two big bolts (right arrows) secure the torque plate to the steering knuckle - don't remove them unless you need to remove the brake disc

Position a drain pan under the brake assembly and clean the caliper and surrounding area with brake system cleaner.

3 On 2WD pick-up models, push the piston back into the bore with a C-clamp to provide room for the new brake pads **(see illustration)**. As the piston is depressed to the bottom of the caliper bore, the fluid in the master cylinder will rise. Make sure it doesn't overflow. If necessary, siphon off some of the fluid.

4 To replace the brake pads on 2WD pick-up models, follow the accompanying photos, beginning with **illustration 3.4a**. Be sure to stay in order and read the caption under each illustration. Work on one brake assembly at a time so that you'll have something to refer to if you get in trouble. Note that the pads on 1-ton calipers have one shim instead of two, and use wire-type anti-squeal springs **(see illustration 3.4p)**.

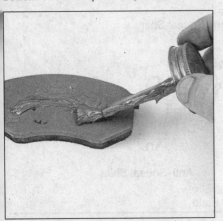

3.4j Apply anti-squeal compound to the backing plates of the new pads

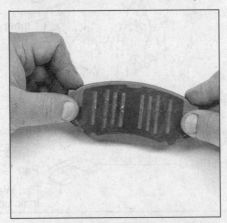

3.4k Install the anti-squeal shim(s) on the new pads

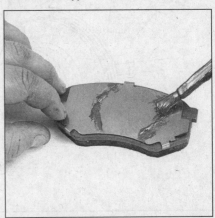

3.4l Apply anti-squeal compound to the outer shims of both brake pads

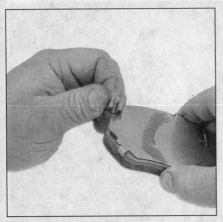

3.4m Install the pad wear indicator plates on the new inner pad

3.4n Install the inner and outer pads in the torque plate, making sure they are properly seated

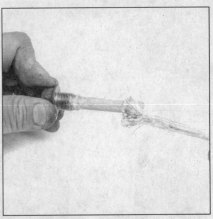

3.4o Apply high-temperature grease to the caliper bolt before installing it; be sure to tighten the bolt to the torque listed in this Chapter's Specifications

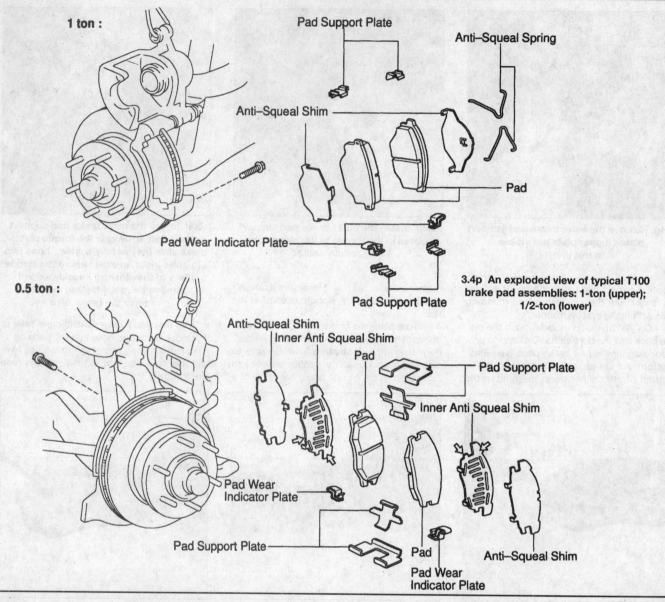

1 ton :

Pad Support Plate

Anti–Squeal Spring

Anti–Squeal Shim

Pad

Pad Wear Indicator Plate

Pad Support Plate

3.4p An exploded view of typical T100 brake pad assemblies: 1-ton (upper); 1/2-ton (lower)

0.5 ton :

Anti–Squeal Shim
Inner Anti Squeal Shim

Pad

Pad Support Plate

Inner Anti Squeal Shim

Pad Wear Indicator Plate

Pad Support Plate

Pad

Pad Wear Indicator Plate

Anti–Squeal Shim

4WD pick-ups and all 4Runners

3.5a Wash the brake assembly with brake system cleaner (see illustration 3.4a), then detach the pin retaining clip

3.5b Pull out the lower pad retaining pin

3.5c Remove the anti-rattle spring

3.5d Remove the upper pad retaining pin, then remove the outer brake pad

3.5e Push the outer pistons back into their bores to provide room for the new pad (replace one pad at a time to prevent the pistons on the opposite side of the caliper from popping out)

3.5f Apply anti-squeal compound to the back of the new pads . . .

5   To replace the brake pads on 4WD pick-up models and all 4Runner models, follow the accompanying photos, beginning with **illustration 3.5a**. Be sure to stay in order and read the caption under each illustration. Work on one brake assembly at a time so you'll have something to refer to if you get in trouble.

6   While the pads are removed, inspect the caliper for brake fluid leaks and ruptures in the piston boot(s). Replace the caliper if it's damaged or leaking (see Section 4). Also inspect the brake disc carefully (see Section 5). If machining is necessary, follow the information in that Section to remove the disc.

7   Before installing the caliper mounting bolt (2WD models), clean and check it for corrosion and damage. If significantly corroded or damaged, replace both of them. Be sure to tighten the caliper mounting bolt to the torque listed in this Chapter's Specifications.

8   Install the brake pads on the opposite wheel, then install the wheels and lower the vehicle. Tighten the lug nuts to the torque listed in the Chapter 1 Specifications.

9   Add brake fluid to the reservoir until it's full (see Chapter 1). Pump the brakes several

3.5g . . . install the anti-squeal shims . . .

3.5h . . . and apply anti-squeal compound to the back of the shim - install the new outer brake pad, repeat the replacement procedure for the inner pad, then install the anti-rattle spring, pad retaining pins and the pin retaining clip

times to seat the pads against the disc, then check the fluid level again.

10   Check the operation of the brakes before driving the vehicle in traffic. Try to avoid heavy brake applications until the brakes have been applied lightly several times to seat the pads.

4.4a Do NOT remove this banjo bolt from the brake caliper unless you intend to replace the caliper; after removal, discard the sealing washers (new ones should be used on installation)

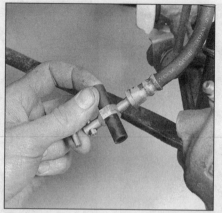

4.4b Using a piece of hose of the appropriate size, plug the banjo fitting to prevent brake fluid from dripping out of the hose and to prevent contaminants from entering the brake system

4.5 To remove the caliper from a 4Runner or any 4WD model, unscrew the tube nut fitting for the brake line (center arrow) and remove the two caliper bolts (upper and lower arrows)

4 Disc brake caliper - removal and installation

Refer to illustrations 4.4a, 4.4b and 4.5
Note: *If caliper replacement is indicated (usually because of fluid leaks, a stuck piston or broken bleeder screw) explore your options. New and factory rebuilt calipers are available on an exchange basis.*

1   Loosen the front wheel lug nuts, raise the front of the vehicle and support it securely on jackstands. Apply the parking brake. Remove the wheels.

2   Remove about two-thirds of the fluid from the master cylinder reservoir and discard it; as the pistons are pushed in for clearance to allow the pads to be removed, the fluid will be forced back into the reservoir. Position a drain pan under the brake assembly and clean the caliper and surrounding area with brake system cleaner.

3   On 2WD pick-up models, push the piston back into the bore with a C-clamp to provide room for the new brake pads **(see illustration 3.3)**. As the piston is depressed to the bottom of the caliper bore, the fluid in the master cylinder will rise. Make sure it doesn't overflow. If necessary, siphon off some of the fluid.

4   On 2WD pick-up models, remove the banjo bolt **(see illustration)**. **Note:** *If you're removing the caliper for access to other components, leave the hose connected.* Discard the two copper sealing washers on each side of the banjo fitting; use new ones when you reattach the brake hose to the caliper. Plug the banjo fitting with a piece of rubber hose **(see illustration)**.

5   On 4WD pick-ups and all 4Runner models, simply unscrew the tube nut fitting and detach the brake line from the caliper **(see illustration)**. **Note:** *Use a flare-nut wrench, if available, to prevent rounding-off the corners of the fitting.*

6   Remove the caliper mounting bolts **(2WD models, see illustration 3.4b; 4WD models, see illustration 4.5)**. If the caliper can't be pulled off on 4WD models, the brake pads are hanging up on the ridge around the circumference of the disc; remove the brake pads (see Section 3).

7   If you're planning to install the same caliper, clean the caliper with brake system cleaner. DO NOT use kerosene or petroleum-based solvents. Carefully inspect the caliper for leaks and damage. Do NOT install a caliper that is leaking or damaged.

8   Install the caliper and tighten the caliper pins or bolts to the torque listed in this Chapter's Specifications.

9   Connect the brake hose to the caliper, using new sealing washers. On 2WD models, make sure the locating lug on the fitting engages with the hole in the caliper. Tighten the banjo bolt to the torque listed in this Chapter's Specifications. On all 4Runners and 4WD models, tighten the brake line fitting securely.

10   Bleed the front brake circuit (see Section 14). If the brake fluid hose was not disconnected (caliper removed for access to other components), the brakes will not require bleeding.

11   Install the wheel and lug nuts, lower the vehicle and tighten the lug nuts to the torque listed in the Chapter 1 Specifications. Check brake operation carefully before placing vehicle into service.

5 Brake disc - inspection, removal and installation

Inspection

Refer to illustrations 5.3, 5.4a, 5.4b, 5.5 and 5.9

1   Loosen the wheel lug nuts, raise the front of the vehicle and support it securely on jackstands. Apply the parking brake. Remove the wheel. On 4WD Tacoma and all 4Runner models, reinstall the lug nuts to hold the disc in place against the hub (washers may have to be used to allow the nuts to apply pressure to the disc).

2   Remove the brake caliper (but don't disconnect the brake line or hose from the caliper) and suspend it out of the way with a piece of wire (see Section 4). **Caution:** *Don't let the caliper hang by the brake hose.* On 2WD models, remove the brake pads (see Section 3).

3   Visually inspect the disc surface for score marks and other damage **(see illustration)**. Light scratches and shallow grooves are normal after use and won't affect brake operation. Deep grooves - over 0.015-inch (0.38 mm) deep - require disc removal and refinishing by an automotive machine shop. Be sure to check both sides of the disc.

4   To check disc runout, place a dial indicator at a point about 1/2-inch from the outer edge of the disc **(see illustration)**. Set the indicator to zero and turn the disc. The indicator reading should not exceed the allowable runout listed in this Chapter's Specifications. If it does, the disc should be refinished by an automotive machine shop. **Note:** *To produce a smooth finish and ensure a perfectly smooth surface - thereby eliminating brake pedal pulsation or any other undesir-*

5.3 The bake pads on this vehicle were obviously neglected - they wore down to the rivets, which cut deep grooves into the disc; if the disc is worn this severely, replace it

5.4a Measure the brake disc runout with a dial indicator; if the reading exceeds the maximum allowable runout limit, the disc must be resurfaced or replaced

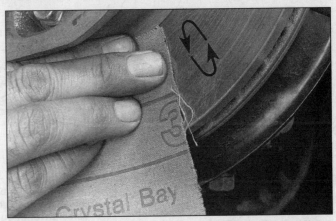

5.4b Using a swirling motion, remove the glaze from the disc surface with sandpaper or emery cloth

able symptoms - the discs should be resurfaced regardless of the dial indicator reading. If you elect not to have the discs resurfaced, deglaze them with sandpaper or emery cloth **(see illustration)**.

5   The disc must not be machined to a thickness less than the specified minimum thickness, which is cast into the disc. Measure disc thickness with a micrometer **(see illustration)**.

Removal and installation

6   On 2WD pick-up models, remove the brake caliper (see Section 4), brake pads (see Section 3) and the torque plate **(see illustration 3.4i)**; it's not necessary to disconnect the brake hose from the caliper on 2WD models. On 4WD pick-ups and all 4Runner models, the brake pads and the caliper can be removed as an assembly (see Section 4).

7   On 2WD pick-up models, the disc is bolted to the backside of the hub. Disc/hub removal and installation is part of the front wheel bearing repack and adjustment procedure (see Chapter 1).

8   On 4WD T100 models, the hub must also be removed and disassembled (see Chapter 1) before the disc can be removed.

9   On 4WD Tacoma and all 4Runner models, remove the lug nuts (installed in Step 1) and pull off the disc **(see illustration)**.

10   While the disc/hub assembly is removed, clean, inspect and repack the wheel bearings (2WD pick-up models and 4WD T100 models, see Chapter 1).

11   On models where the disc is bolted to the hub, tighten the disc-to-hub bolts to the torque listed in this Chapter's Specifications.

12   On 4WD T100 models, reassemble the hub (see Chapter 1).

13   Install the disc/hub assembly and adjust the wheel bearings (2WD pick-ups and 4WD T100, see Chapter 1). On 4WD Tacomas and all 4Runners, simply slide the disc back onto the hub.

14   On 2WD pick-up models, install the torque plate and tighten the torque plate bolts to the torque listed in this Chapter's Specifications. Install the brake pads (see Section 3) and the caliper (see Section 4).

15   On 4WD pick-ups and all 4Runner models, install the caliper and brake pads (see Section 4) and bleed the brakes (see Section 14).

16   Remove the jackstands and lower the vehicle.

6   Drum brake shoes - replacement

Refer to illustrations 6.2, 6.3, 6.4a through 6.4cc, 6.5, 6.7a, 6.7b and 6.7c

Warning: Brake shoes must be replaced on both wheels at the same time - never replace the shoes on only one wheel. Also, brake system dust often contains asbestos, which is hazardous to your health. DO NOT blow it out with compressed air and DO NOT inhale it. DO NOT use gasoline or solvent to remove the dust. Use brake system cleaner or denatured alcohol only.

1   Loosen the wheel lug nuts, raise the rear of the vehicle and support it securely on jackstands. Block the front wheels to keep the vehicle from rolling off the stands. Remove the rear wheels.

2   Remove the brake drum. If the drum is stuck because of corrosion between the axle flange and the wheel studs or brake drum, spray penetrating oil around the flange and studs and allow it to soak in. Tap around the studs and flange with a hammer to break the drum loose, then tap around the back edge of the drum to remove it. If the drum is still stuck, screw a couple of bolts into the

5.5 Measure the brake disc thickness at several points with a micrometer

5.9 To detach the disc from the hub on 4WD Tacomas and all 4Runners, simply pull it off

6.2 If the brake drum is "frozen" onto the wheel studs, it can usually be loosened by applying penetrant to the studs; if that doesn't work, thread a couple of bolts into the holes in the drum and tighten them until they push the drum off

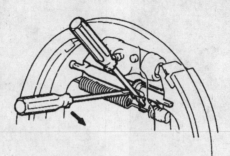

6.3 If the drum binds on the shoes, remove the adjusting hole plug, insert a screwdriver through the hole, pry the adjusting lever off the adjuster wheel, hold it off, insert another screwdriver through the hole and retract the brake shoes by turning the wheel counterclockwise (as seen from the rear of the vehicle, looking forward)

6.4a Wash the brake assembly with brake cleaner; DO NOT blow it out with compressed air!

threaded holes in the drum and tighten them **(see illustration)**. When they come in contact with the axleshaft flange, they'll push the drum off.

3   If the drum is locked onto the shoes

because of excessive drum wear, remove the plug in the access hole in the backing plate, insert a screwdriver through the hole, push the actuator lever off the star adjuster **(see illustration)** and, using another screwdriver

or a brake adjuster tool, back off the adjuster wheel to retract the shoes.

4   Clean the brake assembly with brake system cleaner before beginning work. Follow **illustrations 6.4a through 6.4cc** for the inspection and replacement of the brake shoes. Be sure to stay in order and read the caption under each illustration.

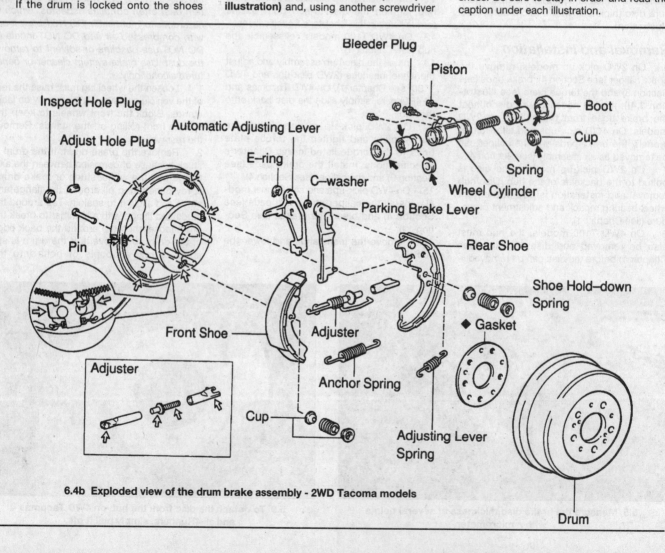

6.4b Exploded view of the drum brake assembly - 2WD Tacoma models

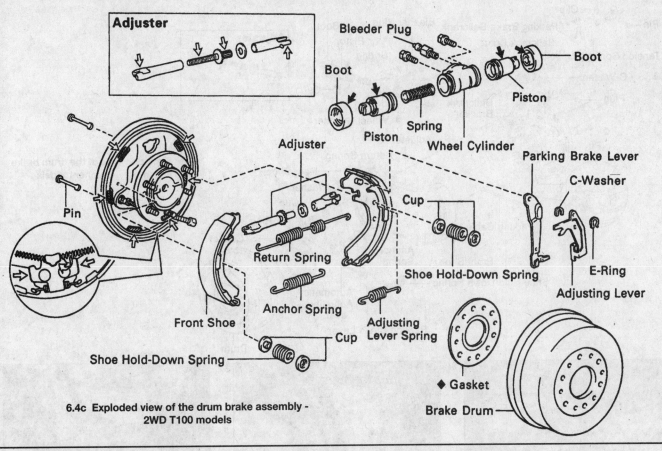

6.4c Exploded view of the drum brake assembly – 2WD T100 models

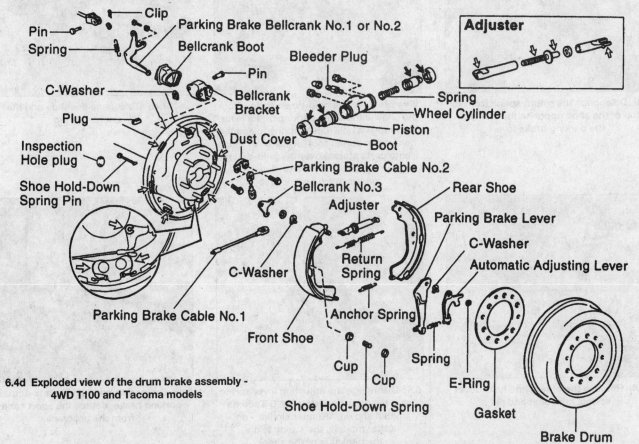

6.4d Exploded view of the drum brake assembly – 4WD T100 and Tacoma models

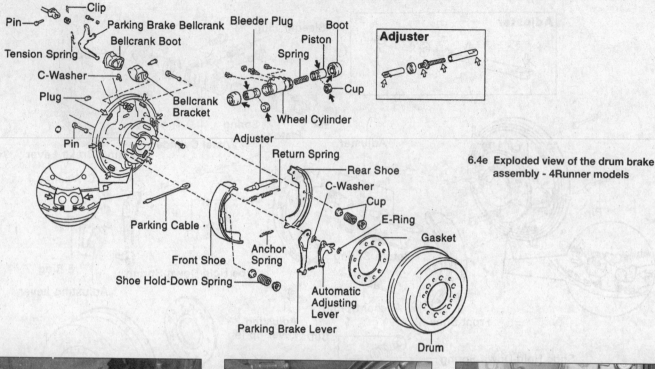

6.4e   **Exploded view of the drum brake assembly - 4Runner models**

6.4f   **Disengage the return spring from the top of the shoe opposite the one with the parking brake lever**

6.4g   **Remove the hold-down spring from the shoe without the parking brake lever. To remove a hold-down spring, place the hold-down spring tool (available at most auto parts stores) over the hold-down spring, push down and give it a quarter-turn and release**

6.4h   **Disengage the shoe and the anchor spring**

6.4i   **Remove the other shoe hold-down spring, cup, seat and pin**

6.4j   **Disengage the adjusting lever spring from the adjusting lever (2WD Tacoma model shown, 4Runner similar - on other models, the spring is on the backside of the shoe)**

6.4k   **On models with a bellcrank-actuated parking brake, detach the short cable from the bellcrank**

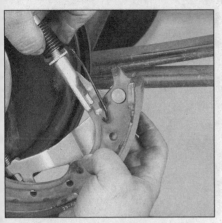

6.4l Remove the adjuster assembly

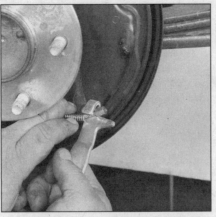

6.4m On 2WD pick-up models, disengage the parking brake cable from the parking brake lever

6.4n Pry off the E-clip that secures the automatic adjusting lever to the pin on the shoe (Note: *On 2WD Tacoma models the parking brake lever assembly mounts to the backside of the rear shoe; on all 4Runners and 2WD T100 models it mounts to the front side of the rear shoe; on 4WD pick-up models it mounts to the front side of the front shoe*)

5   Clean the brake drum and check it for score marks, deep grooves, hard spots (which will appear as small discolored areas) and cracks. If the drum is worn, scored or out-of-round, it can be resurfaced by an automotive machine shop. **Note:** *Professionals recommend resurfacing the drums whenever a brake job is done. Resurfacing will eliminate the possibility of out-of-round*

drums. If the drums are worn so much they can't be resurfaced without exceeding the maximum allowable diameter (stamped into the drum) **(see illustration)**, *new ones will be required. At the very least, if you elect not to have the drums resurfaced, remove the glazing from the surface with sandpaper or emery cloth using a swirling motion.*

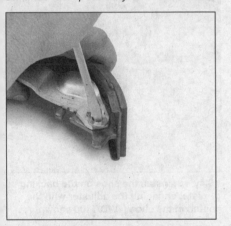

6.4o Pry off the C-clip that secures the parking brake lever to the pin on the shoe

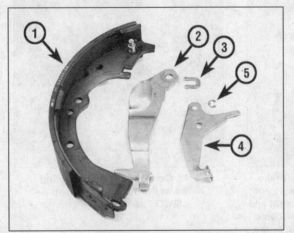

6.4p Parking brake lever/adjuster lever details

1   Brake shoe
2   Parking brake lever
3   C-clip
4   Automatic adjusting lever
5   E-ring

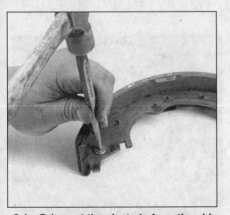

6.4q Drive out the pivot pin from the old brake shoe and drive it into the new shoe (if a new pin comes with the new shoe, use it instead)

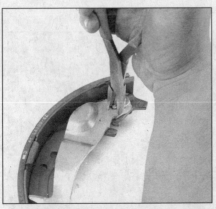

6.4r After installing the parking brake lever on the new brake shoe, squeeze the ends of the new C-clip together

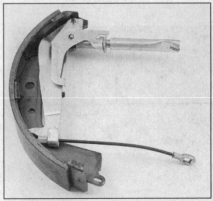

6.4s Install the automatic adjusting lever on the pivot pin, then secure it with a new E-ring. Install the adjusting lever spring (see illustration 6.4j) and if equipped, the short parking brake cable

6.4t Lubricate the brake shoe contact points on the backing plate with high-temperature brake grease. At this time, also clean the adjuster screw and lubricate its moving parts with a light film of high-temperature brake grease

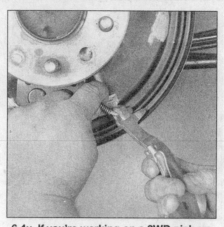

6.4u If you're working on a 2WD pick-up model, reattach the parking brake cable to the parking brake lever

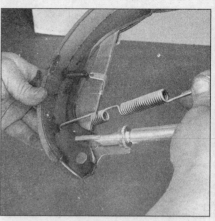

6.4v Attach the adjuster screw assembly and hook the return spring to the shoe (on Tacoma 2WD models the spring wraps around the adjuster; on all other models, make sure the space between the short and long coils is positioned over the adjuster screw star wheel

6.4w Position the shoe/parking brake lever assembly on the backing plate and install the hold-down pin, spring, seat and retainer (4WD T100 shown). On models with a bellcrank-actuated parking brake, attach the short parking brake cable to the bellcrank

6.4x Connect the anchor spring between the bottoms of the shoes (2WD Tacoma shown) . . .

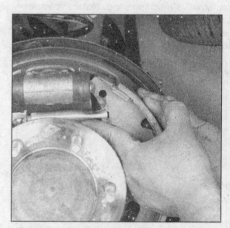

6.4y . . . install the shoe on the backing plate, engaging the adjuster with the notch in the shoe (4WD T100 shown) . . .

6.4z . . . connect the other end of the return spring to the other shoe . . .

6.4aa . . . and install the hold-down spring

6.4bb This is how the assembled brake should look - 2WD Tacoma models

6.4cc On 4WD pick-up models, the brake should look like this when assembled properly

6.5 The maximum diameter of the rear drum is cast into the inside of the drum

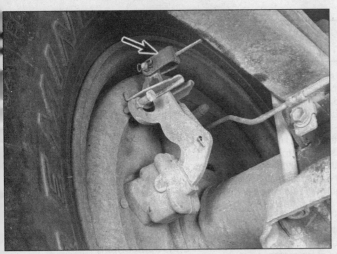

6.7a To disconnect the parking brake cable clevis (arrow) from the bellcrank on a 4WD T100 or Tacoma model (T100 shown here) . . .

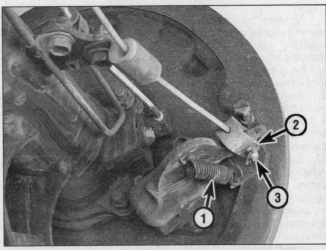

6.7b . . . or on a 4Runner model (shown here), remove the spring (1), remove the retainer clip (2) and pull out the clevis pin (3)

6 Repeat Steps 2 through 5 for the other rear brake assembly.

7 On 4WD pick-ups and all 4Runner

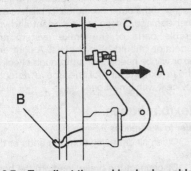

6.7c To adjust the parking brake cable bellcrank on 4WD pick-ups and all 4Runner models, pull the parking brake cable bellcrank in direction A until there is no clearance at B, loosen the bellcrank adjusting bolt locknut and turn the adjusting bolt in or out to bring dimension C within the range listed in this Chapter's Specifications

models, adjust the parking brake cable bellcrank. Disconnect the parking brake cable from the bellcrank **(see illustrations)**. Lightly pull the parking brake cable bellcrank in direction A until there is no clearance at B **(see illustration)**, loosen the bellcrank adjusting bolt locknut and turn the adjusting bolt in or out to bring dimension C within the range listed in this Chapter's Specifications. Tighten the adjusting bolt locknut. Connect the parking brake cable clevis to the bellcrank with the clevis pin and install the clevis pin retainer clip. Hook the tension spring to the bellcrank lever. Repeat this procedure at the other rear brake.

8 On all models, move the parking brake lever back and forth a few times and verify that the adjuster screw turns. Repeat this procedure for the other brake.

9 Install the brake drums. Pump the brake several times, then turn the adjuster star wheel using a screwdriver inserted through the hole in the backing plate until the shoes slightly drag on the drums as the drums are turned. Now, back off the adjuster until the

shoes don't drag on the drums. Install the plug in the brake backing plate.

10 Install the rear wheels, install the lug nuts, lower the vehicle and tighten the wheel lug nuts to the torque listed in the Chapter 1 Specifications.

11 Check the brake pedal position. If the brake pedal goes too close to the floor, further adjustment of the brakes is required. Back the vehicle up, making repeated stops, to actuate the self-adjusters, which work only when the vehicle is in reverse. Test the brakes for proper operation before driving in traffic.

7 Wheel cylinder - removal and installation

Refer to illustration 7.2
Note: *Never replace only one wheel cylinder. Always replace both of them at the same time.*

1 Remove the brake drum and brake shoes (see Section 6).

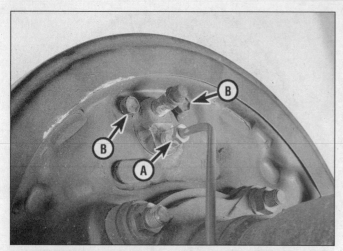

7.2 To remove the wheel cylinder, unscrew the brake line threaded fitting (A) with a flare-nut wrench, then remove the wheel cylinder mounting bolts (B)

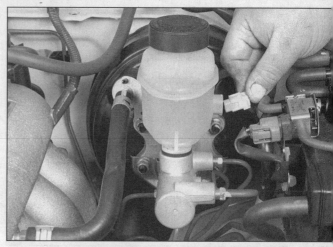

8.2 Unplug the electrical connector for the fluid level warning switch

2   Unscrew the brake line fitting from the rear of the wheel cylinder **(see illustration)**. If available, use a flare-nut wrench to avoid rounding off the corners on the fitting. Don't pull the metal line out of the wheel cylinder - it could bend, making installation difficult.

3   Remove the two bolts securing the wheel cylinder to the brake backing plate.

4   Remove the wheel cylinder.

5   Plug the end of the brake line to prevent the loss of brake fluid and the entry of dirt.

6   Installation is the reverse of removal. Attach the brake line to the wheel cylinder before installing the mounting bolts and tighten the line fitting after the wheel cylinder mountings bolts have been tightened. If available, use a flare-nut wrench to tighten the line fitting.

7   Install the brake shoes and brake drum (see Section 6).

8   Bleed the brakes (see Section 14). Don't drive the vehicle in traffic until the operation of the brakes has been thoroughly tested.

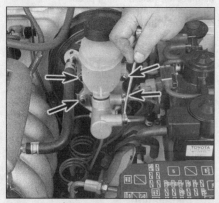

8.3 To detach the master cylinder assembly from the power brake booster, unscrew the brake line threaded fittings with a flare-nut wrench, then remove the master cylinder mounting nuts (arrows); there are four mounting nuts (arrows) on Tacoma and T100 models but only two on 4Runners

8   Master cylinder - removal and installation

Refer to illustrations 8.2 and 8.3

Note: *Before deciding to overhaul the master cylinder, check on the availability and cost of a new or factory rebuilt unit and also the availability of a rebuild kit.*

1   Place rags under the brake line fittings and prepare caps or plastic bags to cover the ends of the lines once they're disconnected. **Caution:** *Brake fluid will damage paint. Cover all painted surfaces and avoid spilling fluid during this procedure.*

2   Unplug the brake fluid level warning switch electrical connector **(see illustration)**.

3   Loosen the tube nuts at the ends of the brake lines where they enter the master cylinder. To prevent rounding off of the flats on these nuts, a flare-nut wrench, which wraps around the nut, should be used **(see illustration)**. Pull the brake lines away from the master cylinder slightly and plug the ends to prevent contamination.

4   Remove the two (4Runner) or four (T100 and Tacoma) master cylinder mounting nuts **(see illustration 8.2)**. Make sure you don't kink the hydraulic lines. Remove the master cylinder from the vehicle.

5   Remove the reservoir cap and discard any fluid remaining in the reservoir.

6   Whenever the master cylinder is removed, the entire hydraulic system must be bled. The time required to bleed the system can be reduced if the master cylinder is filled with fluid and bench bled before the master cylinder is installed on the vehicle.

7   Mount the master cylinder in a vise equipped with soft jaws. The jaws of the vise should be clamping on the flange of the master cylinder. Fill the reservoirs with brake fluid.

8   Hold your fingers tightly over the holes where the brake lines normally connect to the master cylinder to prevent air from being drawn back into the master cylinder.

9   Slowly depress the piston several times to ensure all air has been expelled. A large Phillips screwdriver can be used to push on the piston assembly. Wait several seconds each time for brake fluid to be drawn from the reservoir into the piston bore, then depress the piston again. Be sure your fingers are covering the holes before releasing the piston. When the bleeding procedure is complete, temporarily install plugs in the holes.

10   Carefully install the master cylinder by reversing the removal steps.

11   Bleed the brake system (see Section 14).

9   Brake hoses and lines - check and replacement

1   About every six months, with the vehicle raised and placed securely on jackstands, the flexible hoses which connect the steel brake lines with the front and rear brake assemblies should be inspected for cracks, chafing of the outer cover, leaks, blisters and other damage. These are important and vulnerable parts of the brake system and inspection should be complete. A light and mirror will be needed for a thorough check. If a hose exhibits any of the above defects, replace it with a new one.

Flexible hoses

Refer to illustrations 9.3 and 9.4

2   Clean all dirt away from the ends of the hose.

3   Disconnect the brake line from the hose fitting **(see illustration)**. Be careful not to bend the frame bracket or line. If necessary, soak the connections with penetrating oil.

4   Remove the U-clip from the female fitting at the bracket **(see illustration)** and remove the hose from the bracket.

5   Disconnect the hose from the caliper, discarding the copper washers on either side of the fitting.

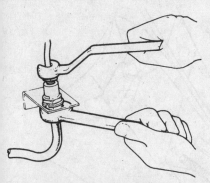

9.3 Hold the hose fitting with a wrench to prevent twisting the line, then loosen the tube nut with a flare-nut wrench to prevent rounding off the corners of the nut

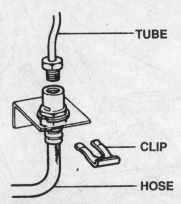

9.4 Once the tube nut has been completely loosened, pull off the clip with a pair of pliers or pry it off with a screwdriver

6   Using new copper washers, attach the new brake hose to the caliper.

7   Pass the female fitting through the frame or frame bracket. With the least amount of twist in the hose, install the fitting in this position. **Note:** *The weight of the vehicle must be on the suspension, so the vehicle should not be raised while positioning the hose.*

8   Install the U-clip in the female fitting at the frame bracket.

9   Attach the brake line to the hose fitting using a back-up wrench on the fitting. Tighten the tube nut securely.

10   Carefully check to make sure the suspension or steering components don't make contact with the hose. Have an assistant push down on the vehicle and also turn the steering wheel lock-to-lock during inspection.

11   Bleed the brake system as described in Section 14.

Metal brake lines

12   When replacing brake lines, be sure to use the correct parts. Don't use copper tubing for any brake system components. Purchase steel brake lines from a dealer parts department or auto parts store.

13   Prefabricated brake lines, with the ends already flared and fittings installed, are available at auto parts stores and dealer service departments. If necessary, carefully bend the line to the proper shape. A tube bender is recommended for this. **Caution:** *Don't crimp or damage the line.*

14   When installing the new line make sure it's well supported in the brackets and has plenty of clearance between moving or hot components.

15   After installation, check the master cylinder fluid level and add fluid as necessary. Bleed the brake system as outlined in Section 14 and test the brakes carefully before placing the vehicle into normal operation.

10   Load sensing proportioning and bypass valve

Description

Refer to illustration 10.1

1   The center of gravity is higher on a truck than a car, and the majority of an unloaded truck's weight is up front. When the brakes are applied, the combination of higher cg and forward weight bias tends to "pitch" the vehicle onto its front tires, simultaneously unloading the rear end. The front brakes therefore require more hydraulic pressure, and the rear brakes require less (or else the rear brakes will lock under heavy braking). This is also true of a car, which is equipped with a proportioning valve to "bias" braking power to the front brakes. But on a truck the forces involved are more extreme, and they change in proportion to the load in the bed: a loaded truck has more weight on the rear end than an unloaded truck. So the vehicles covered by this manual are equipped with a load sensing proportioning and bypass valve (LSP & BV) which alters front/rear braking bias in accordance with the weight of the load **(see illustration). Caution:** *Brake fluid will damage paint. Cover all painted surfaces and avoid spilling fluid during this procedure.*

2   Because of the special gauge set needed to check and adjust the LSP & BV, servicing this unit at home is not recommended. However, if the LSP & BV malfunctions, you can replace it yourself. But you'll have to take the vehicle to a dealer service department or other qualified repair shop to have the unit adjusted. Also, to remove the rear axle, you must disconnect the LSP & BV height sensing rod from the axle. As long as the adjustment isn't changed, disconnecting and reattaching the height sensing rod should not affect the function of the LSP & BV.

Removal and installation

Warning: *If replaced, the valve must be checked and, if necessary, adjusted at a dealer service department or other qualified repair shop equipped with the necessary gauges.*

All models

3   Raise the vehicle and support it securely on jackstands.

T100 and Tacoma models

Refer to illustration 10.4

4   Disconnect the height sensing spring shackle No. 2 from the axle **(see illustration).**

10.1 The load sensing proportioning and bypass valve (LSP & BV) is bolted to the underside of the vehicle (Tacoma unit shown, T100 similar)

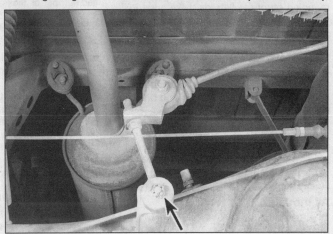

10.4 To disconnect the height sensing spring from the axle, remove the cotter pin and nut (arrow) (T100 shown)

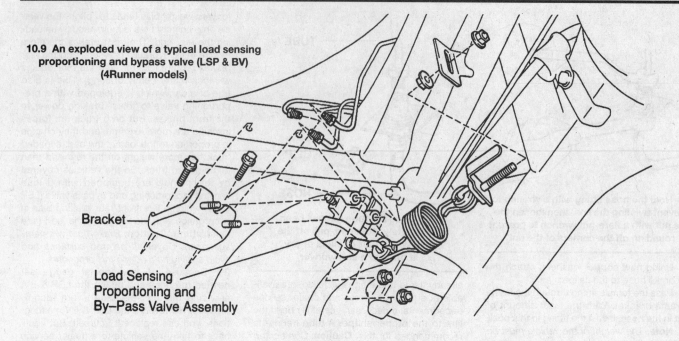

10.9 An exploded view of a typical load sensing proportioning and bypass valve (LSP & BV) (4Runner models)

Bracket

Load Sensing Proportioning and By–Pass Valve Assembly

5   Loosen the tube nuts that connect the brake lines to the LSP& BV valve. Use a flare-nut wrench to prevent rounding off of the flats on these nuts. Pull the brake lines away from the LSP & BV slightly and plug the ends of the lines to prevent contamination.

6   Remove the LSP & BV bracket mounting bolts and remove the LSP & BV and bracket assembly.

7   Unbolt the LSP & BV from the bracket. Disconnect the height sensing spring from the LSP & BV.

8   Installation is the reverse of removal. Be sure to tighten the LSP & BV mounting bolts to the torque listed in this Chapter's Specifications. Proceed to Step 14.

4Runner models

Refer to illustrations 10.9 and 10.13

9   Loosen the tube nuts that connect the brake lines to the LSP & BV valve **(see illustration)**. Use a flare-nut wrench to prevent rounding off of the flats on these nuts. Pull the brake lines away from the LSP & BV slightly and plug the ends of the lines to prevent contamination.

10   Remove the locknut and disconnect the adjusting bolt from the rear suspension arm.

11   Remove the LSP & BV bracket mounting bolts and remove the LSP & BV and bracket assembly.

12   Remove the LSP & BV mounting nuts and separate the LSP & BV from the bracket.

13   Installation is the reverse of removal. Be sure to set the spring length to its initial set length and tighten the locknut **(see illustration)**.

All models

14   Bleed the brake hydraulic system (see Section 14).

15   Have the LSP & BV adjusted at a dealer service department or other qualified repair shop.

11 Parking brake - adjustment

1   The parking brake is hand-operated by a lever under the dash on T100 and Tacoma models and by a lever between the seats on 4Runner models. All parking brake systems are self-adjusting; automatic adjusters in the rear brake drums compensate for brake shoe wear. However, additional adjustment may be needed in the event of cable stretch, which occurs as the vehicle ages. When you pull back on the parking brake handle on T100 models, it should take 11 to 17 clicks to apply the parking brake system; on Tacoma models, it should take 12 to 18 clicks; on 4Runners, the parking brake lever should apply the parking brake cables with seven to nine clicks. If the handle or lever applies the parking brake system in less than the specified number of clicks, the cable is too tight; if it travels more than the specified number of clicks, the cable is too loose.

4Runner models

Refer to illustration 11.4

2   Release the parking brake lever.

3   Remove the center console (see Chapter 11).

4   Loosen or tighten the adjustment nut **(see illustration)** as necessary. Apply the parking brake lever and verify that it applies the parking brakes in the specified number of clicks. If not, repeat this procedure until cable tension is correct.

5   Install the center console.

T100 and Tacoma models

Refer to illustrations 11.7a, 11.7b and 11.8

6   Release the parking brake handle, raise the rear of the vehicle until the wheels are off the ground and support it securely on jackstands.

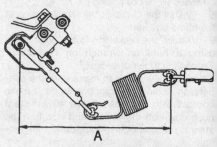

10.13 When installing the LSP & BV on 4Runner models, be sure to set the initial spring length (dimension A) to the length listed in this Chapter's Specifications

7   On 2WD models, cable tension is adjusted at the equalizer, which is located at the junction of the front and rear cables. Using a back-up wrench on the adjuster nut, loosen the locknut **(see illustrations)**, then tighten or loosen the adjuster nut until you feel a slight drag when the rear wheels are turned **(see illustration)**. **Note:** *If the threads appear rusty, apply penetrating oil before attempting adjustment.* Loosen the

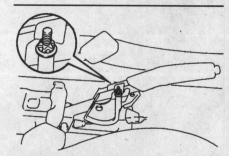

11.4 To adjust the parking brake lever on 4Runner models, turn this adjusting nut in or out until cable tension is correct

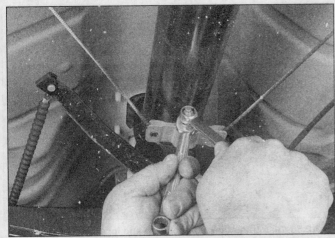

11.7a To loosen the parking brake cable locknut on 2WD pick-up models, hold the adjusting nut with a backup wrench

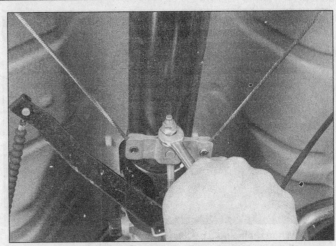

11.7b To adjust the parking brake cable on 2WD pick-up models, turn the adjusting nut until cable tension is correct

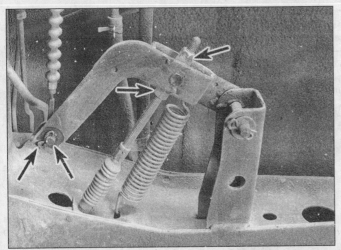

11.8 To adjust the parking brake cable on 4WD pick-up models, loosen one of these adjusting nuts (arrows) and tighten the other, or vice versa, until cable tension is correct; to disconnect the cable from the intermediate lever, remove the retainer clip and pull out the clevis pin (arrows)

12.3 To detach the cable housing from the brake backing plate on 2WD pick-up models, remove these two bolts

12.4 To disconnect a parking brake cable from the equalizer on 2WD T100 and Tacoma models, simply disengage the cable end plug from its slotted hole

adjustment nut until the wheels turn freely again. Apply the parking brake handle and verify that the brakes are applied in the specified number of clicks. If not, repeat this procedure.

8   On 4WD models, cable tension is adjusted at the intermediate lever **(see illustration)**. Tighten one adjusting nut while loosening the other, or vice versa, until you feel a slight drag when the rear wheels are turned **(see illustration)**. **Note:** *If the threads appear rusty, apply penetrating oil before attempting adjustment.* Loosen the adjustment nut until the wheels turn freely again. Apply the parking brake handle and verify that the brakes are applied in the specified number of clicks. If not, repeat this procedure. Verify that the bellcrank stopper screw comes into contact with the backing plate (see Step 8 in Section 6). Apply the parking brake handle and verify that cable tension is now correct. If not, repeat this procedure.

9   Remove the jackstands and lower the vehicle.

12 Parking brake cables - replacement

Refer to illustrations 12.3, 12.4, 12.5a, 12.5b and 12.5c

1   Release the parking brake. Loosen the rear wheel lug nuts. Raise the vehicle and place it securely on jackstands. Remove the wheels.

2   Loosen the adjusting nut to take tension off the cable (see Section 11).

3   On 2WD models, remove the drum brake assembly, disconnect the parking brake cable from the parking brake lever **(see illustration 6.4m)** and detach the cable housing from the brake backing plate **(see illustration)**. On 4WD and 4Runner models, disconnect the parking brake cable from the bellcrank **(see illustration 6.7a or 6.7b)**.

4   On 2WD models, disengage the cable from the equalizer **(see illustration)**. On 4WD models, disengage the cable from the intermediate lever **(see illustration 11.8)**.

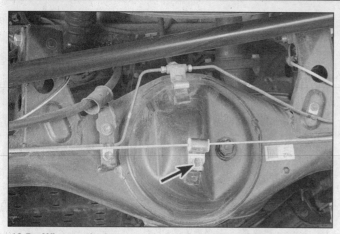

12.5a When replacing a parking brake cable, look for and detach all cable brackets on the axle, such as this one (arrow) on a 4Runner

12.5b Also trace the cable forward and locate and detach all brackets (arrows) bolted to the frame (Tacoma shown, other models use similar cable fasteners)

5   Detach all cable brackets from the frame and/or axle **(see illustrations)**.

6   Installation is the reverse of removal.

7   Adjust the cable when you're done (see Section 11).

8   Remove the jackstands and lower the vehicle.

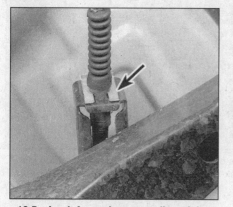

12.5c Look for and remove all retaining clips such as this one (arrow) on a Tacoma (similar retaining clips used on other models)

13   Power brake booster - check, removal and installation

1   The power brake booster unit requires no special maintenance apart from periodic inspection of the vacuum hose and the case.

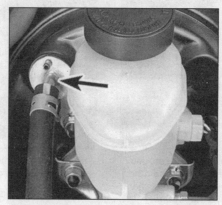

13.7 Detach the intake manifold vacuum hose (arrow) from the power brake booster; inspect the hose for cracks and replace it if necessary

Check

Operating check

2   Depress the brake pedal several times with the engine off and make sure there's no change in the pedal reserve distance (see Section 15).

3   Depress the pedal and start the engine. If the pedal goes down slightly, operation is normal.

Airtightness check

4   Start the engine and turn it off after one or two minutes. Depress the brake pedal slowly several times. If the pedal depresses less each time, the booster is airtight.

5   Depress the brake pedal while the engine is running, then stop the engine with the pedal depressed. If there's no change in the pedal reserve travel (see Section 15) after holding the pedal for 30 seconds, the booster is airtight.

Removal

Refer to illustration 13.7, 13.9 and 13.10

6   Disassembly of the power brake booster unit requires special tools and is not

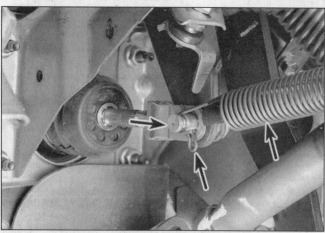

13.9 To disconnect the power brake booster pushrod from the brake pedal, remove this retainer clip, disengage the pedal return spring from the clevis pin and pull out the clevis pin (arrows)

13.10 To detach the power brake booster from the firewall, remove these four nuts (arrows)

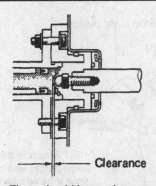

13.13a There should be no clearance between the booster pushrod and the master cylinder piston, but no interference either - if there is interference between the two, the brakes may drag; if there is clearance, there will be excessive brake pedal travel

ordinarily performed by the home mechanic. If a problem develops, install a new or rebuilt unit.

7   In the engine compartment, disconnect the intake manifold vacuum hose from the power brake booster **(see illustration)**.

8   Remove the nuts attaching the master cylinder to the booster (see Section 8). Carefully pull the master cylinder forward until it clears the mounting studs. Be careful not to bend or kink the brake lines.

9   In the passenger compartment, remove the retainer clip **(see illustration)**, disengage the pedal return spring from the clevis pin, pull out the clevis pin and disconnect the power brake pushrod from the top of the brake pedal.

10   Remove the nuts attaching the booster to the firewall **(see illustration)**.

11   Carefully pull the booster unit away from the firewall until the studs clear the holes.

Installation

Refer to illustration 13.13a, 13.13b, 13.13c, 13.13d and 13.14

12   Place the booster in position on the firewall and tighten the retaining nuts to the torque listed in this Chapter's Specifications. Connect the brake pedal. Use a new retainer clip if the old one is distorted. Don't forget to hook up the return spring.

13   If a new power brake booster unit is being installed, check the pushrod clearance **(see illustration)** as follows:

a) *Measure the distance that the pushrod protrudes from the master cylinder mounting surface on the front of the power brake booster, including the new gasket. Jot down this measurement* **(see illustration)**. *This is "dimension A."*

b) *Measure the distance from the mounting flange to the end of the master cylinder* **(see illustration)**. *Jot down this measurement . This is "dimension B."*

c) *Measure the distance from the end of the master cylinder to the bottom of the pocket in the piston* **(see illustration)**. *Jot down this measurement. This is "dimension C."*

d) *Subtract measurement B from measurement C, then subtract measurement A from the difference between B and C. This the pushrod clearance.*

e) *Compare your calculated pushrod clearance to the pushrod clearance listed in this Chapter's Specifications. If necessary, adjust the pushrod length to achieve the correct clearance.*

14   To adjust the pushrod length, hold the serrated part of the pushrod with a pair of pliers and turn the pushrod end with a wrench **(see illustration)**. Recheck the clearance. Repeat this step as often as necessary until the clearance is correct.

13.13b Measure the distance that the pushrod protrudes from the brake booster at the master cylinder mounting surface (including the gasket, if equipped)

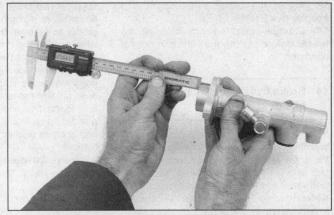

13.13c Measure the distance from the mounting flange to the end of the master cylinder

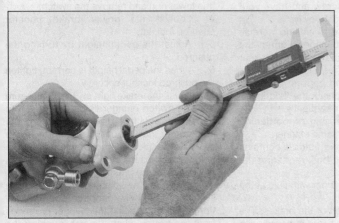

13.13d Measure the distance from the piston pocket to the end of the master cylinder

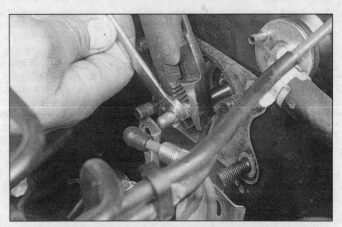

13.14 To adjust the length of the booster pushrod, hold the serrated portion of the rod with a pair of pliers and turn the adjusting screw in or out, as necessary

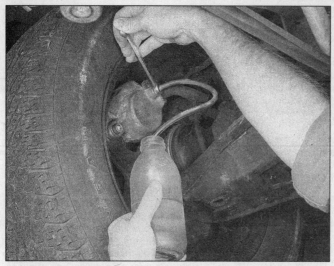

14.8 When bleeding the brakes, a hose is connected to the bleed screw at the caliper or wheel cylinder and then submerged in brake fluid - air will be seen as bubbles in the tube and container (all air must be expelled before moving to the next wheel)

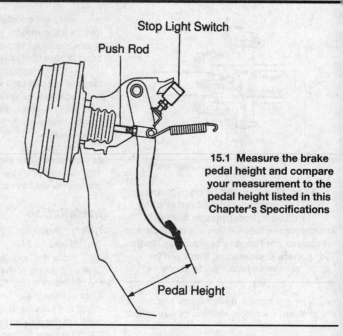

Stop Light Switch

Push Rod

15.1 Measure the brake pedal height and compare your measurement to the pedal height listed in this Chapter's Specifications

Pedal Height

15 Install the master cylinder (see Section 8) and reattach the intake vacuum hose. Make sure the hose is tightly clamped and in good condition.

16 Adjust the brake pedal height and freeplay (see Section 15).

17 Carefully test the operation of the brakes before placing the vehicle in normal operation.

14 Brake hydraulic system - bleeding

Refer to illustration 14.8

Warning: *Wear eye protection when bleeding the brake system. If the fluid comes in contact with your eyes, immediately rinse them with water and seek medical attention.*

Note: *Bleeding the brake system is necessary to remove any air that's trapped in the system when it's opened during removal and installation of a hose, line, caliper, wheel cylinder or master cylinder.*

1 It will probably be necessary to bleed the system at all four brakes if air has entered the system due to low fluid level, or if the brake lines have been disconnected at the master cylinder.

2 If a brake line was disconnected only at a wheel, then only that caliper or wheel cylinder must be bled.

3 If a brake line is disconnected at a fitting located between the master cylinder and any of the brakes, that part of the system served by the disconnected line must be bled.

4 Remove any residual vacuum (or hydraulic pressure) from the brake power booster by applying the brake several times with the engine off.

5 Remove the master cylinder reservoir cover and fill the reservoir with brake fluid. Reinstall the cover. **Note:** *Check the fluid level often during the bleeding operation and*

add fluid as necessary to prevent the fluid level from falling low enough to allow air bubbles into the master cylinder.

6 Have an assistant on hand, as well as a supply of new brake fluid, an empty clear plastic container, a length of plastic, rubber or vinyl tubing to fit over the bleeder valve and a wrench to open and close the bleeder valve.

7 Beginning at the right rear wheel, loosen the bleeder screw slightly, then tighten it to a point where it's snug but can still be loosened quickly and easily.

8 Place one end of the tubing over the bleeder screw fitting and submerge the other end in brake fluid in the container **(see illustration)**.

9 Have the assistant slowly push down on the brake pedal, then hold the pedal firmly depressed.

10 While the pedal is held depressed, open the bleeder screw just enough to allow a flow of fluid to leave the valve. Watch for air bubbles to exit the submerged end of the tube. When the fluid flow slows after a couple of seconds, tighten the screw and have your assistant release the pedal slowly.

11 Repeat Steps 9 and 10 until no more air is seen leaving the tube, then tighten the bleeder screw and proceed to the left rear wheel, the right front wheel and the left front wheel, in that order, and perform the same procedure. Be sure to check the fluid in the master cylinder reservoir frequently.

12 Bleed the load sensing proportioning and bypass valve in the same manner.

13 Never use old brake fluid. It contains moisture which will can boil, rendering the brakes useless.

14 Refill the master cylinder with fluid at the end of the operation.

15 Check the operation of the brakes. The pedal should feel solid when depressed, with no sponginess. If necessary, repeat the entire process. **Warning:** *Do not operate the vehicle*

if you are in doubt about the effectiveness of the brake system. It is possible for air to become trapped in the anti-lock brake system valve assembly, so, if the pedal continues to feel spongy after repeated bleedings or the BRAKE or ANTI-LOCK light stays on, have the vehicle towed to a dealer service department or other qualified shop to be bled with the aid of a scan tool.

15 Brake pedal - adjustment

Refer to illustrations 15.1, 15.9, 15.15 and 15.17

1 Measure the brake pedal height **(see illustration)** and compare your measurement to the pedal height listed in this Chapter's Specifications. If the measured pedal height is not within specification, adjust the pedal height as follows.

2 Unplug the electrical connector from the brake light switch (see Section 16).

3 Remove the brake light switch locknut (the lower nut) and remove the switch.

4 Loosen the power brake booster pushrod locknut.

5 Adjust the pedal height by turning the pushrod.

6 When the pedal height is correct, tighten the pushrod locknut securely.

7 Install the brake light switch. Make sure that the switch plunger lightly contacts the pedal stopper. If it doesn't, back off the adjustment nut (upper nut) to lower the switch's position in the bracket until the plunger touches the stopper.

8 Back off the brake light switch one turn.

9 Measure the distance between the switch and the pedal stopper **(see illustration)** (the distance that the plunger protrudes from the switch when it's just touching the released brake pedal) and compare your measurement to the switch-to-pedal distance

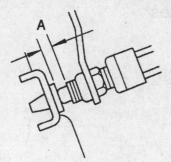

15.9 Measure the distance (dimension A) between the switch and the pedal stopper (the distance that the plunger protrudes from the switch when it's just touching the released brake pedal) and compare your measurement to the switch-to-pedal distance listed in this Chapter's Specifications

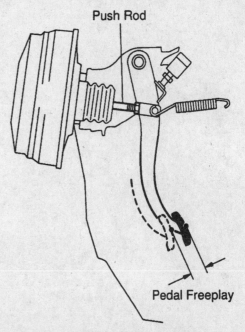

Push Rod

Pedal Freeplay

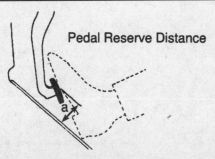

Pedal Reserve Distance

15.17 With the engine running (intake manifold vacuum present), depress the brake pedal, measure the pedal reserve distance (dimension A) and compare your measurement to the pedal reserve distance listed in this Chapter's Specifications.

15.15 Push the pedal down with your hand to the point at which you feel initial resistance, measure the distance between the released pedal and this point and compare your measurement to the pedal freeplay listed in this Chapter's Specifications

listed in this Chapter's Specifications. If the measured distance is not within specification, raise or lower the switch in the bracket as necessary.

10   When the brake light-to-pedal stopper distance is within specification, tighten the brake light switch locknut securely and plug in the switch electrical connector.

12   Verify that the brake lights come on when the brake pedal is applied, and go out when the brake pedal is released.

13   Now measure the brake pedal freeplay (if the brake light-to-pedal stopper distance is correct, pedal freeplay should be correct, but check it anyway, to verify that you have adjusted the pedal height and brake light switch correctly).

14   The engine must be turned off during this check. Depress the brake pedal several times until there is no more vacuum in the power brake booster.

15   Push the pedal down with your hand to the point at which you feel initial resistance. Measure the distance between the released pedal and this point **(see illustration)**. Record your measurement and compare it to the pedal freeplay listed in this Chapter's Specifications.

16   If pedal freeplay is incorrect, readjust the brake light switch. If pedal freeplay is correct, check pedal reserve.

17   Release the parking brake. Start the engine. With the engine running (intake manifold vacuum present), depress the brake pedal and measure the pedal reserve distance **(see illustration)**. Compare your measurement to the pedal reserve distance listed in this Chapter's Specifications.

18   If the pedal reserve distance is correct, the brake pedal is adjusted. If the pedal reserve distance is incorrect, troubleshoot the brake system. Look for a leak.

16 Brake light switch - check and replacement

Check

Refer to illustration 16.1

1   The brake light switch **(see illustration)** is located on the brake pedal bracket. You'll need to remove the trim panel beneath the steering column to get to the switch and connector (see Chapter 11).

2   With the brake pedal in the fully released position, the switch opens the brake light circuit. When the brake pedal is depressed, the switch closes the circuit and sends current to the brake lights.

3   If the brake lights are inoperative, check the fuse and the bulbs (see Chapter 12).

4   If the fuse and bulbs are okay, verify that voltage is available at the switch.

5   If there's no voltage to the switch, search for an open circuit condition between the fuse block and the switch. If there is voltage to the switch, close the switch (depress the brake pedal) and verify that there's voltage on the other side of the switch.

6   If there's no voltage on the other side of the switch, replace the switch. If there is voltage but the brake lights still don't work, look for an open circuit condition between the switch and the brake lights.

Replacement

7   Remove the trim panel below the steering column (see Chapter 11).

8   Unplug the electrical connector from the switch.

9   Remove the locknut (the lower nut) from the switch.

10   Remove the switch from its bracket.

11   Installation is the reverse of removal.

12   Adjust the switch when you're done (see Section 15).

16.1 The brake light switch is located at the top of the brake pedal assembly; to remove it, unplug the electrical connector (upper arrow) on top, then remove the locknut (lower arrow); the upper nut (middle arrow) is the adjustment nut (Tacoma unit shown, others similar)

Notes

Chapter 10
Suspension and steering systems

Contents

Specifications

General

Balljoint stud turning torque	
T100 and Tacoma	
Lower balljoint	
2WD..	17 to 61 in-lbs
4WD..	17 to 34 in-lbs
Upper balljoint	
2WD..	17 to 34 in-lbs
4WD..	4 to 22 in-lbs
4Runner	
Lower balljoint..	0.8 to 21.7 in-lbs
Upper balljoint..	6 to 39 in-lbs
Steering knuckle bushing thrust clearance (4WD T100 models)	
Standard...	0.0039 to 0.0197 inch
Maximum...	0.039 inch
Strut bar length (2WD T100)...	16-21/32 inches

Torque specifications

Ft-lbs (unless otherwise indicated)

Front suspension

Balljoint
  T100 and Tacoma
    Lower balljoint mounting nuts/bolts

2WD	55
4WD	43

    Upper balljoint mounting nuts/bolts

2WD	23
4WD	25
Lower balljoint stud nuts	105

    Upper balljoint stud nuts

2WD	80
4WD	105

  4Runner

Lower balljoint mounting bolts	59
Lower balljoint stud nuts	105
Upper balljoint stud nuts	80

Lower control arm-to-frame pivot bolt(s)/nut(s)
  T100

2WD	152
4WD	145
2WD Tacoma	148
4Runner and 4WD Tacoma	96
Lower suspension arm No. 3 nuts (2WD Tacoma)	111

Shock absorber (T100 and 2WD Tacoma)
  Lower fasteners
    T100

2WD (two bolts)	156 in-lbs
4WD (bolt/nut)	101
Tacoma (two bolts)	29
Upper nut	18

Shock absorber/coil spring (4Runner and 4WD Tacoma)

Lower nut/bolt	101
Upper nuts (three nuts)	47
Damper rod nut	22

Stabilizer bar
  T100
    2WD

Bushing bracket bolts	22
Link upper and lower nuts	108 in-lbs

    4WD

Bushing bracket bolts	22
Link nuts	19

  Tacoma
    2WD

Bushing bracket bolts	22
Link nuts	29

    4WD

Bushing bracket bolts	19
Upper link nuts	22
Lower link nuts	51

  4Runner

Bushing bracket bolts	19
Upper link nut	16 in-lbs
Lower link nut	51

Strut bar (2WD T100 and Tacoma models)
  T100

Front nut	90
Strut bar-to-lower control arm nuts	55

  Tacoma

Strut bar-to-frame nut/bolt	221
Strut bar-to-lower control arm nuts	111

Torsion bar
  Torque arm bolts

2WD	36
4WD	64

Front suspension

Upper control arm

  T100

    2WD

	Ft-lbs (unless otherwise indicated)
Pivot shaft/adjusting shim bolts	71
Front and rear pivot shaft bolts	93

    4WD

Pivot shaft retaining bolts	131
Front and rear pivot shaft nuts	166

  Tacoma

    2WD

Pivot shaft/adjusting shim bolts	94
Front and rear pivot shaft bolts	92

  4Runner and Tacoma 4WD

Pivot bolt/nut	87

Rear suspension

Lateral rod (4Runner)

bolts/nuts	64

Leaf spring (T100 and Tacoma)

  T100

Leaf spring-to-front hanger nuts	67
Shackle-to-frame nuts	67
Shackle-to-spring nuts	67
U-bolt nuts	97

  Tacoma

Leaf spring-to-front hanger nuts	116
Shackle-to-frame nuts	67
Shackle-to-spring nuts	67
U-bolt nuts	90

Shock absorber bolts

T100 and 2WD Tacoma	19
4WD Tacoma	53

  4Runner

Lower bolt	47
Upper bolt	168 in-lbs

Stabilizer bar (4Runner)

Bushing bracket bolts	168 in-lbs
Link nuts	168 in-lbs

Suspension arms (4Runner)

Lower control arm nuts	107
Upper control arm nuts	64

Steering

Steering wheel nut	26
Power steering pump pulley nut	32

Tacoma, 4Runner and 2WD T100

Tie-rod end-to-steering knuckle ballstud nut	53
Intermediate shaft U-joint-to-input shaft pinch bolt	26

Steering gear mounting nuts/bolts

  2WD T100

Left through/bolt and nut	65
Right bracket short bolt (on top)	65
Right bracket long bolt (on front)	108 in-lbs

  2WD Tacoma

Mounting nuts/bolts	148

  4WD Tacoma

Left through/bolt and nut	141
Right bracket nut and bolt	123

  4Runner

Left through/bolt and nut	151
Right bracket nut and bolt	123

4WD T100

Idler arm

Idler arm-to-frame nuts/bolts	105
Idler arm-to-relay rod balljoint stud nut	43

Pitman arm

Pitman arm-to-steering gear nut	130
Pitman arm-to-relay rod balljoint stud nut	67

Torque specifications

Ft-lbs (unless otherwise indicated)

Steering

4WD T100 (continued)

Steering damper

Damper-to-frame nut/bolt 19

Damper-to-relay rod balljoint stud nut 43

Steering gear

Steering gear-to-frame bolts/nuts.. 105

Intermediate shaft U-joint-to-input shaft pinch bolt.......................... 26

Tie-rods

Inner tie-rod-to-relay rod balljoint stud nuts 67

Adjuster tube clamp bolts 16

Tie-rod end-to-steering knuckle balljoint stud nuts 67

---

1   General information

Front suspension

Refer to illustrations 1.2a, 1.2b, 1.3a, 1.3b, 1.3c and 1.3d

The front suspension system is fully independent. The steering knuckles are connected to the upper and lower control arms by balljoints. The control arms are bolted to the frame. All models use a front stabilizer bar to reduce vehicle roll during cornering.

The front suspension on T100 models **(see illustrations)** uses torsion bars instead of coil springs. On 2WD models, the torsion bars are attached to the lower control arms on 4WD models, they're attached to th upper arms. On 2WD models, the lower control arms are positioned by strut bars connected to the frame.

The front suspension on Tacoma an 4Runner models **(see illustrations)** uses co springs and shock absorbers. On Tacoma

1.2a T100 front suspension and steering components (4WD model shown)

1	Steering damper	*5*	Outer tie-rod ends	*9*	Stabilizer bar link nuts
2	Pitman arm	*6*	Steering arms	*10*	Lower control arm
3	Idler arm	*7*	Lower control arm balljoint	*11*	Stabilizer bar mounting clamps
4	Tie-rod adjuster sleeves	*8*	Steering knuckles	*12*	Stabilizer bar

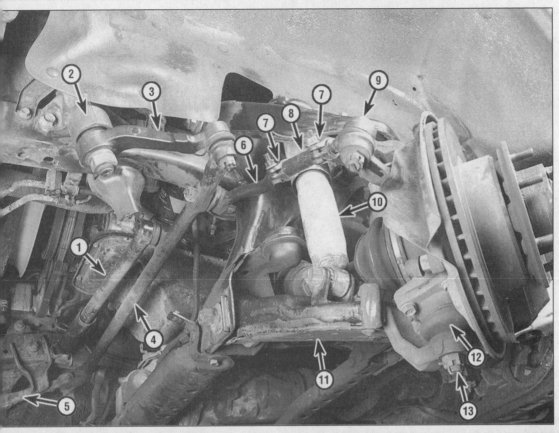

1.2b T100 front suspension and steering components (4WD model shown)

1   Steering damper
2   Steering gearbox
3   Pitman arm
4   Relay rod
5   Idler arm
6   Inner tie-rod end
7   Tie-rod adjuster tube pinch-bolt/clamps
8   Tie-rod adjuster tube
9   Outer tie-rod end
10 Shock absorber
11 Lower control arm
12 Lower balljoint
13 Lower balljoint ballstud

1.3a Tacoma front suspension and steering components (2WD model shown)

1 Steering gear	5 Steering knuckles	8 Stabilizer bar links	11 Stabilizer bar
2 Steering gear dust boots	6 Lower balljoints	9 Strut bars	12 Coil springs
3 Tie-rods	7 Shock absorber-to-lower	10 Stabilizer bar clamps	13 Lower control arms
4 Tie-rod ends	control arm nut and bolt		

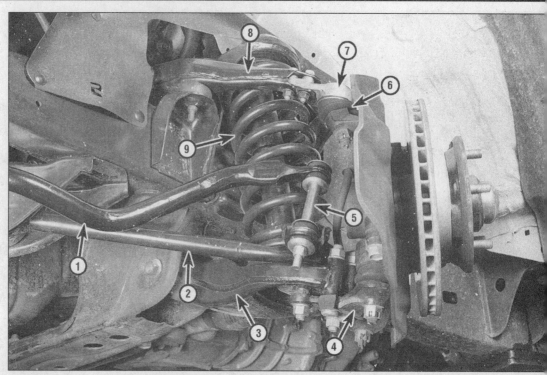

1.3b Tacoma front suspension and steering components (2WD model shown)

1   Stabilizer bar
2   Strut bar
3   Lower control arm
4   Lower balljoint
5   Stabilizer bar link
6   Steering knuckle
7   Upper balljoint
8   Upper control arm
9   Coil spring (shock absorber inside spring)

2WD models, the shocks are installed inside the coil springs, but they're separate components; the coil springs are positioned by spring pockets on the frame and the lower control arms. The shocks are attached to the lower control arms by bolts; the upper end of each shock is attached to a bracket on the frame. On Tacoma 2WD models, the lower control arms are positioned by strut bars connected to the frame. On Tacoma 4WD models and all 4Runner models, the shocks and coils are integral assemblies; the upper ends are bolted to brackets on the frame and the lower ends are bolted to brackets on the lower control arms.

Rear suspension

Refer to illustrations 1.4 and 1.5

The rear suspension on T100 and Tacoma models **(see illustration)** consists of a pair of multi-leaf springs and two shock absorbers. The rear axle assembly is attached to the leaf springs by U-bolts. The front ends of the springs are attached to the frame at the front hangers, through rubber bushings. The rear ends of the springs are attached to the frame by shackles which allow the springs to alter their length when the vehicle is in operation.

The rear suspension on 4Runner models

1.3c 4Runner front suspension and steering components (4WD model shown)

1   Steering gear
2   Steering gear dust boots
3   Tie-rods
4   Stabilizer bar
5   Lower balljoint ballstuds
6   Steering knuckles
7   Lower control arms
8   Coil spring/shock absorber assemblies

1.3d 4Runner front suspension and steering components (4WD model shown)

1 Lower control arm
2 Steering knuckle
3 Lower balljoint ballstud
4 Upper balljoint
5 Upper control arm
6 Coil spring
7 Shock absorber

1.4 Rear suspension components (T100 shown, Tacoma similar)

1 Rear axle
2 Shock absorbers
3 Multi-leaf spring assemblies
4 Lower shock absorber mount/leaf spring seat
5 Leaf spring hanger
6 Leaf spring shackle

1.5 Rear suspension components (4Runner models)

1	*Rear axle*	*3*	*Stabilizer bar clamps*	*5*	*Shock absorbers*
2	*Stabilizer bar*	*4*	*Lower suspension arms*	*6*	*Coil springs*

7   Lateral rod

(see illustration) consists of a pair of coil springs, two shock absorbers, four suspension arms (two lower, two upper), and a lateral rod, which connects the left end of the axle to the right frame rail. A stabilizer bar, bolted to the axle and connected to the frame by a pair of links, reduces vehicle roll during cornering.

Steering

Tacoma, 4Runner and T100 2WD models are equipped with power-assisted rack-and-pinion steering systems. The steering gear is bolted to the back of the crossmember and is connected to the steering knuckles by a pair of tie-rods.

T100 4WD models are equipped with a power-assisted steering gearbox which uses steering linkage consisting of a Pitman arm, idler arm, relay rod, two adjustable tie-rod assemblies (each consisting of an inner tie-rod, adjuster tube and outer tie-rod), and a steering damper. When the steering wheel is turned, the gear rotates the Pitman arm which forces the relay rod to one side. The tie-rods, which are connected to the relay rod by ballstuds, transfer steering inputs to the steering knuckles. The tie-rods are adjustable

and are used for toe-in adjustments. The relay rod is supported by the Pitman arm and idler arm. The idler arm pivots on a bracket bolted to the right frame rail. The steering damper is attached to a bracket on the frame and to the relay rod.

Frequently, when working on the suspension or steering system components, you may come across fasteners which seem impossible to loosen. These fasteners on the underside of the vehicle are continually subjected to water, road grime, mud, etc., and can become rusted or "frozen," making them extremely difficult to remove. In order to unscrew these stubborn fasteners without damaging them (or other components), be sure to use lots of penetrating oil and allow it to soak in for a while. Using a wire brush to clean exposed threads will also ease removal of the nut or bolt and prevent damage to the threads. Sometimes a sharp blow with a hammer and punch is effective in breaking the bond between a nut and bolt threads, but care must be taken to prevent the punch from slipping off the fastener and ruining the threads. Heating the stuck fastener and surrounding area with a torch sometimes helps too, but isn't recommended because of the obvious dangers associated with fire. Long

breaker bars and extension, or "cheater," pipes will increase leverage, but never use an extension pipe on a ratchet - the ratcheting mechanism could be damaged. Sometimes, turning the nut or bolt in the tightening (clockwise) direction first will help to break it loose. Fasteners that require drastic measures to unscrew should always be replaced with new ones.

Since most of the procedures that are dealt with in this Chapter involve jacking up the vehicle and working underneath it, a good pair of jackstands will be needed. A hydraulic floor jack is the preferred type of jack to lift the vehicle, and it can also be used to support certain components during various operations. **Warning:** *Never, under any circumstances, rely on a jack to support the vehicle while working on it. Also, whenever any of the suspension or steering fasteners are loosened or removed they must be inspected and, if necessary, replaced with new ones of the same part number or of original equipment quality and design. Torque specifications must be followed for proper reassembly and component retention. Never attempt to heat or straighten suspension or steering components. Instead, replace bent or damaged parts with new ones.*

2.2a To detach the lower end of the shock absorber from the lower control arm on a 2WD pick-up model, remove these two bolts (arrows) (Tacoma shown, WD T100 similar)

2.2b To detach the lower end of the shock absorber from the lower control arm on a 4WD T100 model, hold the bolt with a wrench, remove the nut and remove the bolt (disc, hub and bearing removed for clarity)

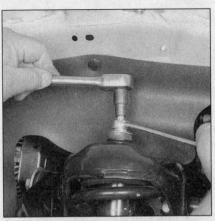

2.3 To detach the upper end of the shock from its mounting bracket, hold the shock damper rod with a wrench or socket and remove the locknut; when installing a new shock, don't forget to install the washer and rubber bushing below the nut, as well as the other washer and bushing below the bracket (2WD Tacoma shown, 2WD/4WD T100 similar)

2 Front shock absorber (T100 and 2WD Tacoma models) - removal and installation

Refer to illustrations 2.2a, 2.2b and 2.3

1 Loosen the front wheel lug nuts. Raise the vehicle and support it securely on jack-stands. Remove the front wheels.

2 Working from underneath the vehicle, remove the two bolts (2WD models) or bolt and nut (4WD models) attaching the lower end of the shock absorber to the lower control arm **(see illustrations)**.

3 Using a wrench or socket to hold the shock absorber damper rod, remove the upper mounting nut **(see illustration)**.

4 Note the order in which the washers and bushings are installed above and below the upper mounting bracket, then pull out the shock from below.

5 Inspect the rubber bushings for cracks, tears and deterioration. If they're worn or damaged, replace them.

6 Installation is the reverse of removal. Be

sure to tighten the upper mounting nut and the lower mounting bolt(s) to the torque listed in this Chapter's Specifications.

3 Front shock absorber/coil spring assembly (4Runner and 4WD Tacoma models) - removal, component replacement and installation

Refer to illustrations 3.2, 3.3, 3.7 and 3.8
Warning: *Before undertaking the following procedure, be aware that disassembling the shock absorber/coil spring assemblies is a potentially dangerous job. Careless or unsafe work can cause serious injury. Use only the highest-quality spring compressor and be sure to follow the spring compressor manu-facturer's instructions. After removing the compressed spring, set it aside in a safe, iso-lated place.*
Note: *If the shock absorber/coil spring assemblies must be replaced, you can save*

time by simply installing new complete shock/coil assemblies. Or, you can replace just the shocks or just the springs. But, to do so, you will have to disassemble the shock absorber/coil spring assemblies. Therefore, before deciding which way you want to go, find out the local cost of each option. You may find that the cost for two assembled complete shock/coil assemblies is only slightly higher than the cost for two new shock absorbers or coil springs.

1 Loosen the front wheel lug nuts. Raise the vehicle and support it securely on jack-stands. Remove the front wheels.

2 Working from underneath the vehicle, remove the nut and bolt attaching the lower end of the shock absorber to the lower con-trol arm **(see illustrations)**.

3 Remove the three nuts that attach the upper end of the shock to the frame bracket **(see illustration)**.

3.2 To detach the lower end of the shock absorber/coil spring assembly from the lower control arm on 4Runner and 4WD Tacoma models, remove this nut (arrow) and bolt

3.3 To detach the upper end of the shock absorber/coil spring assembly from its mounting bracket, remove these three nuts (arrows) (NOT the nut in the middle, which is the damper rod nut; it must never be removed unless the spring is compressed with a spring compressor)

3.7 Install the spring compressor in accordance with the manufacturer's instructions; compress the spring until you can wiggle it before removing the damper rod nut

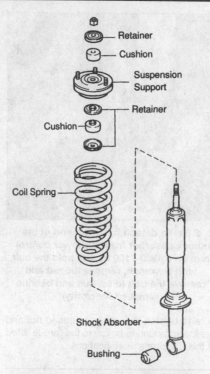

3.8 An exploded view of the shock absorber/coil spring assembly used on 4Runner and 4WD Tacoma models

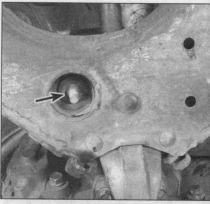

4.2a To detach the lower end of the stabilizer bar link from the lower control arms on a T100 model, remove this nut (arrow)

4   Remove the shock absorber/coil spring assembly.

5   Inspect the shock absorber for leaking fluid, dents, cracks and other damage. Inspect the coil spring for chips and cracks which could cause premature failure. Inspect the spring seats for hardness and general deterioration. If either the shock or the spring is worn or damaged, replace it. If you're installing new complete units, proceed to Step 14; if you're going to install new shocks or coil springs, proceed to the next Step.

6   Secure the shock/coil assembly in a bench vise. If you're planning to reuse the old shock absorbers, line the jaws of the vise with wood or shop rags to protect the shock bodies. And don't tighten the jaws any more than necessary; overtightening the vise may crush the shock body.

7   Install a spring compressor in accordance with the manufacturer's instructions **(see illustration)**. (You can buy a spring compressor at most auto parts stores or rent one from most equipment yards on a daily basis.) Compress the spring far enough to relieve all pressure from the spring seat;

when you can wiggle the spring, it's compressed enough to disassemble the shock/spring assembly. **Warning:** *Don't compress the spring any more than necessary.*

8   Hold the damper rod with a wrench and remove the damper rod nut **(see illustration)**.

9   Remove the upper retainer, upper cushion and suspension support.

10   Remove the compressed spring assembly and set it safely aside.

11   Remove the lower retainers and cushion.

12   Inspect the cushions for cracks and tears and general deterioration. Replace

them if they're damaged. Make sure the retainers are in good condition too. If they're distorted or otherwise damaged, replace them.

13   Reassembly is the reverse of disassembly. Make sure the lower end of the coil spring is correctly seated in the low spot in the lower spring seat. Tighten the damper rod to the torque listed in this Chapter's Specifications before releasing tension on the spring.

14   Installation is the reverse of removal. Be sure to tighten the upper and lower fasteners to the torque listed in this Chapter's Specifications.

4   Front stabilizer bar - removal and installation

Refer to illustrations 4.2a, 4.2b, 4.2c, 4.2d and 4.3

1   Raise the vehicle and support it securely on jackstands.

2   Remove the nuts **(see illustrations)** from the link bolts and remove the link bolts.

4.2b Be sure to note the order in which the washers and rubber bushings are installed on the link

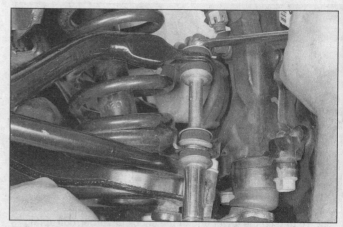

4.2c To disconnect the stabilizer bar link bolt on 2WD Tacoma models, hold the upper end of the link with a wrench and remove the nut at the lower end of the link with a socket

4.2d Stabilizer link fasteners (4Runner and 4WD Tacoma models)

4.3 To separate the stabilizer bar from the frame, remove the bushing clamp bolts (arrows) from both clamps

5.3a If the steering knuckle has a brake hose bracket attached to it, such as this 4WD T100, remove the bracket bolt (arrow) and pull the brake hose clear of the knuckle

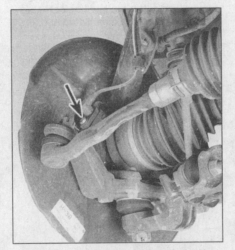

5.3b On vehicles with ABS, remove the front wheel speed sensor retaining bolt (arrow) and detach the sensor from the steering knuckle (4Runner shown, others similar)

5.6a To remove the disc splash shield on a 2WD model, remove these bolts (arrows)

5.6b To remove the disc splash shield on a 4WD model, remove these bolts (arrows)

3   Remove the stabilizer bar bushing bracket bolts and/or nuts **(see illustration)**.
4   Remove the stabilizer bar.
5   Remove the rubber bushings from the stabilizer bar.
6   Inspect the rubber bushings for cracks, tears and deterioration. If they're worn or damaged, replace them.
7   When you install the rubber bushings on the stabilizer bar, be sure to position them so the slits face toward the front of the vehicle (on Tacoma 2WD models, they should face down).
8   Installation is otherwise the reverse of removal. Be sure to tighten all fasteners to the torque listed in this Chapter's Specifications.

5   Steering knuckle - removal and installation

Refer to illustrations 5.3a, 5.3b, 5.6a, 5.6b, 5.7, 5.11a through 5.11g and 5.12

1   Loosen the wheel lug nuts. Raise the front of the vehicle and support it securely on jackstands. Apply the parking brake. Remove the wheel.
2   On 2WD pick-up models, support the lower control arm with a jack and raise it slightly. **Warning:** *The jack must remain in this position throughout the entire procedure.*
3   Detach all brake hose brackets from the steering knuckle **(see illustration)**. On vehicles with ABS, detach the front wheel speed sensor from the steering knuckle **(see illustration)**.
4   Remove the brake caliper and, on 2WD pick-up models, the torque plate (see Chapter 9).
5   Remove the brake disc/hub assembly (see Chapter 1, *Front wheel bearing check, repack and adjustment*). On 4Runners and 4WD Tacoma models, slide the disc off the hub.
6   Remove the disc splash shield **(see illustrations)**. The splash shield retaining ring

on 4WD T100 models is also a seal; discard this part and replace it with a new seal/retainer.

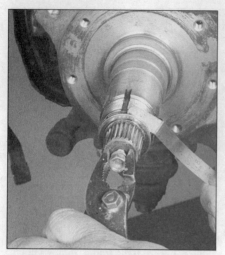

5.7 On 4WD T100 models, pull out on the driveaxle end and measure the thrust clearance between the spacer and the outer thrust bushing

5.11a Here's a typical upper balljoint setup on a 2WD pick-up model: to disconnect the upper end of the steering knuckle from the upper control arm, remove the cotter pin and back off - but don't remove - the castellated nut . . .

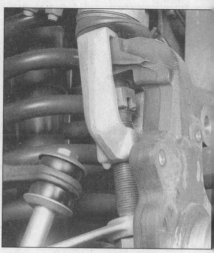

5.11b . . . install a suitable puller and pop the balljoint stud loose from the knuckle (2WD Tacoma shown; T100 similar)

5.11c Here's a typical upper balljoint setup on a 4WD T100 model: to disconnect the upper end of the steering knuckle from the upper control arm, remove the four nuts (arrows) . . .

5.11d . . . and pry the upper balljoint out from under the upper arm

5.11e On 4Runners and 4WD Tacoma models, remove the cotter pin (arrow), back off - but don't remove - the castellated nut, then use a two-jaw puller to separate the ballstud from the upper control arm

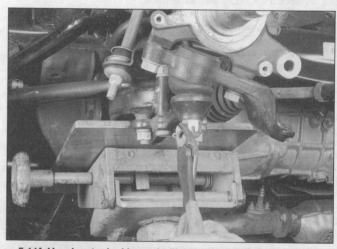

5.11f Here's a typical lower balljoint setup: To disconnect the lower end of the steering knuckle from the lower control arm, remove the cotter pin and back off - but don't remove - the castellated nut . . .

5.11g . . . install a suitable puller and pop the balljoint stud loose from the lower control arm (2WD Tacoma shown, others similar)

5.12 Removing the steering knuckle on a 4WD T100 model .

7 On 4WD T100 models, measure the thrust clearance **(see illustration)** and compare your measurement to the clearance listed in this Chapter's Specifications. If the indicated clearance exceeds the allowable maximum, have the steering knuckle inner and outer bushings replaced by an automotive machine shop.

8 Disconnect the tie-rod end from the knuckle (see Section 21).

9 On 4WD T100 models, disconnect the lower end of the shock absorber from the lower control arm (see Section 2). Remove the snap-ring and spacer from the end of the driveaxle.

10 On 4WD T100 models, disconnect the stabilizer bar link from the lower control arm (see Section 4).

11 Disconnect the steering knuckle from the upper and lower control arms **(see illustrations)**.

12 Remove the steering knuckle **(see illustration)**.

13 Installation is the reverse of removal. Tighten all suspension fasteners to the torque listed in this Chapter's Specifications.

14 On all models except 4Runners and 4WD Tacomas, adjust the front wheel bearings (see Chapter 1).

6 Front hub and bearing assembly (4Runner and 4WD Tacoma models) - replacement

1 Remove the steering knuckle (see Section 6).

2 The front hub and bearing are pressed into the steering knuckle on these models. Take the steering knuckle to an automotive machine shop and have the hub and old bearing pressed out and the new bearing and hub pressed in.

3 Install the steering knuckle (see Section 6).

7 Balljoints - check and replacement

Check

Refer to illustrations 7.5 and 7.10

1 Inspect the upper and lower balljoints for looseness whenever the vehicle is raised for any reason. You can check the balljoints with the suspension assembled as follows.

2 Raise the front of the vehicle and support it securely on jackstands.

3 Wipe the balljoints clean and inspect the seals for cuts and tears. If a balljoint seal is damaged, replace the balljoint.

Lower balljoint (all except 4WD T100 models)

4 On all models except 4WD T100s, place a floor jack under the lower control arm and raise it slightly to unload the balljoint. Position the jack as close to each balljoint as possible. Make sure the vehicle is stable. It should not rock on the stands. **Note:** *The balljoints on 4WD T100s must be checked without a jack supporting the lower control arms.*

5 Pry up on the tire of each wheel **(see illustration)** and have an assistant feel for play in the lower balljoint. If there is significant play, replace the balljoint.

Lower balljoint (4WD T100 models)

6 With the vehicle raised and supported on jackstands and the suspension hanging free, pry up and down on the lower control arm, feeling for play in the balljoint. If there is significant play, replace the balljoint.

Upper balljoint (all except 4WD T100 models)

7 With the vehicle raised and supported on jackstands, and a floor jack supporting the

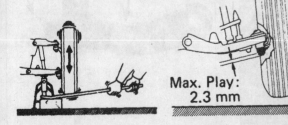

7.5 Check the suspension balljoints for wear by prying up on the tire of each wheel as shown here; note that the lower control arm must be supported by a jack (except on 4WD T100 models) and the tire must be off the ground

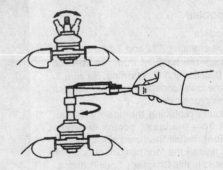

7.10 To bench test a balljoint, flip the balljoint stud back and forth five times, then measure the turning torque on the fifth turn

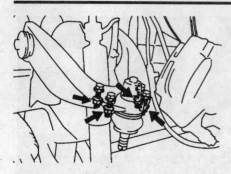

7.12 If you're replacing the upper balljoint on a 2WD T100, remove these four nuts and bolts (arrows) from the upper control arm

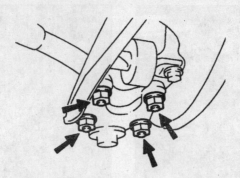

7.13 If you're replacing the lower balljoint on a 2WD T100, remove these four nuts (arrows)

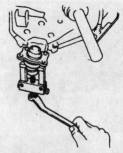

7.17 If you're replacing the lower balljoint on a 4WD T100, remove the four nuts and bolts, then loosen the castle nut and separate the balljoint from the lower arm with a two-jaw puller

lower control arm (slightly raised), pry up and down on the upper control arm while feeling for play in the balljoint. If there is significant play, replace the balljoint.

Upper balljoint (4WD T100 models)

8   With the vehicle raised and supported on jackstands, and the suspension hanging free, pry up on the tire **(see illustration 7.5)** while an assistant feels for play in the upper balljoint. If significant play is felt, replace the balljoint.

All balljoints

9   Balljoints should also be checked whenever they're separated from the steering knuckle, or the steering knuckle is separated from the upper or lower control arm. See if you can turn the ballstud in its socket with your fingers. If the balljoint is loose, or if the ballstud can be turned, replace the balljoint.
10   Toyota also specifies a more accurate version of this bench test. Flip the balljoint stud back and forth five times **(see illustration)**, then install the nut. Using an inch-pound torque wrench, measure the turning torque as follows: turn the nut continuously at a rate of one turn every two to four seconds. On the fifth turn, read the indicated torque and compare it to the acceptable torque range listed in this Chapter's Specifications. If the indicated turning torque is not within the specified range, replace the balljoint.

Replacement

T100 models

2WD models

Refer to illustrations 7.12 and 7.13

11   Detach the balljoint from the steering knuckle (see Section 6). **Warning:** *Be sure to support the lower control arm with a floor jack during this procedure.*
12   If you're replacing the upper balljoint, unbolt it from the upper control arm **(see illustration)**. Install the new balljoint on the arm and tighten the four balljoint nuts to the torque listed in this Chapter's Specifications.
13   If you're replacing the lower balljoint, unbolt it from the lower control arm **(see illustration)**. Install the new balljoint on the

arm and tighten the four balljoint nuts to the torque listed in this Chapter's Specifications.
14   The remainder of installation is the reverse of removal (see Section 6). Be sure to tighten all suspension fasteners to the torque listed in this Chapter's Specifications.

4WD models

Refer to illustration 7.14

15   Detach the balljoint from the steering knuckle (see Section 6).
16   If you're replacing the upper balljoint, unbolt it from the upper control arm **(see illustration 5.11c)**. To separate the balljoint from the steering knuckle, remove the cotter pin and loosen the castle nut, then break the balljoint loose from the knuckle with a pickle-fork tool or other suitable puller. Installation is the reverse of removal. Tighten the four balljoint nuts and the castle nut to the torque listed in this Chapter's Specifications. Insert a new cotter pin in the castle nut, tightening it a bit more to align a slot in the nut with the hole in the ballstud, if necessary.
17   If you're replacing the lower balljoint, detach the balljoint from the lower arm with a puller **(see illustration)**. Installation is the reverse of removal. Tighten the fasteners to the torque listed in this Chapter's Specifications.
18   The remainder of installation is the reverse of removal (see Section 6). Tighten all

suspension fasteners to the torque listed in this Chapter's Specifications.

2WD Tacoma models

Upper balljoint

Refer to illustration 7.17

19   Disconnect the upper end of the steering knuckle from the upper control arm (see Section 6). **Warning:** *Be sure to support the lower control arm with a floor jack during this procedure.*
20   Unbolt the upper balljoint from the upper control arm **(see illustration)**.
21   Installation is the reverse of removal (see Section 6). Tighten the four balljoint retaining nuts, the balljoint stud nut and all other suspension fasteners to the torque listed in this Chapter's Specifications. Be sure to use a new cotter pin.

Lower balljoint

Refer to illustration 7.23

22   Disconnect the lower end of the steering knuckle from the lower control arm (see Section 6). **Warning:** *Be sure to support the lower control arm with a floor jack during this procedure.*
23   Detach the tie-rod end from the steering knuckle arm (see Section 21). Unbolt the lower balljoint from the steering knuckle **(see illustration)**.

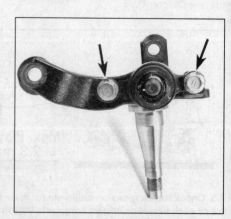

7.20 To detach the upper balljoint from the upper control arm on a 2WD Tacoma, remove these four bolts (arrows) and nuts

7.23 To detach the lower balljoint from the steering knuckle, remove these two bolts (arrows)

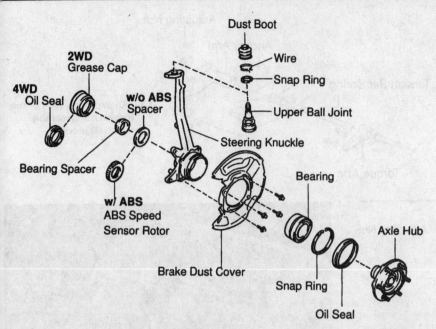

Dust Boot

Wire

Snap Ring

Upper Ball Joint

2WD
Grease Cap

4WD
Oil Seal

w/o ABS
Spacer

Steering Knuckle

Bearing Spacer

Bearing

w/ ABS
ABS Speed
Sensor Rotor

Axle Hub

Brake Dust Cover

Snap Ring

Oil Seal

7.26 An exploded view of the steering knuckle and upper balljoint assembly (4Runner and 4WD Tacoma models)

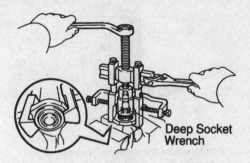

Deep Socket
Wrench

7.27 Use a two-jaw puller and a socket to remove the upper balljoint from the steering knuckle

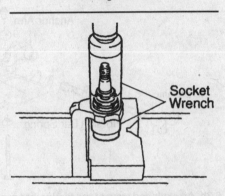

Socket
Wrench

7.28 If you're replacing the balljoint yourself, use a press and two sockets of the proper size to install the new balljoint (4Runner and 4WD Tacoma models)

24   Installation is the reverse of removal (see Section 6). Tighten the two balljoint retaining bolts, the balljoint stud nut and all other suspension fasteners to the torque listed in this Chapter's Specifications. Be sure to use a new cotter pin.

4Runner and 4WD Tacoma models

Upper balljoint
Refer to illustration 7.26, 7.27 and 7.28

25   Remove the steering knuckle (see Section 6).
26   Remove the dust boot wire retainer and dust boot, then remove the snap-ring with a pair of snap-ring pliers **(see illustration)**.
27   Use a two-jaw puller, with the screw of the puller bearing on a large socket that fits over the balljoint, to remove the upper balljoint from the steering knuckle **(see illustration)**. If you don't have the right tool, have the old balljoint removed and the new one installed at an automotive machine shop.
28   If you're replacing the balljoint yourself, use a hydraulic press (or a balljoint press) and two sockets to install the new balljoint **(see illustration)**. This could also be performed with a large vise.

29   Installation is otherwise the reverse of removal. Tighten all suspension fasteners to the torque listed in this Chapter's Specifications.

Lower balljoint
Refer to illustration 7.32

30   Disconnect the tie-rod end from the steering knuckle (see Section 21).
31   Disconnect the steering knuckle from the lower control arm (see Section 6).
32   Unbolt the lower balljoint from the steering knuckle **(see illustration)**.
33   Install the new lower balljoint and tighten the four bolts to the torque listed in this Chapter's Specifications.
34   Installation is otherwise the reverse of removal. Tighten all suspension fasteners to the torque listed in this Chapter's Specifications.

8   Torsion bar (T100 models) - removal and installation

Refer to illustrations 8.2, 8.3a, 8.3b, 8.3c and 8.4

1   Raise the vehicle and support it securely on jackstands. Allow the front suspension to hang free.

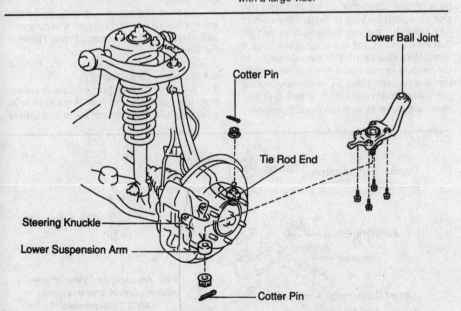

Lower Ball Joint

Cotter Pin

Tie Rod End

Steering Knuckle

Lower Suspension Arm

Cotter Pin

7.32 Installation details of the lower balljoint (4Runner and 4WD Tacoma models)

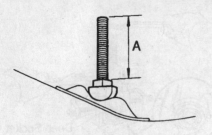

8.2 Measure the exposed part of the torsion bar adjusting bolt before unscrewing it

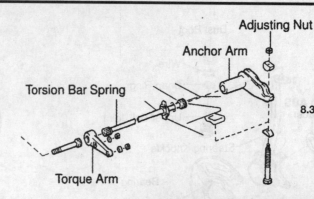

8.3a An exploded view of the torsion bar assembly (2WD models)

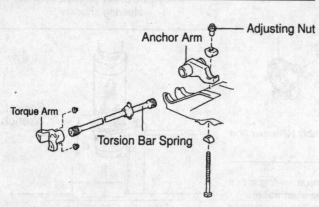

8.3b An exploded view of the torsion bar assembly (4WD models)

8.3c Using a wrench to hold the adjusting nut, loosen and remove the adjusting bolt and remove the anchor arm.

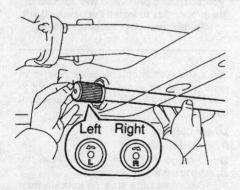

8.4 There are left and right markings on the rear ends of the torsion bars; don't switch the bars - they're not interchangeable

2   Measure the exposed part of the adjusting bolt **(see illustration)**. Record this measurement and save it for reassembly. Failure to tighten the adjusting bolt to the same spot will upset the ride height on that side of the vehicle.

3   Loosen and remove the adjusting nut **(see illustrations)** and remove the anchor arm.

4   Pull the torsion bar out of the torque arm. If the splines are frozen, apply penetrating oil to free them up and try again. If you're removing both torsion bars, be aware that they're not interchangeable; there are left and right markings on the rear ends of the torsion

bars **(see illustration)** so you don't mix them up.

5   If you're replacing the lower control arm on a 2WD model **(see illustration 8.3a)** or the upper control arm on a 4WD model **(see illustration 8.3b)**, remove the torque arm.

6   Installation is the reverse of removal. Be sure to lubricate the splines with multi-purpose grease, don't mix up left and right torsion bars, and be sure to restore the correct ride height by turning the adjusting bolt so that the exposed part is the same length as it was before disassembly. If the ride height of the vehicle is not equal from side-to-side, turn the adjusting bolt as necessary, rolling the vehicle back-and-forth a few feet between adjustments to settle the suspension.

9   Upper control arm - removal and installation

Refer to illustrations 9.8a, 9.8b, 9.8c, 9.9a and 9.9b

Note: *This procedure applies to 2WD and 4WD models.*

1   Loosen the wheel lug nuts, raise the front of the vehicle and support it securely on jackstands. Apply the parking brake. Remove the wheel.

2   Remove the brake caliper and hang it out of the way (see Chapter 9).

3   Disconnect any brake hose brackets from the upper control arm. If the vehicle is equipped with ABS, detach the speed sensor

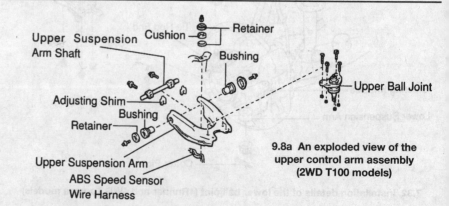

9.8a An exploded view of the upper control arm assembly (2WD T100 models)

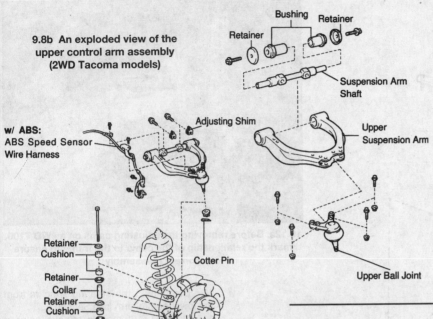

9.8b An exploded view of the upper control arm assembly (2WD Tacoma models)

Bushing
Retainer
Retainer
Suspension Arm Shaft
Adjusting Shim
Upper Suspension Arm

w/ ABS:
ABS Speed Sensor Wire Harness

Retainer
Cushion
Retainer
Collar
Retainer
Cushion
Retainer
Cushion
Cotter Pin
Upper Ball Joint

9.8c Before loosening the pivot shaft retaining bolts (upper arrows), count the number of shims (lower arrows) used at each bolt

harness from the upper arm.

4   On all except 4WD T100 models, position a floor jack under the lower control arm. Raise the jack slightly. **Warning:** *The jack must remain in this position throughout the entire procedure.*

5   On 4WD T100 models, remove the torsion bar (see Section 8).

6   On 2WD Tacoma models, remove the stabilizer link assembly (see Section 4).

7   Disconnect the steering knuckle from the upper control arm (see Section 5).

8   On 2WD pick-up models, note the location and number of shims between the upper control arm pivot shaft and the frame, then remove the pivot shaft bolts and shims **(see illustrations)**.

9   On 4WD T100 models, remove the pivot shaft-to-frame bolts **(see illustration)** and remove the arm from the vehicle. On 4Runners and 4WD Tacoma models, remove the nut, washer and pivot bolt **(see illustrations)**. Remove the arm.

10   Inspect the bushings for wear and deterioration. If they're cracked or damaged, take the arm to an automotive machine shop and have new bushings installed.

11   Installation is the reverse of removal. Be sure to tighten all suspension fasteners to the torque listed in this Chapter's Specifications. **Note:** *The pivot bolt/nut on 4Runners and 4WD Tacomas should be tightened with the vehicle at normal ride height. This can be done after the vehicle has been lowered to the ground (on vehicles with adequate clearance), or can be simulated by raising the lower control arm with a floor jack.*

12   On 2WD pick-up models, its a good idea to have the wheel alignment checked and, if necessary, adjusted.

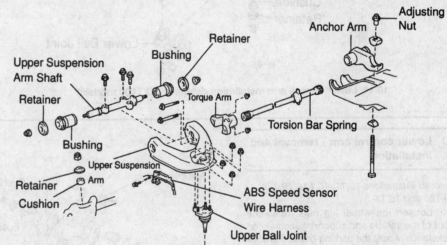

Upper Suspension Arm Shaft
Retainer
Bushing
Retainer
Bushing
Torque Arm
Anchor Arm
Adjusting Nut
Torsion Bar Spring
Upper Suspension Arm
Retainer
Cushion
ABS Speed Sensor Wire Harness
Upper Ball Joint

9.9a An exploded view of the upper control arm assembly (4WD T100 models)

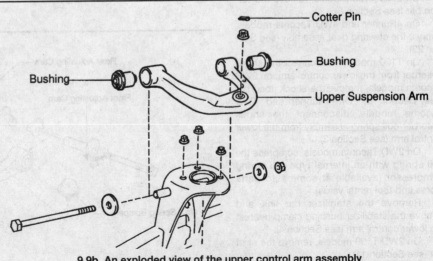

Cotter Pin
Bushing
Bushing
Upper Suspension Arm

9.9b An exploded view of the upper control arm assembly (4Runner and 4WD Tacoma models)

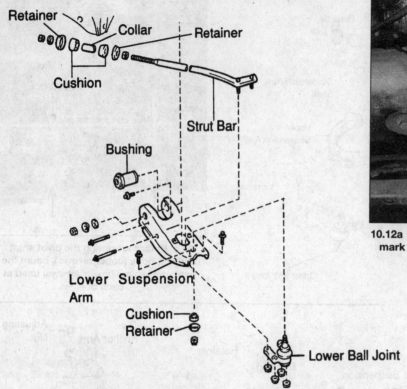

10.12a Before removing the adjusting cams on a 4WD T100, mark the relationship of the cams to the frame to ensure correct reassembly

10.11 Lower control arm installation details (2WD T100 models)

10   Disconnect the steering knuckle from the lower control arm (see Section 5).

11   On 2WD T100 models, remove the pivot bolt nut **(see illustration)** and remove the lower control arm.

12   On 4Runner and 4WD pick-up models, make alignment marks on the front and rear adjusting cams **(see illustration)**, then remove the front and rear nuts and pivot bolts **(see illustrations)** and remove the lower control arm.

10 Lower control arm - removal and installation

Refer to illustrations 10.11, 10.12a, 10.12b, 10.12c and 10.13

1   Loosen the wheel lug nuts, raise the front of the vehicle and support it securely on jackstands. Apply the parking brake. Remove the wheel.

2   On 2WD T100 models, remove the engine under cover.

3   On 2WD T100 models, remove the torsion bar (see Section 8).

4   On 4Runner and 4WD Tacoma models, remove the steering gear assembly (see Section 23).

5   On T100 models, disconnect the shock absorber from the lower control arm; on 2WD Tacoma models, remove the shock absorber (see Section 2). On 4Runner and 4WD Tacoma models, disconnect the shock absorber/coil spring assembly from the lower control arm (see Section 3).

6   On 2WD Tacoma models, compress the coil spring with an internal type coil spring compressor (available at some auto parts stores and tool rental yards).

7   Remove the stabilizer bar link and remove the stabilizer bushing clamp nearest the lower control arm (see Section 4).

8   On 2WD T100 models, remove the strut bar (see Section 11).

9   On 2WD Tacoma models, support the lower control arm with a floor jack.

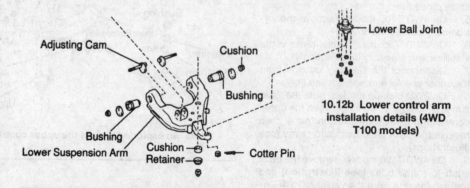

10.12b Lower control arm installation details (4WD T100 models)

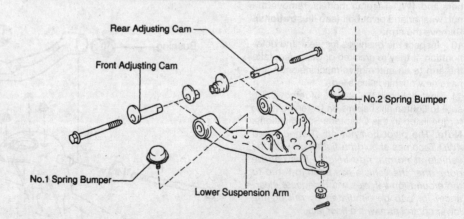

10.12c Lower control arm installation details (4Runner and 4WD Tacoma models)

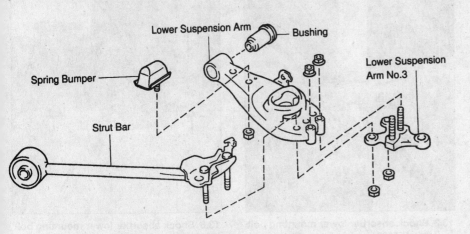

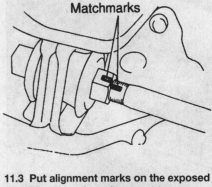

11.3 Put alignment marks on the exposed strut bar threads and rear nut to ensure that correct toe is restored when the strut bar is installed

10.13 Lower control arm and strut bar installation details (2WD Tacoma models)

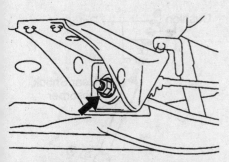

11.4 To detach the front end of the strut bar from the frame, remove this nut (arrow), and remove the washer, retainer and rubber bushing from the front end of the strut bar

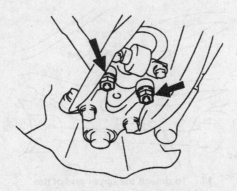

11.5 To detach the strut bar from the lower control arm, remove these two nuts (arrows)

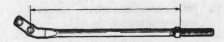

11.8 If you're installing a new strut bar, be sure to set its length to the dimension listed in this Chapter's Specifications by turning the rear nut

8   Installation is the reverse of removal. Make sure you install the retainers, rubber bushings and metal bushing in the correct order (see illustration 10.11). If you're using a new strut bar, be sure set the length to the dimension listed in this Chapter's Specifications by turning the rear nut (see illustration).

Tacoma models

9   Remove the lower control arm and strut bar as an assembly (see Section 10).
10   Unbolt the strut bar from the lower control arm (see illustration 10.13).
11   Installation is the reverse of removal. Be sure to tighten the strut bar fasteners to the torque listed in this Chapter's Specifications.

12   Front coil spring (Tacoma 2WD models) - removal and installation

1   Remove the lower control arm (see Section 10).
2   Remove the compressed coil spring. If you are going to replace the spring, slowly loosen the spring compressor tool until the spring is fully extended. Install the tool on the new spring and compress it sufficiently to allow lower control arm installation.
3   Installation is the reverse of removal. Be sure to tighten all suspension fasteners to the torque listed in this Chapter's Specifications.

13   On 2WD Tacoma models, loosen the lower control arm pivot bolt and nut (see illustration), loosen the forward end of the strut bar from the frame, remove both bolts and remove the lower control arm and strut bar as an assembly. Guide the compressed coil spring out as this is done.
15   If you're replacing the lower arm on a 2WD Tacoma model, remove the strut bar (see Section 11) and lower suspension arm No. 3 (see illustration 10.13) and install them on the new arm. Be sure to tighten the strut-to-lower control arm nuts and the lower suspension arm No. 3 retaining nuts to the torque listed in this Chapter's Specifications.
16   Installation is the reverse of removal. On those models which have adjusting cams, make sure that the alignment marks you made prior to disassembly are lined up. Be sure to tighten all suspension fasteners to the torque listed in this Chapter's Specifications.
Note: *The pivot bolts/nuts should be tightened with the vehicle at normal ride height. This can be done after the vehicle has been lowered to the ground (on vehicles with adequate clearance), or can be simulated by raising the lower control arm with a floor jack.*

11   Strut bar (2WD pick-up models) - removal and installation

T100 models

Refer to illustrations 11.3, 11.4, 11.5 and 11.8
1   Loosen the wheel lug nuts, raise the front of the vehicle and support it securely on jackstands. Apply the parking brake. Remove the wheel.
2   Remove the engine under cover.
3   Put alignment marks on the strut bar and rear nut (see illustration).
4   Remove the nut, washer, retainer and rubber bushing from the front end of the strut bar (see illustration).
5   Remove the two nuts that attach the rear end of the strut bar to the lower control arm (see illustration) and disconnect the strut bar from the lower control arm.
6   Remove the collar (metal bushing) and the other rubber bushing and retainer from the strut bar.
7   Inspect the metal bushing, the washers and the rubber bushings for wear and damage and replace as necessary.

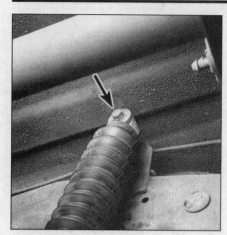

13.2 Shock absorber upper mounting bolt (arrow) (T100 model shown, Tacoma models similar)

13.3 Shock absorber lower mounting bolt (arrow) (T100 model shown, Tacoma models similar)

13.6 Shock absorber lower mounting bolt (right arrow); stabilizer bar bracket bolts (left arrows) (4Runner)

13 Rear shock absorber - removal and installation

1   Loosen the rear wheel lug nuts. Raise the rear of the vehicle and support securely on jackstands. Block the front wheels so the vehicle doesn't roll off the stands. Remove the rear wheels.

Pick-up models

Refer to illustrations 13.2 and 13.3
2   Support the rear axle with a floor jack. Remove the shock absorber upper mounting bolt from the frame **(see illustration)**.
3   Remove the lower mounting bolt from the spring seat **(see illustration)**. Remove the shock absorber.
4   Installation is the reverse of removal. Tighten the mounting bolts to the torque listed in this Chapter's Specifications.

4Runner models

Refer to illustrations 13.6, 13.7 and 13.8
5   Support the rear axle with a floor jack.
6   Disconnect the lower end of the shock absorber from the axle **(see illustration)**.
7   To disconnect the upper end of the shock from the frame, remove the upper mounting nut **(see illustration)**. There's not a lot of room to turn a wrench or socket up top, so hold the nut and turn the shock instead. Remove the shock absorber.
8   Installation is the reverse of removal. Be sure to install the cushions and retainers in the correct sequence up top **(see illustration)** and tighten the upper nut and lower bolt to the torque listed in this Chapter's Specifications.

14 Leaf spring/shackle (pick-up models) - removal and installation

Refer to illustrations 14.2, 14.3, 14.4 and 14.5
1   Raise the rear of the vehicle and support

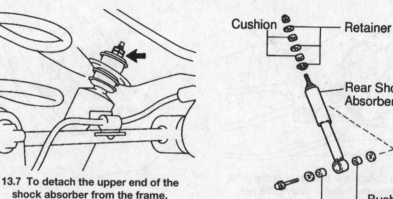

13.7 To detach the upper end of the shock absorber from the frame, remove this nut

it securely on jackstands. Block the front wheels to keep the vehicle from rolling off the stands. Support the axle with a floor jack and raise it just enough to take the weight and relieve the tension on the leaf springs.
2   Remove the four U-bolt nuts and washers **(see illustration)**.
3   Remove the spring seat, U-bolts **(see illustration)**.
4   Remove the nut from the hanger pin bolt **(see illustration)**.
5   Remove the shackle pin nuts, washers and shackle pin **(see illustration)**. Lower the rear of the spring to the ground.
6   Remove the hanger pin bolt, then remove the spring assembly from the vehicle.
7   If the bushings at the ends of the spring are worn or deteriorated, an automotive machine shop or dealer service department can press the old ones out and press new ones in.
8   Installation is the reverse of removal. Gradually tighten the U-bolt nuts in a criss-cross pattern, to the torque listed in this Chapter's Specifications. The hanger pin and shackle pin bolts/nuts should also be tightened to the torque listed in this Chapter's Specifications, but this should be done with the vehicle resting at normal ride height.

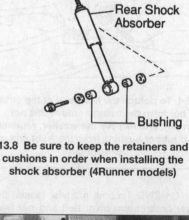

13.8 Be sure to keep the retainers and cushions in order when installing the shock absorber (4Runner models)

14.2 To detach the spring from the axle, remove the four U-bolt nuts (arrows) and washers

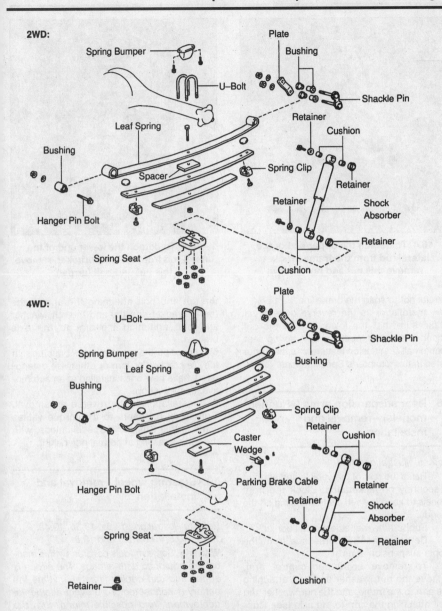

14.3 An exploded view of typical rear leaf spring assemblies

14.4 To detach the front end of the spring from the frame, remove the nut (arrow) from the hanger pin bolt

15 Rear stabilizer bar (4Runner models) - removal and installation

Refer to illustration 15.2

1   Raise the rear of the vehicle and support it securely on jackstands. Block the front wheels to keep the vehicle from rolling off the stands.

2   Remove the stabilizer bar link nuts and remove both links **(see illustration)**.

3   Detach the bushing bracket bolts **(see illustration 13.6)**.

4   Remove the stabilizer bar.

5   Inspect the stabilizer bar bushings and link cushions for cracks, tears and other deterioration. Replace as necessary.

6   Installation is the reverse of removal. Be sure to tighten all fasteners to the torque listed in this Chapter's Specifications.

14.5 To detach the rear end of the spring from the frame, remove the shackle pin nuts (arrows) and pull out the shackle pin

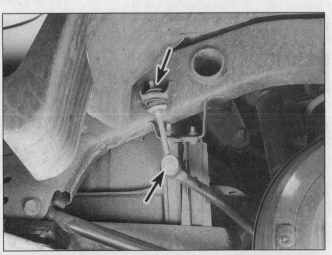

15.2 To remove the stabilizer bar link, remove the upper and lower nuts (arrows) (4Runner models)

16 Lateral rod (4Runner models) - removal and installation

Refer to illustrations 16.4 and 16.5

1   Raise the rear of the vehicle and support it securely on jackstands. Block the front wheels to keep the vehicle from rolling off the stands.

2   Support the rear axle with a floor jack.

3   Disconnect the load sensing proportioning and bypass valve (LSP & BV) from the axle (see Chapter 9).

4   Disconnect the upper end of the lateral rod from the frame bracket **(see illustration)**.

5   Disconnect the lower end of the lateral rod from the axle bracket **(see illustration)**.

6   Remove the lateral rod.

7   Installation is the reverse of removal. Be sure to tighten both nuts to the torque listed in this Chapter's Specifications (the vehicle should be at normal ride height when the bolts are tightened).

17 Rear coil spring (4Runner models) - removal and installation

1   Raise the rear of the vehicle and support it securely on jackstands. Block the front wheels to keep the vehicle from rolling off the stands.

2   Support the rear axle with a floor jack.

3   Run a chain through the coil spring and bolt its ends together to prevent the spring from flying out accidentally as the rear axle is lowered. Make sure there is enough slack in the chain to allow the spring to extend fully.

4   Disconnect the shock absorbers from the axle (see Section 13).

5   Disconnect the stabilizer bar bushing brackets from the axle (see Section 15).

6   Disconnect the lateral rod from the axle (see Section 16).

7   Slowly lower the rear axle housing just far enough to remove the coil spring. Be

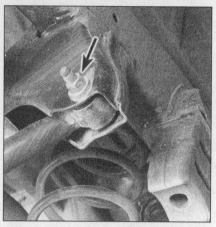

16.4 To detach the upper end of the lateral rod from the frame bracket, remove this nut and bolt (arrow)

16.5 To detach the lower end of the lateral rod from the axle bracket, remove this nut and bolt (arrow)

careful not to snag the brake line.

8   Installation is the reverse of removal. Make sure that the lower end of the coil spring is seated properly on the spring seat. Tighten all suspension fasteners to the torque listed in this Chapter's Specifications.

18 Rear suspension arms (4Runner models) - removal and installation

Refer to illustrations 18.4

1   Raise the rear of the vehicle and support it securely on jackstands. Block the front wheels to keep the vehicle from rolling off the stands.

2   Support the rear axle with a floor jack.

3   Detach the ABS harnesses from the upper suspension arms.

4   To remove an upper control arm, remove the nut, washer and bolt attaching the arm to the frame, and the nut, washer and bolt attaching the arm to the axle **(see illustration)**.

5   To remove a lower control arm, remove

the nut and bolt attaching the arm to the frame bracket and the and the nut, washer and bolt attaching the arm to the axle bracket.

6   Inspect the control arm bushings. If they're cracked or torn or otherwise deteriorated, have new ones installed at an automotive machine shop.

7   Installation is the reverse of removal. Tighten all fasteners to the torque values listed in this Chapter's Specifications, with the vehicle resting at normal ride height.

19 Steering wheel - removal and installation

Refer to illustrations 19.3a, 19.3b, 19.4a, 19.4b, 19.5, 19.6, 19.7 and 19.8

Warning: *Some models covered by this manual are equipped with airbags. The airbag is armed and can deploy (inflate) anytime the battery is connected. To prevent accidental deployment (and possible injury), turn the ignition key to LOCK and disconnect the negative battery cable whenever working near*

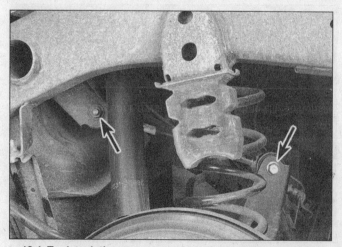

18.4 To detach the upper control arm from the frame and the axle, remove these nuts and bolts (arrows)

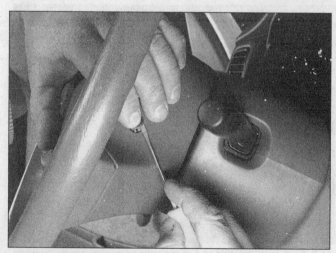

19.3a Pry off these covers on the sides of the steering wheel . . .

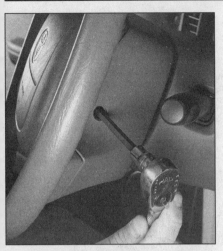

19.3b . . . and, using a Torx bit of the correct size, loosen the Torx screws that retain the airbag module; back off the screws until the grooves in their circumference catch on the screw cases (when you feel the screws "catch," don't force them beyond that point)

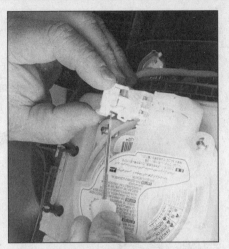

19.4a To unplug the airbag connector, flip up the locking cap . . .

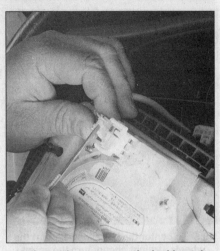

19.4b . . . then pry open the locking tab and pull out the connector

airbag components. After the battery is disconnected, wait at least two minutes before beginning work (the system has a back-up capacitor that must fully discharge). For more information see Chapter 12.

1   Park the vehicle with the front wheels pointed straight ahead and the steering wheel centered. Disconnect both cables from the battery (see Chapter 5). **Caution:** *If the stereo in your vehicle is equipped with an anti-theft system, make sure you have the correct activation code before disconnecting the battery.*

2   On airbag-equipped models, refer to Chapter 12 and disable the airbag system.

3   Pry out the two small covers, one on each side of the steering wheel, and loosen the two Torx screws that retain the airbag module **(see illustrations)**. Back out the screws until the grooves along the screw cir-

cumferences catch on the screw cases.

4   Lift the airbag module off the steering wheel and disconnect the airbag connector **(see illustrations)**. **Warning:** *When handling the airbag module, hold it with the trim side facing away from you. Set the airbag module down in a safe location with the trim side facing up.*

5   Unplug any other electrical connectors, such as the one for the horn **(see illustration)**.

6   Remove the steering wheel retaining nut and mark the position of the steering wheel to the shaft, if marks don't already exist or don't line up **(see illustration)**.

7   Use a puller to detach the steering wheel from the shaft **(see illustration)**. Don't hammer on the shaft to dislodge the wheel. **Warning:** *While the steering wheel is removed, do NOT turn the steering shaft. If the steering shaft is turned, the spiral cable will be un-centered and the harness will break, rendering the airbag inoperative. If the spiral cable is accidentally un-centered, it must be centered before installing the steering wheel.*

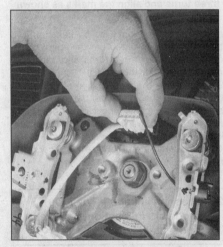

19.5 Unplug any other electrical connectors that would interfere with steering wheel removal

8   Make sure the spiral cable is centered, as follows: Verify that the front wheels are pointing straight ahead. Turn the spiral cable

19.6 Remove the steering wheel nut, then mark the relationship of the steering wheel to the steering shaft

19.7 Use a steering wheel puller to remove the steering wheel

19.8 To center the spiral cable, point the wheels straight ahead, turn the spiral cable housing counterclockwise until it's hard to turn, then turn it clockwise about three turns and align the marks as shown

housing counterclockwise by hand until it becomes hard to turn. Turn the spiral cable clockwise about three turns and align the marks **(see illustration)**.

9   To install the wheel, align the mark on the steering wheel hub with the mark on the shaft and slide the wheel onto the shaft. Install the nut and tighten it to the torque listed in this Chapter's Specifications.

10   Installation is otherwise the reverse of removal.

20   Steering linkage (4WD T100 models) - inspection, removal and installation

Inspection

Refer to illustration 20.1

1   The steering linkage **(see illustration)** connects the steering gear to the front wheels and keeps the wheels in proper relation to each other. The linkage consists of the Pitman arm, the idler arm, the relay rod, two adjustable tie-rods and a steering damper. The Pitman arm, which is fastened to the steering gear shaft, moves the relay rod back-and-forth. The relay rod is supported on the other end by a frame-mounted idler arm. The back-and-forth motion of the relay rod is transmitted to the steering knuckles through a pair of tie-rod assemblies. Each tie-rod is made up of an inner and outer tie-rod end, a threaded adjuster tube and two clamps.

2   Set the wheels in the straight-ahead position and lock the steering wheel.

3   Raise one side of the vehicle until the tire is approximately one inch off the ground.

4   Mount a dial indicator with the needle resting on the front outside edge of the wheel. Grasp the front and rear of the tire and, using light pressure, wiggle the wheel back-and-forth and note the dial indicator reading. The gauge reading should be less

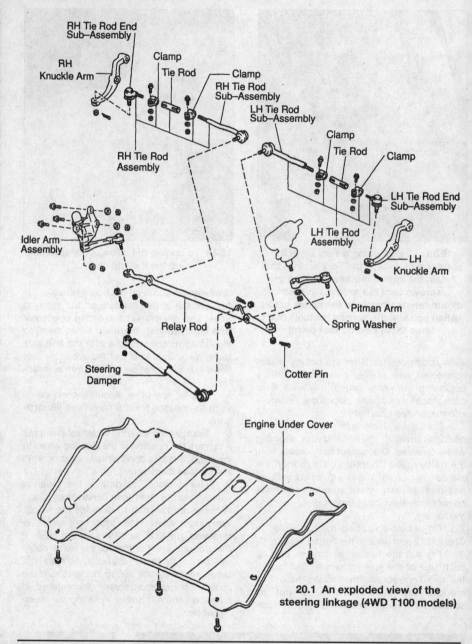

20.1 An exploded view of the steering linkage (4WD T100 models)

than 0.108-inch. If the play in the steering system is more than specified, inspect each steering linkage pivot point and ballstud for looseness and replace parts, if necessary.

5   Raise the vehicle and support it on jackstands. Push up, then pull down on the relay rod end of the idler arm, exerting a force of approximately 25 pounds each way. Measure the total distance the end of the arm travels. If the play is greater than 3/16-inch, replace the idler arm.

6   Check for torn ballstud boots, frozen joints and bent or damaged linkage components.

Removal and installation

Tie-rod

Note: *This procedure covers replacing the tie-rod ends as well as the entire tie-rod. If*

you'll only be replacing a tie-rod end, ignore the steps that don't apply.

7   Loosen the wheel lug nuts, raise the vehicle and support it securely on jackstands. Apply the parking brake. Remove the wheel.

8   Remove the cotter pin and loosen, but do not remove, the castellated nut(s) from the ballstud(s). If only the outer tie-rod end will be replaced, only loosen the outer nut. If only the inner tie-rod end will be replaced, only loosen the inner nut. If the entire tie-rod will be replaced, loosen both nuts.

9   If the outer tie-rod end or the entire tie-rod will be replaced, use a two-jaw puller to separate the tie-rod end from the steering knuckle. Remove the castellated nut and pull the tie-rod end from the knuckle.

10   If the inner tie-rod end or the entire tie-rod will be replaced, separate the inner tie-rod

21.2a Loosen the tie-rod end locknut . . .

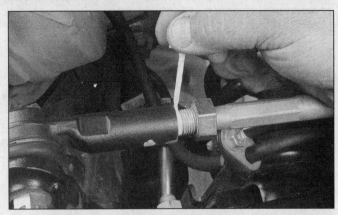

21.2b . . . and mark the position of the tie-rod end on the threaded portion of the tie-rod

end from the relay rod (see Steps 8 and 9).

11   If the inner or outer tie-rod end must be replaced, measure the distance from the end of the adjuster tube to the center of the ball-stud and record it. Loosen the adjuster tube clamp bolts and unscrew the tie-rod end.

12   Lubricate the threaded portion of the tie-rod end with chassis grease. Screw the new tie-rod end into the adjuster tube and adjust the distance from the tube to the ballstud to the previously measured dimension. The number of threads showing on the inner and outer tie-rod ends should be equal within three threads. Don't tighten the clamp yet.

13   Connect the disconnected ballstud nut(s). Tighten the nut(s) to the torque listed in this Chapter's Specifications and install a new cotter pin. If the ballstud spins when attempting to tighten the nut, force it into the tapered hole with a large pair of pliers. If necessary, tighten the nut slightly to align a slot in the nut with the hole in the ballstud.

14   Insert the inner tie-rod end ballstud into the relay rod until it's seated. Install the nut and tighten it to the torque listed in this Chapter's Specifications.

15   Tighten the clamp nuts. The center of the bolt should be nearly horizontal and the adjuster tube slot must not line up with the gap in the clamps.

16   Install the wheel and lug nuts, lower the vehicle and tighten the lug nuts to the torque listed in the Chapter 1 Specifications. Have the front end alignment checked and, if necessary, adjusted.

Idler arm

17   Raise the vehicle and support it securely on jackstands. Apply the parking brake.

18   Loosen but do not remove the idler arm-to-relay rod nut.

19   Separate the idler arm from the relay rod with a two jaw puller. Remove the nut.

20   Remove the idler arm-to-frame bolts.

21   To install the idler arm, position it on the frame and install the bolts, tightening them to the torque listed in this Chapter's Specifications.

22   Insert the idler arm ballstud into the relay rod and install the nut. Tighten the nut to the specified torque. If the ballstud spins when

attempting to tighten the nut, force it into the tapered hole with a large pair of pliers.

Relay rod

23   Raise the vehicle and support it securely on jackstands. Apply the parking brake.

24   Separate the two inner tie-rod ends from the relay rod.

25   Separate the relay rod from the Pitman arm (see Steps 29 and 30).

26   Separate the relay rod from the idler arm (see Steps 18 and 19).

27   Installation is the reverse of the removal procedure. If the ballstuds spin when attempting to tighten the nuts, force them into the tapered holes with a large pair of pliers. Be sure to tighten all of the nuts to the torque listed in this Chapter's Specifications.

Pitman arm

28   Raise the vehicle and support it securely on jackstands.

29   Loosen the relay rod nut from the Pitman arm ballstud.

30   Using a puller, separate the relay rod from the Pitman arm ballstud. Remove and discard the nut - don't reuse it.

31   Remove the Pitman arm nut and washer. Mark the Pitman arm and the steering gear shaft to ensure proper alignment at reassembly time.

32   Remove the Pitman arm with a Pitman arm puller or a two-jaw puller.

33   Check the splines on the Pitman arm for damage. Also check the hole for the relay rod ballstud for elongation. If either of these conditions exist, replace the Pitman arm.

34   Installation is the reverse of removal. Make sure the marks you made on the Pitman arm and Pitman shaft are aligned.

Steering damper

35   Inspect the steering damper for fluid leakage. A slight film of fluid near the shaft seal is normal, but if there's excessive fluid present and it's obviously coming from the steering damper, replace the damper.

36   Inspect the steering damper bushing for excessive wear. If it's in bad shape, replace the damper.

37   To test the damper itself, disconnect it

from the frame or axle end (see next step). Using as much travel as possible, extend and compress the damper. The resistance should be smooth and constant for each stroke. If any binding or unusual noises are present, replace the damper.

38   Remove the damper ballstud-to-relay rod cotter pin, then remove the nut. Separate the damper from the relay rod.

39   Remove the steering damper mounting bolt and nut, then remove the damper.

40   Installation is the reverse of removal. Tighten all the fasteners securely.

---

21   Tie-rod ends - removal and installation

Refer to illustrations 21.2a, 21.2b, 21.3a and 21.3b

1   Loosen the wheel lug nuts, raise the vehicle and place it securely on jackstands. Remove the wheel.

2   Loosen the tie-rod end locknut and mark the position of the tie-rod end on the threaded portion of the tie-rod **(see illustrations)**.

3   Remove the cotter pin and loosen the castle nut from the tie-rod end balljoint stud, then install a puller and separate the tie-rod

21.3a Remove the cotter pin . . .

21.3b ... loosen (don't remove) the castle nut from the tie-rod end balljoint stud, then install a puller and separate the tie-rod end from the steering knuckle

22.4 The outer clamp on the steering gear boot can be removed with a pair of pliers - the inner clamp must be cut off

end from the steering knuckle **(see illustrations)**. Remove the nut and detach the tie-rod end from the steering knuckle arm.

4   Unscrew the old tie-rod end and install the new one. Make sure the new tie-rod end is aligned with the mark you made on the threads of the tie-rod.

5   Installation is the reverse of removal. Be sure to tighten the tie-rod end balljoint nut to the torque listed in this Chapter's Specifications. Tighten the locknut securely.

22   Steering gear boots - replacement

Refer to illustration 22.4

1   If a steering gear boot is torn, dirt and moisture can damage the steering gear. Replace it.

2   Loosen the wheel lug nuts, raise the vehicle and place it securely on jackstands. Remove the front wheels.

3   Remove the tie-rod end and locknut (see Section 21).

4   Remove the boot clamps **(see illustra-**

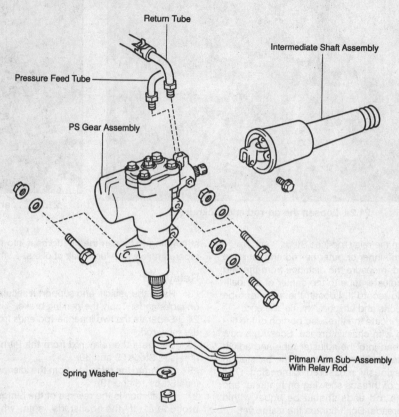

23.2 Installation details of the steering gear (4WD T100 models)

tion) and slide the boot off the tie-rod.

5   Installation is the reverse of removal. Be sure to use new clamps on the boot.

23   Steering gear - removal and installation

Warning: *On models equipped with an airbag, DO NOT allow the steering column shaft to rotate with the steering gear removed or damage to the airbag system could occur. As a method of preventing the shaft from turning, wrap the seat belt around the rim of the steering wheel and buckle the belt in place.*

1   Point the wheels straight ahead. Raise the front of the vehicle and support it securely on jackstands. Apply the parking brake.

4WD T100 models

Refer to illustrations 23.2 and 23.5

2   Place a drain pan under the steering gear. Disconnect the power steering hose fittings **(see illustration)** and cap the ends to prevent excessive fluid loss and contamination.

3   Insert a screwdriver between the two halves of the U-joint plastic shield and pry them apart, then pull out the shield. Mark the relationship of the intermediate shaft lower

universal joint to the steering gear input shaft. Remove the intermediate shaft lower pinch bolt.

4   Disconnect the Pitman arm from the relay rod (see Section 20).

5   Support the steering gear and remove the mounting nuts/bolts **(see illustration)**. Lower the unit, separate the intermediate shaft from the steering gear input shaft and remove the steering gear from the vehicle.

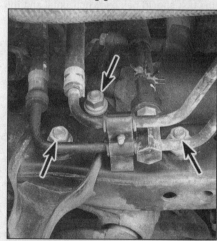

23.5 To detach the steering gear from the frame on a 4WD T100 model, remove these three nuts (arrows) from the left frame rail

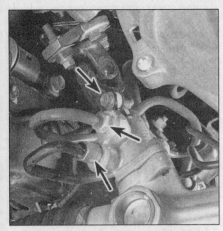

23.17 Mark the relationship of the intermediate shaft U-joint coupler to the steering gear (in the vicinity of the arrows), remove the coupler pinch bolt and unscrew the fittings (arrows) for the pressure and return lines

6   Mark the relationship of the Pitman arm to the shaft so it can be installed in the same position. Remove the Pitman arm nut and washer. Remove the Pitman arm from the shaft with a puller.
7   Slide the Pitman arm onto the shaft. Make sure the marks are aligned. Install the washer and nut and tighten the nut to the torque listed in this Chapter's Specifications.
8   If the steering shaft is accidentally turned while the steering gear is removed, remove the steering wheel and center the spiral cable (see Section 19).
9   Raise the steering gear into position and connect the intermediate shaft, aligning the marks.
10   Install the mounting bolts, washers and nuts and tighten them to the torque listed in this Chapter's Specifications.
11   Install the intermediate shaft pinch bolt and tighten it to the torque listed in this Chapter's Specifications. Install the plastic shield.
12   Connect the power steering hose fittings to the steering gear and fill the power steer-

ing pump reservoir with the recommended fluid (see Chapter 1).
13   Lower the vehicle and bleed the steering system (see Section 20).

Tacoma, 4Runner and 2WD T100 models

Refer to illustrations 23.17, 23.19a, 23.19b and 23.19c

14   Disconnect the left and right tie-rod ends from the steering knuckles (see Section 21).
15   On 4Runner and 4WD Tacoma models,

remove the engine under cover. There are ten bolts on 4Runner under covers and four bolts on Tacoma under covers.
16   On 4Runner models, remove the stabilizer bar (see Section 4).
17   Mark the relationship of the intermediate shaft to the steering gear **(see illustration)** and remove the U-joint coupler pinch bolt.
18   Disconnect the pressure and return lines from the steering gear.
19   To detach the steering gear on 2WD T100 models, remove the two mounting bracket bolts on the right end of the steering gear and the single nut and through-bolt at

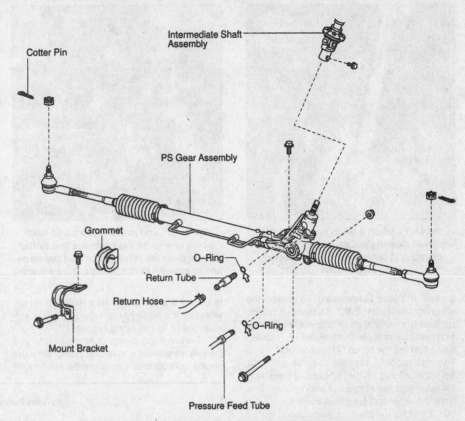

23.19a Installation details of the steering gear (2WD T100 models)

Labels: Cotter Pin, Intermediate Shaft Assembly, PS Gear Assembly, Grommet, Return Tube, O–Ring, Return Hose, O–Ring, Mount Bracket, Pressure Feed Tube

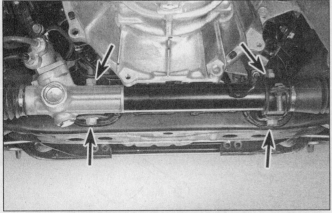

23.19b To detach the steering gear from the frame on 2WD Tacoma models, remove the two vertical mounting bolts and nuts

23.19c To detach the steering gear from the frame on 4Runner and 4WD Tacoma models, remove the single through-bolt and nut (arrow) on the left and the nut, bolt (arrows) and bracket on the right

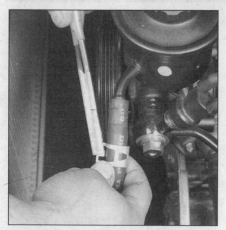

24.4a Position a drain pan under the power steering pump, loosen the hose clamp and detach the power steering fluid return hose . . .

24.4b . . . and remove the banjo bolt which connects the pressure line to the pump; plug the return hose and pressure line to prevent contaminants from entering

24.5 Jam an extension or other tool through one of the pulley holes and wedge it against the pump bracket to immobilize the pulley, then remove the nut and take off the pulley

the left end **(see illustration)**. To detach the steering gear on 2WD Tacoma models, remove the vertical mounting nuts and bolts from each end **(see illustration)**. To detach the steering gear on 4Runner and 4WD Tacoma models, remove the nut and bolt from the bracket on the right end of the steering gear and the single nut and through-bolt from the other end **(see illustration)**.

20   Remove the steering gear assembly.

21   If the steering shaft is accidentally turned while the steering gear is removed, remove the steering wheel and center the spiral cable (see Section 19).

22   Installation is the reverse of removal. Tighten all steering gear fasteners to the torque listed in this Chapter's Specifications.

23   Bleed the power steering system when you're done (see Section 25).

24 Power steering pump - removal and installation

Refer to illustrations 24.4a, 24.4b, 24.5, 24.6a and 24.6b

1   Disconnect the cable from the negative terminal of the battery. **Caution:** *On models equipped with an anti-theft audio system, be sure the lockout feature is turned off before performing any procedure which requires disconnecting the battery.*

2   On T100 and Tacoma models with a V6 engine, remove the air cleaner assembly (see Chapter 4).

3   Remove the serpentine drivebelt (see Chapter 1).

4   Position a drain pan under the power steering pump. Disconnect the pressure and return hoses from the backside of the pump **(see illustrations)**. Plug the hoses to prevent contaminants from entering.

5   If you're replacing the power steering pump, remove the pulley **(see illustration)**. (You can also remove the pulley after removing the pump from the engine, but you'll have

to secure the pump in a bench vise to do so, whereas it's already immobilized while still attached to its mounting bracket.)

6   Remove the pump mounting fasteners **(see illustrations)** and lift the pump from the engine compartment, taking care not to spill

fluid on the painted surfaces.

7   Installation is the reverse of removal. Tighten the pulley nut to the torque listed in this Chapter's Specifications and tighten the pump mounting bolts and nuts securely.

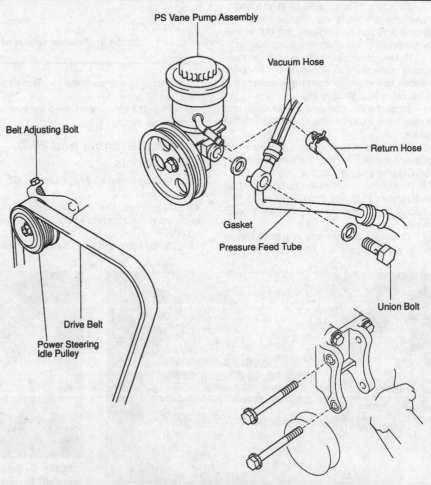

24.6a Power steering pump installation details (typical four-cylinder engine)

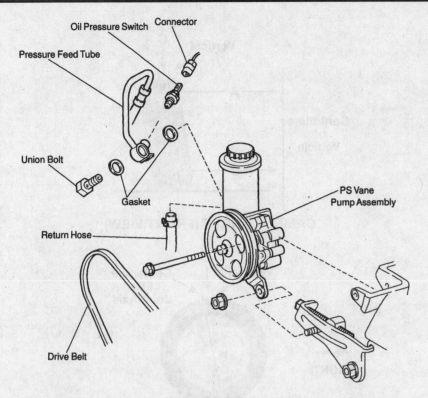

24.6b Power steering pump installation details (typical V6 engine)

Oil Pressure Switch *Connector*
Pressure Feed Tube
Union Bolt
Gasket
Return Hose
Drive Belt
PS Vane Pump Assembly

26 Wheels and tires - general information

Refer to illustration 26.1

All vehicles covered by this manual are equipped with metric-size fiberglass or steel belted radial tires **(see illustration)**. Use of other size or type of tires may affect the ride and handling of the vehicle. Don't mix different types of tires, such as radials and bias belted, on the same vehicle as handling may be seriously affected. It's recommended that tires be replaced in pairs on the same axle, but if only one tire is being replaced, be sure it's the same size, structure and tread design as the other.

Because tire pressure has a substantial effect on handling and wear, the pressure on all tires should be checked at least once a month or before any extended trips (see Chapter 1).

Wheels must be replaced if they're bent, dented, leak air, have elongated bolt holes, are heavily rusted, out of vertical symmetry or if the lug nuts won't stay tight. Wheel repairs that use welding or peening are not recommended.

Tire and wheel balance is important to the overall handling, braking and perfor-

8   Fill the power steering reservoir with the recommended fluid (see Chapter 1) and bleed the system following the procedure described in the next Section.

25 Power steering system - bleeding

1   Following any operation in which the power steering fluid lines have been disconnected, the power steering system must be bled to remove all air and obtain proper steering performance.
2   With the front wheels in the straight ahead position, check the power steering fluid level and, if low, add fluid until it reaches the Cold mark on the dipstick.
3   Start the engine and allow it to run at fast idle. Recheck the fluid level and add more if necessary to reach the Cold mark on the dipstick.
4   Bleed the system by turning the wheels from side-to-side, without hitting the stops. This will work the air out of the system. Keep the reservoir full of fluid as this is done.
5   When the air is worked out of the system, return the wheels to the straight ahead position and leave the vehicle running for several more minutes before shutting it off.
6   Road test the vehicle to be sure the steering system is functioning normally and noise free.
7   Recheck the fluid level to be sure it's up to the Hot mark on the dipstick while the engine is at normal operating temperature. Add fluid if necessary (see Chapter 1).

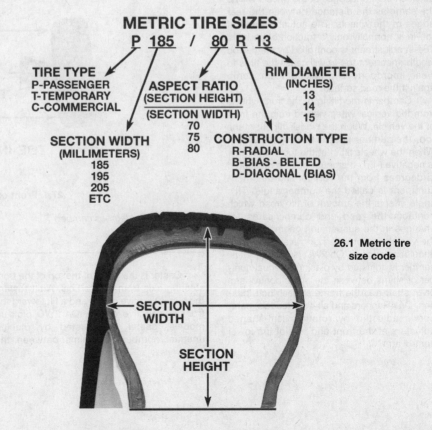

METRIC TIRE SIZES
P 185 / 80 R 13

TIRE TYPE
P-PASSENGER
T-TEMPORARY
C-COMMERCIAL

**ASPECT RATIO
(SECTION HEIGHT)
(SECTION WIDTH)**
70
75
80

**RIM DIAMETER
(INCHES)**
13
14
15

**SECTION WIDTH
(MILLIMETERS)**
185
195
205
ETC

CONSTRUCTION TYPE
R-RADIAL
B-BIAS - BELTED
D-DIAGONAL (BIAS)

26.1 Metric tire size code

SECTION WIDTH

SECTION HEIGHT

mance of the vehicle. Unbalanced wheels can adversely affect handling and ride characteristics as well as tire life. Whenever a tire is installed on a wheel, the tire and wheel should be balanced by a shop with the proper equipment.

27 Front end alignment - general information

Refer to illustration 27.1

A front end alignment refers to the adjustments made to the front wheels so they're in proper angular relationship to the suspension and the ground. Front wheels that are out of proper alignment not only affect steering control, but also increase tire wear.

Getting the proper front wheel alignment is a very exacting process, one in which complicated and expensive machines are necessary to perform the job properly. Because of this, you should have a technician with the proper equipment perform these tasks. We will, however, use this space to give you a basic idea of what is involved with front end alignment so you can better understand the process and deal intelligently with the shop that does the work.

Toe-in is the turning in of the front wheels. The purpose of a toe specification is to ensure parallel rolling of the front wheels. In a vehicle with zero toe-in, the distance between the front edges of the wheels will be the same as the distance between the rear edges of the wheels. The actual amount of toe-in is normally only a fraction of an inch. Toe-in adjustment is controlled by the tie-rod length. Incorrect toe-in will cause the tires to wear improperly by making them scrub against the road surface.

Camber is the tilting of the front wheels from the vertical when viewed from the front of the vehicle. When the wheels tilt out at the top, the camber is said to be positive (+). When the wheels tilt in at the top the camber is negative (-). The amount of tilt is measured in degrees from the vertical and this measurement is called the camber angle. This angle affects the amount of tire tread which contacts the road and compensates for changes in the suspension geometry when the vehicle is cornering or traveling over an undulating surface. On 2WD pick-up models, camber is adjusted by placing an equal number of shims between the upper control arm pivot shaft and the frame at each bolt location. On 4Runners and all 4WD models, camber is adjusted by rotating cam-shaped adjusters at the front and rear of the lower control arm.

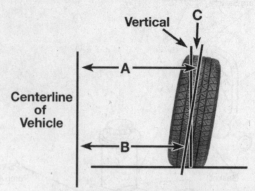

CAMBER ANGLE (FRONT VIEW)

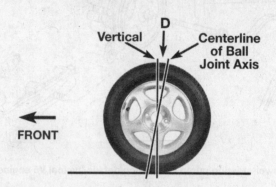

CASTER ANGLE (SIDE VIEW)

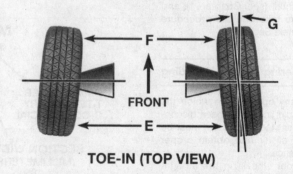

TOE-IN (TOP VIEW)

27.1 Front end alignment details

A minus B = C (degrees camber)
D = degrees caster

E minus F = toe-in (measured in inches)
G = toe-in (expressed in degrees)

Caster is the tilting of the top of the front steering axis from the vertical. A tilt toward the rear is positive caster and a tilt toward the front is negative caster. On 2WD pick-up models, caster is adjusted by placing unequal numbers of shims between the upper control arm pivot shaft and the frame at each bolt location. On 4Runners and all 4WD models, caster is adjusted by rotating cam-shaped adjusters at the front and rear of the lower control arm.

Chapter 11   Body

Contents

1   General information

Warning: *Some models covered by this manual are equipped with airbags. The airbag is armed and can deploy (inflate) anytime the battery is connected. To prevent accidental deployment (and possible injury), turn the ignition key to LOCK and disconnect the negative battery cable whenever working near airbag components. After the battery is disconnected, wait at least two minutes before beginning work (the system has a back-up capacitor that must fully discharge). For more information see Chapter 12.*
Caution: *On models equipped with an anti-theft audio system, be sure the lockout feature is turned off before performing any procedure which requires disconnecting the battery.*

The vehicles covered by this manual are

built with a body-on-frame construction. The frame is a ladder type, consisting of two box steel side rails joined by crossmembers. These crossmembers are welded or riveted to the side rails, with exception of some transmission crossmembers which are bolted into place for easy removal. The vehicle body is secured to the chassis by rubber insulated mounts and can be completely removed from the chassis.

Certain components are particularly vulnerable to accident damage and can be unbolted and repaired or replaced. Among these parts are the doors, seats, tailgate, tailgate glass, bumpers, front fenders and door glass.

Only general body maintenance practices and body panel repair procedures within the scope of the do-it-yourselfer are included in this Chapter.

2   Body - maintenance

1   The condition of your vehicle's body is very important, because the resale value depends a great deal on it. It's much more difficult to repair a neglected or damaged body than it is to repair mechanical components. The hidden areas of the body, such as the wheel wells, the frame and the engine compartment, are equally important, although they don't require as frequent attention as the rest of the body.
2   Once a year, or every 12,000 miles, it's a good idea to have the underside of the body steam cleaned. All traces of dirt and oil will be removed and the area can then be inspected carefully for rust, damaged brake lines, frayed electrical wires, damaged cables and other problems. The front suspension components should be greased after completion

These photos illustrate a method of repairing simple dents. They are intended to supplement *Body repair - minor damage* in this Chapter and should not be used as the sole instructions for body repair on these vehicles.

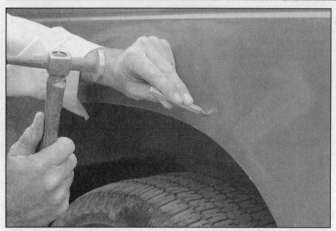

1   If you can't access the backside of the body panel to hammer out the dent, pull it out with a slide-hammer-type dent puller. In the deepest portion of the dent or along the crease line, drill or punch hole(s) at least one inch apart . . .

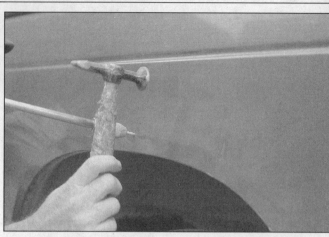

2   . . . then screw the slide-hammer into the hole and operate it. Tap with a hammer near the edge of the dent to help 'pop' the metal back to its original shape. When you're finished, the dent area should be close to its original contour and about 1/8-inch below the surface of the surrounding metal

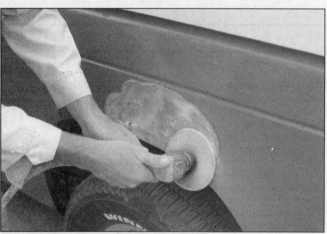

3   Using coarse-grit sandpaper, remove the paint down to the bare metal. Hand sanding works fine, but the disc sander shown here makes the job faster. Use finer (about 320-grit) sandpaper to feather-edge the paint at least one inch around the dent area

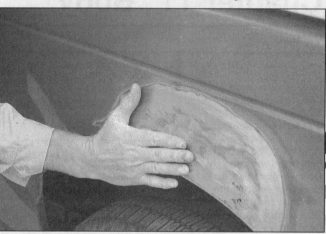

4   When the paint is removed, touch will probably be more helpful than sight for telling if the metal is straight. Hammer down the high spots or raise the low spots as necessary. Clean the repair area with wax/silicone remover

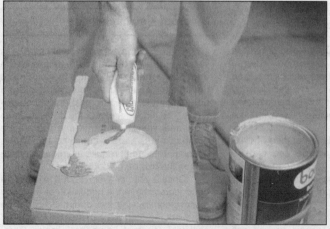

5   Following label instructions, mix up a batch of plastic filler and hardener. The ratio of filler to hardener is critical, and, if you mix it incorrectly, it will either not cure properly or cure too quickly (you won't have time to file and sand it into shape)

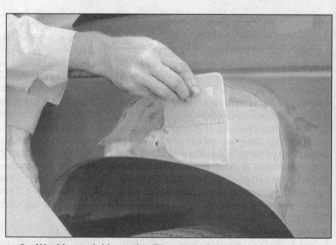

6   Working quickly so the filler doesn't harden, use a plastic applicator to press the body filler firmly into the metal, assuring it bonds completely. Work the filler until it matches the original contour and is slightly above the surrounding metal

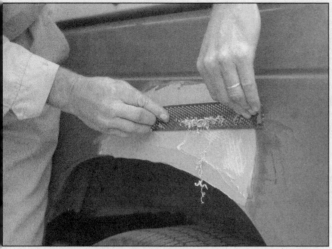

7   Let the filler harden until you can just dent it with your fingernail. Use a body file or Surform tool (shown here) to rough-shape the filler

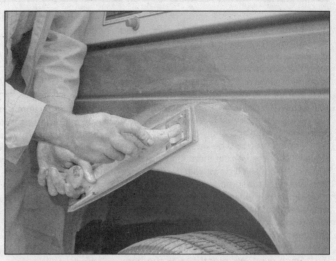

8   Use coarse-grit sandpaper and a sanding board or block to work the filler down until it's smooth and even. Work down to finer grits of sandpaper - always using a board or block - ending up with 360 or 400 grit

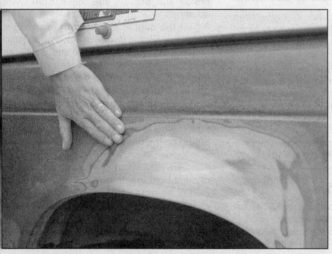

9   You shouldn't be able to feel any ridge at the transition from the filler to the bare metal or from the bare metal to the old paint. As soon as the repair is flat and uniform, remove the dust and mask off the adjacent panels or trim pieces

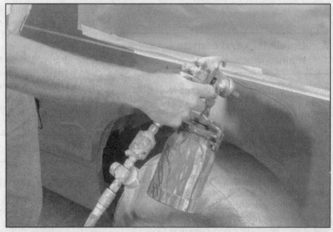

10   Apply several layers of primer to the area. Don't spray the primer on too heavy, so it sags or runs, and make sure each coat is dry before you spray on the next one. A professional-type spray gun is being used here, but aerosol spray primer is available inexpensively from auto parts stores

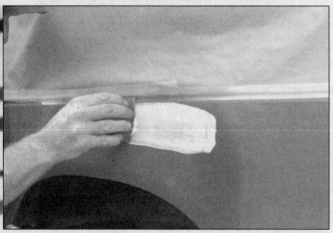

11   The primer will help reveal imperfections or scratches. Fill these with glazing compound. Follow the label instructions and sand it with 360 or 400-grit sandpaper until it's smooth. Repeat the glazing, sanding and respraying until the primer reveals a perfectly smooth surface

12   Finish sand the primer with very fine sandpaper (400 or 600-grit) to remove the primer overspray. Clean the area with water and allow it to dry. Use a tack rag to remove any dust, then apply the finish coat. Don't attempt to rub out or wax the repair area until the paint has dried completely (at least two weeks)

of this job.

3   At the same time, clean the engine and the engine compartment with a steam cleaner or water soluble degreaser.

4   The wheel wells should be given close attention, since undercoating can peel away and stones and dirt thrown up by the tires can cause the paint to chip and flake, allowing rust to set in. If rust is found, clean down to the bare metal and apply an anti-rust paint.

5   The body should be washed about once a week. Wet the vehicle thoroughly to soften the dirt, then wash it down with a soft sponge and plenty of clean soapy water. If the surplus dirt is not washed off very carefully, it can wear down the paint.

6   Spots of tar or asphalt thrown up from the road should be removed with a cloth soaked in solvent.

7   Once every six months, wax the body and chrome trim. If a chrome cleaner is used to remove rust from any of the vehicle's plated parts, remember that the cleaner also removes part of the chrome, so use it sparingly.

3   Upholstery and carpets - maintenance

1   Every three months remove the floor mats and clean the interior of the vehicle (more frequently if necessary). Use a stiff whisk broom to brush the carpeting and loosen dirt and dust, then vacuum the upholstery and carpets thoroughly, especially along seams and crevices.

2   Dirt and stains can be removed from carpeting with basic household or automotive carpet shampoos available in spray cans. Follow the directions and vacuum again, then use a stiff brush to bring back the ÒnapÓ of the carpet.

3   Most interiors have cloth or vinyl upholstery, either of which can be cleaned and maintained with a number of material-specific cleaners or shampoos available in auto supply stores. Follow the directions on the product for usage, and always spot-test any upholstery cleaner on an inconspicuous area (bottom edge of a back seat cushion) to ensure that it doesn't cause a color shift in the material.

4   After cleaning, vinyl upholstery should be treated with a protectant. **Note:** *Make sure the protectant container indicates the product can be used on seats - some products may make a seat too slippery.* **Warning:** *Do not use protectant on vinyl-covered steering wheels.*

5   Leather upholstery requires special care. It should be cleaned regularly with saddle soap or leather cleaner. Never use alcohol, gasoline, nail polish remover or thinner to clean leather upholstery.

6   After cleaning, regularly treat leather upholstery with a leather conditioner, rubbed in with a soft cotton cloth. Never use car wax on leather upholstery.

7   In areas where the interior of the vehicle

is subject to bright sunlight, cover leather seating areas of the seats with a sheet if the vehicle is to be left out for any length of time.

4   Vinyl trim - maintenance

Don't clean vinyl trim with detergents, caustic soap or petroleum-based cleaners. Plain soap and water works just fine, with a soft brush to clean dirt that may be ingrained. Wash the vinyl as frequently as the rest of the vehicle.

After cleaning, application of a high quality rubber and vinyl protectant will help prevent oxidation and cracks. The protectant can also be applied to weatherstripping, vacuum lines and rubber hoses (which often fail as a result of chemical degradation) and to the tires.

5   Hinges and locks - maintenance

Once every 3000 miles, or every three months, the hinges and latch assemblies on the doors, hood and trunk should be given a few drops of light oil or lock lubricant. The door latch strikers should also be lubricated with a thin coat of grease to reduce wear and ensure free movement. Lubricate the door and trunk locks with spray-on graphite lubricant.

6   Body repair - minor damage

Repair of scratches

1   If the scratch is superficial and does not penetrate to the metal of the body, repair is very simple. Lightly rub the scratched area with a fine rubbing compound to remove loose paint and built up wax. Rinse the area with clean water.

2   Apply touch-up paint to the scratch, using a small brush. Continue to apply thin layers of paint until the surface of the paint in the scratch is level with the surrounding paint. Allow the new paint at least two weeks to harden, then blend it into the surrounding paint by rubbing with a very fine rubbing compound. Finally, apply a coat of wax to the scratch area.

3   If the scratch has penetrated the paint and exposed the metal of the body, causing the metal to rust, a different repair technique is required. Remove all loose rust from the bottom of the scratch with a pocket knife, then apply rust inhibiting paint to prevent the formation of rust in the future. Using a rubber or nylon applicator, coat the scratched area with glaze-type filler. If required, the filler can be mixed with thinner to provide a very thin paste, which is ideal for filling narrow scratches. Before the glaze filler in the scratch hardens, wrap a piece of smooth cotton cloth around the tip of a finger. Dip the cloth in thinner and then quickly wipe it along the surface of the scratch. This will ensure

that the surface of the filler is slightly hollow. The scratch can now be painted over as described earlier in this Section.

Repair of dents

See photo sequence

4   When repairing dents, the first job is to pull the dent out until the affected area is as close as possible to its original shape. There is no point in trying to restore the original shape completely as the metal in the damaged area will have stretched on impact and cannot be restored to its original contours. It is better to bring the level of the dent up to a point which is about 1/8-inch below the level of the surrounding metal. In cases where the dent is very shallow, it is not worth trying to pull it out at all.

5   If the back side of the dent is accessible, it can be hammered out gently from behind using a soft-face hammer. While doing this, hold a block of wood firmly against the opposite side of the metal to absorb the hammer blows and prevent the metal from being stretched.

6   If the dent is in a section of the body which has double layers, or some other factor makes it inaccessible from behind, a different technique is required. Drill several small holes through the metal inside the damaged area, particularly in the deeper sections. Screw long, self-tapping screws into the holes just enough for them to get a good grip in the metal. Now the dent can be pulled out by pulling on the protruding heads of the screws with locking pliers.

7   The next stage of repair is the removal of paint from the damaged area and from an inch or so of the surrounding metal. This is easily done with a wire brush or sanding disk in a drill motor, although it can be done just as effectively by hand with sandpaper. To complete the preparation for filling, score the surface of the bare metal with a screwdriver or the tang of a file or drill small holes in the affected area. This will provide a good grip for the filler material. To complete the repair, see the Section on *filling and painting.*

Repair of rust holes or gashes

8   Remove all paint from the affected area and from an inch or so of the surrounding metal using a sanding disk or wire brush mounted in a drill motor. If these are not available, a few sheets of sandpaper will do the job just as effectively.

9   With the paint removed, you will be able to determine the severity of the corrosion and decide whether to replace the whole panel, if possible, or repair the affected area. New body panels are not as expensive as most people think and it is often quicker to install a new panel than to repair large areas of rust.

10   Remove all trim pieces from the affected area except those which will act as a guide to the original shape of the damaged body, such as headlight shells, etc. Using metal snips or a hacksaw blade, remove all loose metal and any other metal that is badly affected by rust. Hammer the edges of the

hole on the inside to create a slight depression for the filler material.

11 Wire brush the affected area to remove the powdery rust from the surface of the metal. If the back of the rusted area is accessible, treat it with rust inhibiting paint.

12 Before filling is done, block the hole in some way. This can be done with sheet metal riveted or screwed into place, or by stuffing the hole with wire mesh.

13 Once the hole is blocked off, the affected area can be filled and painted. See the following subsection on *filling and painting*.

Filling and painting

14 Many types of body fillers are available, but generally speaking, body repair kits which contain filler paste and a tube of resin hardener are best for this type of repair work. A wide, flexible plastic or nylon applicator will be necessary for imparting a smooth and contoured finish to the surface of the filler material. Mix up a small amount of filler on a clean piece of wood or cardboard (use the hardener sparingly). Follow the manufacturer's instructions on the package, otherwise the filler will set incorrectly.

15 Using the applicator, apply the filler paste to the prepared area. Draw the applicator across the surface of the filler to achieve the desired contour and to level the filler surface. As soon as a contour that approximates the original one is achieved, stop working the paste. If you continue, the paste will begin to stick to the applicator. Continue to add thin layers of paste at 20-minute intervals until the level of the filler is just above the surrounding metal.

16 Once the filler has hardened, the excess can be removed with a body file. From then on, progressively finer grades of sandpaper should be used, starting with a 180-grit paper and finishing with 600-grit wet-or-dry paper. Always wrap the sandpaper around a flat rubber or wooden block, otherwise the surface of the filler will not be completely flat. During the sanding of the filler surface, the wet-or-dry paper should be periodically rinsed in water. This will ensure that a very smooth finish is produced in the final stage.

17 At this point, the repair area should be surrounded by a ring of bare metal, which in turn should be encircled by the finely feathered edge of good paint. Rinse the repair area with clean water until all of the dust produced by the sanding operation is gone.

18 Spray the entire area with a light coat of primer. This will reveal any imperfections in the surface of the filler. Repair the imperfections with fresh filler paste or glaze filler and once more smooth the surface with sandpaper. Repeat this spray-and-repair procedure until you are satisfied that the surface of the filler and the feathered edge of the paint are perfect. Rinse the area with clean water and allow it to dry completely.

19 The repair area is now ready for painting. Spray painting must be carried out in a warm, dry, windless and dust free atmo-

sphere. These conditions can be created if you have access to a large indoor work area, but if you are forced to work in the open, you will have to pick the day very carefully. If you are working indoors, dousing the floor in the work area with water will help settle the dust which would otherwise be in the air. If the repair area is confined to one body panel, mask off the surrounding panels. This will help minimize the effects of a slight mismatch in paint color. Trim pieces such as chrome strips, door handles, etc., will also need to be masked off or removed. Use masking tape and several thickness of newspaper for the masking operations.

20 Before spraying, shake the paint can thoroughly, then spray a test area until the spray painting technique is mastered. Cover the repair area with a thick coat of primer. The thickness should be built up using several thin layers of primer rather than one thick one. Using 600-grit wet-or-dry sandpaper, rub down the surface of the primer until it is very smooth. While doing this, the work area should be thoroughly rinsed with water and the wet-or-dry sandpaper periodically rinsed as well. Allow the primer to dry before spraying additional coats.

21 Spray on the top coat, again building up the thickness by using several thin layers of paint. Begin spraying in the center of the repair area and then, using a circular motion, work out until the whole repair area and about two inches of the surrounding original paint is covered. Remove all masking material 10 to 15 minutes after spraying on the final coat of paint. Allow the new paint at least two weeks to harden, then use a very fine rubbing compound to blend the edges of the new paint into the existing paint. Finally, apply a coat of wax.

7 Body repair - major damage

1 Major damage must be repaired by an

auto body/frame repair shop with the necessary welding and hydraulic straightening equipment.

2 If the damage has been serious, it is vital that the structure be checked for proper alignment or the vehicle's handling characteristics may be adversely affected. Other problems, such as excessive tire wear and wear in the driveline and steering may occur.

3 Due to the fact that all of the major body components (hood, fenders, etc.) are separate and replaceable units, any seriously damaged components should be replaced rather than repaired. Sometimes these components can be found in a wrecking yard that specializes in used vehicle components, often at considerable savings over the cost of new parts.

8 Windshield and fixed glass - replacement

Replacement of the windshield and fixed glass requires the use of special fast setting adhesive/caulk materials. These operations should be left to a dealer or a shop specializing in glass work.

9 Hood - removal, installation and adjustment

Note: *The hood is somewhat awkward to remove and install - at least two people should perform this procedure.*

Removal and installation

Refer to illustrations 9.2, 9.3 and 9.4

1 Open the hood and place rags or covers over the windshield and fenders to protect them during the removal procedure.

2 Disconnect the windshield washer fluid lines **(see illustration)**.

3 Mark the relationship of the hood to the hinges **(see illustration)**.

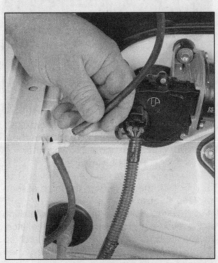

9.2 Before removing the hood, detach the windshield washer fluid line

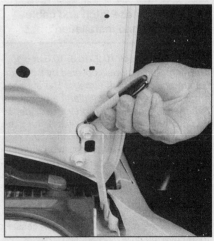

9.3 Before removing the hood hinge bolts, mark the relationship of the hood to the hood hinges

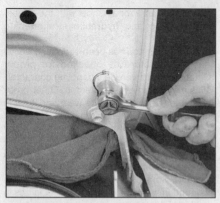

9.4 Place a shop rag under the corners of the hood to protect the paint, then have an assistant support one side of the hood as you remove the bolts from the other side

4   Remove the hood retaining bolts and lift off the hood **(see illustration)**.
5   Installation is the reverse of removal.

Adjustment

Refer to illustration 9.7

6   If necessary after installation, the entire hood latch assembly can be adjusted up-and-down as well as from side-to-side on the upper radiator support so the hood closes securely and is flush with the fenders. To do this, scribe a line around the hood latch mounting bolts to provide a reference point **(see illustration 9.3)**. Then loosen the bolts and reposition the latch as necessary. Following adjustment, retighten the mounting bolts.
7   Finally, adjust the hood bumpers on the radiator support so the hood, when closed, is flush with the fenders **(see illustration)**.
8   The hood latch, as well as the hinges, should be periodically lubricated with white lithium-based grease to prevent sticking and wear.

10 Hood release latch and cable - removal and installation

Refer to illustrations 10.2, 10.3, 10.6 and 10.7
Warning: *Some models covered by this manual are equipped with airbags. The airbag is armed and can deploy (inflate) anytime the battery is connected. To prevent accidental deployment (and possible injury), turn the ignition key to LOCK and disconnect the negative battery cable whenever working near airbag components. After the battery is disconnected, wait at least two minutes before beginning work (the system has a back-up capacitor that must fully discharge). For more information see Chapter 12.*
1   On some models, it may be necessary to remove the grille (see Section 11).
2   Mark the edge of the latch in relationship to the radiator support before un-bolting the latch. Unbolt the latch **(see illustration)**.

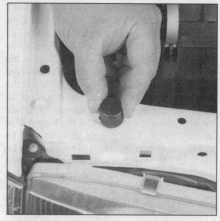

9.7 Screw the hood bumpers in or out to adjust the hood flush with the fenders

10.3 Flip the latch over and pry the end of the cable out of the latch (grille removed for clarity)

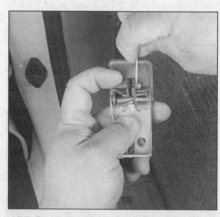

10.7 Pry the cable from the lever bracket, then disengage the cable end from the lever (Tacoma model shown, other models similar)

3   Detach the cable from the latch assembly **(see illustration)**.
4   If you're replacing the latch, installation is the reverse of removal. To adjust the latch, loosen the bolts a little and move the latch up or down, left or right, as necessary, then tighten the bolts securely.
5   If you're replacing the cable, trace the cable back toward the firewall and detach all

10.2 To detach the hood release latch, remove the retaining bolts (arrows) (grille removed for clarity)

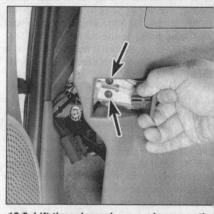

10.6 Lift the release lever and remove the lever retaining screws (arrows)

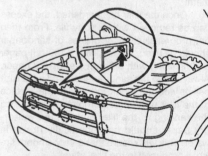

11.1a Plastic grilles are attached to the radiator support by retaining clips - depress each clip (arrow), then pull the grille forward to disengage it from the clips

cable brackets and/or clips in the engine compartment.
6   Working in the passenger compartment, remove the left lower finish panel (see Section 25) and detach the hood release lever from the instrument panel **(see illustration)**.
7   Detach the hood release lever from the cable **(see illustration)**.
8   Attach a piece of string or thin wire to the end of the cable. Pull the cable and grommet into the engine compartment.
9   Installation is the reverse of removal.

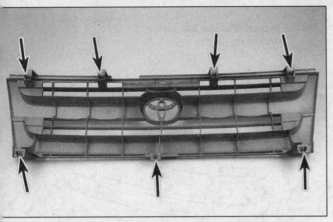

11.1b Most plastic radiator grilles have seven retaining clips (Tacoma model shown, other models similar)

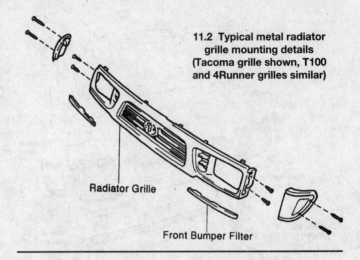

11.2 Typical metal radiator grille mounting details (Tacoma grille shown, T100 and 4Runner grilles similar)

Radiator Grille

Front Bumper Filter

11 Radiator grille - removal and installation

Refer to illustrations 11.1a, 11.1b and 11.2
Warning: *Some models covered by this manual are equipped with airbags. The airbag is armed and can deploy (inflate) anytime the battery is connected. To prevent accidental deployment (and possible injury), turn the ignition key to LOCK and disconnect the negative battery cable whenever working near airbag components. After the battery is disconnected, wait at least two minutes before beginning work (the system has a back-up* capacitor that must fully discharge). For more information see Chapter 12.*

1   Plastic grilles are retained by small plastic clips that are pushed into grommets in the radiator support. To detach the grille on a model with a plastic grille, depress the retaining clips and carefully pry the grille loose at the indicated points **(see illustrations)**.
2   On models with metal grilles, remove the side marker lights, then remove the grille retaining screw(s) and retaining clips **(see illustration)**.
3   Remove the radiator grille from the vehicle.
4   Installation is the reverse of removal.

12 Bumpers - removal and installation

Front

Refer to illustrations 12.3a, 12.3b, 12.3c and 12.3d

1   Remove the radiator grille (see Section 11).
2   Remove the turn signal lights (see Chapter 12).
3   Remove the bumper arm bolts and the bumper-to-body bolts **(see illustrations)**.

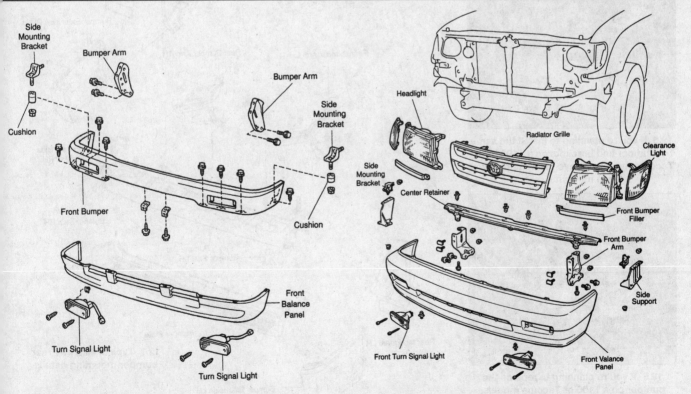

12.3a Typical T100 front bumper mounting details

12.3b Typical Tacoma plastic bumper mounting details

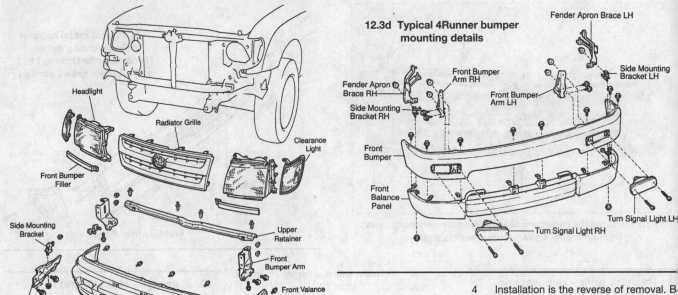

Headlight

Radiator Grille

Clearance Light

Front Bumper Filler

Side Mounting Bracket

Upper Retainer

Front Bumper Arm

Side Support Bracket

Front Valance Panel

Front Bumper Sub–Assembly

Front Turn Signal Light

12.3c Typical Tacoma steel bumper mounting details

12.3d Typical 4Runner bumper mounting details

Fender Apron Brace LH

Fender Apron Brace RH

Front Bumper Arm RH

Side Mounting Bracket LH

Front Bumper Arm LH

Side Mounting Bracket RH

Front Bumper

Front Balance Panel

Turn Signal Light LH

Turn Signal Light RH

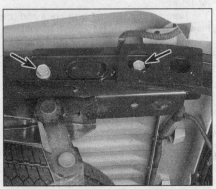

12.5 If you're planning to install the same bumper and brackets on a T100 or Tacoma model, remove the bolts (arrows) from the frame rails

12.6 If you're planning to replace the bumper on a T100 or Tacoma models, remove the bolts securing the bumper to the bumper brackets

4   Installation is the reverse of removal. B sure to tighten all fasteners securely.

Rear

Refer to illustrations 12.5, 12.6 and 12.7

5   If you're planning to install the sam bumper and brackets on a T100 or Tacom model, unbolt the bumper brackets from th

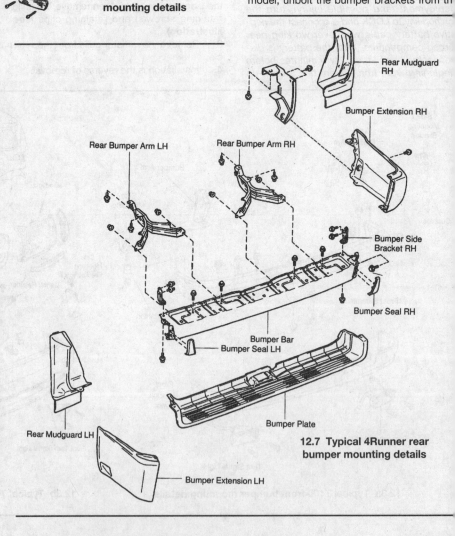

Rear Mudguard RH

Bumper Extension RH

Rear Bumper Arm LH

Rear Bumper Arm RH

Bumper Side Bracket RH

Bumper Seal RH

Bumper Bar

Bumper Seal LH

Bumper Plate

Rear Mudguard LH

Bumper Extension LH

12.7 Typical 4Runner rear bumper mounting details

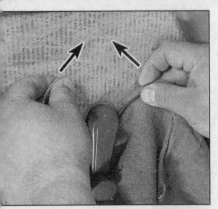

13.2 To remove the manual window regulator handle, work a clean shop rag between the handle and the door as shown, then pull up on the rag to pop off the snap-ring

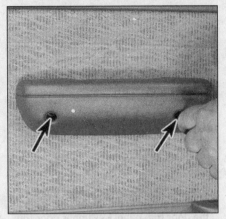

13.3a To remove the armrest, pry off the two small screw covers and remove both screws (arrows)

13.3b On T100 models, remove the screw from the pull handle well

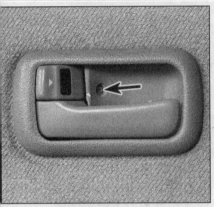

13.4a On T100 models, remove the inside handle trim screw (arrow) and cover

13.4b On 4Runner and Tacoma models, remove the inside door handle retaining screw . . .

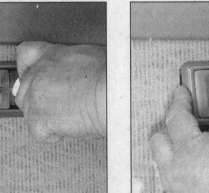

13.4c . . . then slide the handle forward to release it from the door trim panel . . .

frame **(see illustration)**.

6   If you're planning to replace the bumper on a T100 or Tacoma, unbolt it from the bumper brackets **(see illustration)**.

7   If you're replacing the rear bumper or brackets on a 4Runner model, refer to the accompanying exploded view **(see illustration)**.

8   Installation is the reverse of removal. Be sure to tighten all fasteners securely.

13   Door trim panel - removal and installation

Removal

Refer to illustrations 13.2, 13.3a, 13.3b, 13.4a, 13.4b, 13.4c, 13.4d, 13.5, 13.6a, 13.6b, 13.7a, 13.7b, 13.7c, 13.7d and 13.9

1   On models equipped with power windows, disconnect the negative cable at the battery. **Caution:** *On models equipped with an anti-theft audio system, be sure the lockout feature is turned off before disconnecting the battery.*

2   To remove the window regulator handle on models without power windows, work a shop rag between the handle and the door

13.4d . . . and disengage the handle from the control link

trim panel, then pull up on both ends of the rag and pop loose the snap-ring that secures the handle to the regulator shaft **(see illustration)**.

3   Remove the armrest **(see illustration)**. On T100 models, there's no separate armrest, but there's a screw **(see illustration)** inside the pull handle that must be removed.

4   On T100 models, unscrew the handle

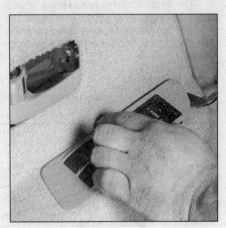

13.5 On models with power windows and/or power door locks, pry out the control panel and unplug the electrical connectors (T100 model shown, other models similar)

trim cover **(see illustration)** and detach it from the door. On other models, remove the inside door handle **(see illustrations)**.

5   To remove the switch control panel on power window equipped vehicles, carefully pry it upward **(see illustration)**, then pull it

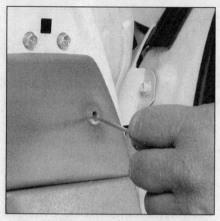

13.6a On most models, you'll find a door trim panel screw just below the mirror

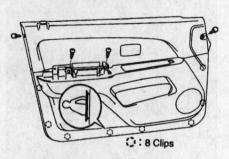

◯ : 8 Clips

13.6b On 4Runner models, there's another screw in the upper rear edge of the door trim panel - 4Runner door trim panels also use eight clips

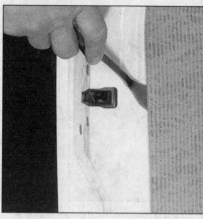

13.7a Insert a putty knife or trim removal tool between the door and the trim panel, then carefully pry the clips out

out and unplug the electrical connector.

6   On most models, there's a trim panel retaining screw below the mirror **(see illustration)**. On 4Runner models, there's another trim panel retaining screw on the upper rear edge of the trim panel **(see illustration)**.

7   On some models, it may be necessary to remove the mirror trim panel (see Section 14) before the door trim panel can be removed. To detach the door trim panel, carefully pry off the retaining clips **(see illustration)**. There are 13 clips on T100 models **(see illustration)**, 12 clips on Tacoma models **(see illustration)** and eight clips on 4Runner models **(see illustration 13.6b)**. On 4Runner rear doors, the trim panel has two clips securing the front and rear edge, two screws in the middle of the panel and seven clips around the outer edge of the panel **(see illustration)**.

8   On T100 models, remove the inside door handle (see Section 22 if necessary).

9   For access to the inner door, carefully peel back the plastic water shield **(see illustration)**.

Installation

10   Before installing the door trim panel,

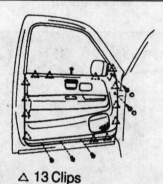

△ **13 Clips**

13.7b On T100 models, the door trim panel is retained by 13 clips

make

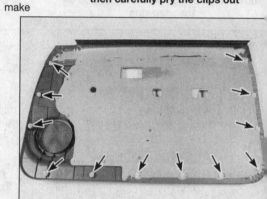

13.7c On Tacoma models, the door trim panel is retained by 12 clips (arrows)

sure the plastic water shield is correctly installed **(see illustration 13.9)**. If the shield is torn, patch it with tape. If the edge fails to adhere to the door anywhere, seal it with a little silicone sealant. Install any grommets, clips or other fasteners which may have fallen out of the trim panel or the door when you removed the panel. On T100 models, install the inside door handle.

11   Place the door trim panel in position push all the clips into their respective grommets until they're fully seated. Install the trim panel retaining screws, if applicable. Don't forget to install any trim panel screws, if applicable.

12   Install the mirror trim panel, if removed.

13   Install the inside door handle. On T100 models, install the inside handle trim cover and screw.

14   Install the armrest. On T100 models.

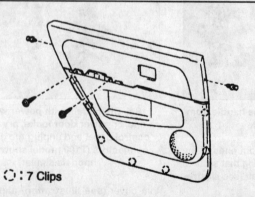

◯ : 7 Clips

13.7d On 4Runner models, the rear door trim panel has two clips securing the front and rear edges, two screws in the middle of the panel and seven clips around the outer edge of the trim panel

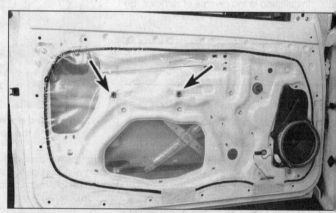

13.9 Before peeling off the water shield on Tacoma and 4Runner models, be sure to remove the two grommets (arrows) - if the shield is torn during removal, repair it with tape or replace it - make sure the shield is sealed all the way around the edge

14.1 Pry off the mirror trim panel

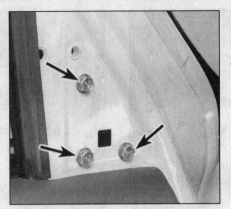

14.2 Remove the mirror retaining bolts
(arrows) - if equipped with power mirrors
unplug the electrical connector
(not shown)

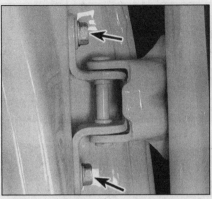

15.4a To detach the door from the body,
scribe or draw alignment marks along the
edges of the hinges, then remove the
upper hinge bolts (arrows) . . .

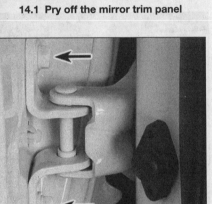

15.4b . . . and the lower bolts (arrows)
(Tacoma model shown, other
models similar)

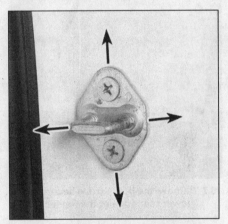

15.7 To adjust the door lock striker,
slightly loosen the screws and tap the
striker up, down or sideways as
necessary until the door lock latch
engages it correctly (Tacoma model
shown, other models similar)

16.3a To remove the trim piece below the
headlight on a Tacoma model, remove
this screw from the inner end . . .

install the pull handle screw.
15   Install the regulator handle or the switch
control panel. Don't forget to plug in all electrical connectors.

14   Outside mirror - removal and installation

Refer to illustrations 14.1 and 14.2
1   Remove the mirror trim panel **(see illustration)**.
2   Remove the mirror-to-door retaining bolts **(see illustration)** and, on power mirrors, unplug the electrical connector.
3   Remove the mirror assembly.
4   Installation is the reverse of removal.

15   Door - removal and installation

Refer to illustrations 15.4a, 15.4b and 15.7
1   Disconnect the negative cable from the battery. **Caution:** *On models equipped with an anti-theft audio system, be sure the lockout feature is turned off before disconnecting the battery.*
2   Remove the door trim panel (see Sec-

tion 13). On doors with power components, unplug all electrical connections (it's a good idea to label all connections to aid the reassembly process) and remove the electrical harness from the door.
3   Open the door all the way and support it on jacks or blocks covered with cloth or pads to prevent damaging the paint.
4   Mark the relationship of the door hinges to the body by scribing or drawing a line around the hinges. With an assistant supporting the door, remove the door hinge bolts **(see illustrations)**, then carefully lift off the door.
5   When installing the door, make sure the hinges are aligned with the outlines you made, then tighten the hinge bolts securely.
6   Installation is otherwise the reverse of removal.
7   If the door does not close properly after installation, slightly loosen the door latch striker bolts **(see illustration)** and carefully tap the striker up, down or sideways as necessary to provide positive engagement with the latch mechanism.

16   Front fender - removal and installation

Refer to illustrations 16.3a, 16.3b, 16.5, 16.6 and 16.7
Warning: *Some models covered by this manual are equipped with airbags. The airbag is armed and can deploy (inflate) anytime the battery is connected. To prevent accidental deployment (and possible injury), turn the ignition key to LOCK and disconnect the negative battery cable whenever working near airbag components. After the battery is disconnected, wait at least two minutes before beginning work (the system has a back-up capacitor that must fully discharge). For more information see Chapter 12.*
Note: *The front fender procedure described below depicts a typical front fender on a Tacoma model. The location and number of fender fasteners on T100 models and 4Runners are similar, but not identical.*
1   Raise the vehicle, support it securely on jackstands and remove the front wheel.
2   Remove the side marker lights (see Chapter 12). Disconnect any other lighting components that interfere with fender removal.
3   If the radiator grille includes the head-

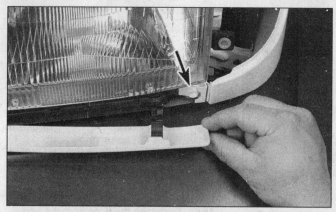

16.3b . . . then disengage the outer end from under the headlight – the bolt (arrow) below the headlight is the front fender bolt

16.5 To detach the upper edge of the fender, remove the bolts (arrows) shown

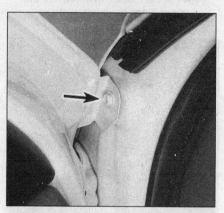

16.6 Open the door and remove the bolt (arrow) securing the upper rear corner of the front fender

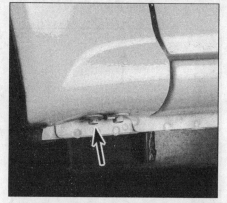

16.7 Remove the bolt (arrow) securing the lower rear edge of the fender

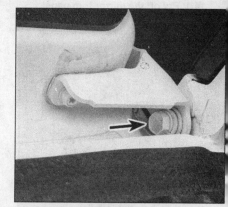

17.1 To detach the entire tailgate assembly from the vehicle, remove the hinge bolts (arrow) (left bolt shown) - be sure to mark the relationship of the hinges to the tailgate if you plan to remove or replace them

light trim, remove the grille (see Section 11). If not, remove the trim piece below the head-lights **(see illustrations)**.

4   Detach the wheel housing splash shields from the fender. The splash shields are attached between the frame and the fender with an assortment of screws and clips; the number and type of fasteners used varies from one model to another.

5   Remove the retaining bolts from the top edge of the fender **(see illustration)**.

6   Open the door and remove the retaining bolt that attaches the upper rear corner of the fender to the body **(see illustration)**.

7   Remove the bolt from the lower rear edge of the fender, right behind the wheel well **(see illustration)**.

8   Remove the fender. It is a good idea to have an assistant support the fender while it's being moved away from the vehicle to prevent damage to the surrounding body panels.

9   If you're planning to replace the fender, remove the molding around the wheel open-ing. The molding on T100 front fenders is attached with six screws and a clip; the front fender molding on Tacoma models has six screws (the mudguard, if equipped, has three bolts). On 4Runner models, the fender mold-ing is attached by five bolts, six clips and two rivets. Drill out the rivet flanges to remove the

rivets. To make sure you don't drill too deep, wrap the drill with tape about 0.20 inch from the tip of the drill.

10   Installation is the reverse of removal. Tighten all fasteners securely.

17   Tailgate and latch (T100 and Tacoma models) - removal and installation

Refer to illustrations 17.1, 17.2, 17.3a, 17.3b, 17.3c and 17.3d

1   To remove the tailgate assembly, simply disengage the two tailgate cables from the tailgate and remove the hinge pivot bolts **(see illustration)**. If you intend to remove the hinges from the tailgate, scribe or draw align-ment marks along their edges to ensure proper realignment.

2   If you want to replace the tailgate latch strikers, mark their relationship to the body, then remove the striker bolts **(see illustra-tion)**. If you want to replace the tailgate cables, simply remove the screw securing each end of the cable.

3   If you want to replace the tailgate handle or the latches, remove the plastic liner **(see illustration)**, if equipped, then remove the service hole cover **(see illustration)**. Disen-gage the latch control rods from the tailgate

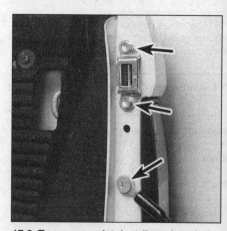

17.2 To remove a latch striker, detach the bolts (arrows) - to replace a tailgate cable remove the screw (arrow) from each end of the cable

handle **(see illustration)**, unbolt the handle from the tailgate or detach the latches from the tailgate **(see illustration)** and pull them out.

4   Installation is the reverse of removal. Tighten all fasteners securely.

17.3a Remove the plastic tailgate liner, if equipped (the number of screws may vary with brand of liner)

17.3b To access the tailgate handle and latch mechanism, remove the service hole cover; there are 12 screws on Tacoma models (shown) but only a couple of screws on T100 covers, which are much smaller (not all screws visible in this photo)

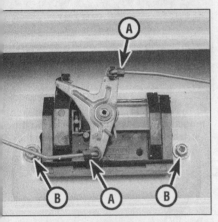

17.3c To remove the tailgate handle, detach the control rods (A) and remove the bolts (B)

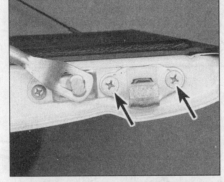

17.3d To remove a latch, detach the two screws (arrows) and pull out the latch (the control rod must be disconnected from the back of the latch mechanism)

18.2a To remove a strut support, simply remove the bolts (arrows) at the top ...

18 Liftgate (4Runner models) - removal, installation and adjustment

Refer to illustrations 18.2a, 18.2b, 18.3, 18.4, 18.6a, 18.6b, 18.6c, 18.7a and 18.7b
Note: *The liftgate is heavy and somewhat*

awkward to remove and install - at least two people should perform this procedure.

1   Disconnect the negative cable from the battery. **Caution:** *On models equipped with an anti-theft audio system, be sure the lock-out feature is turned off before disconnecting the battery.*

2   Open the liftgate and support it

securely. Remove the liftgate struts **(see illustrations)**.

3   Disconnect the wire harness between the liftgate and the body **(see illustration)**.

4   Mark the relationship of the hinges to the liftgate, then unbolt them **(see illustration)**.

5   Installation is the reverse of removal.

6   To replace the lock, you'll have to

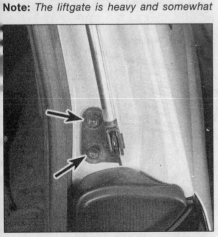

18.2b ... and the bolts (arrows) at the bottom

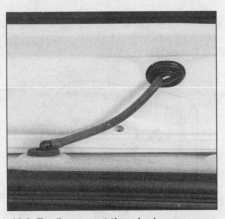

18.3 To disconnect the wire harness, pry out the rubber grommet and unplug the electrical connectors

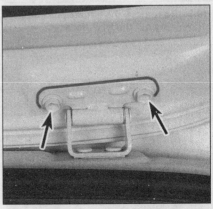

18.4 To detach the liftgate from the body, mark the relationship of both hinges to the body, then remove the bolts (arrows)

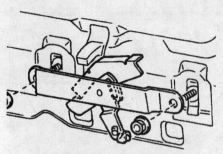

18.6a To detach the lock control bellcrank, remove the two nuts

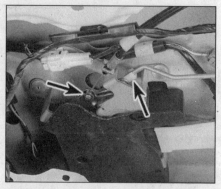

18.6b Disconnect the lock control rod and the release cable (arrows) from the lock

18.6c To detach the latch, remove the bolts (arrows)

 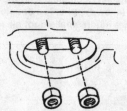

18.7a To adjust the liftgate forward or rearward in relation to the body, remove the hinge-to-body nuts and tap the hinges forward or backward as necessary, then tighten the nuts securely

remove the liftgate trim panel, the service hole plate, the back door glass run, the outer weather-strip, the back door glass, the window regulator, and the glass guide rails (see Section 19). Remove the lock control bell-crank **(see illustration)** and remove the lift-gate remote control. The license plate gar-nish is secured by a nut and five clips.

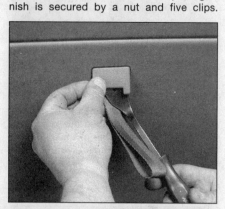

19.3a To remove the liftgate pull handle, pry out the trim piece . . .

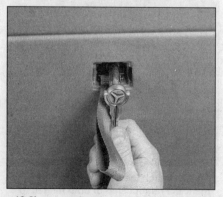

19.3b . . . and remove the retaining bolt

18.7b To adjust the liftgate latch striker, loosen the screws (arrows) and tap the striker as necessary, then tighten the screws securely

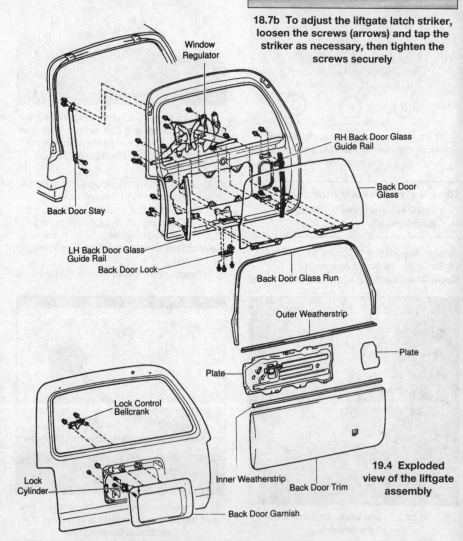

Window Regulator

Back Door Stay

RH Back Door Glass Guide Rail

Back Door Glass

LH Back Door Glass Guide Rail

Back Door Lock

Back Door Glass Run

Outer Weatherstrip

Plate

Plate

Lock Control Bellcrank

Lock Cylinder

Inner Weatherstrip

Back Door Trim

Back Door Garnish

19.4 Exploded view of the liftgate assembly

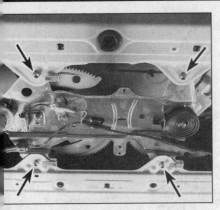

19.6 To remove the window regulator assembly, detach the bolts (arrows)

Remove the nut and pry off the garnish with a scraper. Remove the two key lock cylinder nuts, remove the key lock cylinder and unplug the electrical connector. Then trace the lock control rod and the release cable down to the lock **(see illustration)** and disconnect both of them. Remove the three lock retaining bolts **(see illustration)** from the lower edge of the liftgate and remove the lock. Installation is the reverse of removal.

7　If the liftgate requires adjustment to close properly, there are three adjustments available. To move the liftgate forward or rearward in relation to the body, loosen the nuts that attach the hinges to the body **(see illustration)** and lightly tap the hinges with a small plastic hammer in the direction you want to move the liftgate, then tighten the nuts securely. To adjust the liftgate to the left or right, or up or down, in relation to the body, loosen the hinge bolts on the liftgate **(see illustration 18.4)**, carefully move the liftgate the direction you want to go, then tighten the bolts securely. To adjust the liftgate striker, loosen the striker screws **(see illustration)** and carefully tap the striker with a small plastic hammer until the liftgate lock and the striker are engaging properly, then tighten the striker screws securely.

8　Installation is the reverse of removal.

19　Liftgate glass and regulator (4Runner models) - removal and installation

Refer to illustrations 19.3a, 19.3b, 19.4 and 19.6

1　Disconnect the negative cable from the battery. **Caution:** *On models equipped with an anti-theft audio system, be sure the lockout feature is turned off before disconnecting the battery.*

2　Although it's not absolutely necessary, you may want to remove the liftgate (see Section 18) before removing the liftgate glass. Servicing the liftgate components is easier with the liftgate on the floor.

3　Remove the liftgate pull handle **(see illustrations)**.

4　To remove the trim panel, pry loose

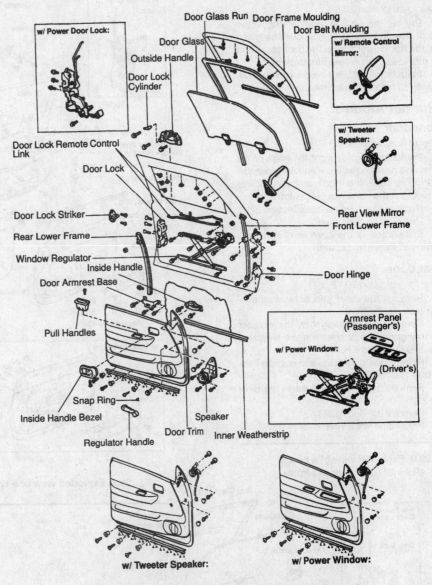

20.4　Exploded view of a typical T100 door assembly

the 10 trim panel clips. To remove the service plate, unplug all electrical connectors and remove the service plate screws **(see illustration)**.

5　Remove the liftgate glass run, the outer weather-stripping and the liftgate glass **(see illustration 19.4)**.

6　Disconnect any remaining electrical connections and remove the window regulator **(see illustration)**.

7　Installation is the reverse of removal.

20　Door window glass - removal and installation

Warning: *Safety glasses and gloves should be worn when performing this procedure.*

1　Lower the glass fully in the door. On models equipped with power windows and/or door locks, disconnect the cable from the negative battery terminal. **Caution:** *On models equipped with an anti-theft audio system, be sure the lockout feature is turned off before disconnecting the battery.*

2　Remove the outside rear view mirror (see Section 14).

3　Remove the door trim panel and water shield (see Section 13).

T100 models

Refer to illustration 20.4

4　Remove the door belt and door frame molding, the door glass run, the inner weatherstrip and the door glass **(see illustration)**.

5　Installation is the reverse of removal. Tighten all fasteners securely.

Tacoma models

Refer to illustration 20.6

6   Pry out the window weatherstrip in the top of the door opening, remove the glass run, the front lower frame, the door glass and the rear lower frame **(see illustration)**.
7   Installation is the reverse of removal. Tighten all fasteners securely.

4Runner models

Front door

Refer to illustration 20.8

8   Pry loose the clips from the edge of the panel and remove the inner and outer weatherstrip, remove the front and rear lower frames, and the glass run **(see illustration)**.
9   Remove the regulator (see Section 21).
10   Remove the door glass.
11   Installation is the reverse of removal. Tighten all fasteners securely.

Rear door

Refer to illustration 20.12

12   Remove the inner and outer weatherstrip **(see illustration)**.
13   Remove the division bar, the quarter window glass, the quarter window weatherstrip and the glass run.
14   Remove the door latch and outside handle (see Section 22).
15   Remove the window regulator (see Section 21).
16   Remove the door glass.
17   Installation is the reverse of removal.

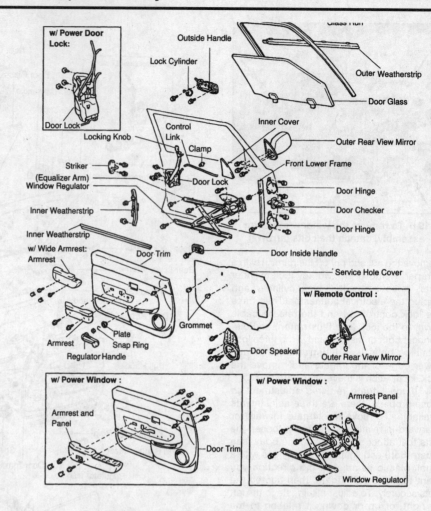

20.6 Exploded view of a typical Tacoma door assembly

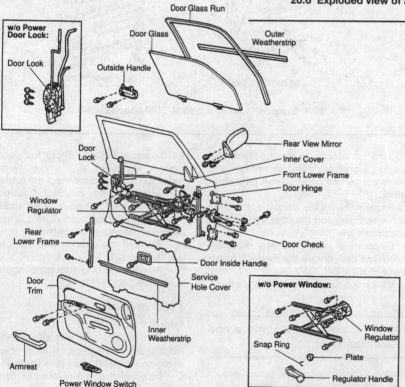

20.8 Exploded view of a typical 4Runner front door assembly

21   Door window regulator - removal and installation

Refer to illustrations 21.4a, 21.4b, 21.4c and 21.5

1   On models equipped with power windows and door locks, disconnect the cable from the negative battery terminal. **Caution:** *On models equipped with an anti-theft audio system, be sure the lockout feature is turned off before disconnecting the battery.*
2   Remove the door trim panel and water shield (see Section 13).
3   Remove the door glass (see Section 20).
4   To remove a manual window regulator (T100 and Tacoma only), remove the five retaining bolts **(see illustrations)**. To remove a power window regulator (except 4Runner rear door), unplug the electrical connector and remove the six retaining bolts **(see illustration)**.
5   To remove the power window regulator from a 4Runner rear door, remove the door latch and outside handle (see Section 22), then unplug the electrical connector, remove the four regulator retaining bolts **(see illus-**

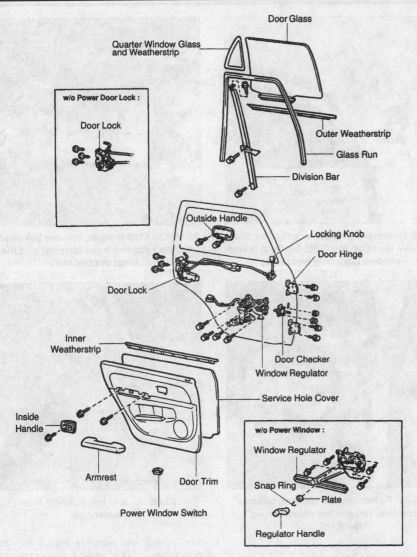

Door Glass

Quarter Window Glass and Weatherstrip

Outer Weatherstrip

Glass Run

Division Bar

w/o Power Door Lock :

Door Lock

Outside Handle

Locking Knob

Door Hinge

Door Lock

Door Checker

Window Regulator

Service Hole Cover

Inner Weatherstrip

Inside Handle

Armrest

Door Trim

Power Window Switch

w/o Power Window :

Window Regulator

Snap Ring

Plate

Regulator Handle

20.12 Exploded view of a typical 4Runner rear door assembly

21.4a To remove a manual window regulator, remove the bolts (arrows) above the service hole . . .

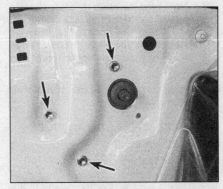

21.4b . . . and the bolts (arrows) surrounding the regulator handle (Tacoma model shown, other models similar)

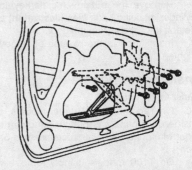

21.4c To remove a power window regulator, remove the six bolts (Tacoma model shown, other models similar)

tration) and pull out the regulator assembly.

6   Installation is the reverse of removal. Lubricate all regulator rollers with multipurpose grease. Tighten all fasteners securely.

22   Door latch, lock cylinder and handles - removal and installation

1   On models equipped with power windows and door locks, disconnect the cable from the negative battery terminal. **Caution:** *On models equipped with an anti-theft audio system, be sure the lockout feature is turned off before disconnecting the battery.*

2   Remove the door trim panel and the plastic water shield (see Section 13).

Door latch

Refer to illustration 22.5

3   Using a flashlight, note how the control

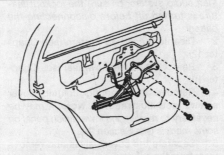

21.5 To detach the power window regulator from a 4Runner rear door, remove the four bolts

rods are connected to the door latch. Disengage the link(s) from the lock.

4   On models with power door locks, unplug the electrical connector from the door latch.

5   Remove the latch retaining screws **(see illustration)** and remove the latch assembly.

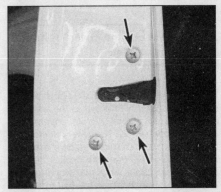

22.5 To detach the latch assembly from the door, remove three screws (arrows)

22.7 Note how the control rods (arrows) are connected to the key lock cylinder and to the outside door handle, then disconnect them (models with power door locks have only one control rod)

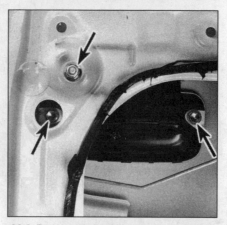

22.8 Remove the small access plug, then remove the retaining bolts (arrows) (some models have only two bolts)

22.11 On T100 models, remove the inside handle retaining bolts (arrows) and the latch control rod

6   Installation is the reverse of removal. Tighten the screws securely.

Outside handle and key lock cylinder

Refer to illustrations 22.7 and 22.8

7   Note how the control rods are connected to the outside door handle and to the key lock cylinder **(see illustration)**. Disengage the link(s) from the handle and/or the lock cylinder.
8   Remove the outside handle/key lock cylinder retaining bolts **(see illustration)** and detach the handle from the door.
9   Installation is the reverse of removal. Tighten the bolts securely.

Inside door handle

Refer to illustration 22.11

10   On Tacoma and 4Runner models, the inside door handle is part of removing the door trim panel removal procedure (see Section 13).
11   On T100 models, simply remove the bolts **(see illustration)** and disconnect the latch control rod from the back of the handle.
12   Installation is the reverse of removal. Tighten the bolts securely.

---

23   Steering column cover - removal and installation

Refer to illustrations 23.4a and 23.4b
Warning: *Some models covered by this manual are equipped with airbags. The airbag is armed and can deploy (inflate) anytime the battery is connected. To prevent accidental deployment (and possible injury), turn the ignition key to LOCK and disconnect the negative battery cable whenever working near airbag components. After the battery is disconnected, wait at least two minutes before beginning work (the system has a back-up capacitor that must fully discharge). For more*

23.4a To remove the steering column covers, remove the screws from the front . . .

information see Chapter 12.
1   Disconnect the negative battery cable.
Caution: *On models equipped with an anti-theft audio system, be sure the lockout feature is turned off before disconnecting the battery.*
2   Disable the airbag system (see Chapter 12).
3   Remove the steering wheel (see Chapter 10).
4   Remove the steering column cover screws **(see illustrations)**. **Note:** *It may be necessary to remove the lower finish panel on some models (see Section 24).*
5   Separate the cover halves and remove them from the column.
6   Installation is the reverse of removal.

---

24   Console - removal and installation

Refer to illustrations 24.3a, 24.3b and 24.3c
Warning: *Some models covered by this manual are equipped with airbags. The airbag is armed and can deploy (inflate) anytime the battery is connected. To prevent accidental*

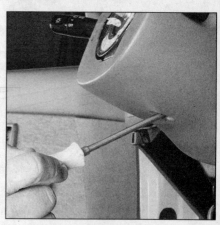

23.4b . . . and the screw(s) from underneath

deployment (and possible injury), turn the ignition key to LOCK and disconnect the negative battery cable whenever working near airbag components. After the battery is disconnected, wait at least two minutes before beginning work (the system has a back-up capacitor that must fully discharge). For more information see Chapter 12.
1   Disconnect the negative battery cable.
Caution: *On models equipped with an anti-theft audio system, be sure the lockout feature is turned off before performing any procedure which requires disconnecting the battery.*

Rear Console Box

24.3a Typical T100 center console mounting details

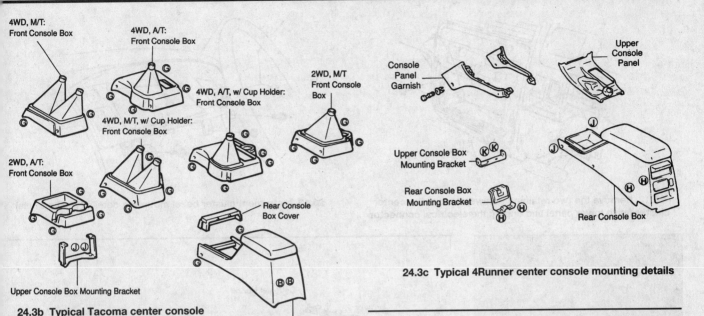

4WD, M/T: Front Console Box

4WD, A/T: Front Console Box

4WD, A/T, w/ Cup Holder: Front Console Box

4WD, M/T, w/ Cup Holder: Front Console Box

2WD, M/T Front Console Box

2WD, A/T: Front Console Box

Upper Console Box Mounting Bracket

24.3b Typical Tacoma center console mounting details

Rear Console Box Cover

Rear Console Box

Console Panel Garnish

Upper Console Panel

Upper Console Box Mounting Bracket

Rear Console Box Mounting Bracket

Rear Console Box

24.3c Typical 4Runner center console mounting details

2   Remove the shift lever knob (see Chapter 7A or 7B); on 4WD models, remove the transfer shift lever knob (see Chapter 7C).

3   Remove the retaining screws and remove the console **(see illustrations)**.

4   Installation is the reverse of removal.

25 Dashboard trim panels - removal and installation

Warning: *Some models covered by this manual are equipped with airbags. The airbag is armed and can deploy (inflate) anytime the battery is connected. To prevent accidental deployment (and possible injury), turn the ignition key to LOCK and disconnect the negative battery cable whenever working near airbag components. After the battery is disconnected, wait at least two minutes before beginning work (the system has a back-up capacitor that must fully discharge). For more information see Chapter 12.*

1   Disconnect the negative battery cable.

Caution: *On models equipped with an anti-theft audio system, be sure the lockout feature is turned off before disconnecting the battery.*

2   Disable the airbag system (see Chapter 12).

3   Remove the steering wheel (see Chapter 10).

4   Remove the steering column cover (see Section 23).

T100 models

Refer to illustrations 25.5, 25.12 and 25.13

5   Remove the front pillar garnish, front door scuff plate and cowl side trim **(see illustration)**.

6   Remove the hood lock release lever (see Section 10).

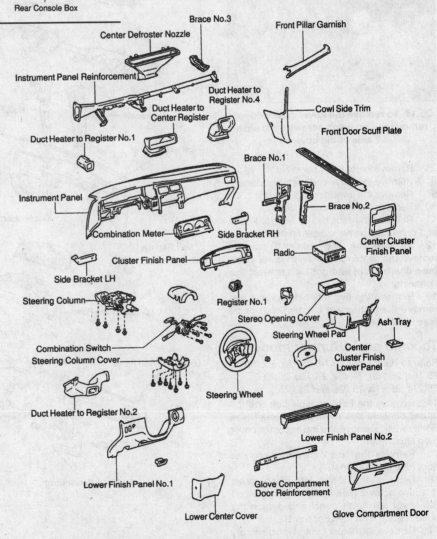

Brace No.3

Center Defroster Nozzle

Front Pillar Garnish

Instrument Panel Reinforcement

Duct Heater to Register No.4

Duct Heater to Center Register

Cowl Side Trim

Duct Heater to Register No.1

Front Door Scuff Plate

Brace No.1

Instrument Panel

Brace No.2

Combination Meter

Side Bracket RH

Cluster Finish Panel

Radio

Center Cluster Finish Panel

Side Bracket LH

Steering Column

Register No.1

Stereo Opening Cover

Ash Tray

Combination Switch

Steering Column Cover

Steering Wheel Pad

Center Cluster Finish Lower Panel

Steering Wheel

Duct Heater to Register No.2

Lower Finish Panel No.2

Lower Finish Panel No.1

Glove Compartment Door Reinforcement

Lower Center Cover

Glove Compartment Door

25.5 Exploded view of typical dashboard trim panels (T100 models)

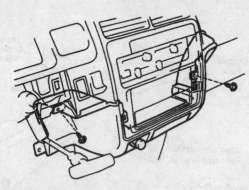

25.12 Remove the two retaining screws, remove the center cluster finish lower panel and unplug the electrical connector

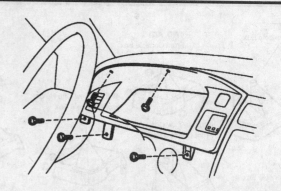

25.13 Instrument cluster bezel mounting details (T100 models)

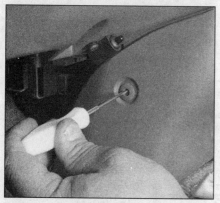

25.14 To remove the lower center cover, remove the retaining screws from each side of the cover

7   Remove lower finish panel No. 1.
8   Remove the glove compartment door.
9   Remove the lower finish panel No. 2.
10   Remove the lower center cover.
11   Remove the four heater control knobs and pry off the center cluster finish panel.
12   Remove the two retaining screws, remove the center cluster finish lower panel **(see illustration)** and unplug the electrical connector.
13   Remove the five retaining screws and remove the instrument cluster finish panel **(see illustration)**.

Tacoma and 4Runner models

Refer to illustrations 25.14, 25.15a, 25.15b, 25.16a, 25.16b, 25.18a, 25.18b, 25.20, 25.21a, 25.21b, 25.22a and 25.22b

14   Remove the front console box and the upper console box mounting bracket (see Section 24). Remove the lower center cover **(see illustration)**.
15   Remove the No. 2 heater-to-register duct **(see illustrations)**.
16   Remove the lower left finish panel retaining screws **(see illustrations)**, pull off the lower left finish panel and detach the hood release lever (see Section 10).
17   Remove the heater control knob and pry off the heater control panel.
18   Remove the center cluster finish panel retaining screws **(see illustrations)**, pull off

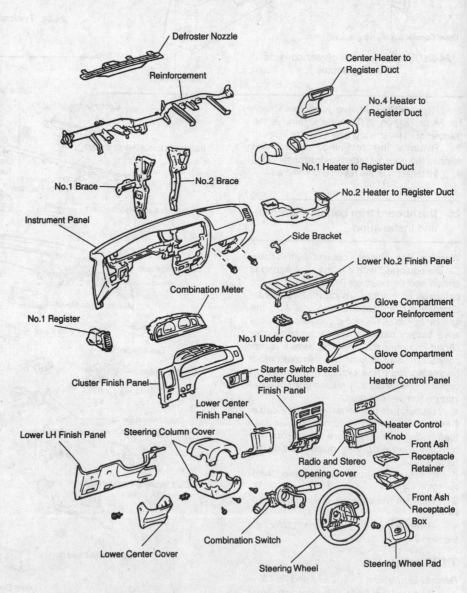

25.15a Exploded view of typical dashboard trim panels (Tacoma models)

Defroster Nozzle
Reinforcement
Center Heater to Register Duct
No.4 Heater to Register Duct
No.1 Brace
No.2 Brace
No.1 Heater to Register Duct
Instrument Panel
No.2 Heater to Register Duct
Side Bracket
Lower No.2 Finish Panel
Combination Meter
No.1 Register
Glove Compartment Door Reinforcement
No.1 Under Cover
Glove Compartment Door
Starter Switch Bezel
Center Cluster Finish Panel
Heater Control Panel
Cluster Finish Panel
Lower Center Finish Panel
Heater Control Knob
Lower LH Finish Panel
Steering Column Cover
Radio and Stereo Opening Cover
Front Ash Receptacle Retainer
Front Ash Receptacle Box
Lower Center Cover
Combination Switch
Steering Wheel
Steering Wheel Pad

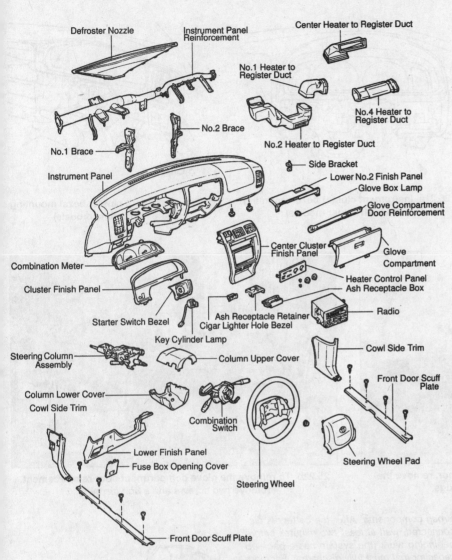

25.15b Exploded view of typical dashboard trim panels (4Runner models)

25.16a To detach the lower left finish panel, remove the retaining screws (arrows) securing the left side of the panel . . .

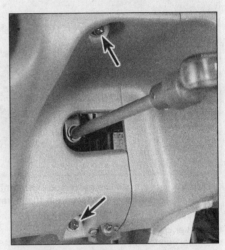

25.16b . . . and the screws (arrows) securing the right side of the panel . . .

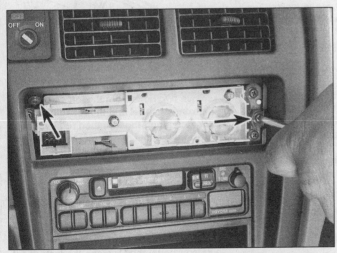

25.18a To remove the center cluster finish panel, remove the retaining screws (arrows) located in the middle of the panel . . .

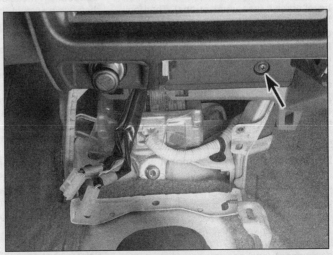

25.18b . . . and at the lower edge (arrow) of the panel - pull off the center cluster finish panel and unplug the electrical connectors

25.20 Pry off the ignition switch bezel and remove it

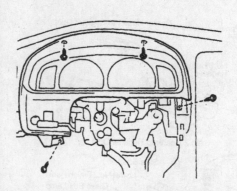

25.21a Instrument cluster bezel mounting details (4Runner models)

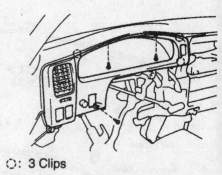

◯: 3 Clips

25.21b Instrument cluster bezel mounting details (Tacoma models)

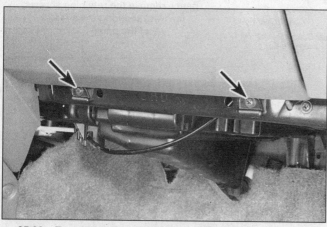

25.22a To remove the glove compartment door, remove the screws (arrows) from the lower edge

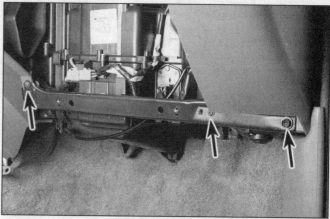

25.22b To remove the glove compartment door reinforcement, remove two screws and a bolt (arrows)

the center cluster finish panel and unplug the electrical connectors.

19 Pry out the cigarette lighter bezel and remove the ashtray and retainer.

20 Pry off the ignition switch bezel **(see illustration)**.

21 Remove the instrument cluster trim bezel screws **(see illustrations)**. Then pull the bezel outward and unplug the electrical connector from the dimmer switch. Remove the instrument cluster trim bezel from the instrument panel. To remove the dimmer switch from the bezel, simply pry off the knob and remove the switch retaining nut.

22 Remove the glove compartment door and the glove compartment door reinforcement **(see illustrations)**.

26 Instrument panel - removal and installation

Warning: *Some models covered by this manual are equipped with airbags. The airbag is armed and can deploy (inflate) anytime the battery is connected. To prevent accidental deployment (and possible injury), turn the ignition key to LOCK and disconnect the negative battery cable whenever working near*

airbag components. After the battery is disconnected, wait at least two minutes before beginning work (the system has a back-up capacitor that must fully discharge). For more information see Chapter 12.

1 Disconnect the negative battery cable.
Caution: *On models equipped with an anti-theft audio system, be sure the lockout feature is turned off before disconnecting the battery.*

2 Disable the airbag system (see Chapter 12).

3 Remove the steering wheel (see Chapter 10).

4 Remove the steering column covers (see Section 23) and all the dashboard trim panels described in Section 25.

5 Remove the heater and air conditioning controls (see Chapter 3).

6 Remove the instrument cluster and radio (see Chapter 12).

7 Unplug all electrical connectors. Mark them to facilitate correct identification when the instrument panel is reassembled.

T100 models

Refer to illustration 26.9

8 Remove register No. 1, duct heater-to-register No. 1, duct heater-to-register No. 2,

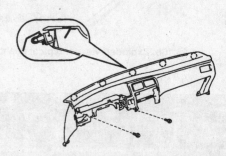

26.9 To remove a T100 instrument panel, remove two bolts from the left side of the instrument panel and the retaining clips located along the top, then remove the instrument panel reinforcement fasteners (not shown)

the glove compartment door reinforcement, braces No. 1 and No. 2 **(see illustration 25.5)**.

9 Detach the instrument panel bolts and clips **(see illustration)**, the reinforcement nuts and bolts, then remove the instrument panel.

10 Installation is the reverse of removal.

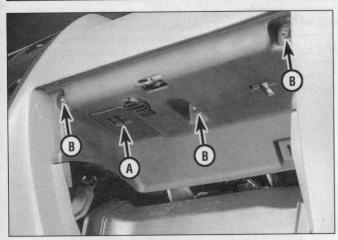

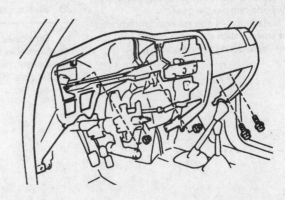

26.13a To detach the instrument panel on Tacoma models, remove the two nuts and two bolts located across the center of the instrument panel, then detach the clips securing the instrument panel at base of the window

26.12 Open the access cover (A) and unplug the passenger side airbag connector if equipped, then remove the glove compartment reinforcement bolts or screws (B)

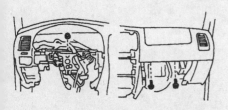

26.13b To detach the instrument panel on 4Runner models, remove the nut and two bolts located across the center of the instrument panel, then detach the clips securing the instrument panel at base of the window

Tacoma and 4Runner models

Refer to illustrations 26.12, 26.13a and 26.13b

11   Remove the No. 1 and No.4 heater-to-register duct **(see illustrations 25.15a and 25.15b)**.

12   Open the access cover in the ceiling of the glove compartment **(see illustration)** and unplug the passenger side airbag connector if equipped. Also remove the glove compartment reinforcement bolts.

13   On Tacoma models, remove the two bolts and two nuts **(see illustration)**. On 4Runner models, remove the single nut and two bolts **(see illustration)**. Remove the instrument panel.

14   Installation is the reverse of removal.

27   Cowl vent grille - removal and installation

Refer to illustrations 27.2a and 27.2b

1   Mark the position of the windshield wiper blades on the windshield with a wax marking pen or pieces of tape.

2   Pry the wiper arm covers up, remove the nuts and detach the wipers **(see illustrations)**.

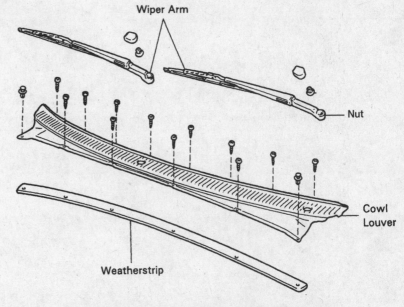

27.2a Cowl vent grille mounting details (T100 models)

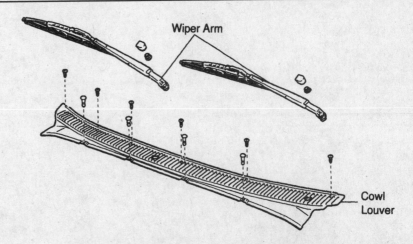

27.2b Cowl vent grille mounting details (Tacoma and 4Runner models)

3   Remove the cowl retaining clips and screws and remove the cowl.

4   Installation is the reverse of removal. Make sure to align the wiper blades with the marks made during removal.

28   Seats - removal and installation

1   On power seat models, disconnect the negative cable from the battery. **Caution:** *On models equipped with an anti-theft audio system, be sure the lockout feature is turned off before disconnecting the battery.*

2   Unplug any electrical connectors.

3   Remove the seat track covers.

4   Remove the seat mounting bolts and remove the seat.

5   Installation is the reverse of removal. Tighten the bolts securely.

Chapter 12
Chassis electrical system

Contents

1 General information

Warning: *Some models covered by this manual are equipped with airbags. The airbag is armed and can deploy (inflate) anytime the battery is connected. To prevent accidental deployment (and possible injury), turn the ignition key to LOCK and disconnect the negative battery cable whenever working near airbag components. After the battery is disconnected, wait at least two minutes before beginning work (the system has a back-up capacitor that must fully discharge). For more information see Section 28.*
Caution: *On models equipped with an anti-theft audio system, be sure the lockout feature is turned off before disconnecting the battery.*

The electrical system is a 12-volt, negative ground type. Power for the lights and all electrical accessories is supplied by a lead/acid-type battery which is charged by the alternator.

This Chapter covers repair and service procedures for the various electrical components not associated with the engine. Information on the battery, alternator, ignition system and starter motor can be found in Chapter 5. It should be noted that when portions of the electrical system are serviced, the negative battery cable should be disconnected from the battery to prevent electrical shorts and/or fires.

2 Electrical troubleshooting - general information

A typical electrical circuit consists of an electrical component, any switches, relays, motors, fuses, fusible links or circuit breakers related to that component and the wiring and electrical connectors that link the component to both the battery and the chassis. To help you pinpoint an electrical circuit problem, wiring diagrams are included at the end of this book.

Before tackling any troublesome electrical circuit, first study the appropriate wiring diagrams to get a complete understanding of what makes up that individual circuit. Trouble spots, for instance, can often be narrowed down by noting if other components related to the circuit are operating properly. If several components or circuits fail at one time, chances are the problem is in a fuse or ground connection, because several circuits are often routed through the same fuse and ground connections.

Electrical problems usually stem from simple causes, such as loose or corroded connections, a blown fuse, a melted fusible link or a bad relay. Visually inspect the condition of all fuses, wires and connections in a problem circuit before troubleshooting it.

If testing instruments are going to be utilized, use the diagrams to plan ahead of time where you will make the necessary connections in order to accurately pinpoint the trouble spot.

The basic tools needed for electrical troubleshooting include a circuit tester or voltmeter (a 12-volt bulb with a set of test leads can also be used), a continuity tester, which includes a bulb, battery and set of test leads, and a jumper wire, preferably with a circuit breaker incorporated, which can be used to bypass electrical components. Before attempting to locate a problem with test instruments, use the wiring diagram(s) to decide where to make the connections.

Voltage checks

Voltage checks should be performed if a circuit is not functioning properly. Connect one lead of a circuit tester to either the negative battery terminal or a known good ground. Connect the other lead to an electrical connector in the circuit being tested, preferably nearest to the battery or fuse. If the bulb of the tester lights, voltage is present, which means that the part of the circuit between the electrical connector and the battery is problem free. Continue checking the rest of the circuit in the same fashion. When you reach a point at which no voltage is present, the problem lies between that point and the last test point with voltage. Most of the time the problem can be traced to a loose connection. **Note:** *Keep in mind that some circuits receive voltage only when the ignition key is in the Accessory or Run position.*

3.1a The passenger compartment fuse/relay block on T100 models is located in the left kick panel (cover removed)

3.1b The passenger compartment fuse/relay block on Tacoma and 4Runner models is located in the left end of the instrument panel (cover removed)

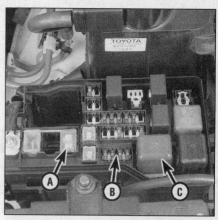

3.1c The engine compartment fuse/relay block is located on the driver's side of the engine compartment - it contains fusible links (A), fuses (B), and relays (C)

Finding a short

One method of finding shorts in a circuit is to remove the fuse and connect a test light or voltmeter in its place to the fuse terminals. There should be no voltage present in the circuit. Move the wiring harness from side-to-side while watching the test light. If the bulb goes on, there is a short to ground somewhere in that area, probably where the insulation has rubbed through. The same test can be performed on each component in the circuit, even a switch.

Ground check

Perform a ground test to check whether a component is properly grounded. Disconnect the battery and connect one lead of a self-powered test light, known as a continuity tester, to a known good ground. Connect the other lead to the wire or ground connection being tested. If the bulb goes on, the ground is good. If the bulb does not go on, the ground is not good.

Continuity check

A continuity check is done to determine if there are any breaks in a circuit - if it is passing electricity properly. With the circuit off (no power in the circuit), a self-powered continuity tester can be used to check the circuit. Connect the test leads to both ends of the circuit (or to the "power" end and a good ground), and if the test light comes on the circuit is passing current properly. If the light doesn't come on, there is a break somewhere in the circuit. The same procedure can be used to test a switch, by connecting the continuity tester to the switch terminals. With the switch turned On, the test light should come on.

Finding an open circuit

When diagnosing for possible open circuits, it is often difficult to locate them by sight because oxidation or terminal misalignment are hidden by the electrical connectors. Merely wiggling an electrical connector on a

sensor or in the wiring harness may correct the open circuit condition. Remember this when an open circuit is indicated when troubleshooting a circuit. Intermittent problems may also be caused by oxidized or loose connections.

Electrical troubleshooting is simple if you keep in mind that all electrical circuits are basically electricity running from the battery, through the wires, switches, relays, fuses and fusible links to each electrical component (light bulb, motor, etc.) and to ground, from which it is passed back to the battery. Any electrical problem is an interruption in the flow of electricity to and from the battery.

3   Fuses - general information

Refer to illustrations 3.1a, 3.1b, 3.1c and 3.3
Caution: *On models equipped with an anti-theft audio system, be sure the lockout feature is turned off before disconnecting the battery.*

1   The electrical circuits of the vehicle are protected by a combination of fuses, circuit breakers and fusible links. The passenger compartment fuse block **(see illustrations)** is located either in the left kick panel (T100 models) or in the left end of the instrument panel (Tacoma and 4Runner models). The engine compartment fuse block **(see illustration)** is located in the left front corner of the engine compartment.

2   Each of the fuses is designed to protect a specific circuit, and the various circuits are identified on the fuse panel itself.

3   Miniaturized fuses are employed in the fuse block. These compact fuses, with blade terminal design, allow fingertip removal and replacement. If an electrical component fails, always check the fuse first. The best way to check the fuses is with a test light. Check for power at the exposed terminal tips of each fuse. If power is present on one side of the fuse but not the other, the fuse is blown. A blown fuse can also be confirmed by visually

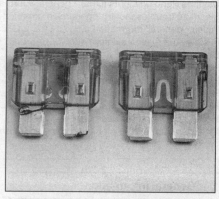

3.3 When a fuse blows, the element between the terminals burns - the fuse on the left is blown, the fuse on the right is good

inspecting it **(see illustration)**.

4   Be sure to replace blown fuses with the correct type. Fuses of different ratings are physically interchangeable, but only fuses of the proper rating should be used. Replacing a fuse with one of a higher or lower value than specified is not recommended. Each electrical circuit needs a specific amount of protection. The amperage value of each fuse is molded into the fuse body.

5   If the replacement fuse fails immediately, don't replace it again until the cause of the problem is isolated and corrected. In most cases, the cause will be a short circuit in the wiring caused by a broken or deteriorated wire.

4   Fusible links - general information

Some circuits are protected by fusible links. The links are used in circuits which are not ordinarily fused, such as the ignition circuit.

A conventional type of fusible link (described below) is used on some early model vehicles, while cartridge type fusible

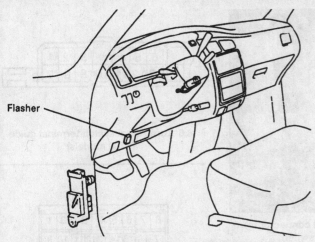

Flasher

7.1a Turn signal and hazard flasher location (T100 models)

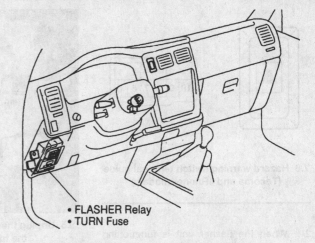

- FLASHER Relay
- TURN Fuse

7.1b Turn signal and hazard flasher location (Tacoma and 4Runner models)

links are used on later models. Cartridge type fusible links are located in the engine compartment fuse block and are similar to a large fuse **(see illustration 3.1c)**, and, after disconnecting the negative battery cable, are simply unplugged and replaced by a unit of the same amperage. Some fusible links are held in place by a screw which must be loosened before removing the link. **Caution:** *On models equipped with an anti-theft audio system, be sure the lockout feature is turned off before disconnecting the battery.*

Conventional type fusible links cannot be repaired. A new link of the same size wire must be installed in its place. The procedure is as follows:

a) *Disconnect the cable from the negative terminal of the battery.* **Caution:** *On models equipped with an anti-theft audio system, be sure the lockout feature is turned off before disconnecting the battery.*

b) *Disconnect the fusible link from the wiring harness.*

c) *Cut the damaged fusible link out of the wiring just behind the connector.*

d) *Strip the insulation back approximately 1/2-inch.*

e) *Position the connector on the new fusible link and crimp it into place.*

f) *Use rosin core solder at each end of the new link to obtain a good solder joint.*

g) *Use plenty of electrical tape around the soldered joint. No wires should be exposed.*

h) *Connect the battery ground cable. Test the circuit for proper operation.*

5 Circuit breakers - general information

Circuit breakers protect components such as power windows, power door locks and headlights.

On some models the circuit breaker resets itself automatically, so an electrical overload in a circuit breaker protected system will cause the circuit to fail momentarily, then come back on. If the circuit doesn't come back on, check it immediately. Once the condition is corrected, the circuit breaker will resume its normal function. Some circuit breakers must be reset manually.

6 Relays - general information and testing

General information

1   Several electrical accessories in the vehicle, such as the fuel injection system, horns, starter, and fog lamps use relays to transmit the electrical signal to the component. Relays use a low-current circuit (the control circuit) to open and close a high-current circuit (the power circuit). If the relay is defective, that component will not operate properly. The various relays are mounted in engine compartment and several locations throughout the vehicle. If a faulty relay is suspected, it can be removed and tested using the procedure below or by a dealer service department or a repair shop. Defective relays must be replaced as a unit.

Testing

2   It's best to refer to the wiring diagram for the circuit to determine the proper hook-ups for the relay you're testing. However, if you're not able to determine the correct hook-up from the wiring diagrams, you may be able to determine the test hook-ups from the information that follows.

3   On most relays, two of the terminals are the relay's control circuit (they connect to the relay coil which, when energized, closes the large contacts to complete the circuit). The other terminals are the power circuit (they are connected together within the relay when the control-circuit coil is energized).

4   The relays are usually marked as an aid to help you determine which terminals are the control circuit and which are the power circuit

(a schematic is molded into the relay cover).

5   Connect a fused jumper wire between one of the two control circuit terminals and the positive battery terminal. Connect another jumper wire between the other control circuit terminal and ground. When the connections are made, the relay should click. On some relays, polarity may be critical, so, if the relay doesn't click, try swapping the jumper wires on the control circuit terminals.

6   With the jumper wires connected, check for continuity between the power circuit terminals as indicated by the markings on the relay.

7   If the relay fails any of the above tests, replace it.

7 Turn signal/hazard flasher and hazard warning switch - check and replacement

Warning: *Some models covered by this manual are equipped with airbags. The airbag is armed and can deploy (inflate) anytime the battery is connected. To prevent accidental deployment (and possible injury), turn the ignition key to LOCK and disconnect the negative battery cable whenever working near airbag components. After the battery is disconnected, wait at least two minutes before beginning work (the system has a back-up capacitor that must fully discharge). For more information see Section 28.*
Caution: *On models equipped with an anti-theft audio system, be sure the lockout feature is turned off before disconnecting the battery.*

Check

Refer to illustrations 7.1a and 7.1b

1   The flasher unit on T100 models is located under the instrument panel, behind the lower left finish panel. The flasher unit on Tacoma and 4Runner models is located in the passenger compartment fuse/relay block **(see illustrations)**.

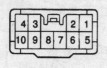

7.8 Hazard warning switch terminal guide (Tacoma and 4Runner models)

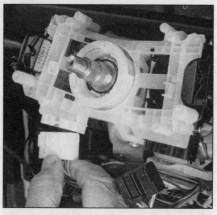

8.5 Unplug the electrical connector from the turn signal switch

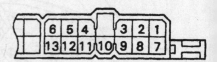

8.6 Turn signal switch terminal guide (T100 models)

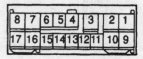

8.8 Turn signal switch terminal guide (Tacoma and 4Runner models)

2   When the flasher unit is functioning properly, an audible click can be heard during its operation. If the turn signals fail on one side or the other and the flasher unit does not make its characteristic clicking sound, a faulty turn signal bulb is indicated.

3   If both turn signals fail to blink, the problem may be due to a blown turn signal fuse (located in the passenger compartment fuse box), a faulty flasher unit, a broken switch or a loose or open connection. If a quick check of the fuse box indicates that the turn-signal fuse has blown, check the wiring for a short before installing a new fuse (see the Wiring Diagrams at the end of this Chapter).

Replacement

Turn signal/hazard flasher

4   To replace the flasher on a T100, remove the left lower finish panel (see Chapter 11) and unplug the flasher. To replace the flasher on a Tacoma or 4Runner, unplug it from the passenger compartment fuse block.

5   Make sure that the replacement unit is identical to the original. Compare the old one to the new one before installing it.

6   Installation is the reverse of removal.

Hazard warning switch

Refer to illustration 7.8

7   Pry the switch out of the dash and unplug it.

8   Using an ohmmeter, verify that there is continuity between terminals 2 and 3 (this is the illumination circuit). Turn the switch Off and verify that there is continuity between terminals 7 and 10. Turn the switch On and verify that there is continuity between terminals 5, 6, and 9, and between terminals 7 and 8 **(see illustration)**.

9   If the hazard warning switch doesn't operate as described, replace it.

8   Turn signal switch - check and replacement

Warning: *Some models covered by this manual are equipped with airbags. The airbag is armed and can deploy (inflate) anytime the battery is connected. To prevent accidental*

deployment *(and possible injury), turn the ignition key to LOCK and disconnect the negative battery cable whenever working near airbag components. After the battery is disconnected, wait at least two minutes before beginning work (the system has a back-up capacitor that must fully discharge). For more information see Section 28.*

Check

Refer to illustrations 8.5, 8.6 and 8.8

1   Disconnect the cable from the negative terminal of the battery. **Caution:** *On models equipped with an anti-theft audio system, be sure the lockout feature is turned off before disconnecting the battery.*

2   Disable the airbag system (see Section 28).

3   Remove the steering wheel (see Chapter 10).

4   Remove the steering column covers (see Chapter 11).

5   Unplug the electrical connector from the turn signal switch/headlight switch **(see illustration)**.

T100 models

6   Using an ohmmeter, check the continuity of the switch terminals **(see illustration)**.

a) *With the turn signal stalk in its "neutral" position, there should be no continuity between any terminals.*

b) *With the turn signal stalk in the "left turn" position, there should be continuity between terminals 3 and 9.*

c) *With the turn signal stalk in the "right turn" position, there should be continuity between terminals 3 and 8.*

7   If the switch doesn't operate as described, replace it.

Tacoma and 4Runner models

8   Using an ohmmeter, check the continuity of the switch terminals **(see illustration)**.

a) *With the turn signal stalk in its "neutral" position, there should be no continuity between any terminals.*

b) *With the turn signal stalk in the "left turn" position, there should be continuity between terminals 1 and 2.*

c) *With the turn signal stalk in the "right turn" position, there should be continuity between terminals 2 and 3.*

9   If the switch doesn't operate as described, replace it.

Replacement

Refer to illustration 8.10

10   Detach the turn signal switch/headlight switch from the switch body **(see illustration)**.

11   Installation is the reverse of removal. Verify that the spiral cable is correctly centered before installing the steering wheel (see Chapter 10).

9   Ignition switch and key lock cylinder - check and replacement

Warning: *Some models covered by this manual are equipped with airbags. The airbag is armed and can deploy (inflate) anytime the battery is connected. To prevent accidental deployment (and possible injury), turn the ignition key to LOCK and disconnect the negative battery cable whenever working near airbag components. After the battery is disconnected, wait at least two minutes before beginning work (the system has a back-up capacitor that must fully discharge). For more information see Section 28.*

Check

Refer to illustrations 9.6, 9.7, 9.10 and 9.11

1   Disconnect the cable from the negative terminal of the battery. **Caution:** *On models equipped with an anti-theft audio system, be sure the lockout feature is turned off before disconnecting the battery.*

2   Disable the airbag system (see Section 28).

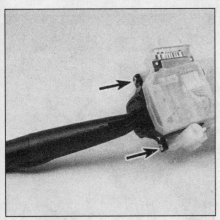

8.10 To detach the turn signal switch from the switch body, remove these two screws (switch body removed from steering column for clarity)

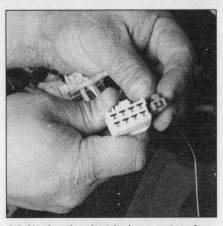

9.6 Unplug the electrical connectors from the ignition switch (Tacoma shown, 4Runner similar; there's only one connector on T100 models)

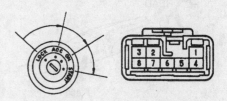

9.7 Ignition switch and key unlock warning switch terminal guide (T100 models)

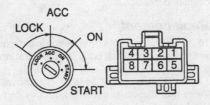

9.10 Ignition switch terminal guide (Tacoma and 4Runner models)

9.11 Key unlock warning switch terminal guide (Tacoma and 4Runner models)

3   Remove the steering wheel (see Chapter 10).

4   Remove the steering column covers (see Chapter 11).

5   Pry off the starter switch bezel (see Chapter 11).

6   Unplug the electrical connectors from the ignition switch **(see illustration)**.

T100 models

7   Using an ohmmeter, check the continuity of the switch terminals **(see illustration)**.

a) *With the key turned to LOCK, there should be no continuity.*

b) *With the key turned to ACC, there should be continuity between terminals 2 and 3.*

c) *With the key turned to ON, there should be continuity between terminals 1, 2 and 3 and between terminals 7 and 8.*

d) *With the key turned to START, there should be continuity between terminals 1, 3 and 6 and between terminals 7 and 8.*

8   Check the continuity of the key unlock warning switch with the switch OFF and the key removed; there should be no continuity. Insert the key and turn the switch ON; there should be continuity between terminals 4 and 5 **(see illustration 9.7)**.

9   If the ignition switch doesn't operate as described, replace it.

Tacoma and 4Runner models

10   Using an ohmmeter, check the continuity of the switch terminals **(see illustration)**.

a) *With the key turned to LOCK, there should be no continuity.*

b) *With the key turned to ACC, there should be continuity between terminals 2 and 3.*

c) *With the key turned to ON, there should be continuity between terminals 2, 3 and 4 and between terminals 6 and 7.*

d) *With the key turned to START, there should be continuity between terminals 1, 2 and 4 and between terminals 6, 7 and 8.*

11   Check the continuity of the key unlock warning switch with the switch OFF and the key removed, there should be no continuity. Insert the key and turn the switch ON, there should be continuity between terminals 1 and 2 **(see illustration)**.

12   If the ignition switch doesn't operate as described, replace it.

Replacement

Refer to illustration 9.15

13   Follow Steps 1 through 6.

14   Insert the key in the ignition switch key lock cylinder and turn the key to ACC.

15   Insert a small screwdriver into the hole in the bottom of the ignition switch casting **(see illustration)** and press the release button while pulling the lock cylinder straight out.

16   Installation is the reverse of removal.

10   Headlight switch - check and replacement

Warning: *Some models covered by this manual are equipped with airbags. The airbag is armed and can deploy (inflate) anytime the battery is connected. To prevent accidental deployment (and possible injury), turn the ignition key to LOCK and disconnect the negative battery cable whenever working near airbag components. After the battery is dis-*

connected, wait at least two minutes before beginning work (the system has a back-up capacitor that must fully discharge). For more information see Section 28.

Check

Refer to illustrations 10.6 and 10.8

1   Disconnect the cable from the negative terminal of the battery. **Caution:** *On models equipped with an anti-theft audio system, be sure the lockout feature is turned off before disconnecting the battery.*

2   Disable the airbag system (see Section 28).

3   Remove the steering wheel (see Chapter 10).

4   Remove the steering column covers (see Chapter 11).

9.15 Insert a small screwdriver into the hole in the bottom of the ignition switch casting and press the release button while pulling the lock cylinder straight out

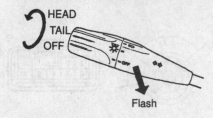

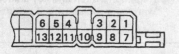

10.6 Headlight control switch terminal guide (T100 models)

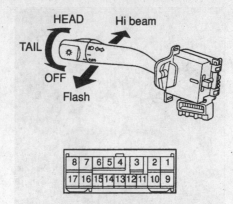

10.8 Headlight control switch terminal guide (Tacoma and 4Runner models)

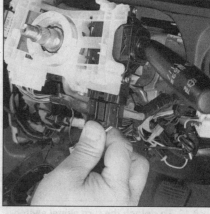

11.5 Unplug the electrical connector from the windshield wiper switch

5   Unplug the electrical connector from the turn signal switch/headlight switch **(see illustration 8.5)**.

T100 models

6   Using an ohmmeter, check the continuity of the switch terminals **(see illustration)**.

a) *With the switch in the OFF position there should be no continuity between any terminals on Low or High beam, but there should be continuity between terminals 5, 12 and 13 with the switch in the FLASH position.*

b) *With the switch in the TAIL position, there should be continuity between terminals 10 and 11 on low beam and on high beam, and there should be continuity between terminals 10 and 11 and between terminals 5, 12 and 13 with the switch in the FLASH position.*

c) *With the switch in the HEAD position, there should be continuity between terminals 4, 10, and 11 and between terminals 6 and 13 on low beam. Continuity between terminals 4, 10 and 11 and between 5 and 13 on high beam. Continuity between terminals 4, 10, and 11, and between terminals 5, 12 and 13 with the switch in the FLASH position.*

7   If the switch doesn't operate as described, replace it.

Tacoma and 4Runner models

8   Using an ohmmeter, check the continuity of the switch terminals **(see illustration)**.

a) *With the light control switch in the OFF position, there should be no continuity between any terminals.*

b) *With the switch in the TAIL position, there should be continuity between terminals 14 and 16.*

c) *With the switch in the HEAD position, there should be continuity between terminals 13, 14 and 16.*

d) *With the headlight dimmer switch on Low beam, there should be continuity between terminals 16 and 17.*

e) *With the switch on High beam, there should be continuity between terminals 7 and 16.*

f) *With the switch on Flash, there should be continuity between terminals 7, 8 and 16.*

9   If the switch doesn't operate as described, replace it.

Replacement

10   Detach the turn signal switch/headlight switch from the switch body **(see illustration 8.10)**.

11   Installation is the reverse of removal. Verify that the spiral cable is correctly centered before installing the steering wheel (see Chapter 10).

w/MIST WIPER

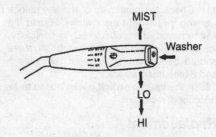

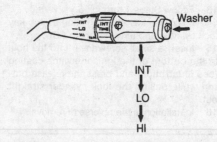

11.6 Windshield wiper and washer switch terminal guide (T100 models)

11   Windshield wiper switch - check and replacement

Warning: *Some models covered by this manual are equipped with airbags. The airbag is armed and can deploy (inflate) anytime the battery is connected. To prevent accidental deployment (and possible injury), turn the ignition key to LOCK and disconnect the negative battery cable whenever working near airbag components. After the battery is disconnected, wait at least two minutes before beginning work (the system has a back-up capacitor that must fully discharge). For more information see Section 28.*

Check

Refer to illustrations 11.5, 11.6, 11.9a and 11.9b

1   Disconnect the cable from the negative terminal of the battery. **Caution:** *On models equipped with an anti-theft audio system, be sure the lockout feature is turned off before disconnecting the battery.*

2   Disable the airbag system (see Section 28).

3   Remove the steering wheel (see Chapter 10).

4   Remove the steering column covers (see Chapter 11).

5   Unplug the electrical connector from the windshield wiper switch **(see illustration)**.

T100 models

6   Using an ohmmeter check the continuity of the switch terminals **(see illustration)**.

Mist-type wiper switch

a) *With the switch in the MIST position, there should be continuity between terminals 4 and 8.*

b) *With the switch in the OFF position, there should be continuity between terminals 7 and 8.*

c) *With the switch in the LO position, there should be continuity between terminals 4 and 8.*

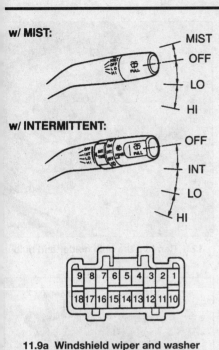

w/ MIST:

MIST
OFF
LO
HI

w/ INTERMITTENT:

OFF
INT
LO
HI

11.9a Windshield wiper and washer switch terminal guide (Tacoma and 4Runner models)

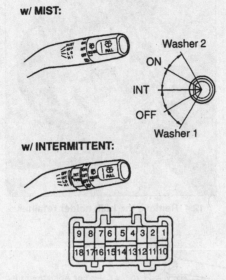

w/ MIST:

Washer 2
ON
INT
OFF
Washer 1

w/ INTERMITTENT:

11.9b Rear window wiper and washer switch terminal guide (Tacoma and 4Runner models)

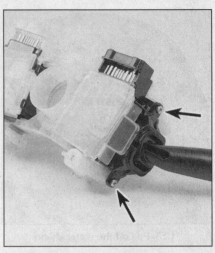

11.12 To detach the windshield wiper and washer switch from the switch body, remove the screws (arrows) (switch body removed from steering column for clarity)

Replacement

Refer to illustration 11.12

12 Detach the windshield wiper switch from the switch body **(see illustration)**.

13 Installation is the reverse of removal. Verify that the spiral cable is correctly centered before installing the steering wheel (see Chapter 10).

---

d) *With the switch in the HI position, there should be continuity between terminals 4 and 9.*

Intermittent-type wiper switch:

a) *With the switch in the OFF position, there should be continuity between terminals 7 and 8.*

b) *With the switch in the INT position, there should be continuity between terminals 7 and 8.*

c) *With the switch in the LO position, there should be continuity between terminals 4 and 8.*

d) *With the switch in the HI position, there should be continuity between terminals 4 and 9.*

7 To check washer switch on both types, verify that there is no continuity with the switch in the OFF position and continuity between terminals 1 and 2 with the switch in the ON position.

8 If the switch doesn't operate as described, replace it.

Tacoma and 4Runner models

9 Using an ohmmeter, check the continuity of the switch terminals **(see illustrations)**.

Mist-type wiper switch

a) *With the switch in the OFF position, there should be continuity between terminals 7 and 16.*

b) *With the switch in the MIST position, there should be continuity between terminals 7 and 17.*

c) *With the switch in the LO position, there should be continuity between terminals 7 and 17.*

d) *With the switch in the HI position, there should be continuity between terminals 8 and 17.*

Intermittent-type wiper switch

a) *With the switch in the OFF position, there should be continuity between terminals 7 and 16.*

a) *With the switch in the MIST position, there should be continuity between terminals 7 and 16.*

c) *With the switch in the LO position, there should be continuity between terminals 7 and 17.*

d) *With the switch in the HI position, there should be continuity between terminals 8 and 17.*

Rear wiper switch

a) *With the switch at the Washer 1 position, there should be continuity between terminals 2 and 12.*

b) *With the switch at the Wiper OFF position, there should be no continuity.*

c) *With the switch at the Wiper INT position, there should be continuity between terminals 2 and 13.*

d) *With the switch at the Wiper ON position, there should be continuity between terminals 2 and 10.*

e) *With the switch at the Washer 2 position, there should be continuity between terminals 2, 10 and 12.*

10 To check washer switch on both types, verify that there is continuity between terminals 2 and 11 with the switch in the ON position.

11 If the switch doesn't operate as described, replace it.

12 Headlight bulb - replacement

Refer to illustrations 12.2, 12.3, 12.4 and 12.5

1 Disconnect the cable from the negative terminal of the battery. **Caution:** *On models equipped with an anti-theft audio system, be sure the lockout feature is turned off before disconnecting the battery.*

2 Unplug the electrical connector from the headlight bulb holder **(see illustration)**. On T100 models, rotate the plastic bulb holder cover counterclockwise and remove it.

12.2 Unplug the electrical connector from the headlight bulb holder

12.3 Pull off the water shield

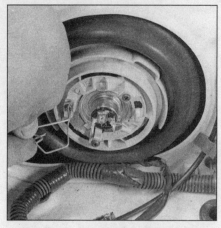

12.4 Remove the bulb holder retainer

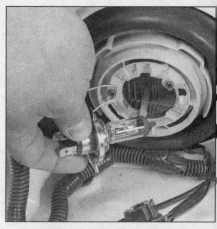

12.5 Remove the bulb holder and bulb

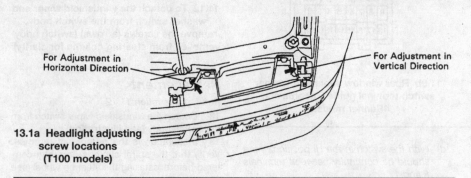

13.1a Headlight adjusting screw locations (T100 models)

For Adjustment in Horizontal Direction

For Adjustment in Vertical Direction

13.1b The headlight adjusting screws on Tacoma and 4Runner models are located on the backside of the headlight housing (headlight housing removed for clarity)

Horizontal

Vertical

3   Pull off the water shield **(see illustration)**.
4   Remove the bulb holder retainer **(see illustration)**.
5   Remove the bulb holder and bulb **(see illustration)**.
6   Installation is the reverse of removal. **Caution:** *Don't touch the bulb with your fingers. If you do, clean it with rubbing alcohol (the oil from your skin can cause the bulb to overheat and fail).*

13   Headlights - adjustment

Refer to illustrations 13.1a, 13.1b and 13.3
Note: *The headlights must be aimed correctly. If adjusted incorrectly they could blind the driver of an oncoming vehicle and cause a serious accident or seriously reduce your ability to see the road. The headlights should be checked for proper aim every 12 months and any time a new headlight is installed or front end body work is performed. It should be emphasized that the following procedure is only an interim step which will provide temporary adjustment until the headlights can be adjusted by a properly equipped shop.*
1   The headlights have two adjusting screws on the headlight housing, one to control up-and-down (vertical) movement and the other to control left-and-right (horizontal) movement **(see illustrations)**.
2   There are several methods of adjusting the headlights. The simplest method requires

13.3 Headlight adjustment details

High-Intensity Area

Floor to Center of Headlamp Lens

Center of Vehicle to Center of Headlamp Lens

Vehicle Centerline

25 FT

Front of Headlamp

a blank wall 25-feet in front of the vehicle and a level floor.
3   Position masking tape vertically on the wall in reference to the vehicle centerline and the centerlines of both headlights **(see illustration)**.
4   Position a horizontal tape line in reference to the centerline of all the headlights.
Note: *It may be easier to position the tape on*

the wall with the vehicle parked only a few inches away.
5   Adjustment should be made with the vehicle sitting level, the gas tank half-full and no unusually heavy load in the vehicle.
6   Starting with the low beam adjustment, position the high intensity zone so it's two inches below the horizontal line and two inches to the right of the headlight vertical line. Adjustment is made by turning the top adjusting screw clockwise to raise the beam and counterclockwise to lower the beam. The adjusting screw on the side should be used in the same manner to move the beam left or right.
7   With the high beams on, the high intensity zone should be vertically centered with the exact center just below the horizontal line. **Note:** *It may not be possible to position the headlight aim exactly for both high and low beams. If a compromise must be made, keep in mind that the low beams are the most used and have the greatest effect on driver safety.*
8   Have the headlights adjusted by a dealer service department or service station at the earliest opportunity.

14.5a To detach the headlight housing, remove the nuts (arrows) on the side . . .

14.5b . . . and the bolts (arrows) on the front of the housing

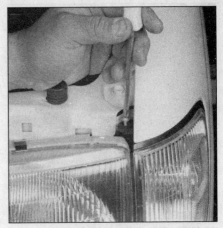

15.2 Remove the upper side marker retaining screw

14 Headlight housing - removal and installation

Refer to illustrations 14.5a and 14.5b
Warning: *Some models covered by this manual are equipped with airbags. The airbag is armed and can deploy (inflate) anytime the battery is connected. To prevent accidental deployment (and possible injury), turn the ignition key to LOCK and disconnect the negative battery cable whenever working near airbag components. After the battery is disconnected, wait at least two minutes before beginning work (the system has a back-up capacitor that must fully discharge). For more information see Section 28.*
1   Disconnect the negative cable from the battery. **Caution:** *On models equipped with an anti-theft audio system, be sure the lockout feature is turned off before disconnecting the battery.*
2   Unplug the electrical connector from the headlight bulb **(see illustration 12.2).**
3   Remove the side marker light (see Section 15).

4   If the radiator grille includes the headlight trim, remove the grille (see Chapter 11). If not, remove the trim piece below the headlights **(see illustrations 16.3a and 16.3b in Chapter 11).**
5   Remove the headlight housing retaining nuts and bolts **(see illustrations)** and pull out the assembly.
6   Installation is the reverse of removal. Check and adjust headlights (see Section 13).

15 Bulb replacement

1   Disconnect the negative cable from the battery. **Caution:** *On models equipped with an anti-theft audio system, be sure the lockout feature is turned off before disconnecting the battery.*

Front side marker lights

Refer to illustrations 15.2, 15.4 and 15.5
2   Remove the upper side marker retaining screw **(see illustration).**

3   Pull out the side marker light housing and unplug the electrical connector.
4   Turn the bulb holder counterclockwise and remove it from the side marker light housing **(see illustration).**
5   To detach the bulb from the bulb holder, pull it straight out **(see illustration).**
6   Installation is the reverse of removal.

Front turn signal lights

Refer to illustration 15.8
7   For your convenience, you may wish to raise the front of the vehicle and support it securely on jackstands. However, it's not essential. Locate the turn signal light in the backside of the bumper. Use a flashlight if necessary.
8   Rotate the bulb holder counterclockwise and remove it **(see illustration). Note:** *Some models may require detaching the lens and removing the bulb from the front of the vehicle.*
9   To remove the turn signal bulb from the holder, turn it counterclockwise and pull it out.
10   Installation is the reverse of removal.

15.4 Turn the bulb holder counterclockwise and remove it from the side marker light housing

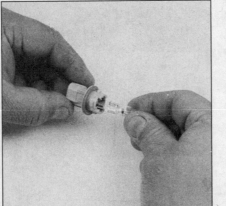

15.5 To detach the side marker bulb from the bulb holder, pull it straight out

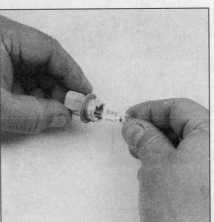

15.8 Rotate the front turn signal bulb holder counterclockwise and remove it from the turn signal housing - rotate the bulb counterclockwise and pull straight out to remove it

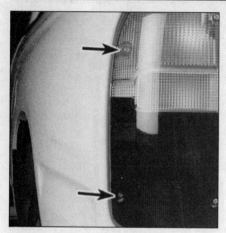

15.11 To detach the tail light lens, remove the screws (arrows)

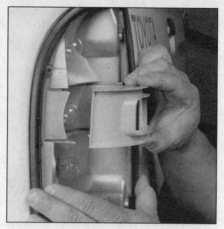

15.13 To replace the turn signal bulb or brake light bulb, simply turn it counterclockwise and pull it out of the tail light housing - to access the back-up light bulb, remove the plastic partition

15.14 To remove the tail light housing, unplug the main connector and detach the housing from the vehicle

Rear tail light/brake light/turn signal

Refer to illustrations 15.11, 15.13 and 15.14

11   Remove the tail light lens (**see illustration**).
12   To replace the turn signal bulb or brake light bulb, simply turn it counterclockwise and pull it out. **Note:** *Some models may require removing the tail light housing and removing the bulbs from the rear of the housing.*
13   To get to the back-up light bulb, remove the plastic partition (**see illustration**).
14   To remove the entire tail light assembly, unplug the main connector and remove it from the vehicle (**see illustration**).
15   Installation is the reverse of removal.

License plate light

Refer to illustration 15.17

16   For your convenience, you may wish to raise the rear of the vehicle and support it securely on jackstands. However, it's not essential. Locate the license plate light in the rear bumper. Use a flashlight if necessary.
17   To remove the bulb holder, turn it counterclockwise and pull it out (**see illustration**).

On 4Runner models, remove the lens retaining screws.
18   To remove the bulb from the holder, pull it straight out (**see illustration 15.5**).
19   Installation is the reverse of removal.

Heater control panel light

Refer to illustration 15.21

20   Remove the dashboard trim panel surrounding the heater and air conditioning control panel (see Chapter 11).
21   Pull out the defective bulb (**see illustration**).
22   Installation is the reverse of removal.

Instrument cluster light bulbs

Refer to illustration 15.24

23   Remove the instrument cluster (see Section 21).
24   Rotate the bulb holder counterclockwise and pull it out of the cluster (**see illustration**).
25   To remove the bulb from the holder, simply pull it straight out (**see illustration 15.5**).
26   Installation is the reverse of removal.

16   Radio and speakers - removal and installation

Warning: *Some models covered by this manual are equipped with airbags. The airbag is armed and can deploy (inflate) anytime the battery is connected. To prevent accidental deployment (and possible injury), turn the ignition key to LOCK and disconnect the negative battery cable whenever working near airbag components. After the battery is disconnected, wait at least two minutes before beginning work (the system has a back-up capacitor that must fully discharge). For more information see Section 28.*

Radio

Refer to illustrations 16.3a, 16.3b and 16.3c

1   Detach the cable from the negative terminal of the battery. **Caution:** *On models equipped with an anti-theft audio system, be sure the lockout feature is turned off before disconnecting the battery.*
2   Remove the center cluster finish bezel (see Chapter 11).

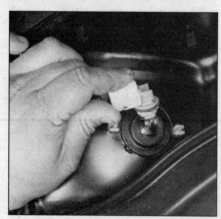

15.17 To remove the license plate bulb holder, turn it counterclockwise and pull it out (Tacoma model shown, T100 similar)

15.21 To replace the heater control panel bulbs, first remove dashboard trim panel, then simply pull the bulb(s) straight out

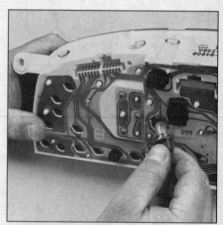

15.24 To remove a bulb from the instrument cluster, rotate the bulb holder counterclockwise and pull it out

16.3a To detach the radio from the instrument panel, remove the mounting bolts (arrows) . . .

16.3b . . . pull out the radio, unplug the antenna lead . . .

16.3c . . . and unplug the electrical connectors (Tacoma model shown, other models similar)

16.7a To remove a door-mounted speaker, remove the retaining screws (arrows), pull off the speaker and unplug the electrical connector (T100 speaker shown, other models similar)

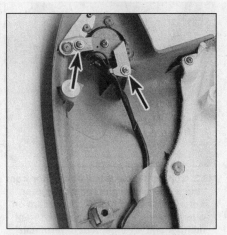

16.7b To remove a door trim panel-mounted tweeter, unplug the electrical connector and remove the speaker retaining screws (arrows)

17.2 Use a small open-end wrench to unscrew the antenna mast

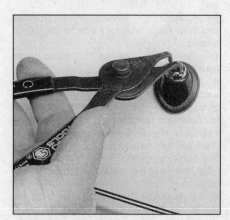

17.3 Use a pair of snap ring pliers or similar tool to loosen and remove the antenna base retaining nut

3   Remove the radio retaining bolts **(see illustration)** and pull out the radio, then disconnect the antenna lead and the electrical connector **(see illustrations)**.
4   Remove the radio from the instrument panel.
5   Installation is the reverse of removal.

Speakers

Refer to illustrations 16.7a and 16.7b
6   All models have at least one speaker in each door. T100 and 4Runner models also have a tweeter in each door trim panel. Some extra cab T100 models are also equipped with a pair of rear speakers. To remove any door-mounted speaker, remove the door trim panel (see Chapter 11).
7   Remove the speaker retaining screws and unplug the electrical connector **(see illustrations)**.
8   To remove a rear speaker on a T100 model, remove the speaker enclosure, unplug the electrical connector and remove the speaker retaining screws.
9   Installation is the reverse of removal.

17 Antenna - removal and installation

Note: *The following procedure applies to conventional external type antennas. It does not apply to the glass-printed antennas used on some 4Runner models. Glass-printed antennas should be serviced by a dealer service department or other qualified repair shop.*
1   Remove the radio and unplug the antenna cable **(see Section 16)**. Trace the routing of the cable and detach all cable clamps and/or clips. Attach about four or five feet of string or wire to the antenna lead to help aid the installation of the new antenna lead.

Fixed antenna

Refer to illustrations 17.2 and 17.3
2   Use a small open-end wrench to unscrew the antenna mast **(see illustration)**.
3   Remove the antenna base retaining nut **(see illustration)**, then detach the antenna

base and pull out the antenna lead until the string or wire is exposed.
4   Attach the string or wire to the new antenna lead and pull the antenna lead back through.
5   Installation is otherwise the reverse of removal.

17.9a On 4Runner models with wheel opening extensions, remove the three fender liner clips (arrows) and pull out the fender liner . . .

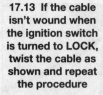

17.13 If the cable isn't wound when the ignition switch is turned to LOCK, twist the cable as shown and repeat the procedure

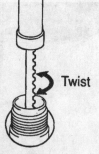

Twist

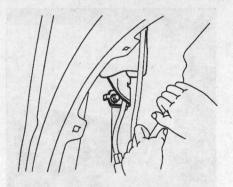

17.9b . . . unplug the electrical connector from the antenna motor and remove the antenna motor retaining bolt (arrow)

18.2 Unplug the electrical connector from the windshield wiper motor (Tacoma motor connector shown, connectors on other models similar but have different number and arrangement of terminals)

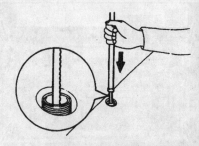

17.12 Install the antenna mast with the teeth on the cable facing forward

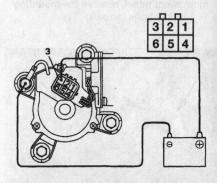

18.4 Connect a lead from the positive battery terminal to motor terminal 3 and the other lead from the negative battery terminal to the motor body and verify that the motor runs at low speed; switch the positive lead to terminal 2 and verify that the motor runs at high speed (T100 models)

Power antenna

Refer to illustrations 17.9a, 17.9b, 17.12 and 17.13

Note: *At least two people should perform this task.*

6   Connect the battery, if disconnected and turn the ignition switch to the LOCK position.

7   Remove the antenna base retaining nut **(see illustration 17.3)**.

8   With one person controlling the ignition switch and the second person holding the antenna mast. Press the AM/FM buttons on the radio and simultaneously turn the ignition switch to the ACC position. The antenna mast will fully extend and be detached from the antenna motor. Remove the antenna mast, but leave the ignition switch in the ACC position.

9   Detach the inner fenderwell from the fender (see Chapter 11) and unbolt the power antenna motor from the fender. Pull out the antenna lead until the string or wire is exposed. On 4Runner models with wheel opening extensions, remove the three fender liner clips **(see illustration)**, pull out the fender liner, unplug the electrical connector from the antenna motor, remove the antenna motor retaining bolt **(see illustration)** and remove the antenna motor.

10   Attach the string or wire to the new antenna lead and pull the antenna lead back into the passenger compartment.

11   Install the power antenna motor.

12   Install the antenna mast with the teeth on the cable facing forward **(see illustration)**.

13   To wind the cable and retract the mast, turn the ignition switch to the LOCK position (if the ignition switch has already been turned from ACC to LOCK, repeat Step 8 first). If the cable isn't wound when the ignition switch is turned to LOCK, twist the cable as shown **(see illustration)**.

14   Install the antenna base retaining nut, even if the mast hasn't fully retracted yet. Press the radio wave band select buttons and the antenna will retract.

15   The remainder of the installation is the reverse of removal.

18 Wiper motor - check and replacement

Check

Refer to illustration 18.2

1   If the wipers work slowly, make sure the battery is in good condition and has a strong charge (see Chapter 1). If the battery is in good condition, remove the wiper motor (see below) and operate the wiper arms by hand.

Check for binding linkage and pivots. Lubricate or repair the linkage or pivots as necessary. Reinstall the wiper motor. If the wipers still operate slowly, check for loose or corroded connections, especially the ground connection. If all connections look OK, replace the motor.

2   If the wipers fail to operate when activated, check the fuse. If the fuse is OK, connect a jumper wire between the wiper motor and ground, then re-test. If the motor works now, repair the ground connection. If the motor still doesn't work, turn on the wipers, unplug the electrical connector from the motor **(see illustration)** and check for voltage at the motor. If there's no voltage at the motor, Check the switch for continuity (see Section 11). If voltage is present at the motor, check the motor as described below.

3   To access the terminals of a rear wiper motor on 4Runner models, remove the liftgate trim panel (see Chapter 11).

T100 and Tacoma models

Refer to illustrations 18.4 and 18.6

4   Using jumper wires, connect one lead from the positive terminal of the battery to terminal 3 and the other lead from the negative battery terminal to the motor body **(see illustration)** and verify that the motor runs at low speed.

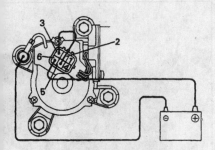

18.6 Bridge terminals 3 and 5, connect the positive battery lead to terminal 6 and the negative battery lead to the motor body, and verify that it stops running at its stop position (T100 models)

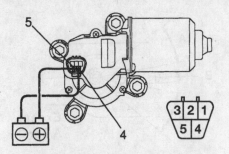

18.8 Using jumper wires, connect the positive battery lead to terminal 5 and the negative battery to the motor body or terminal 4 and verify that the motor runs at low speed (1998 Tacoma models)

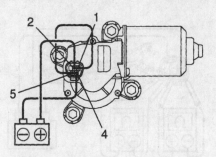

18.10 Bridge terminals 1 and 5, connect the positive battery lead to terminal 2 and the negative battery lead to the motor body or terminal 4, operate the motor at low speed again and verify that it stops running at its stop position (1998 Tacoma models)

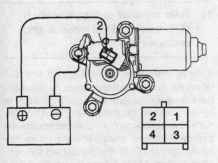

18.12 Connect the positive battery lead to terminal 2 and the negative battery lead to the motor body and verify that the motor runs at low speed (4Runner models)

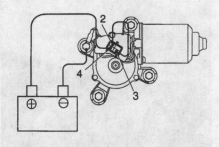

18.14 Bridge terminals 2 and 3, connect the positive battery lead to terminal 4 and the negative battery lead to the motor body, operate the motor at low speed again and verify that it stops running at its stop position (4Runner models)

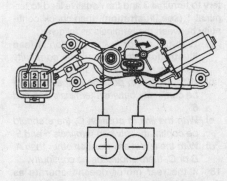

18.16 Connect the positive battery lead to terminal 1 and the negative battery lead to terminal 3 and verify that the rear window wiper motor runs in a clockwise direction; reverse the polarity and verify that the motor runs in a counterclockwise direction (4Runner models)

5   Connect one lead from the positive terminal of the battery to terminal 2 and the other lead from the negative battery terminal to the motor body and verify that the motor runs at high speed.
6   Operating the motor at low speed (see Step 4), disconnect the lead from terminal 3 and stop the motor anywhere except at its stop position, bridge terminals 3 and 5, connect the positive battery lead to terminal 6 and the negative battery lead to the motor body **(see illustration)**, and verify that it stops running at its stop position.
7   If the motor doesn't operate as described, replace it.

Tacoma models (1998)

Refer to illustrations 18.8 and 18.10
Caution: *Perform the following tests quickly (no more than 20 seconds) to protect the coil from overheating and burning out.*
8   Using jumper wires, connect one lead from the positive terminal of the battery to terminal 5 and the other lead from the negative battery terminal to the motor body or terminal 4 **(see illustration)** and verify that the motor runs at low speed.
9   Connect one lead from the positive ter-

minal of the battery to terminal 3 and the other lead from the negative battery terminal to the motor body or terminal 4 and verify that the motor runs at high speed.
10   Operating the motor at low speed (see Step 8), disconnect the lead to terminal 5 and stop the motor anywhere except at its stop position, bridge terminals 1 and 5, connect the positive battery lead to terminal 2 and the negative battery lead to the motor body or terminal 4 **(see illustration)**, operate the motor at low speed again and verify that it stops running at its stop position.
11   If the motor doesn't operate as described, replace it.

4Runner models

Refer to illustrations 18.12 and 18.14
12   Using jumper wires, connect one lead from the positive terminal of the battery to terminal 2 and the other lead from the negative battery terminal to the motor body **(see illustration)** and verify that the motor runs at low speed.
13   Connect one lead from the positive terminal of the battery to terminal 1 and the other lead from the negative battery terminal

to the motor body and verify that the motor runs at high speed.
14   Operating the motor at low speed (see Step 12), disconnect the lead to terminal 2 and stop the motor anywhere except at its stop position, bridge terminals 2 and 3, connect the positive battery lead to terminal 4 and the negative battery lead to the motor body **(see illustration)**, operate the motor at low speed again and verify that it stops running at its stop position.
15   If the motor doesn't operate as described, replace it.

Rear wiper motor (4Runner models)

Refer to illustrations 18.16, 18.17a and 18.17b
16   Using jumper cables, connect one lead from the positive terminal of the battery to terminal 1 and the other lead from the negative battery terminal to terminal 3 **(see illustration)** and verify that the motor runs in a clockwise direction. Reverse the polarity and verify that the motor runs in a counterclockwise direction.

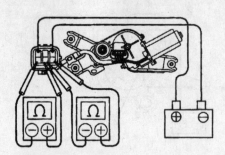

18.17a Connect the positive battery lead to terminal 3 and the negative lead to terminal 1, then check continuity between the specified terminals (4Runner models)

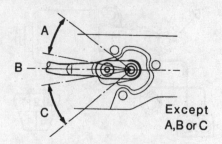

18.17b Motor link positions (4Runner models)

18.20 To remove the windshield wiper motor, remove the mounting bolts (arrows)

17   Connect the positive lead from the battery to terminal 3 and the negative lead to terminal 1 **(see illustration)**, then check continuity between the terminals as follows:

a) *With the motor link in position A* **(see illustration)**, *there should be continuity between terminals 5 and 6.*

b) *With the link in position B, there should be continuity between terminals 4, 5 and 6.*

c) *With the link in position C, there should be continuity between terminals 5 and 6.*

d) *With the link in any position other than A, B or C, there should be no continuity.*

18   If the rear motor doesn't operate as described, replace it.

Replacement

Front wiper motor

Refer to illustrations 18.20, 18.21 and 18.22

19   Remove the cowl (see Chapter 11) and disconnect the electrical connector from the wiper motor.

20   Remove the wiper mounting bolts **(see illustration)**.

21   Pull out the motor and detach the lever arm from the wiper link **(see illustration)**.

22   To remove the wiper linkage, detach the bolts from the cowl **(see illustration)** and remove it through the vent hole.

23   Installation is the reverse of removal.

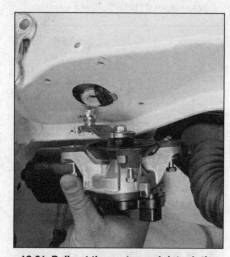

18.21 Pull out the motor and detach the lever arm from the wiper linkage

Rear wiper motor (4Runner models)

24   To detach the wiper arm, flip up the cover and remove the nut.

25   Open the liftgate and remove the trim panel and service hole cover (see Chapter 11).

26   Remove the retaining bolts, unplug the electrical connector, then lift the wiper motor from the vehicle.

27   Installation is the reverse of removal.

19   Rear window defogger switch (4Runner models) - check and replacement

Refer to illustrations 19.3, 19.4, 19.5 and 19.7
Warning: *Some models covered by this manual are equipped with airbags. The airbag is armed and can deploy (inflate) anytime the battery is connected. To prevent accidental deployment (and possible injury), turn the ignition key to LOCK and disconnect the negative battery cable whenever working near airbag components. After the battery is disconnected, wait at least two minutes before beginning work (the system has a back-up capacitor that must fully discharge). For more information see Section 28.*

1   Detach the cable from the negative terminal of the battery. **Caution:** *On models equipped with an anti-theft audio system, be sure the lockout feature is turned off before disconnecting the battery.*

2   Pry the defogger switch out of the dash and unplug it.

3   Verify that there is continuity between terminals 1 and 3 on the relay side of the connector **(see illustration)**. If there isn't, check the bulb.

Relay Side

19.3 To check the rear window defogger indicator bulb, verify that there is continuity between terminals 1 and 3 on the relay side of the connector; if there's no continuity, check the bulb

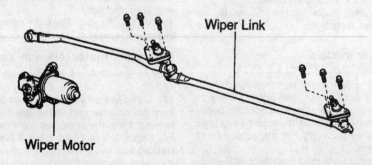

Wiper Link

Wiper Motor

18.22 A typical wiper linkage assembly

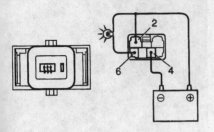

Wire Harness Side

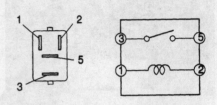

19.4 Check the operation of the defogger timer as indicated

19.5 Defogger timer circuit terminal guide

19.7 Defogger relay terminal guide

20.4 When measuring the voltage at the rear window defogger grid, wrap a piece of aluminum foil around the positive probe of the voltmeter and press the foil against the wire with your finger

20.5 To determine if a heating element has broken, check the voltage at the center of each element - if the voltage is 6-volts, the element is unbroken - if the voltage is 12-volts, the element is broken between the center and the ground side - if there's no voltage, the wire is broken between the center of the wire and the power side

20.7 To find the break, place the voltmeter negative lead against the defogger ground terminal, place the voltmeter positive lead with the foil strip against the heating element at the positive terminal end and slide it toward the negative terminal end - the point at which the voltmeter deflects from 12-volts to zero volts is the point at which the element is broken

Using jumper wires, connect the positive battery lead to terminal 2 and the negative battery lead to terminal 4 on the switch, then connect the positive side of the battery through a 3.4W test bulb to terminal 6 **(see illustration)**. Push the defogger switch on and verify that the indicator light and test bulb light up for 12 to 18 minutes, and then go out. If the switch doesn't operate as specified, replace it.

5   Unplug the electrical connector from the switch and check the switch circuit on the wire harness side as follows:

a) *There should be constant continuity between terminal 4 and ground* **(see illustration)**.

b) *With the ignition switch in LOCK or ACC, there should be no voltage between terminal 2 and ground, and between terminal 6 and ground.*

c) *With the ignition switch in ON, there should be battery voltage between terminal 2 and ground, and between terminal 6 and ground.*

d) *Jump terminals 4 and 6 and verify that the defogger system operates normally.*

6   If the circuit doesn't operate as described, replace the switch.

7   To check the defogger relay (located in the passenger compartment fuse block), verify that there's constant continuity between

terminals 1 and 2 **(see illustration)**. Apply battery voltage between terminals 1 and 2 and verify that there's continuity between terminals 3 and 5.

8   If the relay doesn't operate as described, replace it.

---

20   Rear window defogger (4Runner models) - check and repair

1   The rear window defogger consists of a number of horizontal elements baked onto the glass surface.

2   Small breaks in the element can be repaired without removing the rear window.

Check

Refer to illustrations 20.4, 20.5 and 20.7

3   Turn the ignition switch and defogger system switches to the ON position. Using a voltmeter, place the positive probe against the defogger grid positive terminal and the negative lead against the ground terminal. If battery voltage is not indicated, check the fuse, defogger switch and related wiring.

4   When measuring voltage during the next two tests, wrap a piece of aluminum foil around the tip of the voltmeter positive probe and press the foil against the heating element with your finger **(see illustration)**.

5   Check the voltage at the center of each heating element **(see illustration)**. If the voltage is 6-volts, the element is okay (there is no break). If the voltage is 12-volts, the element is broken between the center of the element and the ground side. If the voltage is 0-volts the element is broken between the center of the element and positive side.

6   If none of the elements are broken, connect the negative lead to a good body ground. the voltage reading should stay the same, if it doesn't the ground connection is bad.

7   To find the break, place the voltmeter negative lead against the defogger ground terminal. Place the voltmeter positive lead with the foil strip against the heating element at the positive terminal end and slide it toward the negative terminal end. The point at which the voltmeter deflects from several volts to zero is the point at which the heating element is broken **(see illustration)**.

20.13 To use a defogger repair kit, apply masking tape to the inside of the window at the damaged area, then brush on the special conductive coating

21.3a To detach the instrument cluster from the instrument panel, remove the retaining screws (arrows) . . .

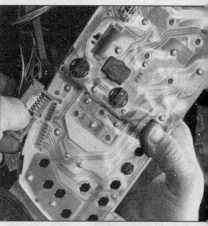

21.3b . . . pull out the cluster and unplug the electrical connectors from the cluster (Tacoma instrument cluster shown, other units similar)

Repair

Refer to illustration 20.13

8   Repair the break in the element using a repair kit specifically recommended for this purpose, such as Dupont paste No. 4817 (or equivalent). Included in this kit is plastic conductive epoxy.

9   Prior to repairing a break, turn off the system and allow it to cool off for a few minutes.

10   Lightly buff the element area with fine steel wool, then clean it thoroughly with rubbing alcohol.

11   Use masking tape to mask off the area being repaired.

12   Thoroughly mix the epoxy, following the instructions provided with the repair kit.

13   Apply the epoxy material to the slit in the masking tape, overlapping the undamaged area about 3/4-inch on either end **(see illustration)**.

14   Allow the repair to cure for 24 hours before removing the tape and using the system.

21   Instrument cluster - removal and installation

Refer to illustrations 21.3a and 21.3b

Warning: *Some models covered by this manual are equipped with airbags. The airbag is armed and can deploy (inflate) anytime the battery is connected. To prevent accidental deployment (and possible injury), turn the ignition key to LOCK and disconnect the negative battery cable whenever working near airbag components. After the battery is disconnected, wait at least two minutes before beginning work (the system has a back-up capacitor that must fully discharge). For more information see Section 28.*

1   Detach the cable from the negative terminal of the battery. **Caution:** *On models equipped with an anti-theft audio system, be sure the lockout feature is turned off before disconnecting the battery.*

2   On T100 models, remove instrument cluster finish panel. On Tacoma and 4Runner models, remove the instrument cluster trim bezel (see Chapter 11).

3   Remove the instrument cluster retaining screws **(see illustration)**, pull out the cluster and unplug the electrical connectors from the cluster **(see illustration)**.

4   Installation is the reverse of removal.

22   Horn - check and replacement

Check

Refer to illustration 22.8

Caution: *On models equipped with an anti-theft audio system, be sure the lockout feature is turned off before disconnecting the battery.*

1   The horn on Tacoma models is located behind the grille, between the radiator and the right headlight. There is an extra horn on T100 and 4Runner models, at the same location on the left side of the radiator.

2   To test the horn, unplug the electrical connector from the horn and connect battery voltage to the two terminals with a pair of jumper wires. If the horn doesn't sound, replace it.

22.8 To detach the horn from the body, remove this bracket bolt (arrow)

3   If the horn does sound, check for voltage at the terminal when the horn button is depressed. If there's voltage at the terminal, check for a bad ground at the horn.

4   If there's no voltage at the horn, check the relay (see Section 6). Note that most horn relays are either the four-terminal or externally grounded three-terminal type.

5   If the relay is OK, check for voltage to the relay power and control circuits. If either of the circuits is not receiving voltage, inspect the wiring between the relay and the fuse panel.

6   If both relay circuits are receiving voltage, depress the horn button and check the circuit from the relay to the horn button for continuity to ground. If there's no continuity, check the circuit for an open. If there's no open circuit, replace the horn button.

7   If there's continuity to ground through the horn button, check for an open or short in the circuit from the relay to the horn.

Replacement

8   To replace a horn, unplug the electrical connector and remove the bracket bolt **(see illustration)**.

9   Unbolt the bracket from the old horn and bolt it onto the new unit.

10   Installation is the reverse of removal.

23   Power mirror control system - description and check

Refer to illustrations 23.7a, 23.7b, 23.7c, 23.12a and 23.12b

1   Most electric rear view mirrors use two motors to move the glass; one for up and down adjustments and one for left-right adjustments.

2   The control switch has a selector portion which sends voltage to the left or right side mirror. With the ignition ON but the engine OFF, roll down the windows and operate the mirror control switch through all func-

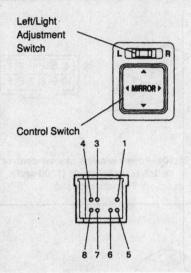

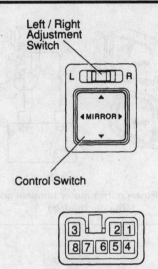

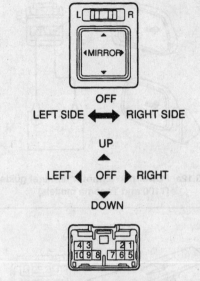

23.7a Power mirror switch terminal guide (T100 models)

23.7b Power mirror switch terminal guide (Tacoma models)

23.7c Power mirror switch terminal guide (4Runner models)

tions (left-right and up-down) for both the left and right side mirrors.

3   Listen carefully for the sound of the electric motors running in the mirrors.

4   If the motors can be heard but the mirror glass doesn't move, there's probably a problem with the drive mechanism inside the mirror. Remove and disassemble the mirror to locate the problem.

5   If the mirrors do not operate and no sound comes from the mirrors, check the fuse (see Chapter 1).

6   If the fuse is OK, remove the mirror control switch from its mounting without disconnecting the wires attached to it. Turn the ignition ON and check for voltage at the switch. There should be voltage at one terminal. If there's no voltage at the switch, check for an open or short in the circuit between the fuse panel and the switch.

7   If there's voltage at the switch, disconnect it. First, verify that there is no continuity when the switch is in the OFF position, then check the switch for continuity in all its operating positions as follows.

T100 models

Left side

a) *With the switch in the UP position, there should be continuity between terminals 3 and 4, and between terminals 1 and 8 (see illustration).*

b) *With the switch in the DOWN position, there should be continuity between terminals 1 and 3, and between terminals 4 and 8.*

c) *With the switch in the LEFT position, there should be continuity between terminals 3 and 4, and between terminals 1 and 7.*

d) *With the switch in the RIGHT position, there should be continuity between terminals 1 and 3, and between terminals 4 and 7.*

Right side

a) *With the switch in the UP position, there should be continuity between terminals 3 and 4, and between terminals 1 and 5.*

b) *With the switch in the DOWN position, there should be continuity between terminals 1 and 3, and between terminals 4 and 5.*

c) *With the switch in the LEFT position, there should be continuity between terminals 3 and 4, and between terminals 1 and 6.*

d) *With the switch in the RIGHT position, there should be continuity between terminals 1 and 3, and between terminals 4 and 6.*

Tacoma models

Left side

a) *With the switch in the UP position, there should be continuity between terminals 2 and 3, and between terminals 1 and 7 (see illustration).*

b) *With the switch in the DOWN position, there should be continuity between terminals 1 and 2, and between terminals 3 and 7.*

c) *With the switch in the LEFT position, there should be continuity between terminals 2 and 3, and between terminals 1 and 8.*

d) *With the switch in the RIGHT position, there should be continuity between terminals 1 and 2, and between terminals 3 and 8.*

Right side

a) *With the switch in the UP position, there should be continuity between terminals 2 and 3, and between terminals 1 and 5.*

b) *With the switch in the DOWN position, there should be continuity between terminals 1 and 2, and between terminals 3 and 5.*

c) *With the switch in the LEFT position, there should be continuity between terminals 2 and 3, and between terminals 1 and 6.*

d) *With the switch in the RIGHT position, there should be continuity between terminals 1 and 2, and between terminals 3 and 6.*

4Runner models

Left side

a) *With the switch in the UP position, there should be continuity between terminals 1 and 9, and between terminals 6 and 10 (see illustration).*

b) *With the switch in the DOWN position, there should be continuity between terminals 1 and 10, and between terminals 6 and 9.*

c) *With the switch in the LEFT position, there should be continuity between terminals 5 and 9, and between terminals 6 and 10.*

d) *With the switch in the RIGHT position, there should be continuity between terminals 5 and 10, and between terminals 6 and 9.*

Right side

a) *With the switch in the UP position, there should be continuity between terminals 6 and 10, and between terminals 7 and 9.*

b) *With the switch in the DOWN position, there should be continuity between terminals 6 and 9, and between terminals 7 and 10.*

c) *With the switch in the LEFT position, there should be continuity between terminals 6 and 10, and between terminals 8 and 9.*

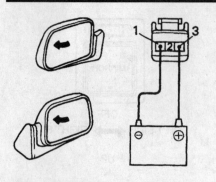

23.12a Power mirror motor terminal guide (T100 and Tacoma models)

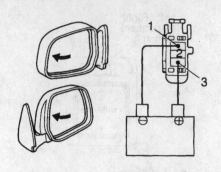

23.12b Power mirror motor terminal guide (4Runner models)

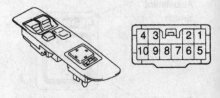

25.10a Power window master control switch terminal guide (T100 and Tacoma models)

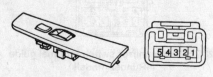

25.10b Passenger window switch terminal guide (T100 and Tacoma models)

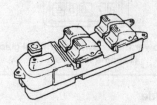

25.10c Power window master control switch terminal guide (4Runner models)

25.10d Passenger window switch terminal guide (4Runner models)

d) *With the switch in the RIGHT position, there should be continuity between terminals 6 and 9, and between terminals 8 and 10.*

8   If the switch does not have the specified continuity, replace it.

9   Re-connect the switch. Locate the wire going from the switch to ground. Leaving the switch connected, connect a jumper wire between this wire and ground. If the mirror works normally with this wire in place, repair the faulty ground connection.

10   If the mirror still doesn't work, remove the mirror and check the wires at the mirror for voltage. Check with ignition ON and the mirror selector switch on the appropriate side. Operate the mirror switch in all its positions. There should be voltage at one of the switch-to-mirror wires in each switch position (except the neutral "off" position).

11   If there's not voltage in each switch position, check the circuit between the mirror and control switch for opens and shorts.

12   If there's voltage, test the mirror motor operation as follows **(see illustrations).**

a) *Using jumper wires, connect the positive lead from the battery to terminal 3 and the negative battery lead to terminal 1 and verify that the mirror turns to the left.*

b) *Reverse the polarity and verify that the mirror turns to the right.*

c) *Connect the positive battery lead to terminal 2 and the negative battery lead to terminal 1 and verify that the mirror turns upward.*

d) *Reverse the polarity and verify that the mirror turns downward.*

13   If the mirror motor fails to operate as described, replace the mirror assembly (see Chapter 11).

24 Cruise control system - description and check

1   The cruise control system maintains vehicle speed with an electrically operated motor located in the engine compartment, which is connected to the throttle lever by a cable. The system consists of the cruise control unit, brake switch, control switches and vehicle speed sensor. Some features of the system require special testers and diagnostic procedures which are beyond the scope of this manual. Listed below are some general procedures that may be used to locate common problems.

2   Locate and check the fuse (see Section 3).

3   Have an assistant operate the brake lights while you check their operation (voltage from the brake light switch deactivates the cruise control).

4   If the brake lights don't come on, or if they stay on all the time, correct the problem and re-test the cruise control.

5   Visually inspect the control cable between the cruise control motor and the throttle linkage for free movement; replace it if necessary.

6   The cruise control system uses a speed sensing device. The speed sensor is located in the speedometer. Check the electrical connectors at the instrument cluster (see Section 21).

7   Test drive the vehicle to determine if the cruise control is now working. If it isn't, take it to a dealer service department or an automotive electrical specialist for further diagnosis.

25 Power window system - description and check

Refer to illustrations 25.10a, 25.10b, 25.10c, 25.10d and 25.12

1   The power window system operates electric motors, mounted in the doors, which lower and raise the windows. The system consists of the control switches, relays, the motors, regulators, glass mechanisms and associated wiring.

2   The power windows can be lowered and raised from the master control switch by the driver or by remote switches located at the individual windows. Each window has a separate motor which is reversible. The position of the control switch determines the polarity and therefore the direction of operation.

3   The circuit is protected by a fuse and a circuit breaker. Each motor is also equipped with an internal circuit breaker; this prevents one stuck window from disabling the whole system.

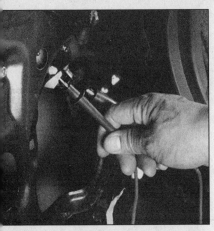

25.12 If no voltage is present at the motor with the switch depressed, check for voltage at the switch

4   The power window system will only operate when the ignition switch is ON. In addition, many models have a window lockout switch at the master control switch which, when activated, disables the switches at the rear windows and, sometimes, the switch at the passenger's window also. Always check these items before troubleshooting a window problem.

5   These procedures are general in nature, so if you can't find the problem using them, take the vehicle to a dealer service department or other properly equipped repair facility.

6   If the power windows won't operate, always check the fuse and circuit breaker first.

7   If only the rear windows are inoperative, or if the windows only operate from the master control switch, check the rear window lockout switch for continuity in the unlocked position. Replace it if it doesn't have continuity.

8   Check the wiring between the switches and fuse panel for continuity. Repair the wiring, if necessary.

9   If only one window is inoperative from the master control switch, try the other control switch at the window. **Note:** *This doesn't apply to the drivers door window.*

10   If the same window works from one switch, but not the other, check the switch for continuity as follows:

T100 and Tacoma models
Master control switch

Driver's switch - window lock and unlock
a) *With the switch in the UP position, there should be continuity between terminals 4 and 6, and between terminals 3 and 9 (see illustrations).*
b) *With the switch in the OFF position, there should be continuity between terminals 3, 4 and 6.*

c) *With the switch in the DOWN position, there should be continuity between terminals 3 and 6, and between terminals 4 and 9.*

Passenger's switch - window unlock
a) *With the switch in the UP position, there should be continuity between terminals 6 and 7, and between terminals 9 and 10.*
b) *With the switch in the OFF position, there should be no continuity.*
c) *With the switch in the DOWN position, there should be continuity between terminals 7 and 9, and between terminals 6 and 10.*

Passenger's switch - window lock
a) *With the switch in the UP position, there should be continuity between terminals 9 and 10.*
b) *With the switch in the OFF position, there should be continuity between terminals 7 and 10.*
c) *With the switch in the DOWN position, there should be continuity between terminals 7 and 9.*

Passenger control switch
a) *With the switch in the UP position, there should be continuity between terminals 1 and 2, and between terminals 3 and 4 (see illustrations).*
b) *With the switch in the OFF position, there should be continuity between terminals 1 and 2, and between terminals 3 and 5.*
c) *With the switch in the DOWN position, there should be continuity between terminals 3 and 5, and between terminals 1 and 4.*

4Runner models
Master control switch

Driver's switch - window lock and unlock
a) *With the switch in the UP position, there should be continuity between terminals 3, 8 and 9, and between terminals 4, 5 and 6 (see illustrations).*
b) *With the switch in the OFF position, there should be continuity between terminals 3, 4 and 5, and between terminals 4, 5 and 6.*
c) *With the switch in the DOWN position, there should be continuity between terminals 6, 8 and 9, and between terminals 3, 4 and 5.*

Front passenger's switch - window unlock
a) *With the switch in the UP position, there should be continuity between terminals 8, 9 and 11, and between terminals 4, 5 and 13.*

b) *With the switch in the OFF position, there should be continuity between terminals 4, 5 and 11, and between terminals 4, 5 and 13.*
c) *With the switch in the DOWN position, there should be continuity between terminals 8, 9 and 13, and between terminals 4, 5 and 11.*

Front passenger's switch - window lock
a) *With the switch in the UP position, there should be continuity between terminals 8, 9 and 11.*
b) *With the switch in the OFF position, there should be continuity between terminals 11 and 13.*
c) *With the switch in the DOWN position, there should be continuity between terminals 8, 9 and 13.*

Rear left passenger's switch - window unlock
a) *With the switch in the UP position, there should be continuity between terminals 8, 9 and 10, and between terminals 4, 5 and 12.*
b) *With the switch in the OFF position, there should be continuity between terminals 4, 5 and 10, and between terminals 4, 5 and 12.*
c) *With the switch in the DOWN position, there should be continuity between terminals 8, 9 and 12, and between terminals 4, 5 and 10.*

Rear left passenger's switch - window lock
a) *With the switch in the UP position, there should be continuity between terminals 8, 9 and 10.*
b) *With the switch in the OFF position, there should be continuity between terminals 11 and 12.*
c) *With the switch in the DOWN position, there should be continuity between terminals 8, 9 and 12.*

Rear right passenger's switch - window unlock
a) *With the switch in the UP position, there should be continuity between terminals 7, 8 and 9, and between terminals 4, 5 and 14.*
b) *With the switch in the OFF position, there should be continuity between terminals 4, 5 and 7, and between terminals 4, 5 and 14.*
c) *With the switch in the DOWN position, there should be continuity between terminals 8, 9 and 14, and between terminals 4, 5 and 7.*

Rear right passenger's switch - window lock
a) *With the switch in the UP position, there should be continuity between terminals 7, 8 and 9.*
b) *With the switch in the OFF position, there should be continuity between terminals 7 and 14.*

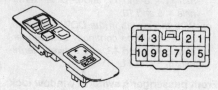

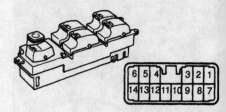

26.3a Driver's side power door lock switch terminal guide (T100 and Tacoma models)

26.3b Passenger's side power door lock switch terminal guide (T100 and Tacoma models)

26.3c Driver's side power door lock switch terminal guide (4Runner models)

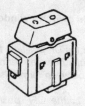

26.3d Passenger's side power door lock switch terminal guide (4Runner models)

c) *With the switch in the DOWN position, there should be continuity between terminals 8, 9 and 14.*

Passenger control switches

a) *With the switch in the UP position, there should be continuity between terminals 1 and 2, and between terminals 3 and 5* **(see illustrations).**
b) *With the switch in the OFF position, there should be continuity between terminals 1 and 2, and between terminals 4 and 5.*
c) *With the switch in the DOWN position, there should be continuity between terminals 1 and 3, and between terminals 4 and 5.*

11 If the continuity is not as specified replace the switch. If the switch tests OK, check for a short or open in the circuit between the affected switch and the window motor.
12 If one window is inoperative from both switches, remove the trim panel from the affected door and check for voltage at the switch and at the motor **(see illustration)** while the switch is operated.
13 If voltage is reaching the motor, disconnect the glass from the regulator (see Chapter 11). Move the window up and down by hand while checking for binding and damage. Also check for binding and damage to the regulator. If the regulator is not damaged and the window moves up and down smoothly, replace the motor. If there's binding or damage, lubricate, repair or replace parts, as necessary.

14 If voltage isn't reaching the motor, check the wiring in the circuit for continuity between the switches and motors. You'll need to consult the wiring diagram for the vehicle. If the circuit is equipped with a relay, check that the relay is grounded properly and receiving voltage.
15 Test the windows after you are done to confirm proper repairs.

26 Power door lock system - description and check

Description

The power door lock system operates the door lock actuators mounted in each door. The system consists of the switches, actuators, a control unit and associated wiring. Diagnosis can usually be limited to simple checks of the wiring connections and actuators for minor faults which can be easily repaired. Since this system uses an electronic control unit, in-depth diagnosis should be left to a dealership service department. The door lock control unit is located behind the instrument panel, to the right of the fuse box.

Power door lock systems are operated by bi-directional solenoids located in the doors. The lock switches have two operating positions: Lock and Unlock. When activated, the switch sends a ground signal to the door lock control unit to lock or unlock the doors. Depending on which way the switch is activated, the control unit reverses polarity to the solenoids, allowing the two sides of the circuit to be used alternately as the feed (positive) and ground side.

Some vehicles may have an anti-theft systems incorporated into the power locks. If you are unable to locate the trouble using the following general Steps, consult a dealer service department or other qualified repair shop.

Check

Refer to illustrations 26.3a, 26.3b, 26.3c, 26.3d, 26.3e and 26.6

1 Always check the circuit protection first. Some vehicles use a combination of circuit breakers and fuses.
2 Operate the door lock switches in both directions (Lock and Unlock) with the engine off. Listen for the click of the solenoids operating.
3 Test the door lock switches for continuity as follows.

T100 models and Tacoma models

Driver's door lock switch

a) *With the switch in the LOCK position, there should be continuity between terminals 1 and 5, and between terminals 2 and 6* **(see illustrations).**
b) *With the switch OFF, there should be no continuity.*
c) *With the switch in the UNLOCK position, there should be continuity between terminals 2 and 5, and between terminals 1 and 6.*

Passenger's door lock switch

a) *With the switch in the LOCK position, there should be continuity between terminals 3 and 4* **(see illustrations).**
b) *With the switch OFF, there should be no continuity.*
c) *With the switch in the UNLOCK position, there should be continuity between terminals 2 and 4.*

4Runner models

Driver's door lock switch

a) *With the switch in the LOCK position, there should be continuity between terminals 2 and 4* **(see illustrations).**
b) *With the switch OFF, there should be no continuity.*
c) *With the switch in the UNLOCK position, there should be continuity between terminals 2 and 3.*

Passenger's door lock switches

a) *With the switch in the LOCK position, there should be continuity between terminals 3 and 4* **(see illustrations).**
b) *With the switch OFF, there should be no continuity.*
c) *With the switch in the UNLOCK position, there should be continuity between terminals 2 and 4.*

Liftgate door lock switch

a) *With the switch in the LOCK position, there should be continuity between terminals 1 and 6, and between terminals 3 and 4 (see illustrations).*
b) *With the switch in the UNLOCK position, there should be continuity between terminals 1 and 3, and between terminals 4 and 6.*
c) *The illumination circuit should have continuity between terminals 2 and 5.*

4 Replace the switch if there's not continuity in both switch positions. If the switch is OK, check the wiring between the switches, control unit and solenoids for continuity. Repair the wiring if there's no continuity.

5 Check for a bad ground at the switches or the control unit.

6 If all but one lock solenoids operate, remove the trim panel from the affected door (see Chapter 11) and check for voltage at the solenoid while the lock switch is operated. One of the wires should have voltage in the Lock position, the other should have voltage in the Unlock position (see illustration).

7 If the inoperative solenoid is receiving voltage, replace the solenoid.

8 If the inoperative solenoid isn't receiving voltage, check the relay or for an open or short in the wire between the lock solenoid and the control unit. **Note:** *It's common for wires to break in the portion of the harness between the body and door (opening and closing the door fatigues and eventually breaks the wires).*

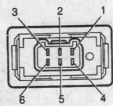

26.3e Liftgate power door lock switch terminal guide (4Runner models)

26.6 Check for voltage at the lock solenoid while the lock switch is operated

---

27 Daytime Running Lights (DRL) - general information

The Daytime Running Lights (DRL) system used on Canadian models illuminates the headlights whenever the engine is running. The only exception is with the engine running and the parking brake engaged. Once the parking brake is released, the lights will remain on as long as the ignition switch is on, even if the parking brake is later applied.

The DRL system supplies reduced power to the headlights so they won't be too bright for daytime use, while prolonging headlight life.

---

28 Airbags - general information

Refer to illustrations 28.1a, 28.1b and 28.1c

Some models are equipped with a Supplemental Restraint System (SRS), more commonly known as an airbag. This system is designed to protect the driver and the front seat passenger from serious injury in the event of a head-on or frontal collision. It consists of an airbag module in the center of the steering wheel and, if equipped, another airbag module on the right side of the instrument panel and a sensing/diagnostic module which is mounted in the center of the vehicle

below the instrument panel. T100 models are equipped with a pair of impact sensors that are located at the front of the vehicle **(see illustrations)**.

Airbag module
Steering wheel-mounted

The airbag inflator module contains a housing incorporating the cushion (airbag) and inflator unit, mounted in the center of the steering wheel The inflator assembly is mounted on the back of the housing over a hole through which gas is expelled, inflating the bag almost instantaneously when an electrical signal is sent from the system. A coil assembly on the steering column under the module carries this signal to the module.

This coil assembly can transmit an electrical signal regardless of steering wheel position. The igniter in the airbag ignites the sodium azide/copper oxide powder, producing nitrogen gas, which inflates the bag.

Instrument panel-mounted

The passenger side airbag is mounted above the glove compartment and designated by the letters SRS (Supplemental Restraint System). It consists of an inflator containing an igniter, a bag assembly, a reaction housing and a trim cover.

The passenger airbag is considerably larger than the steering wheel-mounted unit and is supported by the steel reaction housing. The trim cover has a molded seam which splits when the bag inflates.

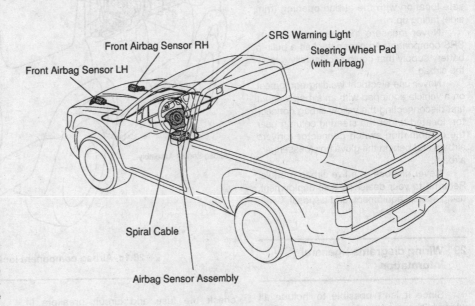

28.1a Airbag component locations (T100 models)

Sensing and diagnostic module

The sensing and diagnostic module supplies the current to the airbag system in the event of the collision, even if battery power is cut off. It checks this system every time the vehicle is started, causing the "AIR BAG" light to go on then off, if the system is operating properly. If there is a fault in the system, the light will go on and stay on, flash, or the dash will make a beeping sound. If this happens, the vehicle should be taken to your dealer immediately for service.

Precautions

Disabling the SRS system

Warning: *Failure to follow these precautions could result in accidental deployment of the airbag and personal injury.*

Caution: *If the stereo in your vehicle is equipped with an anti-theft system, make sure you have the correct activation code before disconnecting the battery.*

Whenever working in the vicinity of the steering wheel, steering column or any of the other SRS system components, the system must be disarmed. To disarm the system:

a) *Point the wheels straight ahead and turn the ignition key to the LOCK position.*

b) *Disconnect the cable from the negative terminal of the battery.*

c) *Wait at least two minutes for the back-up power supply capacitor to be depleted.*

Whenever handling an airbag module, always keep the airbag opening (trim side) pointed away from your body. Never place the airbag module on a bench or other surface with the airbag opening facing the surface. Always place the airbag module in a safe location with the airbag opening (trim side) facing up.

Never measure the resistance of any SRS component. An ohmmeter has a built-in battery supply that could accidentally deploy the airbag.

Never use electrical welding equipment on a vehicle equipped with an airbag without first disconnecting the yellow airbag connector, located under the steering column near the combination switch connector (drivers airbag) and behind the glove box (passengers airbag).

Never dispose of a live airbag module. Return it to your dealer for safe deployment, using special equipment, and disposal.

29 Wiring diagrams - general information

Since it isn't possible to include all wiring diagrams for every year covered by this manual, the following diagrams are those that are typical and most commonly needed.

Prior to troubleshooting any circuits,

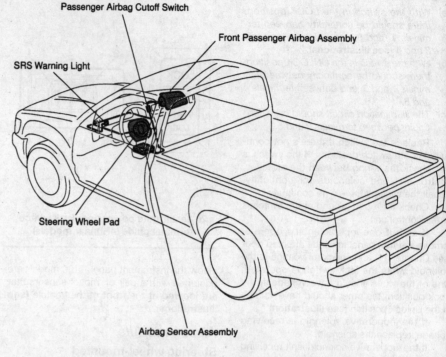

28.1b Airbag component locations (Tacoma models)

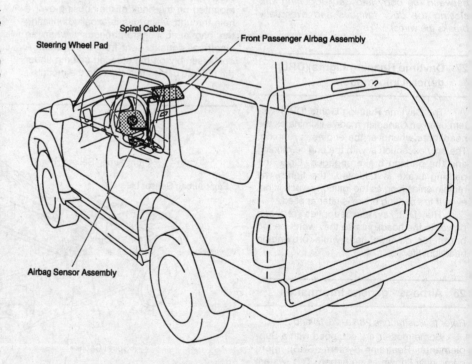

28.1c Airbag component locations (4Runner models)

check the fuse and circuit breakers (if equipped) to make sure they're in good condition. Make sure the battery is properly charged and check the cable connections (see Chapter 1).

When checking a circuit, make sure that all connectors are clean, with no broken or loose terminals. When unplugging a connector, do not pull on the wires. Pull only on the connector housings themselves.

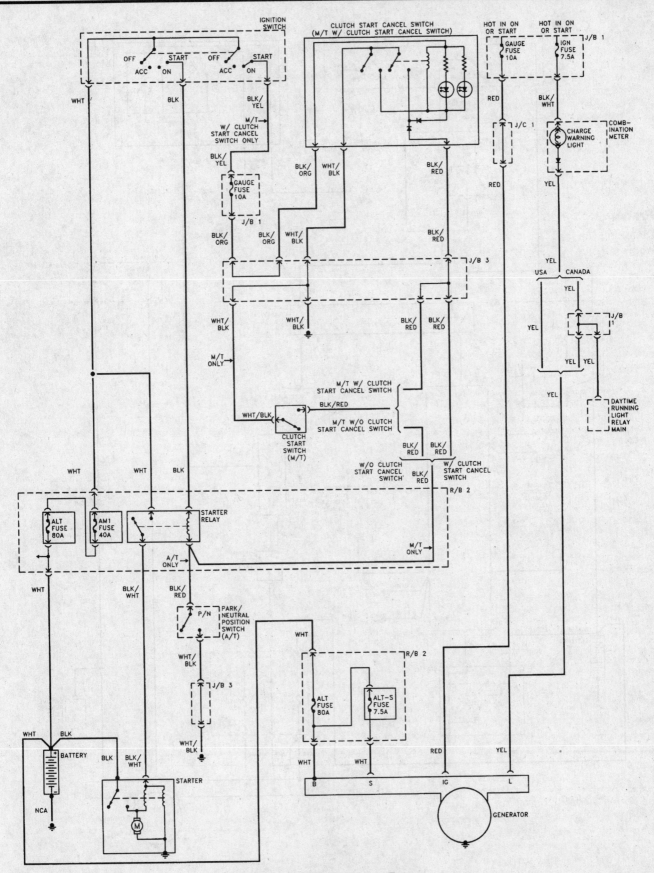

Starting and charging systems - Tacoma

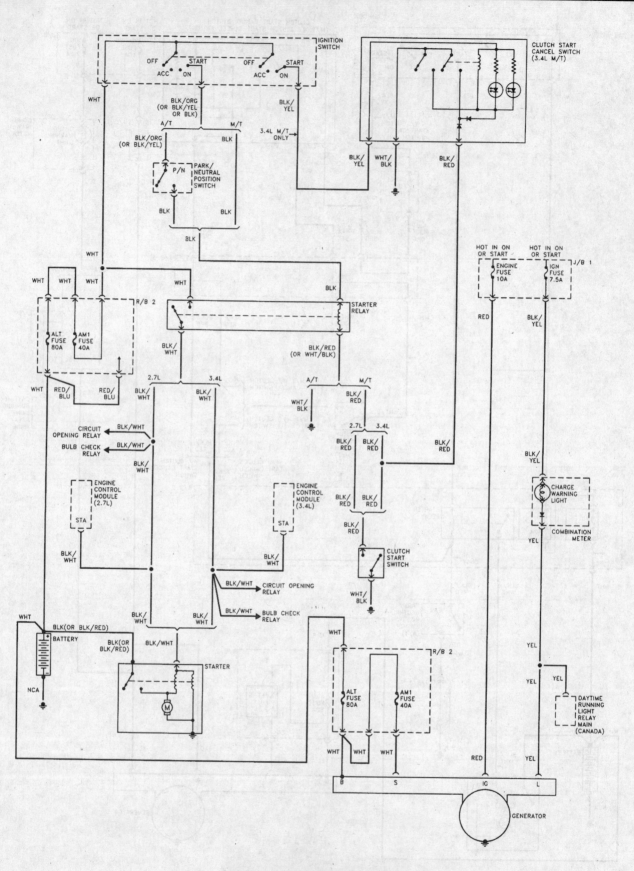

Starting and charging systems - T100

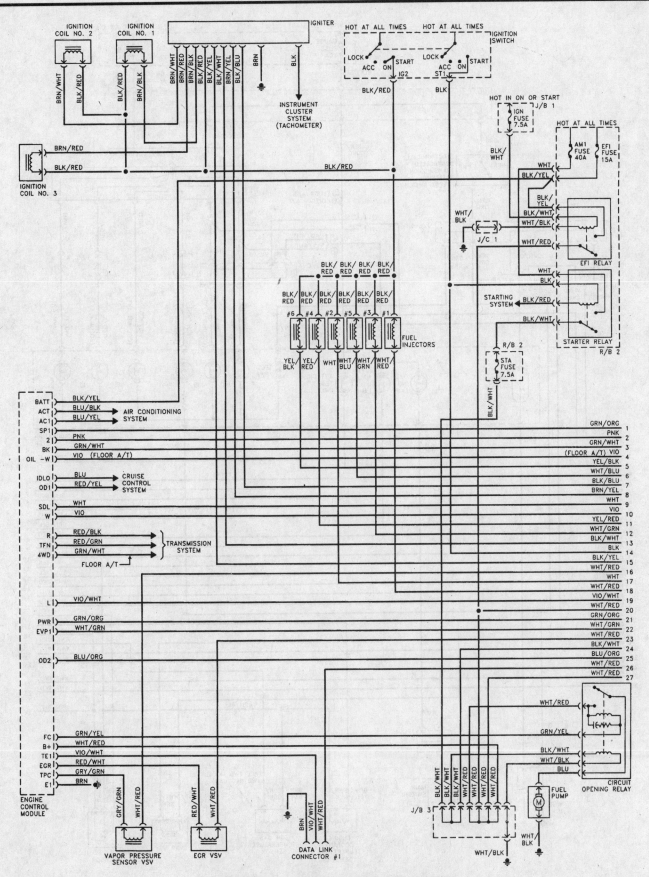

Engine control system - Tacoma 3.4L V6 (1 of 3)

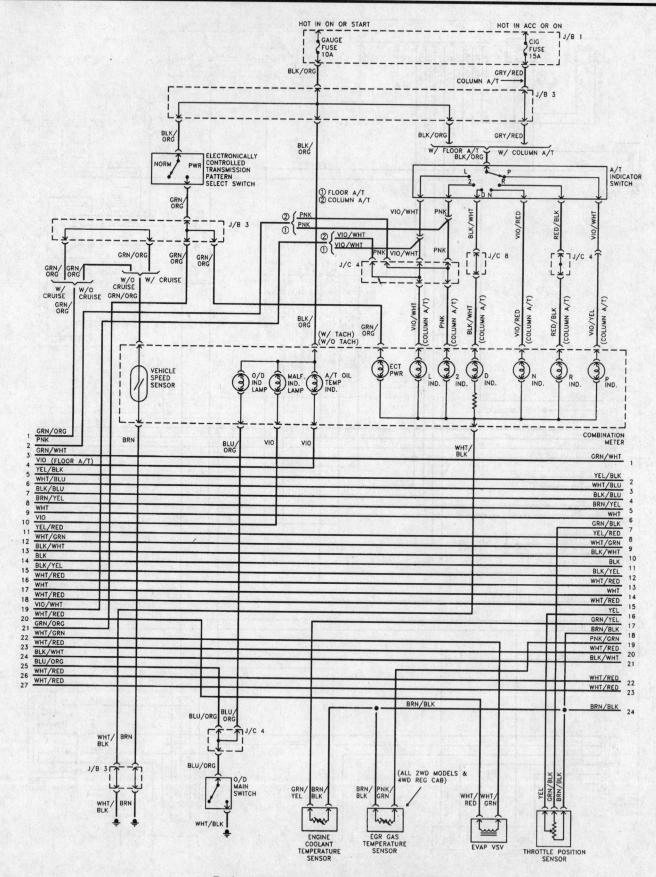

Engine control system - Tacoma 3.4L V6 (2 of 3)

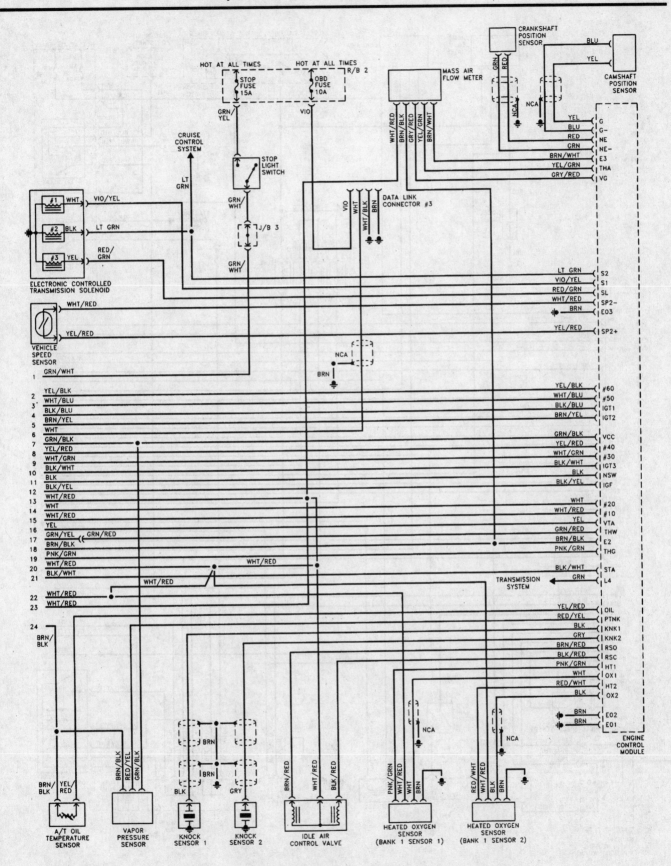

Engine control system - Tacoma 3.4L V6 (3 of 3)

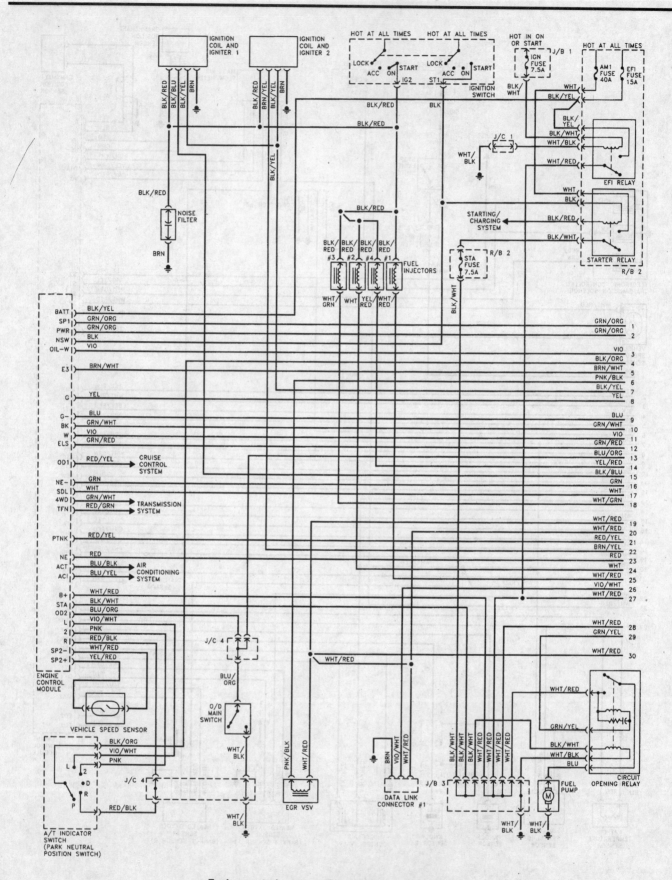

Engine control system - Tacoma four-cylinder (1 of 3)

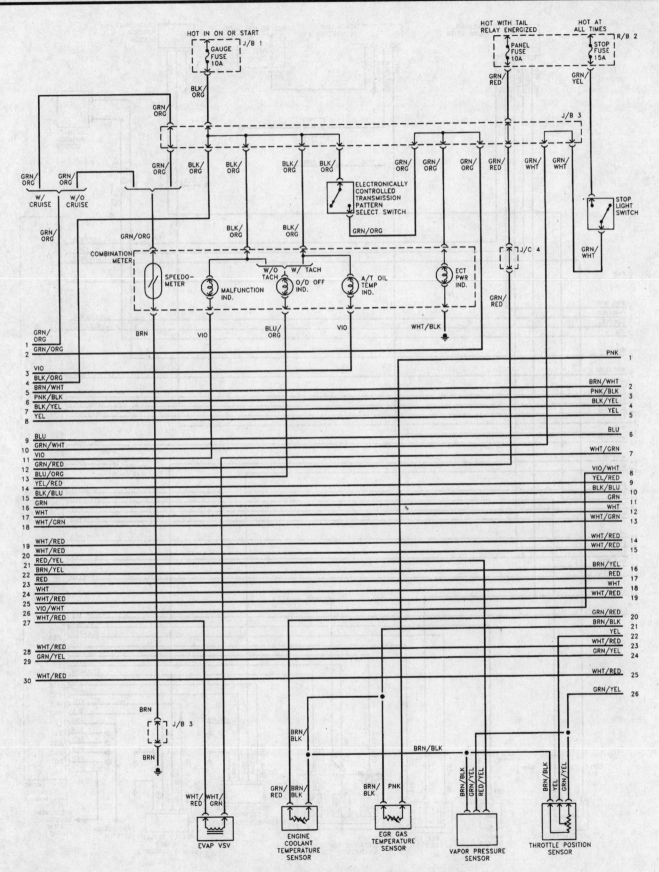

Engine control system - Tacoma four-cylinder (2 of 3)

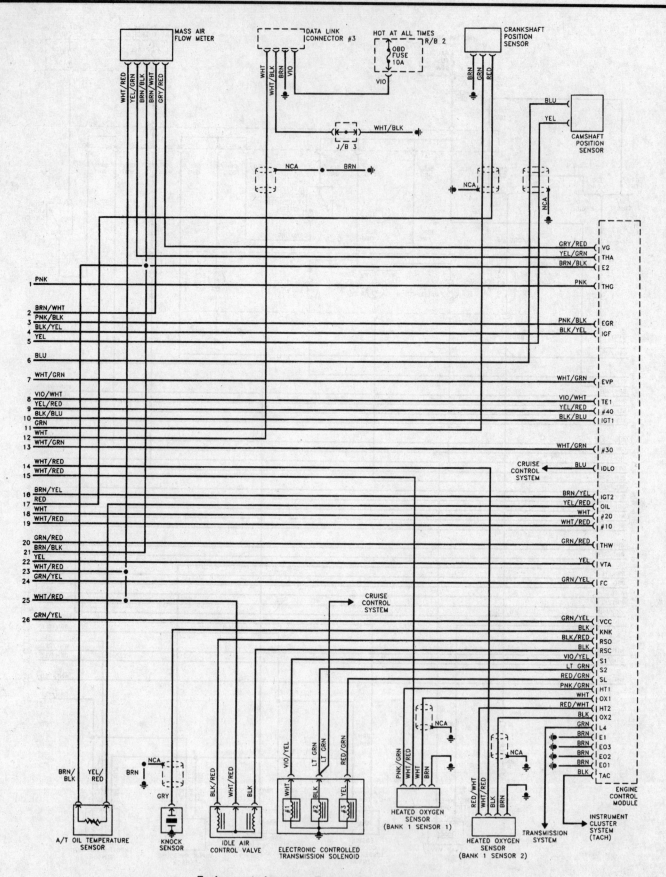

Engine control system - Tacoma four-cylinder (3 of 3)

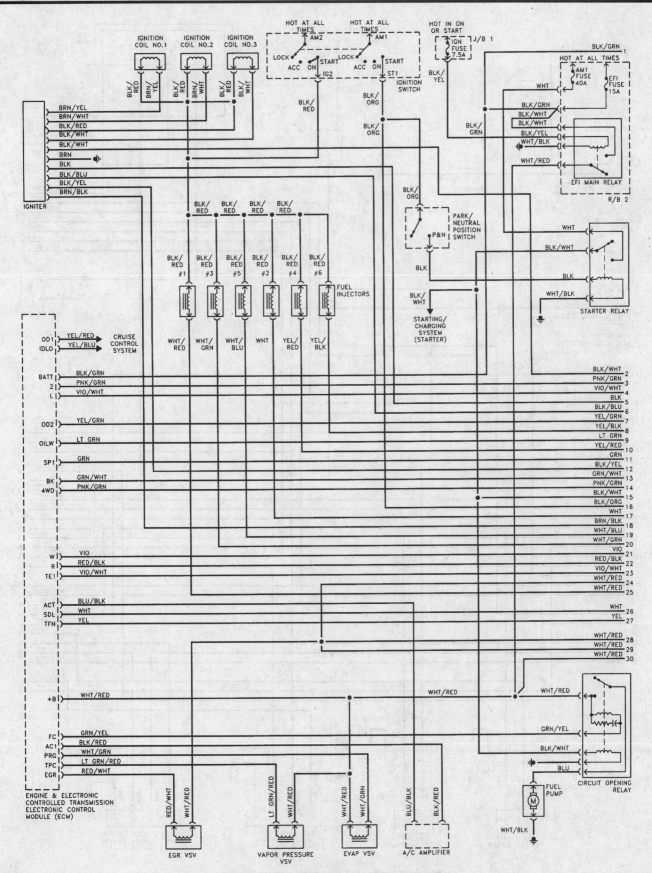

Engine control system - T100 3.4L V6 (1 of 4)

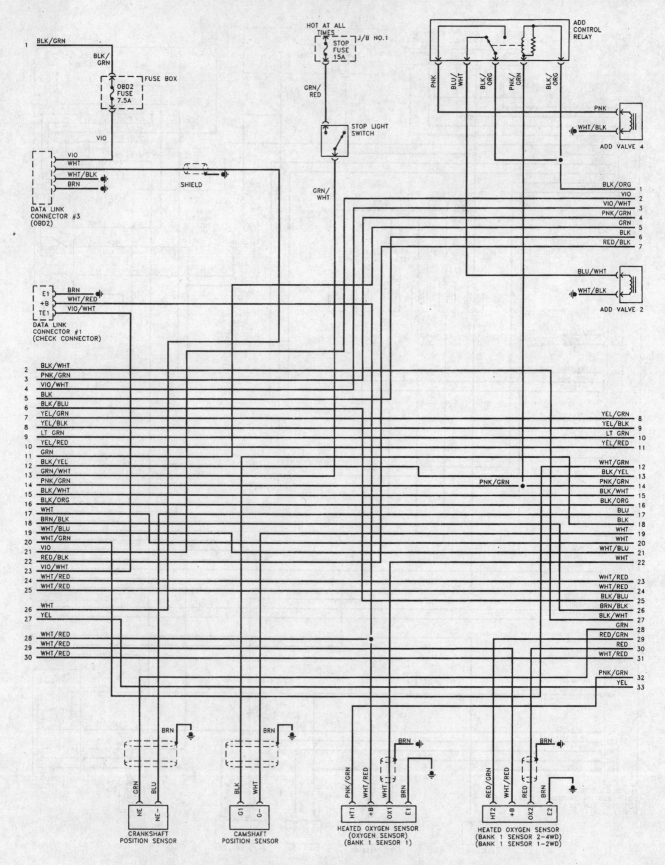

Engine control system - T100 3.4L V6 (2 of 4)

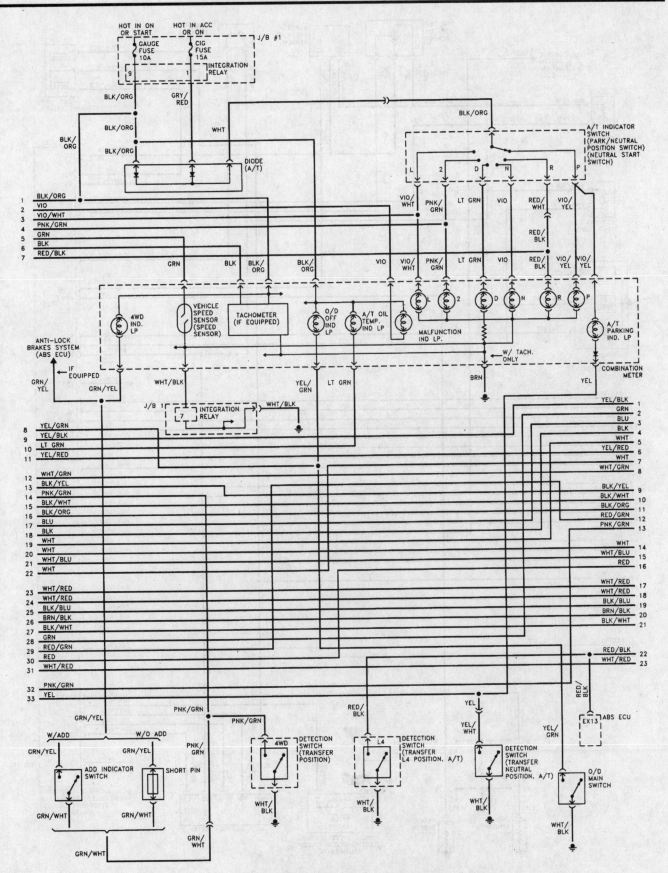

Engine control system - T100 3.4L V6 (3 of 4)

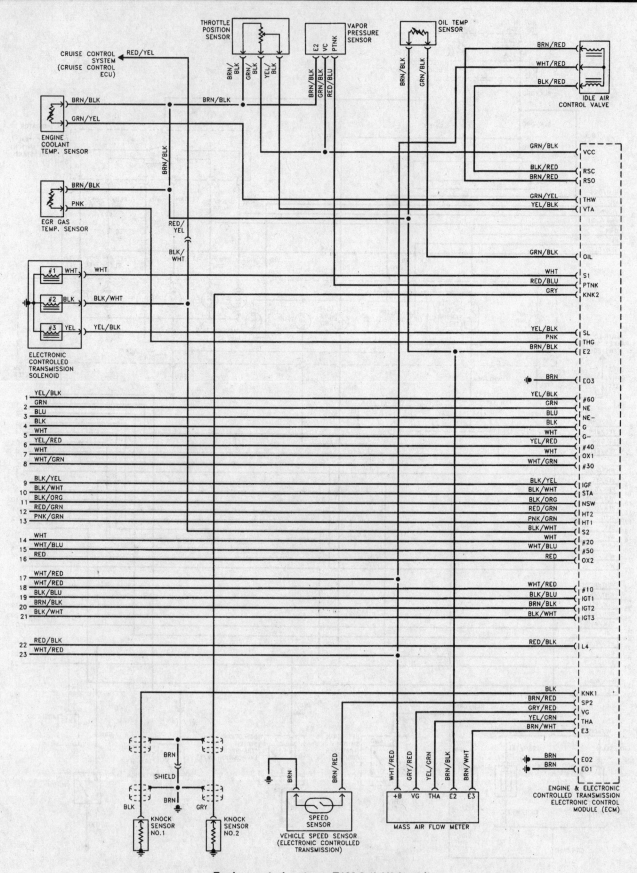

Engine control system - T100 3.4L V6 (4 of 4)

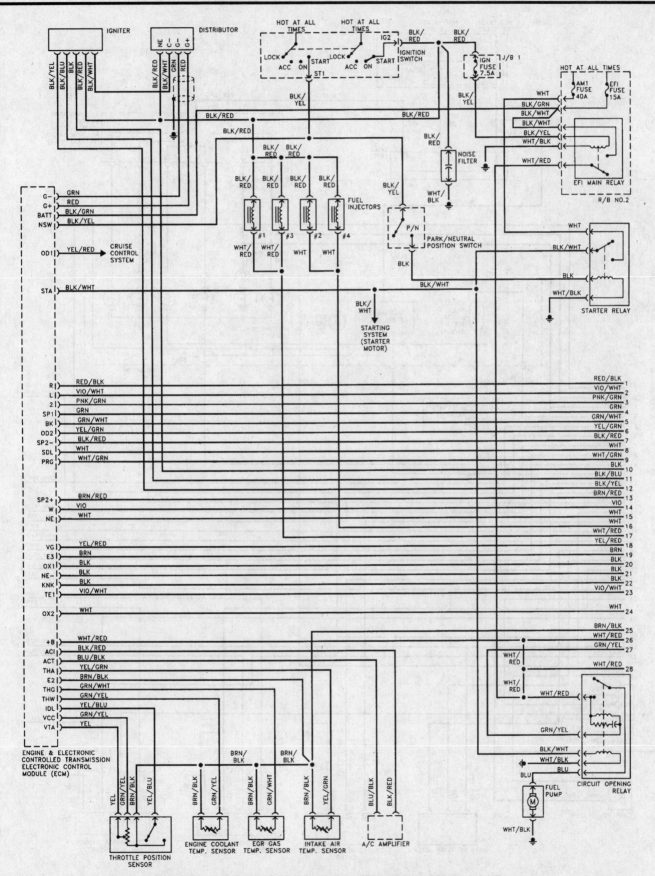

Engine control system - 1995 through 1998 T100 four-cylinder (1 of 3)

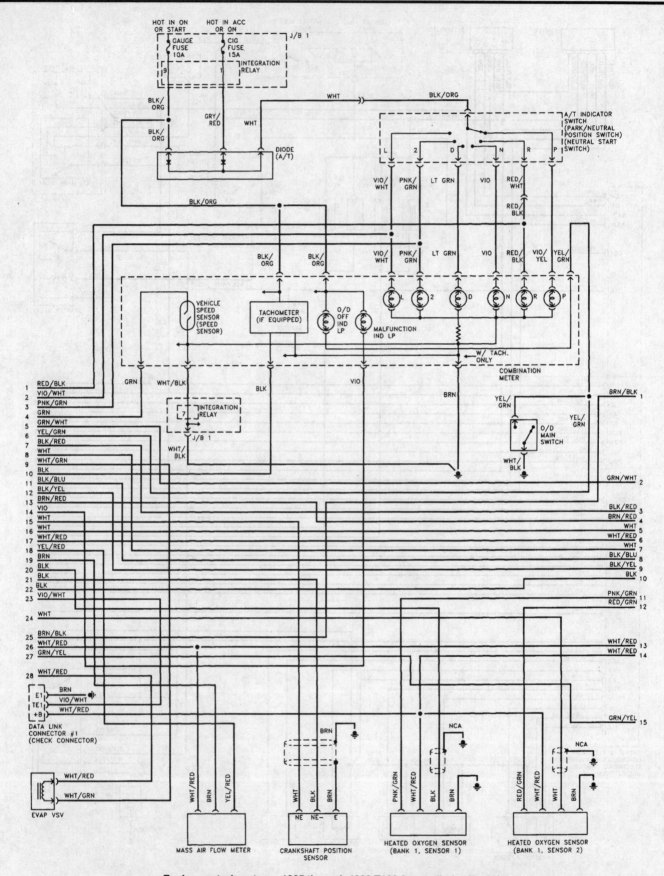

Engine control system - 1995 through 1998 T100 four-cylinder (2 of 3)

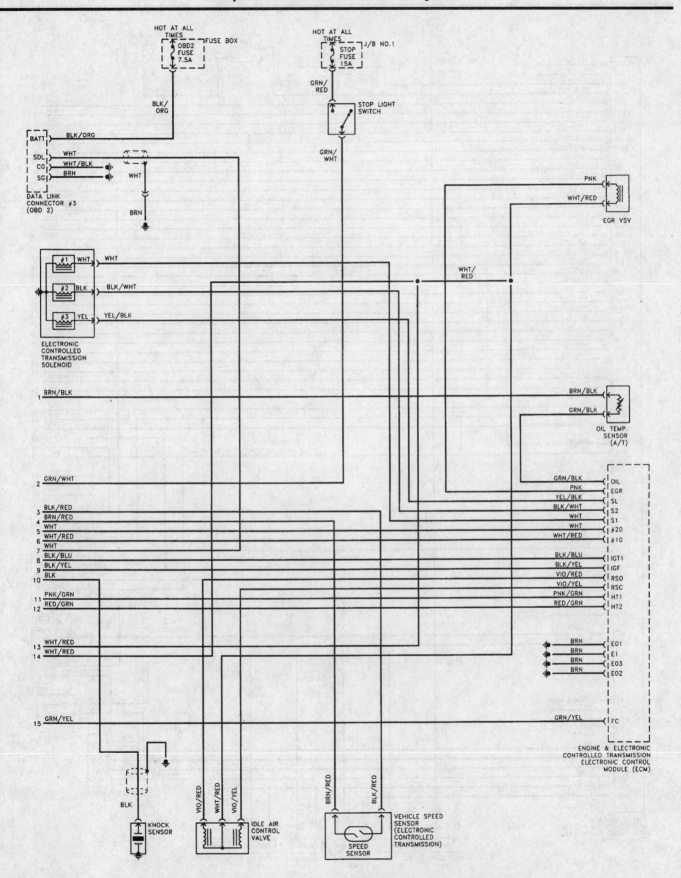

Engine control system - 1995 through 1998 T100 four-cylinder (3 of 3)

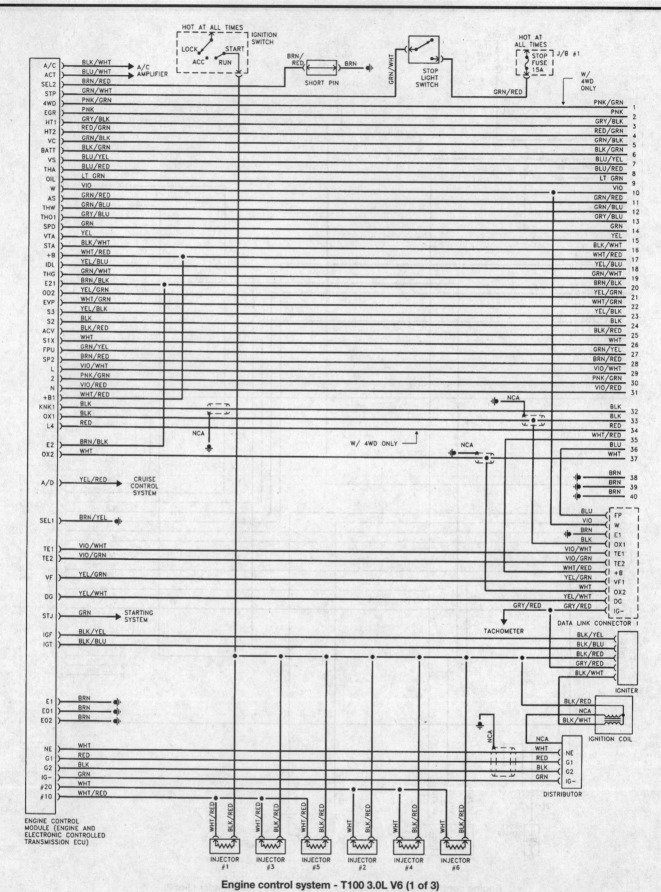

Engine control system - T100 3.0L V6 (1 of 3)

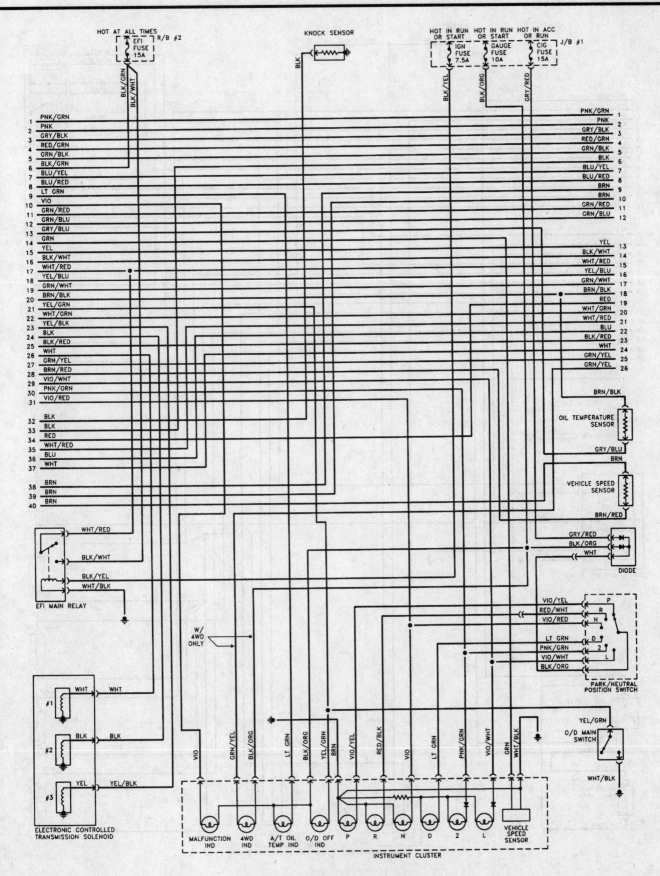

Engine control system - T100 3.0L V6 (2 of 3)

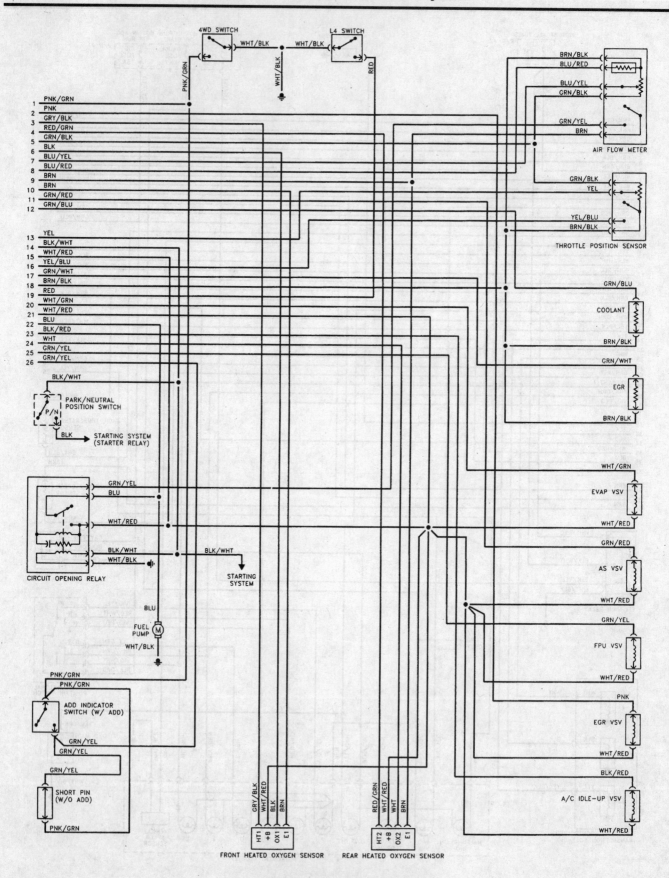

Engine control system - T100 3.0L V6 (3 of 3)

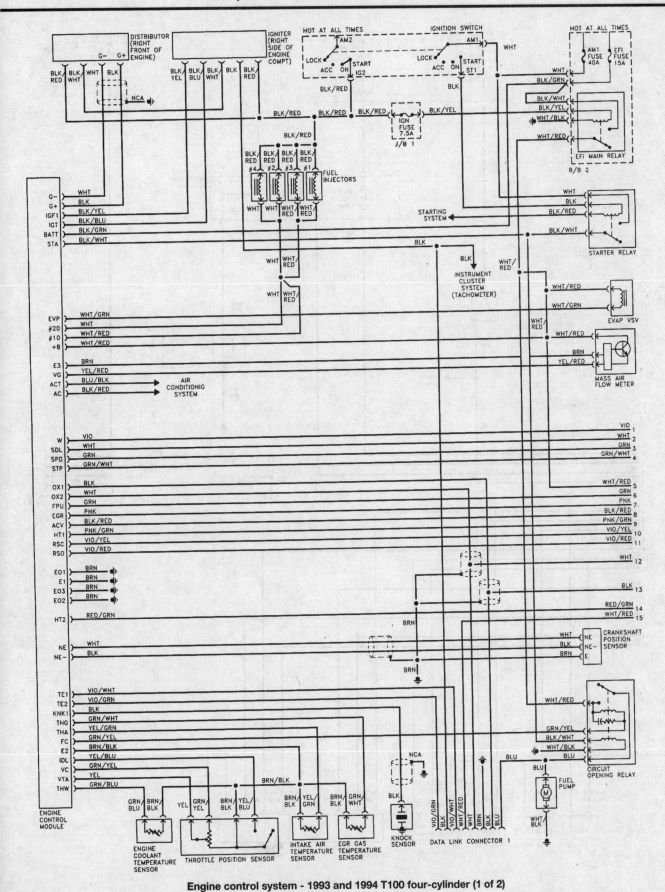

Engine control system - 1993 and 1994 T100 four-cylinder (1 of 2)

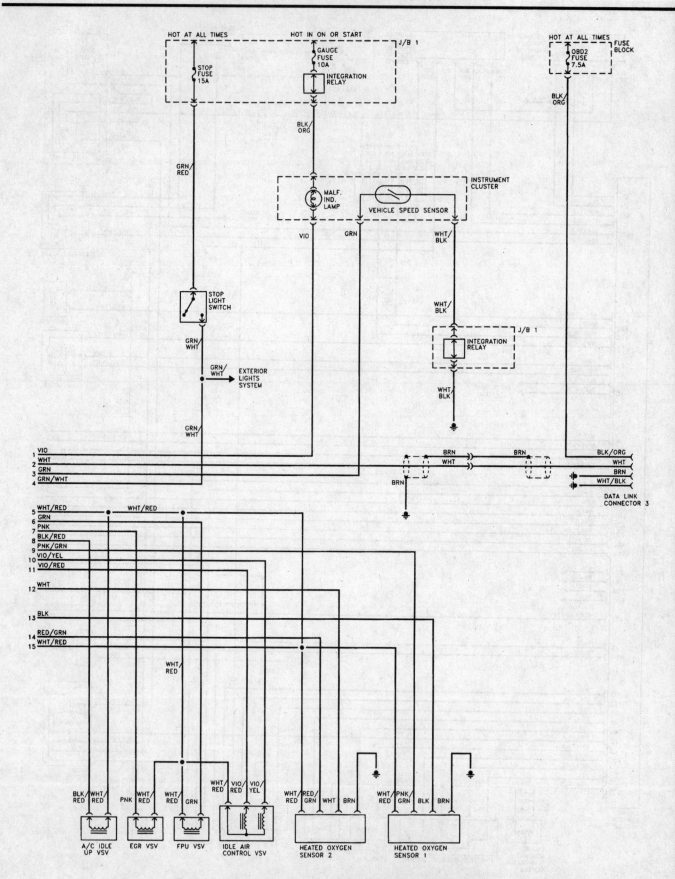

Engine control system - 1993 and 1994 T100 four-cylinder (2 of 2)

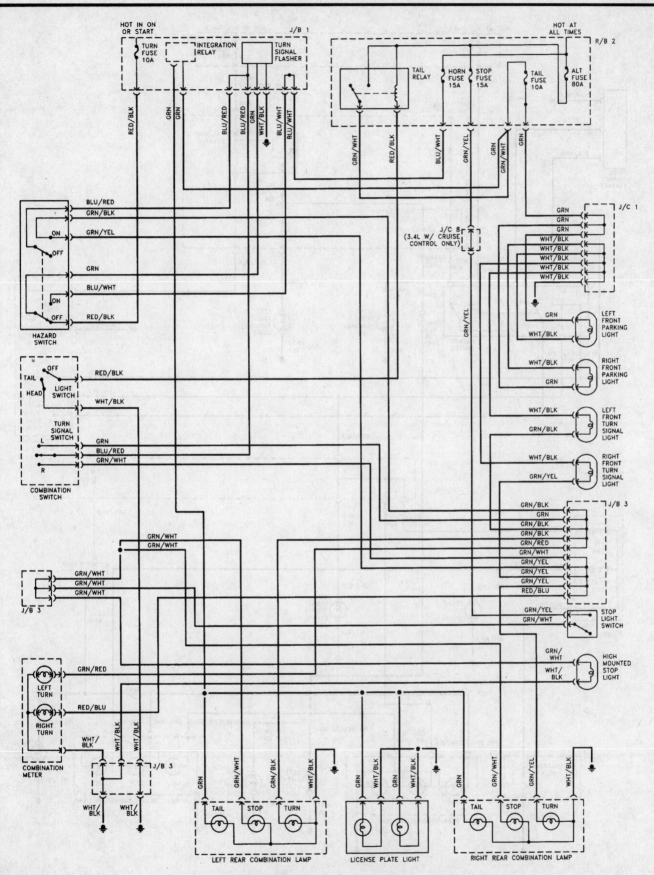

Exterior lighting system (except headlights) - Tacoma

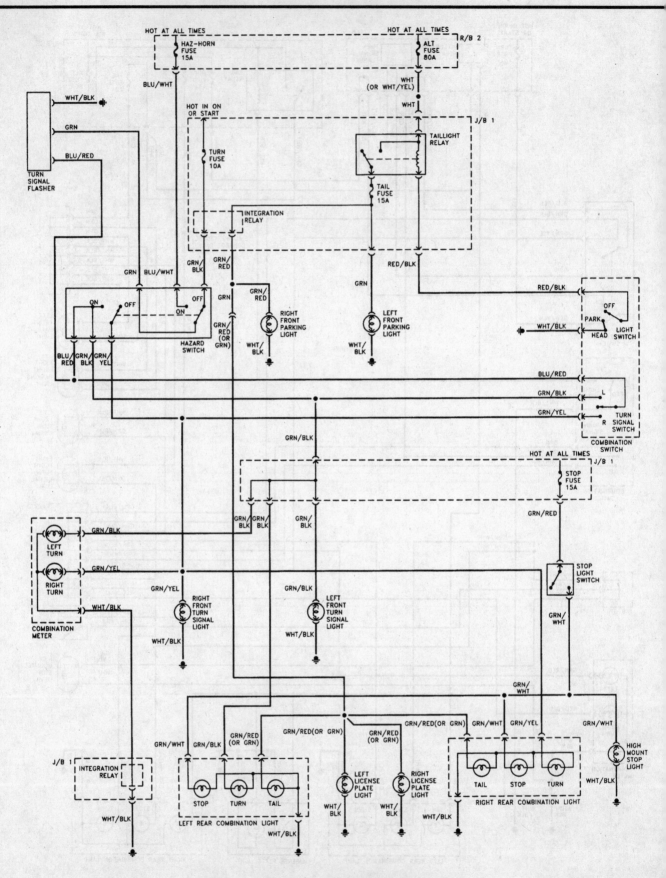

Exterior lighting system (except headlights) - T100

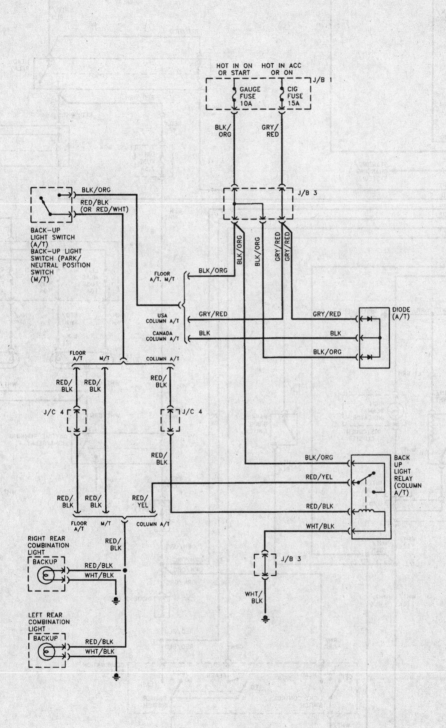

Back-up light circuit (all models)

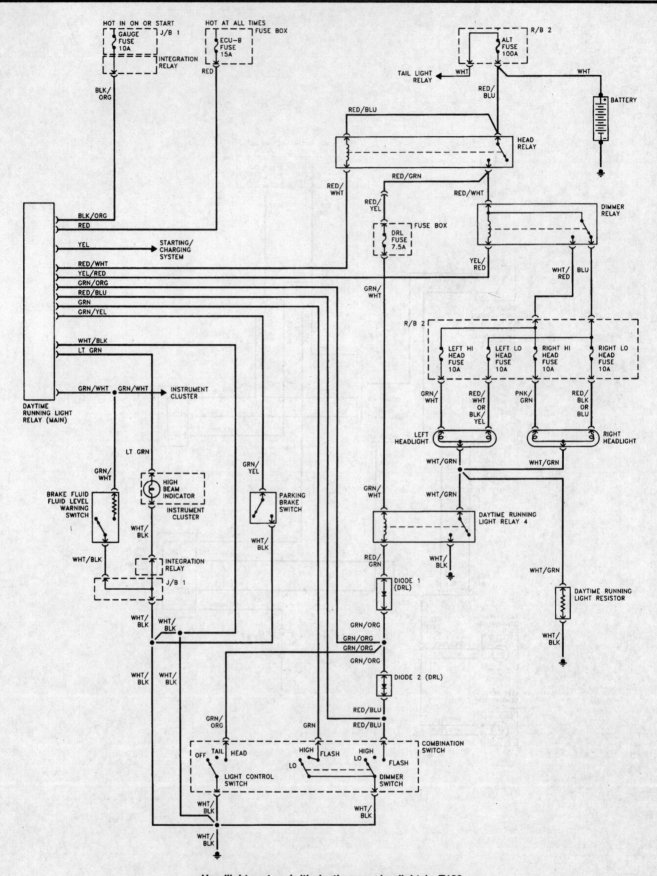

Headlight system (with daytime running lights) - T100

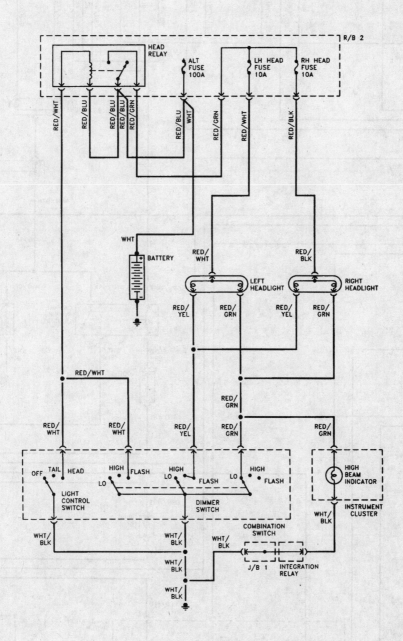

Headlight system (without daytime running lights) - T100

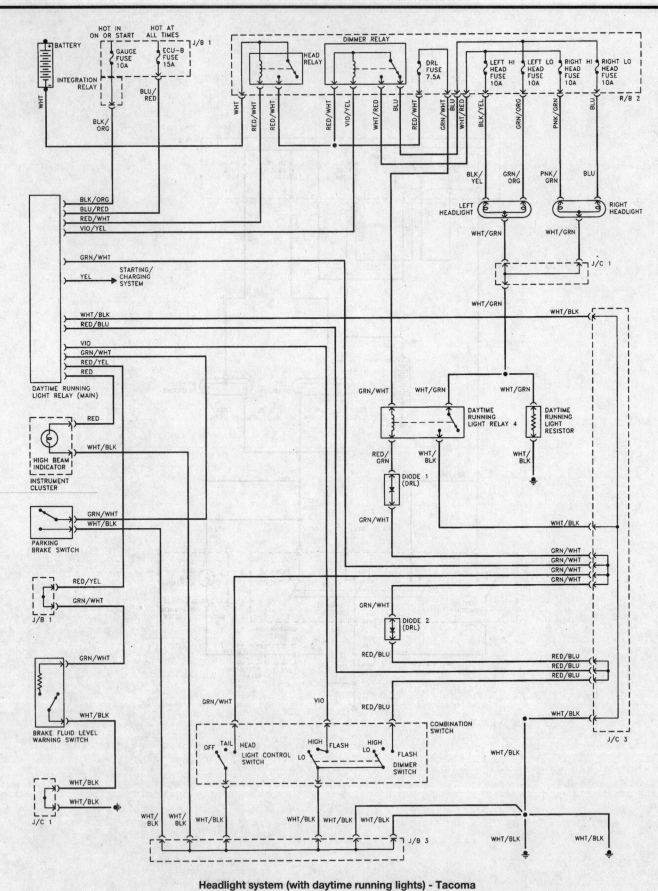

Headlight system (with daytime running lights) - Tacoma

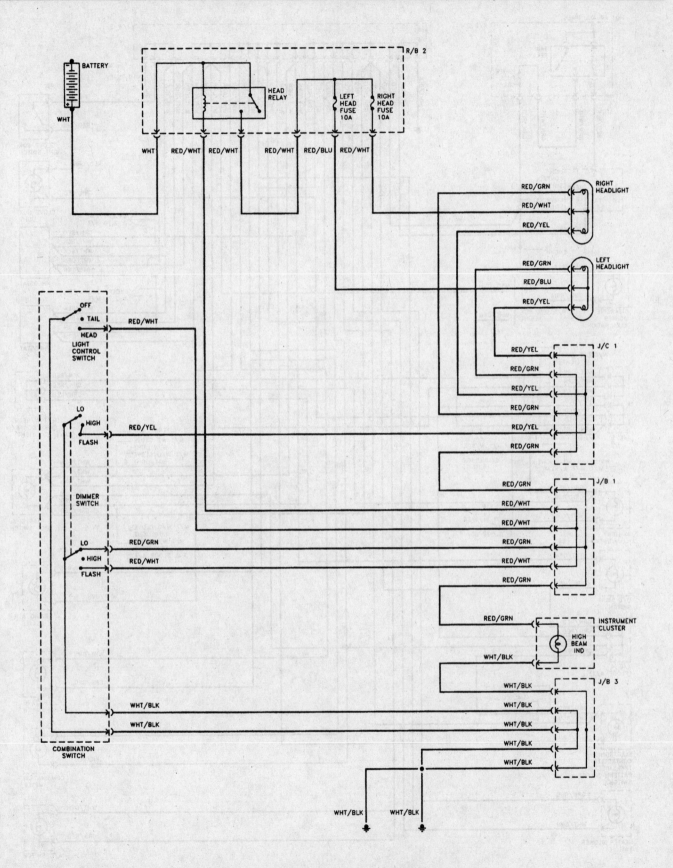

Headlight system (without daytime running lights) - Tacoma

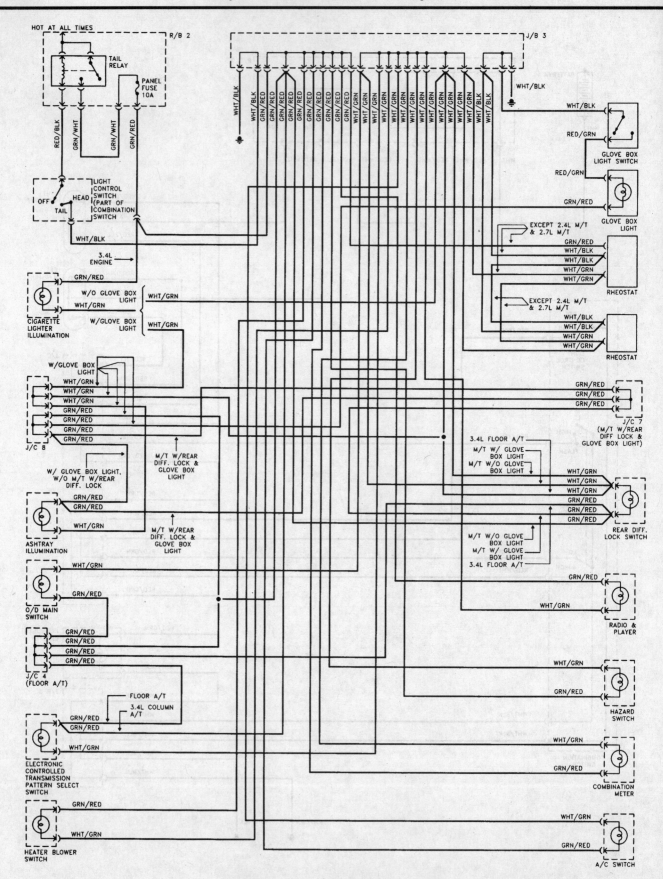

Instrument panel illumination system - Tacoma

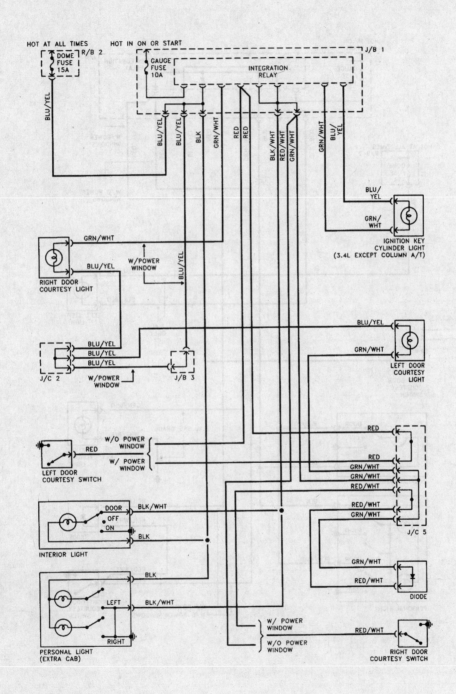

Interior lighting system - Tacoma

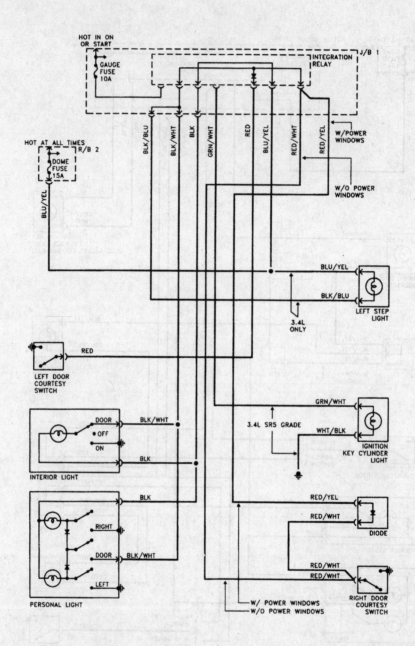

Interior lighting system - T100

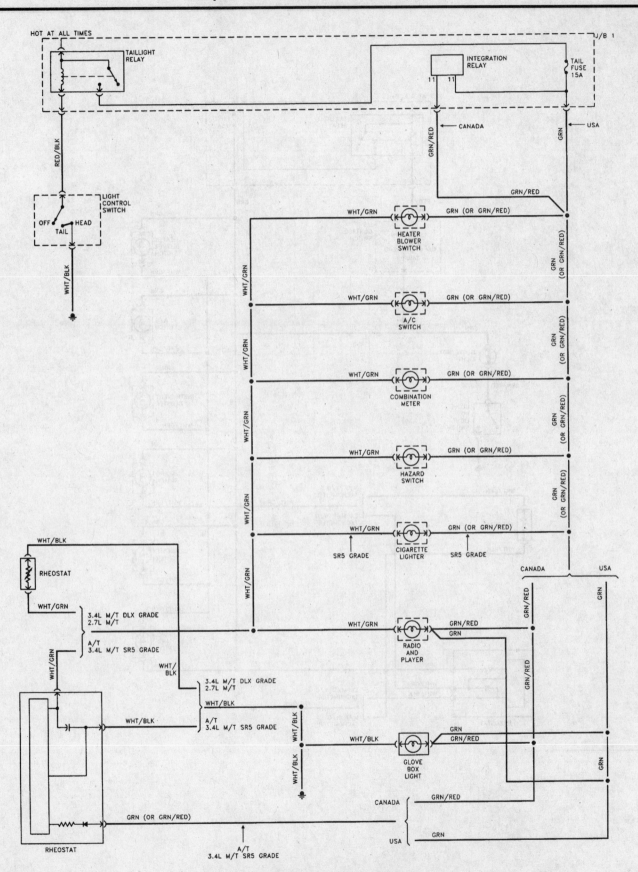

Instrument panel illumination system - 1995 through 1998 T100

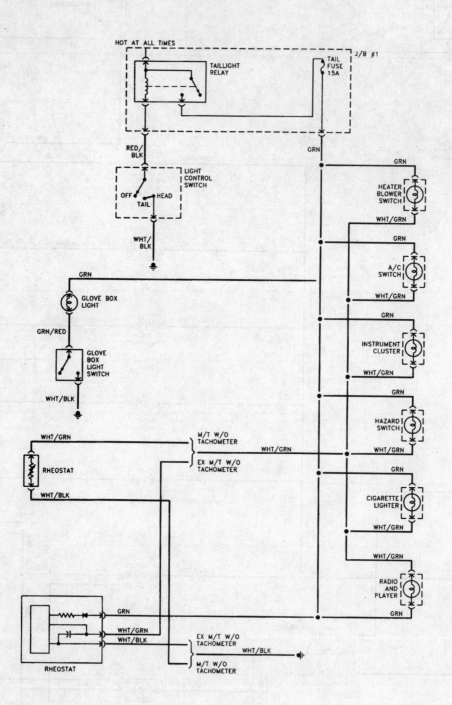

Instrument panel illumination system - 1993 and 1994 T100

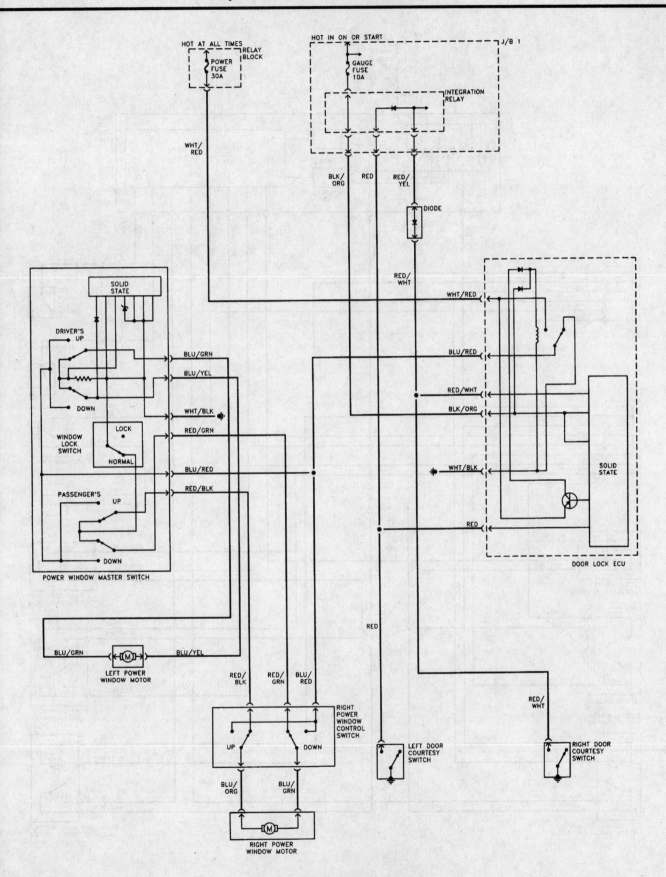

Power window system (all models)

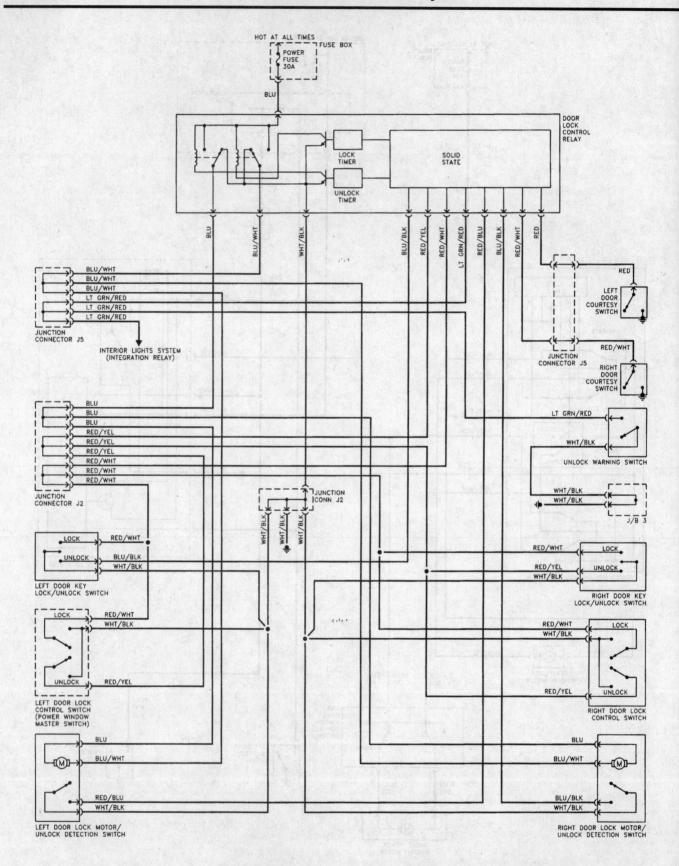

Power door lock system - Tacoma

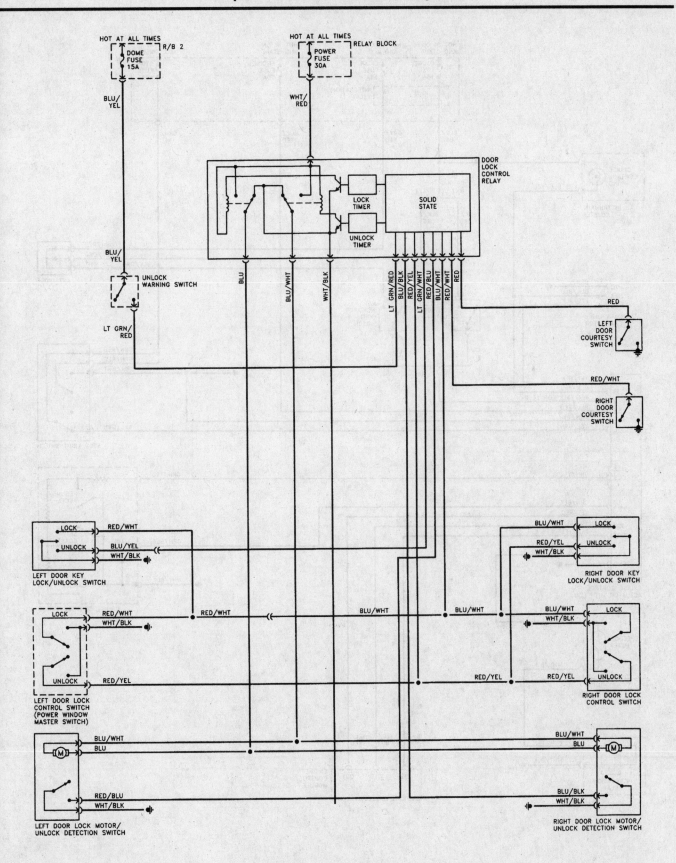

Power door lock system - T100

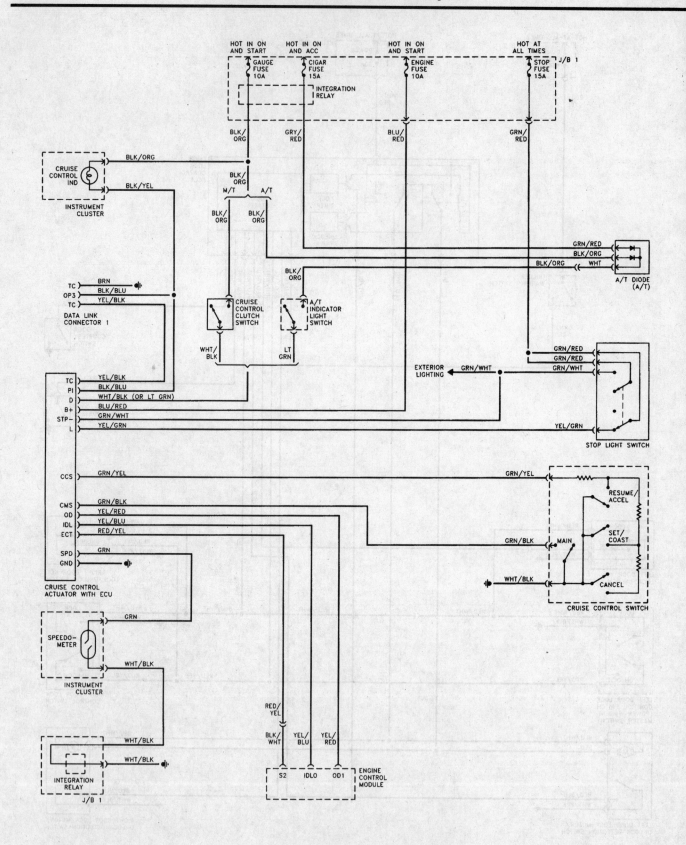

Cruise control system - 1997 and 1998 T100

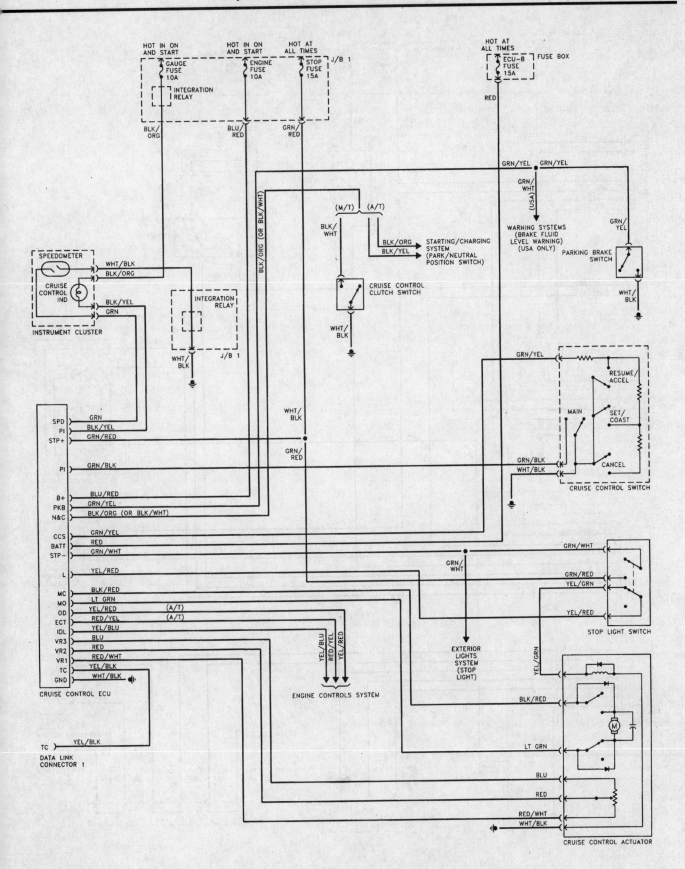

Cruise control system - 1993 through 1996 T100

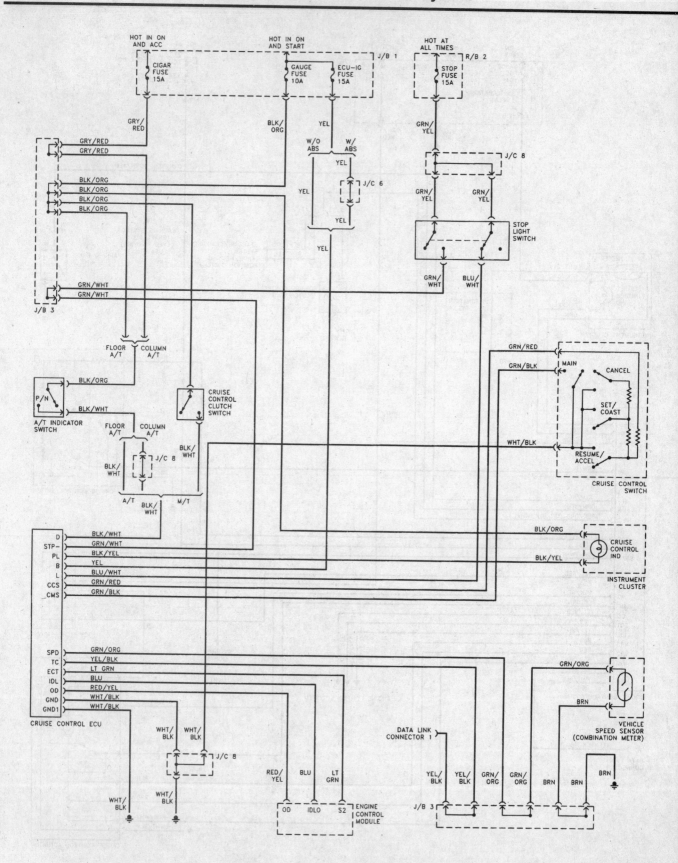

Cruise control system - Tacoma 3.4L V6

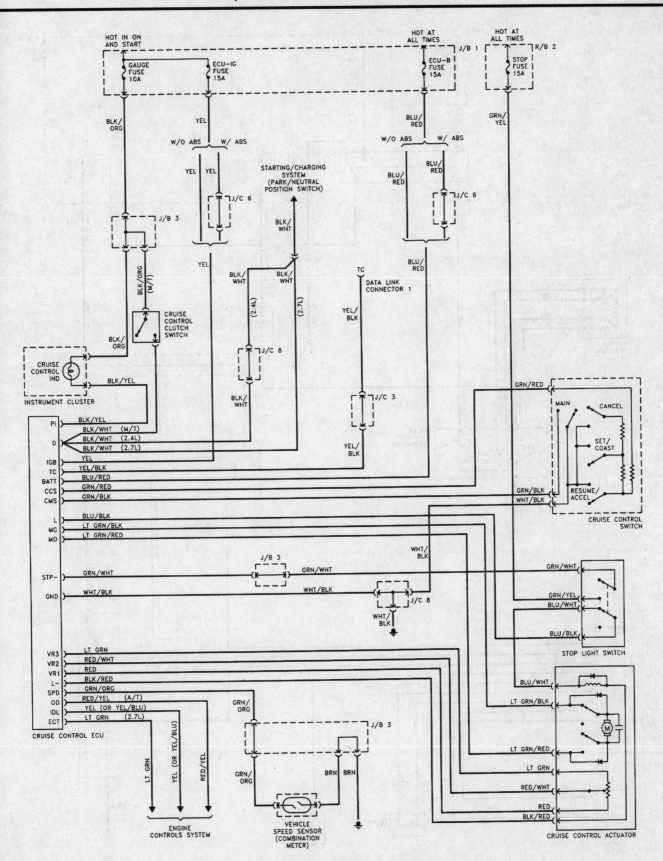

Cruise control system - Tacoma four-cylinder

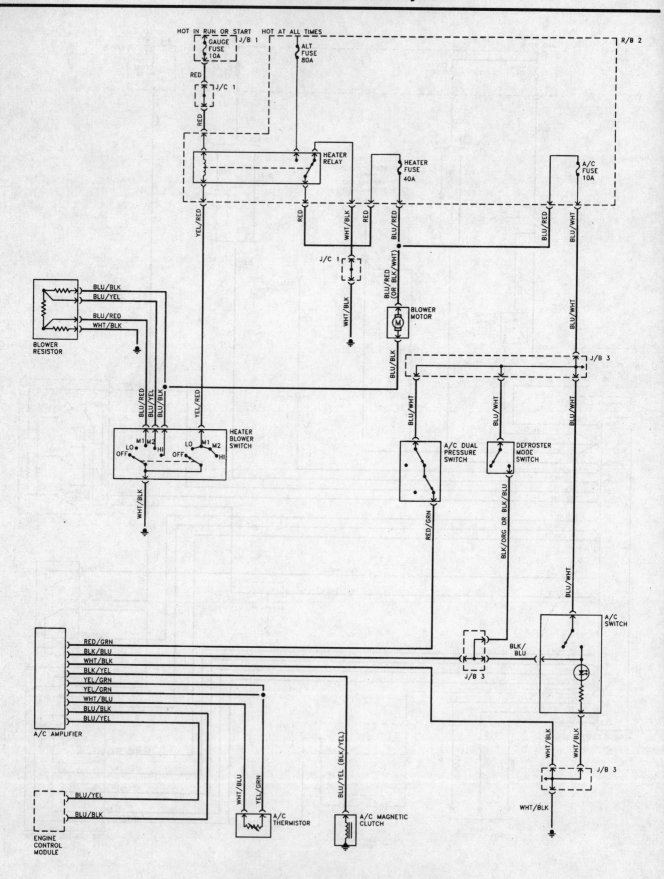

Heating and air conditioning system - 1997 and 1998 Tacoma

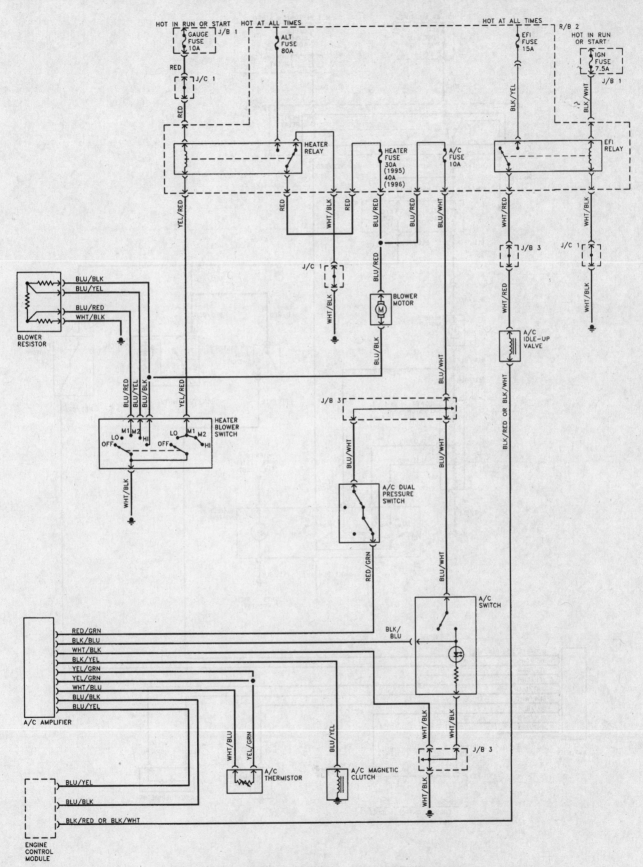

Heating and air conditioning system - 1995 and 1996 Tacoma

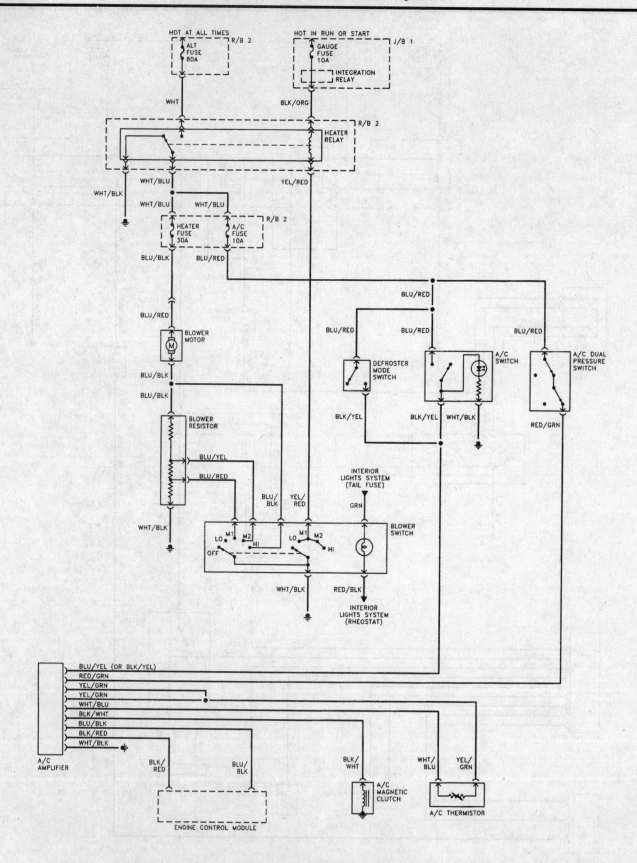

Heating and air conditioning system - T100

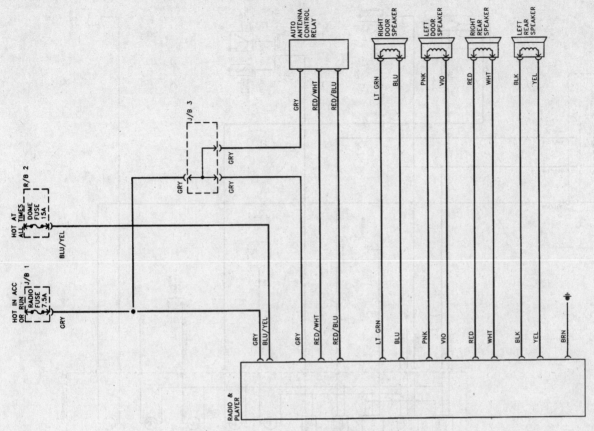

Radio and speakers - Tacoma

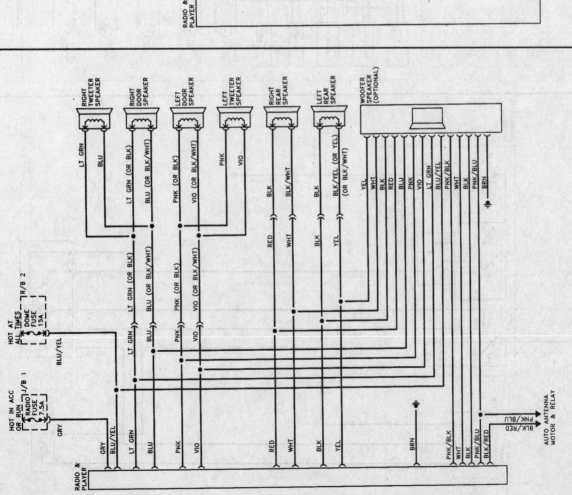

Radio and speakers - T100

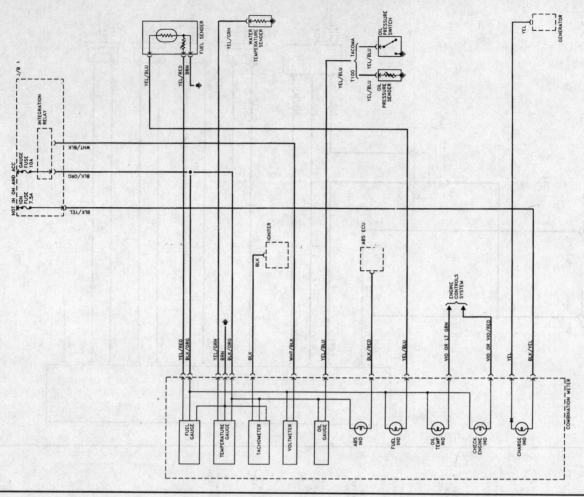

Instrument panel gauges and warning light system (all models)

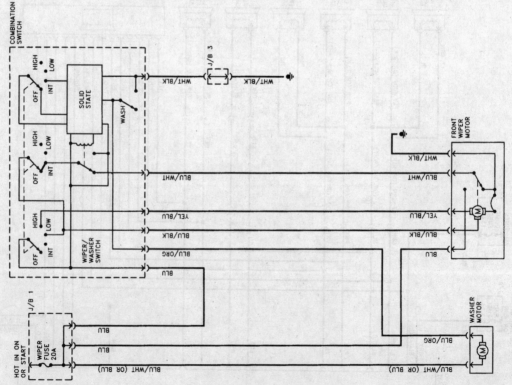

Windshield wiper circuit (all models)